MARKETING STRATEGY
AND **COMPETITIVE**
POSITIONING

Pearson

At Pearson, we have a simple mission: to help people make more of their lives through learning.

We combine innovative learning technology with trusted content and educational expertise to provide engaging and effective learning experiences that serve people wherever and whenever they are learning.

From classroom to boardroom, our curriculum materials, digital learning tools and testing programmes help to educate millions of people worldwide – more than any other private enterprise.

Every day our work helps learning flourish, and wherever learning flourishes, so do people.

To learn more, please visit us at **www.pearson.com/uk**

Seventh edition

MARKETING STRATEGY
AND COMPETITIVE
POSITIONING

Graham Hooley • Brigitte Nicoulaud •
John M. Rudd • Nick Lee

Harlow, England • London • New York • Boston • San Francisco • Toronto • Sydney • Dubai • Singapore • Hong Kong
Tokyo • Seoul • Taipei • New Delhi • Cape Town • São Paulo • Mexico City • Madrid • Amsterdam • Munich • Paris • Milan

PEARSON EDUCATION LIMITED
KAO Two
KAO Park
Harlow CM17 9SR
United Kingdom
Tel: +44 (0)1279 623623
Web: www.pearson.com/uk

First published in 1993 as Competitive Positioning: The key to market success (print)
Second edition published 1998 by Prentice Hall Europe (print)
Third edition published 2004 (print)
Fourth edition published 2008 (print)
Fifth edition published 2012 (print)
Sixth edition published 2017 (print and electronic)
Seventh edition published 2020 (print and electronic)

© Prentice Hall International (UK) Ltd 1993, 1998 (print)
© Pearson Education Limited 2004, 2008, 2012 (print)
© Pearson Education Limited 2017, 2020 (print and electronic)

The Financial Times. With a worldwide network of highly respected journalists, *The Financial Times* provides global business news, insightful opinion and expert analysis of business, finance and politics. With over 500 journalists reporting from 50 countries worldwide, our in-depth coverage of international news is objectively reported and analysed from an independent, global perspective. To find out more, visit www.ft.com/pearsonoffer.

ISBN: 978-1-292-27654-0 (print)
       978-1-292-27657-1 (PDF)
       978-1-292-27655-7 (ePub)

British Library Cataloguing-in-Publication Data
A catalogue record for the print edition is available from the British Library

Library of Congress Cataloging-in-Publication Data
Names: Hooley, Graham J., author. | Nicoulaud, Brigitte, author. | Rudd,
   John M., author.
Title: Marketing strategy & competitive positioning / Graham Hooley,
   Brigitte Nicoulaud, John M. Rudd, Nick Lee.
Other titles: Marketing strategy and competitive positioning
Description: Seventh edition. | Harlow ; New York : Pearson, 2020. |
   Includes bibliographical references and index. | Summary: "Since the
   sixth edition of this book, published in 2017, many economies around the
   world have continued to feel the aftershocks of the deepest recession
   since the Great Depression of the 1930s, which started with the
   well-publicised 'credit crunch'. Despite continuing academic debate
   about the causes and extent, there is now little doubt that climate
   change and global warming is beginning to have a significant impact on
   our physical environment.
Identifiers: LCCN 2019050392 (print) | LCCN 2019050393 (ebook) | ISBN
   9781292276540 (print) | ISBN 9781292276557 (epub) | ISBN 9781292276571
   (PDF)
Subjects: LCSH: Target marketing. | Marketing—Management.
Classification: LCC HF5415.127 .H66 2020 (print) | LCC HF5415.127 (ebook)
   | DDC 658.8/02—dc23
LC record available at https://lccn.loc.gov/2019050392
LC ebook record available at https://lccn.loc.gov/2019050393

10 9 8 7 6 5 4 3 2 1
24 23 22 21 20

Cover: © echo3005/Shutterstock

NOTE THAT ANY PAGE CROSS REFERENCES REFER TO THE PRINT EDITION

BRIEF CONTENTS

CONTENTS

PREFACE

Since the sixth edition of this book, published in 2017, many economies around the world have continued to feel the aftershocks of the deepest recession since the Great Depression of the 1930s, which started with the well-publicised 'credit crunch'. Despite continuing academic debate about the causes and extent, there is now little doubt that climate change and global warming is beginning to have a significant impact on our physical environment. Technology and the ever-growing acceptance and use of social media are having a profound effect on customer expectations, experience and behaviour.

Despite ongoing economic difficulties and turbulence, climate change has not been ignored, and it presents significant challenges and opportunities for businesses. Sustainable energy technologies, such as wind, solar, wave and thermal biomass, are now being pursued more vigorously and attempts to reduce energy consumption (of cars, buildings and airplanes) are creating new business opportunities. Increasingly, companies, public sector organisations, individuals and nations are adopting and implementing measures, such as sourcing more raw materials locally to reduce 'carbon miles' and limiting the use of high-emission travel options to reduce their carbon footprint.

In parallel, a technological revolution is in full swing: driverless cars are a reality, members of the Y generation communicate and share their feedback via social media, customers look for consistent experiences across all shopping channels, and even traditional business models such as the humble taxi have felt disruption – in this case from an app.

Within this context, throughout the seventh edition we have attempted to identify new approaches to doing business that promote sustainability, both for the organisations adopting them and for the environment (economic, social and natural) in which they operate.

Marketing Strategy and Competitive Positioning (7th edition) deals in general with the process of developing and implementing a marketing strategy. The text focuses on competitive positioning at the heart of marketing strategy, and includes in-depth discussion of the processes used in marketing to achieve competitive advantage within the context introduced above.

The text is primarily about creating and sustaining superior performance in the marketplace. It focuses on the two central issues in marketing strategy formulation – the *identification of target markets* and the *creation of a differential advantage*. In doing so, it recognises the emergence of potential new target markets born of the recession, increased concern for climate change and disruption from ongoing technological advances. It examines ways in which firms can differentiate offerings through recognition of environmental and social concerns and innovation.

Topics examined include service quality and relationship marketing, networks and alliances, innovation, internal marketing and corporate social responsibility. Emphasis is placed on the development of dynamic marketing capabilities, together with the need to reassess the role of marketing in the organisation as a critical process and not simply as a conventional functional specialisation.

The structure of the text

Part 1 is concerned with the fundamental changes that are taking place in how marketing operates in organisations, and the increasing focus on marketing as a process rather than as a functional specialisation. The central questions of the market orientation of organisations and the need to find better ways of responding to the volatile markets, lead us to emphasise the market-led approach to strategic management and the framework for developing marketing strategy that provides the structure for the rest of the text. Our framework for strategic marketing planning provides the foundation for two critical issues on which we focus throughout this text – *choice of market targets* and *building strong competitive positions*. Central to this approach is the resource-based view of marketing and the need to develop, nurture and deploy dynamic marketing capabilities.

Part 2 deals with the competitive environment in which the company operates, and draws specifically on recent changes brought about by recession and concerns for sustainability. Different types of strategic environment are first considered, together with the critical success factors for dealing with each type. Discussion then focuses on the 'strategic triangle' of customers, competitors and company in the context of the environment (social, economic and natural) in which the firm operates. Ways of analysing each in turn are explored to help identify the options open to the company. The emphasis is on matching corporate resources, assets and capabilities to market opportunities.

Part 3 examines in more detail the techniques available for identifying market segments (or potential targets) and current (and potential) positions. Alternative bases for segmenting consumer and business markets are explored, as are the data collection and analysis techniques available. Selection of market targets through consideration of the market attractiveness and business strength is addressed.

Part 4 returns to strategy formulation. The section opens with discussion of how to create a sustainable position in the marketplace. Three chapters are concerned with specific aspects of strategy formulation and execution. The chapter on competing through the marketing mix has been retained from the sixth edition, and expanded to reflect increasing use of new media to promote, distribute and create market offerings. The roles of customer service in relationship building and innovation to create competitive advantage are considered in depth.

Part 5 examines implementation issues in more detail. The section includes chapters on strategic customer management and corporate social responsibility, as well as updated chapters on strategic alliances and networks and internal marketing.

Part 6 provides our perspective on future competition and competitors. Various themes from earlier parts of the text are drawn together in order to identify major changes taking place in markets, the necessary organisational responses to those changes, and the competitive positioning strategies that might form the cornerstones of effective marketing in the future.

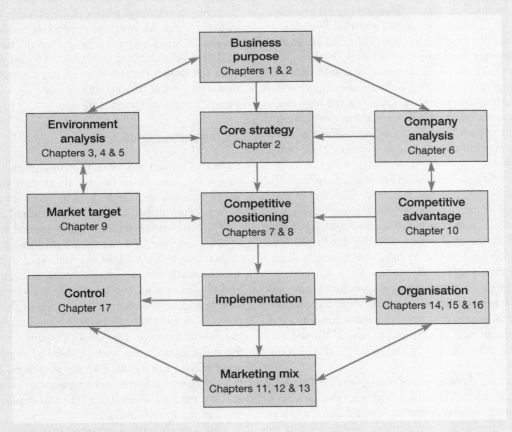

Source: Hooley, Nicoulaud, Rudd and Lee (2019).

New to this edition

- Updated content to reflect ongoing economic turbulence and its impact on business and marketing.
- Coverage of the impact of emerging markets on issues of marketing and innovation, and new realities of competing through services, market analysis and segmentation.
- Increased emphasis on competing through innovation, including new business models/new types of retailing.
- Increased emphasis on competing globally in a digital world.

- Updated vignettes at the beginning of most chapters, and new case studies in many of the chapters.
- Updated online resources, including an Instructor's Manual and PowerPoint slides for instructors, along with additional case studies for students.

This text is ideal for undergraduate and postgraduate students taking modules in Marketing Strategy, Marketing Management and Strategic Marketing Management.

ACKNOWLEDGEMENTS

We wish to acknowledge the support of many friends, colleagues, students and managers who have helped shape our ideas over the years.

More generally, thanks must go to Professor John Saunders, our friend, colleague and co-author of the first three editions of this text. John is an outstanding marketing scholar who has made a very significant contribution to both marketing thought and practice over the years. Much of his contribution to the early editions remains in the current edition and we thank him for his generosity in allowing it to continue to be included. Special thanks also to the late Professor Nigel Piercy. His contribution to the first six editions of the text was, and remains, significant!

We would also like to acknowledge the contributions of a number of outstanding management and marketing scholars with whom we have been fortunate to work and learn from over recent years: Professor Mike Ahearne, Professor Gary Armstrong, George Avlonitis, Rick Bagozzi, Amanda Beatson, Suzanne Beckmann, Jozsef Beracs, Pierre Berthon, Günther Botschen, Amanda Broderick, Rod Brodie, Peter Buckley, John Cadogan, Frank Cespedes, David Cook, David Cravens, Adamantios Diamantopoulos, Susan Douglas, Colin Egan, Heiner Evanschitztky, John Fahy, Krzysztof Fonfara, Gordon Foxall, Mark Gabbott, Brandan Gray, Gordon Greenley, Salah Hassan, J. Mac Hulbert, Peter Leeflang, Ian Lings, David Jobber, Hans Kasper, Costas Katsikeas, Philip Kotler, Giles Laurent, Gary Lilien, Jim Lynch, Malcolm MacDonald, Felix Mavondo, Sheelagh Mattear, Hafiz Mizra, Kristian Müller, Neil Morgan, Hans Muhlbacher, Leyland Pitt, Bodo Schlegelmilch, David Shipley, Stan Slater, Anne Souchon, Jan-Benedict Steenkamp, Vasilis Theohorakis, Rajan Varadarajan, Michel Wedel, David Wilson, Berend Wierenga, Jan Wieseke, Veronica Wong.

More personally:

Professor Brigitte Nicoulaud: My eternal gratitude to my husband Nick for his unwavering and empathetic support, and my mother for having taught me nothing is impossible.

Professor John M. Rudd: My deepest thanks goes to my wife Gail, my children George and Emily and my parents Dorothy and Peter. I quite literally couldn't have done it without you!

Professor Nick Lee: As always, I am deeply appreciative of the inspiration and support I receive from my wife, Laura. I would also like to thank my mother Trecia and my sister Meg for being such great examples for me over the years, and my nephew Brylie for always providing some perspective on life, in that I could always be building Lego or playing a computer game instead. I would also like to thank my wife's parents, Mark and Alison, and brother Huw for their constant kindness and support.

August 2019

PUBLISHER'S ACKNOWLEDGEMENTS

Text credits:

4 John Wiley & Sons: Doyle, P. (2008), Value Based Marketing, 2nd edn, London: John Wiley and Sons; **4-5 The Financial Times Limited:** Alice Hancock (2017) Younger consumers drive shift to ethical products. © The Financial Times Limited 2019. All Rights Reserved; **7 Harvard Business Publishing:** Felton, A.P. (1959), 'Making the marketing concept work', Harvard Business Review, 37(4), 55–65; **7 Pearson Education:** Kotler, P.C., Armstrong, G., Saunders, J.A. and Wong, V. (1996), Principles of Marketing: The European Edition, Hemel Hempstead: Prentice Hall; **7 SAGE Publications:** Ferrell, O.C. and Lucas, G.H. (1987), 'An evaluation of progress in the development of a definition of marketing', Journal of the Academy of Marketing Science, 15(3), 12–23; **7 American Marketing Association:** Definitions of Marketing, American Marketing Association 2003; **7 Marketing Science Institute:** Webster, F.E. (1997), 'The future role of marketing in the organisation', in D.R. Lehmann and K.E. Jocz (eds), Reflections on the Futures of Marketing, Cambridge, MA: Marketing Science Institute, pp. 39–66; **8 American Marketing Association:** Kohli, A.K. and Jaworski, B.J. (1990), 'Market orientation: The construct, research propositions and managerial implications', Journal of Marketing, 54(2), 1–18; **8 American Marketing Association:** Narver, J.C. and Slater, S.F. (1990), 'The effect of a market orientation on business profitability', Journal of Marketing, 54(4), 20–35; **13-14 John Wiley & Sons:** Christensen, C. and Bower, J. (1996), 'Customer power, strategic investment and the failure of leading firms', Strategic Management Journal, 17(3), 197–218; **16 John Wiley & Sons:** Doyle, P. (2008), Value Based Marketing, 2nd edn, London: John Wiley and Sons; **18 John Lewis Partnership plc:** Sir Charlie Mayfield, Chairman of the John Lewis Partnership; **20 Simon & Schuster:** Levitt, T. (1986), The Marketing Imagination, New York: The Free Press; **21 Marketing Science Institute:** Greyser, S.A. (1997), 'Janus and marketing: The past, present and prospective future of marketing', in D.R. Lehmann and K.R. Jocz (eds), Reflections on the Futures of Marketing, Cambridge, MA: Marketing Science Institute; **22 Macmillan Publishers:** Toffler, A. (1981), The Third Wave, William Collins/Pan Books; **25-27 The Financial Times Limited:** from Milne, R. (2015) 'Lego enters a new dimension with its digital strategy', Financial Times, September 27, 2015. © The Financial Times Limited 2019. All Rights Reserved; **28 Pearson Education:** Johnson, G., Scholes, K. and Whittington, R. (2008), Exploring Corporate Strategy: Text and Cases, 8th edn, London: Financial Times/Prentice Hall; **28 Peters, Fraser & Dunlop:** Sir John Harvey Jones, Chairman of Imperial Chemical Industries (ICI) 1982–1987; **28-29 The Financial Times Limited:** Nic Fildes (2017), Three brings Smarty to the low-cost mobile party, © The Financial Times Limited 2019. All Rights Reserved; **30 Eden Project:** Tim Smit, founder and chief executive of the Eden Project in Cornwall; **32 Harvard Business Publishing:** Hamel, G. and Prahalad, C.K. (1989), 'Strategic intent', Harvard Business Review, 67(3), 63–76; **32 Mars, Incorporated and its Affiliates.:** Mars website, https://www.mars.com/global/about-us/five-principles - accessed January, 2019; **33 Sheilas Wheels:** Sheilas Wheels; **35-36 HarperCollins:** Drucker, P. (1973). Management: Tasks, Responsibilities, Practices. New York: Harper & Row; **39 Times Newspapers Limited:** Hurley, James (2019) Fender identifies its customers to stay in tune with the times, March 11 2019, Times Newspapers Limited; **51-52 The Financial Times Limited:** from Mishkin, S. (2014) Amazon eyes online sales boost through "Fire" smartphone, Financial Times, 19 June. © The Financial Times Limited 2019. All Rights Reserved; **56-57 The Financial Times Limited:** Plimmer, Gill. (2018) 'Nimble' consultancy focuses on quick response to disruption, JANUARY 18 2018, © The Financial Times Limited 2019. All Rights Reserved; **56 John Hagel:** Quote by John Hagel; **58 Marketing Science Institute:** Haeckel, S. (1997), 'Preface', in D.R. Lehmann and K.R. Jocz (eds), Reflections on the Futures of Marketing, Cambridge, MA: Marketing Science Institute; **60 International Monetary Fund:** (Figure 3.2) International Monetary Fund (April 2019); **63 Nike, Inc.:** Nike's advertising; **63 Barclays:** (Figure 3.5) Talking About My Generation: Exploring the Benefits Engagement Challenge, September 2013, Barclays; **64 Centaur Media plc:** Lyons, Erin. (2018) Localised marketing, GDPR, digital skills: 5 killer stats to start your week, 24 September 2018, Marketing Week; **67 NCTA:** (Figure 3.6) Infographic: The Growth Of The Internet Of

Things, NCTA, May 5 2014; **69 The Financial Times Limited:** Lewin, J. (2016) Laura Ashley shares fall 9.3% as profits wilt, Financial Times, March 23. © The Financial Times Limited 2019. All Rights Reserved; **69 John Wiley & Sons:** Kotler, P., Kartajaya, H. and Setiawan, I., (2018), 'Marketing 4.0', The Marketing Journal, May 5; **71 The Marketing Journal:** Hagel, J. (2016), 'Strategy made simple, the 3 Core Strategy Questions', The Journal of Marketing, October 27; **71 The Marketing Journal:** Sarkar, C. and Kotler, P. (2019), 'Ecosystem Marketing: The Future of Competition', The Marketing Journal, February 21; **72 Simon & Schuster:** (Figure 3.7) from Competitive Strategy: Techniques for Analyzing Industries and Competitors (by Michael E. Porter, 1998) Reprinted with the permission of Free Press, a Division of Simon & Schuster, Inc., Copyright © 1980, 1998by The Free Press. All rights reserved; **77 iLounge, Inc:** (Figure 3.9) iPodlounge.com; **78 BioAge Group:** (Figure 3.10) US Sales of Hybrids Down 50% in November, 2008, Green Car Congress; **81 Taylor & Francis Group:** (Figure 3.12) O'Shaughnessy, J. (1995), Competitive Marketing, 3rd edn, London: Routledge; **90-93 The Financial Times Limited:** (Case study V3.2 and Figure 3.17 & 3.18) Peter Campbell and Michael Pooler, "Dyson: a British inventor pivots to Asia" in London and Stefania Palma in Sydney OCTOBER 26, 2018. © The Financial Times Limited 2019. All Rights Reserved; **94 Elsevier:** Hill, R. (1979), 'Weak signals from the unknown', International Management, 34(10), 55–60; **94-95 The Financial Times Limited:** from Hale, T. (2015) Amadeus set to soar on airline bookings, Financial Times, 26 February. © The Financial Times Limited 2019. All Rights Reserved; **99 Guardian News & Media:** Heather Tomlinson and Rob Evans "Tesco stocks up on inside knowledge of shoppers' lives" The Guardian, 20 September 2005; **100 Elsevier:** Crouch, S. and Housden, M. (2003), Marketing Research for Managers, 3rd edn, London: Butterworth-Heinemann; **102 John Wiley & Sons:** Bradley, U. (1987), Applied Marketing and Social Research, 2nd edn, Chichester: John Wiley; **109 Pearson Education:** Lilien, G.L., Kotler, P. and Moorthy, K.S. (1992), Marketing Models, Hemel Hempstead: Prentice Hall International; **109 Forbes Media LLC:** Columbus, L. (2016), 'Ten Ways Big Data Is Revolutionizing Marketing and Sales', Forbes, May 9; **111-113 The Financial Times Limited:** (Case Study V4.2 and Figures 4.9 & 4.10) Bradshaw, T. (2018) Amazon and Google lead way on virtual assistant dealmaking at CES, Financial Times, 9 January. © The Financial Times Limited 2019. All Rights Reserved; **114-115 The Financial Times Limited:** from Sherwood, B. (2010) Gatwick seeks greater competition with BAA', Financial Times, 21 June. © The Financial Times Limited 2019. All Rights Reserved; **115 & 137 Hachette:** Clavell, J. (ed.) (1981), The Art of War by Sun Tzu, London: Hodder and Stoughton; **120 McGraw-Hill Education:** (Figure 5.2) Adapted from Lehmann, D.R. and Winer, R.S. (1991), Analysis for Marketing Planning, 2nd edn, Homewood, IL: Irwin; **126 Nike, Inc:** Nike's slogan; **137-139 The Financial Times Limited:** from Whipp, L. and Shotter, J. (2015) Adidas struggles to catch up with Nike's runaway success', Financial Times, 7 August. © The Financial Times Limited 2019. All Rights Reserved; **140 Marketing Director, International Food Marketing Company:** Marketing Director, International Food Marketing Company; **140-141 The Financial Times Limited:** Rachel Sanderson (2017), Moncler scraps catwalk shows for the social media generation, © The Financial Times Limited 2019. All Rights Reserved; **143 Marketing Science Institute:** Day, G.S. (1997), 'Aligning the organisation to the market', in D.R. Lehmann and K.E. Jocz (eds), Reflections on the Futures of Marketing, Cambridge, MA: Marketing Science Institute; **144, 145 Harvard Business Publishing:** Hamel, G. (1996), 'Strategy as revolution', Harvard Business Review, 74 (4), 9 –82; **144 Harvard Business Publishing:** Porter, M.E. (1996), 'What is strategy?', Harvard Business Review, 74(6), 61–78; **146 John Wiley & Sons:** Grant, R.M. (1995), Contemporary Strategy Analysis, 2nd edn, Cambridge, MA: Basil Blackwell; **147 John Wiley & Sons:** Helfat, C.E., Finkelstein, S., Mitchell, W., Peteraf, M.A., Singh, H., Teece, D.J. and Winter, S.G. (2007), Dynamic Capabilities: Understanding Change in Organisations, Oxford: Blackwell Publishing; **148 The Institute for Operations Research and the Management Sciences:** Zollo, M. and Winter, S.G. (2002), 'Deliberate learning and the evolution of dynamic capabilities', Organisation Science, 13(3), 339–51; **151 Interbrand:** (Table 6.1) Interbrand "Best Global Brands" ranking data (2009, 2013, 2018); **154 Mujirushi ryohin:** Mujirushi ryohin; **157 Audi AG:** Audi AG; **161 Institute for Operations Research and the Management Sciences:** Zollo, M. and Winter, S.G. (2002), 'Deliberate learning and the evolution of dynamic capabilities', Organisation Science, 13(3), 339–51; **163 Harvard Business Publishing:** (Figure 6.9) Adapted from Hamel, G. and Prahalad, C.K. (1994), Competing for the Future, Boston, MA: Harvard Business School Press; **164-167 (Case Study 6.1 and Figures 6.10, 6.11 & 6.12) The Financial Times Limited:** Tom Hancock (2019), Why Ford is stalling in China while Toyota succeeds, © The Financial Times Limited 2019. All Rights Reserved; **170-171 The Economist Newspaper Limited:** From The Economist "Why retired people could be ideal customers for self-driving cars" Print edition, Business Feb 21st 2019; **173 Pearson Education:** Kotler, P.C. (1997), Marketing

Management: Analysis, Planning, Implementation and Control, 9th edn, Hemel Hempstead: Prentice Hall International; **174 Jay Reno:** Jay Reno, Feather Furniture Founder; **174 McGraw-Hill Education:** Ries, A. and Trout, J. (1982), Positioning: The Battle for Your Mind, New York: McGraw-Hill; **176 Taylor & Francis Group:** Piercy, N.F. and Morgan, N.A. (1993), 'Strategic and operational market segmentation: A managerial analysis', Journal of Strategic Marketing, 1, 123–40; **179 Centaur Media plc:** Rogers, C. (2017), The Shrinking and Emerging Demographics that Marketers need to know, Marketing Week, 13 March; **179 Elaine Rogrigo:** Danone's Chief Strategy and Insights Officer, Elaine Rogrigo; **181 The Market Research Society:** (Table 7.1) from Occupation Groupings: A Job Dictionary, 6th ed, 2006. ttps://www.mrs.org.uk/pdf/occgroups6.pdf. The Market Research Society; **189 Centaur Media plc:** Rogers, C. (2019), Why behaviour beats demographics when it comes to segmentation, Marketing Week, April 16; **195 The European Marketing Confederation:** McDonald, M. (2017), Market Segmentation: still the bedrock of commercial success, The Marketing Journal, October 17; **196 Laing Henry:** Laing, H. (1991), Brand Advertising Targeting System, London: Laing Henry; **196 Centaur Media plc:** Young, D. (1996), 'The politics behind market segmentation', Marketing News, October 21, p. 17; **196 Harvard Business Publishing:** Shapiro, B.P. and Bonoma, T.V. (1990), 'How to segment industrial markets', in R.J. Dolan (ed.), Strategic Marketing Management, Cambridge, MA: Harvard Business School Press; **199-201 The Economist Newspaper Limited:** The Economist "First-class air travel is in decline" Print edition, International Mar 9th 2019, DUBAI; **202-203 The Financial Times Limited:** Long, C. (2018) Sole woman: Nike embraces female footwear, 28 February. © The Financial Times Limited 2019. All Rights Reserved; **205 Springer Nature:** Palmatier, R. and Sridhar, S. (2017), Marketing Strategy: Based on First Principles and Data Analytics, Palgrave; **206 University of Chicago Press:** Evans, F.B. (1959), 'Psychological and objective factors in the prediction of brand choice', Journal of Business, 32, October, 340–69; **209 Taylor & Francis Group:** (Figure 8.1) Based on Maier, J. and Saunders, J.A. (1990), 'The implementation of segmentation in sales management', The Journal of Personal Selling and Sales Management, 10(1), 39–48; **212 SAGE Publications:** (Table 8.1) Based on Punj, G. and Stewart, D.W. (1983), 'Cluster analysis in marketing research: Review and suggestions for applications', Journal of Marketing Research, 20(May), 135–48; **215 John Wiley & Sons:** Calder, B.J. (1994), 'Qualitative marketing research', in Richard P. Bagozzi (ed.), Principles of Marketing Research, Boston, MA: Blackwell; **217**

Pearson Education: Tull, D.S. and Hawkins, D.I. (1993), Marketing Research: Measurement and Method, 6th edn, Englewood Cliffs, NJ: Prentice Hall; **226-229 The Financial Times Limited:** (VBox 8.2 and Figures 8.9, 8.11 & 8.12) John Gapper (2018) How millennials became the world's most powerful consumers, The Financial Times. © The Financial Times Limited 2019. All Rights Reserved; **227 The Financial Times Limited:** (Figure 8.9) John Gapper (2018) How millennials became the world's most powerful consumers, The Financial Times. © The Financial Times Limited 2019. All Rights Reserved; **230 Hachette:** Clavell, J. (ed.) (1981), The Art of War by Sun Tzu, London: Hodder and Stoughton; **230-231 The Economist Newspaper Limited:** "Harley-Davidson brought low by tariffs and demographics" Sales keep plunging in the home market, The Economist Print edition, Business Feb 2nd 2019, MILWAUKEE; **232 Taylor & Francis Group:** (Figure 9.1) Adapted from Piercy, N.F. (1997), Market-Led Strategic Change: Transforming the Process of Going to Market, 2nd edn, Oxford: Butterworth-Heinemann; **232 The Financial Times Limited:** Porter, quoted in Jackson, T. (1997), 'Dare to be different', Financial Times, June 19. © The Financial Times Limited 2019. All Rights Reserved; **233 Stanley Marcus:** Stanley Marcus of Neimann Marcus; **235 The Marketing Journal:** Sarkar, C. and Kotler, P. (2019), 'Ecosystem Marketing: The Future of Competition', The Marketing Journal, February 21; **235 IDEA BITE PRESS:** Ulwick, A. W., (2016), Jobs to be done: Theory to Practice, Idea Bite Press; **236 The Financial Times Limited:** Miln, R. (2019) Ikea to trial furniture leasing in business overhaul, Financial Times 4 February. © The Financial Times Limited 2019. All Rights Reserved; **236 John Wiley & Sons:** Kotler, P., Kartajaya, H. and Setiawan, I., (2017), Marketing 4.0 Moving from Traditional to Digital, Wiley; **237 The Financial Times Limited:** de Burton, S. (2019) Can hybrid watches hijack the ascent of the smartwatch? Financial Times, 21 March. © The Financial Times Limited 2019. All Rights Reserved; **242 Elsevier:** Piercy, N.F. (1997), Market-Led Strategic Change: Transforming the Process of Going to Market, 2nd edn, Oxford: Butterworth-Heinemann; **242 The National Association of Cider Makers:** National Association of Cider Makers; **243 James Dyson:** James Dyson; **248 Pearson Education:** Kotler, P. and Keller, K. (2016), Marketing Management, 15th edn, Pearson; **249 Glaxo Group Limited:** Lucozade brand slogan; **249 LUCOZADE:** Lucozade brand slogan; **250 Nike, Inc:** Nike Slogan; **251-252 The Financial Times Limited:** Boland, V. and Wild, J. (2014) No-frills Ryanair faces test with Business Plus, Financial Times, 27 August. © The Financial Times Limited 2019. All Rights Reserved; **256 Simon**

& Schuster: Michael Porter "Competitive Advantage: Creating and Sustaining Superior Performance" Free Press (1985); **256-257 The Financial Times Limited:** Jung-a, S. (2015) Samsung to launch new mobile payment service in the US, Financial Times, 25 September. © The Financial Times Limited 2019. All Rights Reserved; **262 Ryanair DAC:** Ryanair Slogan; **267 Steve Jobs:** Quote by Steve Jobs; **270 Heineken N.V:** Heineken N.V; **270 Nike, Inc:** Nike Slogan; **270-271, 273-274 Centaur Media plc:** Vizard, S. (2018), 'Nike 'proud' of Colin Kaepernick ad as campaign drives 'record engagement', Marketing Week, September 26; **271 Industry Dive:** Huff, Travis. (2014) How Starbucks Crushes It on Social Media, Aug. 23 2014, Industry Dive; **272 Audi AG:** Audi Slogan; **273 Centaur Media plc:** Barnett, M. (2018), 'How brands are finally realising the full potential of personalisation', Marketing Week, November 13; **273 The Marketing Journal:** "Scaling Trust: Marketing in a New Key" – An Interview with John Hagel III " The Marketing Journal (2016, January 15); **280 Pelanduk Publications:** Khoo, P.C. (1992), Sun Tzu and Management, Petaling Jaya, Malaysia: Pelanduk; **283 Pearson Education:** Kotler, P. and Keller, K. (2016), Marketing Management, 15th edn, Pearson; **286 The Financial Times Limited:** Reed, J. (2010) Volvo's heart will "remain in Sweden", Financial Times, 29 March. © The Financial Times Limited 2019. All Rights Reserved; **287 President & Fellows of Harvard College:** Culliton, J. (1948), The Management of Marketing Costs, Boston, MA: Harvard University Graduate School of Business Administration, Research Division; **287 Cambridge University Press:** Borden, N. (1964), 'The concept of the marketing mix', Journal of Advertising Research, 4, 2–7; **287 The Financial Times Limited:** Gray, A. (2019) McDonald's to buy AI company Dynamic Yield, Financial Times in New York, 25 March. © The Financial Times Limited 2019. All Rights Reserved; **290 Simon & Schuster:** Rogers, E. (1962), Diffusion of Innovations, New York: The Free Press; **290-291 Simon & Schuster:** Parasuraman, A. and Colby, C.L. (2001), Techno-Ready Marketing: How and Why Your Customers Adopt Technology, New York: Free Press; **295 New Scientist Ltd:** (Figure 11.5) Mullins, J. (2004) The next generation, New Scientist, Reed Business Information Ltd; **295 Statista:** (Figure 11.6) Based on CIPA: StatistaCharts; **296 Statista:** (Figure 11.7) Based on nfoTrends via Bitkom: StatisticaCharts; **297 Newzoo:** (Table 11.1) Martin Armstrong, Feb 16, 2018, Statista, Data taken from Newzoo; **299 Forbes Media LLC:** Morgan, J. (2014), A Simple Explanation of the "Internet of Things", Forbes, 13 May; **299 Harvard Business Publishing:** Dawar, N. (2018), Marketing in the Age of Alexa, Harvard Business Review, May-June; **300 Canalys:** (Figure 11.8) Canalys forecasts, Mobility services, April 2019; **305 Springer Nature:** Simon, H. (2015), Confessions of the Pricing Man: How Price Affects Everything, Springer International Publishing, Switzerland; **307 World Advertising Research Center,:** Maunder, S., Harris, A., Bamford, J., Cook, L. and Cox, A. (2005), 'O2: It only works if it works – how troubled BT Cellnet was transformed into thriving O2', in A. Hoad (ed.), Advertising Works 13: Proving the Effectiveness of Marketing Communications, Henley-on-Thames, World Advertising Research Centre; **310 John Wiley & Sons:** Kotler, P., Kartajaya, H. and Setiawan, I., (2017), Marketing 4.0 Moving from Traditional to Digital, Wiley; **311 Opresnik Management Consulting:** Opresnik, M. O., Kotler, P. and Hollensen, S. (2017), 'Social Media Marketing. A Practioner Guide', 3rd ed., Opresnik Management Consulting, 2019; **311 Springer Nature:** Backaler, J. & Shankman, P. (2018), Digital Influence: Unleash the Power of Influencer Marketing to Accelerate Your Global Business, Palgrave Macmillan; **313 Elsevier:** Verhoef, P.C., Kannan, P.K. and Inman, J.J. (2015), From multi-channel retailing to omni-channel retailing: introduction to the Special Issue on Multi-Channel Retailing, Journal of Retailing, 91(2): 174-81; **313 The Omnichannel Opportunity: Unlocking the power of the connected consumer, Deloitte 2014:** (Figure 11.13) The Omnichannel Opportunity: Unlocking the power of the connected consumer, Deloitte 2014; **317 John Wiley & Sons:** Kotler, P., Kartajaya, H. and Setiawan, I., (2017), Marketing 4.0 Moving from Traditional to Digital, Wiley; **318-319 The Financial Times Limited:** Gray, S. & Walker, K. (2019) How ABB FIA Formula E championship built a fan base from scratch, Financial Times, 10 April. © The Financial Times Limited 2019. All Rights Reserved; **320 The Financial Times Limited:** Howlett, A. (2019) Fitness trackers enter the pet insurance market. Regularly exercised dogs can collar premium discounts for their owners, Financial Times, 27 March. © The Financial Times Limited 2019. All Rights Reserved; **323 Harvard Business Publishing:** Christensen, C., Anthony, S.D. and Roth, E.A. (2004), Seeing What's Next: Using the Theories of Innovation to Predict Industry Change, Boston, MA: Harvard Business School Press; **323 IBM Corporation:** IBM tagline; **323 Elsevier:** Piercy, N.F. (2009a), Market-Led Strategic Change: Transforming the Process of Going to Market, 4th edn, Oxford: Butterworth-Heinemann; **325 Daimler AG:** Daimler slogan; **326 Elsevier:** (Figure 12.2) Adapted from Piercy, N. (2017), Market-Led Strategic Change: Everything Has Changed, But Everything is the Same, Abingdon, UK: Routledge; **327 Harvard Business Publishing:** Christensen, C.M., Kaufman, S.P. and Shih, W.C. (2008), 'Innovation killers', Harvard Business Review, January, 98–105; **327 Bloomberg L.P:** Arndt, M. and Einhorn, B. (2010), 'The 50 most innovative companies', Bloomberg BusinessWeek, April 25, pp. 34–40; **328 Harvard Business Publishing:** Christensen, C.M. (1997), The Innovator's Dilemma: When New Technologies Cause Great Firms to Fail, Boston, MA: Harvard Business School Press; **329 Harvard Business Publishing:** Christensen, C.M. and Raynor, M.E. (2003), The Innovator's Solution: Creating and Sustaining Successful Growth, Boston, MA: Harvard Business School Press; **330 SAGE Publications:** Chandy, R.K. and Tellis, G.J. (1998a), Organising for Radical Product Innovation, Boston, MA: Marketing Science Institute, Report, 98–102; **331 Harvard Business Publishing:** Hamel, G. (2000), Leading the Revolution, Boston, MA: Harvard Business School Press; **332 The Financial Times Limited:** Kay, J. (2009) Innovation is not about wearing a white coat, Financial Times, December 16, p. 17. © The Financial Times Limited 2019. All Rights Reserved; **334 Harvard Business Publishing:** Schmitt, B.H. (2007), Big Think Strategy: How to Leverage Bold Ideas and Leave Small Thinking Behind, Boston, MA: Harvard Business School Press; **334 The Financial Times Limited:** Allison, K. (2008) Apple unveils iPhone grand plan, Financial Times, 10 March, p. 23. © The Financial Times Limited 2019. All Rights Reserved; **334 Pearson Education:** Gratton, L. (2007), Hot Spots: Why Some Companies Buzz With Innovation – And Others Don't, Harlow: FT/Prentice Hall; **335 Harvard Business Publishing:** Ancona, D. and Bresman, H. (2007), X-Teams: How to Build Teams That Lead, Innovate and Succeed, Boston, MA: Harvard Business School Press; **335 The Financial Times Limited:** Mallett, V. and Crabtree, J. (2015) The American connection, Financial Times, May 25, p. 12. © The Financial Times Limited 2019. All Rights Reserved; **338 Bloomberg L.P:** Hamm, S. (2006), 'Speed demons', BusinessWeek, March 27, pp. 67–76; **340 Fortune Media IP:** Morris, Betsy. (2008) What Makes Apple Golden, March 17, 2008, Fortune Media IP; **341 Allen and Hamilton Inc:** (Figure 12.5) Booz, Allen and Hamilton (1982), New Products Management for the 1980s, New York: Booz, Allen and Hamilton Inc.; **352-353 The Financial Times Limited:** Bradshaw, T. and Waters, R. (2014) Apple moves into fashion business with Watch launch, Financial Times, 10 September. © The Financial Times Limited 2019. All Rights Reserved; **354 The Financial Times Limited:** Skapinker, M. (2003) Awkward customers, Financial Times, February 12, p. 12. © The Financial Times Limited 2019. All Rights Reserved; **354-355 The Financial Times Limited:** Fulton, C. (2018) Halfords boosted by fall in new car sales, Financial Times, 4 September. © The Financial Times Limited 2019. All Rights Reserved; **355 Harvard Business Publishing:** Womack J.P. and Jones, D.T. (2005), 'Lean consumption', Harvard Business Review, March, 58–68; **355 Toyota Motor Corporation:** Lexus Slogan; **357 John Lewis Partnership plc:** John Lewis Partnership plc http://www.johnlewispartnership.co.uk/about/our-principles/generating-loyalty-through-choice-value-and-service.html, accessed 2015, October 15; **358 Emerald Publishing Limited:** Coyles, S. and Gokey, T.C. (2005), 'Customer retention is not enough', Journal of Consumer Marketing, 22 (2), 101–5; **361 ROLLS-ROYCE PLC:** ROLLS-ROYCE PLC Slogan; **362 Westburn Publishers Ltd:** Piercy, N.F., Cravens, D.W. and Lane, N. (2010a), 'Marketing out of the recession: Recovery is coming, but things will never be the same again', Marketing Review, 10(1), 3–23; **362 Elsevier:** Piercy, N.F. (2009d), 'Ryanair: The master of non-service strategy', in N.F. Piercy, Market-Led Strategic Change: Transforming the Process of Going to Market, 4th edn, Oxford: Butterworth-Heinemann, pp. 46–48; **362 Ryanair DAC:** Ryanair's slogan; **362 The Financial Times Limited:** Mitchell, A. (2008) If you want to be loved, just do it right, Financial Times, March 27, p. 16. © The Financial Times Limited 2019. All Rights Reserved; **363 John Wiley & Sons:** Price, B. and Jaffe, D. (2008), The Best Service Is No Service: How to Liberate Your Customers From Customer Service, Keep them Happy and Control Costs, San Francisco, CA: Jossey Bass; **365 Elsevier:** (Figure 13.4) Payne, A., Christopher, M., Clark, M. and Peck, H. (1995), Relationship Marketing for Competitive Advantage, Oxford: Butterworth-Heinemann; **369 Penguin Random House:** Kawasaki, G. (2012), Enchantment: The Art of Changing Hearts, Minds and Actions – How to Woo, Influence and Persuade, London: Portfolio/Penguin; **369 Harvard Business Publishing:** Dixon, M., Freeman, K. and Toman, N. (2010), 'STOP trying to delight your customers', Harvard Business Review, July–August, 116–22; **369 The Financial Times Limited:** Skapinker, M. (2003) Awkward customers, Financial Times, February 12, p. 12. © The Financial Times Limited 2019. All Rights Reserved; **370 American Marketing Association (AMA):** (Figure 13.6) Parasuraman, A., Zeithaml, V.A. and Berry, L.L. (1985), 'A conceptual model of service quality and the implications for further research', Journal of Marketing, Fall, 41–50; **373 The Financial Times Limited:** Edmunds, M. (2000) Your wish is on my database, Financial Times, February 28, p. 16. © The Financial Times Limited 2019. All Rights Reserved; **374 Elsevier:** Knox, S., Maklan, S., Payne, A., Peppard, J. and Ryals, L. (2003), Customer Relationship Management: Perspectives from the Marketplace, Oxford: Butterworth-Heinemann; **377 Simon & Schuster:** Berry, L.L. and

Parasuraman, A. (1991), Marketing Services: Competing Through Quality, New York: The Free Press; **379 American Marketing Association (AMA):** (Figure 13.11) Parasuraman, A., Zeithaml, V.A. and Berry, L.L. (1985), 'A conceptual model of service quality and the implications for further research', Journal of Marketing, Fall, 41–50; **381-383 The Financial Times Limited:** Allen, K. (2014) Property portals hand control to homeowners, Financial Times, 22 August. © The Financial Times Limited 2019. All Rights Reserved; **387 Harvard Business Publishing:** Thomas Stewart, writing in the Harvard Business Review in 2006; **387-388 The Financial Times Limited:** Kuchler, H. (2017) Hacker-for-hire company Synack raises $21m, Financial Times, April 2011. © The Financial Times Limited 2019. All Rights Reserved; **389 The Financial Times Limited:** Ward, A. and Waldmeir, P. (2014) Big Pharma fights back from China scandal, Financial Times, April 3, p. 21. © The Financial Times Limited 2019. All Rights Reserved; **389 The Financial Times Limited:** Andrew, J. and Waldmeir, P. (2013) Bribery fears infect drug dealings in China, Financial Times, September 24, 19. © The Financial Times Limited 2019. All Rights Reserved; **391 Harvard Business Publishing:** Levitt, T. (1960), 'Marketing myopia', Harvard Business Review, 38(4), 45–56; **391 Harper & Row:** Drucker, P. (1973), Management: Tasks, Responsibilities and Practices, New York: Harper & Row; **394 Taylor & Francis Group:** Leigh, T.W., and Marshall, G.W. (2001), 'Research priorities in sales strategy and performance', Journal of Personal Selling & Sales Management, 21 (Spring), 83–94; **395 Elsevier:** Ingram, T.N., LaForge, R.W. and Leigh, T.W. (2002), 'Selling in the new millennium: A joint agenda', Industrial Marketing Management, 31, 559–67; **395 Harvard Business Publishing:** Shapiro, B.P., Slywotsky, A.J. and Doyle, S.X. (1998), Strategic Sales Management: A Boardroom Issue, Note 9-595-018, Cambridge, MA: Harvard Business School; **395 Mazur:** Mazur, L. (2000), 'The changing face of sales', Marketing Business, May, 31; **395 Academy of Management:** Homburg, C., Workman, J.P. and Jensen, O. (2000), 'Fundamental changes in marketing organisation: The movement toward a customer-focused organisational structure', Journal of the Academy of Marketing Science, 28(4), 459–78; **397 Harvard Business Publishing:** Shapiro, B.P., Slywotsky, A.J. and Doyle, S.X. (1998), Strategic Sales Management: A Boardroom Issue, Note 9-595-018, Cambridge, MA: Harvard Business School; **397 Oxford University Press:** Piercy, N.F. and Lane, N. (2009a), Strategic Customer Management: Strategizing the Sales Organisation, Oxford: Oxford University Press; **398 Harvard Business Publishing:** Cespedes, F.V. (2014), 'Putting sales at the centre of strategy', Harvard Business Review, October, 23–5; **400 SAMA:** Seidenschwartz, W. (2005), 'A model for customer enthusiasm: Connecting the customer with internal processes', Strategic Account Management Association Conference, February, Paris; **402 Harvard Business Publishing:** Shapiro, B.P., Slywotsky, A.J. and Doyle, S.X. (1998), Strategic Sales Management: A Boardroom Issue, Note 9-595-018, Cambridge, MA: Harvard Business School; **410 IMI plc:** IMI plc (2010), IMI plc – Key Themes, www.imi.plc.uk/about; **414 Elsevier:** Piercy, N.F. and Lane, N. (2006a), 'The underlying vulnerabilities in key account management strategies', European Management Journal, 24(2–3), 151–82; **420-421 The Financial Times Limited:** Manson, K. (2014) Power of the "mummies" key to Nestlé's strategy in DR Congo, Financial Times, 1 October. © The Financial Times Limited 2019. All Rights Reserved; **423 Penguin Random House:** Gibbs, R. and Humphries, A. (2009), Strategic Alliances & Marketing Partnerships: Gaining Competitive Advantage Through Collaboration and Partnering, London: Kogan Page; **423 The Viscount Palmerston:** Attributed to Henry John Temple, Viscount Lord Palmerston 1784–1865, Foreign Secretary and Prime Minister of Great Britain during Queen Victoria's reign; **423 The Financial Times Limited:** Edgecliffe-Johnson, A. (2015) MasterCard cashes in on smart transit, Financial Times, 2 July. © The Financial Times Limited 2019. All Rights Reserved; **426 SAGE Publications:** Miles, R.E. and Snow, C.C. (1984), 'Fit, failure, and the hall of fame', California Management Review, Spring, 10–28; **429 SAGE Publications:** Webster, F.E. (1992), 'The changing role of marketing in the corporation', Journal of Marketing, 56(4), 1–17; **436 Academy of Marketing Science:** Achrol, R. (1997), 'Changes in the theory of interorganisational relations in marketing: Toward a network paradigm', Journal of the Academy of Marketing Science, 25(1), 56–71; **436 Emerald Publishing Limited:** Gummesson, E. (1994), 'Service management: An evaluation and the future', International Journal of Service Industry Management, 5(1), 77–96; **436 Academy of Marketing Science:** Achrol, R. (1997), 'Changes in the theory of interorganisationa relations in marketing: Toward a network paradigm', Journal of the Academy of Marketing Science, 25(1), 56–71; **437 Bloomberg L.P:** Engardio, P. (2009), 'Why NCR said, "let's go back home"', BusinessWeek, August 24 and 31, p. 19; **438 The Financial Times Limited:** Mallaby, S. (2013), 'American industry is on the move' Financial Times, January 9, p. 13. © The Financial Times Limited 2019. All Rights Reserved; **438 American Marketing Association:** Lambert, D.M., Emmelhainz, M.A. and Gardner, J.T. (1996), 'So you think you want to be a partner?', Marketing Management, Summer, 25–41; **442, 444**

Simon & Schuster: Quinn, J.B. (1992), Intelligent Enterprise, New York: Free Press; **444 Emerald Publishing Limited:** Bensimon, S. (1999), 'Strategic alliances', Executive Excellence, 16(10), 9; **445 Emerald Publishing Limited:** Gummesson, E. (1994), 'Service management: An evaluation and the future', International Journal of Service Industry Management, 5(1), 77–96; **447 Elsevier:** (Table 15.1) Cravens, K., Piercy, N. and Cravens, D.W. (2000), 'Assessing the performance of strategic alliances: Matching metrics to strategies', European Management Journal, 18(5), 529–41; **449-451 The Financial Times Limited:** Wright, R. (2014) UPS and FedEx turn focus to consumer behaviour, Financial Times, 12 August. © The Financial Times Limited 2019. All Rights Reserved; **452 Harvard Business Publishing:** Martin, R.L. (2010), 'The execution trap', Harvard Business Review, July–August, 64–71; **452 Harvard Business Publishing:** Nayar, V. (2010), Employees First, Customers Second: Turning Conventional Management Upside Down, Cambridge, MA: Harvard Business Press; **452-453 The Financial Times Limited:** Beesley, A. & Rovnick, N. (2018) Ryanair cancels flights after strike by pilots and cabin crew, Financial Times, 28 September. © The Financial Times Limited 2019. All Rights Reserved; **454 Centaur Media plc:** Croft, M. (2007), 'Training and development: Brand ambassadors', Marketing Week, March 8, p. 39; **455 Hampton Inn hotel:** Hampton Inn hotel Slogan; **456 Elsevier:** Piercy, N.F. (2009), Market-Led Strategic Change: Transforming the Process of Going to Market, 4th edn, Oxford: Butterworth-Heinemann; **458 Emerald Publishing Limited:** Freedman, M. (2003), 'The genius is in the implementation', Journal of Business Strategy, March/April, 26–31; **458-459 Elsevier:** Hrebiniak, L.G. (2006), 'Obstacles to effective strategy implementation', Organisational Dynamics, 35(1), 12–31; **459 John Wiley & Sons:** Alexander, L.D. (1991), 'Strategy implementation: Nature of the problem', in D. Hussey (ed.), International Review of Strategic Management, 2(1), 74; **459 Springer Nature:** Piercy, N.F. (1998), 'Marketing implementation: The implications of marketing paradigm weakness for the strategy execution process', Journal of the Academy of Marketing Science, 26(3), 222–36; **459 The Financial Times Limited:** Kellaway, L. (2015) No need to "lean in" when laziness can be just as effective, Financial Times, February 23, p. 16. © The Financial Times Limited 2019. All Rights Reserved; **460 Centaur Media plc:** Schultz, D.E. (2006), 'Definition of internal marketing remains elusive', Marketing News, January 15, p. 6; **461 Elsevier:** Gummesson, E. (1987), 'The new marketing – developing long-term interactive relationships', Long Range Planning, 20(4), 10–20; **461 Marketing Science Institute:** Gilly, M.C. and Wolfinbarger, M.

(1996), Advertising's Second Audience: Employee Reactions to Organisational Communications, Cambridge, MA: Marketing Science Institute; **462 Southwest Airlines Co:** Southwest Airlines Co; **462 Centaur Media plc:** Bonoma, T.V. (1990), 'Employees can free the hostages', Marketing News, March 19; **463 Elsevier:** Piercy, N.F. (2009a), Market-Led Strategic Change: Transforming the Process of Going to Market, 4th edn, Oxford: Butterworth-Heinemann; **464 Internal Communication Focus:** (Table 16.1) Pounsford, M. (1994), 'Nothing to lose: Is internal communications adding value in today's organisations?', Internal Communication Focus, September, 6–8; **465 Woody Morcott:** Quote by Woody Morcott; **465 Centaur Media plc:** Divita, S. (1996), 'Colleagues are customers, market to them', Marketing News, October 21; **467 Elsevier:** (Figure 16.4) Piercy, N.F. (2009a), Market-Led Strategic Change: Transforming the Process of Going to Market, 4th edn, Oxford: Butterworth-Heinemann; **468 Cengage Learning:** Ulrich, D. (1992), 'Strategic and human resource planning: Linking customers and employees', Human Resource Planning, 15(2), 47–62; **472 Wall Street Journal:** Moroko, L. and Uncles, M.D. (2009), 'Employer branding: Companies have long divided consumers into segments; They should do the same with potential – and current – workers', Wall Street Journal, March 23, R7; **475 Hewlett-Packard Development Company, L.P:** Hewlett-Packard; **476 Marketing Science Institute:** Webster, F.E. (1997), 'The future role of marketing in the organisation', in D.R. Lehmann and K.E. Jocz (eds), Reflections on the Futures of Marketing, Cambridge, MA: Marketing Science Institute, pp. 39–66; **476 Taylor & Francis Group:** Dewsnap, B. and Jobber, D. (2000), 'The sales–marketing interface in consumer packaged goods companies: A conceptual framework', Journal of Personal Selling & Sales Management, 2, 109–19; **476 SAGE Publications:** Workman, J.P., Homburg, C. and Gruner, K. (1998), 'Marketing organisation: An integrative framework of dimensions and determinants', Journal of Marketing, 62(July), 21–41; **476 Harvard Business Publishing:** Cespedes, F.V. (1995), Concurrent Marketing: Integrating Product, Sales and Service, Cambridge, MA: Harvard Business School Press; **477 Harvard Business Publishing:** Shapiro, B.P. (2002), Creating the Customer-Centric Team: Coordinating Sales & Marketing, Harvard Business School, Note 9-999-006; **477 Taylor & Francis Group:** Rouzies, D., Anderson, E., Kohli, A.K., Michaels, R.E., Weitz, B.A. and Zoltners, A.A. (2005), 'Sales and marketing integration: A proposed framework', Journal of Personal Selling & Sales Management, 25(2), 113–22; **478 Simon & Schuster:** Hulbert, J.M., Capon, N. and Piercy, N.F. (2002), Total Integrated

Marketing: Breaking the Bounds of the Function, New York: The Free Press; **478 Harvard Business Publishing:** Shapiro, B.P. (2002), Creating the Customer-Centric Team: Coordinating Sales & Marketing, Harvard Business School, Note 9-999-006; **482-484 The Financial Times Limited:** (Figures 16.7 & 16.8) Milne, R. (2019) Inter Ikea's Torbjorn Loof: making the vision clear, Financial Times, 3 February. © The Financial Times Limited 2019. All Rights Reserved; **485 Bloomberg L.P.:** Porter, M.E. (2010), 'How big business can help itself by helping its neighbors', BusinessWeek, May 31–June 6, p. 56; **485 Harvard Business Publishing:** Porter, M.E. and Kramer, M.R. (2011), 'Creating shared value', Harvard Business Review, January–February, 62–77; **485-486 The Economist Newspaper Limited:** Bartleby "A 25-year battle to improve the image of McDonald's", The Economist Feb 7th 2019; **487 European Commission:** Commission of the European Communities (2001), Green Paper: Promoting a European Framework for Corporate Social Responsibility, Strasbourg: COM, July; **488 Mike Jeffries:** Mike Jeffries, CEO of Abercrombie & Fitch; **489 The Financial Times Limited:** Skapinker, M. (2003) Awkward customers, Financial Times, February 12, p. 12. © The Financial Times Limited 2019. All Rights Reserved; **489 Harvard Business Publishing:** Porter, M.E. and Kramer, M.R. (2011), 'Creating shared value', Harvard Business Review, January–February, 62–77; **491 Harvard Business Publishing:** Heineman Jnr, B.W. (2007), 'Avoiding integrity land mines', Harvard Business Review, April, 100–108; **491 Times Newspapers Limited:** Rushe, D. (2007), 'Starbucks stirs up a storm in a coffee cup', Sunday Times, March 2, 3.7; **492 The Financial Times Limited:** Grande, C. (2007), Ethical consumption makes mark on branding, Financial Times, February 20, p. 24. © The Financial Times Limited 2019. All Rights Reserved; **495 Academy of Management:** Wood, D.J. (1991), 'Corporate social performance revisited', Academy of Management Review, 16(4), 691–718; **495, 496, 508, 509, 510 Harvard Business Publishing:** Porter, M.E. and Kramer, M.R. (2006), 'Strategy and society: The link between competitive advantage and corporate social responsibility', Harvard Business Review, December, 78–92; **497 Profile Books Limited:** Moss Kanter, R. (2009), Supercorp: How Vanguard Companies Create Innovation, Profits, Growth and Social Good, London: Profile Books; **497 The Financial Times Limited:** Skapinker, M. (2010) Long-term corporate plans may be lost in translation, Financial Times, November 23, p. 15. © The Financial Times Limited 2019. All Rights Reserved; **499 Adam Smith Institute:** Adam Smith Institute (2008), Unfair Trade, London: Adam Smith Institute; **506 Bloomberg L.P.:** Capell, K. (2008), 'The wool industry gets bloodied', BusinessWeek, July 14 and 21, p. 31; **510 Harvard Business Publishing:** (Figure 17.4) Reprinted by permission of Harvard Business Review. Responsive and Strategic Corporate CSR, from 'The link between competitive advantage and corporate social responsibility' by Michael E. Porter and Mark R and Kramer, December 2006. Copyright © 2006 by the Harvard Business School Publishing Corporation; all rights reserved; **510 John Wiley & Sons:** Savitz, A. and Weber, K. (2006), The Triple Bottom Line: How Today's Best-Run Companies are Achieving Economic, Social and Environmental Success and How You Can Too, San Francisco, CA: Pfeiffer Wiley; **512 Academy of Management:** Carroll, A.B. (1979), 'A three-dimensional conceptual model of corporate performance', Academy of Management Review, October, 497–505; **513 Westburn Publishers Ltd:** (Figure 17.5) Piercy, N.F. and Lane, N. (2009b), 'Corporate social responsibility: Impacts on strategic marketing and customer value', The Marketing Review, 9(4), 335–60; **515 The Financial Times Limited:** Harvey, F. and Birchall, J. (2007) Walmart in greenhouse gas initiative, Financial Times, September 24, p. 25. © The Financial Times Limited 2019. All Rights Reserved; **515 The Financial Times Limited:** Wiggins, J. (2007) Coke develops a thirst for sustainability, Financial Times, July 2, p. 26. © The Financial Times Limited 2019. All Rights Reserved; **518-519 The Financial Times Limited:** Eley, J. (2019) Iceland Foods takes heat for bold environmental message, Financial times, 14 March. © The Financial Times Limited 2019. All Rights Reserved; **522 Charles Darwin:** Charles Darwin, On the Origin of Species (1853); **522 Niels Bohr:** Niels Bohr (Danish physicist, 1885 - 1962); **522-524 The Financial Times Limited:** (Unbox 18.1 and Figures 18.11 & 18.12) Tim Bradshaw (2019), Apple ready to unveil big bet on television © The Financial Times Limited 2019. All Rights Reserved; **525 Harvard Business Publishing:** Drucker, P. (1997), 'The future that has already happened', Harvard Business Review, 75(5), 20–4; **532 John Wiley & Sons:** Helfat, C.E., Finkelstein, S., Mitchell, W., Peteraf, M.A., Singh, H., Teece, D.J. and Winter, S.G. (2007), Dynamic Capabilities: Understanding Change in Organisations, Oxford: Blackwell Publishing; **533 American Marketing Association:** Brown, A. (1995), 'The fall and rise of marketing', Marketing Business, February, 25–8; **536 Audi AG:** Audi AG; **539 Johnson & Johnson Private Limited:** Listerine slogan; **541 Marketing Science Institute:** Haeckel, S. (1997), 'Preface', in D.R. Lehmann and K.R. Jocz (eds), Reflections on the Futures of Marketing, Cambridge, MA: Marketing Science Institute; **542 Taylor & Francis Group:** Sheth, J.N. and Sisodia, R.S. (eds) (2006), 'The image of marketing', in Does

Marketing Need Reform? Fresh Perspectives on the Future, New York: M.E. Sharpe Inc.; 542 **The Financial Times Limited:** from Gelles, D. (2010) Twitter builds on its character, Financial Times, 15 April. © The Financial Times Limited 2019. All Rights Reserved.

Photo Credits:

4 Getty Images: Jamie McDonald/Staff/Getty Images; **23 Alamy Stock Photo:** Susan E. Degginger/Alamy Stock Photo; **25 Getty Images:** Patrick T. Fallon/Bloomberg/Getty Images; **28 Getty Images:** Matthew Lloyd/Bloomberg/Getty Images; **51 Getty Images:** Justin Sullivan/Getty Images News/Getty Images; 70 **Shutterstock:** Viktoria Kurpas/Shutterstock; **75 Getty Images:** Teh Eng Koon/AFP/Getty Images; **77 Alamy Stock Photo:** Susanne Baumgarten/Vario images GmbH & Co.KG/Alamy Stock Photo; 90 **Alamy Stock Photo:** CARTA image/Alamy Stock Photo; **94 Alamy Stock Photo:** Greg Balfour Evans/Alamy Stock Photo; 105 **Alamy Stock Photo:** Vibrant Pictures/Alamy Stock Photo; 109 **Shutterstock:** mamanamsai/Shutterstock; 111 **Alamy Stock Photo:** Daniel Karmann/dpa picture alliance/Alamy Stock Photo; 114 **Alamy Stock Photo:** Ian Leonard/Alamy Stock Photo; 124 **Dyson Ltd:** Dyson Ltd; 137 **Alamy Stock Photo:** Torontonian/Alamy Stock Photo; 140 **REUTERS:** Charles Platiau/REUTERS; **164 Getty Images:** Bernardo De Niz/Bloomberg/Getty Images; 170 **Voyage:** Luke Beard/Voyage; 180 **Shutterstock:** John Locher/AP/Shutterstock; 182 **Center Parcs Ltd:** Center Parcs Ltd; **199 Getty Images:** Tim Graham/Hulton Archive/Getty Images; 202 **Alamy Stock Photo:** Robert Stainforth/Alamy Stock Photo; 230 **Alamy Stock Photo:** Digital-Fotofusion Gallery/Alamy Stock Photo; 241 **Shutterstock:** Sofiaworld/Shutterstock; **251 Alamy Stock Photo:** Ian G Dagnall/Alamy Stock Photo; **256 Alamy Stock Photo:** Matt Siegel/Reuters/Alamy Stock Photo; 265 **Shutterstock:** Bas Czerwinski/EPA-EFE/Shutterstock; 286 **Alamy Stock Photo:** Oleksiy Maksymenko Photography/Alamy Stock Photo; **287 Getty Images:** Paul Thomas/Bloomberg/Getty Images; 300 **Shutterstock:** Ross D Franklin/AP/Shutterstock; 318 **Getty Images:** FIA ABB Formula E/Handout/Getty Images; 320 **Shutterstock:** Petr David Josek/AP/Shutterstock; 352 **Alamy Stock Photo:** James Copeland/Alamy Stock Photo; 354 **Alamy Stock Photo:** British Retail Photography/Alamy Stock Photo; 381 **Alamy Stock Photo:** Sjscreens/Alamy Stock Photo; 387 **Getty Images:** DragonImages/iStock/Getty Images Plus; 420 **Alamy Stock Photo:** Kumar Sriskandan/Alamy Stock Photo; 423 **Alamy Stock Photo:** Maurice Savage/Alamy Stock Photo; 449 **Alamy Stock Photo:** Johan Nilsson/Epa European Pressphoto agency b.v./Alamy Stock Photo; **452 Getty Images:** John Thys/AFP/Getty Images; 482 **REUTERS:** Anna Ringstrom/REUTERS; 485 **Paul Blow:** Illustration created by Paul Blow; 522 **Getty Images:** Justin Sullivan/Getty Images; **542 Getty Images:** Chip/Bloomberg/Contributor/Getty Images.

PART 1
MARKETING STRATEGY

The first part of this text is concerned with the role of marketing in strategy development and lays the groundwork for analysing the two central issues of competitive positioning and market choices.

Chapter 1 discusses marketing as a process of value creation and delivery to customers that transcends traditional departmental boundaries. We examine the issue of market orientation as a way of doing business that places the customer at the centre of operations, and aligns people, information and structures around the value-creation process. We also recognise and explore the role of organisational resources in creating sustainable competitive advantage. The chapter concludes with a set of fundamental marketing principles to guide the actions of organisations operating in competitive markets, and identifying the role of marketing in leading and shaping strategic management.

Chapter 2 presents a framework for developing a marketing strategy that is adopted throughout the text. A three-stage process is proposed. First, the establishment of the core strategy. This involves defining the business purpose, assessing the alternatives open to the organisation through an analysis of customers, competition and the resources of the organisation, and deciding on the strategic focus that will be adopted. Second is the creation of the competitive positioning for the company. This composes the selection of the target market(s) (which dictates *where* the organisation will compete) and the establishment of a competitive advantage (which clarifies *how* it will compete). Third, implementation issues are discussed, such as the achievement of positioning through the use of the marketing mix and organisation and control of the marketing effort.

The ideas and frameworks presented in Part 1 are used to structure the remainder of the text, leading to a more detailed discussion of competitive market analysis in Part 2, segmentation and positioning analysis in Part 3, the development of competitive positioning strategies in Part 4 and strategy implementation issues in Part 5.

CHAPTER 1
MARKET-LED STRATEGIC MANAGEMENT

> 'The purpose of marketing is to contribute to maximising shareholder value, and marketing strategies must be evaluated in terms of how much value they create for investors.'
>
> Peter Doyle (2008)

Younger consumers drive shift to ethical products

By Alice Hancock in London

From free-range meat to vegan haircare, demand for sustainable goods is rising

In a busy north London supermarket the weekend before Christmas, the meat aisle is a hubbub. Sarah Rymer, 32, picks her way through a shelf of whole chickens. She chooses a free-range bird. 'I've definitely become more conscious of what I buy in the past few years,' she says. 'It can be confusing, but I think it's worth the money.' Ms Rymer is one of an increasing number of shoppers driving the UK's £81.3bn market for ethical products and services. According to not-for-profit consultancy Ethical Consumer, the sector has grown by more than £40bn since 2008, with households spending an average of £1,263 on ethical goods last year. The ethical food and drink market alone was up 9.7 per cent, compared with 5.3 per cent growth in 2015. Businesses are seeing the appeal. For Thanksgiving this year Butterball, the US's largest turkey producer, launched its first organic range in response to increasing consumer demand, while earlier in the year UK sandwich chain Pret A Manger opened its second and third all-vegetarian outlets. Ikea, which says that it uses its sustainable credentials to set it apart from other affordable homeware brands, intends to use only recycled or FSC certified wood by 2020. Big consumer

With consumers showing increasing concern for animal welfare, demand has risen for free-range poultry
Source: Jamie McDonald / Staff/Getty Images.

product groups are making concerted efforts, too. French cosmetics company L'Oréal this month unveiled its first vegan hair colour products, aimed at boosting its flagging professional haircare division. As part of a steady strategy of smaller acquisitions, Unilever bought Sir Kensington, a maker of vegan mayonnaise, and Pukka organic teas. Its sustainable brands – those the company describes as 'combin[ing] a strong purpose delivering a social or environmental benefit' – grew 40 per cent faster than the rest of the business in 2016, it says.

Younger consumers are fuelling this response. YouGov data show that in the past year alone the proportion of 18- to 24-year-olds turning to vegetarianism for environmental or welfare reasons has increased from 9 to 19 per cent. And it is not just in their consumer habits. 'We know that millennials want to work for companies that take this stuff seriously,' says Rob Harrison, director of Ethical Consumer. 'Lots of new start-ups have an ethical mission and it translates across into buying patterns.' He is speaking to me on his Fairphone, marketed as 'the world's first ethical, modular smartphone'. Ben Gleisner is the founder of one such ethically minded start-up. In 2009, while working as an economist in the New Zealand treasury, he identified what he calls a 'massive market failure': businesses, unaware that customers were interested in ethical products did not invest in them, resulting in a 'huge undersupply'. Conscious Consumers, the platform he has set up, provides retailers with data about customers' ethical preferences. Shoppers sign up online and link their credit or debit card to the app. Whenever they spend money at businesses registered with Conscious Consumers, data entered on their profile – from whether they would prioritise buying organic to whether they are interested in climate change or workers welfare – is sent to the retailer. In 2015 Mr Gleisner and his team ran New Zealand's second-biggest crowdfunding campaign and in autumn next year it plans to launch in its first foreign market: the UK. Richard Collier-Keywood, previously managing partner of PwC UK, has come on board as a director. Mr Gleisner says that 16- to 35-year-olds – Generations Y and Z – are the strongest market. 'Generation Z is the most environmentally and socially "aware" consumer market yet. Even more so than millennials,' he says. The sticking point is cost. At higher-end supermarket Waitrose, where Ms Rymer is shopping, an Essential range chicken is £2.40 per kg while a free-range bird is £6.25 per kg – more than double the price. Josie Mallin, 27, who is shopping for a Sunday joint in the more affordable Morrisons supermarket nearby, chooses a standard chicken. 'I try to buy ethically but say a normal chicken is £4 and an organic chicken is £10, I'm going to buy the normal one,' she says.

 Source: from 'Younger consumers drive shift to ethical products', *Financial Times*, 23/12/17 (Hancock, A.).

Discussion questions

1 What issues is Conscious Consumers trying to address?
2 How is the company trying to address them?

Introduction

In the quote that begins this chapter, Professor Peter Doyle highlights that the primary overarching goal for chief executives of commercial companies is to maximise shareholder value. However, is this at odds with the increasing awareness of, and attention to, environmental and social responsibility issues? Surely firms seeking to maximise shareholder value will pay scant regard to the natural and social environment in which they operate, taking what they can, irrespective of the consequences, in order to make a quick buck? Isn't this the essence of market-based capitalism – red in tooth and claw?

Wrong! The essence of the shareholder value approach is the long-term sustainability of the organisation through the creation of *lasting* value. Indeed, Doyle also argues that shareholder value is often confused with maximising profits. Maximising profitability is generally considered to be a short-term approach (and may result in eroding long-term competitiveness through actions such as cost cutting and shedding assets, to produce quick improvements in earnings). Maximising shareholder value, on the other hand, requires long-term thinking, the identification of changing opportunities and investment in the building of competitive advantage.

The role of marketing in the modern organisation poses something of a paradox. As Doyle (2008) again points out, few chief executives come from a marketing background, and many leading organisations have no marketing directors on their boards. Indeed, in many firms, the marketing *function* or *department* has had little or no strategic input, and instead is largely concerned with public relations (PR), advertising or sales support roles. However, there has been a noticeable change over the last decade or so regarding the importance of the *marketing concept* in setting strategic direction and influencing the overall culture of firms. Indeed, marketing is now routinely discussed, and embraced as being influential and important, in sectors that might have previously considered its use as irrelevant – for example in not-for-profit enterprises, such as charities and the arts, political parties and public sector organisations such as universities and the police service.

Managers increasingly recognise that the route to achieving commercial or social objectives lies in meeting the needs and expectations of their customers (goods or services). The concept of the customer has always been strong in commercial businesses, and as supply has outstripped demand in so many industries, so customer choice has increased. Additionally, there has been a vast increase in information available to customers through media sources such as the Internet, and as a result power in the supply chain has shifted dramatically from manufacturer to retailer/supplier, to end customer. In a rapidly changing and increasingly complex world, organisations that don't have customer satisfaction at the core of their strategic decision making will find it increasingly hard to survive.

In the not-for-profit world, the concept of the 'customer' is taking more time to get established but is no less central. Public sector organisations talk in terms of 'clients', 'patients', 'students', 'passengers' and the like. In reality, all are customers, in that they receive some form of benefit through an exchange with an entity or service provider. Where customers can make choices between service providers (within the public sector or outside it), they choose providers who best serve their needs. Some private sector providers have successfully identified areas where customers have not been well served by the public sector, and have provided new choices (in healthcare, education, security services and transport, for example). Additionally, and conversely, where private service providers have not delivered promised levels of service/service improvements, they have been 'taken back' into public hands. For example, in 2019, Her Majesty's Prison (HMP) Winson Green in Birmingham (UK) was returned to public hands from the private provider (G4S) by the Ministry of Justice following a series of high-profile issues, and a very poor report from inspectors.

While organisational structures, operational methods and formal trappings of marketing can, and should, change to reflect new developments and market opportunities, the philosophy and concept of marketing, as described in this chapter, are even more relevant today than ever before.

This first chapter sets the scene by examining the marketing concept and market orientation as the foundations of strategic marketing, the role of marketing in addressing various stakeholders in the organisation, and the developing resource-based marketing strategy approach.

1.1 The marketing concept and market orientation

1.1.1 Evolving definitions of marketing

One of the earliest examples of codification and/or definition in the development of marketing as a discipline was concerned with the marketing concept. Over 50 years ago, Felton (1959) proposed that the marketing concept is:

a corporate state of mind that exists on the integration and coordination of all the marketing functions which, in turn, are melded with all other corporate functions, for the basic
objective of producing long-range profits.

More recently, Kotler *et al.* (1996) suggested that the defining characteristic of the marketing concept is that:

the marketing concept holds that achieving organisational goals depends on determining the needs and wants of target markets and delivering the desired satisfactions more
effectively and efficiently than competitors do.

At its simplest, the marketing concept holds that in increasingly dynamic and competitive
markets, the companies or organisations that are most likely to succeed are those that take
notice of customer expectations, wants and needs, and gear themselves to satisfying them
better than their competitors. It recognises that there is no reason why customers should
buy one organisation's offerings unless they are in some way better at serving their wants
and needs than those offered by competing organisations.

As it probably should, the meaning and domain of marketing remains subject to evolution and discussion. To exemplify this, in 1985 the American Marketing Association (AMA)
reviewed more than 25 marketing definitions before arriving at their own (see Ferrell and
Lucas, 1987):

Marketing is the process of planning and executing the conception, pricing, planning and
distribution of ideas, goods and services to create exchanges that satisfy individual and
organisational objectives.

This has since evolved further, but very much embraces the broad ideas expressed in this
initial definition. The AMA's current definition of marketing (from July 2013) is:

Marketing is the activity, set of institutions, and processes for creating, communicating,
delivering, and exchanging offerings that have value for customers, clients, partners, and
society at large.

Taken together, the definitions position marketing as embedded within an organisation,
and as something that has extensive impact outside the organisation. They also reinforce
the centrality of the marketing concept, value, process, mutually beneficial exchange and
customer relationships. These issues may, or may not, be managed by a marketing department or function. These definitions lead to a model of 'mutually beneficial exchanges' as
an overview of the role of marketing, as shown in Figure 1.1.

Definitions of marketing are, of course, extremely useful. However, the reality of what
marketing means operationally, and in reality, is a far more difficult topic. Webster (1997)
points out that, of all the management functions, marketing has the most difficulty in defining its position in the organisation, because it is simultaneously culture, strategy and tactics.
He argues that marketing involves the following:

- **Culture:** marketing may be expressed as the 'marketing concept' – that is, a set of values
  and beliefs embedded in employees that drives organisational decision making through
  a fundamental commitment to serving customers' needs, as the path to sustained
  profitability.
- **Strategy:** as strategy, marketing seeks to develop effective responses to changing market
  environments by defining market segments, and developing and positioning product
  offerings for those target markets.
- **Tactics:** marketing as tactics is concerned with the day-to-day activities of product management, pricing, distribution and marketing communications such as advertising, personal selling, publicity and sales promotion.

The challenge of simultaneously building a customer (or market) orientation in an organisation (culture), developing value propositions and competitive positioning (strategy) and

Figure 1.1
Mutually beneficial
exchanges

developing detailed marketing action plans (tactics) is complex. It is perhaps unsurprising that the organisational reality of marketing often falls short of the demands suggested previously.

1.1.2 Market orientation

Marketing Science Institute (MSI) studies during the 1990s attempted to identify the specific activities that translate the philosophy of marketing into reality, and hence achieve a market orientation. In one of the most widely quoted research streams in modern marketing that stemmed from the seminal, and still influential, Kohli and Jaworski (1990) study, market orientation was defined in the following terms:

> a market orientation entails (1) one or more departments engaging in activities geared towards developing an understanding of customers' current and future needs and the factors affecting them, (2) sharing of this understanding across departments, and (3) the various departments engaging in activities designed to meet select customer needs. In other words, a market orientation refers to the organisation-wide generation, dissemination, and responsiveness to market intelligence.

This view of market orientation is concerned primarily with the development of what may be called market understanding throughout an organisation, and poses a substantial management challenge.

Another important contribution to this discussion, Narver and Slater (1990), defined market orientation as:

> the organisational culture . . . that most effectively and efficiently creates the necessary behaviours for the creation of superior value for buyers and, thus, continuous superior performance for the business.

From this work a number of components, and in essence the context of marketing, are proposed (see Figure 1.2):

- **customer orientation:** understanding customers well enough to create superior value for them;
- **competitor orientation:** awareness of the short-term and long-term capabilities of competitors;
- **interfunctional coordination:** using all company resources, working together, to create value for target customers;
- **organisational culture:** linking employee and managerial behaviour to customer satisfaction;
- **long-term creation of shareholder value:** as the overriding business objective.

Figure 1.2
Components and
context of market
orientation

To support these ideas, there is a significant and quite compelling amount of support for the view that market orientation is associated with superior organisational performance – that is, financial performance and non-financial performance such as employee commitment and *esprit de corps* (Jaworski and Kohli, 1993; Slater and Narver, 1994; Cano *et al.*, 2004; Kumar *et al.*, 2011).

However, it has also been suggested that there may be substantial barriers to achieving market orientation (Harris, 1996, 1998; Piercy *et al.*, 2002). The reality may be that executives face the problem of creating and driving marketing strategy in situations where the company is simply not market orientated. This is probably at the heart of many strategy implementation problems in marketing (see Chapter 16).

The 'signs' of market orientation can be summarised in the following terms, and underlines the links between them and our approach to marketing strategy and competitive positioning:

- Reaching marketing's true potential may rely mostly on success in moving past marketing activities (tactics) to marketing as a company-wide issue of real customer focus (culture) and competitive positioning (strategy). The evidence supports suggestions that marketing has generally been highly effective in tactics, but only marginally effective in changing culture, and largely ineffective in the area of strategy (Day, 1992; Varadarajan, 1992; Webster, 1997; Varadarajan, 2012).

- One key is achieving understanding of the market and the customer throughout the company, and building the capability for responsiveness to market changes. The real customer focus and responsiveness of the company is the context in which marketing strategy is built and implemented. Our approach to competitive market analysis in Part 2 provides many of the tools that can be used to enhance and share an understanding of the customer marketplace throughout the company.

- Another issue is that the marketing process should be seen as interfunctional and cross-disciplinary, and not simply the responsibility of the marketing department. This is the real value of adopting the process perspective on marketing that is becoming more widely adopted by large organisations (Hulbert *et al.*, 2003). We shall see in Part 4 on competitive positioning strategies that superior service and value, and innovation to build defensible competitive positions, rely on the coordinated efforts of many functions and people within the organisation. Cross-functional relationships are also an important emphasis in Part 5.

- It is also clear that a deep understanding of the competition in the market from the customer's perspective is critical. Viewing the product or service from a customer's viewpoint is often difficult, but without that perspective a marketing strategy is highly vulnerable to attack from unsuspected sources of competition. We shall confront this issue in Part 3, where we are concerned with competitive positions.

- Finally, it follows that the issue is long-term performance, not simply short-term results, and this perspective is implicit in all that we consider when building and implementing marketing strategy.

A framework for executives to evaluate market orientation in their own organisations is shown in Box 1.1. However, it is also important to make the point at this early stage that marketing as organisational culture (the marketing concept and market orientation) must also be placed in the context of other drivers of the values and approaches of the organisation. A culture that emphasises customers as key stakeholders in the organisation is completely consistent and complementary with one that also recognises the needs and concerns of shareholders, employees, managers and the wider social and environmental context in which the organisation operates.

In addition to any discussion of customer focus or market orientation it is worth noting that advocacy of a completely customer-focused approach comes with a health warning. Occasionally these approaches are confused with the notion of 'doing whatever the customers say'. There lies madness! While understanding customers, and potential customers, is clearly important, so are issues of creativity and innovation. Hence it is important for organisations to be market driven, but equally it is important to be market driving – that is, trialling new and possibly edgy (beyond what might be expected) products and services. This is advocated, as asking customers what they want can simply be the wrong question – often they don't know!

Box 1.1	**Market orientation assessment**

1 Customer orientation

	Strongly agree	Agree	Neither	Disagree	Strongly disagree	Don't know
Information about customer needs and requirements is collected regularly	5	4	3	2	1	0
Our corporate objective and policies are aimed directly at creating satisfied customers	5	4	3	2	1	0
Levels of customer satisfaction are regularly assessed and action is taken to improve matters where necessary	5	4	3	2	1	0
We put major effort into building stronger relationships with key customers and customer groups	5	4	3	2	1	0
We recognise the existence of distinct groups or segments in our markets with different needs and we adapt our offerings accordingly	5	4	3	2	1	0

Total score for customer orientation (out of 25)

2 Competitor orientation

	Strongly agree	Agree	Neither	Disagree	Strongly disagree	Don't know
Information about competitor activities is collected regularly	5	4	3	2	1	0
We conduct regular benchmarking against major competitor offerings	5	4	3	2	1	0
There is rapid response to major competitor actions	5	4	3	2	1	0
We put major emphasis on differentiating ourselves from the competition on factors important to customers	5	4	3	2	1	0

Total score for competitor orientation (out of 20)

3 Long-term perspectives

	Strongly agree	Agree	Neither	Disagree	Strongly disagree	Don't know
We place greater priority on long-term market-share gain than on short-run profits	5	4	3	2	1	0
We put greater emphasis on improving our market performance than on improving internal efficiencies	5	4	3	2	1	0
Decisions are guided by long-term considerations rather than short-run expediency	5	4	3	2	1	0

Total score for long-term perspectives (out of 15)

4 Interfunctional coordination

	Strongly agree	Agree	Neither	Disagree	Strongly disagree	Don't know
Information about customers is widely circulated and communicated throughout the organisation	5	4	3	2	1	0
The different departments in the organisation work effectively together to serve customer needs	5	4	3	2	1	0
Tensions and rivalries between departments are not allowed to get in the way of serving customers effectively	5	4	3	2	1	0
Our organisation is flexible to enable opportunities to be seized effectively rather than hierarchically constrained	5	4	3	2	1	0

Total score for interfunctional coordination (out of 20)

5 Organisational culture

	Strongly agree	Agree	Neither	Disagree	Strongly disagree	Don't know
All employees recognise their role in helping to create satisfied end customers	5	4	3	2	1	0
Reward structures are closely related to external market performance and customer satisfaction	5	4	3	2	1	0
Senior management in all functional areas give top priority to creating satisfied customers	5	4	3	2	1	0
Senior management meetings give high priority to discussing issues that affect customer satisfaction	5	4	3	2	1	0

Total score for organisational culture (out of 20)

Summary

From the totals obtained:
Customer orientation (out of 25)
Competitor orientation (out of 20)
Long-term perspectives (out of 15)
Interfunctional coordination (out of 20)
Organisational culture (out of 20)
Total score (out of 100)

Interpretation

- 80–100. This indicates a high level of market orientation. However, scores below 100 can still be improved!
- 60–80. This indicates moderate market orientation. Identify the areas where most improvement is needed.
- 40–60. This shows that there is a long way to go in developing a market orientation. Identify the main gaps and set priorities for action to close them.
- 20–40. This indicates a mountain ahead of you! Start at the top and work your way through. Some factors will be more within your control than others. Tackle those first.

Note: If you scored '0' on many of the scales you need to find out more about your own company!

1.2   The resource-based view of marketing

The dominant view of strategy in the 1980s and early 1990s was proposed by, among others, Michael Porter of the Harvard Business School (Porter, 1980, 1985). This view suggested that the key to strategy lay in industry dynamics and characteristics. While there has since been a great deal of academic discussion and debate on this perspective, it is a view that is fundamental to strategic management theory, and hence worthy of further discussion. Porter suggested that some industries were inherently more attractive than others, and that the factors driving industry competition were key determinants of profitability. Under this

Figure 1.3
Marketing
approaches

approach, the focus for explaining performance differences between organisations shifted from outside the firm (the industries in which it operated) to within the firm itself (its resources and capabilities).

Termed the resource-based view of the firm (Wernerfelt, 1984), with a focus on 'core competencies' (Prahalad and Hamel, 1990), this new approach suggested that performance was essentially driven by the resource profile of the organisation, and that the source of superior performance lay in the possession and deployment of distinctive, hard-to-imitate or protected resources.

Our view on strategy and marketing is that these two approaches can be combined successfully to the benefit of both. They do, however, throw into stark relief the different approaches to strategy in general, and marketing in particular, that are still evident in many organisations today. Three main alternative approaches are apparent (see Figure 1.3):

- **Product push marketing.** Under this approach, firms focus activities on existing products and services, and look for ways to encourage or even persuade customers to buy. This is a myopic interpretation of the resource-based view: we have a resource (our product or service) that we are good at producing, and that is different from what competitors offer. The key notion underpinning this approach is to make customers want what we are good at. Car dealerships and their supply chain present good examples of push marketing. Dealers are often given favourable incentives based on volume targets that culminate in significant financial payments based on numbers of cars sold, as are sales people. In this setting it is very much in everyone's interests to 'push' cars through the supply chain to the customer.
- **Customer-led marketing.** The other extreme is customer-led marketing (Slater, 1998). Under this approach, organisations chase their customers at all costs. The goal is to find what customers want and, whatever it is, give it to them. This can also lead to problems. Being excessively customer led can lead to a short-term orientation, resulting in trivial incremental product development efforts and myopic research and development (R&D) (Frosch, 1996). Christensen and Bower (1996) go further, suggesting that 'firms lose their

position of industry leadership . . . because they listen too carefully to their customers'. (See earlier discussion regarding the importance of organisations being market driven and market driving.)

- **Resource-based marketing.** In this text we advocate a middle ground between these two extremes. Here, firms base marketing strategies on equal consideration of the requirements of the market and their abilities to serve it. Under this approach, a long-term view of customer requirements is taken in the context of other market considerations (such as competitor offerings and strategies, and the realities of the supply chain), together with mapping out the assets, competencies and skills of the organisation to ensure they are leveraged to the full.

Resource-based marketing essentially seeks a long-term fit between the requirements of the market and the abilities of the organisation to compete in it. This does not mean that the resources of the organisation are seen as fixed and static, far from it. Market requirements evolve over time and the resource profile of an organisation must continuously develop to enable it to continue to compete, and to enable it to take advantage of new opportunities. The essential factor, however, is that opportunities are seized where the organisation has an existing or potential advantage through its resource base, rather than just pursued *ad hoc*. These points will be returned to when we discuss the assessment of company marketing resources (Chapter 6) and the criteria for selecting those markets in which to operate (Chapter 9).

First, however, we need to explore how market orientation and marketing resources impact on organisational performance. To do this we introduce the idea of organisational stakeholders.

1.3   Organisational stakeholders

Why do organisations exist? The simple answer, for commercial organisations, may be to earn returns on investments for shareholders and owners of those organisations. For non-commercial organisations, such as charities, faith-based organisations, public services and so on, the answer may lie in the desire to serve specific communities or constituencies. However, organisations, both commercial and non-profit, are rarely driven by such simple goals. Often there are many demands, sometimes complementary, sometimes competing, that drive decisions. For example, James Dyson's decision to move production of his household appliances out of the United Kingdom to Asia in early 2002 for cost reasons (responsibility to shareholders to operate efficiently), resulted in a considerable backlash from the local community and national media over the impact on jobs and livelihoods in the UK (responsibility to employees and the local community).

All organisations serve multiple stakeholders (Harrison and St John, 1994; Mitchell *et al.*, 1997). Some, however, will be given higher priority than others in the way decisions are made and resources allocated (Rowley, 1997; Ogden and Watson, 1999). Research into the transition economies of central and Eastern Europe, for example, found that in many state-owned enterprises (SOEs) the major stakeholders were the employees, and organisational objectives centred on providing continuity of employment (Hooley *et al.*, 2000). This orientation persists in many former SOEs following privatisation and sell-off to the commercial sector, although this is now changing. For many of the commercial firms surveyed in the piece of work cited previously, the prime objectives centred on profitability and short-term return on investment.

The long-term implications of climate change and global warming have led many organisations to begin to recognise the importance of the physical and natural environment in their plans and actions. Indeed, the natural environment could be seen as a further 'stakeholder'. Many organisations have really taken this notion to heart and have embedded this thinking

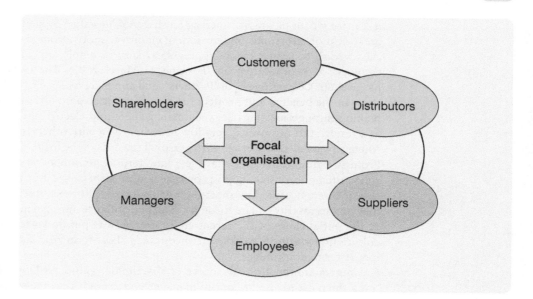

Figure 1.4
Organisational
stakeholders

in how they define themselves. Organisations are increasingly under pressure to assure stakeholders that their actions are sustainable and are having a positive impact on issues such as the environment or society, for example. Related and increasingly widespread terms associated with these important ideas for marketers are 'green marketing', 'cause-related marketing' and 'sustainable marketing'. The 'triple bottom line' is also a term that has become familiar to CEOs the world over, referring to the need for organisations to be seen to improve (or certainly not to have a negative impact on) the overall state of Planet Earth, the human race and financial stakeholders (i.e. shareholders). The rather out-of-date and uninformed 1980s notion of 'greed is good' has now been replaced in many organisations by a more sensible and sustainable mantra that includes a more balanced sentiment at its core. It would be wrong, however, to see this change as a fad or trend, and organisations are increasingly gaining traction with spending customers *because* of their stance on environmental and societal issues. This is the triple bottom line writ large, and companies such as Patagonia, Levi Strauss and McDonald's (with its Ronald McDonald Houses for families of chronically ill children) are great examples of this.

In the context of commercial organisations, a number of primary stakeholders can be identified (see Figure 1.4). These include shareholders and owners, managers, employees, customers, suppliers and the society in which they operate. While a market-orientated culture, discussed earlier, serves to place customers high in the priority ranking, the reality for most organisations is a complex blend of considerations that incorporates all stakeholders.

Doyle (2008) discusses the motivations and expectations of the various stakeholder groups, as follows:

- **Shareholders** may be of two main types. First, there may be individuals with emotional and long-term personal ties to the business. Increasingly, however, shareholders nowadays are financial investors, both individual and institutional, who are seeking to maximise the long-term value of their investments. Paradoxically, this desire for long-term shareholder value may drive many firms to make short-term decisions in order to maximise share price or dividends.

- **Employees** may also have long-term commitment to the firm. Their priorities are generally some combination of compensation (through wages and salaries), job satisfaction and security (of employment). These may be at odds with the value of the firm to shareholders. Few employees would agree that their personal job loss through 'downsizing' is a price worth paying for increasing shareholder value! Some firms, however, put a great deal of effort into understanding employee motivations. For example, Skandia, the Swedish insurance company, regularly surveys employees with a view to aligning employee and corporate goals (*Fortune*, 11 March 2002). The John Lewis Partnership has over 80,000 employees, or 'Partners', and annual revenue of over £10bn; the Partners share in the benefits and profits of the business. It also involves employees in decision making through meetings between management and elected staff representatives and, as a result, staff turnover is very low in comparison with others in the industry.

- **Managers** are also concerned with personal rewards in the form of salaries and prestige. Professional managers may have less long-term commitment to the firm and see their roles as temporary staging posts on their longer-term career journeys. Managerial 'success' is often measured by short-term gains (in sales, for example, or efficiency), which may not necessarily equate to longer-term performance improvement for the firm. Much of the initial cause of the recent credit crunch was put down to the excessive bonus culture in investment banks that encouraged short-term risk taking at the expense of longer-term performance.

- **Customers** are the ultimate source of shareholder value. As Doyle (2008) points out, 'even the most focused financial manager understands that the source of a company's long-term cash flow is its satisfied customers'. There is, however, an inherent danger of pursuing customer satisfaction at the expense of all other considerations. Customers might be 'delighted' by lower prices or higher-quality offerings than competitors, but if the underlying costs exceed the prices that customers are prepared to pay the firm will not remain in business very long. In this respect, the blind pursuit of customer satisfaction may be at odds with longer-term shareholder value creation.

- **Suppliers and distributors** also have a stake in the business. Suppliers rely on the firms they serve to ensure the achievement of their goals. In working with customers, suppliers often seek security, predictability and a satisfactory margin, and some suppliers have tried to ensure these outcomes through embedded and close relationships. For example, Walmart and Proctor and Gamble (P&G) have a very close relationship whereby sales at Walmart are directly linked to order replenishment systems at P&G. Distributors, too, are stakeholders in the business. In the automobile industry, car distributors are normally closely allied to individual car makers through franchise agreements. The success or otherwise of the manufacturer in developing and marketing the right cars for the market impacts directly on the distributor. Again, the distributor may seek predictability and continuity at satisfactory margins.

To these stakeholders identified by Doyle (2008) we would add the following:

- **Society and the community** in which a firm exists can be significantly affected by its actions. Plant closures are an obvious example. When the UK coal industry shrank significantly in the 1970s and '80s the effect on local communities was vast. Mining towns in Yorkshire and the Midlands experienced high rates of unemployment, as job creation initiatives lagged behind jobs lost through pit closures. More recently, Nissan announced that it is likely to close car-making facilities at Swindon in the UK, with the loss of around 3,500 jobs. This announcement has fuelled a significant amount of media speculation about the negative impacts on the local and national economy.

- **The natural (or physical) environment** connects strongly to the earlier discussion about the 'triple bottom line', but has not traditionally been seen as a stakeholder in the conventional use of the term. It is, however, a proxy for future society, as what we do to the environment and the natural resources today will affect future generations. It has been argued that while previous generations may not have completely understood the environmental impact of their actions (in particular the burning of fossil fuels), the implications today are quite clear. Action at national and supranational levels has been, until very recently, fairly elusive (such as the failure of the climate change talks in Copenhagen in December 2009 to result in significant commitment to limit carbon emissions). However, the European Union is leading the way: following the Paris Climate Conference (COP21), held in December 2015, a total of 195 countries agreed to adopt the first ever, universal, legally binding global climate deal. Unfortunately, at the time of writing, President Trump has indicated that the USA is likely to pull out of the Paris accord, dealing a potentially significant blow to the overall aims. On a more positive note, organisations in the private and public sectors are increasingly taking action to reduce emissions and energy consumption, and mitigate their environmental impacts. This makes good commercial sense too! Energy bills for many organisations are the second-highest controllable expense after staff, and customers are increasingly taking interest in the 'green' credentials and practices of the companies they purchase from – and changing consumption habits as a result.

For non-profit organisations, the identification of stakeholders and their requirements may be even more complex:

- **Owners** of the organisation may be hard to identify and their interests difficult to define. For example, who 'owns' the Catholic Church, or Greenpeace, or the Labour Party? Many might argue that the owners are those who support such organisations, the churchgoers, the activists and members. Or are 'employees' (such as the clergy) the owners? In the case of organisations such as the National Health Service (NHS), police service, or some educational establishments, are the owners society in general, the taxpayers, or the government of the day that sets priorities and performance targets?
- **Customers** may be defined as those whom an organisation seeks to serve. The customers of the Catholic Church may be those who attend mass on Sundays. It may also, however, extend to others whom the Church wishes to appeal to and whose behaviour and beliefs it seeks to influence. Who are the customers of the NHS – the patients? Or those who avoid the service through heeding health warnings? Who are the customers of higher education? The students? The parents who fund them? Or the employers who seek their skills on graduation? Who are the customers for the police service? Society in general that needs protection from criminals? The criminals themselves? Or the taxpayers who fund them? Different definitions of 'customers' may result in different interpretations of what their expectations, needs and requirements are or might be. Failure to identify and meet the needs of different customers destroys market position. For example, while doctors and police officers struggle with the idea that they exist to provide customer value, their position is being eroded by the growth of alternative medicine, medical tourism (improving choice) and private security services and systems.
- **Employees,** we might conclude, are relatively easy to identify. Their motivations, however, may be far more complex than in the commercial sector. What motivates nurses to work such long, hard hours for relatively little financial reward? Why do people volunteer to staff charity shops for no payment? Why do activists risk their lives to prevent the dumping of oil platforms or nuclear waste at sea? In the non-profit sector, employees may or may not receive financial rewards. Often their prime motivators are not financial, but centre far more on satisfaction derived from contributing to a cause they cherish or value.
- **Society and community** have perhaps always been high on the list of priorities for many non-profit organisations. Charities exist to serve the society in which they operate (but would they necessarily call them 'customers'?).

While the considerations of many of these stakeholders may be complementary, they may also be in conflict. For example, the desire of shareholders for long-term value creation may be at odds with the demands of suppliers and distributors for continuity, security and satisfactory margins. The demands placed on a firm through being customer led may have significant impacts on the roles and activities of managers and employees, not all of them welcome. This confusion may be compounded when individual stakeholders assume more than one role. For example, managers and employees may also be shareholders in commercial organisations. They could also, from time to time, be their own customers!

In any organisation there will be a blend of orientations towards the various stakeholders. We would argue, however, that a strong orientation towards the market, as discussed at the outset of this chapter, can be a unifying force that helps achieve other stakeholder goals.

1.3.1 The contribution of marketing to stakeholder objectives

There is increasing evidence that firms that do well in the marketplace also do well financially, adding to the value of the firm for shareholders. Homburg and Pflesser (2000), for example, have shown that firms adopting a market-orientated culture perform better financially than those that do not. Many other studies have also shown direct links between market orientation, customer satisfaction and firm financial performance (see Lafferty and Hult, 2001, for a summary).

Figure 1.5 shows the effects of market-orientated culture on firm activities and performance. The degree of market orientation, as discussed previously, is a deeply embedded cultural aspect of any firm. Where market orientation is high, all organisational functions are focused on their contribution to the creation of superior customer value. This, in turn, affects the way those functions are managed, and the priorities they pursue. For example, human resource management and training is often directed towards customer awareness and service, and reward structures are designed to encourage customer satisfaction generation. Where market orientation is high, employee job satisfaction and commitment have also been demonstrated to be high (see Piercy *et al.*, 2002), creating a motivated workforce focused on the needs of customers (see Heskett *et al.*, 2003). To illustrate this notion, Sir Charlie Mayfield, Chairman of the John Lewis Partnership, stated, 'The John Lewis Partnership faces similar challenges to other major retailers but in one respect our response is very different. That's the energy and passion of our Partners who, as co-owners of our business, drive our work to operate an ever-more sustainable and responsible business.'

High levels of market orientation also lead organisations to emphasise the development of marketing assets, such as company and brand reputation (Aaker, 1991), market innovation capabilities (Slater and Narver, 1995; Han *et al.*, 1998), customer relationship management skills (Gummesson, 1999) and satisfied and well-motivated staff. Well-developed marketing resources (both assets and capabilities) have been shown to lead to superior market performance, help create satisfied and loyal customers (Heskett *et al.*, 2003) and also increase sales volume and market share. Reputational assets, such as well-known and respected brands, together with well-developed marketing capabilities such as market innovation skills, also affect market performance directly.

Figure 1.5 Marketing and performance outcomes

The link between market performance and financial performance is also well established. Customer satisfaction and loyalty leads to greater sales volume and market share, which, in turn, leads to financial performance. One suggested route is through the impact of economies and advantages of scale. A second route, explained in detail by Doyle (2008), suggests that shareholder value is determined by anticipated future cash flows, adjusted for the cost of capital. In this view, the crucial task of management is to maximise the sum of future cash flows, and hence maximise shareholder value. Marketing's contribution will be to develop strategies that deliver enhanced cash flows through, for example, successful new product launches or the creation of strong brands that can command high margins and market shares. Under this view, the focus of marketing is on developing and protecting assets (such as brands or market share) that have the potential to deliver enhanced cash flows in the future. Doyle sees the role of marketing as driving value creation through the optimum choice of markets and target segments in which to operate, the creation of a differential (or competitive advantage) in serving those targets and the development of an appropriate marketing mix for delivery.

In summary, marketing can contribute to satisfying the needs of employee and managerial stakeholders through providing security, compensation and job satisfaction. Where the firm is better at serving its customers and more adept at winning orders in the face of competition, it is more likely to survive into the future. There is also evidence that where firms are more market orientated, employees derive more satisfaction from their jobs (Slater and Narver, 1995). This, in turn, can lead to a virtuous circle of improvement, as happy, motivated staff generate increasingly satisfied customers, so that organisational performance improves and staff become more satisfied – and so on. Similarly, the most effective route to achieving the profit and performance desires of supply chain partners is through market success. Heightened success through partnerships and alliances can serve to bond organisations together, creating more stability and predictability in the supply and distribution chain. Nonetheless, concerns of customers and employees for the environment, for social justice, for fair employment and other social priorities have led to renewed emphasis on corporate social responsibility and good corporate citizenship. However, importantly (as we shall see in Part 5), thinking has changed from altruistic behaviour to meet moral obligations, to pursuing social initiatives as part of the value proposition and a source of competitive advantage (see Chapter 17).

1.4   Marketing fundamentals

Building on the marketing concept outlined previously, the considerations of alternative stakeholders and the logic of resource-based marketing, we can distil a set of basic and very pragmatic marketing principles that serve to guide marketing thought and action. Each of these may seem quite intuitive, however recognition and application of them can (and has) revolutionised how organisations respond to, and interact with, their customers.

Principle 1: focus on the customer

This first principle of marketing goes back to the marketing concept itself and recognises that the long-term objectives of the organisation, be they financial or social, are best served by achieving a high degree of customer focus – but not a blind focus! From that recognition flows the necessity for a close investigation of customer wants and needs, followed by a clear definition of if and how the company can best serve them.

It also follows that the only arbiters of how well the organisation satisfies its customers are the customers themselves. The quality of the goods or services offered to the market will be judged by customers on the basis of how well their requirements are satisfied. A quality product or service from the customers' perspective is one that satisfies or is 'fit for purpose', rather than one that provides unrequired 'bells and whistles', or luxuries.

Adopting a market-led approach poses some very basic questions (Levitt, 1986). The most important of these include:

- What business are we in?
- What business could we be in?
- What business do we want to be in?
- What must we do to get into or consolidate in that business?

The answers to these fundamental questions can often change a company's outlook and perspective. In Chapter 2 we discuss more fully business definition, and show how it is fundamental to setting strategic direction for an organisation.

Principle 2: only compete in markets where you can establish a competitive advantage

Market selection is one of the key tasks for any organisation – that is, choosing where to compete and where to commit resources. Many factors will come into the choice of market, including how attractive the market appears to the firm. Especially important in competitive markets is the question 'do we have the skills and competencies to compete here?'. The corporate graveyard is littered with firms that were seduced into markets that looked attractive, but when competition got tough they found they had no real basis on which to compete or gain advantage. Many of the dot.com failures of the early 2000s were firms that saw opportunity but did not really have the skills and competencies to establish advantage over other dot.coms, or over 'bricks-and-mortar' firms. In the eyes of customers, no additional value was being created.

Principle 3: customers do not buy products

The third basic marketing principle is that customers do not buy products, they buy what the product can do for them. To put this another way, customers buy relief from the problem a product solves. Customers are generally less interested in the technical features of a product or service than in what benefits they get from buying, using or consuming the product or service.

For example, the do-it-yourself (DIY) enthusiast putting up bookshelves will assemble the tools for the job. One of these could be a drill bit to make the holes in which to screw the shelf supports, on which to place the shelf. However, the DIY enthusiast does not want a quarter-inch drill bit, but a quarter-inch hole. The drill bit is merely a way of delivering that benefit (the hole) and will only be the solution to the basic need until a better method or solution is invented. We can go further – what is really wanted is storage for books (or, indeed, alternative ways of storing knowledge and information in electronic media). Competition will come not only from other manufacturers of drill bits, but from laser techniques for making holes in the wall, wall designs that incorporate shelving studs in their design, adhesives that support shelves or alternative ways of storing and accessing books, such as the Amazon Kindle e-reader. This is the difference between an industry (firms with similar technologies and products) and a market (customers with a similar problem to solve or a need to meet). In this sense, white goods manufacturers may see themselves as an industry (they all produce white boxes with electric motors), but the different markets they serve are the laundry market, the food-storage market and so on. Similarly, gardeners don't really want a lawnmower, but rather grass that is 1 inch high. Hence, a new strain of grass seed that is hard-wearing and only grows to 1 inch in height could provide very substantial competition to lawnmower manufacturers, as could artificial grass substitutes.

This is far from academic theorising, however, as in grocery retailing the notion of 'category management' is often used. Here, retailers define categories around customer needs, not manufacturers' brands. The challenge to manufacturers is to prove to the retailer what their products and brands add to the overall value of the category. Putting category definition at its simplest:

The manufacturer makes	*potato crisps.*
The retailer merchandises	*salty snacks.*
The customer buys	*lunch!*

Looking at a market from the customers' perspective may suggest a very different view of market opportunities and the threats to a competitive position. It is critical that marketers view products and services as 'bundles of benefits', or a combination of attractions that all give something of value to the customer. One mission for the marketing executive is to ensure that the organisation gears itself to solving customers' problems, rather than exclusively promoting its own current (and often transitory) solutions.

Principle 4: marketing is too important to leave to the marketing department (if there is one)

It is increasingly the case that marketing is everyone's job in an organisation. If we adopt the cultural stance explored earlier, then this is understandable as the actions of all can impact on the overall satisfaction derived by the customer.

In an early work by King (1985), he highlights a number of misconceptions as to what marketing is. One of the most insidious misconceptions he terms 'marketing department marketing'. This is where an organisation employs marketing professionals who are good at analysing marketing data and calculating market shares to three decimal points, but who have very little impact on products and services. Here, the marketing department is seen as the only department where 'marketing is done', so other departments can get on with their own agenda and pursue their own goals.

As organisations become flatter, reducing layers of bureaucracy, and continue to break down spurious functional barriers between departments, it becomes increasingly obvious that marketing is the job of everyone. It is equally obvious that marketing is so central to both survival and prosperity, that it is far too important to leave only to the marketing department.

However, it is also clear that we must avoid simply stating that marketing is 'everyone's job' and leaving it at that. If marketing is everyone's job, then the important issues of accountability and responsibility become problematic to a degree, and marketing may well become 'no one's job'. Greyser (1997) points to the need for simultaneous upgrading of market orientation and downsizing of the formal marketing function as two sides of the same issue:

> While the marketing function ('doing marketing') belongs to the marketing department, becoming and being marketing-minded is everybody's job. What happens when (almost) everybody is doing that job? As companies have become more marketing-minded, there have been substantial reductions in the formal 'marketing departments' which do marketing. In short, a corollary of the trend to better organisational thinking about marketing is the dispersion of the activity of marketing, e.g. via task forces.

Principle 5: markets are heterogeneous

Most markets are not homogeneous, and are made up of different individual customers, submarkets or segments. While some customers, for example, may buy a car for cheap transport from A to B, others may buy for comfortable travel, or safe travel, or energy efficient travel, and still others may buy for status reasons or to satisfy and project their self-image. Products and services that attempt to satisfy a segmented market through a standardised product almost invariably fall between two or more stools and become vulnerable to more clearly targeted competitors.

Picking up on Principle 2, it is evident that a simple way of segmenting markets is on the basis of the benefits customers get in buying or consuming the product or service. Benefit segmentation (see Chapter 7) has proved to be one of the most useful ways of segmenting markets, for the simple reason that it relates segmentation back to the reasons for the existence of the segments in the first place – the different benefit requirements.

Market heterogeneity has another effect. Concentration in the customer base, facilitated by mergers and acquisitions and attrition rates, has become a daily reality for companies in business-to-business marketplaces. The emergence of powerful, well-informed and dominant customers underlines the importance of strategic sales capabilities and strategic account management approaches to give specialised attention to customers who can leverage the seller's dependence on them. It is difficult to consider marketing strategy in business-to-business markets without recognising the deep-seated implications of this factor. (We devote Chapter 14 to this topic.)

Principle 6: markets and customers are constantly changing

It is a truism that the only constant is change. Markets are dynamic, and virtually all products have a limited life that expires when a new or better way of satisfying the underlying want or need is found; in other words, until another solution or benefit provider comes along.

The fate of the slide rule, and before that logarithmic tables, at the hands of the pocket calculator is a classic example of where the problem (the need for rapid and easy calculation) was better solved through a newer technology. The benefits offered by calculators far outstripped the slide rule in speed and ease of use. But pocket calculators themselves are now superseded by applications (apps) on mobile telephones, which provide all the functionality of the high-specification technical calculators of a few years ago.

The recognition that products are not omnipotent, and that they follow a product life-cycle pattern of introduction, growth, maturity and decline, has led companies to undertake more long-term planning activity to ensure that by the time current breadwinners die, there are new products in the company's portfolio to take their place.

Also evident is the need for constant product and service improvement. As customer expectations change, usually becoming more demanding in the benefits they expect from a given product or service, so organisations need to upgrade their offerings continuously to retain, let alone improve, position.

There are two main processes of improvement. The first is through innovation, where a relatively large step is taken at one point in time. The advent of the pocket calculator was a significant innovation that virtually wiped out the slide rule industry overnight! Other step changes in technology, such as the advent of digital television and radio, the MP3 player and music streaming, have changed whole industries in a similarly short period of time.

The second approach to improvement is a more continuous process whereby smaller changes are made but on an insistent basis. This approach has been identified as a major contributor to the success of Japanese businesses in world markets during the 1960s, '70s and '80s. The Japanese call continuous improvement *kaizen*, and see it as an integral part of business life. Increasingly, organisations are attempting to marry the benefits of step-change innovation with continuous (*kaizen*) improvement. Figure 1.6 illustrates this process diagrammatically.

The impact of technological change is always felt significantly in the computer industry. It is sometimes hard to remember that computers were invented *after* the Second World War, as they are now such a pervasive and integral part of our business and home lives. Toffler (1981) noted in *Computer World* magazine:

> If the auto industry had done what the computer industry has done over the last thirty years, a Rolls Royce would cost $2.50, get around 2,000,000 miles to the gallon and six of them would fit on the head of a pin!

If that was true, then just think what the analogy would be today!

The challenges raised by economic recession also hasten change in many markets. Increasingly price-sensitive customers shop around more now, using the greater amount of information available online, and have become more deal-conscious. However, despite this turbulence and disruption, firms with strong relationships with customers are able to weather the economic storm far more effectively.

Figure 1.6 Product and process improvement

Global warming and climate change are creating markets for new products too. New versions of old products, such as wind turbines and hybrid or electric cars, are being developed and marketed. Concerns about rising sea levels are affecting how new homes are built; for example, on the north-west coast of the Netherlands, homes increasingly are being built on 'rafts' that rise or fall with changes in sea level. Some of them are really nicely designed and allow you to see the raft structure quite clearly.

Well-designed raft houses in the Netherlands represent market opportunities in the face of global warming and climate change

Source: Susan E. Degginger / Alamy Stock Photo.

1.5   The role of marketing in leading strategic management

In order for strategic management to cope with the changing marketing environment, there is a need for it to become increasingly market led. In taking a leading role in the development and implementation of strategy, the role of marketing can be defined as shown in Figure 1.7. That role is threefold.

Figure 1.7 The role of marketing in the organisation

1.5.1 Identification of customer requirements

The first critical task of marketing is to identify the requirements of customers and to communicate them effectively throughout the organisation. This involves conducting or commissioning customer research to uncover, first, who the customers are and, second, what will give them satisfaction.

Who the customers are is not always obvious. In some circumstances, buyers may be different from users or consumers; specifiers and influencers may also be different. Where services are funded by central government, for example, suppliers may be forgiven for the (mistaken) view that central government is their customer.

Customers *expect* a degree of benefit from purchasing or using a product or service. However, they may actually *want* something more, but believe they have to settle for second best because of budget or other constraints. The organisation that can give customers something closer to what they want than what they expect has an opportunity to go beyond customer satisfaction and create 'customer delight'.

Customer expectations, wants and needs must be understood and clearly communicated to those responsible for designing the product or service, those responsible for creating or producing it and those responsible for delivering it. (Identifying what customers require is discussed in Chapter 4.)

1.5.2 Deciding on the competitive positioning to be adopted

Recognising that markets are heterogeneous and typically made up of various market segments, each having different requirements from essentially similar offerings, requires firms to decide clearly which target market, or markets, they will serve.

Two main factors influence those decisions. First, how attractive the alternative potential targets are and, second, how well the company can hope to serve each potential target relative to competition – in other words, the relative strengths or competencies it can bring into play in serving the market. (These two related issues are discussed at length in Part 4.)

1.5.3 Implementing the marketing strategy

The third, and arguably the most difficult, key task of marketing is to marshal all the relevant organisational resources, and to plan and execute the delivery of customer satisfaction. This involves ensuring that all members of the organisation are aware of what is expected, and are coordinated in their efforts to satisfy customers, and that no actual or potential gaps exist between offer design, production and delivery. (Chapters 14, 15 and 16 address implementation and coordination issues more fully.)

Summary

This chapter has reviewed the marketing concept and demonstrated its importance in providing a guiding approach to doing business in the face of increasingly competitive and less predictable marketing environments. This approach we term 'market-led strategic management'. A number of marketing principles were discussed, together with the role of marketing in strategic management. The remainder of Part 1 presents a framework for developing a market-led approach.

Case study

LEGO builds new dimension with digital vision

By Richard Milne, Nordic correspondent

Danish group launches toys-to-life game, giving children the opportunity to put physical playthings into virtual worlds

Imagine Homer Simpson driving the Batmobile down the Yellow Brick Road. Or Superman steering a DeLorean time machine through Middle-earth.

What was once fantasy will become reality this week when LEGO and Warner Bros launch their big-budget game 'LEGO Dimensions'.

It marks a crucial step in the Danish toy-maker's digital strategy. The game – whose starter pack will be priced at a hefty $100 – pushes it into a new segment: the toys-to-life category, worth $700m a year in the USA alone.

'LEGO is the archetypal toys-to-life experience. We are just pushing those digital borders continually so we remain present and relevant in all the environments where children want to play', says John Goodwin, the finance director.

Toymakers have been hit hard by the emergence of smartphones and tablets, as children spend increasing amounts of time in digital play on such devices. LEGO has managed to buck that trend, largely thanks to the strength of its physical products as it became the world's biggest toymaker by sales in the first half of this year.

But, while it has developed a successful line in video games through Warner's TT Games, the

Source: Bloomberg/Getty Images.

privately-owned Danish company has struggled in other digital ventures with a number of flops.

'I don't think they have conquered the digital world. It's hard to point to something digital that they have done that is successful. But what you are seeing now is the first attempts for LEGO to create some kind of hybrid physical–digital experience', says David Robertson, co-author of *Brick by Brick: How LEGO Rewrote the Rules of Innovation and Conquered the Global Toy Industry* (2014).

That increases the pressure all the more on 'LEGO Dimensions', a sprawling game that cost the same as a blockbuster film to develop and features different brands including *Doctor Who, Back to the Future* and *Ghostbusters*.

For their $100, players will get a game for Sony's PlayStation, Microsoft's Xbox or Nintendo's Wii, alongside almost 300 LEGO pieces used to create a controller, as well as three characters: Batman, Gandalf from *Lord of the Rings* and Wyldstyle from *The Lego Movie*. Additional kits featuring other characters – from the Wicked Witch in *The Wizard of Oz*, Scooby Doo and Wonder Woman through to Krusty the Clown – will cost $15–30 and unlock new games levels and include vehicles for game play.

The game works by recognising which characters and vehicles are placed on a controller and making them part of the action, which takes place over 14 levels – one for each brand involved. Typical LEGO flourishes are included, such as an ability to rebuild each vehicle in three different ways.

'I wanted to make a game like this eight years ago. With my own kids, I could see how they would play with LEGO Batman and Gandalf together. When I saw toys-to-life, I knew this was the mechanism', says Jon Burton, the founder of British developer TT Games.

The game, which took 160 people three years to develop, is launching in a crowded marketplace. Activision Blizzard's 'Skylanders' game has dominated the toys-to-life category since it launched in 2011, but has been joined by Disney's 'Infinity' (which features *Star Wars* figures) and Nintendo's 'Amiibo' lines.

Liam Callahan, an analyst at market research group NPD, says the toys-to-life sector was worth $710m in the USA in the year to the end of August, up 6 per cent on the previous year. He argues that, even though the price is high and there is plenty of competition, 'LEGO Dimensions' should be a success thanks to the toymaker's brand and the huge number of other brands and characters involved in the game. 'Our research shows that the main market for these types of games are young males; but with the range of toys for "LEGO Dimensions", there may be a wider age and gender for main consumer as well as a cross-generational appeal for families', he adds.

Mr Burton says that the broad pitch is deliberate as he pushed to include levels from 'Portal', a puzzle video game, and *Back to the Future* to appeal to adults as well as children. 'There is a bigger market for this toys-to-life than just 6 to 12-year-olds', he adds.

Mr Goodwin is eager to underline that LEGO is not betting the company on 'Dimensions'. But he is keenly aware of the importance of the toymaker making a success of its digital offering.

'What is obvious is the digital and physical is something of a distinction we make but children don't . . . From a LEGO brand point of view, we continue to be anchored in the physical brick experience. But we are going to explore more ways that you can build strong linkages between the physical and digital worlds', he says.

LEGO took the decision to concentrate on the physical brick when it neared financial collapse in 2004. As part of its recovery under chief executive Jørgen Vig Knudstorp, over-diversification was diagnosed as one of its ills and its video games development arm was sold off.

Mr Burton, who was also an executive producer of *The Lego Movie*, says each company decided to focus on what they were best at: 'They handle bricks, we handle the digital side.'

Another recent collaboration is 'LEGO Worlds', a game still only in limited beta release that many see as the toymaker's answer to 'Minecraft'. Players can build worlds, buildings and figures using LEGO bricks with nearly all the freedom of the physical world, while new ideas are being incorporated according to what LEGO's online community suggests.

Mr Goodwin and Mr Burton say there is more to come, especially around making the digital experience more 'real'. The toys-to-life category works by the controller reading a chip in a character's base, meaning that if Batman is placed on Superman's base the machine will still think it is Superman. Similarly, only the exact model or vehicle will be imported into the game, not whatever the player imagines. Mr Goodwin hopes that will change one day.

Mr Robertson says that LEGO's great success has been building a range of products and experiences around the physical brick – so that children cannot just play with the products but also watch a television show, go to an event or see a display in a toy shop. Its digital push should be seen in that light, he argues, although he also says LEGO could gradually develop into more of a digital company. 'Maybe you and I might be talking in 2020 about what is the core of LEGO: is it physical or digital?'

Mr Goodwin dismisses such talk, arguing that if you 'put bricks in front of kids they just love to build'.

Losing strategies: award-winning games but not sales winners

Success is far from guaranteed for 'LEGO Dimensions', as some of the toymaker's previous digital efforts show. 'LEGO Universe', an ambitious and costly attempt to replicate the experience of playing with bricks in a game, developed by dozens of workers, was killed off within months of its launch in 2010.

At about the same time, a single Swedish computer enthusiast working part-time developed 'Minecraft', which became one of the biggest-selling games of all time and is, in Jon Burton's words, 'a digital version of LEGO'.

John Goodwin says that failure led to LEGO realising it needed to be more agile when dealing with digital products rather than physical ones: 'Other companies put their games out in beta [an early development stage] and constantly reiterate it. That's not part of our DNA. We have a tendency to want to have perfection by the time it gets into consumer hands.'

More recently, 'LEGO Fusion' won a string of awards in the USA but it was unsuccessful in grabbing children's attention and that too was discontinued. It allowed players to create two-dimensional models with physical bricks that they then imported into the game using a smartphone or tablet camera. 'One product was unusable, one was not fun', summarises David Robertson, a professor at the Wharton School in Pennsylvania.

Mr Goodwin adds, somewhat ruefully: 'It's not about winning awards, it's about delighting consumers constantly and we weren't able to do that.'

 Source: from 'Lego enters a new dimension with its digital strategy', *Financial Times*, 27/09/2015 (Milne, R.).

Discussion questions

1 Evaluate and comment on LEGO's market orientation using the market orientation assessment form (see Box 1.1) to support your analysis.

2 Which of the three approaches to marketing presented in this chapter do you think best describes LEGO's approach? Why?

3 What marketing principles are in evidence in this case?

CHAPTER 2
STRATEGIC MARKETING PLANNING

'Strategy is the matching of the activities of an organisation to the environment in which it operates and to its own resource capabilities.'

Johnson, Scholes and Whittington (2008)

'Planning is an unnatural process; it is much more fun to do something. The nicest thing about not planning is that failure comes as a complete surprise, rather than being preceded by a period of worry and depression.'

Sir John Harvey Jones, Chairman of Imperial Chemical Industries (ICI) 1982–1987

Three brings Smarty to the low-cost mobile party

By Nic Fildes

New UK mobile phone service gives discount to customers who do not use all their data

Three is set to go downmarket with the launch of a new mobile phone service that will give discounts to customers who do not use up all their data.

The imminent launch of Smarty is the first time that Three has delivered a sub-brand to the market. The move represents a push to attract a different segment of customers – those looking for cheaper deals than they can get through the main Three brand, which has almost 9m customers.

A website for Smarty offering 'simple and honest' mobile phone services has appeared online, with only details in the small print of the privacy policy revealing that Three is behind the new service. A source briefed on the new brand said it would initially only be open to a limited number of people. Three itself declined to comment.

The new SIM-only network is targeted at a low-spending demographic that does not want to sign up for pricey data contracts. The move to offer discounts on bills if a user does not use their data allotment

Source: Bloomberg / Contributo/Getty Images.

is similar to moves by Sky and Virgin Media to add more mobile customers – by allowing users to roll over unused data capacity between months.

The Smarty launch also comes ahead of a new range of Vodafone packages due to be launched in the second half designed to stimulate growth in the UK market and reposition the brand.

Other telecoms companies have established sub-brands. O2 owns the GiffGaff service and half of Tesco Mobile, while BT also operates under both the EE and Plusnet brands. Sub-brands can be used to target different customer segments but can also prove an expensive distraction. Vodafone, for example, is set to close down the Talkmobile brand it acquired from Carphone Warehouse to save costs.

The launch of the low-cost service comes amid a fierce debate about the impending spectrum auction, which will free up more airwaves for mobile phone companies to improve 4G networks and launch 5G in the future.

Three, part of the CK Hutchison conglomerate, has threatened to launch a judicial review of the process after Ofcom refused to introduce a 30 per cent cap on the amount of airwaves any operator can own. Three has argued that there is a spectrum imbalance, with EE, part of BT, and Vodafone controlling the majority of the airwaves between them and leaving Three and O2 constrained by their smaller spectrum holdings.

 Source: from 'Three brings Smarty to the low-cost mobile party', *Financial Times*, 10/08/17 (Fildes, N. Telecoms Correspondent).

Discussion questions

1 Why is Three launching a sub-brand?
2 How is Three trying to compete?

Introduction

The essence of developing a marketing strategy for any organisation is to ensure that organisational capabilities are matched to the current market environment, and that they continue to be matched in future. For a commercial organisation, this means ensuring that resources and capabilities match the needs and requirements of the competitive markets in which it operates. For a not-for-profit organisation, such as a charity or a public utility, it means achieving a fit between its abilities to serve and the requirements of the publics or causes it seeks to serve. At the heart of strategy lies a need to assess critically the organisation's resource profile (often referred to as strengths and weaknesses) and the environment it faces (often referred to as opportunities and threats).

Strategic planning attempts to answer three basic questions:

1 What is the business doing now?
2 What is happening in the environment?
3 What should the business be doing?

Strategy is concerned primarily with effectiveness (doing the right things) rather than efficiency (doing what you do well). The vast bulk of management time is, of necessity, concerned with day-to-day operations management. A time audit for even senior management will often reveal a disproportionate amount of time spent on routine daily tasks, with the more difficult and demanding task of planning further into the future relegated to a strategy conference, 'away day' or 'retreat' perhaps once a year. In many successful companies, however, thinking strategically, or sitting back from the present concerns of improving what you do now and questioning what it *is* you are doing, is a constant process.

Fundamental to strategic thinking is the concept of 'strategic fit', shown diagrammatically in Figure 2.1. For any strategy to be effective, it needs to be well tuned both to the needs and requirements of customers (the market conditions in which it is implemented), and to the resources and capabilities of the organisation seeking to implement it. No matter how well-crafted and articulated a strategy might be, if it is not focused on meeting the needs of customers, it is doomed to failure. Similarly, if the organisational resources necessary for successful implementation are unavailable, success will be elusive.

As with the adoption of a marketing philosophy throughout the organisation, the adoption of strategic thinking goes beyond the remit of marketing management alone. All senior

Figure 2.1
Strategic fit

executives in the company or organisation have a responsibility for developing the strategic profile of the company and giving it a strategic focus. Strategic planning and strategic marketing planning share many activities, although strategic planning has more breadth and covers all business activities. A market orientation must permeate the whole of an organisation, but the strategic marketing plan is just one of several functional plans that feed into the overall strategic plan of a company. Marketing management, however, with its specific responsibility for managing the interface between the organisation and its environment (both customers and competitors), has an increasingly important role to play in overall strategy development.

Marketing strategy should be set in the context of overall corporate strategy. Once the overall direction of the organisation has been decided, with appropriate input from all relevant stakeholders, marketing strategy will need to be aligned to ensure that direction is achieved.

2.1   Defining the business purpose or mission

For many organisations, a useful starting point in strategy formulation is to define a mission or purpose. Tim Smit, co-founder and executive vice chair of Eden Project Ltd in Cornwall, UK, set out to build the biggest global eco-brand and to change the way people think about themselves and their relationship with the planet on which they live (see **www.edenproject. com/eden-story/about-us/sir-tim-smit-kbe**). The mission was stated as 'to promote the understanding and responsible management of the vital relationship between plants, people and resources leading to a sustainable future for all'. The Millennium Commission weighed in with £37.5 million of Lottery funding to single Eden out as the landmark project of the far southwest, and its subsequent contributions brought the total to just over £56 million (**www.edenproject.com/eden-story/about-us/our-funding**). Other major sources of funding included the EU and Southwest Regional Development Agency (£50 million between them) and £20 million of commercial loans, in order to create a complex of greenhouse domes (or biomes) and an Outdoor Garden covering the 11.5 hectares of a disused clay pit at St Austell. Importantly, it gave the people working on the project a worthwhile set of objectives to strive for, and to commit to. Since opening to the public in 2001, Eden has attracted more than 18 million visitors and inspired an economic renaissance in Cornwall by contributing more than 1.7 billion to the local economy.

Defining the business purpose or mission requires a company to ask the fundamental questions first posed by Levitt over half a century ago (see Levitt, 1960):

- What business are we in?
- What business do we want to be in?

Many years ago, so marketing folklore has it, a new managing director took over at Parker Pens. One of his first actions was to assemble the board of directors, stand before them holding the top-of-the-range Parker of the day and ask, 'Who is our greatest competitor?'.

The first answer to emerge from the board was Shaeffer. Shaeffer produced a pen very similar to the Parker. It had a good reputation for quality, had a similar stylish finish and was similarly priced at the top end of the market. The new managing director was not, however, impressed with this answer. 'We certainly compete to some extent with Shaeffer, but they are by no means our major competitor.'

A newer member of the board then suggested that the major competitor might be Biro-Swan, the manufacturers and marketers of a range of ballpoint pens. While these retailed considerably cheaper than the Parker, he reasoned that they were used for the same purpose (writing) and hence competed directly with Parker. The business definition was now changing from 'quality fountain pens' to 'writing implements' and under this definition pencils could also be considered as competitors, as could the more recent developments in the market of fibre-tip pens and rollerball pens. 'Your thinking is getting better', said the MD, 'but you're still not there.'

Another board member then suggested that perhaps the major competitor was the telephone – something that had gained widespread use in recent years. Under this view of the market they were in 'communications' and competing with other forms of communication including the written word (perhaps competing here with typewriters and, more recently, word processors) and other (verbal) means of communication. 'More creative thinking', said the MD, 'but you still haven't identified the main competitor.'

Eventually the MD gave his view of the major competitor. To an astonished board he announced, 'Our major competitor is the Ronson cigarette lighter!'. When asked to explain his reasoning, he defined the market that the company was in as the 'quality gift market'. Analysis of sales of Parker pens showed that the majority of purchases were made by individuals buying them as gifts for other people. When they considered what to buy, often a major alternative was a quality cigarette lighter and hence the definition of the market. (Story courtesy of Graham Kenwright.)

This definition, or view, has implications for the way in which this product might be marketed. Packaging assumes a more important role, as does the development and maintenance of a superior quality image. Price is perhaps less important than might have been thought under alternative market definitions. Distribution (through the outlets where potential customers buy gifts) also becomes more important.

This example serves to illustrate how asking a basic question such as 'Who is our major competitor?' or 'What market are we in?' can affect the whole strategic direction of the company.

2.1.1 Mission formulation and statement

Formulating the mission into a brief and concise statement that can be communicated across the organisation can help engender a sense of common purpose, and provide guidelines for how decisions will be made and resource allocations prioritised in the future. Poorly constructed statements, especially those offering nothing more than 'motherhood and apple pie', can cause more damage than good, by creating derision among employees, managers and even customers.

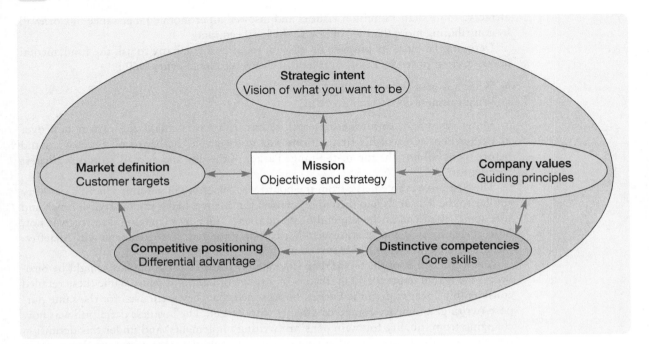

Figure 2.2 Components of mission

Hooley *et al.* (1992) discuss the elements that go to make up an effective statement of mission, and these are shown in Figure 2.2. An effective mission statement needs to spell out the following:

1 The **strategic intent** (see Hamel and Prahalad, 1989), or vision of where the organisation wants to be in the foreseeable future. Hamel and Prahalad cite examples of strategic intent for Komatsu (earthmoving equipment manufacturers) as being to 'encircle Caterpillar', and for the American Apollo space programme as 'landing a man on the moon ahead of the Soviets'. However, strategic intent need not be as inherently competitive as these examples. It might focus on the achievement of a set of worthy social goals, or improving quality of life for particular groups of people or animals.

2 The **values of the organisation** should be clearly stated and communicated in order to set an ethical and moral tone that guides operations. Mars (confectionery) articulates five 'principles' that guide the actions and decision making of its employees. These are:

Quality: The consumer is our boss, quality is our work and value for money is our goal.
Responsibility: As individuals, we demand total responsibility from ourselves; as associates, we support the responsibilities of others.
Mutuality: A mutual benefit is a shared benefit; a shared benefit will endure.
Efficiency: We use resources to the full, waste nothing and do only what we can do best.
Freedom: We need freedom to shape our future; we need profit to remain free.
(Mars, 2019)

Clearly, once value statements are articulated, it is important that they guide the actions of organisational stakeholders. If not then there is little point in spending time and effort in producing them. Additionally, certain stakeholders may become cynical about the underlying business ethos driving an organisation that might do this.

Similarly, assertions about concern for the environment in mission statements can sound hollow if not followed up with deeds and actions.

3 The **distinctive competencies of the organisation** should articulate what differentiates the organisation from others of its kind – what its distinctive essence is. This is a difficult but necessary thing for many organisations. It seeks to spell out the individuality of the organisation, and clarify why it exists as a separate entity and what is special about it.

4 **Market definition**, in terms of major customer targets that the organisation seeks to serve, and the functions or needs of those customers that will be served. At launch, the insurance company Sheila's Wheels (now part of the esure Group plc) focused on the needs of a specific target market that was reflected in its brand name and its business purpose: 'a car insurance company designed for the female driver'. However, of late, its targeting has softened and widened somewhat, to indicate that it is 'dedicated to helping young families' (**www.sheilaswheels.com**).

5 Finally, the mission should spell out where the organisation is, or intends to be, **positioned** in the marketplace, and should reflect or indicate its uniqueness and distinctiveness. This is the result of bringing together market definition and distinctive skills and competencies.

In a classic academic marketing paper, Ted Levitt (1960) provided many examples of companies adopting a myopic view in defining their businesses. The railroads believed they were in the railway business, not transportation, and failed to take note of alternative means of transport. The oil industry believed they were in the business of producing oil, not in the business of producing and marketing energy. In defining the business, it is necessary to understand the total product or service that customers are buying and what benefits it delivers, and avoid the trap of concentrating too much on the physical features offered.

The second question posed at the start of this section – 'What business do we want to be in?' – is often more difficult to answer. It requires a thorough analysis of the options open to the organisation and an understanding of how the world in general, and the company's markets in particular, are changing.

2.2   The marketing strategy process

Once the purpose of the organisation is defined, the marketing strategy can be crafted to help achieve that purpose. We can view the development of marketing strategy at three main levels: the establishment of a core strategy; the creation of the company's competitive positioning; and the implementation of the strategy (see Figure 2.3).

The establishment of an effective marketing strategy starts with a detailed and creative assessment both of the company's capabilities – its strengths and weaknesses relative to the competition – and the opportunities and threats posed by the environment. On the basis of this analysis, the core strategy of the company will be selected, identifying marketing objectives and the broad focus for achieving them.

At the next level, market targets (both customers and competitors) are selected and/or identified. At the same time, the company's differential advantage, or competitive edge, in serving the customer targets better than the competition is defined. Taken together, the identification of targets and the definition of differential advantage constitute the creation of the competitive positioning of the organisation and its offerings.

At the implementation level, a marketing organisation capable of putting the strategy into practice must be created. The design of the marketing organisation can be crucial to the success of the strategy. Implementation is also concerned with establishing a mix of products, price, promotion and distribution that can convey both the positioning and the products and services themselves to the target market. Finally, methods of control must be designed to ensure that the strategy implementation is successful. Control concerns both the efficiency with which the strategy is put into operation, and the ultimate effectiveness of that strategy. Each of the three main levels of strategy is now considered in more detail.

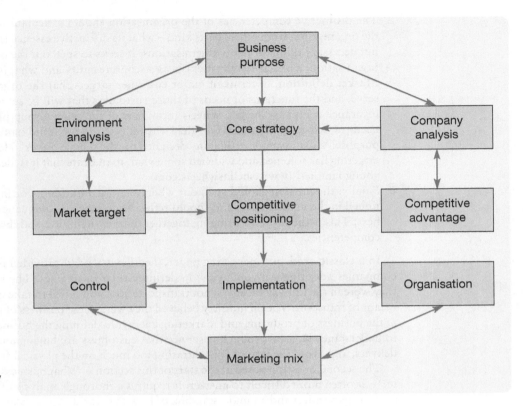

Figure 2.3 The marketing strategy process

2.3 Establishing the core strategy

The core strategy is both a statement of the company's objectives and the broad strategies it will use to achieve them. To establish the core strategy requires a detailed analysis of the resources available and the market in which the organisation will operate, both within the context of achieving the overall business purpose or mission.

2.3.1 Analysis of organisational resources

Any organisation could create a long list of the resources it has at its disposal. Not all of those resources, however, will be equally useful in crafting or implementing a marketing strategy. Similarly, if it is sufficiently self-critical, any organisation could list many weaknesses, but not all of those will be fatal in competitive terms. In defining the core strategy, organisations attempt to define the distinctive resources (assets and capabilities) that serve to define the organisation. This helps to set the bounds on what options are currently open to the organisation and to identify where its strengths can be utilised to the full, while minimising vulnerability to its weaknesses. Core competencies or core skills may result from any aspect of the operation. They may stem from the skills of the workforce in assembling the product effectively or efficiently, from the skills of management in marketing or financial planning, or from the skills of the R&D department in initiating new product ideas or creating new products on the basis of customer research. What is important from a marketing strategy perspective, however, is whether they can be utilised in the marketplace to provide superior customer value.

The distinctive competencies of the company may lie in its marketing assets of image and market presence, or its distribution network or after-sales service. The crucial issue in identifying distinctive competence is that it must be something exploitable in the marketplace. Distinctive technological skills in producing a product are of little value if there is no demand for that product. Hence, an important role of marketing management is to assess the potential distinctive competencies of the organisation in the light of exploitability in the market.

The counterbalance to distinctive competencies or exploitable strengths are weaknesses relative to the competition. Where, for example, competitors have a more favourable or protected supply of raw materials, or a stronger customer loyalty, the company must be fully aware of its limitations and generate strategies to overcome or circumvent them. Structural weaknesses – those inherent in the firm's operations, brought about by its very mode of doing business – may be difficult or even impossible to eliminate. Strategies should be developed to shift competition away from these factors, and to make them less important to competitive success. Other weaknesses may be more easily avoided once they have been identified, or even changed to strengths by exploiting them in a different way.

The product portfolio

A key aspect of understanding an organisation's resources is to undertake a portfolio analysis of the various offerings it has available on the market.

For some time, being 'one or two in all we do' has been the driving philosophy of General Electric (GE), the American conglomerate whose activities range from power stations to LEDs. GE's businesses are amazingly diverse, and until quite recently one of its most successful subsidiaries was the manufacture of electric light bulbs – a very mature, high-volume and low-priced commodity. In 2016, however, GE announced that it was no longer going to produce traditional electric light bulbs and instead was going to focus on LEDs – a market where it had had a lot of early success. Other divisions in GE make domestic electrical appliances of all types, medical equipment including body scanners, renewable energy, and one of the most successful parts of the company is market leader in the military and commercial aero engine markets. It is clear that different businesses within the company are operating in different markets, with different opportunities and threats, and utilising different corporate skills and resources. It is therefore important to ensure that appropriate objectives and strategies are formulated for each business unit, and that these support each other to ensure sustainability of the corporate entity. The process of balancing activities across this variety of business units involves portfolio planning, which is the subject of this chapter.

Consider, for example, the challenges that managing a group of businesses such as those owned by Virgin presents. Virgin's operations include travel, communications, entertainment, financial services, hospitality, retail, aerospace and a host of other areas. It is an example of growth through collaboration and of portfolio management, with both successes and failures.

Portfolio analysis is the foundation for making important choices for investment and for strategic direction. These examples underline the importance of portfolio issues and the central role of marketing variables, as opposed to purely financial criteria, in making portfolio choices.

More than four decades ago, one of the founding fathers of management theory Peter Drucker, identified seven types of businesses that still have resonance today (see Figure 2.4):

1 **Today's breadwinners** – the products and services that are earning healthy profits and contributing positively to both cash flow and profits.
2 **Tomorrow's breadwinners** – investments in the company's future. These are the products and services that may not yet be making a strong financial contribution to the company, but that are in growth or otherwise attractive markets and are expected to take over the breadwinning role in the future, when today's breadwinners eventually fade.
3 **Yesterday's breadwinners** – the products and services that have supported the company in the past, but are not now contributing significantly to cash flow or to profits. Many companies have a predominance of businesses of this type, indicating that they have been slow to invest in future developments.

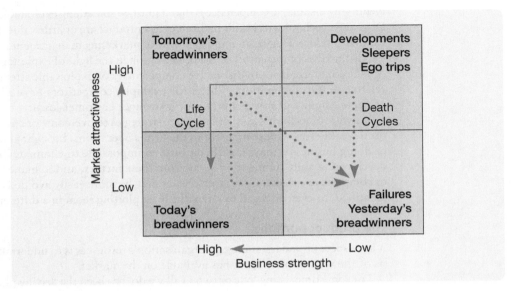

Figure 2.4 Product types in the portfolio

4 **Developments** – the products and services recently developed that may have some future, but where greater investment is needed to achieve that future.

5 **Sleepers** – the products and services that have been around for some time, but have so far failed to establish themselves in their markets or, indeed, their expected markets have failed to materialise. These are allowed to remain in the portfolio, in the hope that one day they will take off.

6 **Ego trips** – the products and services that have strong product champions among influential managers, but for which there is little proven demand in the marketplace. The company, because of the involvement of powerful managers, continues to put resources into these products in the hope of their eventually coming good.

7 **Failures** – the products and services that have failed to play a significant role in the company's portfolio and have no realistic chance of doing so. These are kept on the company's books largely through inertia. It is easier to do so than admit defeat and withdraw or divest them.

The product life cycle (or death cycle) provides a link between the businesses identified by Drucker (see Figure 2.4). As they stand, developments, sleepers or ego trips contribute little to the company, but it is hoped that they may one day do so. The markets they are in may be highly attractive but, because of underinvestment, the company has little ability to serve them. If left alone as they are, with no extra investment, these businesses will follow the death cycle and become failures.

Strategically, a company faces a dilemma with these businesses. If left alone they are unlikely to succeed, so a choice has to be made between investing in them, or getting out. In even the largest companies it is impossible to pursue all attractive markets, so the first portfolio decision is one of double or quits. If the choice is to invest, then the aim is to build the business until it is strong enough to become one of tomorrow's breadwinners. This usually means achieving some degree of market dominance in a growth sector. If successfully managed, the product will mature to become one of today's breadwinners and, as it ages, one of yesterday's. As with all things, the difficulty in the portfolio is not starting ventures, but knowing when to kill them and when to concentrate resources where success can be achieved.

Portfolio planning

Any diversified organisation needs to find methods for assessing the balance of businesses in its portfolio and to help guide resource allocation between them. A number of portfolio planning models are available in the management literature to facilitate this process. The earliest and most basic model was the Growth–Share Matrix, developed by the Boston Consulting Group. More sophisticated models have been developed by consultants Arthur D. Little and McKinsey, as well as by organisations such as Shell and General Electric. All, however, share a number of key objectives (Grant, 1995):

1 **Development of business strategies and allocation of resources** (both financial and managerial). By assessing the position of a business in its industry, together with the prospects for that industry over the medium to long term, investment priorities can be set for individual businesses. Those businesses that are strong in attractive markets are likely to be self-sustaining financially. They will, however, require attentive management to ensure they continue to achieve their potential. Hold or build strategies will typically be indicated. Weak businesses in attractive markets may require further investment to build a position for the future. Products in declining sectors may be less deserving of resource allocation unless turnaround strategies are likely to reverse market trends. In declining markets, products are often managed for cash flow, to enable resources to be reallocated to areas of the portfolio with more potential.

2 **Analysing portfolio balance.** In addition to suggesting strategies for individual businesses, portfolio analysis assists assessment of the overall portfolio balance in terms of cash flow, future prospects and risk (see Figure 2.5). Cash flow balance is achieved where investments in businesses with potential are met through surpluses from current or past breadwinners. The extent to which the cash flow is out of balance suggests opportunities for expansion or acquisition or the need to raise capital from external investors (see Figures 2.6 and 2.7). For example, in the first financial quarter of 2019, Apple reported that it had $245 billion cash on hand. Here, ability to mitigate threats, capitalise on opportunities and generally manage the balance of a business portfolio competing in turbulent markets is significant, and likely not to depend on external sources on funding.

Additionally, a crucial element of portfolio planning is to help assess the future prospects of the organisation as a whole. Too heavy a dependence in the portfolio on yesterday's products may indicate a healthy current cash flow, but unless that is invested in tomorrow's products the longer-term future may be in doubt. Too many future investments without a solid-enough current cash generation may suggest an overstretched portfolio. Finally, assessing the risks associated with individual businesses enables a firm to spread its overall risk, ensuring not all its ventures are high risk but allowing some more risky ventures to be balanced by perhaps less rewarding but more predictable activities.

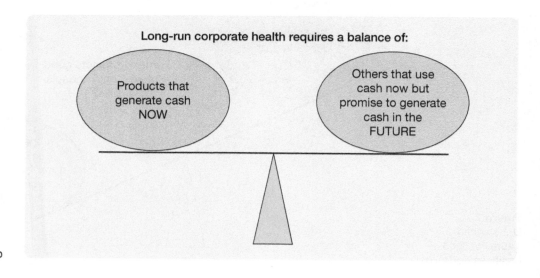

Figure 2.5
Balancing the
business portfolio

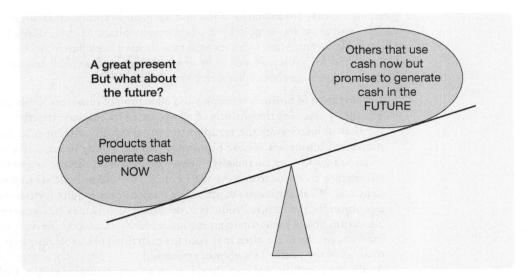

Figure 2.6
Unbalanced,
present-focused
business portfolio

Strengths and weaknesses can only be determined effectively through a systematic and comprehensive audit of the firm's resources and their utilisation relative to the competition. (Chapter 6 describes in more detail how this can be accomplished.)

2.3.2 Analysis of the markets served

An analysis of the markets in which the company operates, or wishes to operate, can serve to throw into focus the opportunities and threats facing the company. Those opportunities and threats stem from two main areas: the customers (both current and potential) and competitors (again both current and potential).

Most markets segment in one way or another. They consist of heterogeneous customers, or customers with varying needs and wants. Asking 'How is the market segmented?' can provide valuable insights into customer requirements and help in focusing on specific market targets.

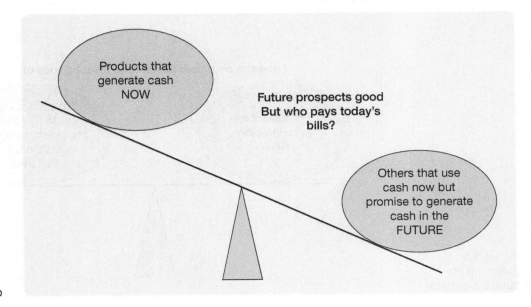

Figure 2.7
Unbalanced,
future-focused
business portfolio

In an effort to create a deeper understanding of its customer base, the world-famous Fender guitar company recently reviewed and refreshed the data it had on the guitar market and customers in general. The insights from that process revolutionised the company and allowed it to more closely align marketing operations with the needs and wants of customer segments. Indeed, a great deal of 'new' information became available to the company on which to base decisions and actions. For example, it found that 45 per cent of its guitars were sold to first-time, relatively affluent buyers, 95 per cent of whom subsequently gave up playing within a year. As a result, Fender launched 'Fender Play', a video-based online subscription service that helps people learn to play. At the time of writing there are 100,000 subscribers to this innovation. Andy Mooney (CEO of Fender), when discussing the opportunity revealed by the data, stated that Fender 'saw there was a viable opportunity to do online learning. If we could reduce the abandonment rate by only 10 per cent we could double the size of the industry' (interview from *The Times*, March 2019).

In the 1990s, Sega and Nintendo were hugely successful in developing the computer games market with relatively cheap games consoles and addictive software, before late entrant Sony eventually became market leader with its PlayStation. Forecasters and market watchers have for some time predicated a decline in the game console market, largely due to the increased power, utility, availability and relative low cost of PCs. However, the market has remained remarkably resilient and has continued to grow through excellent advertising, significant levels of innovation in games and games consoles and new and attractive packaging and income models in the industry. The 'Fortnite' video game phenomenon, currently played by millions of young people all over the world, uses a format whereby the game is available free to download, but 'in-game' purchases and lucrative merchandising have delivered enviable returns through an increasingly 'industry standard' operating model.

Having examined the current and potential segmentation of the market, the next step in assessing alternatives is to search for untapped, or under-tapped, opportunities in the market. In the food market, for example, changes in eating habits are currently taking place. Some of the most significant are the increased emphasis on convenience foods, the trend towards healthier eating and vegetable-based diets and an increase in demand for gluten-free food. These changes open up new and significant opportunities to those willing and able to take advantage of them.

Market opportunities are created through changes (as with increased health awareness and its impact on eating habits), or through the inability of competitors to serve existing needs. This might be because companies cannot serve them (they do not have the skills and competencies to do so) or they choose not to serve them for one reason or another.

Timing in recognising and capitalising on opportunities is of great importance (Abell, 1978). The concept of 'strategic windows' focuses on the fact that there are limited periods during which the fit between the requirements of the market and the capabilities of the firm is at an optimum. Investment, therefore, should be timed to coincide with periods when strategic windows open and, conversely, disinvestment should be considered once a good fit is no longer apparent.

In addition to considering the opportunities open to the organisation, it is important to examine the threats facing it. These stem from two main sources: changes in the market-place that the firm is not aware of, or capable of keeping up with; or competitive activity designed to change the balance of power within the market.

A changing world requires constant intelligence gathering on the part of the organisation, to ensure that it can keep abreast of customer requirements. Keeping up with technological developments can be particularly important in many markets, as new innovations can change the shape of a competitive landscape very rapidly if unaddressed. This is not to say that every change must be responded to, however, as this would create a chaotic and completely reactive business model. Organisations should be aware of 'what's out there', and regularly discuss any changes and developments in light of the possible or actual impact on their business. In the early 1970s, the advent of digital watches caused severe (albeit relatively temporary) problems for Swiss watch manufacturers and, today, music downloads and streaming services are reshaping the music industry. Changes also occur in customer tastes, which manifest in the products and services demanded. The fashion industry is one where tastes change incredibly rapidly, and fashions come and go – a phenomenon driven by designers and marketers. In such settings, particularly, but nevertheless in many modern markets where tastes change quickly, keeping up with market knowledge is crucial. (Chapter 4 deals in more detail with customer analysis.)

The second major type of threat an organisation may face is from competition. Increasing competition, both from domestic and international sources, is the name of the game in most markets. As competitors become more sophisticated in seeking out market opportunities and designing marketing programmes to exploit them, so incumbent companies need to improve marketing activities, products and services. In the United Kingdom, many industries have not responded adequately to increased international competition, and have suffered the consequences; high-profile examples would be the once world-leading car and aircraft manufacturing industries. It is telling that in the highly competitive laptop computer market, the first 'lightweight' computers demanded by business users weary of carrying heavier machines did not come from existing PC manufacturers, but from Sony – leveraging its core competence of making things smaller. In more sophisticated marketing companies, rigorous competitor analysis commands almost as much time as customer analysis and self-evaluation. Substantial effort is directed towards identifying competitors' strengths and weaknesses and likely strategies (see Chapter 5).

2.3.3 SWOT analysis

The previous analysis of organisational strengths and weaknesses (*internal focus*) can then be combined with analysis of the market (*external focus*) to create a SWOT (strengths, weaknesses, opportunities and threats) analysis (see Figure 2.8).

The purpose of SWOT is twofold. First, it seeks to identify the most significant factors, both internal and external, affecting the organisation and its markets. It provides a quick, executive summary of the key issues. Second, by looking at where strengths and weaknesses align with opportunities and threats, it can help strategy formulation (see Figure 2.9). The organisation can begin to see where its strengths might be best deployed, both offensively and defensively, as well as where its weaknesses leave it vulnerable to market change or competitor action.

	Internal	External
Good points	**Strengths** What are we good at relative to competitors?	**Opportunities** What changes are creating new options for us?
Danger points	**Weaknesses** What are we bad at relative to competitors?	**Threats** What emerging dangers must we avoid or counter?

Figure 2.8 SWOT analysis

Figure 2.9
SWOT strategic
implications

2.3.4 Core strategy

Using the previous analysis, the company seeks to define key factors for success (KFS), sometimes termed 'critical success factors', in particular markets. KFS are those factors that are crucial to doing business in a particular industry, and are identified by examining differences between industry 'winners' and 'losers'. They often represent the factors where the greatest leverage can be exerted – that is, where the most effect can be obtained for a given amount of effort.

In the grocery industry, for example, KFS might centre on relationships between manufacturer and retailer. The power of the major multiples (in the UK, the top three retailers, Tesco, Sainsbury's and Asda, account for just under 60 per cent of sales) is such that if a new food product does not obtain distribution through the major outlets, a substantial amount of the potential market is unavailable, thus severely impacting on the overall viability of that product. In commodity markets, where price is often considered the only real means of product differentiation, a KFS might be production process efficiency.

A further consideration when setting the core strategy for a multi-product or multi-divisional company is how the various corporate activities add up – the role in the company's overall business portfolio of each activity (see Chapter 6).

Having identified corporate capabilities, market opportunities and threats, the key factors for success in the industry in which the firm operates and the role of the particular product or business in the company's overall portfolio, the company sets its marketing objectives. The objectives should be for both the long and short term. Long-term objectives indicate the future overall destination of the company – its long-term goals. To achieve those long-term goals, however, it is usually necessary to translate them into shorter-term objectives, a series of which will add up to the longer-term goals. Long-term objectives are often set in terms of profit or market domination for a firm operating in the commercial sector. Non-profit-making organisations, too, set long- and short-term goals. The long-term goal of Greenpeace, for example, is to help save the world's environment.

Often, short-term and long-term goals can become confused, or conflict. There is also the danger that setting them in isolation can result in a situation where the attainment of the short-term goals does nothing to further the long-term objectives and may, in some instances, hinder them. For example, a commercial company setting long-term market domination goals might find short-term profit maximisation at odds with this. Many managers are judged on their annual performance, as opposed to performance over the long term. Hence, they might be encouraged to pursue short-term objectives at the expense of building a stronger market position over a longer timescale (see the discussion in Chapter 1 on stakeholder motivations).

The core strategy of the organisation is a statement of how it intends to achieve its objectives. If, for example, the long-term objective is to be market leader in market X, with a share of market at least twice that of the nearest competitors, the core strategy may centre on using superior technology to achieve this, or lower prices, or better service or quality. The core strategy will take advantage of the firm's core competencies and bring them to bear wherever possible on the KFS to achieve the corporate objectives of the company.

The core strategy pursued may vary at different stages of the product's or service's life cycle. Figure 2.10 shows alternative ways in which a company may go about improving the performance of its products or services. These are choices of strategic focus.

A basic choice appears to exist (more on this later) between attempting to increase sales and improving the level of profitability achieved from existing sales (or even reduced sales in a declining market). When the objectives are to increase sales, again two fundamental approaches may be taken: either to expand the total market (most easily, though not exclusively, achieved during the early growth stages of the life cycle); or to increase share of the existing market (most often pursued during the late-growth/maturity phases).

Expand the market

Market expansion can be achieved by attracting new users to the product or service, identifying new uses for the product, or by developing new products and services to stimulate the market. New users can be found through geographical expansion of the company's operations, both domestically and internationally. For example, Asda in the UK (now owned by Walmart, the large American multinational retailer), pursued new customers when it expanded operations to the south, from its Yorkshire home base. Conversely, Sainsbury's attacked new markets in the north of England from its 'traditional' south-east stronghold. More recently, Aldi and Lidl have been very successful in moving into the UK from a European base. Alternatively, new segments with an existing or latent need for the product may

Figure 2.10 Strategic focus

be identifiable. Repositioning Lucozade as a high-energy sports-type drink found a new segment for a product once sold exclusively to parents of sick children as a recuperative aid.

The spectacular growth of 'no-frills' airlines is founded not only on taking market share, but also on growing the market so that more people fly more often. Ryanair, in particular, with carefully chosen routes where it is the only flyer, has on occasion experienced fourfold traffic growth.

Many manufacturers of off-road vehicles have been incredibly successful in attracting new users, who would have otherwise purchased cars. Through advertising that has extolled the adventurous credentials of such vehicles and the safety features of the higher driving position and robust design, despite many of them never being used for more than shopping trips or taking children to school, the market for 4×4s (or sport utility vehicles – SUVs) has expanded hugely over the past decade. Companies such as Volvo, Jaguar, BMW and Porsche have all successfully developed and launched new products into the market, although latterly emissions concerns regarding diesel engines have slowed growth somewhat. Battery technology and lighter/leaner models seem to be the way forward for manufacturers, with significant investment in this direction already evident.

For some products it may be possible to identify new uses. Head & Shoulders shampoo is a good example of this. Originally it was positioned as an anti-dandruff/'medicated' product, but more recently the overall conditioning and 'look' of hair washed in Head & Shoulders has been featured more heavily. Celebrity endorsements have also been used to reposition the brand as being more youthful and vibrant in order to attract new users. Among household cleaners, Flash was originally marketed as a product for cleaning floors, but now is also promoted as an all-purpose product for general cleaning, and for baths and basins.

Increase share

Increasing market share, especially in mature markets, usually comes at the expense of existing competition. The *main* routes to increasing market share include: a) winning competitors' customers; b) merging with (or acquiring) the competitors; or c) entering into strategic alliances with competitors, suppliers and/or distributors. In order to win customers from competitors, a company must offer something that is currently unavailable through another supplier. Another way to look at this, is that the company must create a perception in the mind of the customer that what they offer is currently unavailable from another supplier. This may come about through identification of competitor weaknesses, or through better exploitation of the company's own strengths and competencies. Each of the elements of the marketing mix (products, price, promotion and distribution) may be used to offer the value-added proposition to the customer, to induce switching.

Increasing usage rate may be a viable approach to expanding the market for some products. For example, breakfast cereals might be promoted as healthy snacks to be eaten at any time of day, and not just at breakfast. Alternatively, they might also be promoted as food that can help as part of a calorie-controlled diet, such as Kellogg's Special K. Of late, many organisations have introduced loyalty schemes, designed to reward repurchase and 'loyalty' in order to increase purchase frequency, share of 'purse' and customer retention.

Improving profitability

With existing levels of sales, or even reduced levels, profitability can be increased through improving margins. This is usually achieved by increasing price, reducing costs or doing both of these things. In a multi-product firm, it may also be possible through 'weeding' of the product line – that is, removing poorly performing products and concentrating effort on the more financially viable. The longer-term positioning implications of this weeding should, however, be carefully considered prior to wielding the axe. It may be, for example, that maintenance of seemingly unprofitable lines is essential to allow the company to continue to operate in the market as a whole, or in its own specifically chosen niche of that market.

They may be viewed as the ground stakes in the strategic game, essential to reserve a seat at the competitive table.

Earlier we said that it 'appears' a choice exists between the options, and this is true to a large extent. But it is useful for us to reflect on what choosing between the options outlined implies for the strategic direction of a business, and in 'the real world' it is likely that more than one of these options is desirable for the senior management team, who are often under pressure to increase sales *and* improve productivity. The specific nuances of a particular company strategy (and associated organisational politics) are somewhat beyond the bounds of this text; however, it is worth noting that initiatives to improve productivity in one part of the organisation may not act in isolation from a 'sales drive' in another part. This said, what is clear is that the overarching notion of strategic focus (and choosing one option) is still very much relevant and important for organisations wishing to improve market position.

2.4　Creation of the competitive positioning

The competitive positioning of the company is a statement of market targets (*where* the company will compete) and differential advantage (*how* the company will compete). The positioning is developed to achieve the objectives laid down under the core strategy. For a company whose objective is to gain market share, and the broad approach to that is to win competitors' customers, for example, the competitive positioning will be a statement of exactly how and where in the market that will be achieved.

2.4.1 Market targets

While the discussion of core strategy required an analysis of customers and competitors to identify potential opportunities and threats, competitive positioning selects those targets most suited to utilising the company's strengths and minimising vulnerability due to weaknesses.

A number of factors should be considered in choosing a market target. Broadly, they fall into two categories: assessing market attractiveness and evaluating the company's current or potential strengths in serving that market (see Porter, 1987).

Market attractiveness consists of many (possibly conflicting) factors, and it is important that a sensible, rounded and structured review is undertaken. Other things being equal, however, a market will generally be more attractive if the following hold:

- It is large.
- It is growing.
- Contribution margins are high.
- Competitive intensity and rivalry are low (and the current incumbents do not provide high levels of satisfaction).
- There are high entry and low exit barriers.
- The market is not vulnerable to uncontrollable events.

Markets that possess all these features do not exist for long, if at all. They are, almost by definition, bound to attract high levels of competition and hence become less attractive to other entrants over time. For small or medium-sized companies, small and/or static markets that do not attract more powerful competitors may be more appealing. In a market where high entry barriers (such as proprietary technology, high switching costs, etc.) can be erected, the company will be better able to defend its position against competitive attack (see Chapter 10).

To a greater or lesser extent, all markets are vulnerable to external and uncontrollable factors such as general economic conditions, government legislation or political change. However, some markets are more vulnerable, and this is especially true when selecting among international market alternatives. In the UK, companies can seek help and advice from the government in the form of the Department for International Trade (see **www.gov. uk/government/organisations/department-for-international-trade**).

Domestically, companies must balance the power of various pressure groups in determining market vulnerability. A company's strengths, and potential strengths, in serving a particular market should be considered relative to customer requirements and competitor strengths. Other things being equal, the company's existing strength in a market will be greater where (relative to the competition) the following hold:

It commands a high market share.
It is growing faster than the market.
It has unique and valued products or services.
It has superior-quality products.
It has better margins.
It has exploitable marketing assets.
It can achieve production and marketing efficiencies.
It has protected technological leadership.

As with assessing market attractiveness, it is unlikely that in any market a particular company will enjoy all these favourable characteristics. In any situation, the management will have to assess the relative importance of each aspect of strength in evaluating overall strength in serving that market (target market selection is covered in more detail in Chapter 9).

Having selected the market target, or targets, on the basis of market attractiveness and current or potential business strength in serving the market, the company creates its differential advantage, or competitive edge, in serving that market.

2.4.2 Differential advantage

A differential advantage can be created out of any of the company's strengths, or distinctive competencies relative to the competition. The essential factors in choosing how to create the advantage are that it must be on a basis of value to the customer (e.g. lower prices, superior quality or better service), and should be using a skill of the company that competitors will find hard to copy.

Porter (1980) argues that competitive advantage can be created in two main (though not exclusive) ways: through cost leadership or differentiation (see Figure 2.11).

Cost leadership

The first type of advantage involves pursuing a cost leadership position in the industry. Under this strategy, the company seeks to obtain a cost structure significantly below that of competitors, while retaining products on the market that are in close proximity to competitors' offerings. With a low-cost structure, above-average returns are possible despite heavy competition.

Cost leadership is attained through aggressive construction of efficient scale economies, the pursuit of cost reductions through experience effects, tight cost and overhead control, and cost minimisation in R&D, services, salesforce and advertising, etc. The cost leadership route is the one followed aggressively by Ryanair in the budget airline market, for example.

Cost leaders typically need high market shares to achieve the above-average economies, and favourable access to raw materials. If, for example, efficient production processes or superior production technology enabling cheaper production were identified as company

Figure 2.11
Routes to
competitive
advantage

strengths or distinctive competencies, they could be effectively translated into a competitive advantage through cost leadership. Similarly, if backward integration (merger with, or acquisition of, suppliers) has secured the relatively cheaper supply of raw materials, that asset could also be converted into a competitive advantage.

This strategy is particularly suitable in commodity markets, where there is little or no differentiation between the physical products offered. Where products are highly differentiated, however, the strategy has a major disadvantage in that it does not create a reason why the customer should buy the company's offering. Low costs could be translated into lower price, but this would effectively be a differentiation strategy (using price as the basis on which to differentiate).

Differentiation

The second approach to creating a competitive advantage is differentiation, creating something that is seen as unique in the market. Under this strategy, company strengths and skills are used to differentiate the company's offerings from those of its competitors along some criteria that are valued by consumers.

Differentiation can be achieved on a variety of bases – for example design, style, product or service features, price, image, etc. The major advantage of a differentiation strategy, as opposed to a cost leadership strategy, is that it creates a reason why the customer should buy from the company rather than from its competitors. While cost leadership creates an essentially financially based advantage for the company, differentiation creates a market-based advantage (see Figure 10.3 in Chapter 10).

Products or services that are differentiated in a valued way can command higher prices and margins, and thus avoid competing on price alone. An example of this would be products labelled as 'Fairtrade'. These are differentiated by the way in which suppliers are rewarded for their efforts. Generally, the prices charged to retail customers are higher than for non-Fairtrade products in the same category, but a growing segment of consumers are prepared to pay higher prices for these goods, to be assured that producers in developing countries are not being exploited.

Differentiation and cost leadership

The two strategies are not mutually exclusive, and could be pursued simultaneously. Car manufacturers, for example, constantly seek to drive cost from their businesses (often working with suppliers); however, they are also adept at advertising and branding activities (linked closely with design) that clearly differentiate their products from competitors'. Furthermore, differentiation, especially through superior quality, can often result in lower unit costs through gains in market share and attendant economies of scale and/or experience effects.

Each of the two basic approaches to creating a differential advantage has its attendant risk. Cost leadership may be impossible to sustain due to: a) competitor imitation (using, for example, similar technology and processes); b) technological change, which may make it cheaper for later market entrants to produce the products or services; or c) competitors finding and exploiting alternative bases for cost leadership (see the discussion of cost drivers in Chapter 10). Cost leadership is also a risky strategy where there is a high degree of differentiation between competitive offerings. Differentiation creates reasons for purchase, while cost leadership does not. In addition, cost leadership typically requires minimal spending on R&D, product improvements and image creation, all of which can leave the product vulnerable to competitively superior products.

Differentiation as a strategy is also open to a variety of risks. If differentiation is not based on distinctive marketing assets, it is possible that competitors will try to imitate. For example, low price positioning might seem attractive in harsh economic times, but unless costs are also low comparably with competitors, it could spark costly price wars that seriously erode or eliminate margins. This risk can be minimised by building differentiation around competencies or marketing assets that the company alone possesses, and that competitors cannot copy. In addition, the basis for differentiation may become less important to customers over time, or possibly new bases for differentiation become more important. These latter points, however, can be mitigated through customer and competitor monitoring and benchmarking. A further danger of a differentiation strategy is that the costs of differentiating may outweigh the value placed on it by customers, and as such this would be an untenable approach.

For cost leadership and differentiation approaches that seek an 'industry-wide' appeal, there is the added risk that focusers or nichers in the market (competitors that focus activities on a selected segment or segments) may achieve lower costs, or more valued differentiation, in specific segments. Thus, in markets where segmentation is pronounced, both the basic approaches carry high risks. (Chapter 10 explores further these approaches to creating a defensible position in the marketplace.)

2.5   Implementation

Once the core strategy and the competitive positioning are selected, the task of marketing management is to implement those decisions through marketing effort. Three basic elements of implementation – marketing mix, organisation and control – are discussed next.

2.5.1 Marketing mix

The marketing mix of products, price, promotion and distribution is the means by which the company translates strategy from a statement of intent into effort in the marketplace. Each element of the mix should be aligned (and designed) to deliver the positioning required by the strategy.

Viewed in this light, it is evident that decisions on elements of the mix, such as pricing or advertising campaigns, cannot be considered in isolation from the strategy being pursued. For example, a premium positioning that might differentiate a company's offerings from the competition in terms of high product quality, could be destroyed through charging too low a price. Similarly, to achieve such a positioning, the product itself will have to deliver the quality claimed, and the promotions will have to communicate premium quality. The distribution channels selected, and the physical distribution systems used or created, must also ensure that the products or services get to the target customers. In this way, elements of the mix are integrated to deliver a consistent and targeted message to the markets/desired customers.

Where elements of the mix contradict each other, the positioning achieved will be confused, and as a result will confuse customers.

2.5.2 Organisation

How the marketing effort and the marketing department are organised will have an effect on how successfully the strategy is implemented.

At a very basic level, it is essential for the required humans (people) and financial resources to be available. However, the ways in which these resources are organised (organisational form) can also affect ability to implement strategy effectively. The more 'traditional' organisational structures often found in marketing are **functional** and **product (brand) management**.

Within a **functional organisation** structure, the marketing department consists of specialists in various marketing activities who report to a coordinator (in effect) of marketing activity, often entitled 'manager' or 'director'. Typical functions include sales management, advertising and promotions management, market research and new product development. An extension of the functional design is a geographic organisation where, within the functions given previously as examples (such as sales management), managers are responsible for specific geographic markets. Functional structures offer simplicity, and are designed to foster high levels of expertise in each function. They are also, and often, the first step for organisations wishing to adopt a higher and more active profile for the marketing function as a whole. They are most applicable where the number and complexity of products or services the company has on the market are limited.

Within a **product (or brand) management** structure (originally pioneered by Procter & Gamble in 1927 for a then-ailing Camay soap brand), responsibility for all marketing activities of a particular product rests with one product manager. In diversified companies (suggesting some degree of scale) with many different products, the system has the major advantage of locating responsibility of the mix of marketing activities around one individual, hence making a consistent and coordinated approach more likely. Additionally, and in larger companies, product managers are able to call on the talents of functional specialists as and when necessary.

Dramatic changes in the marketing environment have caused many companies to rethink the role of the product manager. Today's consumers have more information and benefit from more choice than ever before and, as a result, consumer marketing companies are shifting away from 'national' advertising and favouring price and point-of-sale promotions, as well as a focus on the digital space for communication with (and to) customers. Brand managers have traditionally focused on long-term, brand-building strategies that target mass audiences, but today's marketplace realities often demand shorter-term, sales-building strategies designed for local markets.

A second significant force affecting brand management is the growing power of retailers. Larger and arguably more powerful retailers now demand more trade promotions and support from suppliers, in exchange for scarce shelf space. The move towards more trade promotion and support though retail channels leaves marketing budgets stretched, and certainly less money for national advertising – traditionally the brand manager's primary marketing tool. The use of digital tools and channels has also been a 'game changer', and this is discussed further, and in more depth, later in this text.

Other companies adopt a **category management** approach. Under this system, brand managers report to a category manager who has total responsibility for an entire product category. For example, Heinz, Unilever, L'Oréal and Proctor and Gamble have all traditionally adopted a category management approach, as it offers a number of important advantages over alternative approaches. First, category managers have broader planning perspectives than brand managers, as rather than focusing on specific brands, they can shape a company's entire category offering. Second, it better matches the buying processes of retailers. Recently, retailers have tended to make individual buyers responsible for all suppliers in a specific product category, and hence a category management system connects far more strongly with this new retailer 'category buying' system.

For companies that sell one product line to many different types of market that have different needs and preferences, a **market management organisation** might be most effective. Many companies are organised along market lines. A market management organisation is similar to the product management organisation. Market managers are responsible for developing long-range, annual plans for sales and profits in their markets. This system's main advantage is that the company is organised around the needs of specific customer segments.

Increased attention is also being given to organisational approaches based on key processes of value creation and delivery, rather than traditional structures and mechanisms. Traditional organisational approaches are often seen as too slow, unresponsive and cumbersome to deal with rapidly changing markets, new Internet-based competition and strategies depending on alliances and partnering. For example, a **venture marketing organisation** is one such approach (Aufreiter *et al.*, 2000). It was this approach that allowed Starbucks to take its Frappucino from a line manager's idea to a full national launch in less than a year. In its first year, Frappucino contributed 11 per cent of Starbucks' US sales. More generally, the pressure is towards a more effective integration of company resources around value creation, regardless of traditional organisational structures (Hulbert *et al.*, 2003). Additionally (and as discussed briefly in Chapter 1), organisations are trying to dismantle functional boundaries and bring teams together to focus on customer outcomes. For example, Annhauser-Busch InBev and Johnson & Johnson have implemented cross-functional working teams (or squads/tribes) in order to align their internal structures and employee skills more closely with the competitive and market issues faced.

Whatever the organisational structure, individuals are needed with the necessary skills to carry out various marketing tasks. Two sources of personnel emerge: those internal to the company or those brought in from outside. When entering new markets, bringing in external expertise can be a shortcut to developing the knowledge needed in-house. Skills can be improved and extended through training programmes held within a company or through outside training agencies.

2.5.3 Control

As the marketing strategy is executed, an important role of the marketing department is to monitor and control the effort. Marketing managers, after all, have a vested and significant interest in being able to justify and quantify the outcomes of their actions and expenditure (Hanssens and Dekimpe, 2012).

Performance can be monitored in two main ways: on the basis of market performance and on financial performance. Market performance measures such things as sales, market share, customer attitudes and loyalty. Changes in these over time can then be related back to the original objectives of the strategy being pursued. However, performance measures should include factors other than those used to set objectives, to ensure that pursuit of those objectives has not lost sight of the wider implications. For example, a strategic objective may be to reduce costs, but no one monitors customer satisfaction or complaints. As a result, the company reduces costs (and achieves an objective), but loses customers and puts its future in jeopardy. This is, of course, an extreme example to illustrate the idea of casting a wide net of control variables in order to capture unintended outcomes (as far as is possible, of course).

Financial performance is measured by monitoring product contribution relative to resources employed to achieve it. Often a basic conflict between marketing and financial performance arises. Where marketing objectives are long-term market domination, then short-term financial performance may have to suffer slightly. Where managers are rewarded (promoted/given bonuses) on the basis of short-term financial performance, it is highly likely that long-term marketing objectives will be sacrificed for short-term profit.

Much attention has focused on the development of 'marketing metrics' as a better way of linking marketing activities and financial returns to the business (Ambler, 2000; Moorman and Lehman, 2004). Ambler reports that the most important marketing metrics used by companies are:

- relative perceived quality;
- loyalty/retention;
- total number of customers;
- customer satisfaction;
- relative price (market share/volume);
- market share (volume or value);
- perceived quality/esteem;
- complaints (level of dissatisfaction);
- awareness;
- distribution/availability.

Ambler argues that linking marketing to business performance requires such metrics to be reported to top management regularly, and that they should be compared with forecasts and with competitors, with the drivers of buyer behaviour clarified and monitored.

Marketing in the digital era has introduced a whole new lexicon of outcome/performance variables for marketers and business managers to consider, with 'Downloads', 'Likes', 'Share of voice' and the like, increasingly discussed, debated and scrutinised. Additionally, the ability of marketers to collect and track data relating to customer behaviour as a result of marketing activity is greatly enhanced. The important thing to remember is that the metrics used (whether complex or not) should be meaningful and useful, and designed to help managers make better decisions about the markets within which they choose to compete, and the ways in which they deploy their marketing assets and strategies.

A final important element in implementation is contingency planning – that is, answering the question 'What will we do if. . . ?'. Contingency planning asks marketers to consider, anticipate (as much as is possible) and, in doing so, attempt to mitigate competitive reactions to their plans. This is termed 'scenario planning'.

Summary

Strategic marketing planning involves deciding on the core strategy, creating competitive positioning for both the company and its offerings, and implementing that strategy.

This is as true of the one-product firm as it is for the large multi-national containing many different businesses. For the conglomerate business, however, there is an added dimension of portfolio planning, in order to ensure that the mix of businesses within the total corporation is aligned and suitable for achieving overall corporate objectives.

Case study

Amazon eyes online sales boost through 'Fire' smartphone

By Sarah Mishkin in Seattle

Source: Justin Sullivan/Getty Images News/Getty Images.

Amazon has a decent shot at shaking up a smartphone market controlled by Samsung and Apple as well as selling more of everything to its customers with its new Fire smartphone, unveiled on Wednesday in Seattle.

But first, it has to find a way to convince consumers to buy the phone.

'Is it a good product and a neat idea? Yup. Will it be a success? Question mark,' says Mohan Sawhney, a management professor at Northwestern University who has studied Amazon.

Another question is just what constitutes success: muscle in on the smartphone market or driving more sales of the multitude of products sold via Amazon?

The phone is likely to funnel users towards buying more from Amazon, says Michael Graham, an internet analyst at Canaccord Genuity. Getting users of its hardware to buy more goods from its online store is how Amazon profited from the Kindle line of tablet and e-readers, in spite of selling many of those at or below cost.

The phone also comes with a free year of Amazon Prime membership, worth $99, allowing unlimited free shipping and a catalogue of digital music, movies and television shows. Users can store in Amazon's cloud an unlimited number of photos that they take with the device.

Prime users are more lucrative for Amazon than regular customers, says Mr Graham, and Firefly could encourage phone owners to use Amazon, rather than use search engine Google, as their main place to search for purchases.

But the challenge, says James McQuivey, an analyst with Forrester, is that entry into the phone market is tough to crack. Buying a phone typically means locking into a two-year contract, or paying more for a faster upgrade. The difficulty convincing consumers to wager on whether they will like a new device in two years had stymied many purchases – some early phones from Microsoft sold fewer than 20,000, he says.

Bringing more users into Prime and trying to sell more Amazon goods 'are shrewd and calculated moves, and the phone in theory could be a tremendous extension of that strategy, but you've got to get people to want one', he says. 'I'm not sure [the Fire] will impress consumers to the tune of millions of them running out to buy it.'

The Fire starts with a 32GB model that sells for $199 on a two-year contract through AT&T, the only US carrier offering the device. Without a contract, it costs $649.

That places the Fire on par with Apple's iPhone and Samsung's high-end Galaxy line of devices – a part of the market that is increasingly competitive as sales slow and users are reluctant to switch from familiar brands and operating systems. Many other would-be contenders, including HTC, Motorola and Nokia have struggled to gain market share.

To help Amazon succeed where others failed, Jeff Bezos, Amazon's chief executive, brought to the launch in a Seattle warehouse a device that mixes content, customer services and hardware.

Best known for its online shopping mall, Amazon also controls a global network of warehouses, one of the world's largest commercial cloud storage operations, and has access to a growing catalogue of digital music, movies and films – expanded weekly with the launch of a Spotify-like music streaming service.

The Fire sports a 3D display that uses four infrared cameras to track users' head motion and pivot games or maps in line with how the viewer is looking at them. It also has a visual search tool named Firefly.

With Firefly, a user can point the phone's camera at anything from a book to a shaker of salt or a poster and either extract and save information – such as an email address – or navigate directly to a product page on Amazon to buy it.

'What we saw was an opportunity to prove some new capabilities that really hadn't been done before in premium smartphones,' says Ian Freed, Amazon's vice-president for the Fire phone. 'We've seen innovation stagnate a bit over the past two to three years.'

Analysts with Jefferies, the brokerage, estimate that Foxconn, the phone's manufacturer, will produce roughly 200,000 phones a month in the coming months.

Amazon decline to comment on plans to launch the phone in Europe, but people familiar with the company say it is holding discussions with Vodafone and O2 in the UK about possibly launching there.

By December or January – after the big back to school and holiday sales – it should be clear how well the phone is doing in the US, says Mr McQuivey. If Amazon reduces the price or adds more benefits, such as an additional year of Prime membership, it would be a sign that the initial launch underwhelmed the market and a rethink was needed.

'There are levers that Amazon could still pull if it needs to,' he says.

 Source: from 'Amazon eyes online sales boost through "Fire" smartphone', *Financial Times*, 19/06/2014 (Mishkin, S.).

Discussion questions

1 What is driving Amazon's entry into the smartphone market? Is it an ego trip?

2 How does it fit in Amazon's vision 'to be earth's most customer-centric company; to build a place where people can come to find and discover anything they might want to buy online'?

3 What strategic focus does the move signify? What alternatives are open to Amazon and how could Amazon pursue them?

PART 2
COMPETITIVE MARKET ANALYSIS

Part 2 examines the analysis of competitive markets in finer detail.

Chapter 3 commences with a discussion of the changing market and competitive environment facing many firms and organisations in the 2020s. Frameworks, such as PEST analysis for analysing change in the broader macro-environment, are introduced and strategies for operating in changing markets discussed. The chapter then focuses on the competitive, or industry, environment. This begins with a discussion of the Five Forces Model of industry competition and an introduction of the product life cycle, followed by a review of strategic groups and industry evolution. Environmental stability is assessed, together with SPACE analysis. Finally, the Advantage Matrix is reviewed as a means of assessing the key characteristics of an industry when forming strategy.

Chapter 4 considers customer analysis. Information requirements are first discussed, followed by sources of customer information. The variety of marketing research techniques available to aid customer analysis is examined. The discussion then turns to the processes by which customer data are collected and how those data can be turned into information to aid marketing decision making.

Chapter 5 addresses competitor analysis. Following a discussion of competitive benchmarking, the dimensions of competitor analysis are discussed, together with techniques for identifying competitor response profiles. The chapter concludes with a review of sources of competitor information.

Chapter 6 is concerned with the internal analysis of an organisation's resources, assets and capabilities that can be leveraged in its target markets. Starting from a broad, resource-based view of the firm and the identification of its core competencies, the chapter moves to the more detailed issues of auditing resources and itemising specific marketing assets, such as brands, reputation, supply chain strengths and partnerships. The chapter concludes with a framework to build a profile of a company's marketing capabilities.

CHAPTER 3

THE CHANGING MARKET ENVIRONMENT

> 'Because knowledge changes so rapidly, knowledge flow is more important than knowledge stock.'
>
> John Hagel

'Nimble' consultancy focuses on quick response to disruption

By Gill Plimmer

Profile: Adaptive Lab founder says CEOs struggle to act on new technology threats

Newspapers are struggling, taxi ranks are being replaced by Uber drivers and the hotel industry has been rattled by Airbnb. Yet, getting businesses to adapt quickly to embrace and compete with disruptive technologies can be surprisingly difficult.

James Haycock, managing director and founder of Adaptive Lab, set up the London-based consultancy in 2009 to help businesses adjust to new technology and the accompanying shifts in customer behaviour and regulation.

'The chief executives of these companies are waking up terrified that they are going to be eaten up by disruptive technologies,' says Mr Haycock. 'But for all the meetings they hold, they actually struggle to act. We try to package the new ways of working used by start-ups and take them to larger businesses. The idea of experimentation is really important to us.'

He points to Airbnb, the room-sharing service, as an example of good practice. Its founders slept in some of their clients' houses to get first-hand experience of the service they were offering.

'There's a lot of talk in business about being customer-obsessed and prioritising decisions about what customers need, but in fact in many cases the actual priority is to deliver to shareholders. We try to get them to address how they can better serve customer needs and put themselves in their shoes,' says Mr Haycock.

The firm was 'frequently recommended' by clients and peers in the digital transformation category of the UK's Leading Management Consultants, compiled by the FT and Statista, and 'recommended' in the financial institutions and services sector.

One of Adaptive Lab's main findings was that customers did not always want additional programmes, they simply wanted existing services to function as they should.

'When we worked with credit card companies, we brought in customer research,' Mr Haycock says. 'We found out that customers didn't want value-added programmes – they just wanted the corporate credit card programme to work properly,' he adds.

He points to a brand called Smarty, created for Three, the mobile phone company, after its research found customers wanted greater simplicity and transparency of contracts – 'a very simple and straightforward plan'. The phone service provides discounts to customers who do not use up all their data.

Working with Saberr, an artificial intelligence company, Adaptive Lab helped to design a strategy that included a simplified, viable product with which Saberr could go to market quickly. This has resulted in Coachbot, a digital team coach that is being piloted in the NHS and at Unilever and Logitech.

Other clients include Barclays, Santander, Lloyds, Standard Life, Vodafone, TalkTalk, Asos and Tesco. It is also working with Konica Minolta, a manufacturer of photocopiers and office equipment.

The business, which employs around 50 staff, has grown quickly. In the past four years, sales have doubled every year, and it is aiming to increase revenues by 40 per cent next year.

'Big companies are so ingrained in what they do, they don't ask, "why do we do it like this?" We try to help them act a little more nimbly,' he says. 'It's a matter of when, not if, banking will be reinvented, so we are helping them to figure out how.'

The foreign exchange market is one part of banking that is being transformed, with new online businesses such as TransferWise stealing market share from the large lending institutions.

'They are really eating into the margins of the foreign currency market,' says Mr Haycock. 'The banks may have invited them in and held meetings but they haven't shaken up the business to adapt. Even though they are aware of the new entrants and scanning them they don't necessarily take them as seriously as they should,' he adds.

Mr Haycock is convinced that Adaptive Lab offers something fresh in the overcrowded consultancies market. The bigger consultancies can take up to two years to come up with a plan, he says – far too long to get competitive advantage.

'Although big consultancies say they are agile, they take a long time to deliver. They will say, "this is a big programme of work so we need a big business case",' he says. 'From a [large] consultancy's perspective, the more bodies on a project the better for the longer term.'

 Source: from '"Nimble" consultancy focuses on quick response to disruption', *Financial Times*, 18/01/18 (Plimmer, G.).

Discussion questions

1 What changes in the market environment has Adaptive Lab exploited?
2 What is Adaptive Lab's competitive advantage over larger consultancy firms?

Introduction

Of central importance in developing and implementing a robust marketing strategy is awareness of how the environment in which marketing takes place is changing. At its simplest, the marketing environment can be divided into the competitive environment (including the company, its immediate competitors and customers) and the macro-environment (the wider social, political and economic setting in which organisations operate). Competition between firms to serve customers is the very essence of modern, market-led economies. Since the middle of the twentieth century, competition has been intensifying as firms seek to create competitive advantage in ever-more crowded markets and with increasingly demanding customers. This chapter provides a number of tools for understanding the competitive environments in which firms operate and recognising the opportunities and threats they present. It can provide no simple rules for achieving competitive success, but can explain the forms of industry environment that exist, the competition within them and when and why certain strategies succeed.

It should be borne in mind, however, that **industries** and **markets** are not the same thing – industries are collections of organisations with technologies and products in common, whereas markets are customers linked by similar needs. For example, white goods firms comprise an industry – companies that make refrigerators, washing machines and so on. On the other hand, laundry products constitute a market – the products and services customers use to clean their clothes. This distinction is important for two reasons. First, if we only think about the conventional industry we may ignore the potential for competition for our customers from companies with different products and technologies that meet the same need, not to mention the so called 'disruptors'. For example, conventional taxi companies were wrong-footed by Uber's entry into the market, building upon the sharing economy.

Second, there are signs that many companies are having to abandon traditional industry definitions under pressure from distributors and retailers. For example, **category management** in grocery retailing is fundamental, the retailers being concerned with managing a category of products that meet a particular need, such as laundry, meal replacement or lunch, not with individual products or brands. The effects of category management can be bizarre – Walmart discovered, for example, a relationship between the purchase of disposable nappies and beer on Friday evenings. The explanation was that young fathers were being told by their partners to stock up on nappies on the way home from work. They reasoned this was a good opportunity (or reason?) to stock up on beer as well. These products are now merchandised together on Fridays. The point is that we should temper any conclusions we draw about the industry by recognising that markets may change in ways that invalidate conventional industry definitions.

Systematic analysis of the business environment typically commences at the macro level, highlighting aspects of the broader environment that may impinge on the specific markets the firm operates in. At a more specific industry level, however, the identification of the forces driving competition within industries can be a useful starting point. We then go on to discuss strategic groups, which provide a useful basis for understanding opportunities and threats facing individual firms. It is within those strategic groups that firms compete to grow, survive or decline.

3.1   A framework for macro-environmental analysis

Here we deal with the nature of change in the macro-environment and examine its impact on organisational marketing strategies.

The importance of understanding the macro-environment is twofold. First, we should recognise the marketing impact of change in the business environment and be in a position to respond. But, second, we should also be alert to the fact that the nature of the change facing organisations is itself changing. For example, Haeckel (1997) already noted in the 1990s that of all the pressures driving companies to revitalise their marketing processes:

> the leading candidate is a change in the nature of change: from continuous (but incremental) to discontinuous [because] when discontinuous change makes customer requests unpredictable, strategic leverage shifts from efficiency to flexibility and responsiveness – and to investments that enable a firm to sense unanticipated change earlier and co-ordinate an unprecedented response to it faster.

Many changes are taking place in the environment in which marketing operates, and some important examples are summarised briefly in the text that follows (see also Kotler *et al.*, 2017). However, this can never be a comprehensive list for the reasons Haeckel identified previously. For our purposes, change is discussed under three main headings. Taken together these are often referred to as PEST analysis (see Figure 3.1) – political and economic, social (including legal, cultural and environmental) and technological environments. We discuss the political and economic environments together as the interplay between the two often makes it difficult to disentangle their individual impacts. A political change here can

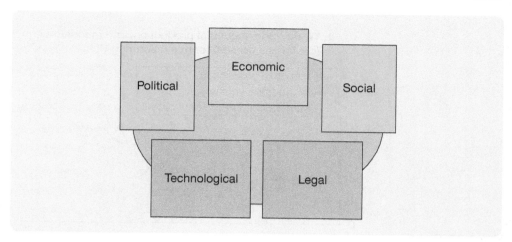

Figure 3.1 PEST
analysis of the
macro-environment

create an economic effect there, and changes in the economy may well precipitate political action or change.

3.2   The economic and political environment

The global economic recession of 2008–10 was the deepest since the Great Depression of the 1930s, and its impact is still felt today. Triggered by a financial crisis brought about through unsustainable lending practices by banks, the credit crunch rapidly spread to the 'real' economy as firms of all sizes in developed economies found it increasingly difficult to raise operating funds. Similarly, consumer credit dried up significantly, reducing spending power of consumers. In the UK, the *Financial Times* index of 100 leading shares (the FTSE 100) plunged from a high of 6,500 before the recession to a low of 3,500 in March 2009. As businesses struggled to survive and unemployment rose, government tax takings fell significantly and governments around the world found that they had to increase their borrowing to record levels to keep services operating.

In attempts to bolster their economies, governments adopted massive fiscal stimulus packages and reduced interest rates to record-low levels. In November 2008, China had pumped $586bn into a stimulus package and in April 2009 Japan followed suit with a $153bn package. In 2009, the USA passed the American Recovery and Reinvestment Act, committing £787bn to boosting the US economy.

The impact of these economic shocks was to be felt for many years to come. While the private sector recession may have been declared officially over by January 2010 in most developed countries, the public sector recession was just starting. In attempts to rebalance the books and reduce national debt levels, governments began to raise taxes, cut public sector spending, or combinations of these actions.

Even before the credit crunch, however, many of the developed economies were experiencing a slowing of economic growth. While economic growth is undoubtedly cyclical, the indications are that the developed economies are unlikely to see again the rates of growth experienced in the first few decades after the Second World War. Many organisations will have to learn to live with low growth in their once-buoyant markets. Where growth objectives once dominated management thinking, other criteria (such as profitability) are now becoming more important. Economic growth is of particular concern to companies. In April 2019 the IMF cut its global growth to its lowest pace since the 2008 crisis, to just 3.3 per cent. Other measures of economic activities have softened (illustrated by Figure 3.2), thus creating challenges for business.

Figure 3.3 shows a number of key considerations of which firms need to be aware when assessing the political and economic environments in which they operate.

Figure 3.2 Global activity downturn

Source: International Monetary Fund (April 2019).

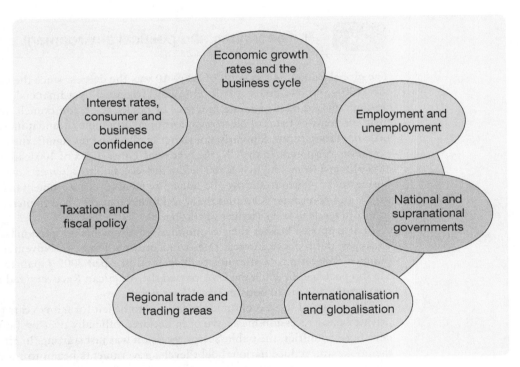

Figure 3.3 The economic and political environment

The European Single Market and its enlargement

January 1992 saw the realisation of the dream of many Europeans with the creation of the European Single Market. The Single Market of over 320 million consumers was created to allow the free flow of products and services, people and capital between the member states. As such, it was intended to improve economic performance by lowering costs of trading across national borders within the European Union (EU), and to encourage economies of scale of operation rivalling the US internal market. By January 2002, a single European currency, the euro, had been introduced into the euro-zone (all but a handful of the EU member states), further facilitating trade and exchange across the old political borders.

However, it also had its problems. With economies in the zone operating at different speeds, and facing different levels of public sector debt but without the freedom to set separate exchange or interest rates, difficulties began to emerge. In early 2010 the Greek economy (within the euro-zone) caused particular concern, followed by Spain and Portugal, as debt levels rose and the countries' credit ratings were lowered, casting a doubt on the survival of the euro-zone.

In October 2002, a referendum in the Irish Republic paved the way for the enlargement of the European Union through the accession of ten new states in May 2004: the three Baltic states of Latvia, Lithuania and Estonia, plus Hungary, Poland, the Czech Republic, Slovakia, Cyprus, Malta and Slovenia. That enlargement had significant implications for many organisations, both commercial and non-commercial, as Europe expanded. The population of the European Union rose by around 20 per cent, while GDP rose by only 5 per cent (Fishburn and Green, 2002). Significant differences in labour costs, for example, were likely to raise questions of location for many firms. Hourly labour costs ranged from €3.70 to €40.10 across the 28 EU member states in 2013, for example.

More significantly, in June 2016, the UK voted to leave the European Union and as of May 2019 was still in the process of deciding how to leave the block. This decision has had a major impact on the short-term economic prospects of both the UK and the EU, and has been accompanied by a growing resentment of globalisation and the rise of populist parties.

Internationalisation and globalisation

While Western, developed economies have struggled to maintain momentum during the recession, the inexorable rise of China and India as the economic super powers of the future has continued. By 2050 it is estimated that the population of India will overtake China at around 1.6 billion in each, compared with 700 million in Europe and 400 million in the USA. While Western economies stagnated or declined during the recession, the Chinese economy continued to grow, albeit at a slower rate than previously. Growth in 2015 was estimated at 3.3 per cent compared with 13 per cent in 2007 (and an average for the previous 30 years of over 10 per cent). Early in 2019, China's economic growth was reported to be at its slowest in over 25 years (growing at 6.6 per cent in 2018 compared to 7.3 per cent three years earlier), contributing to a reduced growth rate in other world economies.

The last decade of the 1900s saw dramatic changes in East–West relationships. The dismantling of the Berlin Wall, the liberalisation of the economies of central Europe (Poland, Hungary, the Czech Republic, Slovakia) and the break-up of the Soviet Union signalled many potential changes in trading patterns.

While the political barriers have been coming down in Europe, there is some concern that the emergence of regional trading blocs ('free trade areas') will have a dramatic impact on the future of free world trade. The European Single Market post-1993, closer economic relations in the Asia Pacific region (Australia, Singapore, Thailand and South Korea – the Trans-Pacific Partnership signed in January 2016) and the North American Free Trade Alliance zone (the United States, Canada and Mexico) were emerging as massive internal markets where domestic-based, 'international' trade was becoming freer.

However, US President Donald Trump's trade agenda is very different. His 'America First' priority has led to threats (and imposition of tariffs) on allies, of withdrawing from the WTO, use of tariffs and sanctions as a national security tool and a focus on bilateral agreements that do not fit into a global free-trade economy. It may be that these policies are only short term, but there are concerns over their long-term impact.

3.3   The social and cultural environment

Coupled with the changing economic environment has been a continuous change in social attitudes and values that are likely to have important implications for marketing management (see Figure 3.4). Examples include the following.

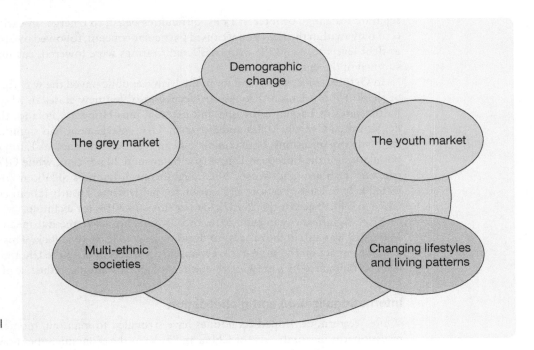

Figure 3.4 The social and cultural environment

Demographic change

The Western 'demographic time bomb' has started to have an impact on diverse businesses. With generally better standards of living, life expectancy has increased across the world and is set to continue increasing: for example, by 2030 life expectancy is set to exceed 90 in South Korea.

The grey market

In the developed West, the over-60s age group currently makes up around 23 per cent of the population, and is predicted to rise to nearer one-third by 2050 (and projected to grow by 56 per cent between 2015 and 2030 worldwide). These 'grey' consumers are relatively rich.

The over-50s own around three-quarters of the world's financial assets and control half of the discretionary budget. Perhaps surprisingly, however, around 90 per cent of consumer advertising is aimed at the under-50s. Marketers are increasingly coming to recognise the potential value of this market and to target more offerings and promotions towards them (Fishburn and Green, 2002).

Barratt Developments in the United Kingdom, for example, has been particularly quick to capitalise on this change in the demographic profile and has specialised in providing retirement homes for the elderly. Demographic changes of this type vary significantly between countries and regions throughout the world, and warrant serious study as a fundamental influence on demand for different products and services. In Japan, for example, it is predicted that by 2030 around 37 per cent of the population will be older than 65, compared with 5 per cent in 1950 and 19 per cent in 2000.

There are also significant financial implications of the greying of Western society. Increased longevity, coupled with economic slowdown, has led to significant challenges to pension funds. Many defined benefit (final salary pension, or career average) schemes have been underfunded and forced to change terms and conditions for members. This could have significant implications for the purchasing power of tomorrow's pensioners.

The youth market

At the other end of the spectrum, the youth market has also become more affluent and poses new opportunities for marketers. Fashion and music industries have been quick to recognise this new-found affluence.

Related to this youth market has been the emergence of 'generations'. The 'Generation X' consumer is cynical, world-weary and hostile to business values and traditional advertising and branding, and will reject many conventional product offers. The pay-off in understanding the values and preferences of this type of consumer has been substantial for companies such as Nike in clothing and footwear and Boss in fragrances and clothing – these consumers react positively to pictures of athletes vomiting on their sports shoes at the end of the race, and Nike's advertising copy: 'We don't sell dreams. We sell shoes . . . Don't insult our intelligence. Tell us what it is. Tell us what it does. And don't play the national anthem while you do it.' Marketers are also now targeting 'Generation Y' (or Millennials), and anticipating how 'Generation Z' will consume. Generation Y was entering the workforce in the mid-2010s and is the one that mostly populates social media channels and as such possesses substantial influence. These consumers also react differently to advertising appeals than their parents, the baby boomers (Loroz and Helgeson, 2013) and have different communication preferences (see Figure 3.5).

Multi-ethnic societies

Many Western societies are becoming increasingly multi-ethnic. In the United Kingdom, for example, by 2011 ethnic minorities represented 12.1 per cent of the population, and forecasts predict the number will reach 20 per cent by 2051. This group spends some £10 billion a year, and includes many socially mobile and affluent groups. As well as being a target for specialised products and services, ethnic minorities are increasingly vocal about what they object to in conventional marketing and advertising. For example, some brands have been labelled as 'ethnically insensitive', such as Persil's TV advertisement showing a Dalmatian dog shaking off its black spots, or McDonald's TV advertisement showing a stereotypical young black man listening to very loud music while driving. On the other hand, some marketers have earned praise for being 'ethnically sensitive': for example, BT's radio

Characteristics	Maturists (pre–1945)	Baby Boomers (1945–1960)	Generation X (1961–1980)	Generation Y (1981–1995)	Generation Z (Born after 1995)
Formative experiences	Second World War Rationing Fixed gender roles Rock 'n' Roll Nuclear families Defined gender roles– particularly for women	Cold War Post-war boom 'Swinging Sixties' Apollo moon landings Youth culture Woodstock Family-oriented Rise of the teenager	End of Cold War Fall of Berlin Wall Reagan/Gorbachev Thatcherism Live Aid Introduction of first PC Early mobile technology Latch-key kids Rising levels of divorce	9/11 terrorist attacks PlayStation Social media Invasion of Iraq Reality TV Google Earth Glastonbury	Economic downturn Global warming Global focus Mobile devices Energy crisis Arab Spring Produce own media Cloud computing WikiLeaks
Percentage in UK workforce	3%	33%	35%	29%	Currently employed in either part-time jobs or new apprenticeships
Aspiration	Home ownership	Job security	Work–life balance	Freedom and flexibility	Security and stability
Attitude towards technology	Largely disengaged	Early information technology (IT) adaptors	Digital immigrants	Digital natives	'Technoholics' – entirely dependent on IT: limited grasp of alternatives
Attitude towards career	Jobs are for life	Organisational – careers are defined by employers	Early 'portfolio' careers – loyal to profession, not necessarily to employer	Digital entrepreneurs – work 'with' organisations not 'for'	Career multitaskers – will move seamlessly between organisations and 'pop-up' businesses
Signature product	Automobile	Television	Personal computer	Tablet/smartphone	Google Glass, graphene, nano-computing, 3-D printing, driverless cars
Communication media	Formal letter	Telephone	E-mail and text message	Text or social media	Hand-held (or integrated into clothing) communication devices
Communication preference	Face-to-face	Face-to-face ideally, but telephone or email if required	Text messaging or e-mail	Online and mobile (text messaging)	Facetime
Preference when making financial decisions	Face-to-face meetings	Face-to-face ideally, but increasingly will go online	Online – would prefer face-to-face if time permitting	Face-to-face	Solutions will be digitally crowdsourced

Figure 3.5 Differences between generations

Source: adapted from Barclays.

advertisements in Hindi to promote long-distance phone calls, and W.H. Smith for stocking ethnic greetings cards (Dwek, 1997).

Changing living patterns and lifestyles

There has also been an increase in single-person households, predicted by Euromonitor to be the fastest-growing household profile worldwide (not just in the West) between 2014 and 2030. This is leading to the development of smaller goods or services targeted at singles, such as Daewoo's mini washing machine and Cerca Travel's two-day 'solo wedding' packages for single women.

A further development has been the significant growth in the number of women in employment, be it full- or part-time. This has led to changes in household eating patterns, with an emphasis on convenience foods and cooking. It has, in turn, led to increased markets for products to make cooking and meal preparation easier and quicker, such as the KitchenAid or Kenwood multifunction food processors that can do everything from food preparation to cooking, or recipe boxes that can be bought in the supermarket or delivered to people's homes.

Coupled with greater concern for the environment is greater concern for personal health. There has been a dramatic movement in the grocery industry, for example, towards healthier food products, such as wholemeal bread, bran-based cereals, 'superfoods' and vegan food (for being kinder to the planet). This movement, originally dismissed by many food manufacturers as a passing fad among a minority of the population, has accelerated with the marketing of organically produced products and low-sugar, salt-free products, free from additives, colourings and preservatives (the British government imposed a tax on sugar in March 2016). Fitness products in general, from sportswear and exercise machines to the membership of gyms and leisure clubs, have enjoyed very buoyant markets. By 2014, over 22 per cent of household expenditure in the United Kingdom was spent on leisure activities and products.

Also of relevance to the overall economic conditions in which organisations operate is the political environment. In the USA, a Democrat, Barack Obama, was returned to the White House in 2008, and in the UK the May 2010 election resulted in the first coalition government (between the Conservative and Liberal Democrat parties) in over 60 years. Such political leaders and their parties set the economic agenda – more or less taxation, more or less public spending, more or less investment, more or less public ownership. This, in turn, creates opportunities and challenges for all sectors of the economy. For example, Donald Trump, a Republican, was elected in the USA in 2016 with a completely different economic agenda from his predecessor and, as mentioned previously, the world is seeing a rise in 'populist' parties with more protectionist agendas.

3.3.1 Social, cultural and environmental pressures on organisations

Customers are becoming increasingly demanding of the products and services they buy. Customers demand, and expect, reliable and durable products with quick, efficient service at reasonable prices. What is more, there is little long-term stability in customer demand. Competitive positions are achieved through offering superior customer value, yet without constant improvement 'value migration' will occur – buyers will migrate to an alternative value offering (Slywotzky, 1996).

Companies are well advised to recognise that how customers see value can change. Indeed, brand values are becoming more and more relevant to purchasing decisions. In the UK, one in four people believe that brands' values are just as important as the products themselves. This group expects brands to take a stand on social matters and will reward companies that do:

- 90 per cent would try a company's product for the first time if they took a stand;
- 83 per cent would switch to a competitor if no stand was taken;
- 83 per cent would pay a premium for a socially aware company's products;
- 73 per cent would share the company's information on social media (*Marketing Week*, 24 September 2018).

A second major trend, exacerbated by the recession and looking set to continue, is that customers are less prepared to pay a substantial premium for products or services that do not offer demonstrably greater value. While it is undeniable that well-developed and managed brands can command higher prices than unbranded products in many markets, the differentials commanded are now far less than they were, and customers are increasingly questioning the extra value they get for the extra expense. The sophisticated customer is less likely to be attracted to cheap products with low quality, but is also unlikely to be won by purely image-based advertising. The implications are clear – differentiation needs to be based on providing demonstrably superior value to customers.

Increased questioning of the industrial profit motive as the prime objective for commercial enterprises has grown. Some are going further in explicitly measuring their performance through the 'triple bottom line' (TBL) of People, Planet and Profit. The phrase originated in the early 1990s (Elkington, 1994) and recognises that business has responsibilities not only to shareholders but also to other stakeholders affected directly or indirectly by the business. 'People' relates to the human capital in the company – both the people working in the organisation and the community in which a company conducts its business. Fairtrade practices, for example, seek to ensure farmers and producers of foodstuffs receive fair recompense for their labours. 'Planet' relates to the natural capital the organisation uses and its attempts to minimise environmental impact. Organisations practising a TBL approach endeavour to minimise their ecological footprint through controlling use of energy, switching to renewable energy sources where possible and reducing manufacturing waste. 'Profit' is the net economic value created by the organisation and goes beyond the internal profit created by a firm to encompass the economic impact the organisation has on its wider economic environment and society. In short, the triple bottom line approach aims at creating sustainable businesses in a more sustainable environment.

A further social/cultural change has been in attitudes to, and concern for, the physical or natural environment. Environmental pressure groups impact on businesses, so much so that major oil multinationals and others spend large amounts on corporate advertising each year to demonstrate their concern and care for the environment. The activities of groups such as Greenpeace have begun to have a major impact on public opinion and now affect policy making at the national and international levels. It is to be expected that concern for the environment will increase and hence will be a major factor in managing that prime marketing asset – company reputation. The significance of the impact on business is underlined by the three-year 'Save The Arctic' campaign of Greenpeace and others against Shell's drilling there. In September 2015, Shell announced it was withdrawing its plan. In April 2019, Extinction Rebellion, established in the UK in 2018 as a socio-political movement against climate change, blocked streets in London over several days, creating transport difficulties. The group was joined by a teenage Swedish climate activist, Greta Thunberg, in asking for action. This led the leader of the opposition to force a vote on whether the UK should be the first country to declare an environmental emergency.

Many car manufacturers are also now offering hybrid or totally electric cars. The entry of BMW in 2014 into the electric car market gave it a more 'mainstream' status.

3.4   The technological environment

The latter part of the twentieth century saw technological change and development impact on virtually every industry sector. A number of these significant developments are discussed next.

There has been a shortening of commercialisation times of new inventions. Photography, for example, took over 100 years from initial invention to commercial viability. The telephone took 56 years, radio 35 years, television 12 years and the transistor only 3 years.

Looked at another way, the telephone took 40 years to reach 10 million users worldwide, the television 18 years, the personal computer 15 years and the World Wide Web only five.

This shortening of commercialisation times has, in turn, led to a shortening of product life cycles, with products becoming obsolete far more quickly than previously. In the Japanese electronics industry, for example, the time between perception of a need or demand for a new product and shipment of large quantities of that product can be under five months. Computer integration of manufacturing and design is helping to shorten product development times. It has been estimated that in automobiles this has been in the order of 25 per cent.

Through technological changes, whole industries or applications have been changed dramatically almost overnight. In 1977–78 cross-ply tyre manufacturers in the United States lost 50 per cent of the tyre market to radials in just 18 months (Foster, 1986b).

Newer technology has a major impact on particular aspects of marketing. The advent of the microcomputer and its wide availability to management initially led to increased interest in sophisticated market modelling and decision support systems. Increased amounts of information can now be stored, analysed and retrieved very much more quickly than in the past. Now, the impact of the Internet revolution can be felt in customer experience and relationship management and all elements of the marketing mix. For example, virtual products take over from their physical equivalent: in March 2016 the British newspaper *The Independent* ceased to exist in paper form, and social media have transformed how companies communicate with their audiences. Audi has opened virtual showrooms in major world cities and customers are looking for a seamless omni-channel experience when they shop online instead of in a physical store. In April 2019, South Korea was the first country to achieve substantial deployment of 5G – the next generation of advanced wireless systems. This technology is expected to speed the development and spread of the Internet of Things, smart cities and a connected life.

Innovative marketing research companies have been quick to seize on the possibilities afforded by the new technology for getting information to their clients more quickly than competitors. Suppliers of retail audits (see Chapter 6) can now present their clients with online results of the audits completed only 24 hours previously. In a rapidly changing marketplace, the ability to respond quickly, afforded by almost instantaneous information, can mean the difference between success and failure.

The 'data warehouses' created by the capture of customer data are increasingly a major marketing resource for companies, which has the potential for achieving stronger and more enduring relationships than competitors. Examples include: the data collected by retailers such as Tesco and Sainsbury's through their loyalty card schemes; the customer information held by airlines to monitor the purchase behaviour of their frequent flyer customers; and the customer data gained through the direct marketing of products such as financial services.

Even the small business (if it invests in the modest costs of establishing a website) can access markets throughout the world at almost no cost. This changes fundamentally the costs of market entry and the competitive structures of the markets affected.

3.4.1 Technological pressures on organisations

Technology continues to develop at a bewildering pace, affecting not just the high-tech industries such as telecommunications and personal computers, but also other industries that make use of the new technologies. Bill Gates, writing in *The World in 2003* (Fishburn and Green, 2002), goes so far as to predict that computers *per se* will soon disappear. Increasingly, they will be integrated into other products. It has been estimated that people in the United States already interact with 150 embedded 'computer' systems every day (in products such as mobile phones, petrol pumps and retail point-of-sale systems), utilising 90 per cent of the microprocessors currently in use – now referred to as the Internet of Things (IoT). The number of connected devices is expected to reach 75.44 billion by 2025 and an estimated 125 billion by 2030. This explosion of connected devices is represented in Figure 3.6.

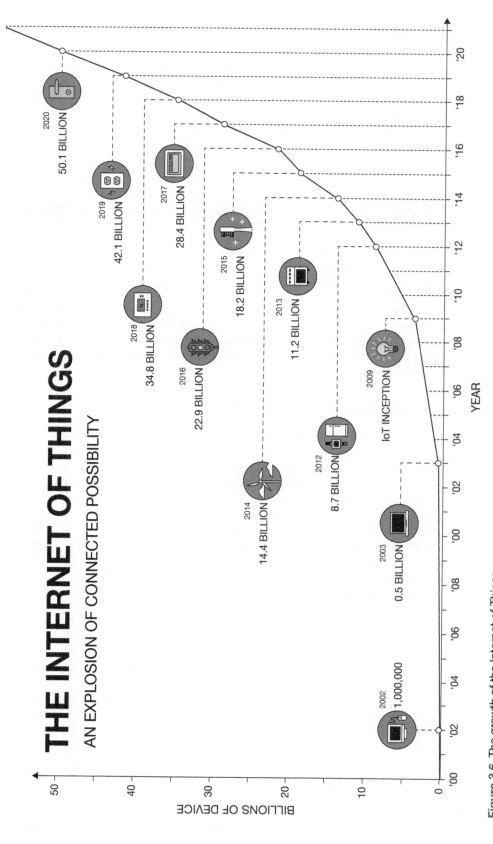

Figure 3.6 The growth of the Internet of Things
Source: NCTA (5 May 2014).

Changes in the way in which computer chips are made are likely to further boost computer power and lower costs. The newer laser-assisted direct impact technique allows minute features to be stamped on to molten silicon. As of 2017, the highest number of transistors per chip is over 30 billion, to be found in an IBM chip. Moore's law (the doubling of transistor counts every two years) is still valid 50 years on.

Time and distance are shrinking rapidly as firms use the Internet to market their offerings to truly global markets. One result is that cross-national segments are now emerging for products and services, from fast foods, through books and toys, to computers and automobiles.

3.5 Changes in marketing infrastructure and practices

In addition to the changes noted previously, there are several important changes taking place in the general marketing environment and in marketing practices.

In many markets increased levels of competition, both domestic and international, are reaching unprecedented levels. In the three years following the start of the global recovery in 2010, Britain's exports increased by 14.7 per cent in terms of value, and volumes rose by 7.2 per cent. Exports increased to a record £304.3 billion in 2013, up from £300.5 billion in 2012, according to the Office for National Statistics. HSBC had forecast that UK exports would increase by 5 per cent between 2016 and 2020 and then decrease to 4 per cent between 2020 and 2030.

3.5.1 Globalisation of markets

Many markets are global in nature and no business, however big or small, is exempt from global competition. The reasoning centres on the impact of technology on people throughout the world. Technology has made products more available and potential consumers more aware of them. Over the years we have witnessed a move towards gigantic, world-scale markets where economies of scale in production, marketing and distribution could be vigorously pursued. The result has been significantly lower costs, creating major problems for competitors that do not operate on a global scale. Many of these cost advantages have been realised as companies operating within the EU's Single Market rationalise their production and distribution facilities. This is one of the reasons cited for Japanese car companies stopping investing in the UK two years after the Brexit referendum. Similarly, Dyson has decided to move its headquarters from the UK to Singapore to 'future-proof" the company and to be close to what it sees as a critical future market.

The counter-argument to the globalisation thesis is that markets are becoming more fragmented, with consumers more concerned to express their individuality than to buy mass-produced, mass-marketed products. In addition, there is little evidence of the existence of widespread preference for the cheapest products available. The demand for low prices, relative to other product benefits and extras, is not proven in many markets. Each market should be examined individually and the factors likely to affect it explored.

Whether one subscribes to the globalisation argument or not, one factor is clear: organisations ignore international competition at their peril. The UK motorcycle industry is a textbook example of a once-supreme industry now virtually non-existent because of its failure to recognise and respond to the threat posed by cheap, good-quality, Japanese motorbikes.

At the same time as markets are becoming more global, so the existence of distinct market segments is becoming clearer. The most successful firms are those that have recognised this increasing importance of segmentation and positioned their companies so as to take best advantage of it.

Founded in 1953 by Bernard and Laura Ashley, the Laura Ashley company was based on a quintessentially British design concept, characterised by the long flowing skirts and romantic floral designs that were the foundation of the company's success in the 1960s and 1970s. With its Victorian- and Edwardian-style designs, Laura Ashley wallcoverings were favoured in locations such as the British Embassy in Washington and at Highgrove, home of the Prince of Wales, and its floral smocks and chintzes were favoured by the young Princess Diana. From its early designs for women's clothes the company expanded rapidly into fabrics, wallcoverings and paints, linked by the central design concept. Manufacturing plants were established in Wales, and by 1997 the company operated more than 400 retail stores worldwide covering dozens of countries, including more than 150 in the United States. By 1997 the company had sales of £320 million, but was issuing repeated profit warnings, and its shares had lost three-quarters of their value in 12 months. The loss-making manufacturing units started to declare redundancies. The death of the founder in 1985 had marked a turning point. The loss of vision for the company at that point was accompanied by losses in most of the following 12 years. Ann Iverson (then chief executive) faced the problem of turning the company around and reclaiming its position with the affluent 35–50-year-old female fashion buyer. City commentators pointed to the strength of new competitors such as Ralph Lauren in this core market and concluded that 'its management must decide what to be, preferably before the money runs out' (*Daily Telegraph*, 1997; Olins, 1997a). Unfortunately, the company incurred heavy losses in 1998 and was bought the same year by MUI Asia Ltd, but initially the company still had no focus. Over the years, until 2015, fashion's share of the overall business decreased to 17 per cent. Despite a commitment to increasing brand awareness, ensuring global relevance of the products and growth, the company reported a four-year-low profit (March 2016) of £19.4m and sales down to £289.5m. This was attributed to the franchise business, with the UK business remaining strong. Laura Ashley's chairman said: 'We remain optimistic for the future and are confident that the strength of the brand and the enduring appeal of our product ranges mean we are well positioned for continued growth' (*Financial Times*, 2016, March 23).

3.5.2 The role of marketing

The role of marketing in the modern corporation has been subject to far-reaching reappraisal. Kotler *et al.* (2018) argue a new approach to marketing that brings together online and offline in a systematic way:

> The concept focuses on how, in the times of a digital economy boom, offline touch serves as a major differentiation in an increasingly online world. It also encompasses how style blends with substance, in that even as brands need to adopt flexible and adaptive styles in view of fast-changing technological developments, the brand's core, authentic character is ever more important. Brands need to come across as true to their identity and authentic in their messages – this perceived substance is a valuable asset in an increasingly transparent world. And finally, Marketing 4.0 is about balancing machine-to-machine (M2M) with human-to-human (H2H). As connected devices become more commonplace on the back of artificial intelligence and IoT, resulting in greater marketing productivity, they need to go hand-in-hand with human-to-human connectivity in order to strengthen customer engagement.

> Moving towards Marketing 4.0 requires balancing our use of machines and devices with human contact to strengthen customer engagement.

Source: Viktoria Kurpas/Shutterstock.

The marketing function has a major role to play in keeping a company up to date with changes in its broader environment and the competitive environment. However, the way that role is fulfilled is likely to reflect major forces of change in the environment, such as: increasingly sophisticated customers; the move from an emphasis on single sales transactions to long-term customer relationships; the role of information technology (IT) in changing how markets and organisations work; and the development of the network organisation, consisting of a group of companies collaborating to exploit their core competencies, linked together by a mix of strategic alliances, vertical integration and looser partnerships.

3.6   New strategies for changing macro-environments

In reaction to the changes mentioned previously, a number of critical issues are emerging for marketing management and theory.

First, and central to developing a sustainable competitive advantage in rapidly and often unpredictably changing circumstances, is the ability to learn fast and adapt quickly (Dickson, 1992). A major challenge for any organisation is to create the combination of culture and climate to maximise learning (Slater and Narver, 1995).

Slow to change has been the high-street retailer W.H. Smith. Almost every UK high street and rail station has a W.H. Smith retail outlet, selling magazines and newspapers, books, stationery, cassettes/compact discs and videos. Its bookstalls first appeared in 1792, and W.H. Smith had a market value of £1.1 billion in 1997, with 10 million customers a week buying in its stores. However, during the 1980s and 1990s, W.H. Smith's traditional core market was attacked by strong competitors. On the one side there was a growth in specialist retailers such as Dillons, and on the other was a dramatic expansion by the main supermarket groups in selling books, newspapers and music/videos. W.H. Smith had bought its own specialists, such as Dillons and Our Price, but the commercial position of the core retail chain continued to decline. Many of the peripheral businesses were sold by Bill Cockburn, the chief executive, who spent the mid-1990s trying to position the company as a 'world-class retailer' before resigning in 1996. Management at the problematic retail chain claim that W.H. Smith is a middle-of-the-market variety chain, serving consumers who are not Dillons customers or Tesco customers. The retail business is struggling to find a role and has been left behind by market change. Analysts suggest that the underlying retail concept and trading format has had its day, leaving the business with no credible growth strategy in its core business (Olins, 1997b; Weyer, 1997). The chain is now divided into two businesses: travel and retail. While the travel business has been steadily growing over the past few years, the retail side has continued to shrink. This is explained by the move from paper to digital. The company is also criticised for pursuing a defensive strategy and poor shopping experience, putting in doubt its sustainability (Lynn, 2015).

In increasingly demanding, crowded and competitive markets there is no substitute for being market orientated. This does not, however, imply oversophisticated marketing operations and elaborate marketing departments. Staying close to the customer, understanding their needs and requirements and marshalling the firm's resources, assets and capabilities to deliver superior value is what counts. Here, the resource-based view of the firm (see Hamel and Prahalad, 1994) can add important new insights into achieving the necessary fit between firm and market (Day, 1994).

The shift from transactions-based marketing to relationship marketing has intensified in many markets as firms seek to establish closer bonds with their customers (Gummeson, 2008). They will need to realise, however, that for any relationship to last requires benefits on both sides. Too many early attempts at 'relationship building' have been simply mechanisms to buy temporary loyalty. Relationship building will need to become far more sophisticated.

Firms are also increasingly practising 'multi-mode marketing' – pursuing intense relationship-building strategies with some customers, less intense strategies with others and arm's length strategies with yet others, depending on the long-term value of the customer and their requirements.

3.6.1 Marketing strategies

To suggest that firms need to develop new strategies in increasingly turbulent and complex times may not go far enough. The problem may not just be that we need to develop new strategies, but that we have to develop wholly new approaches to strategy. For example, John Hagel (co-chairman for Deloitte LLP's Centre for the Edge) challenges conventional marketing thinking along the following three core strategy questions:

- **What's my differentiation?** Hagel urges marketers to identify ways to differentiate in a meaningful way that avoids confrontation with competitors. That requires a deep contextual understanding of the target market and how it and its needs evolve and will evolve. Differentiation has always been critical, but what is different now is the vast array of choices that people face. Hagel also warns marketers against superficial differentiation via features and to include experiences and/or help customers achieve self-actualisation or self-transcendence (Almquist *et al.*, 2016).
- **How can I maximise my leverage?** Hagel, here, is referring to the increasing imperative of doing more with less: 'the real power of leverage can only be realized in dynamic ecosystems where the focus is on how to build relationships that help all participants to learn faster by working together'. Delivering more with fewer resources can itself be a differentiator.
- **How will we measure success?** Here, Hagel is not merely referring to financial KPIs but critically softer, qualitative ones such as customer churn rate or how long it takes to introduce new offerings. For example, marketing analytics and consumer insight allow ideas to be tested very quickly. He further clarifies that 'the real question is the relative trajectory of performance. How rapidly are we improving on relevant metrics relative to others in similar arenas?' (Hagel, 2016)

Sarkar and Kotler's 'ecosystem marketing' concept reinforces the influence of ecosystems in strategic marketing thinking. They see its advantages as being:

- it accelerates the time to market/value;
- it positions the company effectively *vis-à-vis* its competitors;
- it improves the efficiency of marketing campaigns;
- it improves visibility and awareness with key stakeholders;
- it helps establish category leadership.

In marketing terms, maximising leverage will involve four interrelated ecosystems: that of the company, competitors, the category and customers (see Sarkar and Kotler, 2019).

These approaches combine to make strategic planning in general, and marketing planning in particular, more difficult now than they have ever been before. They also make them more vital activities than they have ever been before. Strategic marketing planning today attempts to build flexibility into the organisation to enable it to cope with this increased level of complexity and uncertainty and to take full advantage of the changing environment. At the heart of that planning process is the creation of a strong competitive position and a robust marketing strategy – the subject of the remainder of this text.

3.7 The Five Forces model of industry competition

Porter (1980) suggested that five main forces shape competition at the level of strategic business units and that a systematic analysis of each in turn can help managers identify the keys to competitiveness in their particular industry. The five forces are shown in Figure 3.7.

The Five Forces model is not merely of use to commercial organisations. It can also be used by organisations in the public and not-for-profit sectors to better understand their customers, suppliers and other organisations with whom they may be competing for support (financial or otherwise). We discuss each of the five forces in turn.

3.7.1 Rivalry among existing companies

A prime source of competition in any industry is among the existing incumbents. This rivalry is likely to be most intense where a number of conditions prevail:

- **Where the competitors in the industry are roughly evenly balanced** in terms of size and/or market share. The UK chocolate market is a case in point, where three rivals (Cadbury, Nestlé and Mars) all command roughly equal market shares. Competition between them for an extra percentage point of the market is intense, leading to high levels of advertising spend, strong price competition and continuous launch of new products.

Figure 3.7 Five forces driving competition

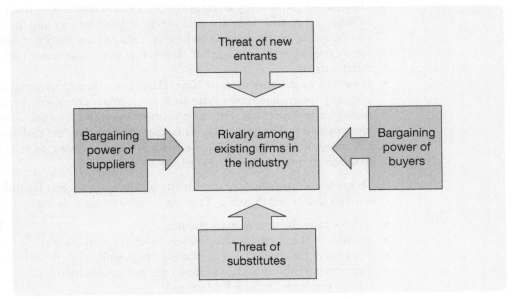

- **During periods of low market growth**, especially during the mature and decline stages of the product life cycle. Under such conditions, individual company growth is achieved only at the expense of competitors, and hence rivalry intensifies. The mobile telephone market is a case in point, where growth slowed in the early 2000s and existing firms such as Ericsson and Nokia found themselves with excess production capacity and entered into increased price competition to secure sales.
- **Where exit barriers are high.** If firms find it difficult to exit a market once they have entered, they are more likely to compete hard for success. High initial investments may create psychological (or egotistical) barriers to exit, high costs of redundancy (monetary or social) may deter exit, or e-market presence may be necessary to enable the firm to compete in more lucrative segments (for many state-owned mail services the cost of remaining in business is to continue to deliver mail to expensive-to-reach, out-of-the-way places).
- **Where product differentiation is low.** In markets where customers see little variation across products, where intrinsic quality and external value are perceived to be similar, competition for sales tends to be more intense. The prime reason is that customer switching costs are low – the cost (financial, inconvenience, etc.) to a customer of changing from one supplier to another.
- **Where fixed costs are relatively high.** High fixed costs relative to variable costs require greater sales volume to cover them. Until that volume is achieved, rivalry can be intense. In power supply industries the fixed costs of power generation are substantial compared with the variable costs of supplying power, leading to intense rivalry among generators.

3.7.2 The threat of market entry

In addition to considering existing rivals, organisations should also consider the potential for new entrants to emerge. The airline industry, for example, has seen a number of low-cost 'no-frills' entrants such as easyJet and Ryanair enter the market. A number of conditions make market entry more likely. Entry barriers can be low where the following hold:

- **Costs of entry are low.** The Internet has meant that many industries that once required substantial capital and investment for market entry are now more vulnerable to entry by lower-resourced competitors. Amazon.com, for example, entered into book retailing online with modest capital but without the need to invest in substantial bricks and mortar in the way that existing book retailers had.
- **Existing or new distribution channels are open to use.** Johnson and Scholes (1988) point out that entering the market for beer in Germany, the United Kingdom and France is hindered by the system of financing of bars and pubs by the large brewers. This 'tied system' has guaranteed access to the market for the large brewers but restricted access to new and small brewers, essentially acting as a barrier to market entry.
- **Little competitive retaliation is anticipated.** The expectation of retaliation by existing incumbents can be one of the most significant deterrents to market entry – for example, Accor Hotels' main focus on the markets where they are leaders such as in Europe, rather than China where their main competitors are strong. Conversely, where incumbents are considered weak, or lacking in resolve to defend their markets, the likelihood of new entrance is greater. The financial state of the large airline carriers in the late 1980s and 1990s meant that they were not in a strong position to see off the low-cost entrants that undercut their fares significantly. They had little leeway to retaliate, and the new entrants knew it. This battle is ongoing: recently British Airways has started to charge for on-board meals.
- **Differentiation is low.** When differentiation between the offerings of existing incumbents is low, there is likely to be more scope for new entrants to offer something unique and valued in the market.

- **There are gaps in the market.** In markets where the existing incumbents are not adequately serving the wants and needs of customers, there is more opportunity for entrants to establish themselves in underserved, or neglected, segments of the market. Highly segmented markets, in particular, where existing firms are slow to recognise diversity in customer requirements, provide tempting opportunities for new entrants.

3.7.3 The threat of substitutes

New entrants may use the existing technology of the industry, or they may attempt to revolutionise the market through leapfrogging. Indeed, technological substitution may come from new entrants or from existing firms doing things in new ways. Substitution can increase competitiveness of an industry for a number of reasons:

- **By making existing technologies redundant.** Classic examples include: the decimation of the slide rule industry by the advent of pocket calculators; apps or even artificial intelligence; the overtaking of mechanical timepieces by electronic technologies and, now, wearable technologies; and the advent of digital television replacing analogue. Where technologies are changing rapidly, competition between firms to stay ahead also tends to be intense.
- **By incremental product improvement.** Even where industries are not revolutionised overnight by step-changes in technology, existing market offerings may become quickly dated. Technological development in the computer industry, for example, proceeds apace, with personal computers becoming out of date almost as soon as they have been shipped! The advent of email as a means of communication has not made the letter obsolete, but it has had a significant impact on postal services. Email is simply a letter posted down the telephone wires rather than in a letterbox. More recently Facebook, Instagram and Snapchat have replaced SMS and email as a communication medium favoured by young people.

3.7.4 Bargaining power of suppliers

The balance of power between the members of an industry, its suppliers and its customers can significantly affect the level of competitiveness experienced by all. Where suppliers and/or customers have greater power than the members of the industry, competition within the industry for scarce suppliers or scarce customers tends to be more intense. Suppliers tend to have more bargaining power where the following hold:

- **Suppliers are more concentrated than buyers.** Where there are few organisations capable and willing to supply, their power over their buyers tends to be greater. Similarly, where buyers are more fragmented, and purchase in relatively small quantities, their power relative to their suppliers is likely to be low.
- **Costs of switching suppliers are high.** If the supplier provides a key ingredient for the purchaser that is difficult or costly to source elsewhere, their bargaining power is likely to be greater. Where the supplier provides commodity products that can be easily purchased elsewhere, they will have less bargaining power. Recently, Sainsbury's and Asda, two major supermarket chains in the UK, attempted to merge in an effort to increase their bargaining power with suppliers and drive costs down. In their view that would have helped them to be more competitive against the discounters such as Aldi and Lidl. However, the merger was blocked by the CMA (Competition and Markets Authority) because it was felt that the two chains combined would result in higher product prices and a reduction in quality and choice for the customer.
- **Suppliers' offerings are highly differentiated.** Where suppliers' products are distinct and different, either through tangible differences in standards, features or design, or through less tangible effects such as branding and reputation, they are likely to hold

more bargaining power. The power of Intel, for example, as a supplier of computer chips (which are increasingly commodity products) is enhanced through the reputation and branding of Intel among the ultimate customers for computers. This pull-through effect enhances the power of Intel in supplying to computer manufacturers and assemblers.

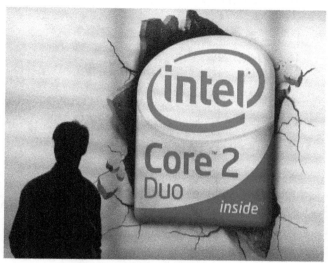

Source: TEH ENG KOON/AFP/Stringer/Getty Images.

3.7.5 Bargaining power of buyers

The buyers or customers of the output from an industry also exert pressures that can affect the degree of competition within it. Buyers tend to be more powerful in the supply chain where the following is true:

- **They are more concentrated than sellers.** Fewer buyers than sellers, especially where individual buyers account for large volumes of purchases and/or the sellers produce relatively small amounts each, means greater bargaining power for the customer. In grocery retailing, for example, a handful of major multiples command such a large percentage of total sales that they can practically dictate terms to their suppliers.
- **There are readily available alternative sources of supply.** Especially in the supply of commodity products or services, it may be relatively easy for buyers to buy elsewhere.
- **Buyer switching costs are low.** Where the inconvenience or cost of switching suppliers is low, greater power resides with the buyer, who can 'shop around' more to get better deals.

3.7.6 Competitiveness drivers

Taken together, these five forces offer a useful framework for assessing the factors likely to drive competition. They also suggest ways in which the players in the industry – current incumbents, suppliers and buyers – might seek to alter the balance of power and improve their own competitive position. We can summarise as follows. Where the following industry characteristics are present, expect greater levels of competition:

There is little differentiation between market offers
Industry growth rates are low
High fixed costs need to be recovered
High supplier switching costs
Low buyer switching costs
Low entry barriers
High exit barriers

As we shall see later (Chapter 10), one of the most successful ways of countering a highly competitive environment is to differentiate your offering from that of competitors, in a way that is of value to customers. That creates buyer switching costs, higher entry barriers and helps create a defensible position in the market irrespective of industry growth rates or costs of supply.

The product life cycle (PLC) is an insightful tool into an industry's competitive environment (Cravens and Piercy, 2012) and market dynamics. Its premises are that:

- All products have a limited lifespan until a better solution to the customer's problems comes along.
- Life cycles of products follow more or less predictable patterns or phases (see Figure 3.8).
- Market conditions, opportunities and challenges vary over the life cycle.
- Strategies need to adapt over the life cycle (see Chapter 11).

Each of the four key stages of the product life cycle (introduction, growth, maturity and decline) will be introduced here.

Introduction stage

The product is launched into the market and generally sales are slow to pick up because customers and distribution have to be found and convinced. If the product is new to the world (as was the first iPad) it will face little or no competition and the company will have a pioneer advantage and appeal to innovators. If it is an addition (such as the Samsung Edge in the smartphone market) it will be targeted at a new segment and fit the 'ideal' of that segment better than alternative solutions. The key question here has to do with how quickly competitors will launch a variant. This is normally the stage for build strategies (see Chapter 10).

Investment costs are likely to be very high prior to launch. The Airbus A380 is a good case in point (see Figure 3.9).

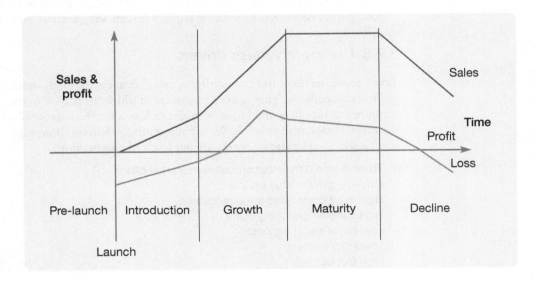

Figure 3.8 The product life cycle

Airbus A380's development costs were €11bn!

Source: Susanne Baumgarten/Vario images GmbH & Co.KG/Alamy Stock Photo.

Growth stage

The growth stage is characterised by a rapid increase in sales as the product starts to attract different types of customers and repeat purchases may start (see Figure 3.9). Critically, it is at this stage that competitors assess the product's market and profit potential and decide on their competitive moves. They may decide to modify or improve their current offerings, or enter the market with their own new products (for example, Microsoft Zunes as the 'iPod killer'). If not, they may use the other elements of the mix to detract attention from the product, such as an advertising campaign or a price promotion. It is possible that defensive attacks may be required to prevent the curve from flattening.

Maturity stage

At this stage, the rate of growth slows down significantly. This stage tends to last longer than the previous ones and is probably the most challenging one. It is a fact of life for most marketers that the markets they have to deal with are mature! This is a stage of severe

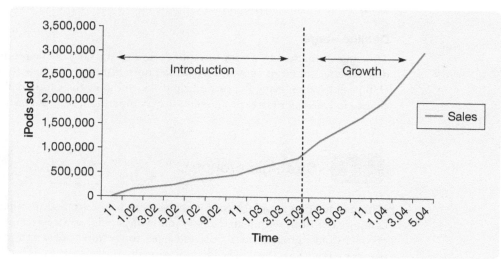

Figure 3.9 Sales of iPods

Source: iPodlounge.com. Data are for every two months from November 2001 to May 2004. Thus 11 is November 2001, 1.02 is January 2002, etc.

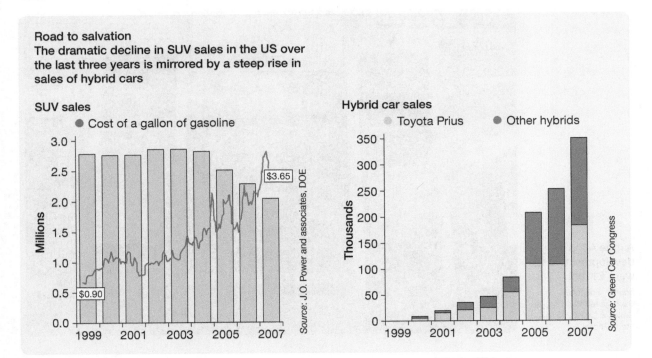

Road to salvation
The dramatic decline in SUV sales in the US over the last three years is mirrored by a steep rise in sales of hybrid cars

Figure 3.10 US car sales

competition, market fragmentation and declining profits, due to over-capacity in the industry. Indeed, competitors will try to uncover untapped niches and/or enter price wars. This leads to a clear-out and the weaker competitors will exit, possibly becoming suppliers to the stronger ones or being bought by them (as has been the case in the car industry). The survivors will be companies supplying the bulk of the market, or competing on a high-volume–low-margin basis, or market nichers. Many firms will try to buck the trend and revamp their PLCs (not always successfully, as both KitKat and Barbie experienced after unsuccessfully launching new variants of their products), or expand the market by creating a new segment, and hence extra demand overall, as Swatch did.

Mature markets are also likely to see a degree of product substitution, where one product form gives way to another. One example is the US car market, where increasing gasoline prices, coupled with increasing concern over emissions, has led to a decline in the sports utility vehicle (SUV) market but a rapid increase in sales of hybrid cars (see Figure 3.10).

Decline stage

This stage is marked by a slow or rapid decline of the sales of the product. Decline may be due to better solutions supplanting weaker ones (for example, new technology such as the USB flashdrive replacing floppy and zip disks, and now the Cloud replacing flashdrives), a change in consumer tastes or an increase in competition, be it domestic or international.

3.9   Strategic groups

Within industries, a useful basis for analysis can be the strategic group. A strategic group is composed of firms within an industry following similar strategies aimed at similar customers or customer groups. Coca-Cola and Pepsi, for example, form a strategic group in the soft drinks market (Kay, 1993). The identification of strategic groups is fundamental to industry analysis because just as industries can rise or fall despite the state of the overall business environment, so strategic groups with the distinctive competencies of their members can defy the general fluctuations within an industry.

Indeed, understanding the dynamics of existing strategic groups can be productive to understanding their vulnerability to competitive attack. For example, pursuing the Coca-Cola and Pepsi illustration, these firms compete on the basis of massive advertising spend on image and packaging to position against each other. They will respond to each other's advertising and promotion with anything except one thing – price. Coca-Cola and Pepsi have experienced price wars and they do not like them. This made the big brands highly vulnerable to attack by cheaper substitutes. Since 2014, Sainsbury's own labels outsell brands, and Waitrose recently de-listed most of its Tropicana and Copella lines to replace them with own-label juices.

The separation of strategic groups within a market depends on the barriers to mobility within the industry. For instance, all the companies within the UK shipbuilding industry tend to compete with each other for high value-added defence contracts, but their lack of cheap labour and resources means that they are not in the same strategic group as the Korean or Japanese suppliers or bulk carriers. Other barriers may be the degree of vertical integration of companies, as in the case of British Gypsum and its source of raw materials for making plasterboard within the United Kingdom, or Boots Pharmaceuticals with its access to the market via the Boots retailing chain. At a global level, geopolitical boundaries can also cause differences. For instance, the fragmented buying of the European military and the small production runs that result tend to position European defence contractors in a different strategic group from their US counterparts. Similarly, the differences in technology, reliability and safety standards form barriers between Russian and Western aerospace manufacturers.

As well as the barriers surrounding them, strategic groups also share competitive pressures. Within the US defence industry, firms share similar bargaining power with the Pentagon and influence through the political lobbying system. This can help protect them from non-US suppliers, but does not give them an advantage within their home market. The threat from substitutes or new entrants may also provide a unifying theme for strategic groups. Within the smartphone industry, suppliers of low-cost (or at least lower-cost) products such as Chinese brand PlusOne are creating intense competition with more established brands such as Samsung and Apple. Companies within the higher value-added mainframe businesses are under less threat from low-cost mainframe manufacturers, but are being squeezed by increasingly sophisticated and networked PCs. Finally, strategic groups often share common competitors because they are often competing to fulfil similar market needs using similar technologies.

The map of strategic groups within the US car market shows their dynamics (see Figure 3.11). The presentation is simplified into two dimensions for ease of discussion, but in reality a full analysis may use more. In this case, the strategic groups show their clear geographical and historic origins. The 'Big Three' – GM, Ford and Fiat Chrysler – though badly affected by the recession, remain dominant in supplying a broad range of cars with high local content (and even more so under President Trump). In this they retain some technological and styling expertise in the supply of regular and luxury sedans, but until recently had the common basic defence of promoting import restrictions.

Another group is the 'Faded Champions', which were once the major importers into the US market. Both are European companies whose US ventures have either seen better days, in the case of Volkswagen/Audi, or much better days, in the case of the now-extinct Rover Group. Once suppliers of a relatively broad range of vehicles, both these companies retreated towards the luxury car sector, where they appeared to have little competitive edge. When Rover was acquired (and then rapidly sold off again) by the German luxury car manufacturer BMW, it reconfirmed its positioning at the cheaper end of the market, complementary to (rather than in direct competition with) the BMW range. The demise of the Faded Champions in the United States is not due to the Big Three, but rather to the entry of the 'Samurai' group into the US market. Initially, the quality and low cost of the

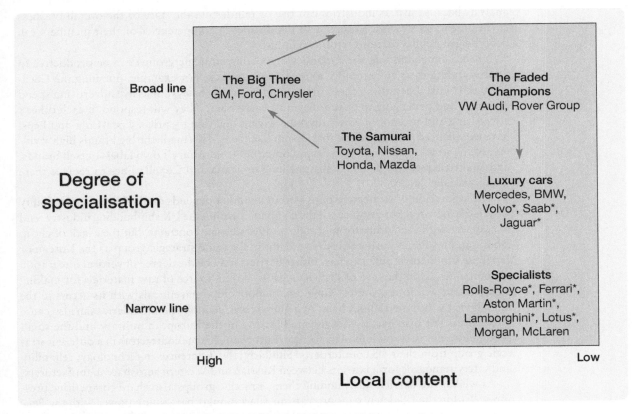

Figure 3.11 Map of strategic groups in the US automobile market

Note: * Brands now owned by large-scale American or European manufacturers.

Japanese strategic group gave them an advantage over the European broad-range suppliers, but now the Japanese are gaining even more power by becoming local manufacturers and therefore overcoming the local content barriers.

High European labour costs have meant that the European companies operate in strategic groups selling high added-value luxury cars or specialist cars, the luxury cars being supplied by relatively large-scale manufacturers with moderately wide product ranges (such as the German firm Mercedes-Benz), or specialist manufacturers producing the very expensive, small-volume products (the British Morgan cars, for instance).

The strength of the barriers surrounding the industry is reflected by recent shifts that have taken place. Although the Samurai have never successfully attacked the hard core of the Big Three, they have continued to nibble away at the weaker imports: first the Faded Champions by introducing cheap, reliable family cars; and more recently against the luxury car makers with the advent of the Lexus and other luxury offerings. Even though they are very large, the Big Three have found it difficult to defend their position by developing their own luxury cars and so have been seeking to defend their flanks against the Samurai by purchasing European manufacturers such as Jaguar, Volvo, Lamborghini, Aston Martin and Lotus. After years of the Big Three and the Samurai avoiding direct competition, the luxury car market has become the point where the two meet. Although the Samurai have not found it appropriate to purchase European companies in order to overcome entry barriers to those sectors (with the exception of Toyota, which has bought, and sold, Lotus), so distinct are the luxury car markets that both Honda and Toyota launched totally new ranges with new brand names and distribution systems to attack the market (the Acura and the Lexus).

With the luxury car market already being fought over, the next stand-up battle between the Big Three and the Samurai is in the specialist market, where the Americans have again been purchasing European brands and the Japanese have been aggressively developing 'Ferrari bashers'. Although the one-time distinct strategic groups are becoming blurred as the main protagonists enter new markets, it is to be noted that in all cases the strategy involves establishing distinct business units with the skills appropriate for the strategic groups being fought over. Examination of the US automobile market shows that even when markets are mature, there can be areas of rapid growth and competition, such as the luxury car and specialist markets. And the different expertise and situations of the strategic groups means that the protagonists from the different groups may well compete in different ways.

The inability of companies to understand the differences in strategic groups is one that causes the frequent failures of companies entering new markets by acquisition. Although the broad business definition, the products being sold and the customers may be similar within the acquired and acquiring company, where the two are in different strategic groups there can be major misunderstandings. Although having great expertise in the domestic market, many UK retailers have found international expansion very difficult because of the competition they face in the new markets and their failure to understand the strategic groups they are entering. Examples include Boots' acquisition in Canada and Dixons' in the USA where, although their international diversification was into the same industries as those with which they were familiar in the United Kingdom, those skills that allowed them to beat competition within their strategic groups at home did not transfer easily internationally. Were the companies facing the same competition within the European markets it is likely that their ventures would have been more successful. In a sense, that is what the Japanese have been doing, as their industries have rolled from country to country across the world, where their major competitors are their own compatriots whom they have faced in many markets in the past.

3.10 Industry evolution and forecasting

The critical issues to be addressed within an industry depend on its evolutionary stage. Porter (1980) discusses the evolution of industries through three main stages: emergence, transformation to maturity and decline (see Figure 3.12). These stages follow in much the

Stage	Issues	Strategies
Emergence	Technological uncertainty Commercial uncertainty Customer uncertainty Channel uncertainty	Locate innovators and early adopters Establish standard Reduce switching cost risk Encourage trial
Transition to maturity	Slow growth, falling profits Excess capacity, intense competition Increased customer power Extended product line	Marketing mix marketing Customer retention, segmentation Efficiency focus Coordination
Decline	Substitution by newer technologies Demographic change	Focus or divest

Figure 3.12 Industry evolution

Source: Adapted from O'Shaughnessy (1995).

same way as products are represented as following more or less identifiable life cycle stages (see O'Shaughnessy, 1995, for a comparison of the product life cycle and Porter's Industry Evolution Model). However, industry evolution is to the product what the product life cycle is to the brand. For example, whereas in the music industry the product life cycle may relate to downloadable music, vinyl records or CDs, industry evolution embraces the transition from cylinders to 78s, 45s, vinyl albums, 8-track cartridges, cassettes, compact discs, digital audio tape and subsequent digital technologies.

Uncertainty is the salient feature within emerging industries. Recent developments in broadcasting show this most clearly. There is no technological uncertainty about the basic technologies involved in achieving the direct broadcasting of television programmes by cable or satellite, but there are vast uncertainties about the combination of technologies to be used and how they should be paid for. In the early 1980s the discussion was about cable and the terrific opportunities offered for industrial redevelopment by cabling declining UK cities such as Liverpool. In the USA, many cable channels emerged but with no particular standard and with numerous channels that had a short life. In only a few years the vast infrastructure requirements of cable have been replaced by the equally capital-intensive but more elegant solution of satellite television. Even there, however, there has been uncertainty about whether to use high-, low- or medium-powered satellites and the means of getting revenue from customers. In the United Kingdom, to that brawl has been added uncertainty concerning British regulations, those of the European Union and the activities of the broadcasting channels, which were once the oligopolistic suppliers. It is not surprising that with this uncertainty consumers have shown reluctance in adopting the new viewing opportunities open to them. However, with the recent advent of the connected home via Smart TVs or new technologies such as Amazon Fire Stick, Google Chromecast and Apple TV, as well as fast broadband, consumers are quickly switching to SVOD (subscription video on demand) and catch-up TV services.

The high losses that can be associated with the emergent stage of an industry are shown by the losses incurred by the pioneers of the competing technologies in the video industry. Out of three competing video disc and video cassette recording technologies in the mid-1980s, only one – VHS – survived into the twenty-first century (to then be replaced by DVD and Blu-Ray). Two of the losers in that earlier round (Philips with the laser disc and V2000 VCRs, and Sony with the BetaMax format) managed the emergence of laser-based reproduction in the late 1980s and 1990s more carefully. The two industry leaders collaborated in the development of a compact disc (CD) standard and licensed the technology widely in order to accelerate its diffusion and reduce customer uncertainty. With the establishment of a single technology, the compact disc was less prone to the software shortages that made video discs so unattractive to customers. Customers still faced potentially high switching costs if they traded-in their existing album collection for CDs, but the impact of this was reduced by focusing on segments that were very conscious of hi-fi quality and were heavy users. The CD was also capable of being integrated into existing hi-fi systems and quickly became an established part of budget rack systems.

In the transition to maturity, uncertainty declines but competition intensifies. Typically, the rapid growth, high margins, little competition and apparent size of industries within the late stage of emergence attract many competitors. Those who sought to avoid the uncertainty in the early stages now feel the time is right for them to enter the market. This decision usually coincides with a transition to maturity within a marketplace where competition increases, profits fall, growth slows and capacity is excessive as more producers come on stream. Also, by now a dominant design has typically emerged, and hence competitors are forced to compete on a basis of price or the extended/augmented product. In technological terms, there is a switch to process technology; in marketing terms, a switch from entrepreneurship to the management of the marketing mix – that is, towards efficiency, coupled with the careful identification of market segments with a marketing mix to address them. Not unexpectedly, companies that fail to notice this transition from entrepreneurial to more bureaucratic management find things difficult.

An industry's decline is usually caused by the emergence of a substitute, or a demographic shift. Two main strategies are usually appropriate: either divest, or focus on the efficient supply of a robust segment. Although the basic options are few, industries often find this decision a difficult one because of the vested interests within the sector declining. It is extraordinary that at this last stage there seem to be more organisational choices about how to implement the basic strategies than at any other stage in an industry's evolution. At a clinical level, there can be the decision to divest or milk a company within a declining sector. There is the option of carefully nurturing a long-lasting, lingering target market; or for the entrepreneurial zest of an opportunist who can take advantage of the shifting needs. There is certainly much money to be made in the remnants of industries, as AEM (a subsidiary of RTZ) has found. It specialises in aviation engineering and maintenance of products that are no longer the main focus of the leading airframe and aero engine manufacturers.

Industry evolution shows the violent shifts that occur within an industry as it progresses from stage to stage. Not only do the major issues change, but the management tasks and styles appropriate are equally shifting. Industry evolution also shows that their very success can lead to failure for some firms that do not adapt their approaches and styles to changing conditions. Firms that have been highly successful in entrepreneurial mode during emergence may find it difficult to make the transition to a more bureaucratic way of operating. Similarly, those that have learned to live with stability and maturity may find difficulty in managing the business during industry decline, where a highly focused, cost-restrained way of operating is appropriate. Understanding the stage of industry evolution is essential if a company is to avoid managing in an environment with which it is unfamiliar, with an inappropriate management style.

3.11   Environmental stability

A limitation of Porter's Industry Evolution Model is the rigid association of technological and marketing uncertainty with only the emerging stage of an industry. This may not be so. For instance, the UK grocery trade has certainly been mature for generations, but the growth of supermarkets and hypermarkets, the removal of retail price maintenance and the move towards out-of-town and online shopping have meant the market has faced great turbulence, despite its maturity. Ansoff's (1984) theory is that environmental turbulence is fundamental to understanding industries, but it should not be seen as relating only to the early stages of industry life cycle.

A distinction is drawn between marketing and innovation turbulence (see Table 3.1). The reason for this is apparent when one considers many industries, such as the automobile industry, where competition has been rapidly changing but for which the competing technologies have changed little. The determinants of environmental turbulence parallel industry evolution in relating uncertainty to the stage of the product life cycle for both marketing and innovation turbulence. However, along with the emerging stage, decline and the transition from stage to stage can spell danger for the unwary company. And in some markets, the antecedents of marketing and innovation turbulence are quite different.

Figure 3.13 provides a mechanism for combining two dimensions of turbulence and shows how two strategic groups in the same industry can be facing different environments. Within the UK food-retailing trade, the environment for the leading grocers, such as Sainsbury's and Tesco, is *developing* in terms of both marketing and innovation. The shift out of town is continuing for larger outlets (though there are signs that concerns for the environmental impact of out-of-town shopping may lead to a slow-down of this trend), as is the move towards larger establishments; but the pattern is well understood, as is the position of the main protagonists within the industry. Similarly, major changes with electronic point-of-sale (EPOS) and stock control technologies have been absorbed by this sector and

Table 3.1 Determinants of environmental turbulence

Association of high marketing turbulence	Association of high innovative turbulence
High % of sales spent on marketing	High % of sales spent on R&D
Novel market entrant	Frequent new products in the industry
Very aggressive leading competitor	Short product life cycles (PLCs)
Threatening pressure by customers	Novel technologies emerging
Demand outstripping industry capacity	Many competing technologies
Emergence, decline or shifting stage of PLC	Emergence, decline or shifting stage of PLC
Low profitability	Low profitability
High product differentiation	Creativity is a critical success factor
Identification of latent needs a critical success factor	

are now a well-established part of their activities. The same applies to the move online and click-and-collect services. The intersection of the developing market turbulence and developing innovation turbulence not surprisingly indicates that the overall environmental turbulence is appropriately classified as developing.

The situation of the leading grocers in Figure 3.13 contrasts with the convenience stores, which form another strategic group within the same industry. Although their innovation turbulence is similar to leading grocers, they face *discontinuous marketing* turbulence. This is due to their not yet having faced the shift from in-town to out-of-town shopping, and their existence within the emergent phase of an industry in which many new entrants are appearing. Although in the same industry as the leading grocers, the convenience stores face *changing environmental* turbulence.

Ansoff draws broad strategic and managerial conclusions from the differences in environmental turbulences that companies face. Whereas, he suggests, the leading retailers see the need to be *reactive* in terms of their strategic thrust and have the ability to adapt, he would suggest that the convenience stores need a more dynamic management style, where they *anticipate* shifts in the environment and look for synergistic opportunities. Within that context, the convenience stores have concentrated on a series of goods for which their position is critical, such as alcoholic beverages, milk and soft drinks, which constitute a very large proportion of their sales.

From a marketing point of view, there is great importance in correctly assessing environmental turbulence. A firm must try to match its capability to appropriate environments, or develop capabilities that fit new ones. The Trustee Savings Bank (TSB) and many other retailing banks in the United Kingdom have shown the dangers of believing their resources can enable them to operate in unfamiliar style. TSB, in particular, almost epitomised custodial management, where it provided an efficient service in a standard way to a very stable market for a long time. Even more than other banks, it meant the company was built around closed systems and operations where there was little need for entrepreneurship. The privatisation of TSB gave it a dangerous combination of a large amount of money and wider opportunities, together with a massively changed banking environment. Two almost inevitable developments have occurred: (a) the bank has shown its inability to manage businesses with a more dynamic environment; and (b) it has found itself unable to work out what to do with its cash mountain. A solution was eventually found in the merger with Lloyds Bank, which could provide the necessary capabilities. However, in 2009 the

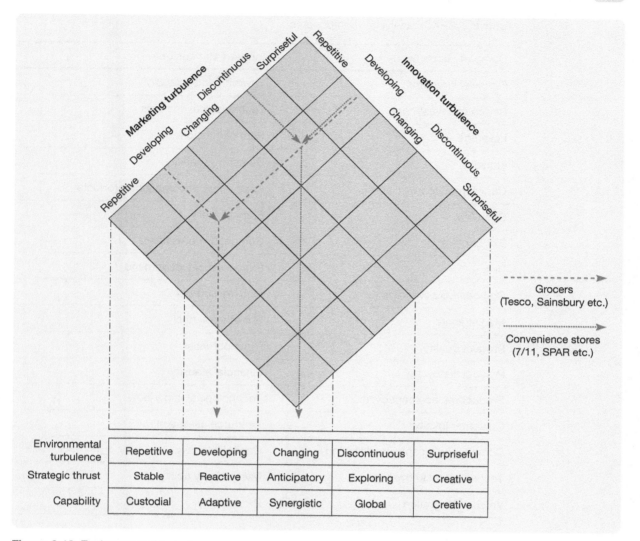

Figure 3.13 Environmental turbulence
Source: Based on Ansoff (1984) Figure 3.4.5, p. 222.

European Commission ruled that the British Government's 43.4 per cent stake in the group represented state aid and so the group was split up in 2015.

3.12   SPACE analysis

SPACE (strategic position and action evaluation – Rowe *et al.*, 1989) analysis extends environmental analysis beyond the consideration of turbulence to look at industry strength and relates this to the competitive advantage and financial strength of a company. Like Shell's Directional Policy Matrix and other multidimensional portfolio planning devices, it is a method of summarising a large number of strategic issues on a few dimensions. One of the dimensions is environmental stability (see Table 3.2), which includes many of the facets of environmental turbulence. However, with SPACE analysis environmental instability is seen as being counterbalanced by financial strength, a company with high liquidity, or access to other reserves being able to withstand environmental volatility.

Table 3.2 SPACE analysis – components

Company dimensions	Industry dimensions
Financial strengths	*Environmental stability*
Return on investment	Technological changes
Leverage	Rate of inflation
Liquidity	Demand variability
Capital required/available	Price range of competing products
Cash flow	Entry barriers
Exit barriers	Competitive pressures
Risk	Price elasticity of demand
Competitive advantage	*Industry strength*
Market share	Growth potential
Product quality	Profit potential
Product life cycle	Financial stability
Product replacement cycle	Technological know-how
Customer loyalty	Resource utilisation
Competition's capacity utilisation	Capital intensity
Technological know-how	Market entry ability
Vertical integration	Productivity

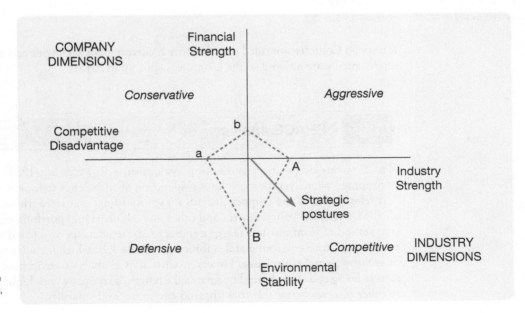

Figure 3.14
SPACE analysis
map

Source: Based on Rowe
et al. (1989) Exhibit 6.10,
p. 145.

Industry strength is the second environmental dimension considered. This focuses on attractiveness of the industry in terms of growth potential, profitability and the ability to use its resources efficiently. For a company within the industry, these strengths are no virtue unless a company has a competitive advantage. SPACE analysis, therefore, opposes industry strength by competitive advantage (see Figure 3.14) to provide a gauge of a company's position relative to the industry.

Rating a company and the industry on each of the four dimensions gives the competitive profile abAB in Figure 3.14. The example clearly shows a company in a weak position: moderately high environmental instability is not balanced by financial strength, and the competitive advantage of the company is not great compared with the overall industry strength.

The relative size of the opposing dimension gives a guide to the appropriate strategic posture of a firm. For example, from Figure 3.14, A + a and B + b show the overall weight of the SPACE analysis to be towards the bottom right-hand quadrant. This indicates a **competitive posture**, which is typical of a company with a competitive advantage in an attractive industry. However, the company's financial strength is insufficient to balance the environmental instability it faces. Such firms clearly need more financial resources to maintain their competitive position. In the long term this may be achieved by greater efficiency and productivity, but likely is the need to raise capital or merge with a cash-rich company.

Firms that find their strategic posture within the **aggressive quadrant** are enjoying significant advantages, yet are likely to face threats from new competition. The chief danger is complacency, which prevents them gaining further market dominance by developing products with a definite competitive edge. The excessive financial strength of these companies may also make it attractive for them to seek acquisition candidates in their own or related industries.

A **conservative posture** is typical of companies in mature markets, where the lack of need for investment has generated financial surpluses. The lack of investment can mean that these companies compete at a disadvantage, and lack of opportunities within their existing markets makes them vulnerable in the long term. They must, therefore, defend their existing products to ensure a continued cash flow while they seek new market opportunities.

Companies with a **defensive posture** are clearly vulnerable. Having little residual strength to combat competition, they need to foster resources by operating efficiently and be prepared to retreat from competitive markets in order to concentrate on ones they have a chance of defending. For these, it just appears to be a matter of time before either competition or the environment gets the better of them.

3.13   The Advantage Matrix

Once strategic groups within a market have been identified, it becomes apparent that the groups have differing levels of profitability. For instance, in the machine tool industry, conventional lathes are almost a commodity and are frequently produced at low cost in the emerging economies. But in another part of the industry, say flexible manufacturing systems, profits can be quite high for those companies with special skills. Recognition of this pattern led the Boston Consulting Group (1979) to develop the Advantage Matrix, which helps to classify the competitive environments that can co-exist within an industry. The framework identifies two dimensions: the number of approaches to achieving advantage within a market, and the potential size advantage. In Figure 3.15, the quadrants of the Advantage Matrix show how relationships between relative size and return on assets for companies can differ.

The **stalemate** quadrant represents markets with few ways of achieving advantage and where the potential size advantage is small. Companies in such a strategic group would therefore find trading akin to a commodity market. These can be relatively complex products, as in the case of desktop computers, where the technologies are well known, product

Figure 3.15 The Advantage Matrix

Source: Based on unpublished material from the Boston Consulting Group.

designs are convergent despite constant technological improvement and similar sources of supply are used by everyone. Both large and small manufacturers are using overseas suppliers, and consumers are well able to compare product with product. Attempts to differentiate the market, as tried by IBM with its PS/2, have failed. Therefore, competitors are forced to compete mainly on the basis of efficient manufacturing and distribution.

The **volume** quadrant represents markets where the opportunities for differentiation remain few, yet where potential size advantages remain great. This has occurred within some of the peripheral markets that support desktop computers. In particular, the printer industry has come to be dominated by Canon, Hewlett-Packard and IBM. The reason for this is the convergence in needs of users of printers and the mass production of the intrinsically mechanical printer units. Unlike microcomputers, where the manufacturing process is one of assembly of basically standard components in a very fixed fashion, as any user of printers will know there are numerous ways of solving the printing and paper-feed problems. This results in an industry where large economies of scale can be achieved by a few dominant suppliers. Where there are markets of this form, battles to achieve volume and economies of scale are paramount. Dominant companies are likely to remain dominant for some time once their cost advantage is achieved, although there is always a threat from a new technology emerging that will destroy the cost advantage they have fought to obtain. In this way, Hewlett-Packard joined the band of leaders within the printer market by becoming the industry standard in the newly emerged market for laser printers.

Specialised markets occur when companies within the same market have differing returns on scale. This occurs most conspicuously among suppliers of software for microcomputers. Within the overall market for software there are clear sub-sectors with dominant leaders. It is also apparent that the market leaders, because of their familiarity and proven reliability, are able to charge a price premium. Microsoft Office, for example, is fast establishing leadership of the integrated office software sector at prices ahead of its major competitors. Within the games sector, Atari is less able to command premium prices, although its dominance does mean it is reaping size advantages within its own segments. The result in these specialised markets is therefore a series of experience curves being followed by different companies. Within these specialised markets, the most successful companies will be those that dominate one or two segments. Within the market for microcomputer software, this has often meant that they will be the companies creating a new generic class of product, as Microsoft achieved with its Windows products – making the IBM PC as user friendly as its Apple Mac rival.

Fragmented markets occur when the market's requirements are less well defined than the stalemate, volume or specialised cases. Several parts of the computer peripheral market conform to this pattern. In contrast to the demand for printers, the specialised users of plotters have a wide variety of requirements and the opportunities for colour and high resolution mean that an unlimited variety of differentiated products can be made. Similarly, in the provision of accounting software, alternative specifications are numerous and therefore many different prices and products co-exist in the same market. Where this fragmentation has occurred, success depends on finding niches where particular product specifications are needed. Each niche provides little opportunity for growth; therefore, a company hoping to expand depends on finding a multiplicity of niches where, hopefully, some degree of commonality will allow economies to be achieved.

Summary

Several broad conclusions can now be drawn and their implications for marketing management identified.

First, in many industries the days of rapid domestic growth are gone forever. In those where high rates of growth are still possible, competition is likely to be increasingly fierce and of an international nature. It is no longer sufficient for companies to become marketing orientated – that is taken for granted. The key to success will be the effective implementation of the marketing concept through clearly defined positioning strategies.

Second, change creates opportunities for innovative organisations and threats for those who attempt to hold it back. It is probable that there will be a redefinition of 'work' and 'leisure', which will provide significant new opportunities to those companies ready and able to seize them. The changing demographic profile, particularly in terms of age, marital status and income distribution, also poses many opportunities for marketing management.

Third, the speed of change in the environment is accelerating, leading to greater complexity and added 'turbulence', or discontinuity. Technological developments are combining to shorten product life cycles and speed up commercialisation times. The increasing turbulence in the market makes it particularly difficult to predict and, as a result, planning horizons have been shortened. Where long-range plans in relatively predictable markets could span 10–15 years, very few companies today are able to plan beyond the next few years in any but the most general terms.

Fourth, successful strategies erode over time. What has been successful at one point in time, in one market, cannot guarantee success in the future in the same or other markets.

A systematic analysis of the competitive or industry environment in which an organisation operates consists of four main components: (1) an analysis of the five forces driving industry competition (rivalry among existing incumbents, the threat of entry and of substitution and the bargaining power of buyers and of suppliers); (2) the recognition of the strategic groups within a market that can allow a company to address its efforts towards specific rather than general competitors; (3) the recognition of the different competitive environments and scale economies that can exist within the sub-markets in which the strategic clusters operate; and (4) the degree of turbulence within markets. Through understanding these, a company can identify the sort of competition that is likely to exist within chosen segments and the types of strategy that are likely to lead to success. From the study of turbulence, they can also find a guide to necessary orientation of the company and the blend of custodial management and entrepreneurial flair that will be needed to manage the venture. Just as segmentation allows a company to direct its resources towards fulfilling a particular set of customer needs, the industry analysis helps a company to build its defences towards a specific group of competitors, and build its strengths in accordance with the type of market it faces.

At the outset we noted, however, that studying the industry alone is not enough – it may blind us to changes in the sources and types of competition we will face in the future and fundamental changes in the structure of markets. To our analysis of industry we must add our understanding of customers and competitors, as well as our real capabilities as an organisation. These are the topics of the chapters that follow.

Case study

Dyson: A British inventor pivots to Asia

By Peter Campbell and Michael Pooler in London and Stefania Palma in Sydney

With one eye on the Chinese market, the British company is set to produce electric cars in Singapore. Will the £2bn gamble pay off?

James Dyson churned out 5,126 prototypes before perfecting the final version of the machine that would make his name and fortune. A quarter of a century after that bagless vacuum cleaner went on sale, his eponymous company's attempt to enter the automotive arena with a series of electric cars from 2021 will allow for far fewer trials.

The privately held British engineering group has bet its future on breaking into one of the world's most competitive markets, pitting the entrepreneur against corporations like Volkswagen, Toyota and General Motors.

Its £2bn gamble shifted up a gear this week, with the announcement that its first automotive manufacturing plant will be in Singapore, the city-state which has not made cars since Ford closed a plant there in 1980.

Singapore's trade links with China, the world's largest electric car market, as well as its abundance of engineering graduates, helped it overtake other shortlisted contenders that included Britain, home to Dyson's headquarters.

Though genuinely considered, the UK was always regarded as a long shot and the decision has inevitably sparked questions over the country's ability to safeguard its car industry as Britain prepares to leave the EU.

Such is the ambition of Sir James, arguably Britain's most famous inventor and a vocal supporter of Brexit, that he believes Dyson cars will eventually outgrow the company's range of hairdryers, vacuums and air filters and come to define the brand.

Source: CARTA image / Alamy Stock Photo.

'If they make an executive decision that they will develop a product in a certain category, then they go all in,' says a former Dyson research engineer.

But the scale of the challenge is enormous. Established players still find making cars at a profit fiendishly difficult. The biggest newcomer in the field, Elon Musk's Tesla, has burnt through billions of dollars of cash with only a handful of quarterly positive earnings to show for it.

Commercial failure, big cost overruns or even just unexpected hiccups on production lines could end up threatening the company that Sir James has built into an empire with £3.5bn of revenue.

'I think Dyson is underestimating the scale of the challenge, both in developing a new car and building it successfully,' says David Bailey, a professor of economics and industrial policy at Aston University.

'It is going to be a lot more expensive than they anticipate. It will gobble up a lot of resources,' he adds.

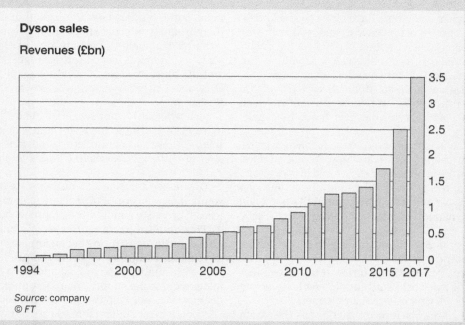

Dyson sales

Revenues (£bn)

Source: company
© FT

Dyson sales

Source: Peter Campbell and Michael Pooler, "Dyson: a British inventor pivots to Asia" in London and Stefania Palma in Sydney OCTOBER 26, 2018.

Dyson's interest in cars goes back to the cyclone principle it uses in its vacuum cleaners to suck up dirt. In the 1990s, Sir James suggested this could be used to extract fumes from diesel exhausts, but his approaches to car makers were rebuffed.

Today, the company can boast success in almost every product category it has entered with the notable exception of its washing machines, which sold at a loss and were discontinued.

Sceptics say there is a huge difference between high-end domestic appliances and an automotive industry undergoing radical shifts amid the rise of electric propulsion technology, artificial intelligence and new ownership models. Yet with far fewer moving parts than traditional internal combustion engine cars, battery-powered vehicles are easier to design and produce, opening the door to new entrants, from California's Tesla to Croatia's Rimac.

In China alone, which Dyson sees as its biggest target market, there are more than 300 registered electric car start-ups, many with rich backers and ambitious founders. They include names such as Lucid, Byton and Nio, which is backed by the internet group Tencent and recently listed on the New York Stock Exchange.

'We know it is a crowded market,' Sir James said last year. 'But if you produce a product that has technology that is genuinely better, and a performance and product that people want, you can make money.'

Tesla has sought to cement a position by attacking the inefficiencies it saw in established manufacturers, from overreliance on suppliers to the traditional dealership model. Dyson is applying a similar disruptive mentality.

'Dyson thinks, like Musk, the incumbent industry doesn't know what it's doing,' says one person who has worked on the project. 'That's quite a risk.'

The company's notorious secrecy – it took more than a year to agree a confidentiality agreement with one supplier on the project – means few details have been revealed about its maiden four-wheeler to roll off the production line in just three years. Scheduled to be the first in a planned series of three models, it will be pitched to the upper end of the market and produced in a small batch of several thousand, according to people familiar with the plans.

Unlike Tesla, which has suffered manufacturing problems, the British group already makes millions of products a year, and sources around 4bn parts annually from across the globe.

'He's not a Silicon Valley start-up, he understands manufacturing,' says one supplier.

Dyson believes that its specialisms, in areas such as electric motors, batteries and aerodynamics, will give it the edge over companies with a century's worth of experience in car making. But to succeed, it will need to cast off some of its reluctance to collaborate with component providers.

Its fans and air purifiers have given Dyson knowledge in the physics of air flow, an important area for electric vehicles because drag is a key factor in battery range, the distance that an electric vehicle can eke out of its 'tank' before needing to recharge.

For instance, a Tesla Model S can travel 300 miles on a full battery, in part because of its sleek design. But when carrying bicycles, the distance falls significantly.

Most established car brands have distinctive grills, which allow cooling air to flow into the hot engines. Keeping the same design for their electric cars allows models to be recognised by the motoring public – an Audi electric car will still look like an Audi – but it will bring aerodynamic trade-offs that will hamper the cars' range.

That should give those starting from scratch an automatic head start.

Dyson's other forte is batteries. It already makes 7 per cent of the world's lithium ion cells, to power devices such as its cordless floor cleaners.

However, it may be forced to scale back the extent of its technological ambitions – at least for now. The company originally intended for its cars to be powered by cells developed in-house as part of a £1bn investment, but has now admitted that it could buy them from an external supplier.

Many car makers already buy-in their batteries to avoid being locked into a single battery type and the huge expense of building a cell production site, says Chris Robinson, a senior analyst at Lux Research.

'One alternative [for Dyson] could be licensing its [battery] material to have someone else make it for them – a contract manufacture,' he adds. 'There are a lot of battery factories in China and elsewhere in Asia.'

Dyson's reluctance to collaborate with other companies – borne out of years of defending its intellectual property – makes this approach unlikely.

This mindset played a crucial role in its decision not to build in Britain, because many of the UK government-funding channels require collaboration with smaller partners, an approach designed to foster a domestic supply chain. Britain may need to change this approach to win future work.

'Where we are falling down is not having any capital money to put into these things,' says one government figure. 'Other states cheat the system and find ways around that, but we don't.'

China dominates sales of battery electric vehicles

Breakdown by region, unit sales (m)

China accounts for over half of BEV sales and its market share is expected to increase tp 65%

Rest of world   Asia ex-China   Europe   US   China

Source: Frost & Sullivan
© FT

China dominates sales of battery electric vehicles

Source: Peter Campbell and Michael Pooler, "Dyson: a British inventor pivots to Asia" in London and Stefania Palma in Sydney OCTOBER 26, 2018.

Singapore's incentives include tax breaks for five years, which can be extended, and R&D grants that can cover up to 30 per cent of the cost of projects that involve product, application or process development, according to the Singapore Economic Development Board. They also offer expensive land at discounted rates, says a person with experience of Singapore's economic planning. 'They definitely would have given [Dyson] a favourable tax break,' they add.

Dyson refuses to reveal the scale of its investment, though the EDB's Kiren Kumar says the company would double its 1,000-strong workforce in the country through the investment.

Advanced manufacturing is a priority for Singapore, which deems it a way to raise productivity at a time when the city-state has struggled to maintain high levels of efficiency.

For Dyson, which says its Singapore investment was premised on market access rather than incentives, no amount of government support can remove the need to pour its own resources into the venture.

Sir James has ruled out an initial public offering to fund the project. Earnings before tax at Weybourne Group, the holding entity for Dyson's commercial interests, rose 27 per cent to £801m last year, while revenue jumped two-fifths to £3.5bn.

Its debt levels are low by the standards of industrial companies, giving it room to borrow significantly, while the core business generates cash.

But still, Sir James is acutely aware of the challenge he has taken on. 'Investing in new technologies requires many leaps of faith and huge financial commitment over long periods,' he told a *Financial Times* dinner this year. 'En route, there can be multiple sleepless nights and lots of frustration,' he said before adding that, at heart, 'Dyson was never a vacuum cleaner company'.

Source: from 'Dyson: A British inventor pivots to Asia', *Financial Times*, 26/10/18 (Campbell P, Pooler, M. and Palma, S.).

Discussion questions

1 What environmental factors are behind Dyson's move into the electric car market and its decision to move its operations to Singapore?

2 What does Sir James means by 'Dyson was never a vacuum cleaner company'?

3 Use the Five Forces model to establish how competitive the electric car industry sector is.

CHAPTER 4

CUSTOMER ANALYSIS

'When the future becomes less visible, when the fog descends, the forecasting horizon that you can trust comes closer and closer to your nose. In those circumstances being receptive to new directions becomes important. You need to take account of opportunities and threats and enhance an organisation's responsiveness.'

Igor Ansoff, quoted by Hill (1979)

Amadeus set to soar on airline data sales

By Thomas Hale in Madrid

Amadeus, the Spanish company that provides the technology behind airline flight bookings, is set to report results in stark contrast to the airlines it serves, as it benefits from a 40 per cent share of a growing air travel market.

On Friday, the group's full-year results are expected to show the effect of its expansion from flights into hotel reservations and the growth of its IT solutions business. Its share price has been charting a sustained upwards trajectory for much of the last five years, hitting an all-time high on Monday this week, for a market capitalisation of more than €16bn.

Amadeus makes most of its money through its global flight distribution system, which manages transactions between customers and about 120 of the world's airlines, many of which take place on online price comparison websites. Its growth is therefore linked directly to an increase in global air traffic.

Source: Greg Balfour Evans/Alamy Stock Photo.

But despite Amadeus being recognised by Bloomberg as the eleventh-largest software company in the world, and second in Europe, Luis Maroto, group chief executive, struck a cautious tone when asked about his company's future prospects.

'It's nothing new', he said. 'Travel is very much linked to economy. . . This is coming more from Asia due to the size of the populations there', he adds.

However, analysts suggest that much of Amadeus' value lies in what it can glean from the billions of transactions it processes: a perspective on the purchasing habits of consumers.

Improved personalisation – from the interrogation of 'big data' – enables airlines to tailor their products and services to the personal whims of individual consumers.

Amadeus has already begun to sell aggregated user information to airlines, revealing customers' search habits. It provides a growing revenue stream for the company. Mr Maroto has said this will form part of the business model in future.

The company, however, faces certain challenges. It competes mainly with other global distribution services, including US group Sabre and UK-based Travelport, both of which listed last year. 'Sabre and Travelport are trying to gain market share', noted Gonzalo Sanz, an analyst at Mirabaud Securities.

Airline companies have also attempted to provide their own IT infrastructure, which threatens to cut Amadeus out of the loop and reduce the number of transactions flowing through its system.

On this front, though, analysts have suggested the tide may be turning in Amadeus' favour. Last summer, Ryanair, which had previously refused to place itself on global distribution platforms, relented and announced a partnership with the company.

 Source: from 'Amadeus set to soar on airline bookings', *Financial Times*, 26/02/2015 (Hale, T.).

Discussion questions

1 Where does most of Amadeus' value lie?
2 What information do companies need to have about their customers?

Introduction

Information is the raw material of decision making. Effective marketing decisions are based on sound information; the decisions themselves can be no better than the information on which they are based. Marketing research is concerned with the provision of information that can be used to reduce the level of uncertainty in decision making. Uncertainty can never be eliminated completely in marketing decisions, but by the careful application of tried-and-tested research techniques it can be reduced.

The first section of this chapter looks at the information needed about customers in order to make effective marketing decisions. This is followed by a brief discussion of the various research techniques available for collecting data from the marketing environment. The use of these techniques in a typical marketing research study aimed at creatively segmenting a market and identifying current and potential product/service positions is then discussed. The chapter concludes with a discussion of how marketing-related information can be arranged within an organisation and the development of marketing decision support systems (MDSS).

4.1   What we need to know about customers

Information needed about customers can be broadly grouped into current and future information. The critical issues concerning current customers are: (1) Who are the prime market targets?; (2) What gives them value?; (3) How can they be brought closer?; and (4) How can they be better served?.

For the future, however, we also need to know: (1) How will customers and their needs and requirements change?; (2) Which new customers should we pursue?; and (3) How should we pursue them?.

4.1.1 Information on current customers

The starting point is to define who the current customers are. The answer is not always obvious as there may be many actors in the purchase and use of a particular product or service. Customers are not necessarily the same as consumers. A useful way to approach customer

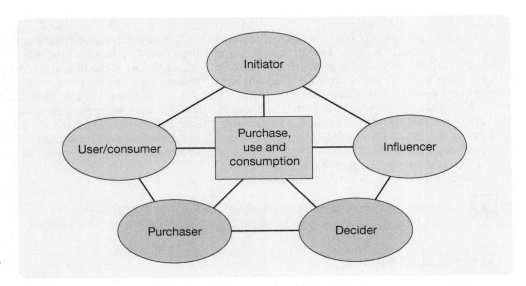

Figure 4.1 Who is the customer?

definition is to recognise five main roles that exist in many purchasing situations. Often several, or even all, of these roles may be conducted by the same individuals, but recognising each role separately can be a useful step in more accurately targeting marketing activity (see Figure 4.1).

The roles are as follows:

1 **The initiator.** This is the individual (or individuals) who initiates the search for a solution to the customer's problem. In the case of the purchase of a chocolate bar, it could be a hungry child who recognises her own need for sustenance (or pleasure!). In the case of a supermarket, the reordering of a particular line of produce nearing sell-out may be initiated by a stock controller, or by an automatic order processing system.

2 **The influencer.** Influencers are all those individuals who may have some influence on the purchase decision. A child may have initiated the search for a chocolate bar, but the parents may have a strong influence (through holding the purse strings) on which product is actually bought. In the supermarket, the ultimate customers will have a strong influence on the brands ordered – the brands they buy or request the store to stock will be most likely to be ordered.

3 **The decider.** Taking into account the views of initiators and influencers, some individuals will actually make the decision as to which product or service to purchase. This may be back to the initiator or the influencer in the case of the chocolate bar. In the supermarket, the decider may be a merchandiser whose task it is to specify which brands to stock, what quantity to order and so on.

4 **The purchaser.** The purchaser is the individual who actually buys the product or service. They are, in effect, the individual that hands over the cash in exchange for the benefits. This may be the child or parent for the chocolate bar. In industrial purchasing, it is often a professional buyer who, after taking account of the various influences on the decision, ultimately places the order, attempting to get the best value for money possible.

5 **The user.** Finally, comes the end user of the product or service – the individual who consumes the offer. For the chocolate bar, it will be the child. For the goods in the supermarket, it will be the supermarket's customers.

What is important in any buying situation is to have a clear idea of the various actors likely to have an impact on the purchase and consumption decision. Where the various roles are undertaken by different individuals, it may be necessary to adopt a different marketing approach to each. Each may be looking for different benefits in the purchase and consumption process. Where different roles are undertaken by the same individual, different approaches may be suitable depending on what stage of the buy/consume process the individual is in at the time (see Figure 4.2).

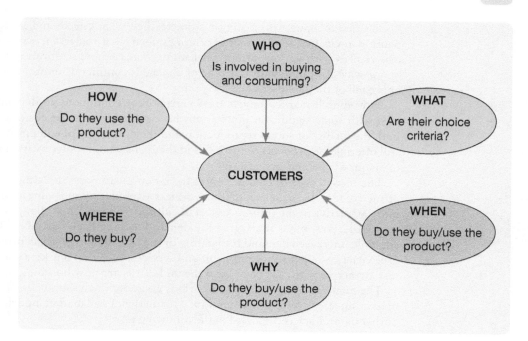

Figure 4.2
Understanding
customers – the
key questions

A central theme of this text is that most markets are segmented; in other words, different identifiable groups of customers require different benefits when buying or using essentially similar products or services. Identifying who the various customers are and what role they play then leads to the question of what gives them value. For each of the members of a decision-making unit (DMU), different aspects of the purchase and use may give value.

For example, in the child's purchase of a chocolate bar, a number of benefits may emerge. The child/initiator/decider/user gets a pleasant sensory experience and a filled stomach. The parent/influencer gets a feeling of having steered the child in the direction of a product that is delicious and good value for money. In a business purchase, such as a tractor, the users (drivers) may be looking for comfort and ease of operation, the deciders (top management) may be looking for economical performance, while the purchaser (purchasing officer) may be looking for a bulk purchase deal to demonstrate their buying efficiency. Clearly, the importance of each actor in the decision needs to be assessed and the benefits each gets from the process understood.

Having identified the motivators for each actor, attention then shifts to how they can be brought closer to the supplier. Ways of offering increased benefits (better sensory experiences, enhanced nutritional value, better value for money) can be examined. This may involve extending the product service offering through the 'augmented' product (see Levitt, 1986).

For business purchases, a major route to bringing customers closer is to develop mutually beneficial alliances that enhance value for both customer and supplier. A characteristic of Japanese businesses is the closeness developed with suppliers so as to ensure continuity of appropriate quality supply of semi-finished material 'just in time' for production purposes.

Better service is at the heart of improving customer relations and making it difficult for customers to go elsewhere. Surveys in the United States have shown that, of lost business, less than 20 per cent is down to poor products and only 20 per cent down to (relatively) high prices. The major reason for losing business is predominantly poor service – more than 50 per cent of cases.

4.1.2 Information on future customers

The issues discussed thus far have been concerned with today's customers. Of importance for the future, however, is how those customers will change. There are two main types of change essential to customer analysis.

The first is changes in existing customers: their wants, needs and expectations. As competition intensifies, so the range of offerings open to customers increases. In addition, their experiences with various offers can lead to increased expectations and requirements. A major way of dealing with this type of change is continuous improvement (or the *kaizen* approach of the Japanese).

In the mobile market (tablets and smartphones), continuous product improvements coupled with some significant innovations have served to increase customer expectations of both the quality of sound reproduction and the portability of equipment. A manufacturer still offering the products of the 2000s in the 2020s would soon find its customers deserting in favour of competitors' offerings.

The second type of change comes from new customers emerging as potentially more attractive targets. Segments that may be less attractive at one point in time might become more attractive in the future. As social, cultural and economic change has affected living standards, so too has it affected the demand for goods and services. There is now, for example, increased demand for healthy or organically grown fresh produce, vegan food, green energy-generation equipment and services, such that markets that might have been less attractive in the 2000s or even the mid-2010s are now booming or starting to grow.

The main ways in which organisations go about analysing their customers is through marketing research (to collect relevant data on them) and market modelling (to make sense of that data). Each is discussed in the following text.

4.2   Marketing research

The use of marketing research services by a variety of organisations, from commercial firms to political parties, has increased dramatically in recent years. Globally, the market research industry was worth $76 billion in 2017 according to Esomar (**www.esomar.org**). Not only large companies and organisations benefit from marketing research. It is possible, through creative design of research studies, for organisations with smaller budgets to benefit from marketing research studies. Commercial research organisations will conduct studies for clients costing as little as £2,000, depending on the research being undertaken. See **www.marketresearchworld.net** for a wealth of information on the types of research available and the methodologies used. It is worth noting that the advent of the digital world has opened the way for new marketing research methods and approaches.

Figure 4.3 shows the range of marketing research activities engaged in by research agencies (Harrison *et al.*, 2016). Some companies, such as Kantar TNS (**www.tnsglobal.co.uk/**), offer a wide variety of services. Others specialise in particular types of research (such as qualitative research). For a comprehensive listing of companies in the United Kingdom providing marketing research services, and where appropriate their specialisations, see **www.mrs.org.uk/researchbuyersguide**, and for worldwide see **https://directory.esomar.org/**. Each type of research is discussed in the following sections.

4.2.1 Company records

An obvious, but often under-utilised, starting point for gathering marketing data is through the effective use of the company's own records. Often, large amounts of data that can be used to aid marketing decisions (both strategic and tactical) are held in unlikely places within the company (such as in the accounts department). Data on factors such as who purchases and how much they purchase may be obtained from invoice records. Similarly, purchase records may show customer loyalty patterns, identify gaps in customer purchasing and highlight the most valuable customers.

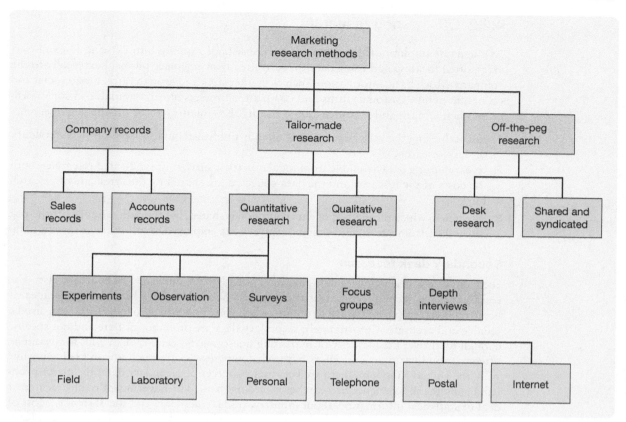

Figure 4.3 Marketing research methods

The value of internally collected data is dependent, however, on how they are collected in the first place. Unfortunately, sales data are often not collected or maintained in a form that facilitates use for marketing decision making. As a general rule, it is desirable to collect routine data on as detailed a basis as possible to allow for unforeseen data analysis requirements. For example, sales records should be filed by customer, customer type, product, product line, sales territory, salesperson and detailed time period. Data of this type would allow the isolation of profitable and unprofitable customers, territories and product lines, and identify trends in the marketplace.

In direct marketing it is said that the best customer prospects are often existing customers. Adequate sales records should reveal frequencies of purchase, latent and lapsed customers, and may suggest alternative products that could be of interest. In the mail order business, catalogue companies keep records of the types of product customers have bought from them. This enables additional catalogues, more specialist in nature, to be targeted at the most likely prospects.

The British supermarket Tesco successfully uses its loyalty card – Clubcard – to build profiles of its customers so that it can 'generate a map of how an individual thinks, works and, more importantly, shops. The map classifies consumers across 10 categories: wealth, promotions, travel, charities, green, time poor, credit, living style, creature of habit and adventurous' (*The Guardian*, 20 September 2005). Amazon uses the data it collects to make tailored suggestions to its customers about what books they might enjoy reading, shows they might want to watch and products they might want to buy.

4.2.2 Off-the-peg research

As the name implies, off-the-peg research consists of tapping into existing research services, often locating and using data that are already in existence but held externally to the company. Much basic information, such as market sizes and growth rates, broad social and economic trends, customer firms and competitor firms, is already available in some form or another. Crouch and Housden (2003) classify three main types of off-the-peg research:

1 research using the very large body of already published data, usually termed secondary or desk research;
2 research using data available from regular market surveys of syndicated research – both the costs of the research and the data collected are shared by the syndicate of research buyers;
3 research in which the method of data collection is shared, but the data are not – off-the-peg research instruments, such as omnibus surveys, are employed to collect client-specific data.

Secondary desk research

Secondary desk research uses data that have already been published by someone else. The researcher is a 'secondary' user of the research. Secondary data have the advantages of being relatively cheap and quick to obtain (when you know where to look!), and can also be reliable and accurate. Unfortunately, secondary data are often out of date and not specific enough to answer the majority of marketing questions. Secondary data will, for example, often tell you how many customers buy each competitor's offering but won't tell you why.

In the United Kingdom, there are very many sources of secondary data; the major problem facing the inexperienced researcher is finding them. The government publishes a great deal of statistical information about industry, trade, commerce and social trends. Most of these data are free, or charged for at the cost of publishing only. The starting point for identifying relevant government statistics is **www.gov.uk/search/research-and-statistics?content_store_document_type=upcoming_statistics**. Increasingly, it is possible to use commercial online information services, such as Harvest (**http://harvest.sourceforge.net/**), to search through alternative sources and to scan quickly what data are already available.

Secondary data vary dramatically in quality, both from country to country and from supplier to supplier within a particular country. In assessing the accuracy of secondary data, the following questions should be borne in mind:

1 Who collected the data and why? (Are they likely to be biased in their reporting?)
2 How did they collect the data? (Sample or census? Sampling method used? Research instruments?)
3 What level of accuracy do they claim? (Does the methodology support the claim?)
4 What use did they put the data to? (Is its use limited?)

Primary research

Primary, or field, research is undertaken where the secondary sources cannot provide the detail of information required to solve a particular problem or to sufficiently aid the decision making. Primary research involves the collection of new data, often directly from customers, or from distribution intermediaries (such as retailers or wholesalers).

Syndicated research

Syndicated research occurs where a group of research buyers share the costs and the findings of research among themselves. The majority of such syndicated research services are conducted by the larger marketing research agencies and the results are sold to whoever will buy.

In the United Kingdom, syndicated research is carried out in a wide variety of markets, though primarily in consumer markets. Typical examples include the Target Group Index

(TGI) of Kantar Media (**www.djsresearch.co.uk/glossary/item/TGI-Target-Group-Index**) and the various media research services, including audience measurement for publishers at PAMCo (**https://pamco.co.uk**) and the television viewing survey, BARB (**www.barb.co.uk**).

There are a great many sources of syndicated research covering a wide variety of markets. They have the major advantages that the methodology is usually tried and tested, the samples are often bigger than individual companies could afford to survey on their own and they are considerably cheaper than conducting the research for one company alone. The disadvantages are that the data are limited in their usefulness to monitoring sales over time, identifying trends in markets and competitors and tracking advertising and other promotional activity. They do not allow further probing of motivations for purchase, nor indeed any additional, company-specific questioning.

Shared research

The final type of research to be classified as off the peg is research where some of the costs and fieldwork are shared by a number of companies but the results are not. Omnibus surveys are regular research surveys that are being undertaken using a predetermined (off-the-peg) sampling frame and methodology. Individual clients then 'buy a seat' on the omnibus by adding their own questions. These are asked, along with the questions of other clients, and the results tabulated against such factors as social class, ACORN (A Classification of Residential Neighbourhood) category, age and so on.

Kantar Public UK (formerly BMRB Omnibus), for example, has a range of omnibus surveys including weekly face-to-face interviews with 2,000 adults (age 15 +), interviews with 1,000 young people (aged 7–19) monthly, mobile phone-based surveys of 500 adults (aged 16–49) and 1,000 Internet users (aged 16–64) surveyed online (**www.tns-bmrb.co.uk/**). Omnibus research has the major advantages of low cost (as the fieldwork costs are shared by all participating companies) and added flexibility, in that each client can ask his or her own questions of a typically large sample of respondents. The number of questions that can be added to an omnibus is, however, generally limited to between six and ten, and, because the respondent will be asked questions about a variety of product fields in the same interview, questions are best kept short and factual to avoid respondent fatigue.

In summary, there is a wide variety of off-the-peg sources from which the company or organisation wishing to conduct market or social research can choose. They have the advantages over conducting primary research in that they have established methodologies and are relatively quick and cheap to tap into. The disadvantages lie in the scope and number of questions that can be asked. Before undertaking costly primary research, however, marketing managers are well advised to examine the possibilities that off-the-peg research offers.

4.2.3 Tailor-made research

Tailor-made research, in contrast to off-the-peg, provides the organisation undertaking the research with the flexibility to design the research to exactly match the needs of the client company. Depending on those needs, there is a variety of techniques available (see Figure 4.3). The techniques are broadly categorised as qualitative and quantitative.

In qualitative research, emphasis is placed on gaining understanding and depth in data that often cannot be quantified. It is concerned with meaning rather than numbers, usually involving small samples of respondents but probing them in depth for their opinions, motivations and attitudes. Quantitative research, on the other hand, involves larger samples, more structured research instruments (questionnaires and so on) and produces quantifiable outputs. In major studies, both types of technique may be used together. Qualitative research is often used in the early, exploratory stages of research (see Figure 4.4), and quantitative research then used to provide quantification of the broad qualitative findings.

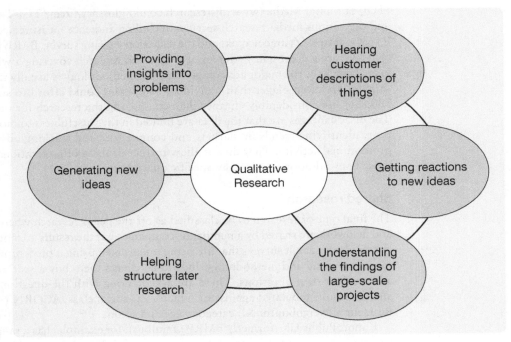

Figure 4.4 Uses of qualitative research

Qualitative techniques

Qualitative techniques are essentially unstructured or semi-structured interviewing methods designed to encourage respondents to reply freely and express their real feelings, opinions and motivations. There are two main techniques used in qualitative research: the group discussion (variously termed focus group or group depth interview) and the individual depth interview.

Group discussions usually take the form of a relaxed, informal discussion among seven to nine respondents, with a group leader or moderator ensuring that the discussion covers areas relevant to the research brief. The discussions are typically held in the moderator's home (in the case of consumer studies) or in a hotel room (for industrial groups). The advantage of the group set-up is that it encourages interaction among the participants, which can generate broader discussion than a one-to-one interview-and-answer session. Its value as a research technique rests with the quality of the group moderator (usually a trained psychologist) and their ability to encourage wide-ranging but relevant discussions of the topics of interest. Products can be introduced into the group for trial and comment in an informal setting conducive to evaluation.

Group discussions were used effectively in the development of the advertising message 'naughty but nice' for fresh cream cakes (see Bradley, 1987). A series of group discussions discovered feelings of guilt associated with eating fresh cream cakes and that the advertising could capitalise on this by emphasising the sheer pleasure of cream cakes and the slightly naughty aspects of eating them. Feelings and emotions of this sort could not have been obtained from quantitative research. The relaxed, informal settings of the group discussion were essential to obtaining the clues that led to the advertising copy development.

The depth interview takes place between one interviewer (again, often a trained psychologist) and one respondent. It is used extensively for deeper probing of motivations, especially in areas of a confidential nature, or on delicate subjects where it is necessary that rapport and trust is built up between the interviewer and the respondent. Many of the techniques used in depth interviews have been developed from clinical psychology, including the use of projective techniques such as word associations and Kelly repertory grids (see Chapter 8, page 223).

Qualitative research is often used as preliminary research prior to a more quantitative investigation. In this context, it can help in the wording of questions on a further questionnaire, indicate what questions to ask and elicit important product and brand features and image dimensions. Qualitative research is also used on its own in motivation studies, for the development and pre-testing of advertising messages, for package design evaluation, for concept testing and new product testing. The major limitation of qualitative research is that its cost and its nature make it impossible to employ large samples and hence it can be dangerous applying the findings to large populations on the basis of the small sample involved.

Quantitative techniques

Quantitative research techniques include surveys, observation methods and experimentation of one type or another.

Surveys are a vast subject in themselves. There are four main types of survey, depending on how the interviews are conducted: personal interviews are where the interviewer and the respondent come face-to-face for a question-and-answer session; telephone interviews, an increasingly used research technique, are conducted over the telephone; postal surveys use the mail services to send self-completion questionnaires to respondents; and surveys on the Internet. Figure 4.5 shows the main uses to which surveys are put.

Each technique has its advantages and drawbacks. Personal interviews are the most expensive to conduct, but offer the greatest flexibility. They are particularly useful where respondents are asked to react to attitudinal statements and more complex questions that may require some clarification by the interviewer.

Telephone interviews are particularly useful when data are required quickly. They do not entail the costs of physically sending interviewers into the field, can be closely controlled and the data collected entered directly onto a computer for analysis. The majority of opinion polls are now conducted in this manner, facilitating next-day reporting in the sponsoring newspapers. The drawbacks of telephone interviews are that more and more people screen their calls, so that respondents are harder to reach and the interview is less personal than a face-to-face encounter, requiring it to be kept relatively short. It is not possible to show prompts and other stimuli during a telephone conversation.

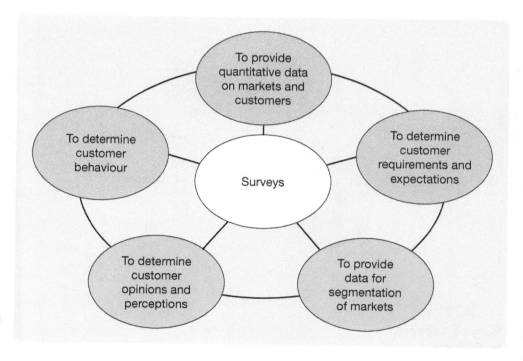

Figure 4.5 Uses of surveys

Postal surveys are the cheapest method of all. They are useful in locating geographically dispersed samples and for situations where the questionnaire is long and detailed. Response rates, however, can be low and there is little control over who responds. The lack of personal contact requires a very clearly laid out questionnaire, well pre-tested to ensure clarity.

Internet-based surveys, either mobile or online, are fast growing. Mobile surveys via apps are particularly apt in reaching people who may not normally participate in research.

Observation techniques can be particularly useful where respondents are unlikely to be able or willing to give the types of information required. Crouch and Housden (1996) cite the example of research into what items a shopper has taken from a supermarket shelf, considered for purchase but not bought. Direct questioning after the shopping trip is unlikely to produce accurate data as the respondent simply will not remember, but observation of shopping behaviour in the store can provide such data.

Observation can be conducted by individuals (as in the case of the supermarket behaviour noted previously, or observation of traffic density on particular roads), or by instruments designed to monitor behaviour. The prime example of the latter is the 'PeopleMeter' recording device used in television viewing research. A black box is attached to the television sets of a sample of viewers and records when the set was turned on and what channel it was tuned to. Each individual in the household has a code key that is activated when they are in the room. Data are transmitted from the home to the research company via the telephone network overnight, enabling rapid analysis of viewing data. PeopleMeters have been widely adopted throughout the developed and developing world as a method of monitoring TV viewing and audiences.

The final type of quantitative research of interest here is experimentation. Experiments are either carried out in the field or in-house (in a laboratory). Field experiments take place in the real world, and the subjects of the experiments typically do not know that they are part of an experiment. The prime example is test marketing, where a new product will be marketed in a limited geographic region prior to a decision on whether to launch the brand nationally or internationally. In-house experiments are conducted in a more controlled but less realistic setting, where the respondents know they are taking part. Figure 4.6 shows the main uses for experiments in marketing.

Figure 4.6 Uses of experimentation

Following positive response to a social media consultation asking its customers how the company could develop vegetarian food, Pret a Manger launched a test marketing campaign in April 2016 called 'Not just for veggies' to test a vegetarian product line presented in a 'Little Veggie Pop-up' and one outlet in Soho, London. It then introduced 'Veggie Fridges' containing the most popular vegetarian and vegan dishes introduced during the campaign, but withdrew them after three months having discovered that customers were more likely to choose a vegetarian option if it was presented alongside meat offerings. However, the popularity of the 'Veggie Pret' shop, originally only temporary, has led the company to open more around the UK and further afield, including the USA and Hong Kong.

Source: Vibrant Pictures/Alamy Stock Photo.

Full-scale testing is also an example of co-creation via social media, but full-blown test marketing experiments can suffer from a number of problems. They can be costly, time-consuming and alert the competition to changes in marketing strategy or new products about to be launched. As a result, there has been an increase in other, smaller-scale testing methods.

Simulated supermarket tests make grocery products available in a simulated environment. They can be helpful in estimating trial rates, testing purchase intents created by exposure to test advertisements and testing individual elements of the marketing mix, such as packaging, pricing and branding. Supermarket panels, recruited from the shoppers of a particular chain, have their purchases recorded through laser scanning and related to purchase card numbers. These panels can be particularly useful in the limited market testing of new brands.

As with off-the-peg research, the variety of tailor-made research available is very wide. There are a great many market research agencies with varying expertise and skills. While it is still true to say that the majority of expenditure on marketing research comes from the larger, fast-moving consumer goods companies, it is possible for smaller companies to take advantage of the research services and sources available (especially off-the-peg research).

Market research techniques are also increasingly being used to investigate non-commercial problems. Research was used heavily, for example, to investigate drug abuse by young people prior to an advertising campaign designed to tackle the problem. The Oxfam charity has used survey research to help it understand the motivations behind charity donations and to help identify 'prime donor segments'. During the run-up to the 2015 general election in the UK, both major political parties spent heavily on market and opinion research to gauge the mood of potential voters. Opinion poll results (sponsored by the media and political parties) were published almost daily in the three-week run-up to the election. In the event, the polls got the results wrong, prompting an investigation that concluded that there was an under-representation of certain groups in the surveys.

In the context of competitive positioning, market research provides the raw data with which it is possible to segment the market creatively, and it can help to identify current and potential product positionings. For example, Customer Care Research (**www.customer-care-research.com/**), which draws on the techniques mentioned previously but follows the story of a purchase (a case study), is helping marketers refine their positions in 'job-to-be-done' segments. One such marketer discovered that his milkshakes were not just competing with other milkshakes but also with doughnuts, bagels, bananas and, more importantly, boredom, and was then able to improve his product to do the job better (see Christensen *et al.*, 2007; Berstell and Nitterhouse, 2005).

4.3   The marketing research process

A typical segmentation and positioning research project might combine the use of several of the techniques already described to investigate a particular market. Figure 4.7 shows the various stages.

Problem definition

The first step is to define clearly the problem to be tackled. Typically, a series of discussions between marketing research personnel (internal or external to the company) and marketing decision makers are necessary to ensure that the research project is tackling the correct issues.

Exploratory research

As part of problem definition, and as a starting point in the research process itself, exploratory research will be used to identify information gaps and specify the need for further research.

Initially, secondary sources can be utilised: company records can be employed, alongside off-the-peg desk research, to quantify the market and draw its preliminary boundaries.

Qualitative research might then be used to explore with customers and/or potential customers why and how the particular product was/should be used. At this stage, group discussions

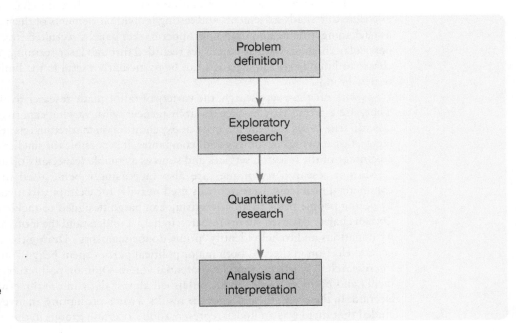

Figure 4.7 Stages in a comprehensive marketing research project

may be relevant in many consumer markets. In industrial markets, while group discussions are successfully employed, a preferred route is often personal depth interviews with key customers.

In a segmentation and positioning study, the focus of this qualitative research will be to identify the prime motivators to purchase (the major benefits being sought) and any demotivators. The research should also seek to identify relevant competitors and explore their strengths and weaknesses in serving the market. Finally, hypotheses about how the market could be segmented should be developed; these can be researched further during the later stages of the research project.

Quantitative research

While qualitative research will help in formulating hypotheses about how the market is segmented and what factors influence purchase, because of the small and normally non-representative samples involved it is unlikely to be adequate in itself for segmentation purposes. Typically, it will be followed by a quantitative study (a personal survey most often) utilising a sufficiently large and random sample to enable market segment sizes to be estimated and strength of opinions to be gauged.

Such a quantitative study might ask respondents to evaluate competing products on a series of attributes that have been identified as important during the qualitative research. Further, respondents could be asked to rate how important to them personally each attribute is and to express what characteristics their 'ideal' product would have. Background customer characteristics could also be collected to enable any market segments uncovered to be described in ways helpful to further marketing activity (see Chapter 7).

Experimentation might also be used in the quantitative phase of a segmentation and positioning study. Product samples might be placed with existing and potential customers to gauge reaction to new or improved products. Conjoint analysis experiments might be used to estimate reaction to hypothetical product combinations.

Analysis and interpretation

Following data collection, statistical techniques and models can be employed to turn the data generated into meaningful information to help with the segmentation. Factor analysis might be used to reduce a large number of attitudinal statements to their underlying dimensions, or underlying factors. Cluster analysis could be used to group respondents on the basis of several characteristics (attitudes, likes, dislikes or background demographics) into meaningful segments. Perceptual mapping techniques could be employed to draw models of customer perceptions on two, three or more relevant dimensions. (These techniques are discussed in more detail in Chapter 8.)

Finally, the results will be presented to and discussed with the senior marketing decision makers to aid their interpretation of the market in which they are operating.

The essence of a successful research project is to use the data-gathering and analysis techniques that are relevant both to the product type being investigated and the stage in the research project where they are being employed. By utilising innovative techniques and looking at markets afresh, it is often possible to gain new insights into market structure and hence aid the sharpening of target market definition.

The final section in this chapter looks at how information is organised within the company.

4.4   Organising customer information

Information is organised within the company through the marketing information system (MIS). This system may be formally structured, physically consisting of several personnel and a variety of computer hardware and software, or it may be a very informal collection of reports and statistics piled on an executive's desk, or even contained in their head!

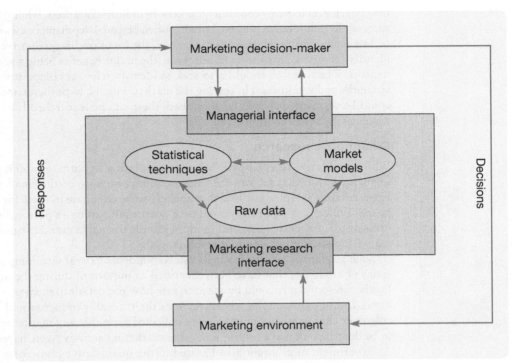

Figure 4.8
Marketing decision
support systems

Conceptually, however, the system can be represented as shown in Figure 4.8 (developed from Little, 1979). The information system has five basic components: a market research interface concerned with collecting and gathering raw data from the marketing environment; the raw data collected through the market research interface; statistical techniques that can be used to analyse, synthesise and collate the raw data, to turn them into information; market models that utilise both the raw data and statistical techniques to describe the marketplace, to simulate it or to predict it; and finally a managerial interface that allows the decision maker access to the information and models to aid their decision making.

Raw data

As discussed previously, data come into the system from a variety of sources, from internal and external, secondary and primary sources. The data are stored in various forms (on paper, in people's heads, on computer). Increasingly, data are being stored on machine-readable media or the Cloud. The enhanced availability of computer hardware and software has made it increasingly possible to store large amounts of data in a form that is readily accessible and easily analysed.

Statistical techniques

The processes available to synthesise and summarise the raw data are called statistics. A wide variety of statistics is available, but often the most important are the simple ones that allow data to be summarised (such as averages, means, standard deviations, ranges, etc.), so that many small, often diverse observations can be condensed into a few important numbers. (For a comprehensive review of statistical techniques available to analyse marketing data, see Field, 2017; Tabachnik & Fidell, 2014; Hair *et al.*, 2018.)

Market models and marketing analytics

A model is a representation of the real world. Most managers have an implicit model in their own minds of the markets in which they operate. For example, they can give an expectation of the effect of changing price on sales of the product based on their experiences.

This is essentially their internal model of the price/sales relationship. In examining data through the use of statistical techniques, the analyst may wish to test out the model of the market he or she already has. Alternatively, the objective may be to build a new model of the market to help managerial understanding of the forces that affect demand and overall company performance. There are models covering all parts of marketing activity. Lilien *et al.* (1992) undertook a comprehensive review of these attempts 'to bring order to the chaos of collected facts'.

Marketing analytics enables marketers to evaluate their marketing initiatives by the systematic use of processes and technologies. It is seen as a way to measure ROI and is used for a variety of purposes, from customer acquisition to omnichannel marketing and marketing mix strategies (see Sorger, 2013). Artificial intelligence is used more and more to enhance marketing analytics. For example, predictive analysis can be used to predict purchasing patterns and deep learning (through learning to recognise sophisticated objects) in order to understand customer brand perception and usage through images.

Currently, customer analytics (48 per cent), operational analytics (21 per cent), fraud and compliance (12 per cent), new product and service innovation (10 per cent) and enterprise data warehouse optimisation (10 per cent) are among the most popular Big Data uses in sales and marketing (Columbus, 2016).

Another example of the use of Big Data is customer value analytics (CVA), which enables marketers to deliver consistent customer experiences across all channels.

Big Data
Source: mamanamsai/Shutterstock.

Managerial interface

If the information system is to be of value to the marketing decision maker, they must have access to that system in such a way as to facilitate and encourage easy use. The interface between the manager and the MIS can consist of an individual (a marketing information officer), a report or set of reports produced on a regular or intermittent basis, or, increasingly commonly, a computer terminal or a microcomputer. With the relevant software to facilitate use of the MIS, direct, 'hands-on' access for the decision maker can encourage wider use of the system and experimentation with the various models developed.

Marketing decision support systems

In the 1990s there was a change in emphasis in marketing from information systems (MIS) to marketing decision support systems (MDSS). The distinction may seem merely one of semantics but is, in fact, fundamental. While MIS placed emphasis on provision of information, primarily in the form of facts and figures, MDSS changed the emphasis to aiding decision making through the provision of question-and-answer facilities. In other words, MDSS allows analysis rather than merely retrieval of information.

Decision support systems can have several types of output. These have been grouped into data-orientated and model-orientated:

1   **Data-orientated decision support systems** focus on data retrieval and simple analysis using statistical techniques. These can include, for example, straightforward data retrieval of such items as stock levels. Systems of this type are effectively information systems rather than decision support systems, as defined previously.
2   **Model-orientated decision support systems,** on the other hand, focus on simulation and representation of aspects of the real world. Accounting models, for example, calculate the consequences of planned actions on the financial performance of the company. Representational models estimate the consequences of action of one type or another. An advertising model may estimate the effects of running a particular advertising campaign. Optimisation models provide guidelines for action by generating the optimal solutions consistent with a series of constraints. For example, given an advertising budget, a target audience and a required average viewing frequency, an optimisation model could be used to select the most effective combination of media and insertions.

Implementation of MDSS in marketing has been slower than predicted, but with the advent of PCs and user-friendly programs, and increased storage and programming capabilities allowing for almost instant management information, the use of decision support systems in marketing is now well established. Several characteristics of MDSS are worth noting:

- MDSS support decisions! They are not merely data retrieval systems, but are actively designed to help managers make better decisions. In addition, they support, rather than replace, managerial decision making.
- MDSS are essentially interactive. They allow the manager to ask questions, receive inputs and experiment with decisions to estimate the likely outcomes. As such, they are more effective where a manager has the scope to use the system directly.
- MDSS should be flexible and easy to use. Ease of use is a major characteristic essential to gaining widespread use of an innovation such as MDSS poses in many organisations. Flexibility is desirable to allow the system to respond to a variety of information and decision support needs.

Expert systems for marketing decision support

Developments in computer hardware and software offer exciting opportunities for marketing management. The developments in expert systems and artificial intelligence that enable not only the modelling of marketing phenomena but also the decision-making processes of 'experts' in the field promise to revolutionise the whole area of decision support.

The directions in which these developments will move are still evolving at present (Wierenga, 2010). What is certain, however, is that marketing decisions will become more data based (there is already a data explosion in marketing) and there will be an increased need to organise those data in meaningful ways to enable them to be used quickly and effectively. In particular, increased computing and modelling power will enable decisions to be tested in simulated environments prior to implementation in the real world.

Summary

Understanding customers is central to developing a coherent positioning strategy. This chapter has examined, first, the types of information about customers that can be useful in determining competitive position and, second, the marketing research methods available for collecting that information. The process typically undertaken to identify potential market segments and their needs was then discussed. Finally, developments in organising and presenting data were examined.

Case study

Amazon and Google lead way on virtual assistant dealmaking at CES

By Tim Bradshaw in Las Vegas

Technology groups look to build alliances to distribute Alexa and Assistant platforms

It is often said that the most interesting part of the Consumer Electronics Show is not the technology on show but the conversations that happen behind closed doors.

At this year's CES, deal making has taken centre stage as tech companies, carmakers, appliance manufacturers, chip providers and start-ups race to strike alliances for the 'internet of things' era.

Nowhere is that more obvious than in the world of virtual assistants, with Amazon and Google leading the way on recruiting partners to help them distribute and activate their artificial intelligence platforms.

After focusing on 'smart home' technology last year, Amazon is now moving on to the car. The US company has struck deals with Panasonic, one of the largest players in in-car infotainment systems, Chinese electric car start-up Byton and Toyota, which showed off a futuristic, versatile autonomous vehicle called 'e-Palette' that the ecommerce group plans to use for package deliveries.

Amazon is also trying to diversify the types of products that incorporate its digital assistant, bringing its Alexa service to cookers from Whirlpool and GE, as well as Bluetooth-enabled portable devices such as headphones, smartwatches and even smartglasses from New York-based Vuzix.

Cue robots, which function as a teaching assistant, on display at the wide-ranging CES
Source: dpa picture alliance/Alamy Stock Photo.

'We basically envision a world where Alexa is everywhere,' Priya Abani, Amazon's director of AVS enablement, told *Wired* magazine.

Although Amazon does not have its own public presence on the show floor, it has rented a sizeable private space in Las Vegas's Venetian hotel for meetings with partners.

Google, by contrast, is unmissable to CES attendees: advertising for Assistant appears on giant digital billboards up and down the Las Vegas Strip, its branding is plastered inside and outside the city's monorail train carriages, and it will for the first time in several years have a huge booth at the

Consumers flock to smart speakers

Voice-enabled speaker users, US only (m)

Source: Tim Bradshaw in Las Vegas "Amazon and Google lead way on virtual assistant dealmaking at CES",
Financial Times, JANUARY 9, 2018.

convention centre when the show officially opens on Tuesday.

On Monday evening, the company announced a wave of new integrations for its Assistant, which the internet group says now works with more than 1,500 devices. Additions to that line-up include voice-activated speakers and headphones from LG and JBL, and television sets from Sony and TCL.

Google is also using its existing network of Android devices to push out its Assistant, including to millions of cars from the likes of Ford, GM, Volkswagen and Volvo.

After Amazon released its first Echo speakers with screens a few months ago, Google is playing catch-up by teaming with JBL, Lenovo, LG and Sony on 'smart displays', which can show YouTube clips, show images stored in Google Photos and make video calls.

Amazon may have beaten Google to the idea of giving a virtual assistant a screen, but it was Chinese internet group Baidu that first launched that combination at CES a year ago.

On Monday, Baidu launched three new smart speakers running its DuerOS conversational AI platform. These include the pop-in Aladdin smart dome light, an unusual combination of ceiling lamp and projector aimed at the Japanese market, and the Little Fish VSI Smart Speaker, a countertop-sized touchscreen device which resembles Amazon's Echo Show.

Kun Jing, general manager of Baidu's Duer division, said that adding a display to a smart speaker made a 'very big difference' to how often customers use its virtual assistant, compared with voice-only devices.

'The most efficient way for people to communicate with the device is to use our voice but the most efficient way for the computer to communicate back to us is a screen,' he said.

Despite the frantic deal making, not all electronics groups are eager to get into bed with Amazon and Google.

Samsung, in its CES presentation on Monday, made no mention of Alexa or Google Assistant, instead pushing its own digital helper Bixby into its smart TVs, Gear smartwatches and connected cars through its Harman subsidiary.

HS Kim, president and head of Samsung's global consumer products division, said the Bixby's 'next-level intelligence' would 'intuitively understand you and figure out what you need before you even have to ask'. By 2020, all Samsung connected devices will be imbued with Bixby's intelligence, he promised.

For mobile market leaders Samsung, Google and Apple, mastering digital assistants that are

Rise in connected TV popularity

Source: Tim Bradshaw in Las Vegas "Amazon and Google lead way on virtual assistant dealmaking at CES", Financial Times, JANUARY 9, 2018.

used beyond the smartphone is becoming vital as consumers' usage habits change. A survey by consultancy Accenture found that almost two-thirds of customers who own smart speakers use their smartphones less often for entertainment, and more than half use their mobiles less for ecommerce and search queries.

That same trend leaves Baidu and Amazon, who were slower than their rivals to adopt mobile devices, with the most to gain from virtual assistants – as long as they can find enough device partners to help distribute them.

'I believe [the smartphone] is the wrong device for a voice platform because it's fundamentally a finger-first device,' Qi Lu, Baidu's chief operating officer, told reporters at CES on Monday.

 Source: from 'Amazon and Google lead way on virtual assistant deal making at CES', *Financial Times*, 09/01/18 (Bradshaw, T.).

Discussion questions

1 What type of customer information will AI platforms be able to gather?

2 What methods are currently used to gather this type of information?

3 What stages should companies follow when conducting market research?

CHAPTER 5
COMPETITOR ANALYSIS

Two brief notes for consideration on the *nature of competition*:

In the final of the men's 100 metres at the World Athletics Championship in 2009, Tyson Gay clocked a time of 9.71 seconds for the 100 metres. This was his personal best at that moment, and faster than any man, in any other round of the tournament. However, running in the same race was a man by the name of Usain Bolt (you may have heard of him), who ran 9.58 seconds, won the gold medal and also set new world and tournament record times.

Two walkers were out backpacking together in the woods. They rounded a bend in the trail, and came face to face with the largest and most angry looking grizzly bear. Instantly one of the walkers drops to his knee, pulls out his running shoes from his backpack, and begins removing his hiking boots. The other walker stares at this and says, 'What are you doing? There is no way you can outrun a bear that size!' Not looking up from tying his laces, the kneeling hiker replies, 'I don't have to be faster than the bear, I only have to be faster than you.'

The key takeaway from these stories is that *performance should always be evaluated relative to the competition* (see Sabnis and Grewal, 2012).

Gatwick seeks greater competition with BAA

By Bob Sherwood, London and South-East correspondent

Gatwick Airport signalled the first moves to increase competition among London's airports on Monday with the launch of a new brand identity and advertising campaign.

The marketing drive, part of a £1bn scheme to improve London's second airport, is an attempt to create a 'challenger brand' to BAA, the operator that owns Heathrow and was recently forced to sell Gatwick as part of a shake-up ordered by competition authorities.

On the first day of its busy summer season, Global Infrastructure Partners, which bought Gatwick last December, unveiled a new signature-style logo and a campaign aimed at giving Gatwick a friendlier image.

Source: Ian Leonard/Alamy Stock Photo.

It will start running an advertising campaign on Wednesday with the slogan: 'Your London airport'.

The push to win passengers from Heathrow and Stansted is just the kind of move the Competition Commission hoped to stimulate when it ordered BAA, the dominant airport operator, to sell Gatwick and Stansted airports, as well as either Glasgow or Edinburgh.

The plan to differentiate Gatwick from BAA airports heralds the roll-out of a £1bn investment programme to overhaul the airport's facilities. While Heathrow's image was dented by the so-called 'Heathrow hassle' factor of delays and outdated facilities, Gatwick has also suffered from similar complaints.

Stewart Wingate, Gatwick's chief executive, said the new owner had accelerated the delivery of new facilities and introduced plans for faster check-in facilities and new security lanes.

A new inter-terminal transit will open in July and an extension to the airport's north terminal will create a plaza for passengers. There will also be a new check-in system, allowing passengers to tag their bags themselves and drop them more quickly, and a 'fast-track' system aimed at reducing the queues for security screening.

Gatwick said the programme would mean improvements to almost every part of the airport including 'the South Terminal departure lounge, entrance forecourts, immigration hall, baggage systems and the North Terminal Interchange'.

The airport hopes to increase passenger figures from 33m to more than 40m by 2018.

Mr Wingate said the new brand was important not just to attract new passengers but also to 'galvanise our staff internally now that we are competing with BAA'.

He said: 'This is an important milestone as we compete to make Gatwick London's airport of choice for passengers and airlines. We want it to be something fresher, a lot more innovative and creative.'

While the sell-off of Gatwick prompted speculation that a new owner might attempt to win permission for a second runway at Gatwick, the coalition government has expressly ruled out new runways at London airports. Mr Wingate said that although an area of land for a possible second runway had been safeguarded, Gatwick's focus at the moment was solely on the one existing runway and two terminals.

 Source: from 'Gatwick seeks greater competition with BAA', *Financial Times*, 21/06/2010 (Sherwood, B.).

Discussion questions

1 What are the issues that Gatwick is trying to address?
2 How is Gatwick addressing these issues?

Introduction

Sun Tzu (see Clavell, 1981, for a very accessible translation), the great fourth-century BC Chinese general, encapsulated the importance of competitor analysis:

> If you know your enemy as you know yourself, you need not fear the result of a hundred battles. If you know yourself but not the enemy, for every victory you gain you will suffer a defeat. If you know neither the enemy nor yourself, you will succumb in every battle.

Some of the ideas expressed in Sun Tzu's writing are equally valid and applicable in modern business markets. However, one of the main issues facing business strategists today is the degree of complexity faced in some competitive markets, and it is now possible that in a modern business, the main competitor, customer and collaborator are the same company! For example, in the construction industry, many large capital projects require firms that might normally be seen as competitors to collaborate for mutual benefit. The complexity, and hence ambiguity, faced by executives in many modern markets underlines the importance of identifying and understanding competitors.

Without knowledge of competitors' strengths and likely actions (or reactions), it is impossible to identify a central component of marketing strategy – a group of customers where an organisation possesses competitive advantage over the competition. Similarly, since competitive advantage is a relative concept, a company that has poor understanding of its competitors can have no real understanding of itself. Several studies demonstrate a positive link between a clear understanding of competitor strategies and actions, and corporate performance (see, for example, Kapelianis *et al.*, 2005).

In the 1980s and '90s, when Japanese companies sought to compete more effectively with US-based rivals, they very much embraced Sun Tzu's obsession with enemy (or competitor) analysis. During this time, the commitment of Japanese companies to gathering information was a major distinguishing feature of their business strategies. As one example, Lehmann and Winer (1991) report that one Mitsubishi intelligence unit in the USA filled two entire floors of an office building in New York. Indeed, as long ago as the early 1980s, *Business Week* described how Japanese companies had established 'surveillance posts' throughout the heartland of the US computer industry in California's Silicon Valley, monitoring US technology development by hiring American software experts. Of course, this is not just limited to Japanese companies, and today most successful organisations invest significant amounts annually in order to gather, analyse, interpret and act on market-based data.

This chapter provides a framework for the essential activities of gathering, disseminating and acting on competitor intelligence. It covers four areas:

1 benchmarking against rivals;
2 the dimensions of competitor analysis;
3 the choice of 'good' competitors;
4 the origins, sources and dissemination of competitive information.

5.1 Competitive benchmarking

Competitive benchmarking is the process of measuring your company's strategies and operations against 'best-in-class' companies, both inside and outside your own industry. The purpose is to identify certain practices and methodologies that can be adopted and/or adapted to improve overall performance. Benchmarking usually involves four main steps.

5.1.1 Identifying who to benchmark against

Industry leaders are obvious firms with whom to compare activities. Central to such an analysis is identifying the key factors to their success in the market. What is it they do differently from others? What makes the difference to their operations? Why are they 'winners'?

In organisations traditionally viewed as 'non-profit', such as hospitals and universities, benchmarking also takes place. For hospitals, the 'best in class' might be considered those with the lowest mortality rates, or highest patient throughput, or of late those with the highest patient satisfaction scores. For universities, 'best in class' might be those with the best research reputations, highest employability rates for graduates, highest students' satisfaction scores or those most able to attract the best students.

Benchmarking can also be undertaken against lower-ranked competitors in a market. New entrants or smaller, more focused firms may have particular strengths from which larger and more established organisations might learn. These strengths may be in a particular aspect of their operations rather than their operations in total. One firm may be a leader, for example, in terms of customer service, while another may be the best in the industry at cost control.

Organisations can also benchmark specific activities (such as procurement and purchasing) against organisations outside their immediate competitive space, leading to change and innovation opportunities. For example, when Xerox wanted to improve order processing and warehousing, it benchmarked itself against L.L. Bean (a mail-order company), which was believed to be far more 'cutting edge' than Xerox's traditional competitors (Swain, 1993). Many companies now look to organisations such as Amazon and UPS as exemplars for order processing and warehouse management. This illustrates one of the issues and potential dangers with benchmarking. If everyone within a particular competitive space only benchmarks with each other, then necessary change is often missed, as incumbents tend to think and act (and are organised) in very similar ways. Here, the wrong benchmark 'set' is used. These markets tend to open themselves up to smaller and more innovative challengers, who recognise the need for change and the competitive opportunity that exists.

5.1.2 Identifying what aspects of business to benchmark

All aspects of business across the value chain are candidates for benchmarking. Scarce resources and time constraints generally dictate the selection of a few key central processes for detailed benchmarking. These will initially centre on key factors for success in the industry. Initial focus will also typically be on processes that account for significant costs, make a significant impact on customer satisfaction and show greatest room for improvement. Subsequent analyses should be broadened, in an attempt to create fresh competitive advantages in new areas of operation.

5.1.3 Collecting relevant data to enable processes and operations to be compared

Operational data on one's own organisation are likely to be easily available, relative to that of competitors. Three main sources of competitor information for benchmarking that are important and useful are published sources, data sharing and interviews (Swain, 1993):

- **Published sources** include company reports, technical (trade) reports, industry studies and surveys commissioned by governments or industry associations. For example, in consumer goods markets, *Which?* provides comprehensive and useful reports that compare product performance from a customer perspective. Obviously, websites and web forums are excellent sources of data; however, the quality and usefulness of these sources can vary, depending on the sector or industry. Increasingly, customers seeking information about products and services turn to customer reviews for trusted and hopefully helpful insights and feedback into the experiences of others. Well-known examples of such advice, or 'reviews' as they are often called, can be seen on websites such as Amazon and TripAdvisor, but there are many, many more, of course.
- **Data sharing** can take place in industry forums such as conferences, through discussions in formal and informal settings. Indeed, in most industries it is common for employees of competing firms to meet from time to time, and exchange information with each other either consciously or subconsciously. This does not necessarily imply particularly sinister or unsavoury practices, more information exchanges (often within broader general discussions) between interested, knowledgeable and well-informed professionals.
- **Direct interviews** might occur with customers, distributors, former employees of competitors, regulators and government officials. Informed sources, such as those listed, may also be useful in collecting data on competitor operations for benchmarking purposes. Customers that have defected to a close competitor are also a great source of comparative data, and competitors' customers in particular are a rich source of information on competitor processes. Questioning customers on the levels of service received, for example, or the manner in which complaints are handled, can identify the underlying processes used to deliver a particular service.

5.1.4 Comparison with own processes

The final stage in the benchmarking process is to compare and contrast the processes of those identified as 'best in class' organisations with the firm's own processes, in order to identify actions and processes to measure and monitor improvement.

Once benchmarking is complete, and actions identified, a number of options are likely to be apparent. First, the firm may conclude that its own operations are actually very good (even when compared to 'best in class'), and that it will continue to support and improve them. Alternatively, the firm may conclude that its processes are inadequate or suboptimal in some way, and there is a need for change. This may involve setting up new processes that mirror those of the best practices identified, or it may involve adopting best practice processes from other industries, to enable the firm to 'leapfrog' the competition and gain competitive advantage through market-leading process innovation. One consideration, of course, is the resources available to the organisations considering change (can we do this?), and the underlying strategy of what they are trying to achieve (should we do this?). Any changes, based on benchmarking data, must still 'fit' with the strategy of the organisation. A poor reason for change is to replicate competitors without an underpinning strategic rationale, and to illustrate this we can briefly reflect on customer relationship management (CRM) systems. Traditionally, these have a high failure rate in many industries, generally attributable to organisations implementing change (in this case buying and implementing a new CRM system) without embedding the change within a broader strategic objective or rationale. As such, at best, they are an expensive and somewhat novel technological 'bolt-on', rather than a means to achieve a higher order strategic goal.

Whether new processes are proposed or existing processes reinforced, measurable targets should be set that enable the firm to assess progress towards better and improved practices. Targets should be specific and achievable within specified timeframes – for example, 'we aim to answer 95 per cent of telephone calls within 20 seconds'. Additionally, and importantly, consideration should also be given to those tasked with achieving new targets. Have they ever performed at this level previously? Do they, or will they, require training and/or incentives in order to perform at this level? The alignment of resources with strategic aims is important. If those tasked with delivering them see them as unrealistic or unachievable, then they are unlikely to commit, and hence the new goals are unlikely to be met – possibly delivering a damaging competitive blow at an organisational level.

Beyond the benchmarking value of competitor analysis, a clearer picture of competitor strategies, strengths and weaknesses also helps firms develop effective competitive strategies. We now discuss the main processes involved in competitor analysis for the purposes of strategy formulation.

5.2 The dimensions of competitor analysis

In the medium term, the focus of competitor analysis must be firms within the same strategic group as the company concerned. In the longer term, however, there is a danger of the analysis being constrained and possibly limited or myopic. Hence, the entire industry should be explored for competitors with the necessary resources or the need to overcome entry barriers to the incumbent's strategic group. Regardless of whether entry barriers are high, if the incumbent's strategic group shows high profits or growth potential beyond the rest of the market, it is likely to attract new entrants.

The UK financial services sector is an example of where conventional competitors have lost business to the entry of new-style competitors. Well-known examples of this are: a)

Direct Line Insurance (UK-based insurance services based on telemarketing and direct marketing); and b) banking facilities and other financial services offered by major UK-based supermarkets such as Sainsbury's, Tesco and Marks and Spencer (exploiting their customer base and existing retail locations). It follows that a second source of threat could be potential entrants into an industry, or possibly substitutes. Part of EMI's failure in the whole body scanner market was its neglect of new entrants attracted by its success. Rather than build defences or foster coalitions against an almost inevitable onslaught, the company chose to continue to exploit the market as if it was the sole supplier. Perhaps the greatest failing was its falling behind in product quality and its inability to develop a support network for its product (Kay, 1993).

In the longer term, substitutes are the major threat to an industry. These deliver new processes and products with advantages that undermine established competitors' capabilities and sources of advantage. They are also likely to attract new and hungry competitors, willing to question conventional industry practices. When the mighty IBM entered the PC market it was successful relative to target competitors (Apple and Hewlett-Packard), but had great difficulty in handling new competition (at the time, Toshiba and Dell), which its standardised PC attracted. A more recent example is that of downloads that have revolutionised the music industry, and largely precipitated the demise of pre-recorded CDs, with Apple (originally a computer company) becoming the key player. At the time of writing, it is likely that a similar phenomenon will occur in video games – a sector that has moved from hardware-based games (a game is purchased and them loaded onto a piece of hardware such as a PC or an Xbox), to downloadable games (a game is downloaded straight onto a console such as PlayStation), and is now set to enter cloud-based, subscription-type arrangements, where gamers pay a monthly fee for access to unlimited gaming content (for example Apple Arcade and Google Stadia) through devices such as laptops, desktops and phones and tablets.

Competitor analysis, therefore, involves evaluating a series of concentric circles of adversaries: innermost are the direct competitors within the strategic group; next come companies within the industry that are driven to overcome the entry barriers to the strategic group; and then the outermost potential entrants and substitutes (see Figure 5.1).

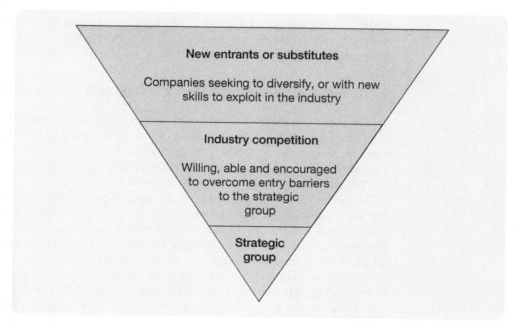

Figure 5.1 The targets of competitor analysis

Figure 5.2 The components of competitor analysis

Source: adapted from Lehmann and Winer (1991).

Figure 5.2 highlights four main stages of competitor analysis. These are:

1   **Assessing competitors' current and future objectives:** understanding what a competitor is trying to achieve can give clues as to the direction it will take, and the aggressiveness with which it will pursue that direction.
2   **Assessing the competitors' current strategies:** understanding the strategies used by competitors in pursuit of their goals and objectives, the firm can identify opportunities and threats arising from competitor actions.
3   **Assessing competitors' resources:** understanding the asset and capability profile of competitors shows what they are currently able to do. While competitor assets and capabilities might not be fully deployed, understanding presents clues as to how competitors might move in future, or how they might react to threats.
4   **Predicting competitors' future strategies:** understanding the previous three analyses starts to answer perhaps the most fundamental question in competitor analysis – that is, what is the firm likely to do in the future?

Each of these stages is now discussed in detail. In particular, potential sources of information are suggested, and ways in which the analyses might be conducted. The aim of the analysis is not to describe competitors, but to present insights into their future intentions and, importantly, what competitors are likely to do in response to competitive actions.

5.2.1 Assessing competitors' current and future objectives

Understanding the goals or objectives of competitors guides strategy development on three levels (see Figure 5.3). Goals can indicate where the company is intending to develop and in which markets, either by industry or internationally, any major initiatives can be expected. The areas of expansion could indicate markets that are to be particularly competitive, but may simultaneously signify companies not so committed.

Where the intention is profitable co-existence, then it is often better to compete in areas that are deemed of secondary interest to major companies, rather than trying to compete directly. Such was the opportunity created when General Motors and Ford once declared that the small car markets in the United States and Europe were intrinsically unprofitable, and therefore of little interest to them. Interestingly, both are now actively pursuing this market as a competitive response to pressure from governments and environmental lobbyists. This has led to massive investment in hybrid and electric cars from all main manufacturers and new-entrant challenger brands, such as Tesla. Additionally, and contributing to this change, there has been a large reduction in demand from customers for the once-dominant diesel engine. This illustrates that goals should change and adapt to

<table>
<tr><td>Assess competitors' current and future objectives</td><td>● What are they trying to achieve?
● Why are they trying to achieve it?
● Are they satisfied with their achievements?</td></tr>
</table>

Key indicators:
Stated goals   *Market assumptions*
Ownership   *Investment priorities*

Figure 5.3
Competitor
objectives

competitive circumstances, and be monitored for relevance when combined with overall strategic direction.

Goals may also give a guide to the intensity of competitor activity and rivalry. When the likes of Procter & Gamble or General Electric declare they are only interested in being the number one, or the strong number two, in markets in which they operate, it is likely that they will compete very hard in every new market they enter.

Finally, a company's goals can indicate the type of trade-off it is likely to make when faced with adversity.

Goals can have implications across the portfolio of a company's activities. When competing against a diversified company, ambitious goals in one sector may indicate commitment to another sector is diminishing. Equally, very large and diversified companies may often be unable to take advantage of huge financial strengths, because of an unwillingness to make strategic shifts in resources. Equally, financially driven companies may be unwilling to take risks on new ventures, preferring instead to 'pick the bones' of organisations damaged by taking the initial risk.

Competitor goals, objectives and strategic direction are best revealed through observing activities pursued, and by reviewing various pronouncements made in company reports and press releases and the like. For example, decisions to build additional production facilities are a clear signal of growth objectives. The recruitment of staff with particular skills (identified through observation of recruitment advertisements) can indicate new directions in which a competitor may go.

Reward structures for staff can also indicate objectives, although these are less easy to access by a competitor. Where sales staff commission is calculated as a percentage of sales, for example, this suggests that sales volume (rather than profitability) is a key objective.

The ownership structure of the competitor can also be indicative of future goals. Competitors owned by employees and/or managers may give higher priority to providing continuity of employment or good employee working conditions, rather than those owned by conventional shareholders. Likewise, competitors run through the public sector may set higher priorities on social goals as opposed to profitability (although not always). Competitors owned as part of a diversified conglomerate might focus on short-term cash generation, rather than long-term market position objectives.

Underlying assumptions

Assumptions that a firm holds about itself, and the market it operates in, affect the goals and objectives it sets and can be a source of opportunity or threat. Examples of flawed assumptions and their dire consequences are manifold, and litter the history of businesses and organisations. For example, in the 1960s, Cunard assumed that as the cost of transatlantic travel was so high people would want a leisurely crossing (getting the most out of their investment), rather than spending a large amount of money in flying across the Atlantic in just a few hours. The result of this faulty logic by Cunard, and other operators of passenger liners, was a massive increase in the tonnage of liners constructed in what turned out to be the last few years of their useful life. Similarly, Dunlop's assumption that it was pre-eminent in tyre rubber technology meant that it neglected Michelin's development of steel-braced radials. The result was what can only be termed a catastrophic decline in its own market share, accompanied by a decline in the total market size that occurred because of the *longer life* of Michelin's new development. Having assumed pre-eminence in an established market, Dunlop's position was intractable through an inability to develop new products.

Dunlop and Cunard were not atypical in their inability to see changing market conditions, and there is a tendency for incumbent companies to be dismissive of new entrants and new technologies as being of little significance or maybe catering for some faddish segment of the market. Such was the case of the Swiss watch industry when faced with competition from Japanese digital alternatives. An evaluation, or possibly an estimation, of assumptions made by competitors can be of major strategic significance, in addition to an understanding held by those conducting the analysis. This said, there is a clear gap between the need to, and the ability of, firms to question their own assumptions. It is possible that awareness of this notion is enough to provoke an interesting and revealing discussion.

Analyses of how major firms react to technological threats show they are rarely able to change their historic orientation. O'Shaughnessy (1995) explains how incumbents often avoid problems rather than taking evasive action. He suggests that there is a tendency for firms to force the evidence to fit preconceptions; to become deaf to any evidence at odds with their beliefs; to predict the most feared competitive action as a defence in case there is any future post-mortem after such action occurs; and to predict that competitive action will be that to which the manager's favourite strategy is an effective counter-strategy, as a way of getting support for that strategy.

5.2.2 Assessing competitors' current strategies and activities

Assessing the current strategy involves asking the basic question: 'What exactly is the competitor doing at the moment?' (see Figure 5.4). This requires making as full as possible a statement of what each competitor is trying to do and how they are trying to achieve it. This is a complex activity, to which the components of marketing strategy (outlined in Chapter 2) can give some structure.

Three main sets of issues need to be addressed with regard to understanding competitor strategies. First, identification of the market or markets they operate in (their selection of target markets). Second, identification of the way they operate in those markets (the strategic focus they are adopting with regard to the type of competitive advantage they are trying to convey). Third, the marketing mix adopted, in order to enable the desired competitive

Figure 5.4
Competitor
strategies

Assess competitors' current strategies	• What target markets are they pursuing? • What is their strategic focus? • What marketing mix do they use? • How do they organise their marketing?

Key indicators:
Advertising media and messages   *Price levels charged*
New product introduction rates   *Distribution channels used*
Recruitment advertisements

positioning to be achieved. Beyond these three core elements of strategy, it can also be helpful to assess the organisation of the marketing effort – the structures adopted – to facilitate implementation of the strategy.

Competitors' target markets

The broad markets, and more specific market segments that competitors compete in, can often be inferred from an analysis of the products and services they are offering, together with the ways in which they price, promote and distribute them. These elements of the marketing mix are generally highly visible aspects of a firm's activities and available for competitors to analyse.

The features built into products, and the type/extent of service offered, are good indicators of the types of customer competitors seek to serve. In the car industry, for example, those with the necessary funds to purchase the latest incarnation of the Rolls Royce Phantom can display a specially commissioned and bespoke piece of artwork from their favourite artist across the front console of their car, in a space Rolls Royce designed into the car, called 'the gallery'. No such option is available for those purchasing, for instance, the Tata Nano – arguably one of the cheapest cars in the world. Prices charged, and the overall pricing strategy, are also indicators of the target market. In grocery retailing, for example, Aldi and Lidl have consistently pursued a minimum-range/low-price strategy in an attempt to attract price-sensitive grocery purchasers, rather than compete directly with industry leaders such as Tesco and Sainsbury's on quality and service, although this is changing. Aldi, in particular, has been extremely successful at eroding market share from the larger and more embedded players in the UK grocery retailing market.

Advertisements and other promotional materials can also give clues as to the target markets aimed for. The wording of advertisements indicates the values the advertiser is attempting to convey and imbue in the product/service offered. For example, Volvo advertising has, until recently, focused largely on safety and has appealed to safety-conscious, largely middle-class families. BMW advertising concentrates on technical quality, the pleasure of driving and, more recently, the efficiency of its engines, suggesting a younger target market. The media in which the advertisements appear, or the scheduling adopted, can also give indications of the target market aimed for. Similarly, the distribution channels the competitor chooses to use to link customers physically with offerings may give clues as to the target markets.

Competitors' strategic focus

Most successful companies attempt to build strategies on the differential advantage they have over others in the market. This is an important consideration in two ways: it is necessary to base differential advantage on customer targets, and avoid basing competitive strategy on trying to build strengths where competitors are relatively and traditionally very strong. For instance, in the jewellery trade it is possible to compete through design or distribution, but impossible to compete with De Beers through securing one's own supply of uncut diamonds.

There are two main routes to creating a competitive advantage. The first is through *low costs* relative to competitors. The second is through providing *valued uniqueness, differentiated products and services* that customers will be willing to pay for.

Indicators of competitors adopting a low-cost focus include attention to overheads in the balance sheet, the vigour with which they pursue low-cost factor inputs and the tight financial controls they exert on all functions and activities. The cost leadership route is a tough one for any firm to follow successfully and requires close, relentless attention to all cost drivers. As noted previously, in the UK grocery market Aldi and Lidl have adopted this rigorous approach, restricting product lines and providing a largely 'no-frills' service. Ryanair, in the budget airline sector, has also been successful in pursuing this approach – an approach well matched to an extremely price-sensitive segment.

Providing something different, but of value, to customers is a route to creating competitive advantage that all players in a market can adopt. The creative aspect of this strategy is to identify those differentiating features on which the firm has, or can, build a defensible edge. Signals of differentiation will be as varied as the means of differentiation. Greater emphasis on customer service, added features to the product, special deals for volume or continued customer loyalty schemes are all means of differentiation. All are highly visible to competitors and indicate the basis on which a given supplier has chosen to compete.

Competitors' supporting marketing mix

As discussed previously, analysis of the marketing mix adopted by competitors can give useful clues as to the target markets at which they are aiming and the competitive advantage they are seeking to build with those targets. Analysis of marketing mix elements can also show areas where the competitor is vulnerable to attack.

Detailed analysis of competitors' products and services, particularly through the eyes of customers, can be used to highlight weaknesses. It is after examining how vacuum cleaners typically lost suction as their bags filled, that James Dyson developed the bagless vacuum cleaner and revolutionised that particular sector.

Analysis of competitor pricing strategies may identify gaps in the market. For example, a firm marketing vodka in the United States noted that the leader offered products at a number of relatively high price points, but had left other price points largely vacant. This enabled the firm to position its offerings in a different market sector.

The Dyson Small Ball Vaccuum Cleaner
Source: Dyson Ltd.

Both the message and the media used by competitors warrant close analysis. Some competitors may be better at exploiting new advertising techniques or media, whereas others may be more adept at public relations. Again, analysis will show where competitors are strong and where they are vulnerable.

Finally, understanding the distribution strengths and weaknesses of competitors can also identify opportunities. Dell, for example, decided to supply direct to businesses, rather than distribute through office retail stores where its established competitors were already strong. At the time this was considered an innovative and insightful competitive move.

Competitors' marketing organisation

Consideration of a competitor's marketing organisation is important because of the way that it can dictate strategy. For a long time, Procter & Gamble's brand management structure was considered a marketing ideal. This was probably the case when the US market was dominant and lessons learned there were relatively easily transferred downstream, to less developed parts of the world. However, with the United States' relative economic decline compared with the rest of the world, Unilever's more flexible structure allowed it to transfer ideas across boundaries more easily and be more flexible to emerging local needs. Indeed, Procter & Gamble itself has now moved away from its 'ideal' product management structure.

Understanding the organisational structure of competitors can provide clues as to how quickly, and in what manner, competitors are likely to respond to environmental change or competitive actions. Competitors where responsibility for products is clearly identified are often able to respond more quickly than those where responsibility is vague or confused. Firms organised around markets, rather than products, are most likely to spot market changes early and be in a position to lead change rather than simply react to it.

The relative position of marketing within the organisational structure can also provide clues to future strategy. In many companies, marketing is considered to be a part of sales (often sales support), and responsible for advertising, lead generation and other promotional activities. In these cases, marketing is not generally considered to be part of the strategic decision-making process. In other firms, marketing may be seen as a guiding philosophy that will ensure a far more market-responsive set of actions, based on a deep knowledge of customer tastes, preferences and behaviours. Clues to the position of marketing may lie in the background of the CEO, the visibility within the firm of senior marketing executives and possibly their previous career tracks.

A useful tool that can be applied to analyse the activities of competitors is the value chain.

Value-chain analysis

Porter (1985) identifies five primary activities that add value to the final output of a company (see Figure 5.5). Areas where value is destroyed or eroded can also be identified through this technique.

1 **Inbound logistics** involves managing the flow of products into the company. Attention to just-in-time manufacturing has shown how important this can be to the efficient operation of a company and how by management of its suppliers and their quality a company can add to the quality of its final products.
2 **Operations** have, for some time, been seen as a central activity of businesses. These comprise the processes whereby the inbound items are changed in form, packaged and tested for suitability for sale. Traditionally, this has been seen as the area where value is added to a company's products. At this stage, value can be added beyond the normal capital and manpower inputs by the maintenance of high quality, flexibility and design.
3 **Outbound logistics** carry the product from the point of manufacture to the buyer. They therefore include storage, distribution, etc. At this stage, value can be added through quick and timely delivery, low damage rates and the formulation of delivery mechanisms that fit the operations of the user. The reverse is clearly also true and can destroy value.

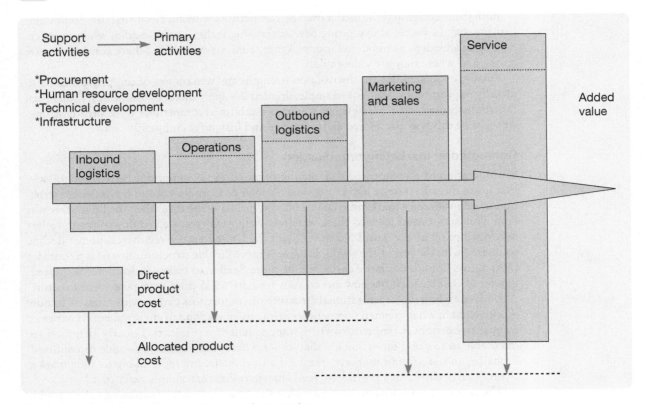

Figure 5.5 The value chain and direct product costing

Much of Amazon's success is based on effective logistics and innovation in this important area. Through a network of delivery teams and drivers, Amazon established a solid reputation for reliable and timely delivery of orders. Not content with this, however, Amazon has recently invested in innovations designed to further enhance customer experience and alleviate concerns, such as Amazon Key (allowing delivery personnel to access customer homes to make secure deliveries) and Amazon Prime Air (drones delivering small packages within 30 minutes of a customer ordering) – although the latter, at the time of writing, is still at the test stage.

4   **Marketing and sales** activities inform buyers about products and services, provide buyers with a reason to purchase and can be a significant value-add when used effectively. Nike is a business widely acknowledged for its advertising prowess. In 1988, Nike's 'Just Do It' campaign was launched – words that are still used and have great resonance today. At the time, Nike's total sales were around the $800 million mark, but within a decade sales had surpassed $2 billion, and they were a world-leading company. Equally, great sales activities can add value in competitive markets. Those organisations able to integrate these two vital areas are likely to create (or 'add') a great deal of value in those areas.

5   **Service** includes all the activities required to keep the product or service working effectively for the buyer, after it is sold and delivered. This can involve training, return of goods policies, a consultation hotline and other facilities. Since customer satisfaction is central to achieving repeat sales and word-of-mouth communication from satisfied customers, after-sales service is clearly a major part of added value. The Ritz Carlton hotel chain is famous for excellent customer service, delivered in part through front-line employees empowered to make decisions that directly enhance customer satisfaction and experience.

In support of the primary activities of the value chain, Porter (1985) also identified support activities. These are procurement, human resource development, technological development and infrastructure. Each, of course, feeds into the stages of the primary activities of the value chain.

There are several ways in which analysis of the value chain can provide an insight into competitors:

- It can reveal cost advantages that competitors may have because of their efficient manufacture, inbound or outbound logistics. It may also reveal why, with better marketing, sales and service, a company making intrinsically similar products may be achieving higher added value through its operations.
- Many conventionally orientated companies perceive operations as their primary source of added value and therefore leave opportunities for competitors that take a more extended view of the value they can add in the customers' eyes.
- Where the value added is costed effectively, it can help locate economical ways of adding value to the customer. There are numerous ways of achieving this, such as: the efficient management of single sourcing and just-in-time inbound logistics; total quality being incorporated in the operations, thus reducing the service requirements and maybe adding to the appeal of the marketing and sales activity by offering extended warranties; well-targeted marketing and sales activities that ensure that maximum perceived added value is communicated to the customer while incurring lower marketing and sales activity than if blanket sales activity was attempted.

A company's assumptions about how costs are allocated across products, and elements of the value chain, can provide clear competitive guidelines. For instance, many companies add most of their overheads to manufacturing operations where inputs can usually be measured. This occurs despite products having vastly different inbound logistics, outbound logistics, marketing, sales and service expenditures. The result can be that the final price of the products in the marketplace has little bearing on the overall inputs and the value chain.

Similarly, where overheads are allocated equally across products, direct product pricing can show where some products are being forced to carry an excessive burden of overheads, thus allowing a competitor to enter the market and compete effectively on price. When a company is competing in many different markets, it is likely that allocated product costs are completely out of line with some of the markets in which it is competing, acting as an overall constraint upon its intention to support those products. IBM once encountered this problem in its PC marketing, where margins were incapable of carrying the allocated overheads coupled to its mainframe and mini-PC business, making it uncompetitive on price (there were also some quality issues at the time). This became particularly apparent with IBM's misguided venture into the home computer market with the 'Peanut', launched with an inappropriate and uneconomical performance-to-price ratio, and also not helped by particularly strong competitors such as the Commodore 64 and an early Apple offer.

5.2.3 Assessing competitors' capability profiles

The previous discussion has highlighted what the competitor is seeking to achieve and what it may be doing now. Also critical, of course, are the degrees of freedom open to the competitor. What might it do in future?

The assessment of a competitor's resources involves looking at its strengths and weaknesses. Whereas a competitor's goals, assumptions and current strategy would influence the likelihood, time, nature and intensity of a competitor's reactions, its resources, assets and capabilities will determine its ability to initiate and sustain moves in response to environmental or competitive changes (see Figure 5.6).

Competitor resource profiles (see Section 5.1 on benchmarking) can be built in much the same way as a firm conducts an analysis of its own assets and capabilities. A useful starting point is to profile competitors against the key factors for success in the particular industry. Among these could be operational areas (such as research and engineering, or financial

Figure 5.6
Competitor
resources

strength) or generic skills (such as the company's ability to grow, quick response capability, ability to adapt to change, staying power or innovativeness).

Lehmann and Winer (1991) suggest concentrating the analysis on five key competitor abilities:

1 **Ability to conceive and design.** Assessing the ability of a competitor to innovate will help the firm predict the likelihood of new products being brought to market, or of new technologies being employed to 'leapfrog' existing products. Indications of this type of ability come from assessing technical resources (such as patents and copyrights held), human resources (the calibre of the creative and technical staff employed) and funding (both the total funds available and the proportion devoted to research and development, relative to industry average).

2 **Ability to produce.** In manufacturing industries, this will include production capacity and utilisation, while in service industries capacity to deliver the service will be critical. Firms with slack capacity should have more opportunities to respond to increased demand. Similarly, service firms that can manage resources flexibly by, for example, calling on temporary but sufficiently skilled and motivated staff may enjoy more flexibility than those with a fixed staff with rigid skills. Ability to produce is signalled by physical resources (such as plant and equipment) together with human resources (including the skills and flexibility of the staff employed).

3 **Ability to market.** Despite strong innovation and production abilities, a competitor may be relatively weak at marketing its products or services to customers. Assessing marketing capability is best accomplished through examining the elements of the marketing mix. Central to this analysis, however, will be the assessment of the skills of the people involved in sales, marketing, advertising, distribution and so on. Also important will be the funds available and devoted to marketing activities. How well does the competitor understand the market? The answer to this question may lie in the extent and type of marketing research being undertaken.

4 **Ability to finance.** Financial resources act as a constraint in any organisation. Due to the recent economic crisis, access to finance has been a major issue for small to medium-sized enterprises, in particular in the UK and Europe. A rise in the number of web-based crowd funding platforms has allowed firms that would not be able to access finance through traditional routes (such as banks) to raise funds for investment in products and services and also start-up proposals. Examination of published accounts can reveal liquidity and cash flow characteristics of competitors where available. Again, however, such hard data should be supplemented with assessments of the qualities and skills of the human resources available within finance.

5 **Ability to manage.** The characteristics of key managers can send clear messages on strategic intentions. Indicators include the previous career paths and actions of powerful managers, the reward systems in place, the degree of autonomy allowed to individual managers and the recruitment and promotions policies of the firm.

Figure 5.7 shows a summary sheet that a company has used to assess the relative capability of 'self' against three competitors: A, B and C. In this case, six dimensions have been determined as critical, and the company has rated itself and the three competitors on each key factor using a scale ranging from −2 (very poor) to +2 (very good). The result is a set of profiles that suggest the companies are quite similar in their overall capabilities and average scores, and which clearly identify the company as being on a par with competitors A and B overall. However, the total score should not be allowed to cloud the differences of the main protagonists in the market, because their relative strengths clearly show that they may move in different directions given similar opportunities. For instance, Company A could build on its European strength in marketing applied technology, whereas Company B may be forced to depend on differentiation achieved through technological breadth and strength in R&D to maintain its market position. However, if the technology or market shifts in a direction that requires major expenditures, Company B may be weaker compared with A or 'self'. An inspection of the competitive capabilities also suggests that, although Company C looks weak overall, it could be a good acquisition by 'self'. Although weak in the financial and technological areas, it has a strong European marketing presence and therefore may be capable of providing 'self' with rapid access to the European markets.

5.2.4 Predicting competitors' future strategies

The ultimate aim of competitor analysis is to determine a competitor's response profile – that is, a guide to how a competitor might behave when faced with various environmental and competitive changes. This covers such questions as:

- **Is the competitor satisfied with its current position?** One that is satisfied may allow indirect competitors to exploit new markets without being perturbed. Alternatively, one

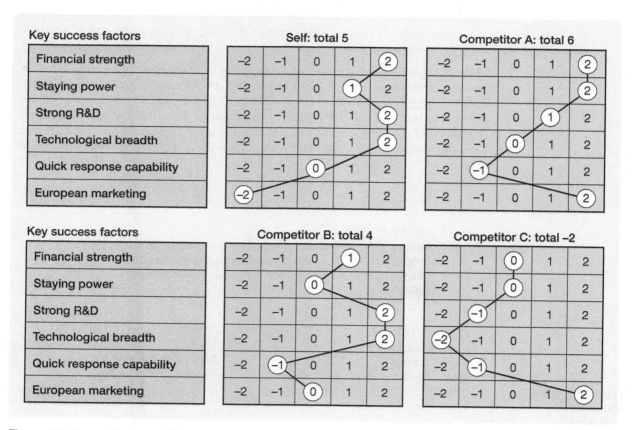

Figure 5.7 Competitor capabilities

that is trying to improve its current position may be quick in chasing market changes or be obsessed by improving its own short-term profits performance. Knowledge of a company's future goals will clearly play an important part in answering this question.

- **What likely moves or strategy shifts will the competitor make?** History can provide some guide as to the way that companies behave. Goals, assumptions and capabilities will also give some guidance as to how the company can respond effectively to market changes. After looking at these, a company may be able to judge which of its own alternative strategies is likely to result in the most favourable reaction on the part of the competitors.

- **Where is the competitor vulnerable?** It takes no great insight to realise that it would be foolish for a company to take on a market leader in the areas where it is strongest. Much better to compete against large and relatively successful competitors in niche markets where large scale is a disadvantage – for example, in rapidly changing markets where bureaucracy may lead to inflexibility in responding to niche competition. Complacency of leaders in markets can provide major opportunities for the well-informed and targeted niche competitor. The leader's feeling of invulnerability may be its weakness, and one that could lead to its downfall. In truth, businesses, like armies, cannot defend themselves on all flanks, from all positions, at all times. No company is ever all-powerful at all places. In the past, the Virgin brand has been particularly skilful, and relatively successful, at identifying opportunities in markets where existing competitors had key vulnerabilities – for example, attacking financial services suppliers through branding, high value and product simplicity in its direct marketing strategy.

- **What will provoke the greatest and most effective retaliation by the competitor?** Market leaders may accept some peripheral activity from competitors, perhaps because of relatively low margins, anti-trust laws or maybe the scale involved relative to their entire business. However, other competitor actions might provoke intense retaliation, and taking a look back in time might present some insights into what stimuli provokes a particular response. For example, Rolls-Royce has learned to expect intense reaction whenever competing in the US market for aero engines. There is little sense, even for the most powerful businesses, in antagonising strong competitors when less 'sensitive' routes to success are available.

Besides providing a general guideline, a competitor's response profile depends on obtaining a view of how a competitor is likely to respond, given various stimuli (see Figure 5.8). Porter (1980) suggests examining the way a competitor may respond to the feasible strategic moves by a firm and feasible environmental changes. This first involves assessing the vulnerability of a competitor to the event, then the degree to which the event will provoke retaliation by the competitor and, finally, the effectiveness of the competitor's retaliation to the event.

Predict competitors' future strategies	• What might the competition do? • What under-utilised resources do they have? • How will they react to our actions?

Key indicators:	
Past strategies	*Past successes and failures*
Past reactions	*Changes in ownership*
Recent resource acquisitions	

Figure 5.8 Future competitor strategies

The aim is to force a company to look beyond its own moves and towards those of its competitors and, like a great player of chess, think several moves ahead. It involves a firm thinking of its moves in a broad, strategic framework rather than the incremental manner in which strategies often emerge. Alternatively, by following a series of seemingly small incremental shifts in pricing and promotion, a firm could be seen as attacking a particular market, and incur the wrath of major players. It is clearly better for A to consider the alternative moves carefully rather than make a series of moves, each one of which makes local sense, without regard to B's counter-moves and the long-term consequences of incremental action.

5.3 Choosing good competitors

When a company enters a market it also, in effect, chooses its competitors. In the selection of new opportunities, therefore, it is important to realise that not all competitors are equal. Just as markets can be attractive and a company's strengths can fit those markets, so competitors can be attractive or unattractive. Porter (1985) lists the characteristics that make a good competitor. In Figure 5.9 these features are organised to show how certain features of competitors can make them attractive.

Companies that have reached competitive maturity understand the market they operate in and will enhance, rather than destabilise, the environment of the strategic group. A good competitor can help promote industry stability by understanding the rules that govern the market, and by having realistic assumptions about the industry and its relative position in it. In this way, a good competitor is unlikely to embark on strategies that are unprofitable and that may result in zero-sum competition, such as precipitating price wars or other unprofitable practices.

A good competitor can support the industry structure, if it invests in developing its own product and enhancing quality differentiation and market development, rather than confrontational price-cutting or promotional strategies. In that way, barriers to entry are enhanced as the overall quality of incumbent competition is heightened. Additionally, the overall impact of a competitor or new entrant is diminished, as a far clearer segmentation and positioning landscape exists. The global pharmaceutical industry tends to have this structure, where legislation and the clear differentiation of drugs allows a relatively large number of medium-sized companies to survive in many leading markets.

A further advantage of a company that is competitively mature is that it provides steady pressure on competitors to become more operationally efficient. It provides respectability

	Balance	Strength	Weakness
Competitive maturity	• Understand the rules • Realistic assumptions • Support industry structure	• Credible/viable • Know the industry costs	• Clear weaknesses • Limited strategic concept
Reconcilable goals	• Moderate strategic stake • Accept current profitability • Desire cash generation	• Comparable ROI targets	• Short time horizons • Risk averse

Figure 5.9 Good competitors

and standards, and ensures that the market does not become too 'comfortable' for the incumbents. The danger, then, as many state monopoly industries have shown, is that once protection is removed or competition is allowed to emerge, companies find themselves too weak or rigid to change and compete effectively. There is much speculation around this issue currently in the UK. At the time of writing, it is still unclear as to what shape 'Brexit' will take, and what ultimately it will mean to UK plc. However, some commentators speculate that the main challenge for many UK-based companies will be to what extent they will be able to compete effectively in a non-EU trading environment. Market pressure increases further when the leading competitor has a thorough understanding of industry costs and therefore sets standards for cost-efficient services.

Finally, the existence of the credible and viable large company within a particular strategic group can act as a deterrent to other entrants. A good competitor, therefore, can provide both pressure to keep competitors lean and an 'umbrella' under which the industry can develop steadily.

A good competitor is a company that has a clear understanding of its strengths and weaknesses, and is likely to leave opportunities for others in the market. Additionally, it will have reconcilable goals that make it comfortable within the market it operates, less likely to make massive strategic shifts and tolerant of moderate intrusion. Where its strategic stake is moderate, a good competitor may not see market dominance, or the maintenance of its own market position, as a principal objective. If under pressure, it may even be willing to retreat from a market when faced with greater opportunities elsewhere.

Moderation in the level of profitability desired is also an advantageous characteristic of a competitor. A company that accepts current levels of profitability is likely to seek stability rather than new opportunities.

The desire of a competitor to maintain cash flow can have a further impact on industry stability. Most ventures that involve destabilising an industry depend on investing in research and development, marketing and/or construction of a new cost-cutting plant. A company with strict cash requirements is therefore less likely to embark on such costly ventures.

The reconcilable goals of a good competitor can also provide beneficial and steady pressure on competitors within an industry. If a competitor has comparable return-on-investment targets to its stakeholders, it will face similar competitive pressures to the rest of the industry. In contrast, a state-owned competitor (that is not likely to face the same profitability requirements), or one that is funded from markets with different expectations, can be unhealthy. Within the European Union, the British Steel Corporation (now part of Tata Steel, following a succession of takeovers and mergers) faced a regulated market against European competitors, heavily subsidised by state governments. Rather than competing with these, however, it chose to concentrate on speciality steels, where the competitors were often in the private sector and therefore faced similar expectations.

A feature of many Western companies that makes them good competitors for competitors from other parts of the world (the East in particular) is their short time-horizon. This means that when faced with adversity or competitive pressure from 'the East', Western companies often cut-back investment to maintain short-term profitability, or attempt a fast route to corporate success rather than investing in internal growth – the latter being a longer-term approach. Risk aversion can also lead to a competitor being more attractive. Where there is fear of making errors there are likely to be followers within an industry, which may allow more agile companies a chance to gain advantage when the market changes.

Clearly, finding a market in which competitors are good on all fronts is unlikely, just as it is impossible to find a market that is completely attractive and consistent with a company's own strengths. But by examining competitors, and looking for markets where they tend to be good rather than wayward, a company is likely to face a more stable environment and one in which opportunities are there to be taken.

The diversity of competition makes it difficult to draw generic classes of companies that are likely to be good competitors. Some groups can be identified as likely to be good or bad competitors, but in all these cases there will be exceptions to the rule. Porter (1985) identifies smaller divisions of diversified firms as one likely group of good competitors. These may not be viewed as essential to the long-term corporate strategy, and they often face tough profitability targets. In a global sense, this is still particularly true of US multinationals, which have shown a remarkable willingness to retreat home when faced with adversity. They are also prone to particularly tough profitability objectives, with little support in, or understanding of, overseas markets. Part of this stems from the belief that what is good enough for the home market is good enough for overseas subsidiaries and that all the major lessons can be learned at home (Wright *et al.*, 1990). There is now a general recognition that things are 'different' in non-home markets, but the incidence of organisations failing, or not realising their potential, is still quite high. Much of this is related to a relative lack of flexibility and adaptability on the part of the non-home market entrant, where assumptions are made about the effectiveness of systems, processes and organisational cultures in different international contexts.

Another group of potentially good competitors can be old established companies with a dynastic interest in the industry. This can be because the companies are strong and set high standards but are careful (as in the case of Sainsbury's in the UK), or because they are moderate in their expectations (as many UK manufacturing companies have been).

Among groups that are more difficult to compete with, and hence not 'good competitors' for the incumbent firm, could be new entrants from other industries that break the mould of established competition in the markets. They could also be new market entrants that have made major investments and therefore have a large stake in terms of ego and money in making a venture a success. By not fully understanding the market, they may destabilise competition and also be willing to accept zero, or low, profits for a long time.

Of course, the issue here is not whether they are good or bad from an ethical point of view. They are just bad competitors to compete with, although the new standards they bring to an industry and the services they provide to the consumer can do great good for the consumers and the economies concerned. Moreover, they *are* good at competing, just not good to be competing *against*. Marc Andreessen, founder of Netscape (the Internet's first commercial browser), is reported to have said: 'Everyone should be in a business once in their lives that competes with Microsoft, just for the experience.' He added that once was enough though (*The Economist*, 9 March 2002).

5.4	Obtaining and disseminating competitive information

It has been said that the inability of commanders to obtain and use military intelligence is one of the major reasons for displays of military incompetence (Dixon, 1976). The same is true of competitive intelligence. Also, given the competitive nature of both war and commerce, it is not surprising that the means of gathering information on an enemy or the competition are similar in both method and ethics; in both cases, the legality or otherwise of methods has not been a barrier to their use. The final section of this chapter draws together the alternative means of gathering competitive information (see Figure 5.10). In doing so, it follows a sequence of declining morality, but seeks to make no judgement about the ethics of many approaches mentioned.

At the most basic level, a company can collect **published statistical information** on competitors and markets. Many companies will have such information on their records from market studies or from published sources on public companies. A problem with many of these sources is their disaggregation and the frequent inconsistency between various government statistics and those provided by a range of market research companies. Increasingly, use of the Internet can provide much background information. Search engines allow investigators to search very wide sources rapidly to obtain up-to-date information on competitors and markets.

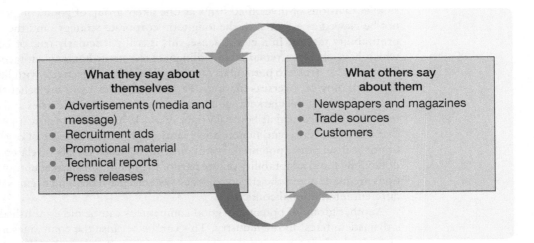

Figure 5.10
Sources of
competitor
information

A company's own **publicity material**, such as brochures, corporate magazines and websites, can also be a source of useful background information. Sales brochures show the range of products on offer, and sometimes include price lists, while websites often give more insight into the strategies and philosophies of firms. Typically designed with customers or employees in mind, these publications need critical scrutiny but can be a mine of useful background information.

A company's own **propaganda** – in other words, its public relations activities – can add texture to background statistical information. The need to communicate to shareholders and intermediaries in markets means that frequent marketing or technological initiatives are broadcast widely. A danger here, clearly, is the credibility of the public relations involvement of the competitors. Investigative journalism can lead to more open disclosures, but here again the press usually is dependent on the goodwill of a company to provide information. Nevertheless, such sources can give a splendid feel for a company's senior executives. In that light, it can be akin to the information that great generals try to gather on each other. Organisational activity through social media is another great source of data that present insights on strategic and tactical issues, customer initiatives and feedback and other more general activity.

An increasingly frequent source of information on a company is **leakages**. These are typically (but not always) unsanctioned information leakages from employees that get into the hands of the media. Since these often have to be newsworthy items, such information is usually limited in context but, once again, can give texture to background information. Firms that are more aggressive seekers of information may take positive steps in precipitating the giving of information: for instance, grilling competitors' people at trade shows or conferences, or following plant tours and being a particularly inquisitive member of a party. Increasingly, trawling social media is also being used as a source of competitive data (Marshall *et al.*, 2012). The social media feeds of those employed by organisations can be a good source of information, and an area that increasingly is being used to present competitive insights. Organisations, of course, are becoming far more aware of this issue and many now have quite strict controls on the private/personal social media activity of employees.

A company can gather information from **intermediaries** or by posing as an intermediary. Both customers and buyers have regular contact with competitive companies and can often be a source of valuable information, particularly with salespeople or buyers from a researching company with whom they have regular contact. It is also possible to pose as a potential buyer, particularly over the phone, to obtain factual information such as price, or to obtain performance data.

Many industries have policies of not recruiting between major companies or, as in the United States, have regulations regarding the nature of an individual's work after they have moved from one company to another. However, a company would be naive if it did not thoroughly debrief **competitors' former employees** if they did join the company. For instance, for a long time Procter & Gamble and Unilever in the UK have provided excellent and highly regarded training grounds for marketing people. When their employees move, they carry with them a great deal of useful information on their previous employers' products, methods and strategies. Many such large employers are very aware of this and often request that people who are leaving must clear their desks and leave within minutes once their intention to move is known. Even if competitors' employees are not eventually recruited, the interviewing process itself can often provide useful information, particularly since the person being interviewed may be eager to impress the potential employer.

Surveillance is widely used within counter-espionage, but is less common as a means of gathering competitive business information. Some of the methods used can be quite innocuous, such as monitoring competitors' employee advertisements or studying aerial photographs. Others are very sensible business practices, such as reverse engineering – that is, tearing apart the competitors' products for analysis. Less acceptable, and certainly less hygienic, is the possibility of buying a competitor's rubbish to sift for useful memoranda or components. Bugging is a controversial means of surveillance that is becoming more common now that equipment is inexpensive, reliable and small enough to be concealed. It is certainly not uncommon for competitors in retail environments to visit competing stores regularly, in order to gather information on promotions, point-of-sale materials and messaging, innovations and customer service practice.

Dirty tricks have always been a danger of test marketing, but with the availability of mini-test markets a new dimension has emerged. Their speed means that while a company is test marketing products over a matter of months, a competitor can buy supplies, put them through a mini-test market, find their market appeal and maybe experiment with alternative defensive strategies, all before the test-marketed product is launched fully.

A final means of gathering information is the use of **double agents**, either placed in a competitor's company purposefully or recruited on to the payroll while still working for the competitor. One can easily imagine how invaluable such people could be over the long term. We know that such individuals are common within military espionage, although few examples have come to light in business circles.

5.4.1 Disseminating competitor intelligence

Intelligence itself is an essentially valueless commodity. It becomes valuable only when it reaches the right people within the organisation and is subsequently acted on. If no one is analysing, discussing and taking action on data collected, then it is a costly and unproductive exercise. Successful dissemination, however, requires two things. First, the destination must be clearly identified, and the question 'who needs to know this?' answered. Second, data must be presented in a manner that a recipient can understand and assimilate. Too many competitive intelligence reports, such as market research reports, are far too detailed and cumbersome for busy executives to extract and use the relevant information.

Bernhardt (1993) suggests the use of a hierarchical approach to dissemination. For senior management (including CEOs and strategy formulation groups), intelligence should be limited to that which is of high strategic value. There is little point burdening top managers with the minutiae of everyday operations. Indeed, too much operational detail in their menu of intelligence may mask the really important issues they need to act on.

Information to senior managers should include special intelligence briefings, typically one- or two-page reports, identifying and summarising specific issues and showing where more detailed information can be obtained. Senior managers may also require regular (monthly or quarterly, depending on the rate of change in the industry and market) intelligence briefings, which address regularly occurring issues systematically so that trends can be identified and priorities made.

Middle and junior managers at a more operational level may require more detailed information to enable them to formulate tactical decisions. Here, more detailed profiles of competitor products and services are required, together with detailed analysis of competitor marketing mix strategies. Increasingly, middle management is becoming conversant with database manipulation, enabling managers to directly interrogate intelligence data rather than simply relying on information specialists to extract and present relevant information (see Fletcher, 1996).

Summary

Just as understanding markets is fundamental to business success, so is a good understanding of competitors, their strengths, weaknesses and likely responses to competitive moves. This chapter suggests that the focus of competitor analysis should be on immediate strategic groups, but should not neglect other firms with the potential to overcome entry barriers. It provides frameworks for analysing competitors, and suggests the importance of thinking through a range of likely responses and the implications of such. It also suggests that when entering markets and instituting strategies, firms should be looking for 'good' competitors that can stabilise markets, provide opportunities and apply some competitive pressure to ensure an efficient and effective market. Finally, suggestions regarding methods of gathering and disseminating competitive information are made across an ethical spectrum. Ultimately, the goal is to learn from competitors, their successes and their mistakes, as well as working out how to compete more effectively (see Figure 5.11).

While equally as important as market information, data on competitors are rarely gathered systematically or comprehensively and discussed in organisations. There are a multitude of date sources that have the potential to be of interest, but there is little chance that this will be done effectively on an *ad hoc* basis. Hence, there is a compelling reason for incorporating competitive information gathering within any robust marketing information system. Also of importance is to have people responsible for ensuring the systems maintenance, and that the information generated is summarised in a useful format and discussed in a systematic and timely fashion. In competitive strategy, just as in war, it is impossible to exaggerate the

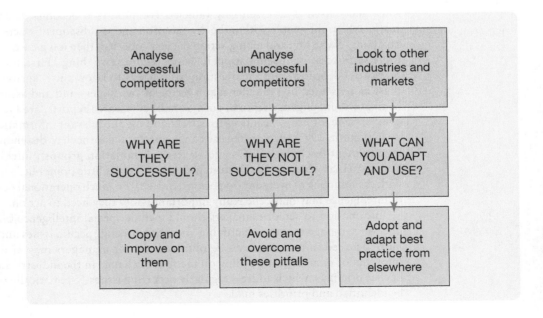

Figure 5.11
Learning from competitors

importance of gathering information on the adversaries a company faces. As Sun Tzu states: 'An army without spies is like a man without ears or eyes', and because of this, 'to remain in ignorance of the adversary's condition simply because one grudges the outlay of a few hundred ounces of silver in honours and emoluments, is the height of inhumanity.'

Case study

Adidas kicks off US drive to close in on Nike

By Lindsay Whipp in Chicago and James Shotter in Frankfurt

A German sporting goods company is focusing on the global 'epicentre' of the sneaker market to catch up with its rival.

They say a picture paints a thousand words but sometimes a number does it even better.

Nike, the US sporting goods behemoth whose swoosh logo is as instantly recognisable as its name, together with its Jordan brand have built up a share of nearly 60 per cent of the US trainers market. Adidas has just 4.4 per cent.

The German group is far more competitive in sports apparel and markets outside the US. The duo are neck-and-neck in western Europe, Adidas is a long way ahead in Russia, and Nike has a narrow lead in China.

Source: Torontonian/Alamy Stock Photo.

But Nike's dominance in the world's most important sneaker market gives it a painfully sharp edge on Adidas, which is pushing a new strategy to claw back share across key sportswear segments, with a strong emphasis on the US. With such a big gap to close in trainers, Adidas has a mammoth task on its hands.

Outside the US there is much greater parity between Nike and Adidas. 'But the US is the epicentre of the global sneaker/"athleisure" market', says Matt Powell, sports industry analyst at research firm NPD, which calculated the market share data. 'Ultimately to win globally, sneaker brands must win in the US. Nike has a deep and rich understanding of the US sneaker consumer.'

Nike has been a runaway success over the past five years. It is the world's biggest sportswear company by sales and in the year to June 2015 revenues rose 10 per cent, to $30.6bn. Adidas, meanwhile, reported a 6 per cent rise in revenues on a currency-neutral basis to €14.5bn, for the full year 2014.

Profit at Nike has risen at a double-digit rate – and that is despite its overseas business grappling with a strong dollar that has made prices less competitive.

Adidas will need to add sales at a brisk pace to even maintain the existing gap with Nike.

The western European market shows how tough this race will be. Over the past three years, the sales growth of the Nike brand has outstripped that of the German group's Adidas and Reebok brands by roughly 10 percentage points on average, once currency fluctuations are excluded, according to UBS analysts.

The result is that Adidas and Nike are now level in the region that has traditionally been the German company's stronghold. Euromonitor, a market research provider, calculates that both groups had a 12.8 per cent share of the western European sportswear market in 2014.

'Alarmingly for Adidas, Nike has caught up in its core western Europe market, and may overtake it in the short term', says Natasha Cazin, senior analyst at Euromonitor International.

Even maintaining the dead heat in which Adidas now finds itself with Nike could be hard, says Zuzanna Pusz, an analyst at Berenberg. 'Adidas is doing fine in western Europe, but they should be as they are spending 14 per cent of their sales on marketing', she says. 'The question is whether this is sustainable.'

A recent survey by analysts at UBS also found signs of Nike's surge, particularly among the young. The survey looked at how many times consumers 'liked' Facebook pages associated with different sports brands, and found that Nike was far ahead of its rivals in all the big European markets – and recently overtook Adidas in Germany.

UBS also found that the perception of Nike's brand exceeded that of Adidas in London and Paris, two of the six cities around the world that Adidas is targeting as part of its efforts to regain ground on its US rival.

'Adidas undoubtedly needs to improve brand perceptions among younger consumers. But the good news is that we think it has a big opportunity to achieve this by placing a bigger focus on social media, leveraging its sponsorship asset base, and creating more relevant product for the target teenager', the analysts wrote.

Adidas's recent overhaul of its football boot offering – it replaced its famous Predator and F50 lines with two newcomers, Ace and X – is seen as one way in which it can renew its appeal among teenagers.

The company has also taken steps to improve its position in the fast-growing area of fitness tracking, snapping up app developer Runtastic. Ms Pusz says focusing on sports software is the right way to go, but adds that Adidas is playing catch-up instead of setting the pace.

Nike is already by far the trendsetter in its home market. Not only does it have the financial clout when it comes to endorsements, it was quick off the mark in recognising the importance of social media and advertisements uploaded on YouTube. During the recent women's World Cup in Canada, although Adidas was the main sponsor, Nike emerged victorious in terms of social media engagement. Its 'No Maybes' campaign was 121 per cent more associated with the World Cup than Adidas, according to Amobee Brand Intelligence.

But it is an area again where it has the potential to catch up and win over more millennials. It plans to improve marketing, be more innovative with its products and bring them more quickly to market. 'Adidas has made the right decisions to move global product and marketing to the US', NPD's Mr Powell says. 'Hopefully they will develop a less European-centric point of view.'

It helps Adidas that the so-called athleisure wear trend is only growing stronger. As more people wear casual sports clothes in situations – even work – that were previously considered more formal, there is room for many companies to expand.

This also means there are more companies to overtake it. Under Armour, a relative newcomer, last year sold more trainers, tracksuits and T-shirts than Adidas in the US.

And fashion is fickle. Some analysts question whether sports brands really benefit by overly focusing on chasing trends or working with celebrities – as Adidas is doing with Kanye West after the pop star dropped his relationship with Nike. Paul Swinland of Morningstar, Inc. says that for a company whose *raison d'être* is performance – which breeds loyalty – chasing fashion ultimately only gives short-term gains and is 'off brand'.

As Adidas works its new strategy in the US, Nike's challenge is maintaining the pace of growth investors have come to expect. 'They've gotten such strong growth in apparel and basketball, it just can't go on forever; you can't have 15–20 per cent growth forever', Mr Swinland says.

Yet being Nike's rival must feel a lot tougher. 'Impossible is nothing', or so goes Adidas's well-known slogan. It will be hoping it does not prove itself wrong.

Rivals take different approaches.

When Adidas and Nike make headlines in China, it is often because workers at one of their suppliers in the 'world's workshop' have gone on strike in manufacturing centres such as Dongguan. But as Adidas seeks to make up ground on Nike, the two companies are paying attention to China as an important market in its own right.

In announcing its second-quarter results on Thursday, Adidas highlighted a 19 per cent increase in its Greater China sales.

With second-quarter revenues of €564m ($615m), Greater China is Adidas's third-largest market, after western Europe and North America. But it is also the German company's second-most profitable one, with a second-quarter gross margin of 59 per cent.

Similarly, Nike's Greater China earnings in the three months to the end of June ($266m) were almost as big as western Europe's ($277m), despite a much smaller revenue base – $829m in Greater China compared with $1.2bn in western Europe.

Reflecting the wealth disparities that make China both a manufacturing powerhouse and coveted market, a pair of Nike's LeBron basketball trainers sell for the equivalent of $275 compared with a monthly minimum wage in Dongguan of $210.

Analysts say that Adidas and Nike have adopted different approaches to the China market. 'Nike has gone through the basketball route, focusing on celebrity endorsements, while Adidas has taken a more grassroots focus aimed at youth culture', says Matthew Crabbe, a retail analyst with Mintel.

Both will have to contend with a tougher retail climate as China's economy is now growing at its slowest annual rate for 25 years.

 Source: from 'Adidas struggles to catch up with Nike's runaway success', *Financial Times*, 07/08/15 (Whipp, L. and Shotter, J.).

Discussion questions

1 Why is Adidas focusing on the US market?

2 Why has Adidas seemingly lost ground to Nike?

3 Should Adidas only benchmark itself against Nike? What steps should it follow when conducting benchmarking activities?

CHAPTER 6
UNDERSTANDING THE ORGANISATIONAL RESOURCE BASE

'The most important assets a company has are its brand names. They should appear at the head of the assets list on the balance sheet.'

Marketing director, international food marketing company.

Moncler scraps catwalk shows for the social media generation

By Rachel Sanderson in Milan

Luxury fashion group to target millennials with 'flash' events and online collections

Moncler, the luxury goods company behind €1,000 puffa jackets, is closing its twice-yearly catwalk shows as smartphones revolutionise the industry with consumers clamouring to see new fashions more frequently online.

The decision by Remo Ruffini, founder and chief executive of Moncler, who in 10 years turned Moncler from a bombed-out French skiwear brand into a company with a market value of near €6bn, also will result in the exit of designers Thom Browne and Giambattista Valli.

In an interview with the *Financial Times*, Mr Ruffini, 56, said the pair had done 'an amazing job' in the past eight years but consumers' changing shopping habits meant he needed 'a new and different energy'.

After ending the Gamme Rouge and Gamme Bleu catwalk shows following this winter's collections,

Instead of fashion shows, Moncler will stage one-off spectacular events that target social media

Source: © Reuters.

Mr Ruffini said his biggest stores would become the venues for more frequent launches of new designs, as often as every two months.

'I believe in creating a new energy for the consumer at the sales points and communicating as fast as possible,' said Mr Ruffini at Moncler's newly opened flagship store in Milan, which is designed to feel like an Alpine chalet.

Instead of fashion shows, Moncler will stage one-off spectacular events that target social media. The group is holding a 'flash art' event in Hong Kong this week, which will see 12,000 Moncler mascots in different locations around the city. The event has been organised with Instagram and other social media in mind.

Mr Ruffini said he was also considering plans to create the 'kind of energy' found in upscale multi-brand stores such as Los Angeles-based Maxfield and London's Dover Street Market, 'where you find designers one next to another'. Nonetheless, he denied market speculation he plans to acquire luxury rivals.

Mr Ruffini, a university drop out, built Moncler's success by spotting the trend for luxury casual wear. 'Casualisation' is one of the main trends driving growth in the €250bn luxury industry, according to Bain & Company.

The move by Moncler follows a week of C-suite turmoil across the industry as brands seek new managers to adapt their businesses to millennial and Generation Z shoppers, who it is estimated will make up nearly half of luxury consumers by 2025.

LVMH, the world's largest luxury goods group, last week announced the exit of Sidney Toledano, long-time chief executive at Dior, to bring in Fendi chief Pietro Beccari; at Italy's Tod's, billionaire founder Diego Della Valle handed over operational management to former LVMH and Bulgari manager Umberto Macchi di Cellere; and Swiss group Richemont elevated Jerome Lambert to chief operating officer and named Emmanuel Perrin, a former director at Cartier, as head of distribution for its watch brands.

Mr Ruffini says one of the biggest tests for the industry is adapting to the Chinese social media platform WeChat, where shopping is integrated within the chat platform. If technology in the US and Europe is moving fast, 'in China they are going incredibly fast,' he said.

 Source: from 'Moncler scraps catwalk shows for the social media generation', *Financial Times*, 13/11/17 (Sanderson. R.).

Discussion questions

1 Why is Moncler closing its twice-yearly catwalk?

2 What have been, and are, the implications for the company's resources?

Introduction

The attractiveness of opportunities open to a firm depends on the resources available to exploit them. Organisational resources include both tangible and intangible assets, capabilities and competences. This is the base from which organisations build their competitive position, and any marketing strategy needs to be firmly grounded in these resources. Strategies that are not built on resource strength are unlikely to be sustainable in the longer term, and under-utilised resources represent potential wastage. To succeed in a particular market, the firm will need specific resources – the key factors for success in that market. If it does not have these, or cannot acquire them, the strategy is likely to fail at the implementation stage.

This chapter is structured around the following issues, which provide a framework for assessing organisational resources:

- the role of marketing resources in creating differentiation;
- insights from the resource-based view (RBV) of the firm, and in particular the more recent emphasis on dynamic capabilities;
- creating and exploiting marketing assets;
- deploying dynamic marketing capabilities;
- developing and exploiting the resource portfolio.

This is shown schematically in Figure 6.1, starting from the most general issues and moving progressively to the more specific.

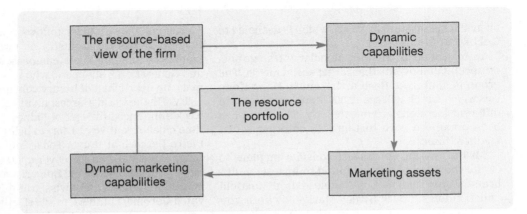

Figure 6.1
Understanding
the organisational
resource base

6.1   **Marketing resources as the foundation for differentiation**

While any organisation could produce a long list of the resources at its disposal, what is important is to identify those resources that can help create a competitive advantage, and ideally an advantage that can be sustained into the foreseeable future – a sustainable competitive advantage (SCA). Theories developed in the strategic management field can be helpful. Strategic management theorists have shown that a sustainable competitive advantage can be achieved when distinct resources are employed that are resistant to competitor imitation or duplication. The resources that will most likely create sustainable advantage have a number of key characteristics. First, they enable the provision of competitively superior value to customers (Barney, 1991, 1997; Slater, 1997). Second, they are resistant to duplication by competitors (Reed and DeFillippi, 1990; Hall, 1992, 1993). Third, their value can be appropriated by the organisation (Collis and Montgomery, 1995).

Resources, such as brand reputation, relationships with customers, effective distribution networks and the competitive position occupied in the marketplace, are potentially significant advantage-generating resources. These have been termed marketing resources as they relate directly to marketing activities and are directly leveraged in the marketplace. Their role in generating value for customers is clear. But how easy are they to protect against competitor imitation (and hence erosion of that advantage)? Some resources, such as capital, plant and machinery, are inherently easier for competitors to copy than others, such as company reputation, brand reputation and competitive position created and reinforced over time. Many marketing resources, as we shall see, are intangible in nature and hence more difficult for competitors to understand and replicate.

The ways in which resources can be protected from duplication have been termed isolating mechanisms (Reed and DeFillippi, 1990), as they serve to isolate the organisation from its competition, creating a competitive barrier. Isolating mechanisms operate at three main levels:

● First, for a competitor to imitate a successful marketing strategy it must be able to identify the resources that have been dedicated to creating and implementing that strategy in the first place. The competitive position created, for example, will include a complex interplay of resources, creating difficulties for competitors in identification. Lippman and Rumelt (1982) refer to this problem for competitors as 'causal ambiguity', which can be created through tacitness (the accumulated skill-based resources resulting from learning by doing and managerial experience), complexity (using a large number of interrelated resources) and specificity (the dedication of certain resources to specific activities). For example, a firm enjoying the resource of close relationships with key customers might offer more of a challenge for a competitor to copy than one selling cut-price bargains. The former will require superior customer linking skills, such as customer relationship management (tacit skills), together with the technical skills to serve customer needs. The latter may be based on an effective cost-control system that could be relatively easily installed by a competitor.

- Second, should a competitor overcome the identification barrier, it would still need to acquire the resources necessary for imitation of the strategy. Some resources, such as corporate culture or market orientation, may take time to develop (referred to as being 'path-dependent' because they require the firm to go down a particular path to develop them), while others may be uneconomic to acquire, or may even be protected in some way (for example, through patents or copyrights). If resources have transaction costs associated with their acquisition, there is likely to be a continuing barrier to duplication. Even where acquisition is theoretically possible, some resources may be less effective in the competing firm (for example, managers may be less effective working in one environment than another).

- Third, most resources depreciate over time as competitors are eventually likely to find ways of imitating successful strategies. This is especially true in rapidly changing markets (such as where technology is changing swiftly). Again, some resources may depreciate less quickly than others. Reputation, for example, has potential for a longer period of advantage generation than, say, rapidly depreciating plant and machinery. We say potential because we should always remember that reputations take time to build but could be destroyed overnight if mishandled. BP, the multinational oil and gas producer, suffered a significant amount of reputational and also financial damage (through large reductions in share price) following the Deepwater Horizon oil rig disaster in 2010. It took some time for them to recover from this, and some commentators suggest that they still have not fully recovered their original position.

In the analysis of resources, therefore, the important question to always bear in mind is: does this resource contribute to the creation of a sustainable competitive advantage for the organisation? Where it does, or it could be leveraged to, the resource should be recognised as the potential source of an effective marketing strategy and protected from both external recognition and internal myopia.

We discuss the types of resources organisations may have at their disposal, and how these can be identified. In common with current usage, we use the terms 'resources', 'assets', 'competencies' and 'capabilities' interchangeably. Conceptually, however, resources could be considered the generic term, while assets and capabilities are different types of resource.

6.2   Value-creating disciplines

Day (1997) points out that

> Every business acquires many capabilities that enable it to move its products through the value chain. Only a few of these need to be superior to competition. These are the distinctive capabilities that support a value proposition that is valuable to customers and hard for competitors to match.

In fact, different ways of delivering superior customer value require quite different resources. For example, Treacy and Wiersema (1995) point to three different 'value disciplines', each of which excels at meeting the distinctive needs of one customer type, and each of which requires different resource capabilities (see Figure 6.2):

- **Operational excellence** – providing middle-of-market products at the best price with the least inconvenience. Examples include no-frills mass-market retailers such as Aldi and Lidl in the retail sector in the UK, and fast food outlets such as McDonald's, Burger King

Figure 6.2 Value disciplines

and KFC. This strategy requires an organisation to achieve, or at the very least strive for, excellence in the core processes of order fulfilment, supply-chain management, logistics, service delivery and transaction processing.

- **Product leadership** – offering products that push the boundaries of product and service performance: Intel is a product leader in computer chips, as is Nike in athletic clothing and footwear. A prime example is Hewlett-Packard's computer printer business that once achieved market dominance through major technology advances, rapid product variations, continuous price reductions and a willingness to attack competitors. The core processes that underpin this strategy include market sensing (of latent customer needs), openness to new ideas, fast product development and launch, technology integration and flexible manufacturing. Management and structure will probably be decentralised, team-orientated and loose-knit.

- **Customer intimacy** – delivering what specific customers want in cultivated relationships. The core requirements are flexibility, a 'have it your way' mindset, mastery of 'mass customisation' to meet the distinct needs of micro-segments of the market and the ability to sustain long-term customer relationships.

Hamel (1996) notes that, in an effective strategy-making process, 'you can't see the end from the beginning'. Organisations need to be flexible enough to change established beliefs about corporate capabilities, as marketing strategy options emerge from analysis (and vice versa); if necessary, they need to be able to rethink the attractiveness of strategy options as a result.

In seeking to define key resources, however, Porter (1996) points to the dangers of the 'competitive convergence trap'. Porter argues that the danger inherent in the pressure on companies to improve operational efficiency is not simply that we substitute operational efficiency for strategy, but that competing companies become more and more similar: 'The more benchmarking companies do, the more they look alike . . . Continuous improvement has been etched on managers' brains. But its tools unwittingly draw companies towards imitation and homogeneity.' When we attempt to assess corporate capabilities, our search should be for sources of competitive differentiation and advantage in activities and areas that matter to customers, not simply sources of operational efficiency.

We should also be aware that how we group, categorise or label what we see as an organisation's resources can be critical. Strategy does not consist of mere operational improvement, neither does it consist of focusing simply on a few core competencies (especially if they are the same things our competitors would claim as their own competencies). Real sustainable advantage comes from the way the various resources fit together, creating a unique resource base for a unique competitive strategy. Porter illustrates this with the example of the car hire business. Companies such as Hertz and Avis are brand leaders, but profitability is generally low – these firms are locked into an operational effectiveness competition, offering the same kinds of cars at the same kinds of airports with the same kind of technology. Enterprise, on the other hand, achieves superior performance in this same industry with smaller outlets that are not at airports, little advertising and generally slightly older cars. Enterprise does everything differently. Enterprise employs more experienced staff and operates a business-to-business sales force – it specialises in temporary car replacement for those whose own vehicle is off the road and has turned its back on the business travel market at major airports. The point is that, on its own, each of the Enterprise capabilities is unremarkable, but together they comprise a powerful route to a differentiated competitive position and superior performance (Porter, quoted in Jackson, 1997).

In reviewing resources, managers need to search for advantage from the way things fit together, not just the individual resources available. Indeed, the critical question may be how capabilities can be managed successfully across alliances of companies.

An important consideration is whose view of resources to follow – much in this area is subjective and judgemental. Indeed, Hamel (1996) suggests that 'the bottleneck is at the top of the bottle'. Senior managers may tend to defend orthodoxy because it is what they know, and what they have built their careers on: 'Where are you likely to find people with the least diversity of experience, the largest investment in the past, and the greatest reverence for strategic dogma? At the top.' (Hamel, 1996).

New perspectives on the resources of the organisation may come from surprising places. Hamel describes how in one company the idea for a multi-million-dollar opportunity came from a twenty-something secretary, and in another some of the best ideas about an organisation's core competencies came from a forklift operator, while in an accounting company the partners learned about virtual reality from a junior employee aged 25.

At the very least, when we are attempting to assess resources we should include the views of those who run the business, and outsiders who may have insights that are valuable.

6.3 The resource-based view of the firm

Two main themes dominated thinking about marketing strategy during the 1990s and influenced much of what is taught today – the notion of market orientation and the resource-based view (RBV) of the firm. While the market orientation literature emphasises the superior performance of companies with high-quality, organisation-wide generation and sharing of market intelligence leading to responsiveness to market needs, the RBV suggests that high-performance strategy is dependent primarily on historically developed resource endowments (see Grant, 2005).

There is, however, a potential conflict between these two approaches in the sense that one advocates the advantages of outward-looking responsiveness in adapting to market conditions, while the other is inward-looking, emphasising the rent-earning characteristics of resources (Amit and Shoemaker, 1993) and the development of corporate resources and capabilities (Mahoney, 1995). Quite simply, from a marketing viewpoint, if strategy becomes too deeply embedded in existing corporate capabilities, it runs the risk of ignoring the demands of changing, turbulent marketing environments (it is too embedded and inflexible – systemically broken, in effect). Yet, from a resource-based perspective, marketing strategies that are not based on a company's distinctive competencies are likely to be ineffective and unsustainable.

However, we argue that competitive positioning provides a way of reconciling this potential conflict. We argue that competitive positioning provides a definition of how the firm will compete by identifying target markets and the competitive advantage that will be pursued in serving these target markets. The attractiveness of markets will depend, in part, on the resources available to the firm to build a strong competitive position. Similarly, the positioning perspective recognises that for corporate resources to be leveraged for economic benefit requires their application in the marketplace. However, it also recognises that, if that application is to be sustainable in the face of competition from rivals, the competitive advantage must be built on the firm's distinctive resources (Hamel and Prahalad, 1994). Indeed, market orientation itself may be considered a key corporate resource, accumulated and learned over a substantial time period.

This iterative relationship between the pressures of market orientation and the RBV and the linkage in competitive positioning is shown in Figure 6.3. In this simplified view, the issue becomes one of responding to markets through applying organisational resources to the opportunities and customer needs identified. The outcome is competitive positioning. However, the theories of the RBV of the firm are worth consideration as a further source of insight into assessing corporate capabilities as a basis for competitive positioning.

6.3.1 Theoretical foundations

The RBV is still present in modern strategy literature (see Grant, 2005 for summaries of the main theory). The central tenet of the RBV is that for strategy to be sustainable, it must be embedded in the firm's resources and capabilities. Indeed, the potential incompatibility with the principles of market orientation is illustrated by Grant's (1995) view that:

> In general, the greater the rate of change in a company's external environment, the more it must seek to base long-term strategy upon its internal resources and capabilities, rather than upon an external market focus.

Grant uses the example of typewriter manufacturers faced with the PC revolution of the 1980s. He suggests there were only two available strategies: pursue the traditional market and attempt to acquire the technology for word processing; or seek other markets where existing competencies and capabilities could be exploited. The move of Olivetti from typewriter to PC is an example of the first strategy. The move of other companies into the printer market to exploit existing resources is an example of the second strategy.

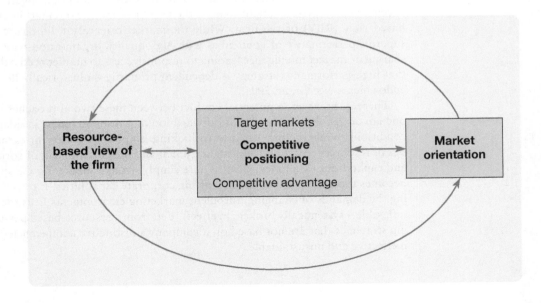

Figure 6.3
Competitive
positioning

However, to assume that these are the only strategies, or that they are mutually exclusive, is somewhat limited.

Notwithstanding this limitation in perspective, the RBV offers a number of useful insights into the nature of corporate resources. There are a number of different views of how to define and classify resources:

- anything that can be thought of as a strength or weakness of a firm (Wernerfelt, 1984);
- stocks of available factors that are owned or controlled by the firm (Amit and Shoemaker, 1993);
- a bundle of assets, capabilities, organisational processes, firm attributes, information and knowledge (Barney, 1991).

However, one particularly useful framework for marketing purposes was proposed by Day (1994) in distinguishing between a company's *assets* and its *capabilities*. In Day's terms, organisational assets are the endowments a business has accumulated, such as those resulting from investments in scale, plant, location and brand equity, while capabilities reflect the synergy between these assets and enable them to be deployed to the company's advantage. In these terms, capabilities are complex bundles of skills and collective learning, which ensure the superior coordination of functional activities through organisational processes.

In essence, the RBV places central emphasis on the role of assets and capabilities in creating competitive advantage. The theory recognises that resources are heterogeneous across firms and that there are barriers to acquisition or imitation that can provide individual firms with ways of defending the advantage created in the short to medium term. Sustainable competitive advantage, the theory suggests, lies in the possession of resources that exhibit certain characteristics: value, rarity, inimitability and non-substitutability (VRIN).

Barriers to imitation, referred to in the literature as isolating mechanisms, include *causal ambiguity* (difficulty in identifying how an advantage was created), *complexity* (arising from the interplay of multiple resources), *tacitness* (intangible skills and knowledge resulting from learning and doing), *path dependency* (the need to pass through critical time-dependent stages to create the advantage), *economics* (the cost of imitation) and *legal barriers* (such as property rights and patents) (Lippman and Rumelt, 1982; Dierickx and Cool, 1989; Reed and DeFillippi, 1990; Hooley *et al.*, 2005).

A major criticism of the RBV, however, has been that it neglects the influence of market dynamism (Priem and Butler, 2001; Wang and Ahmed, 2007). The more rapidly markets change, the more there is a need for firms to renew their resources and develop new capabilities (Ambrosini, Bowman and Collier, 2009). This notion has been explored further in organisational research into flexibility (Rudd *et al.*, 2008), adaptation and adaptability, and also dynamic capabilities. The latter is discussed more fully in the following section.

6.3.2 Dynamic capabilities

In response to the concerns mentioned previously, recent research broadly in the RBV tradition has focused on dynamic capabilities (see Teece, Pisano and Shuen, 1997; Bowman and Ambrosini, 2003; Ambrosini and Bowman, 2009). For a review of the field of dynamic capabilities, see the special issue of *British Journal of Management* edited by Easterby-Smith, Lyles and Peteraf (2009).

Dynamic capabilities are defined as 'the capacity of an organisation to purposefully create, extend, or modify its resource base' (Helfat *et al.*, 2007).

This view recognises that as markets change and become more globally integrated, new forms of competition emerge and new technologies are employed and firms cannot rest on their existing capabilities alone (Winter, 2003; Wang and Ahmed, 2007). Firms need to actively seek to recreate themselves through extending and modifying their operations.

It is noticeable that the new focus on dynamic capabilities recognises the need for firms to understand market dynamics more explicitly than the original RBV perspective. From a marketing perspective, dynamic capabilities help firms to identify market opportunities and subsequently enter new businesses through the creation of new products and improved services (Teece *et al.*, 1997; Helfat *et al.*, 2007).

Teece *et al.* (1997) suggest that dynamic capabilities have both a coordinating/integrating role and a learning role. The coordination/integration role enables firms to integrate external activities. These activities are related to the capabilities of market-driven organisations that among others need to excel in understanding customer needs and requirements, customer linking and new product development processes (Day, 1994). A customer-linking capability enables the firm to gain the 'inside track' (Penrose, 1959) by establishing a relationship with customers that may enable joint problem-solving activities and the rapid assimilation of new and previously unexploited skills (Zander and Zander, 2005). Product development routines are known to require the integration of diverse skills and know-how from inside and outside the firm. This also suggests that, besides their customer-linking abilities with customers, firms must be able to enhance their knowledge creation process by being capable of developing networks and strategic alliances throughout the value chain (Eisenhardt and Martin, 2000).

Learning enables new opportunities to be identified and can stimulate experimentation and innovation (Bowman and Ambrosini, 2003). More specifically, learning is a core element of dynamic capabilities since it is a 'collective activity through which the organisation systematically generates and modifies its operating routines in pursuit of improved effectiveness' (Zollo and Winter, 2002).

It has been suggested by some researchers (such as Ahuja and Katila, 2004) that dynamic capabilities are idiosyncratic and highly dependent on the specific firm–market context. Others, however (such as Eisenhardt and Martin, 2000), seek commonalities across firms. The most recent conceptualisations of dynamic capabilities focus on 'fit' – both technical fit and evolutionary fit. Helfat *et al.* (2007) define technical fit as how effectively a capability performs its intended function (its quality) when normalised (divided) by its cost, and evolutionary fit as how well a dynamic capability enables an organisation to make a living by creating, extending or modifying its resource base. In this sense, evolutionary fitness includes not only technical fitness but also understanding of competition and market conditions.

Evolutionary fit is central to marketing thinking, ensuring not only that the market offerings are technically fit for purpose, but also that they match changing market requirements in the light of customer and competitor change.

Wang and Ahmed (2007) suggest that resources can usefully be considered at four levels. For our purposes, these are conflated to three main levels and types of resource. Figure 6.4 shows these levels in a marketing context:

- At the base level are marketing assets – the resource endowments the organisation has built or acquired over time. Where these exhibit VRIN characteristics (that is, create value for customers, are rare or unique to the firm, are inimitable or difficult/expensive for other firms to imitate or acquire, and are non-substitutable or easily replaced), they can form the basis of a competitive advantage. Most assets, however, depreciate over time unless they are constantly renewed and refreshed.
- Capabilities, the second level of resources of the firm, are the processes that are used to deploy assets effectively in the marketplace. Wang and Ahmed (2007) differentiate between capabilities, which are used to undertake routine tasks, and core capabilities, which are strategically important to creating competitive advantage at a point in time. Core capabilities typically require the bundling together of other capabilities. For example, Zara in the fashion industry has core capabilities in responsiveness to customers, which in turn requires capabilities such as advanced information systems, just-in-time production processes and stock-control processes. Core capabilities, therefore, integrate

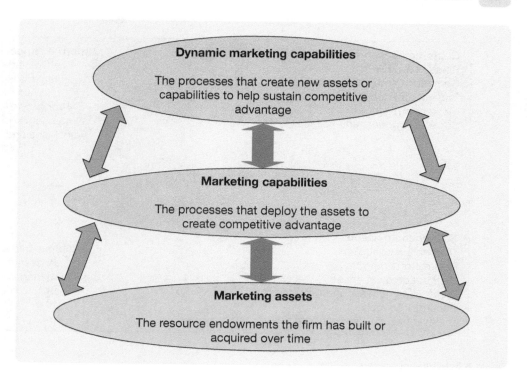

Figure 6.4
Marketing
resources

assets and capabilities to enable the firm to move in its chosen strategic direction. Zara's continuing success is based on being responsive to an inherently fast-paced market, with fast-moving customer tastes. Its retail stores get two deliveries of stock every week, and new products that are designed in Spain are on the shelves within three weeks: an incredibly agile and customer/market-focused business model. It has been suggested, however, that core capabilities can become core rigidities for organisations if (or when) markets change, and they can lock firms into processes that may become less and less relevant (Leonard-Barton, 1992; Tallman, 2003).

- Dynamic capabilities are the third and highest level of firm resources. They are the capabilities that create new assets and/or new capabilities in response to, or indeed to lead, change in the marketplace (see Ambrosini, Bowman and Collier, 2009).

We now go on to discuss marketing resources in more detail. First, we consider marketing assets, then we go on to discuss marketing capabilities, and finally we focus on dynamic marketing capabilities.

6.4   Creating and exploiting marketing assets

The term 'marketing assets' was first used in a series of articles in *Marketing* magazine by Hugh Davidson in 1983. Marketing assets are essentially resources – normally intangible – that can be used to advantage in the marketplace. Davidson also presented the following example of this.

In the early 1980s, the brand share of Kellogg's Corn Flakes, while still in the low twenties percentage, was in long-term decline. The company had spare capacity but did not produce corn flakes for private-label store brands. Kellogg solved this problem by launching Crunchy Nut Corn Flakes, which used the Kellogg name and the corn flakes plant. It was priced at a heavy premium, but it gained 2–3 per cent market share, mainly incremental to

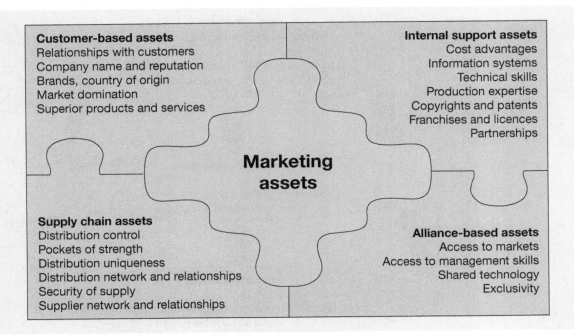

Customer-based assets
Relationships with customers
Company name and reputation
Brands, country of origin
Market domination
Superior products and services

Internal support assets
Cost advantages
Information systems
Technical skills
Production expertise
Copyrights and patents
Franchises and licences
Partnerships

Marketing assets

Supply chain assets
Distribution control
Pockets of strength
Distribution uniqueness
Distribution network and relationships
Security of supply
Supplier network and relationships

Alliance-based assets
Access to markets
Access to management skills
Shared technology
Exclusivity

Figure 6.5 Marketing assets

the share of other Kellogg's brands, at very attractive margins. The new product exploited the existing brand name, flake technology and plant, but did so in a way that attracted new customers at high margins.

A wide variety of company properties can be converted into marketing assets. As shown in Figure 6.5, they can be usefully grouped into:

- customer-based and reputational assets;
- supply chain assets;
- internal or marketing support assets;
- alliance-based assets.

6.4.1 Customer-based marketing assets

Customer-based marketing assets are those assets of the company, either tangible or intangible, valued by the customer or potential customer. Often, they exist in the mind of the customer and they are essentially intangible in nature. They may, however, be one of the most critical issues in building a defensible competitive position in the marketplace.

Company name and reputation

One of the most important customer-based assets a company can possess is its reputation or image. Companies such as Mercedes, BMW, Jaguar Land Rover and Rolls-Royce have a clear image, supplying a particular set of customer benefits (reliability, durability, prestige, overall quality) in the markets in which they operate.

Company name confers an asset on all products of the company where it is clearly identified. Indeed, in many cases where the company identity is a strong asset, it has been converted into a brand name for use on a wide variety of products (for example, Marks and Spencer and Sainsbury are not only company names, but also brands with strong customer franchises). As previously mentioned, however, image and reputation can also be a liability and may negatively impact on how customers view products and services marketed by such companies (see Chapter 17 for more detailed consideration of this issue).

Also important is how firms deal with bad publicity. The reputation of the US tyre manufacturer Firestone was badly damaged by a very 'public' argument with Ford over the cause of 170 traffic deaths and hundreds of accidents in the US involving the Ford Explorer SUV, fitted with Firestone tyres. Ford eventually recalled 13 million tyres at a cost of $3 billion (*Marketing Business*, July/August 2001).

Skoda cars were best known in Britain in the mid-1990s as the butt of bad jokes. For example, 'What do you call a Skoda with twin exhaust pipes?'. Answer: 'A wheelbarrow'. The jokes merely reflected widespread and erroneous beliefs that the cars were of poor quality. In 1995, Skoda was preparing to launch a new model in the UK and did 'blind and seen' tests of the consumers' judgement of the vehicle. The vehicle was rated as better designed and worth more by those who did not know the manufacturer. With the Skoda name revealed, perceptions of the design were less favourable and estimated value was substantially lower. Subsequent advertising made a joke of this image, showing customers happy with the cars but embarrassed at buying a Skoda. By also showing that Skoda had the strength of VW behind it (visually shown in poster advertisements as a VW shadow behind the Skoda) following acquisition, positive brand values were steadily built. Lidl has recently done something very similar in a recent television campaign. In it, a market stall is seen selling (what seem like) artisan products at very low prices. Indeed, some of the customers remark on the low price for the quality of products on sale. The customers are then told that the products they have been raving about are all from Lidl – and of course they are very surprised. Surprise would seem an erroneous reaction; however, this highlights a skewed reputation (or perception), as the quality of the products on offer at Lidl is clearly very high.

This leads us from company name and reputation to brands.

Brands

The identity and exploitation of brands remain central to many views of marketing. For example, Interbrand annually reports the most valuable brand names in the world. The top ten results are presented in Table 6.1 (and are regularly updated by the company on their website at **http://www.interbrand.com/best-brands**). Building brand value takes time and

Table 6.1 The global top ten brands

Rank	2009	2013	2018	2018 value ($US bn)
1	Coca-Cola	Apple	Apple	214.4
2	IBM	Google	Google	155.5
3	Microsoft	Coca-Cola	Amazon	100.7
4	General Electric	IBM	Microsoft	92.7
5	Nokia	Microsoft	Coca-Cola	66.3
6	McDonald's	GE	Samsung	59.8
7	Google	McDonald's	Toyota	53.4
8	Toyota	Samsung	Mercedes	48.6
9	Intel	Intel	Facebook	45.1
10	Disney	Toyota	McDonald's	42.9

Source: Interbrand 'Best Global Brands' ranking data (2009, 2013, 2018).

effort, and it is noticeable how many of the leading brands in the table have been able to retain their position, or close to, over many years. The presence of web/technology-based organisations on this list is noticeable, and perhaps unsurprising.

For companies where corporate identity is a liability or a non-existent asset, more emphasis is placed on building or acquiring individual brand names as assets. Beechams (now GlaxoSmithKline or GSK), for example, deliberately set out to acquire brands with a marketable reputation. The Bovril brand was originally purchased to ease the company's launch into the stock cube market (Bovril being an established brand property in the similar meat extracts market). Companies with little customer-based corporate identity, such as RHM (acquired by Premier Foods), develop various brands into major assets. The Bisto brand, famous as the UK market leader in gravy making, has been used to good effect in a move into the soups and sauces market.

Branding operates at the level of the individual, too. For example, sportsmen and sportswomen have begun to take out patents on their names and nicknames, as they are used in merchandising and advertising. Famous footballers such as David Beckham, Alan Shearer, Paul Gascoigne and Ryan Giggs have all registered surnames, and in some cases nicknames ('Gazza', 'Giggsy'), as brands. Partially facilitated by social media, individual branding has led to some very impressive financial outcomes for certain individuals. Tiger Woods (for those not into sport, he is a really famous golfer) has amassed a huge personal fortune, mainly through 'off-the-golf-course' sponsorship deals following impressive tournament victories. For example, in 2011 Tiger Woods had an estimated income of around $64 million, of which 'only' £2 million was from his tournament earnings; the rest was earned largely from endorsements of golf-related products (source *Golf Digest*, 2012). Clearly, Tiger's undoubted ability on the golf course allowed him to leverage his personal brand and public profile to great effect (and gain) off the golf course also. Tiger is not alone, however, and those with far smaller celebrity media profiles (and hence weaker personal brands) generate significant income from book launches, perfumes and a host of money-making satellite projects.

Of course, the overall power and worth of personal brands are closely linked to the performance and the behaviour of the individual concerned. Tiger Woods lost a number of sponsors (Accenture, AT&T, Buick and Gillette) following a spate of well-publicised problems in his personal life. However, Nike, Tiger's main sponsor, did not abandon him, and their loyalty may well be rewarded handsomely. At the time of writing, Tiger Woods has just won The Masters golf tournament in the USA – one of only four 'major' tournaments that happen every year in golf, and his first major tournament win in over a decade. While past performance is no guarantee of future success, commentators suggest that the brand value accrued to Nike as a result of media exposure of their brand in the final round was around $22.5 million dollars! The longer-term impact on sales of other products endorsed by Woods could clearly be very significant.

Brands can be particularly powerful marketing assets for a number of reasons:

- **Brands are difficult to build** – the leverage highlighted previously for the Tiger Woods brand was not built overnight. It was built over many years, and the same is true for successful and profitable commercial brands.
- **Brands add value for customers** – in most taste tests where products are unknown to the tasters, consumers tend to prefer Pepsi to Coca-Cola. However, when tasters are aware of the drinks they are tasting, then more prefer Coca-Cola than Pepsi. Hence, soft drink preferences are based on brand image and not just taste.
- **Brands create defensible competitive positions** – during periods of supermarket price competition, it is not uncommon to see huge discounting on products such as baked beans, with own-label baked beans often being priced as low as 3 pence a can. It is interesting to note that during these periods of discounting, Heinz customers are very loyal indeed and continue to purchase Heinz regardless of the much cheaper alternatives. Even though these brand-loyal customers are happy to pay around nine times as much as other makes, Heinz has, in the past, been able to actually increase its prices during periods of heavy price competition.

- **Brands build customer retention** – research sponsored by the US Coalition for Brand Equity shows that brand loyalty makes customers less sensitive to competitors' promotions and more likely to try new products and services from that brand. A study of 400 brands over eight years by Information Resources found that with successful brands, 30 per cent of the sales increase attributable to new advertising came from new customers, but 70 per cent came from the increased loyalty of existing customers (Kanner, 1996).
- **Brands can transform markets** – the British financial services sector has long been associated with weak branding and low brand awareness. More recently, however, this sector has seen an influx of new (to this sector) brand names such as Mondo, Virgin, Metro Bank, Tesco Bank and Atom Bank. To a greater or lesser extent, all have taken market share away from incumbents through leveraging their brands and substantial databases.
- **Brands perform financially** – research study after research study highlights the importance of investment in brands. Those companies that invest in building and maintaining their brands, especially in an economic downturn, outperform those that do not.
- **Brands can cross national borders** – global brands are becoming increasingly common, and many firms are attempting to standardise branding across international markets as customers become more global. The scale economies of such are very attractive to organisations seeking cost reduction in competitive markets. The key here is not to assume homogenous customer groups across national boundaries and to ensure that local nuances are well catered for (via advertising and positioning of brands). For example, Coca-Cola recently implemented the largest change in its history when it moved to a 'one brand' approach in all operating regions across the globe. Previously to this, Coca-Cola brands had been marketed separately, with each brand having its own distinct personality in all markets. For example, Diet Coke featured a stereotypical male model in most advertising, designed to target its predominantly female market – something that seems a really out-of-date idea through a modern lens.

Company and brand are not the only influences on customer perceptions of offerings. The origin of the product may also have a significant impact.

Country of origin (COO)

For companies operating in international markets, the identity of the home country can contribute either as an asset or a liability. Japanese firms, for example, collectively enjoy a good reputation for quality and value for money. British-made goods, such as Barbour, Burberry and Church's shoes, have enjoyed a revival in the USA due to the favourable image of Britain in this market. Other examples of COO effects include:

- French wine enjoys a strong international reputation, allowing premium pricing. The use of French words (such as *château* and *appellation d'origine contrôlée*) on labels serves to reinforce the origin. Indeed, wine from specific regions within France can also command a premium even before the wine is sampled. It is noteworthy that wines from Australia depend more on promoting the grape variety (Pinot Noir, Shiraz, Chardonnay), while French wines promote the region of origin.
- New Zealand successfully promoted itself as a tourist destination following the success of the *Lord of the Rings* movies, which were filmed there. The emphasis has now shifted to marketing the country's foods and wines. In 2006, Bacardi paid around $90 million for the luxury vodka brand '42 Below'. Originally it was marketed based on New Zealand's reputation for purity, and had gained significant market share on this basis.

Increasingly, consumers in developed markets are concerned about the 'carbon footprint' of their purchases and are starting to question some of their purchasing habits (for example, buying items that have travelled long distances at the expense of the environment).

The value of image of home country, company or brand should not be underestimated. Image often takes a long time to build up, but can be destroyed very quickly by mistakes or mishaps. For example, French wine suffered significantly in the US market when France did not support the US-led invasion of Iraq in 2003, and some argue that it has not fully recovered. Conversely, it is often more difficult, though not impossible, for competitors to destroy a company's image-based assets than, say, copy its technology or imitate its products.

Market domination

In addition to image, the domination or apparent domination of the market can constitute an asset. Market presence or domination is used by Interbrand as one of the criteria for valuing brands. Market leaders typically enjoy good coverage of the market, wide distribution and good shelf positions. In addition, market leaders are often believed by consumers to be better in some way than the rest of the market (why else would they be market leader unless they were the best?). Simply being there and highly visible may confer an asset on the product. There is, however, a counter-argument emerging. There is some evidence of an increasing desire among more affluent consumers to demonstrate their independence and sophistication by not buying the same goods and services that others buy. In some product areas this could lead to the situation where being popular and widely used actively discourages some customers who wish to feel they are different from the mass.

For example, in Japan there has been a surge in the sales of unbranded goods in an attempt by conspicuous consumers to stand out from the crowd. The very successful Seibu retail stores, based in Tokyo, selling only *Mujirushi ryohin* ('no brand/good quality') products, are an example of a retailer that has taken advantage of this. The company's labels say only what materials are used and the country of manufacture. The clothes have simple designs, plain colours, high quality and reasonable pricing. Seibu's parent group has also developed the no-brand idea for tinned food and household items in its Seiyu supermarkets.

Superior products and services

It is still worth saying that having superior products and services on the market – products that are, or are believed to be, better in some way (cheaper, better quality, more stylish and up to date) than the competitors' – can be a marketing asset for the company. Unique products or services, until they are imitated, can provide marketing assets, so long as customers want them and are prepared to pay for them.

6.4.2 Supply chain assets

Assets based in the supply chain are concerned with the manner in which the product or service is conveyed to the customer. They include the distribution network, its control and its uniqueness and pockets of strength.

Distribution network

The physical distribution network itself can be a major asset. In the car hire business, for example, Hertz owes much of its success to a very wide network of pick-up and drop-off centres, especially in the USA. This wide network ensures availability of the required services in the right place, increasing convenience of use for Hertz's customers.

Distribution control

Investments in dominating some or all of the channels for a product can be a powerful asset. Mars launched the Mars Ice-Cream Bar as a child's treat, and then transformed it into an adult indulgence – a strategy since imitated by countless competitors. However, while having limited success, this product has not lived up to expectations in terms of overall sales growth. The Unilever-owned competitor Walls exercises a high degree of control over an important distribution channel: small convenience stores. Indeed, Walls owns the freezers and display cabinets in many of these outlets, and does not share them with competitors. The critical marketing asset here is distribution channel control. Coca-Cola has a very similar approach with its wide distribution of chiller units in retail outlets. These very attractive units do not stock competitor products as a rule, and hence in many locations Coke occupies/'owns' retail space that is at a premium.

Pockets of strength

Selective but close relationships between a company and its distribution outlets can lead to pockets of strength. Where a company is unable, through size or resource constraints, to serve a wide market, concentrating effort, either geographically on specific regions of the market (William Morrison's supermarkets were particularly strong in Yorkshire but spread nationally through acquisition of the Safeway chain of stores) or through specific outlets, can enable a pocket of strength to be developed.

Companies adopting the latter approach of building up a strong presence with selective distributors, or even end users in many industrial markets, often achieve that pocket of strength through key account marketing – that is, giving full responsibility for each key account development to a specific, normally quite senior, executive. Pockets of strength typically are built up on the basis of strong relationships with those selected distributors and hence require a proactive relationship marketing strategy to ensure their development (see Chapter 15).

Distribution uniqueness

Further distribution-based assets can be built through uniqueness, reaching the target market in a novel or innovative way. For instance, Ringtons sells tea, coffee and other related household items, door to door, in the north of England (http://www.ringtons.co.uk), and the Avon Cosmetics company has built a strong door-to-door business in cosmetics sales (https://www.avon.uk.com).

Similarly, Dell computers has achieved a uniquely strong position in the personal computer market by using a direct distribution approach, which enables most of the computers sold to be built to the specifications of the customer, while at the same time giving Dell a much faster stock-turn than most competitors.

Delivery lead-time and security of supply

Delivery lead-time is a function of at least three main factors – physical location, order through production systems and company delivery policy. In an increasing number of situations, the ability to respond quickly at no compromise to quality is becoming more important. Deliberately creating a rapid-response capability can constitute a significant marketing asset.

Similarly, where the supplier's offering is on the critical path of the customer company, the ability to guarantee supply can be a major asset, particularly in volatile markets. As with lead-time, that ability will be a function of several factors, but perhaps central is the desire on the part of the supplier to meet agreed targets.

The competitive success of fashion clothing retailers such as Primark, Zara and Hennes & Mauritz (H&M) is in large part based on supply chain strengths. These companies identify fashion catwalk trends and have them in stores in as little as two weeks, sourced from low-cost suppliers, at attractive high-street prices. While they have different competitive positions, they all have efficient supply chains and the ability to manage a high velocity of stock movement, rather than focusing purely on stock levels. They are operationally incredibly fast, and their customers expect no less.

Supplier network

At the other end of the supply chain, well-developed or unique links with key suppliers can be important marketing assets. These can help to secure continuity of supply of raw or semi-finished materials at required standards for negotiated prices.

6.4.3 Internal marketing support assets

A resource becomes an asset when actively used to improve the organisational performance in the marketplace. Consider the following examples.

Cost advantages

A competitive cost advantage brought about by employing up-to-date technology, better capacity utilisation, economies of scale, or experience curve effects, can translate into lower prices for products and services in the marketplace. Where the market is price-sensitive, for example, with commodity items a lower price can be a major asset. In other markets where price is less important, cost advantages may not translate into marketing assets, but may be used to provide better margins.

Information systems and market intelligence

Information systems and systematic marketing research can be valuable assets in that they keep the company informed about customers and competitors. Information is a major asset that many firms guard jealously, but until it is utilised to make better decisions, it not a marketing asset as such. This is an important point, as many organisations collect huge amounts of data, but do not utilise them effectively (or at all), which is largely a waste of time, coupled with the additional problem of missing emerging competitive trends.

When used well, data can be utilised to create a closer bond between corporation and customer. Customer experiences can be tailored to give the impression that an individual customer is 'known' and valued by a particular company. We all have examples of this, and you may well be thinking of one right now, but the underlying idea is the same (for example, Virgin Atlantic 'knows' which newspapers and seats frequent fliers prefer, and Amazon always seems to 'know' the kinds of things you are looking for when you log on).

As well as understanding customers better than competitors do, the owners of data warehouses can create marketing strategies that exploit this resource as a differentiating capability; they simply know customers and their markets 'better' than competitors. Of course, they still have to *do something* with this knowledge, and one of the key challenges for data-rich organisations is how well (or possibly how quickly) ideas developed through insights provided by data are converted into actions.

Existing customer base

A major asset for many companies is their existing customer base. Particularly where a company is dealing with repeat business, in consumer and industrial markets, the existence of a core of satisfied customers can offer significant opportunities for further development. The development of the direct marketing industry (accounting for around half of all marketing expenditure in the USA) is symptomatic of this notion. Where customers are satisfied with previous company offerings, they are more likely to react positively to new offers. Hence, where (good) relationships exist with customers, these can be nurtured by managers to develop markets and serve as a barrier to competitive entry.

The converse is also true. Where a customer has been dissatisfied with a product or service, they may not only be negative towards new offers, but also may act as 'well poisoners' in relating their experiences to other potential customers. There is an old marketing adage: 'Each satisfied customer will tell three others; each dissatisfied customer will tell 33!' Of course, in the digital and social media world this is more like 33,000, thus compounding problems at an almost exponential rate.

The issue of customer retention and customer loyalty has become extremely important (and we will consider this in more detail in Chapter 14).

Technological skills

The type and level of technology employed by the organisation can be a further asset. Technological superiority can aid cost reduction and/or improve product quality. For example, the spectacular growth of a company such as Amersham plc (now part of GE Healthcare), a company focused on high-technology medical products, was largely based on its ability to stay ahead of competitors in terms of new product development, but also its capability of distributing highly toxic and radioactive substances safely throughout the world. In the automotive industry, German manufacturers BMW, Audi and Mercedes-Benz have positioned themselves at the high-quality end of the market, through superior design, technical engineering excellence and comprehensive quality controls. The underlying ethos of this position was encapsulated in the famous Audi slogan 'Vorsprung durch Technik' (leading through technology), emphasising the German/engineering heritage of the cars (country-of-origin effect).

Production expertise

Production know-how can be used to good effect as a marketing asset. Mars, for example, is particularly good at producing high-quality nougat, and a great deal of effort has been put into quality control at Mars and developing production processes as a core competence. These efforts have been turned into a marketing asset in a number of leading products such as Mars Bar, Milky Way, Topic and Snickers, all of which are nougat-based.

Copyrights and patents

Copyright is a legal protection for musical, literary or other artistic property, which prevents others using the work without payment of an agreed royalty. Patents grant persons the exclusive right to make, use and sell their inventions for a limited period. Copyright is particularly important in the film industry to protect films from illegal copy ('pirating'), and patents are important for exploiting new product inventions. The protection of copyrights and patents, in addition to offering the holder the opportunity to make and market the items protected, allows the holder to license or sell those rights to others. They therefore constitute potential marketing assets of the company.

Franchises and licences

The negotiation of franchises or licences to produce and/or market the inventions or protected properties of others can also be valuable assets. Retailers franchised to use the 'Mitre 10' name in hardware retailing in New Zealand, for example, benefit from the strong national image of the licensor and extensive national advertising campaigns.

Similarly, in many countries American Express cards and products are marketed under licence to the American Express Company of the USA. The licence agreement is a significant asset for the licensee.

Partnerships

Increasingly, companies are going to market using collaborative or alliance-based strategies (as we shall see in more detail in Chapter 15). We should not neglect the importance of existing partnerships as marketing assets, and also the management capability to manage marketing strategy in alliance-based networked organisations.

Corporate culture

One of the resources that is hard for competitors to imitate, and can be particularly distinctive of a company, is its culture. The formation of culture and the capacity to learn are complex issues, and for many successful companies culture represents a unique resource. For example, Hewlett-Packard (HP) has a culture that encourages teamwork and cross-functional and cross-divisional working. This has allowed HP to use its core technologies in many diverse products – printers, plotters, computers, electronic instruments – and to make these products compatible. Competitors can certainly imitate HP's technology relatively easily, but it is far less straightforward to imitate the culture and organisation that underpins HP's marketing effectiveness.

6.4.4 Alliance-based marketing assets

All the assets discussed previously can be held internally in the firm itself, or gained through strategic alliances and partnerships. Although there are strategic risks involved, alliances can be seen as one way of increasing a company's pool of assets and capabilities without incurring the expense and loss of time in developing them in-house. The importance of strategic alliances and different forms of partnership is discussed in detail in Chapter 15, but for present purposes we should note the significance of such alliance-based marketing assets as:

- **Market access** – for example, alliances with local distributors are frequently the only way open to the exporter to enter protected overseas markets.
- **Management skills** – partnerships may bring access to abilities not held in-house, both in technology management and marketing management.
- **Shared technology** – alliances are often the basis for sharing and combining technologies to create market offerings with higher customer value, which neither partner could achieve alone.
- **Exclusivity** – partnerships may create monopolistic conditions.

6.5 Developing marketing capabilities

All the marketing assets in the world, however, are of little value if they are not actively exploited in the marketplace. The processes and practices that deploy marketing assets are marketing capabilities.

Marketing capabilities are effectively implementation capabilities – the ability to implement marketing mix activities, such as promotions, personal selling, public relations, price deals, special offers to customers, packaging redesign and so on. While the marketing mix is discussed in more detail in Chapter 11, we now briefly describe the main operational marketing capabilities (see Figure 6.6).

6.5.1 Product and service management capability

Managing existing products, including the ability to influence others in the organisation where their activities impact on customer satisfaction, is basic to effective marketing. This involves the marshalling of all resources (which may cut across traditional organisational boundaries) to deliver customer value. Many firms, following the early examples of Procter & Gamble and Unilever, have designed their organisational structures around the products and services they offer (brand, product and category managers) to ensure that diverse activities such as product design, packaging, pricing, promotions and distribution networks

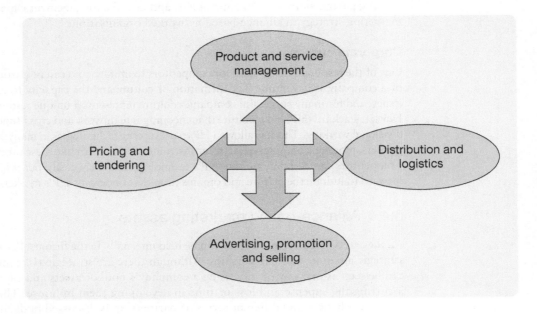

Figure 6.6
Marketing
capabilities

employed all combine effectively. For example, Mercedes cars are clearly positioned as luxury vehicles, and are often sold into the corporate or fleet market. It is important that all aspects of the marketing are drawn together (price relatively high to denote quality and exclusivity, features to support luxury, distribution through reputable dealers located in business centres), in order to reinforce the positioning of the car.

6.5.2 Advertising, promotion and selling capability

Effective communications with customers, both current and prospective, take a variety of forms including advertising, public relations, direct marketing, sponsorship and selling (see Chapter 11). Managing the communications process and campaigns, deciding on the mix of approaches to use and evaluating communications effectiveness are important marketing capabilities.

Increasingly, companies are outsourcing many of these activities to enable them to buy in best practice and expertise from outside. Design consultancies, PR agencies, packaging specialists and the like are emerging as service providers to marketers in these specialist areas of implementation. Within the focal firm, the competencies required are increasingly in the selection, management and coordination of specialist outside suppliers.

6.5.3 Distribution capability

Distribution capability is the ability to employ existing channels and/or develop new distribution methods for servicing customer needs. The logistics of delivery can be critical to distribution. A major factor in the success of Amazon as an online retailer, for example, has been its capability to accurately and consistently deliver goods bought online to customers through third-party delivery agents such as FedEx. Effective distribution management includes competence for efficient management of traditional distribution channels, but also developing and managing franchising networks and newer electronic channels. This is a broad capability drawing on several organisational competencies such as logistics, production line planning and fleet management. With the growth in mobile, tablet and online retailing, clothing companies such as Charles Tyrwhitt, Hawes and Curtis and TM Lewin have built effective and efficient distribution channels in order to make it very easy for customers to buy from them. These companies also have a very substantial high-street presence that also benefits from their effective distribution and logistics operations.

6.5.4 Pricing and tendering capability

Pricing decisions are notoriously difficult. Price too high and sales are likely to be low, price too low and the returns to the firm may not provide enough of a margin to enable it to survive or invest in the future. Pricing decisions involve many considerations, including costs of production of physical products or delivery of services, the prices charged by competitors, demand elasticity and the position in the market targeted. Managing price changes is also a skilled capability requiring judgement about timing, and effective communications. Tendering decisions, used extensively in the construction industry for example, involve a degree of estimation as to who else will tender, and what price they will go in at. Pricing capabilities draw on competencies not only in marketing, but also in finance and operations management.

6.6	**Dynamic marketing capabilities**

As noted previously, the emphasis in the resource-based strategy literature is now on the creation and exploitation of dynamic capabilities (see Bruni and Verona, 2009). While dynamic capabilities in general are the ability to create new resources in changing markets, dynamic marketing capabilities are the ability to create new marketing resources to identify, respond to and exploit change. Ensuring evolutionary fit between market needs in a dynamic competitive environment and market offers is the essence of effective strategic marketing.

Following the typology suggested by Wang and Ahmed (2007), we group dynamic capabilities into three main types: absorptive capability, adaptive capability and innovative capability (see Figure 6.7).

6.6.1 Absorptive marketing capabilities

Absorptive capabilities are the processes that enable firms to recognise the value of new information from the market and to assimilate it. These processes focus on knowledge acquisition and assimilation.

Market-sensing capability

The capability to understand what is happening in the external environment with respect to demand, customers, competitors and wider macro-environmental change is essential to crafting an effective strategy in a changing market (see Foley and Fahy, 2004).

Specific market-sensing capabilities include the ability to undertake (or effectively commission) marketing research and competitor analysis, and the ability to ensure dissemination of the resulting information throughout the organisation as a basis for decision making.

Market sensing is not limited, however, to the conduct of formal market research. Famously, Akio Morita, founder of Sony, sensed that there was a potential market for the Walkman when the market research told him otherwise. Market sensing implies being close to the customer and experiencing products and services in the same way that the customer experiences them. Firms operating in business-to-business (B2B) markets may have particular customers that they are especially close to with whom they will discuss new product development opportunities.

Learning capability

Learning processes enable firms to maintain long-term competitive advantages over rivals (Dickson, 1992). In fact, continuous learning is essential for surviving in dynamic and competitive environments as it makes the firm receptive to acquiring and assimilating external

Figure 6.7
Dynamic marketing capabilities

knowledge (Zahra and George, 2002). Learning enables new opportunities to be identified and allows for repetition and experimentation, enabling firms to integrate information from the external environment. More specifically, learning is a core element of dynamic capabilities since it is a 'collective activity through which the organisation systematically generates and modifies its operating routines in pursuit of improved effectiveness' (Zollo and Winter, 2002). Prior research has suggested that there are a variety of mechanisms that may be employed to access external knowledge (Almeida *et al.*, 2003). These activities are related to the capabilities of market-driven organisations, that, *inter alia*, need to excel in 'outside-in' capabilities such as customer linking (Day, 1994).

6.6.2 Adaptive marketing capabilities

Adaptive capabilities focus on the firm's ability to identify and capitalise on emerging market opportunities. Adaptation implies doing things differently in response to external stimuli.

Market-targeting and positioning capabilities

Market-targeting and positioning capabilities encompass the ability to identify alternative opportunities and then select appropriate market targets, where the firm's resources and capabilities are aligned for the best effect. Positioning is not just a marketing decision, however. In aligning resources and capabilities with changing markets, the competencies of all aspects of the business (including operations, finance and R&D), as well as marketing, need to be taken into account.

As markets change, so the positioning adopted may need to change.

Customer relationship management

Customer relationship management is the ability to acquire, retain, expand and (where necessary) delete customers. Strategic account management skills are becoming increasingly important in business-to-business markets, together with the increased focus in many markets on relationship building through customer service. Direct marketing also has a role to play here. (Because of the increasing importance of customer relationship management, we devote Chapter 14 to discussing this in depth.)

6.6.3 Innovative marketing capabilities

New-product and service-development capabilities

The ability to innovate and develop the next generation of goods and services is the life-blood of any organisation. Effective new-product development requires both an outside-in (customer-sensing) capability and appropriate R&D skills. It relies on interdisciplinary inputs from marketing, R&D, finance, operations and other functional disciplines.

6.7	Resource portfolios

Under the resource-based view of the firm (RBV), organisations are seen as collections of resources, assets and capabilities. These can then be viewed as a portfolio that is available for deployment. When developing strategy, the two key questions are: how can we exploit our capabilities more fully and what new capabilities will we need to build to enable us to compete in the future?

The interdependence of capabilities and their potential for combination can be the essence of their value.

Hamel and Prahalad (1994) suggest that, increasingly, firms will define themselves more as portfolios of competencies than as portfolios of products or strategic business

Figure 6.8
The resource portfolio

units. Indeed, the roots of successful market offerings essentially lie in created and acquired competencies, and the key to future strategy is to further develop, extend and deepen them so that they are available for configuration and deployment in new and innovative ways.

Figure 6.8 shows one way of summarising the portfolio of resources an organisation has at its disposal. Two dimensions have been chosen, to reflect how far resources contribute to creating value for customers (vertical) and where these resources are superior or inferior to those of competitors (horizontal). Four types of resource can be identified:

- **Crown jewels.** These are the resources where the organisation enjoys an edge over its competitors: they are instrumental in creating value for customers. As the source of differentiation, these resources need to be guarded and protected to maintain the competitive edge. At the same time, however, managers need to constantly question whether these resources alone can ensure continued success. The danger lies in resting on the laurels of the past while the world, and customer requirements, move forward.
- **Black holes.** Black holes are resources where the organisation has an edge, but which do not contribute to customer value creation. These may be resources that provided customer value in the past but are no longer important. The world and customers may have moved on, rendering them less important at best, and obsolete at worst. Managers need to take a long hard look at black hole resources and assess the costs of maintaining them. It could well be that some pruning, or downsizing, of such resources will free up efforts and even cash that can then be deployed more effectively elsewhere.
- **Achilles' heels.** Where competitors are strong but the organisation is weak, but at the same time the resources are important in customer value creation, the clear implication is that such resources need to be strengthened. These are resource deficiencies that could prove fatal if not corrected.
- **Sleepers.** Finally, resources that neither constitute a competitive advantage nor are important in customer value creation could be termed sleepers. They are unimportant today, but managers do need to watch that they do not become more important in the future.

The resource portfolio model offers a useful summary of the organisation's resources, and can be used to highlight areas for attention and development.

While the emphasis so far has been on identifying existing resources, organisations also need to ensure they are developing and nurturing the resources that will be required in the future. This involves a degree of forecasting how markets and customers will change over time. Figure 6.9 shows four strategies for development.

The two dimensions shown in Figure 6.9 represent choices open to the organisation in developing and exploiting both the markets in which it operates and the resources it employs.

In the lower-left quadrant, the focus is on utilising existing resources as effectively as possible in existing markets. The 'fill the gaps' strategy involves looking for better ways of serving existing customers, using the existing strengths of the organisation. In many ways this may be seen as a defensive strategy used to protect existing positions from competitor encroachment.

In the top-left quadrant, the organisation retains its focus on existing markets and customers but recognises that the resources it will need to serve them in the future will need to change. This requires the 'next generation' of resources to be built and nurtured. Many traditional bricks-and-mortar firms have found that to continue to serve their existing customers, they need to develop online services including mobile and tablet offerings (see Chapter 14). This often requires a new set of capabilities to be developed, not just those associated with web-based technology. These new resources do not necessarily enable the firm to reach new customers or markets, but they are required to enable it to continue to serve its existing client base. Under this strategy, the organisation stays with the markets that it knows and the customers it has built relationships with, but recognises that it must adapt to continue to serve them effectively.

In the bottom-right quadrant, the organisation seeks new markets and customers where it can 'exploit current skills' more effectively. However, this quest for new customers or new markets is guided by the existing capabilities of the organisation. The acquisition of the UK retailer Asda by the American firm Walmart is a case in point. This enabled Walmart to exploit its existing merchandising and purchasing capabilities in the new markets of the UK.

Finally, at top right, the organisation looks to serve new customers with new resources through 'diversified opportunities'. This option takes the organisation simultaneously away from its existing markets and its existing resources – a more risky strategy and one that should not be pursued lightly. Firms that take this route often do so through acquisition or merger.

Figure 6.9
Developing
and exploiting
resources

Source: Adapted from
Hamel and Prahalad,
1994.

Summary

We started this chapter with a summary of the resource-based view of the firm and the development of ideas surrounding dynamic capabilities. Our focus on competitive positioning (that is, the choice of target markets and the competitive advantage exploited) provides a mechanism for reconciling the *internal* focus of the RBV with the *external* focus demanded in dynamic markets through the development of dynamic marketing capabilities.

The practical reality faced in building robust marketing strategies is that each company has its own unique strengths and weaknesses with respect to the competition, and its own distinctive capabilities. While the overarching imperative is customer focus, a key factor for competing successfully in ever-more competitive markets is to achieve an evolutionary fit between capabilities and the environment.

At a fundamental level, each organisation needs to understand its resource base. These are the skills and processes at which the company excels, and that can produce the next generation of products or services. At the next level, the organisation should be aware of its exploitable marketing assets. The resource-based marketing approach encourages organisations to examine systematically their current and potential assets in the marketplace and to select for emphasis those where they have a defensible uniqueness. Assets built up with customers in the marketplace are less prone to attack by competitors than low prices or easily imitated technologies.

Case study

Why Ford is stalling in China while Toyota succeeds

By Tom Hancock in Harbin

US car group suffered plummeting sales in 2018 as Japanese rival enjoyed bumper year

As Chinese workers returned to duty following a Lunar New Year break, the Changan Ford plant in the north-eastern city of Harbin remained empty, with staff on an extended vacation until March.

'It's a much longer break than last year, which was about a week,' said a security guard at the joint-venture plant, which opened in 2017 after a $1.1bn investment and can produce up to 200,000 Focus models a year.

Ford is one of several car makers cutting production in China, the world's largest car market where passenger vehicle sales fell 4 per cent to 23m last year, their first annual decline in almost three decades.

China accounts for 30 per cent of global car sales, and foreign brands make up two-thirds of the market. That means multinationals' joint ventures with Chinese car makers are heavily exposed to the downturn.

But not all have fared badly. Sales at Toyota's joint venture with Guangzhou Automobile surged nearly 35 per cent last year, while BMW's venture with Brilliance Auto saw a 20 per cent sales rise.

A Chinese worker at a Ford plant: Ford was late to set up in China, which has hit performance and caused layoffs
Source: Bloomberg / Contributor/Getty Images.

Their differing fates show a range of factors – from investment in new models, competitive exposure to local brands, dealer relations, after sales service, and quality perceptions – can determine a brand's success or failure in China.

With Beijing unwilling to offer large subsidies to car buyers and analysts forecasting a further decline in the market this year, it is crucial for investors to pay attention to factors behind the success and failure of different brands in the downturn.

China car sales fall

Source: Tom Hancock (2019), Why Ford is stalling in China while Toyota succeeds, Financial Times.

Ford: slow to bring new models to market

Ford had a late start in China, compared with rivals GM and Volkswagen. Slowed by years of corporate indecision and the impact of the 2008 financial crisis, it did not begin to make a mark on the market until 2012.

Its two joint ventures saw strong demand among consumers for the Escort, Focus and Edge brands. Ford's China sales in the four years to 2016 doubled to reach more than 1.2m. The Focus and Escort qualified for government subsidies on vehicles with engines of 1.6 litres or below introduced at the end of 2015.

But sales began to decline at its main joint venture, Changan, in 2017 as the subsidies began to be reduced, and plunged 54 per cent last year after they were eliminated. Analysts said the company was slow to bring new models to the market.

Two former workers told the *Financial Times* the tougher market conditions have led to hundreds of staff being laid off at the Changan Ford factory in Chongqing since December.

'Their problem is really the model cycle, the majority of their cars are in year five or six, that's when the sales drop rapidly,' said Jochen Siebert of consultancy JSC Automotive.

Ford remedied the problem last year, launching new saloon and hatchback versions of the redesigned Focus car, but by then the market was in a slump, making it harder to attract new buyers.

One consolation is that because of its late entry, China is a much smaller part of Ford's worldwide sales than for GM and Volkswagen, for which China is their biggest market. Ford's high-end Lincoln brand has fared less badly, reflecting stronger demand for premium vehicles.

PSA Group: mid-range brand suffers

The French owner of the Peugeot and Citroën brands saw sales at its joint venture with Dongfeng fall 44 per cent last year, with the fastest losses for its 408 and 308 brands.

Peugeot has also suffered from having older models but were also hit by their mid-range price position during last year's downturn, analysts said. Less well-off consumers refrained from buying cars or switched to second-hand models last year as subsidies were cut and economic growth slowed.

'Any car company that has many cars below Rmb150,000 suffered from the general market downturn,' said Mr Siebert. Because of an increasing supply of high-quality second-hand cars, 'in five years, almost no one will want to buy a new car for Rmb100,000 because they will realise they have a better option,' he added.

Analysts said PSA had been squeezed by increasing competition from local brands, such as Geely and BYD, which have moved up the value chain into mid-range cars, selling for about Rmb120,000 ($17,906), hiring teams of overseas designers to make their vehicles more attractive.

Chinese brands, particularly Geely, are taking market share from the less distinctively defined global brands. 'We can specifically point to Ford and Peugeot,' said Michael Dunne, an industry analyst and former GM executive. 'There's no doubt the Chinese brands are coming up so the global brands must move upscale or move out.'

Tougher local competition has also hit South Korea's Hyundai, whose sales last year barely grew from their six-year-low of 785,000 in 2017 when a diplomatic spat between Beijing and Seoul hit sales of South Korean consumer products.

'PSA is in the middle of the market and is squeezed by both ends as premium brands lower prices in the downturn,' said UBS analyst Paul Gong, a risk he added applies to other mass-market brands such as VW.

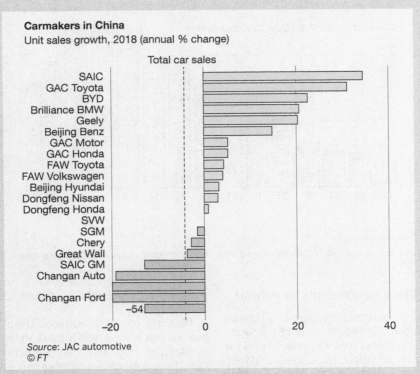

Carmakers in China
Unit sales growth, 2018 (annual % change)

Source: JAC automotive
© FT

Carmakers in China
Source: Tom Hancock (2019), Why Ford is stalling in China while Toyota succeeds, Financial Times.

JLR: popularity hit by repeated safety recalls

Britain's Jaguar Land Rover should have been well placed in a market where sales of more expensive, larger-engine vehicles have been strongest. But its sales fell 23 per cent in China last year.

Also a latecomer to the market, locally assembled products such as the Land Rover Evoque and Discovery, and Jaguar models helped the company raise its Chinese sales to 150,000 in 2017. It modified interiors to meet local tastes.

Analysts said JLR's reputation had suffered from repeated safety recalls in China – reportedly covering more than 100,000 vehicles in 2017. In January it recalled 68,828 vehicles in China over an engine safety hazard.

The brand received a four-star rating in a 2018 survey of Chinese customer satisfaction with post-sales service by JD Power, but that compared with peers such as Audi who gained five stars.

When sales began to fall, JLR continued with ambitious production targets, pushing inventory on to dealers who had to make stiff price cuts.

'Some car companies choose to revise down annual targets to help dealers, while others continue to push inventory, which makes dealers suffer,' said Patrick Yuan, an analyst at investment bank Jefferies. 'The relationship should be a partnership. They cannot fight each other.'

JLR began to cut production last year, and in January vowed to 'work closely with retailers in China to respond to the present market conditions'.

Toyota: reputation for quality boosts sales

Selling a record 1.5m vehicles in China last year, Japan's Toyota has defied the downturn, and it is targeting 7 per cent growth this year. Its Corolla model, which sells for about Rmb150,000, accounts for the bulk of its sales.

The brand has a strong reputation for quality in China and has consistently brought new products to the market, analysts said.

'Toyota stands out as an exception,' said Mr Dunne. 'They consistently deliver high-quality products, good service, and high resell value. The fundamental things that make Toyota a strong company are standing out in a tough market.'

The overall decline in car sales last year was partly because of consistently rising petrol prices, a trend that has benefited Toyota because of its strong fuel-economy and as consumers become more canny.

'Once you start to replace your second or third car, you probably realise that quality and fuel consumption are very important. In this regard Japanese cars do very well,' said Yale Zhang, founder of consultancy AutoForesight.

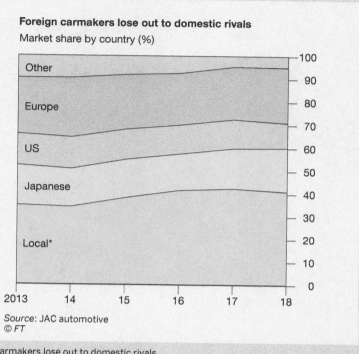

Foreign carmakers lose out to domestic rivals
Market share by country (%)

Source: JAC automotive
© FT

Foreign carmakers lose out to domestic rivals

Source: Tom Hancock (2019), Why Ford is stalling in China while Toyota succeeds, Financial Times.

Mercedes, BMW and Audi: wealthy continue to buy premium brands

About 3m premium vehicles were sold last year, as wealthier consumers have been less affected by the economic slowdown. Beijing Benz, a joint-venture between Daimler, which owns Mercedes-Benz, and BAIC Motor, saw 15 per cent sales growth last year. Volkswagen-owned Audi saw 11 per cent growth to 661,000 vehicles. Top-range brands face almost no local competition.

The premium players have concentrated on China's wealthiest first-tier cities, where car sales rose last year, whereas mid-range brands may have opened too many dealerships in lower-tier cities, where the market shrank.

'The mass-market brands have tried to have dealerships everywhere and in the end that might be a mistake,' said Mr Siebert. While not all brands can switch to luxury, they can learn from premium brands' investment, after-sales service and spending on training for dealer staff, he added.

BMW in October said it would take advantage of Beijing's abolition of joint venture requirements in the car sector in 2021 by buying a majority stake in its partner Brilliance Automotive. Mid-range brands could attempt to follow suit as they try to repeat the success of the luxury groups.

'Staying in a joint-venture operating at 50 per cent capacity and losing money is no fun in China,' said Mr Dunne. But many are partnered with stronger companies than Brilliance, who are likely to resist, leaving companies looking for alternatives.

'You could see a world in which Ford says let's allow the joint-venture to sustain itself, but we will set our sights on going it alone, or getting new partners.'

 Source: from 'Why Ford is stalling in China while Toyota succeeds', *Financial Times*, 04/03/19 (Hancock, T.).

Discussion questions

1 Why are foreign car manufacturers losing out to domestic rivals in China?
2 What are some of the resources required by foreign car manufacturers to succeed in China?
3 What resources have helped Ford succeed to start with in China and what new resources does the company need to develop/acquire to succeed in the future?

PART 3
IDENTIFYING CURRENT AND FUTURE COMPETITIVE POSITIONS

Part 3 addresses in more detail the issues and techniques behind segmentation and positioning research.

Chapter 7 discusses the underlying principles of competitive positioning and market segmentation, and their impact on the choice of target markets. The chapter continues by discussing in detail the logic of segmentation as an approach to identifying target markets, and by comparing the alternative bases for segmenting both consumer and business markets. The chapter closes by considering the benefits of identifying and describing market segments, but also the importance of integrating market segment-based strategies with corporate characteristics and competencies, as well as external factors.

Chapter 8 examines the techniques of segmentation and positioning research in detail. Two fundamentally different approaches are discussed. Under the first, termed *a priori*, the bases for segmenting are decided in advance and typically follow product/brand usage patterns or customer demographic characteristics. The second approach, *post hoc* or cluster based, searches for segments on the basis of a set of criteria, but without preconceived ideas as to what structure in the market will emerge. The chapter then discusses methods for collecting segmentation data (relating back to the marketing research methods discussed in Chapter 4), ways of analysing those data to identify and describe market segments, and addresses the issue of validating empirically the segmentation structure uncovered. The chapter next discusses both qualitative and quantitative approaches to positioning research. In the former, the use of focus groups and depth interviews to identify images and positions is examined. The chapter concludes with a discussion of quantitative approaches to creating perceptual maps.

Chapter 9 discusses choice of target market following the analysis of options. Two key dimensions are suggested for making the selection of target markets. First, the relative attractiveness of each potential segment. This will be dependent on many factors, including size, growth prospects, margins attainable, competitive intensity and so on. The second key dimension is the strength of the organisation in serving that potential target market. This is determined by the resources of the organisation, its current and potential marketing assets and the capabilities and competencies it can call on and deploy relative to competitors.

CHAPTER 7

SEGMENTATION AND POSITIONING PRINCIPLES

'Focussed competitors dominate their target segments – by fending off broad-coverage competitors who have to compromise to serve the segment, and out-performing rivals with the same focus . . . Focussed strategies also gain meaning from the differences between the segments covered and the rest of the market.'

G.S. Day (1994)

It takes a village: Why retired people could be ideal customers for self-driving cars

Autonomous vehicles come to retirement communities

New technologies, from the Walkman to the iPhone, have tended to be adopted first by the young. But when it comes to self-driving cars, the most logical early adopters are the retired. That, at least, is the conclusion reached by Voyage, a start-up based in Silicon Valley. It is testing its autonomous vehicles (AVs) in The Villages, a retirement community in Florida with a population of 125,000 people. Retirement towns are ideally suited to AVs for three reasons, says Oliver Cameron, Voyage's CEO.

Print edition | Business Feb 21st 2019
Source: Luke Beard/Voyage.

First, the environment is simpler and easier for an AV to navigate than a bustling city centre. Speed limits are lower, road layouts are less complex and there are fewer other vehicles.

Second, there is strong demand for mobility. Active retirees want the ability to get around but they may not want the expense and hassle of owning a car. For residents who are unable or have lost the confidence to drive, summoning a vehicle when needed has obvious appeal. Prototype AVs have attracted criticism and outright hostility from locals in some parts of America. Voyage has been warmly welcomed in The Villages, says Mr Cameron.

Third, there is a clear road to a large market. The Villages is America's largest retirement community and one of the fastest-growing residential areas in the country. 'We expect it to be the first city in the world to adopt AVs as the primary means of transport,' says Mr Cameron. The number of such communities is growing fast as America ages.

There are other reasons why retirement communities and AVs fit together neatly. People generally prefer to retire to warm, sunny regions, so there is little risk of snow confusing an AV's sensors. Because the roads are private property, there are fewer reporting requirements on AV operators and the regulatory situation is much simpler. And because everyone is retired, demand for rides is consistent throughout the day, which should make it easier to handle peaks without the need for a large fleet.

Voyage is now operating six prototype AVs in The Villages, with safety drivers on board for the time being to monitor performance and handle unexpected situations. It is also testing in a retirement community in San José. As part of its deal to become the exclusive provider of AV services in these places, Voyage granted a 0.5% stake in the firm to the owners of the two communities. That helps align incentives, says Mr Cameron. The final pricing model has yet to be decided. But he favours monthly contracts covering a certain number of trips (just as mobile-phone plans provide set amounts of calls and data).

Replacing car ownership for the aged may be easier than providing ride-sharing for young urbanites. 'The state of the art in AVs is not ready for downtown San Francisco,' says Mr Cameron. A 93-year-old woman who rode in one of Voyage's cars told him that she recalls travelling in a horse-drawn cab as a young girl. In old age, some people retreat into their past. But some Americans in retirement may already be living in the future.

Source: from *The Economist* print edition | Business (21/02/19).

Discussion questions

1 How could the market for self-driving cars be segmented?

2 Why are retirement towns suited for autonomous vehicles?

Introduction

Our approach to marketing analysis so far has rested largely on the identification and exploitation of key differences – in marketing capabilities and competitive strengths, for example. Our attention now focuses on two particularly important areas of differentiation: the differences between alternative market offerings as far as customers are concerned. That is, the **competitive positioning** of suppliers, products, services and brands and the differences between customers – in terms of their characteristics, behaviour and needs – that are important to marketing decision makers in developing strong marketing strategies and **market segmentation**.

The distinction between competitive positioning and market segmentation is illustrated in Figure 7.1, which suggests that the key issues are as follows:

- **Competitive positioning:** concerned with how customers perceive the alternative offerings on the market, compared with each other – for example, how do Audi, BMW and Mercedes medium-price saloon cars compare in value, quality and 'meaning' or image?
- **Market segmentation:** described as how we as marketers can divide the market into groups of similar customers, where there are important differences between those groups – for example, what are the characteristics of medium-price saloon car buyers that relate to their product preferences and buying behaviour?
- **Customer needs:** while positioning and segmentation are different concepts, ultimately they are linked by customer needs, in the sense that the most robust form of segmentation focuses on the customer benefits that matter most to different types of customer, while the strongest competitive positions to take are those where customers recognise that a supplier or product is the one they choose because it best meets their needs.

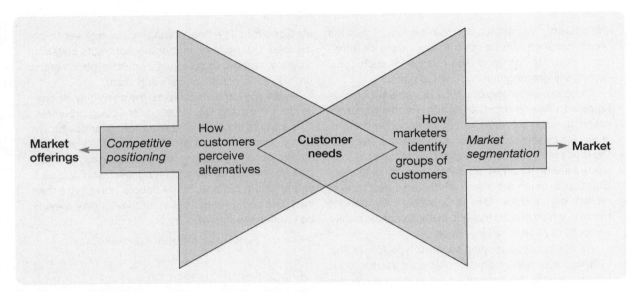

Figure 7.1 Competitive positioning and market segmentation

In this sense, positioning and segmentation are distinct parts of the strategy process and provide us with some extremely powerful tools; but, ultimately, they are linked by the central issue of focusing on satisfying the customer's needs in ways that are superior to competitors.

Operationally, positioning and segmentation may be linked in the way shown in Figure 7.2. This suggests that the sequence in planning can be the following:

- **Market segmentation:** identifying the most productive bases for dividing a market, identifying the customers in different segments and developing segment descriptions.
- **Choice of target markets:** evaluating the attractiveness of different market segments, parts of segments (niches) or groups of segments, and choosing which should be targets for our marketing.
- **Competitive positioning:** identifying the positioning of competitors (in the market and in target segments or niches), to develop our own positioning strategy.
- **Iteration:** understanding competitors' positioning and that the possible positioning strategies open to us should influence our thinking about the attractiveness of different market segments and the choice of market targets, and may change the way we segment our market, leading to revised target choices and positioning approaches.

Figure 7.2 Stages in segmentation and positioning

While they are distinct strategy concepts, there are important similarities between positioning and segmentation. Both start as issues of perception – how customers compare and understand alternative market offerings and how marketers understand the customer benefits different buyers seek from products and services. But both also are susceptible to rigorous research-based analysis.

We approach these issues in the following way. The role of this chapter is to distinguish between positioning and segmentation, and to clarify the underlying concepts and principles. From this foundation we move to an evaluation in Chapter 8 of the technical aspects of developing positioning and segmentation models. The implications for developing marketing strategies are found in Chapter 10 (on creating sustainable competitive advantage in target markets) and Chapter 18 (on the integration of positioning and segmentation to build robust marketing strategies for the future).

7.1 Principles of competitive positioning

Competitive positioning as an issue in developing marketing strategy has been defined in the following terms:

> Positioning is the act of designing the company's offering and image so that they occupy a meaningful and distinct competitive position in the target customers' minds.
> *(Kotler, 1997)*

The essential principle of competitive positioning is that it is concerned with how customers in different parts of the market perceive the competing companies, products/services or brands. It is important to bear in mind that positioning may apply to any of these levels:

- **companies:** for example, in grocery retailing in the United Kingdom the major competitors include Tesco, Sainsbury's and Asda, and positioning is based on these identities;
- **products and services:** positioning also applies at the level of the product, as shown in the example of Apple smartphones compared with similarly priced products from Samsung and Google;
- **brands:** competitive positioning is perhaps most frequently discussed in terms of brand identities: Coca-Cola versus Pepsi, and so on.

Indeed, some cases show the importance of these levels as they relate to each other – Virgin, for example, is a company that stands for certain values in customers' minds, which translates to the company's simplified financial services products, and provides the brand identity for diverse products and services.

Competitive positioning may be seen in some ways as the outcome of companies' attempts to create effective competitive differentiation for their products and services. However, Kotler (1997) suggests that not all competitive differences will create a strong competitive position; attempts to create differentiation should meet the following criteria:

- **importance:** a difference should create a highly valued benefit for significant numbers of customers;
- **distinctive and pre-emptive:** the difference cannot be easily imitated or performed better by others;
- **superior:** the difference should provide a superior way for customers to obtain the benefit in question;
- **communicable:** the difference should be capable of being communicated to customers and understood by them;
- **affordable:** the target customers can afford to pay for the difference;
- **profitable:** the difference will command a price adequate to make it profitable for the company.

One way of describing the outcome of the search for differences that matter to target customers, and how we perform them in a distinctive way, is the concept of the value proposition – the promise made to customers that encapsulates the position we wish to take compared with competitors. For example, Feather Furniture in the USA is a brand that aims to tap into the opportunities of the rental market. Founder Jay Reno launched the subscription-based furniture rental company in April 2017 to alleviate the pain points of those who find themselves in a temporary situation, while making it a cheaper and more sustainable (by not throwing away furniture) way of furnishing a home for a period of time.

Feather's main audiences are millennial renters and start-ups. Jay Reno spotted the opportunity from the fact that in the USA people move on average 12 times while at college, so 'it just doesn't make sense to own a bunch of things when you're moving constantly', he explains. There are 75 million millennials in the USA, making up 30 per cent of the market, according to Reno. So purely positioning itself to target this demographic rather than the wider population works for the company. 'There's this period of time which makes a lot of sense for someone like them [millennials] to use us', he says. 'It's definitely not a narrow market.'

A competitive position may be built on any dimensions of product or service that produce customer benefits in the market, but an important emphasis in positioning is that what matters is customer perception.

In fact the term 'positioning' was brought to prominence by Ries and Trout (1982) to describe the creative process, whereby:

> Positioning starts with a product. A piece of merchandise, a service, a company, or even a person . . . But positioning is not what you do to a product. Positioning is what you do to the mind of the prospect. That is, you position the product in the mind of the prospect.

The Ries and Trout approach to the 'battle for your mind' is highly orientated towards marketing communications and brand image while, as we have seen, competitive positioning is somewhat broader in recognising the impact of every aspect of the market offering that is perceived by customers as important in creating distinctive value. One way of summarising the underlying thinking is to focus on customer benefits and positioning in the customer's mind:

> You don't buy coal, you buy heat; you don't buy circus tickets, you buy thrills; you don't buy a paper, you buy news; you don't buy spectacles, you buy vision; you don't sell products, you create positions.

The importance of clear and strong competitive positioning is underlined by Kotler's (1997) warning of the major positioning errors (see Figure 7.3) that can undermine a company's marketing strategy:

- **Under-positioning:** when customers have only vague ideas about a company or its products, and do not perceive anything special about it, the product becomes an 'also-ran'.

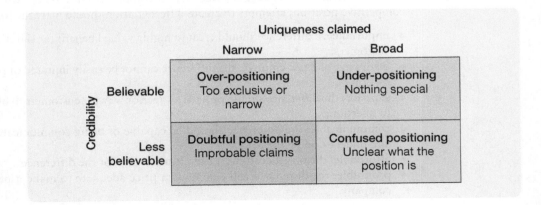

Figure 7.3
Positioning risks and errors

- **Over-positioning:** when customers have too narrow an understanding of the company, product or brand – for example, Mont Blanc sells pens that cost several thousand pounds, but it is important to that company for the consumer to be aware that a Mont Blanc pen can also be purchased for around £200.
- **Confused positioning:** frequent changes and contradictory messages may simply confuse customers about a company's positioning: Weight Watchers' rebranding exercise in late 2018 from a weight loss company to a wellness company, and the accompanying change of name to WW, initially confused typical customers who simply wanted to lose weight while failing to attract a new segment.
- **Doubtful positioning:** the claims made for the company, product or brand may simply not be accepted, whether or not they are true – for example, Coca Cola had to withdraw its Dasani brand of water from the UK having positioned it as 'pure, still water' when, in fact, it was purified tap water and shown to contain bromate, which is linked to increased risk of cancer. Dasani remains the number one brand of bottled water in the USA.

In essence, positioning is concerned with understanding how customers compare alternative offerings on the market and building strategies that describe to the customer how the company's offering differs in important ways from those of existing or potential competitors. Together with market segmentation, competitive positioning is central to the development of effective marketing strategies (see Chapter 10).

These characteristics of competitive positioning can be compared with the principles of market segmentation.

7.2   Principles of market segmentation

Two major features of modern markets are the extent to which they are capable of being segmented (because of growing differences between customers and their demands to be treated as individuals) and the existence of the vastly superior technologies of communication, distribution and production, which allow the pursuit of segmentation strategies. In some cases, this leads to 'micro-segmentation' or 'one-to-one marketing', in which each customer is treated as a different segment.

Where there are differences in customer needs or wants, or in their attitudes and predispositions towards the offerings on the market, between groups or individuals in the market, then there are opportunities to segment the market – to subdivide the larger market into smaller groups (segments) that provide market targets.

The history of thinking about market segmentation can be traced at least as far back as W.R. Smith (1956), who distinguished between strategies of product differentiation (applying promotional techniques to influence demand in favour of the product) and market segmentation (adjusting market offerings in various ways to more closely meet the requirements of different customers). Baker (1992) acknowledges this as the first coherent statement of a distinctive marketing view of market structure, representing a compromise between the economist's view of markets as single entities and the behavioural scientist's focus on individual buyer differences. Seen in this light, segmentation is a logical extension of the marketing concept and market orientation (see Chapter 1).

7.3   The underlying premises of market segmentation

Let us first consider the underlying requirements for market segmentation and take an overview of segmentation issues.

7.3.1 Underlying requirements for market segmentation

Three basic propositions underpin market segmentation as a component of marketing strategy:

1 For segmentation to be useful, customers must **differ from one another** in some important respect, which can be used to divide the total market. If they were not different in some significant way, if they were totally homogeneous, then there would be no need or basis on which to segment the market. However, in reality, all customers differ in some respect. The key to whether a particular difference is useful for segmentation purposes lies in the extent to which the differences are related to different behaviour patterns (different levels of demand for the product or service, or different use/benefit requirements) or susceptibility to different marketing mix combinations (different product/service offerings, media, messages, prices or distribution channels) – that is, whether the differences are important to how we develop a marketing strategy.

2 The operational use of segmentation usually requires that segment targets can be **identified by measurable characteristics** to enable their potential value as a market target to be estimated and for the segment to be identified. Crucial to utilising a segmentation scheme to make better marketing decisions is the ability of the marketing strategist to evaluate segment attractiveness and the current or potential strengths the company has in serving a particular segment. Depending on the level of segmentation analysis, this may require internal company analysis or external market appraisal. (The external market evaluation of segments and selection of market targets are discussed in Chapter 9.)

3 The effective application of segmentation strategy also requires that selected segments be **isolated** from the remainder of the market, enabling them to be targeted with a distinct market offering. Where segments are not distinct they do not form a clear target for the company's marketing efforts.

For any segmentation scheme to be useful it must possess these three characteristics.

7.3.2 Major issues in market segmentation

By way of overview, our general understanding of the issues to be addressed in studying and applying market segmentation falls into the following four areas, suggested by Piercy and Morgan (1993):

1 the methodology of market segmentation;
2 the criteria for testing segments as robust market targets;
3 the strategic segmentation decision itself;
4 the implementation of segmentation strategy in the company.

The methodology of market segmentation

The methodological tools available for use in developing segmentation schemes are concerned with two issues. First, there is the question of the choice of the variables or customer characteristics with which to segment the market – the 'bases' of market segmentation. Second, there is the related question of the procedures or techniques to apply to identify and evaluate the segments of the market. The bases for segmentation are considered in the next section of this chapter, and the techniques of market segmentation analysis are discussed in Chapter 8.

Testing the robustness of segments

If segments can be identified using the bases and techniques chosen, then there is the question of how they should be evaluated as prospective targets. In a classic paper, Frank *et al.* (1972) suggested that to provide a reasonable market target a segment should be measurable, accessible, substantial and unique in its response to marketing stimuli. These criteria remain the basis for most approaches (for example, see Kotler and Keller, 2016). In fact, evaluating market segments may be more complex than this suggests.

Strategic segmentation decision

If the market is susceptible to segmental analysis and modelling, and attractive segments can be identified, then the decision faced is whether to use this as the basis for developing marketing strategies and programmes, and whether to target the entire market or concentrate on part of it. (These issues of strategy are discussed in Chapter 9.)

Implementation of segmentation strategies

Finally, there is the question of the capabilities of the organisation for putting a segmentation approach into effect and, indeed, the extent to which corporate characteristics should guide the segmentation approach in the first place. These questions are considered at the end of this chapter.

7.4 Bases for segmenting markets

Some of the major issues in market segmentation centre on the bases on which the segmentation should be conducted and the number of segments identifiable as targets in a particular market. The selection of the base for segmentation is crucial to gaining a clear picture of the nature of the market – the use of different bases can result in very different outcomes. In fact, the process of segmentation and the creative selection of different segmentation bases can often help to gain new insights into old market structures that in turn may offer new opportunities – this is not merely a mechanical piece of statistical analysis.

In addition to choosing the relevant bases for segmentation, to make the segments more accessible to marketing strategy the segments are typically described further on common characteristics. Segments formed, for example, on the basis of brand preference may be further described in terms of customer demographic and attitudinal characteristics to enable relevant media to be selected for promotional purposes and a fuller picture of the chosen segments to be built.

In the next section we examine the major bases used in consumer markets, and in the following section we turn to industrial and business-to-business markets.

7.5 Segmenting consumer markets

The variables used in segmenting consumer markets can be broadly grouped into three main classes:

1 background customer characteristics;
2 customer attitudes;
3 customer behaviour.

The first two sets of characteristics concern the individual's predisposition to action, whereas the final set concerns actual behaviour in the marketplace.

7.5.1 Background customer characteristics for segmenting markets

Often referred to as classificatory information, background characteristics do not change from one purchase situation to another. They are customer-specific but not specifically related to their behaviour in the particular market of interest. Background characteristics can be classified along two main dimensions (see Figure 7.4).

The first dimension is the origin of the measures. The measures may have been taken from other disciplines and are hence not marketing specific but believed to be related

	Objective measures		Subjective measures
Non-marketing specific	**Demographics** Sex, age, geography, subculture, etc. **Socio-economics** Occupation, income, education	Psychographics	**Personality inventories**
Marketing specific	**Consumer life cycle** **ACORN** **Media usage**		**Lifestyle**

Figure 7.4
Background customer characteristics

to marketing activity. Non-marketing-specific factors include demographic and socio-economic characteristics developed in the fields of sociology and demography. Alternatively, measures may have been developed specifically by marketing researchers and academics to solve marketing problems. Typically, they have been developed out of dissatisfaction with traditional (sociological) classifications. Dissatisfaction with social class, as a predictor of marketing behaviour, for example, has led to the development of lifestyle segmentation and geodemographic segmentation such as the ACORN (A Classification Of Residential Neighbourhoods) and related classification schemes.

The second dimension to these characteristics is the way in which they are measured. Factors such as age or sex can be measured objectively, whereas personality and lifestyle (collectively termed 'psychographics') are inferred from often subjective responses to a range of diverse questions.

The commonest variables used are as follows.

Demographic characteristics

Measures such as age and gender of both purchasers and consumers have been one of the most popular methods for segmenting markets:

- **Gender:** a basic approach to segmentation of the market for household consumables and for food purchases is to identify 'housewives' as a specific market segment. For marketing purposes, 'housewives' can include both females and males who have primary responsibility for grocery purchase and household chores. This segmentation of the total potential market of, say, all adults will result in a smaller (around half the size) identified target. Many segmentation schemes use gender as a first step in the segmentation process, but then further refine their targets within the chosen gender category – by social class or age. In some markets, the most relevant variable is gender preference (such as the gay market) for certain products and services.

- **Age:** age has been used as a basic segmentation variable in many markets. The market for holidays is a classic example, with holiday companies tailoring their products to specific age groups, such as silver surfers, or even generations – from baby boomers to millennials to Generation Z. In these segmentation schemes, it is reasoned that there are significant differences in behaviour and product/service requirements between the demographic segments identified.

Cadbury Schweppes, for example, has developed new products aimed at young drinkers in pubs. One such product, Viking, is a chocolate-based energy snack that is marketed in Australia as 'the bar with horns'.

The main reasons for the popularity of age and gender as segmentation variables have been the ease of measurement of these characteristics (they can be objectively measured) and their usefulness for media selection purposes. Widely available syndicated media research studies present data on viewing and reading habits broken down by these characteristics. Matching media selected to segments described in these terms is, therefore, quite straightforward.

Age may also combine with other characteristics, such as life stage and socio-economics. This is the approach that Thomas Cook follows with their portfolio:

- Sunwing family resorts are aimed at middle-aged people;
- Suprime (high-end, adult only) hotels target older demographics than Sunwing;
- Manos (smaller authentic hotels) appeal to the millennials (Rogers, 2017).

Danone is another example of a company the has moved away from demographics and segments its market by what it calls 'tribes'. The company identified 16 tribes for its water brand Volvic in the UK and served each a short-form bumper ad on YouTube, which delivered a 40 per cent lift in ad recall. Tribes are people united by their passion points. They are defined by Danone's chief strategy and insights officer, Elaine Rogrigo, as 'people with meaningful similarities, but also people that we can find online and offline' (**https://www.youtube.com/watch?v=FWrPd0MNUlc**).

- **Geographic location:** geographic segmentation may be a useful variable, particularly for small- or medium-sized marketing operations that cannot hope to attack a widely dispersed market. Many companies, for example, choose to market their products in their home country only, implicitly excluding worldwide markets from their targets. Within countries it may also be possible to select regional markets where the company's offerings and the market requirements are most closely matched. Haggis, for example, sells best in Scotland, while sales of jellied eels are most successful in the East End of London.
- **Subculture:** each individual is a member of a variety of subcultures. These subcultures are groups within the overall society that have peculiarities of attitude or behaviour. For a subculture to be of importance for segmentation purposes, it is likely that membership of the subculture has to be relatively enduring and not transient, and that membership of the subculture is of central importance in affecting the individual's attitudes and/or ultimate behaviour.

   The major subcultures used for segmentation purposes are typically based on racial, ethnic, religious or geographic similarities. In addition, subcultures existing within specific age groupings may be treated as distinct market segments. For example, targeting 'micro-communities' has become important in relationship marketing – one Canadian bank has focused to great effect on the tightly knit but affluent Filipino community in Canada (Svendsen, 1997).

The major drawback of all these demographic characteristics discussed as bases for segmenting markets is that they cannot be guaranteed to produce segments that are internally homogeneous but externally heterogeneous in ways that are directly relevant to the marketer. Within the same demographic classes there can be individuals who exhibit very different behavioural patterns and are motivated by quite different wants and needs. Similarly, there may be significant and exploitable similarities in behaviour and motivations between individuals in different demographic segments. As a consequence, a generally low level of correspondence between demographics and behaviour has been found in the academic marketing research literature. Although still used due to their relative ease of measurement, demographics may be losing their popularity among some practitioners as the most common forms of segmentation owing to the wealth of customer data available to brands. Procter & Gamble (P&G), for example, has shifted the focus of its segmentation strategy by combining anonymous audience data covering 90 per cent of the US population with purchase data and analytics. This has allowed P&G to move from its traditional, generic demographic targets (for example, women or people aged between 25 and 60) to what its chief brand officer, Mark Pritchard, refers to as more than 350 precise 'smart audiences', which include first-time mums, new home owners and first-time washing machine owners.

Source: John Locher/AP/Shutterstock.

Socio-economic characteristics

Factors such as income, occupation, terminal education age and social class have been popular with researchers for similar reasons to demographics: they are easy to measure and can be directly related back to media research for media selection purposes. More importantly, the underlying belief in segmenting markets by social class is that the different classes are expected to have different levels of affluence and adopt different lifestyles. These lifestyles are, in turn, relevant to marketing-related activity, such as propensity to buy certain goods and services. Socio-economic measures are best seen in the use of social class groups.

Marketing researchers use several social class stratification schemes. The scheme used in the United Kingdom by the Market Research Society is presented in Table 7.1.

For many marketing purposes, the top two and bottom two classes are combined to give a four-group standard classification by social class: AB, C1, C2, DE. In the United States, several alternative social class schemes have been used for segmentation purposes (see Frank *et al.*, 1972). The most widely adopted, however, is that proposed by Warner, 1960 (see Table 7.2).

Social class has been used as a surrogate for identifying the style of life that individuals are likely to lead. The underlying proposition is that consumers higher up the social scale tend to spend a higher proportion of their disposable income on future satisfactions (such as insurance and investments), while those lower down the scale spend proportionately more on immediate satisfactions. As such, socio-economic class can be particularly useful in identifying segments in markets such as home purchase, investments, beer and newspapers.

The financial services industry makes extensive use of socio-economic groups for marketing, such as developing pensions and life assurance products aimed at particular social groups. One company is launching an occupational annuity to pay a higher pension to those in stressful or unhealthy jobs. Premiums and terms for private health insurance are partly determined by social class groupings (Gardner, 1997).

However, as with the demographic characteristics discussed previously, it is quite possible that members of the same social class have quite different purchase patterns and

Table 7.1 UK socio-economic classification scheme

Occupation groups		
	A	Approximately 3 per cent of the total population. These are professional people, very senior managers in business or commerce or top-level civil servants. Retired people, previously grade A, and their widows.
Non-manual	B	Approximately 20 per cent of the total population. Middle-management executives in large organisations, with appropriate qualifications. Principal officers in local government and civil service. Top management or owners of small business concerns, educational and service establishments. Retired people, previously grade B, and their widows.
	C1	Approximately 28 per cent of the total population. Junior management, owners of small establishments, and all others in non-manual positions. Jobs in this group have very varied responsibilities and educational requirements. Retired people, previously grade C1, and their widows.
Manual	C2	Approximately 21 per cent of the total population. All skilled manual workers, and those manual workers with responsibility for other people. Retired people, previously grade C2, with pensions from their job. Widows, if receiving pensions from their late husband's job.
	D	Approximately 18 per cent of the total population. All semi-skilled and unskilled manual workers, apprentices and trainees to skilled workers. Retired people, previously grade D, with pensions from their job. Widows, if receiving a pension from their late husband's job.
	E	Approximately 10 per cent of the total population. All those entirely dependent on the state long term, through sickness, unemployment, old age or other reasons. Those unemployed for a period exceeding six months (otherwise classify on previous occupation). Casual workers and those without a regular income. Only households without a chief income earner will be coded in this group.

Source: The Market Research Society.

Table 7.2 The Warner index of status characteristics

Class name	Description	Consumption characteristics
Upper-upper	Elite social class with inherited social position	Expensive, irrelevant, but purchase decisions not meant to impress; conservative
Lower-upper	Nouveau riche; highly successful business and professional; position acquired through wealth	Conspicuous consumption to demonstrate wealth, luxury cars, large estates, etc.
Upper-middle	Successful business and professional	Purchases directed at projecting successful image
Lower-middle	White-collar workers, small business people	Concerned with social approval; purchase decisions conservative; home and family orientated
Upper-lower	Blue-collar workers, technicians, skilled workers	Satisfaction of family roles
Lower-lower	Unskilled labour, poorly educated, poorly off	Attraction to cheap, 'flashy', low-quality items; heavy exposure to TV

reasons for purchase. Consider, for a moment, your peers – people you work with or know socially. The chances are they will be classified in the same social class as you. The chances are also that they will be attracted to different sorts of products motivated by different factors and make quite different brand choices.

Concern has been expressed among both marketing practitioners and academics that social class is becoming increasingly less useful as a segmentation variable. Lack of satisfaction with social class in particular and other non-marketing-specific characteristics such as segmentation variables has led to the development of marketing-specific measures such as stage of customer life cycle, geodemographics (such as the ACORN classification system) and the development of lifestyle research.

Consumer life cycle

Stage of the family life cycle, essentially a composite demographic variable incorporating factors such as age, marital status and family size, has been particularly useful in identifying the types of people most likely to be attracted to a product field (especially consumer durables) and when they will be attracted. The producers of baby products, for example, build (e)mailing lists of households with newborn babies on the basis of free gifts given to mothers in maternity hospitals. These lists are dated and used to direct advertising messages for further baby, toddler and child products to the family at the appropriate time as the child grows.

Center Parcs
Source: Center Parcs Ltd.

Stage of family life cycle was first developed as a market segmentation tool by Wells and Gubar (1966) and has since been updated and modified by Murphy and Staples (1979) to take account of changing family patterns. The basic life cycle stages are presented in Table 7.3.

In some instances, segmentation by life cycle can help directly with product design, as is the case with package holidays. In addition to using age as a segmentation variable, holiday firms target very specifically on different stages of the life cycle, from the Club Med emphasis on young singles, to Center Parcs family holidays, to coach operators' holidays for senior citizens.

In the United Kingdom, the Research Services Ltd marketing research company has developed a segmentation scheme based on a combination of consumer life cycle, occupation and income. The scheme, termed SAGACITY, defines four main life cycle stages (dependent, pre-family, family and late), two income levels (better off and worse off) and

Table 7.3 Stages of the family life cycle

Stage	Financial circumstances and purchasing characteristics
Bachelor Young, single, not living at parental home	Few financial burdens, recreation orientated; holidays, entertainments outside home
Newly wed Young couples, no children	Better-off financially, two incomes; purchase home, some consumer durables
Full nest I Youngest child under 6	Home purchasing peak; increasing financial pressures, may have only one income earner; purchase of household 'necessities'
Full nest II Youngest child over 6	Financial position improving; some working spouses
Full nest III Older married couples with dependent children	Financial position better still; update household products and furnishings
Empty nest I Older married couples, no children at home	Home ownership peak; renewed interest in travel and leisure activities; buy luxuries
Empty nest II Older couples, no children at home, retired	Drastic cut in income; medical services bought
Solitary survivor Still in labour force	Income good, but likely to sell home
Solitary survivor Retired	Special needs for medical care, affection and security

two occupational groupings (white collar and blue collar – ABC1 and C2DE). On the basis of these three variables, 12 distinct SAGACITY groupings are identified with different aspirations and behaviour patterns (see Crouch and Housden, 1996).

Some analysts have pointed out that the Baby Boomer generation has made a significant impact on marketing to the over 50s (Paul Fifield in *Marketing Business*, January 2002). Thirty years ago the 'Boomers' changed the way marketers dealt with the youth market, as they demanded more individualised and tailored products and services. Having now raised families and paid off mortgages they are approaching the 'empty nester' stage of the life cycle, but are likely to have very different expectations from previous generations of 50+ consumers. Generally fitter, well educated and more affluent, they pose very significant marketing opportunities for the future.

ACORN and related classificatory systems

As a direct challenge to the socio-economic classification system, the geodemographic ACORN system was developed by the CACI Market Analysis Group (**http://www.caci. co.uk/acorn-classification.aspx**). The system is based on population census data and classifies residential neighbourhoods into 36 types within 12 main groups (see Table 7.4). The

Table 7.4 ACORN – a classification of residential neighbourhoods

ACORN group	Description
A	Agricultural areas
B	Modern family housing, higher incomes
C	Older housing of intermediate status
D	Poor-quality older terraced housing
E	Better-off council estates
F	Less well-off council estates
G	Poorest council estates
H	Multiracial areas
I	High-status, non-family areas
J	Affluent suburban housing
K	Better-off retirement areas

groupings were derived from a clustering of responses to census data required by law on a ten-yearly basis. The groupings reflect neighbourhoods with similar characteristics.

Early uses of ACORN were by local authorities to isolate areas of inner-city deprivation (the idea came from a sociologist working for local authorities), but it was soon seen to have direct marketing relevance, particularly because the database enabled postcodes to be ascribed to each ACORN type. Hence its use particularly in direct mail marketing.

Other 'geodemographic' data sources are provided by such firms as Eurodirect, who developed CAMEO (**https://www.cameodynamic.com**), and Experian, with their MOSAIC classification system (**http://strategies.experian.co.uk/**).

Personality characteristics

Personality characteristics are more difficult to measure than demographics or socio-economics. They are generally inferred from large sets of questions, often involving detailed computational (multivariate) analysis techniques.

Several personality inventories have been used by segmentation researchers. Most notable are the Cattell 16-Personality Factor Inventory (see, for example, Oxx, 1972) and the Jackson Personality Inventory (see Kinnear et al., 1974). Both were developed by psychologists for reasons far divorced from market segmentation studies and have, understandably, achieved only varied levels of success when applied to segmentation problems.

Perhaps the main value of personality measures lies in creating the background atmosphere for advertisements and, in some instances, package design and branding. Research to date, however, primarily conducted in the United States, has identified few clear relationships between personality and behaviour. In most instances, personality measures are most likely to be of use for describing segments once they have been defined on some other basis. As with the characteristics discussed, behaviour (and reasons for behaviour) in personality-homogeneous segments may be diverse.

Lifestyle characteristics

In an attempt to make personality measures developed in the field of psychology more relevant to marketing decisions, lifestyle research was pioneered by advertising agencies in the United States and the United Kingdom in the early 1970s. This research attempts to isolate market segments on the basis of the style of life adopted by their members. At one stage these approaches were seen as alternatives to the social class categories discussed previously.

Lifestyle segmentation is concerned with three main elements: activities (such as leisure activities, sports, hobbies, entertainment, home activities, work activities, professional work, shopping behaviour, housework and repairs, travel and miscellaneous activities, daily travel, holidays, education and charitable work); interaction with others (such as self-perception, personality and self-ideal, role perceptions as mother, wife, husband, father, son, daughter, etc. and social interaction, communication with others and opinion leadership); and opinions (on topics such as politics, social and moral issues, economic and business–industry issues and technological and environmental issues).

A typical study would develop a series of statements (in some instances over 200 have been used) and respondents would be asked to agree or disagree with them on a five- or seven-point agree/disagree scale. Using factor analysis and cluster analysis, groups of respondents are identified with similar activities, interests and opinions. Examples include the following:

- In early lifestyle studies, Segnit and Broadbent (1973) found six male and seven female lifestyle segments on the basis of responses to 230 statements. These have been used to segment markets by publishers of newspapers (such as the *Financial Times* and *Radio Times*) and manufacturers (Beechams used the technique successfully to segment the shampoo market in the mid-1970s).
- Martini advertising has been directed at individuals on the basis of what lifestyle they would like to have. It appeals to 'aspirational lifestyle' segments.
- Ford Motor Company identified four basic lifestyle segments for its cars: traditionalists (who go for wood, leather and chrome); liberals (keen on environmental and safety features); life survivors (who seek minimum financial risk by going for the cheapest options); and adventurers (who actually like cars and want models to suit their own self-images) (*The Economist*, 30 September 1995).
- Marketing strategy at the House of Fraser department stores group relied on attracting three types of women clothes shoppers to the stores: the 'Follower of Fashion', the 'Smart Career Mover' and the 'Quality Classic – The Woman of Elegance'. The company deliberately decided not to target the 'Young Mum' and other buyers. In the mid-1990s there was some concern that House of Fraser products and merchandising did not attract the target segments (it was found that they tended to shop at House of Fraser only for the concession areas such as Oasis, Alexon and Morgan) (Rankine, 1996).
- B&Q, the UK DIY store, targeted style-conscious consumers with its portfolio of bedroom and office furniture branded 'it'. The range, created by interior designer Tara Bernerd, was modular, allowing customers to choose according to their taste and the dimensions of their home (*Marketing*, 24 January 2002).
- HelloFresh, the meal-kit company started in 2011 in Berlin, has more than 2 million active customers worldwide in 2019, which makes it market leader in the USA (with a 40 per cent share), UK, Germany, the Netherlands, Switzerland, Australia and five other countries (with a 70 per cent share). Its sales grew 43 per cent in the final quarter of 2018. The concept is to deliver to subscribers ready-portioned ingredients accompanied by recipe cards showing them how to prepare the meal at home. Meal-kits are viewed as healthier alternatives to take-aways and will appeal to people with busy lifestyles. Target consumers tend to be described as busy professionals and working parents who want to give their families healthy meals from scratch and need a helping hand in doing so. HelloFresh's vice-president argues that the concept is a response to modern lifestyles where time is precious. Unsurprisingly, its website's strapline is 'dinner is solved'.

The most significant advantages of lifestyle research are for guiding the creative content of advertising and customer acquisition. Because of the major tasks involved in gathering the data, however, it is thought unlikely that lifestyle research will supplant demographics as a major segmentation variable.

Summary of background customer characteristics

The background customer characteristics discussed previously all examine the individual in isolation from the specific market of interest. While in some markets they may be able to discriminate between probable users and non-users of the product class, they can rarely explain brand choice behaviour. Members of the same segments based on background characteristics may behave differently in the marketplace for a variety of reasons. Similarly, members of different segments may be seeking essentially the same things from competing brands and could be usefully grouped together. While traditionally useful for the purposes of media selection and advertising atmosphere design, these characteristics are often too general in nature to be of specific value to marketers. They are essentially descriptive in nature. They describe who the consumer is, but they do not uncover the basic reasons why the consumer behaves as they do.

7.5.2 Customer attitudinal characteristics for segmenting markets

Attitudinal characteristics attempt to draw a causal link between customer characteristics and marketing behaviour. Attitudes to the product class under investigation and attitudes towards brands on the market have both been used as fruitful bases for market segmentation.

Benefit segmentation

Classic approaches (such as Haley, 1968, 1984) examine the benefits customers are seeking in consuming the product. Segmenting on the basis of benefits sought has been applied to a wide variety of markets, such as banking, fast-moving consumer products and consumer durables. The building society investment market, for example, can be initially segmented on the basis of the benefits being sought by the customers. Typical benefits sought include high rates of interest (for the serious investor), convenient access (for the occasional investor) and security (for the 'rainy day' investor).

Nokia recognised that phones were seen by many customers as fashion accessories. The Nokia 5510, for example, was aimed at fashion-conscious young people who used their phones for text messaging and music. While the market in the late 1990s was dominated by first-time purchasers of phones, replacement purchases in Western Europe accounted for 60 per cent of sales in 2001 and were predicted to rise to nearer 99 per cent by 2006. The Samsung A400 phone had a flip-up lid in a red 'feminine' version, called the 'Ladyphone', with special features such as a biorhythm calculator, a 'fatness' function that calculates height-to-weight ratio and a calorie count function that estimates calories burnt for everyday activities such as shopping, cleaning and cooking. Nokia even launched a subsidiary named 'Vertu', which marketed platinum-cased handsets with sapphire crystal screens for the very rich (they retail at $21,000) (*Economist*, 26 January 2002). However, the company was later sold, and stopped trading altogether in 2017.

Benefit segmentation takes the basis of segmentation right back to the underlying reasons why customers are attracted to various product offerings. As such, it is perhaps the closest means yet to identifying segments on bases directly relevant to marketing decisions. Developments in techniques such as conjoint analysis make them particularly suitable for identifying benefit segments (Hooley, 1982).

Perceptions and preferences

A second approach to the study of attitudes is through the study of perceptions and preferences. Much of the work in the multi-dimensional scaling area (Green *et al.*, 1989) is primarily concerned with identifying segments of respondents who view the products on offer in a similar way (perceptual space segmentation) and require from the market similar features or benefits (preference segmentation). (This approach to market segmentation is discussed further in Chapter 8, where we are concerned with segmentation research.)

Summary of attitudinal bases for segmentation

Segmentation on the basis of attitudes, both to the product class and the various brands on offer, can create a more useful basis for marketing strategy development than merely background characteristics. It gets closer to the underlying reasons for behaviour and uses them as the basis for segmenting the market. The major drawback of such techniques is that they require often costly primary research and sophisticated data analysis techniques.

7.5.3 Customer behavioural characteristics for segmenting markets

The most direct method of segmenting markets is on the basis of the behaviour of the consumers in those markets. Behavioural segmentation covers purchases, consumption, communication and response to elements of the marketing mix.

Purchase behaviour

Study of purchasing behaviour has centred on such issues as the time of purchase (early or late in the product's overall life cycle) and patterns of purchase (the identification of brand-loyal customers):

- **Innovators:** because of their importance when new products are launched, innovators (those who purchase a product when it is still new) have received much attention from marketers. Clearly, during the launch of new products the isolation of innovators as the initial target segment could significantly improve the product's or service's chances of acceptance on the market. Innovative behaviour, however, is not necessarily generalisable to many different product fields. Attempts to seek out generalised innovators have been less successful than looking separately for innovators in a specific field. Generalisations seem most relevant when the fields of study are of similar interest.
- **Brand loyalty:** variously defined, brand loyalty has also been used as a basis for segmentation. While innovators are concerned with initial purchase, loyalty patterns are concerned with repeat purchase. As such, they are more applicable to repeat purchase goods than to consumer durables, though they have been used in durables markets (see the VW example that follows). As with innovative behaviour, research has been unable to identify consumers who exhibit loyal behaviour over a wide variety of products. Loyalty, as with innovativeness, is specific to a particular product field.

    Volkswagen, the German automobile manufacturer, has used loyalty as a major method for segmenting its customer markets. It divided its customers into the following categories: first-time buyers; and replacement buyers − (a) model-loyal replacers, (b) company-loyal replacers and (c) switch replacers. These segments were used to analyse performance and market trends and for forecasting purposes.

    In the context of e-marketing, companies such as Site Intelligence have devised methods of segmenting website visitors and purchasers using combinations of behavioural (visits) and demographic characteristics.

Consumption behaviour

Purchasers of products and services are not necessarily the consumers, or users, of those products or services. Examination of usage patterns and volumes consumed (as in the heavy user approach) can pinpoint where to focus marketing activity. There are dangers, however, in focusing merely on the heavy users. They are, for example, already using the product in quantity and therefore may not offer much scope for market expansion. Similarly, they will either be current company customers or customers of competitors.

Cook and Mindak (1984) have shown that the heavy user concept is more useful in some markets than in others. In the soap market they note that heavy users of soap account for

75 per cent of purchases. However, heavy users account for nearly half the population and constitute a very diverse group. By contrast, bourbon whiskey is consumed by around 20 per cent of adults only, and the heavy users account for 95 per cent of consumption, making this a much tighter target market.

In the latter case, brand-loyalty patterns may be set and competition could be fierce. Companies may be better advised to research further the light or non-users of the product to find out why they do not consume more of the product. In the growth stage of the product life cycle the heavy user segment may well be attractive, but when the market reaches maturity it may make more sense to try to extend the market by mopping up extra potential demand in markets that are not adequately served by existing products.

Product and brand usage has a major advantage over many other situation-specific segmentation variables in that it can be elicited, in the case of many consumer products, from secondary sources. The 'heavy users' of beer, for example, can be identified through the Target Group Index (TGI – see Chapter 4) and their demographic and media habits profiled. For this main reason, consumption is one of the most popular bases for segmenting consumer markets in the UK.

Communication behaviour

A further behavioural variable used in consumer segmentation studies has been the degree of communication with others about the product of interest.

Opinion leaders can be particularly influential in the early stages of the product life cycle. Recording companies, for example, recognise the influence that disc jockeys have on the record-buying public and attempt to influence them with free music and other inducements to play their CDs. In many fields, however, identifying opinion leaders is not so easy. As with innovators, opinion leaders tend to lead opinion only in their own interest areas. A further problem with satisfying opinion leaders is that they tend to have fairly strong opinions themselves and can often be a very heterogeneous group (disc jockeys providing a good example).

In addition to information-giving behaviour (as displayed by opinion leaders), markets could be segmented on the basis of information-seeking behaviour. The information seekers may be a particularly attractive segment for companies basing their strategy on promotional material with a heavy information content.

Response to elements of the marketing mix

The use of elasticities of response to changes in marketing-mix variables as a basis for segmentation is particularly attractive as it can lead to more actionable findings, indicating where marketing funds can best be allocated. Identifying, for example, the deal-prone consumer or the advertising-responsive segment has immediate appeal. There are, however, methodological problems in research in identifying factors such as responsiveness to changes in price.

Relationship-seeking characteristics

A related characteristic for segmentation that is attracting some attention in the light of the move towards relationship marketing (see Chapter 4) is the relationship requirements of customers. One initial model suggests that the relationship-seeking characteristics of customers differ in the type of relationship customers want with suppliers (for example, long term versus short term and transactional) and the intimacy customers want in the relationship (for example, close or distant). This suggests the potential for segmenting markets into such groups as the following, and linking this to other variables:

- **relationship seekers:** who want a close, long-term relationship with the supplier or retailer;
- **relationship exploiters:** who want only a short-term relationship with the supplier, but are happy with a close relationship, which they will exploit for any advantages on offer;

- **loyal buyers:** who want a long-term relationship, but at a distance;
- **arm's-length transaction customers:** who do not want close relationships with suppliers and will shop around for the best deal because they see no value in a long-term relationship.

An example of an integrated study of consumer characteristics on a global scale is work done by the US agency Roper Starch (Shermach, 1995). International business has much interest in whether consumer segments cut across national boundaries and may be more useful than traditional geographical approaches to planning marketing. The study identified the following segments from 40,000 respondents in 40 countries:

- **deal-makers:** well educated, aged in their early 30s, with average affluence and employment (29 per cent of the sample);
- **price-seekers:** a high proportion of retirees and lowest education level with an average level of affluence and more females than males (23 per cent of the sample);
- **brand loyalists:** mostly male, aged in their mid-30s, with average education and employment, and the least affluent group (23 per cent of the sample);
- **luxury innovators:** the most educated and affluent shoppers, mostly male, in professional and executive employment; they seek new, prestigious brands (21 per cent of the sample).

The proportions of consumers in these groups varies in interesting ways across the geographic areas: deal-makers predominate in the United States, Asia, Latin America and the Middle East; price-seekers exist mainly in competitive developed markets such as Europe and Japan. Although producing only stereotypes, the study suggests that consumer behavioural and purchase characteristics may be stronger predictors of purchase behaviour than the traditional country–market definitions used in export and international marketing.

Summary of behavioural bases for segmentation

Many variables have been tested as bases for consumer segmentation, ranging from behaviour, to attitudes, to background characteristics. The most often-used characteristics are product and brand usage and demographics/socio-economics, primarily because of the ease of obtaining this sort of data from secondary sources. Ultimately, however, for a segmentation scheme to be useful to marketing management it should seek not only to describe differences in consumers but also to explain these differences. In this respect, the development of consumer insights supported by sophisticated data analytics helps companies refine the way they segment the market and improves the effectiveness of their marketing strategies. 'Regardless of the approach to segmentation marketers choose to take, the strategy first and foremost must be objective led. Whether looking at a specific demographic, or focusing on a behavioural insight, attitude or life stage, the key is to be clear about what you want to achieve and resist trading in stereotypes' (Rogers, 2019).

7.6	Segmenting business markets

As with consumer markets, a wide variety of factors has been suggested for segmenting business markets, but in fact business segmentation variables can be considered under the same headings as those for consumer markets:

- background company characteristics;
- attitudinal characteristics;
- behavioural characteristics.

It should be noted, however, that market segmentation is substantially less well developed in business marketing than consumer marketing, which may affect both the acceptability of different approaches to companies and the availability of information and support to use a particular approach. It should also be noted that in business-to-business marketing it is far more common to find a one-to-one relationship between supplier and customer. In this situation, the segmentation approach may best be applied inside the customer organisation. The following segmentation structure utilises the model developed in Shapiro and Bonoma (1990).

7.6.1 Background company characteristics

Demographic characteristics of companies can be a useful starting point for business segmentation; indeed, they characterise the approaches most commonly used by business marketing companies. Factors that can be considered here include demographics such as industry type, customer size and location, but also operating variables such as customer technology and capabilities, different purchasing policies and situational factors including product application.

Industry type

Factors such as the Standard Industry Classification (SIC) provide a first stage of analysis, both for identifying target industries and subdividing them into groups of companies with different needs or different approaches to buying. This may be the basis for vertical marketing to industry sectors. Retailers and hospitals, for example, both buy computers, but they have different applications and different buying strategies.

Company size

Size may also be highly significant if, for instance, small companies have needs or buying preferences that are distinctly different from those of larger companies. Typical measures would be variables such as number of employees and sales turnover. Size may be very significant because it impacts on issues such as volume requirements, average order size, sales and distribution coverage costs and customer bargaining power, which may alter the attractiveness of different segments as targets. Company size may be analysed alongside other demographics. Companies, for example, selling ingredients for paint manufacture in the United Kingdom could initially segment the market by SIC to identify paint manufacturers, then by size of company as indicated by number of employees (there are only seven companies employing more than 750 employees and together they account for over 60 per cent of the paint market).

Customer location

The geographic location of customers may be a powerful way of segmenting the market for a business product for several reasons. Domestically, location will impact on sales and distribution costs and competitive intensity may vary if there are strong local competitors in some regions. Increasing concerns over the carbon footprint of sourcing are leading some firms to concentrate their supply, where possible, more locally. For example, leading supermarkets such as Waitrose have developed policies to source as many fresh food products locally as possible.

Product demand may vary also – the demand for chemicals for water softening in operating cooling equipment in factories will vary according to local water hardness conditions. Internationally, product preferences may also be different by location – medical diagnostic products are sold to the National Health Service in the United Kingdom, but to private testing agencies and medical practices in the United States, and to hospital laboratories in the developing world, all of whom display very different product and price requirements.

Company technology

The customer's stage of technology development will impact directly on its manufacturing and product technology, and hence on its demand for different types of product. Traditional factories operating mixed technologies and assembly methods require different product and sub-assembly inputs (such as test equipment, tooling, components) compared with the auto-mated production unit. High-technology businesses may require very different distribution methods – Tesco requires suppliers to have the capability to cooperate in electronic stock control and cross-docking to avoid retail stockholding. Increasingly, high-technology firms require that their suppliers are integrated to their computer systems for all stages of the purchase process.

Customer capabilities

Business customers may differ significantly in their internal strengths and weaknesses, and hence their demand for different types of product and service. For example, in the chemicals industry customers are likely to differ in their technical competencies – some will depend on their suppliers for formulation assistance and technical support far more than others. For many years in the computer business, Digital Equipment specialised in selling mini-computers to customers who were able to develop their own software and systems, and did not need the full-service offering of IBM and others; it targeted a segment on the basis of the customers' technical strength in computing.

Purchasing organisation

How customers organise purchasing may also identify important differences between custom-ers. For example, centralised purchasing may require suppliers to have the capability to operate national or international account management, while decentralised purchasing may require more extensive field sales operations. Depending on a supplier's own strengths and weak-nesses, the purchasing organisation type may be a significant way of segmenting the market. IBM, for example, has always maintained a strong position in companies with a centralised IT department, while other suppliers have focused on companies where IT is less centralised.

Power structures

The impact of which organisational units have the greatest influence may also be effective in segmenting a market to identify targets matching a supplier's strengths. Digital Equipment traditionally targeted engineering-led customers, where its strengths in engineering applica-tions gave it a competitive edge.

Purchasing policies

The way different customers approach purchasing may also be a source of targeting informa-tion. Customers might divide, for example, into those who want a lease-based deal versus those who want to purchase; those with affirmative action policies versus those dominated by price issues; those who want single supply sources versus those who want to dual-source important supplies; public sector and similar organisations where bidding is obligatory versus those preferring to negotiate price; those actively pursuing reductions in their sup-plier base compared with others. Indeed, the model proposed previously, of the customer's relationship requirements as a basis for segmenting, may be even more useful in the business market, where the demand for partnership between suppliers and customers characterises many large companies' approaches to purchasing.

Product application

The product application can have a major influence on the purchase process and criteria and hence supplier choices. The requirements for a small motor used in intermittent service for a minor application in an oil refinery will differ from the requirements for a small motor in continuous use for a critical process.

7.6.2 Attitudinal characteristics

It is possible also to segment business markets on the basis of the benefits being sought by the purchasers. As we saw, benefit segmentation in the consumer market is the process of segmenting the market in terms of the underlying reasons why customers buy, focusing particularly on differences in why customers buy. Its strength is that it is segmentation based on customer needs. In the business market, the same logic applies to the purchasing criteria of different customers and product applications.

This may be reflected, for example, in urgency of order fulfilment – the urgency of a customer's need to keep a plant in operation or to solve a problem for its own customers may change both the purchase process and the criteria used. Urgent replacements may be bought on the basis of availability, not price. A chemical plant needing to replace broken pipe fittings will pay a premium price for a supplier's applications engineering, flexible manufacturing capacity, speed of delivery and installation skills, while a plant buying pipe fittings to be held in reserve would behave quite differently.

One corporate bank struggled to find a way of segmenting the UK market for corporate financial services; they concluded that the most insightful approach was to examine their customers' own strategies as a predictor of financial service product need and purchasing priorities.

An added complication in business markets, however, is the decision-making unit (DMU) (see Chapter 4). For many business purchases, decisions are made or influenced by a group of individuals rather than a single purchaser. Different members of the DMU will often have different perceptions of what the benefits are, both to their organisation and to themselves.

In the purchase of hoists, for example, the important benefit to a user may be lightness and ease of use, whereas the purchasing manager may be looking for a cheaper product to make their purchasing budget go further. Architects specifying installations for a new plant may perceive greater benefit in aesthetically designed hoists while maintenance personnel may look for easy maintenance as a prime benefit.

Benefit segmentation is at the centre, however, of conventional wisdom on selling in business markets. Here the emphasis is on selling benefits rather than features of the product or service. In communicating with the different members of the DMU, different benefits may be emphasised for each.

7.6.3 Behavioural characteristics

Behavioural issues relevant to segmenting business markets may include buyers' personal characteristics and product/brand status and volume.

Buyers' personal characteristics

Although constrained by company policies and needs, business products are bought by people in just the same way that consumer products are. Business goods markets can be segmented by issues such as the following:

- **buyer–seller similarity:** compatibility in technology, corporate culture or even company size may be a useful way of distinguishing between customers;
- **buyer motivation:** purchasing officers may differ in the degree to which they shop around and look at numerous alternative suppliers, and dual-source important products and services, as opposed to relying on informal contacts for information and remaining loyal to existing personal contacts;
- **buyer risk perceptions:** the personal style of the individual, intolerance of ambiguity, self-confidence and status within the company may also provide significant leverage.

For example, for many years in the computer industry IBM focused on IT buyers in major corporates, providing training information and career development support, to build the 'IBM closed shop' where other suppliers were largely excluded.

Product/brand status and volume

The users of a particular product, brand or supplier may have important things in common that can make them a target. For example, customers may differ in the rate and extent of the adoption of new safety equipment in plants. Companies loyal to a specific competitor may be targeted – for instance, to attack that competitor's weaknesses in service or product. Current customers may be a different segment from prospective customers or lost customers.

High-volume product users may be different from medium and low users in how they purchase. Even more than in consumer markets, the 80/20 rule (80 per cent of sales typically being accounted for by only 20 per cent of customers) can dominate a business market. Identifying the major purchasers for products and services through volume purchased can be particularly useful. Also of interest may be the final use to which the product or service is put. Where, for example, the final consumer can be identified, working backwards can suggest a sensible segmentation strategy.

The paint market, for example, can be segmented at various levels. At the first level it can be divided into 'decorative paints' (mainly used on buildings) and 'industrial paints' (used in manufactured products). General industrial paints by volume represented 33 per cent of the UK market, the automobile industry 5 per cent, professional decorative 42 per cent and DIY decorative 22 per cent. Demand for vehicle paints relates to automobile sales (derived demand) and relates closely to demand in this market. In the general industrial paints sector, there are various specialist segments such as marine coatings. Here, ultimate product use dictates the type of paint and its properties and is the basic method for segmentation.

7.6.4 Summary of bases for segmenting business markets

The segmentation bases available for business marketing follow business buying behaviour, as those in consumer marketing follow consumer buying behaviour. Because of the presence, however, of particularly large individual customers in many business markets, usage-based segmentation is often employed. For smaller companies, geographic segmentation may be attractive, limiting their markets to those that are more easily served. Ultimately, however, in business and consumer markets the basic rationale for segmentation is that groups of buyers exist with different needs or wants (benefits sought) and it is segmentation on the basis of needs and wants that offers the closest approach to implementing the marketing concept.

| 7.7 | **Identifying and describing market segments** |

It will be clear that the first task the manager faces is to decide on what bases to segment the market. If product usage or background characteristics are selected, in many markets the segmentation can be accomplished from secondary sources (for example, from TGI or AGB/TCA in UK consumer markets, or from SIC or Kompass in business markets). Where segmentation is based on attitudes, however, there will often be insufficient data available from secondary sources. In these cases, primary research will be necessary.

A typical primary research segmentation study could include initial qualitative research to identify major benefits to users and purchasers of the product or service under consideration. This would be followed by quantitative research to estimate the size of the potential segments and to describe them further in terms of other background characteristics. This methodological approach is described in the seminal work by Haley (1968).

7.7.1 First-order and second-order segmentation

There is a frequent misconception among marketing managers as to what constitutes a market segment.

In consumer marketing, in particular, many managers will describe the segmentation of their market and their selected market targets in terms of customer background characteristics. Thus, for example, a marketer of quality wines might describe the segmentation of the market in terms of social class, the prime target being the ABC1 social classes. From our previous discussion, however, it can be seen that this way of segmenting the market is adequate only if all members of the ABC1 group purchase quality wine for the same reasons and in the same way. Where use/benefits of wine purchase differ substantially within a given social class, there is the opportunity to segment the market in a more fundamental way.

In reality, the most fundamental way of segmenting markets is the market-orientated approach of grouping together customers who are looking for the same benefits in using the product or service. All other bases for segmenting markets are really an approximation of this. The wine marketer assumes that all ABC1s have similar benefit needs from the wines they purchase. Hence use/benefit segmentation can be referred to as **first-order segmentation**. Any attempt to segment a market should commence by looking for different use/benefit segments.

Within identified use/benefit segments, however, there could be large numbers of customers with very different backgrounds, media habits, levels of consumption and so on. Particularly where there are many offerings, attempting to serve the same use/benefit segment concentration on sub-segments within the segment can make sense. Sub-segments, for example, who share common media habits, can form more specific targets for the company's offerings. Further segmentation within use/benefit segments can be termed **second-order segmentation**. Second-order segmentation is used to improve the ability of the company to tailor the marketing mix within a first-order segment.

In the wine example, the marketing manager may have identified a first-order segmentation in terms of the uses to which the wine was being put (as a meal accompaniment, as a home drink, as a social drink, as a cooking ingredient). The quality-level of the wine might suggest use in the first segment as a meal accompaniment. Further research would then reveal within this segment further benefit requirements (such as price bands individual customers are prepared to consider, character of the wine preferred, etc.).

Having further refined the target through matching the company's offerings to specific customer group requirements, the marketer may still find a wide variety of potential customers for their wines. Within the identified first-order segment, sub-segments based on demographic characteristics could be identified (for example, AB social class, aged 35–55, male purchaser), thus enabling a clearer refinement of the marketing strategy.

7.8   The benefits of segmenting markets

There are a number of important benefits that can be derived from segmenting a market, which can be summarised in the following terms:

- Segmentation is a particularly useful approach to marketing for the smaller company. It allows target markets to be matched to company competencies (see Chapter 6), and makes it more likely that the smaller company can create a defensible niche in the market.
- It helps to identify gaps in the market – that is, unserved or underserved segments. These can serve as targets for new product development or extension of the existing product or service range.
- In mature or declining markets it may be possible to identify specific segments that are still in growth. Concentrating on growth segments when the overall market is declining is a major strategy in the later stages of the product life cycle.
- Segmentation enables the marketer to match the product or service more closely to the needs of the target market. In this way, a stronger competitive position can be built (see Jackson, 2007, for the importance for companies of determining their strategic market position). This is particularly important in the Internet age, where companies compete in a large and heterogeneous community (see Barnes *et al.*, 2007).
- The dangers of not segmenting the market when competitors do so should also be emphasised. The competitive advantages noted previously can be lost to competitors if the company fails to take advantage of them. A company practising a mass-marketing

strategy in a clearly segmented market against competitors operating a focused strategy can find itself falling between many stools.

- Malcolm McDonald, after over 40 years of research into the link between long-term financial success and marketing strategies, maintains that 'market segmentation is one of the most fundamental concepts of marketing and is the key to successful business performance' (McDonald, 2017), hence shareholder value – particularly in a world where such value is increasingly intangible coming, in particular, from brands and customer relationships. He argues that this demonstrates how critical customer selection is. Indeed, this is supported by Christensen, who attributed the failure of 90 per cent of 30,000 new product launches in the USA to inadequate market segmentation (Christensen *et al.*, 2005). (For a comprehensive review of market segmentation, please see McDonald and Dunbar, 2012.)

7.9   Implementing market segmentation

It should also be noted that there is evidence that companies often struggle with the implementation of segmentation-based strategies, and fail to achieve the potential benefits outlined previously (see Piercy and Morgan, 1993; Dibb and Simkin, 1994) – this is the difference between segmentation as a normative model and as a business reality (Danneels, 1996).

7.9.1 The scope and purpose of market segmentation

There is growing recognition that conventional approaches may pay insufficient attention to identifying the scope of market segmentation (Plank, 1985). Indeed, a seminal paper by Wind (1978) proposed that in selecting segmentation approaches it is necessary to distinguish between segmentation that has the goal of gaining a general understanding of the market and use for positioning studies, and segmentation concerned with marketing programme decisions in new product launches, pricing, advertising and distribution. These are all valid and useful applications in segmentation analysis, but they are fundamentally different.

7.9.2 Strategic, managerial and operational levels of segmentation

One approach to making the scope of market segmentation clearer is to distinguish between different levels of segmentation, in the way shown in Figure 7.5 (Piercy and Morgan, 1993).

This approach is similar to the first-order and second-order segmentation distinction made previously, but goes further in relating the levels of segmentation to organisational issues as well as customer issues. The nature of the different levels of segmentation can be described as follows:

- **Strategic segmentation** is related to management concerns for strategic intent and corporate mission, based on product/service uses and customer benefits.
- **Managerial segmentation** is concerned primarily with planning and allocating resources such as budgets and personnel to market targets.
- **Operational segmentation** focuses on the issue of aiming marketing communications and selling efforts into the distribution channels that reach and influence market targets (and their subdivisions).

These differences are important to gaining insight into what segmentation can contribute to building marketing strategy and competitive positioning, but also to understanding the sources of implementation problems with segmentation-based strategies. For example, when the manager responsible for marketing replacement car exhausts to car owners groups

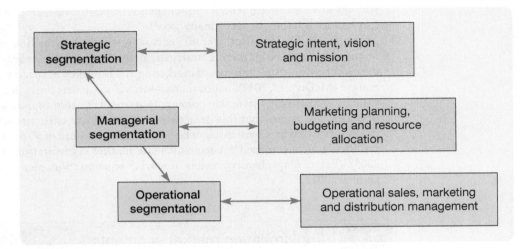

Figure 7.5 Levels of segmentation

their customers in terms of their fears, ignorance and transport dependence, rather than their requirements for different product specifications and engineering, they are concerned with creating a new understanding of the market (strategic segmentation), not a model for the detailed application of marketing resources (operational segmentation). When the corporate banker looks at the corporate banking market in terms of the strategic financial services needs of customers, based on their own corporate strategies (Carey, 1989), the goal is to create a framework for strategy, not a mechanism for advertising and salesforce allocation.

On the other hand, when advertisers and sales managers describe buyers in terms of socio-economic groups, geographic location or industrial sector, they are concerned with the effective targeting of advertising, sales promotion, selling and distribution resources, rather than describing customer benefit-based market segments. Market segmentation studies that describe consumer groups in terms of their media behaviour – for example, as 'mainstream media rejecters', 'genteel media grazers', '30-somethings' and so on (Laing, 1991) – are concerned with operational effectiveness, not strategic positioning.

Confusing these very different roles for segmentation may be why segmentation is sometimes seen as a failure in organisations:

> Failed segmentation efforts tend to fall into one of two categories: the marketer-dominated kind, with little data to support its recommendations, or the purely statistical type that identifies many consumer differences that aren't germane to the company's objectives.
>
> *(Young, 1996)*

The implication is that clarifying the role and purpose of an approach to segmentation may be important to avoid unrealistic expectations. However, it is clear that segmentation-based strategies do sometimes fail at the implementation stage.

7.9.3 Sources of implementation problems

The recognition of implementation problems with segmentation-based strategies may be traced back over the years: Wind (1978) noted that little was known about translating segment research into marketing strategies; Young *et al.* (1978) accused marketers of being preoccupied with segmentation technique rather than actionability; Hooley (1980) blamed segmentation failures on the use of analytical techniques for their own sake and poor communication between managers and marketing researchers; Shapiro and Bonoma (1990) wrote: 'Much has been written about the strategy of segmentation, little about its implementation, management and control', and this would still seem a valid conclusion.

Piercy and Morgan (1993) attempted to catalogue the sources of implementation failure with segmentation-based strategies, and these issues provide a further screening device for evaluating the suitability of a segmentation model generated through market research. Issues to assess include the following:

- **Organisation structure:** companies tend to organise into functional departments and sub-units of one kind or another, depending on their task allocation and how they deal with the outside world. A customer-benefits approach to establishing market targets may cut across these internal divisions – they may not 'fit' with the jurisdiction of departments or regional organisations for sales and marketing. Segment targets that fall between departments and regions may be neglected and lack 'ownership', and the strategies built around them will fail. We need to map carefully how segment targets will match the internal organisation structure.

- **Internal politics:** Young (1996) argues that strategic segmentation is essentially a cross-functional activity, requiring expertise and involvement by many functional specialists. If functions cannot collaborate or work together because people are vying for power and withholding their knowledge and expertise, the segmentation strategy is likely to fail. If our segmentation-based strategy relies on internal collaboration and cooperation, we need to be sure this can be achieved, or the strategy will fail.

- **Corporate culture:** In some circumstances, customer-benefit segmentation is unacceptable to people inside an organisation, because it is not how they understand the world. Organisations dominated by strong professional groups frequently have struggles with customer-benefit segments – examples are traditional financial service companies and professional service firms such as law and accountancy.

- **Information and reporting:** Novel segmentation schemes may not fit with existing information systems and reporting systems. This may mean it is difficult to evaluate the worth of segment targets, or to allocate responsibilities and monitor performance in doing business with them.

- **Decision-making processes:** If segmentation schemes identify new market targets that are not recognised in plans (they are not currently part of the served market, they are spread across existing segment targets for which responsibility has been allocated, or they are subsumed within an existing segment), then they may be ignored in the planning process and when plans are implemented. Similarly, segment targets that are not recognised by existing resource allocation processes may face difficulty in getting a marketing budget. We should examine carefully how a new segmentation approach can be integrated with planning and budgeting and in evaluation systems.

- **Corporate capabilities:** It is all too easy for marketing researchers and analysts to develop attractive market targets, but a company may have little basis for achieving a competitive advantage simply because it lacks the capabilities for dealing with this type of customer (see Chapter 6).

- **Operational systems:** Segmentation strategy may fail because it underestimates the problems faced at the operational level in translating segmentation strategy into effective reality. Can salespeople deal with this target customer? Do we have access to the distribution channels we need? Do we have the expertise to develop and operate segment-based advertising and promotion? Do we have market research organised around the segment targets so that we can identify them, measure opportunities and evaluate progress? Do we have the technical facilities to price differently to different customer types if this is required? We should look very carefully at the operational capabilities we have in sales, advertising, promotion and distribution, and question their ability to adapt to a new segmentation-based strategy.

Many of these issues are covert and hidden inside the organisation, yet to ignore them is to place the strategy at risk. One proposal is that in addition to the conventional evaluation of market targets, each potential target should be tested for internal compatibility, as suggested in Figure 7.6.

Figure 7.6 Market segment attractiveness and organisational resource strength

This analysis may suggest that some market targets are unattractive because they have a poor 'fit' with the company's structures and processes, or even that the company is not capable of implementing a segmentation-based strategy at the present time, or it may identify the areas that need to be changed if the segment target is to be reached effectively.

Summary

In increasingly fragmented markets, marketers in both consumer and business markets are turning more and more to segmentation methods to identify prime market targets. In approaching market segmentation, companies must confront the sometimes quite sophisticated methodology of segmentation, test the market targets identified and make the strategic segmentation decision of how to use a segmentation model in developing their market strategy.

This suggests that one of the major decisions faced is 'what bases to segment on?'. We have seen that there are a great many potential bases for segmentation in consumer and business markets, and for product and service (and non-profit) marketing.

Arguably, the segmentation approach closest to extending the marketing concept is use/benefit segmentation – originally suggested 50 years ago by Haley (1968). While it does require considerable primary investigation, understanding the benefits customers derive in buying and/or consuming products and services is central to designing an integrated marketing strategy.

There are substantial potential benefits to be gained from basing marketing strategy on rigorous market segmentation. However, the organisational issues impacting on the implementation of segmentation-based strategies should also be evaluated to test for the internal compatibility of segment targets and the costs of organisational change that may be involved in segmentation-based marketing strategies.

The next chapter, on segmentation research, concentrates on the methodology for developing bases for segmentation.

Case study — Turning right: First-class air travel is in decline

Executives are flying business class; plutocrats are taking private jets

Dubai is often called a 'Disneyland for the rich'. At the city's airport the three first-class lounges of Emirates, the United Arab Emirates' flag-carrier, do not disappoint. Each one is as big as the terminal's concourse, built to accommodate thousands of passengers. But every day only a hundred or so enter each first-class lounge. Instead of the overpriced fast-food on offer in the public concourse, a maze of restaurants and bars serve free caviar and champagne. In their duty-free sections no knock-off cigarettes or booze are in sight. Think instead Bulgari necklaces and whisky at $25,000 a bottle. The facility is so large, its manager admits, that the most common reaction heard from new arrivals is, 'Oh my God, where is the lounge?'

Source: Tim Graham/Hulton Archive/Getty Images.

Yet the rows of hundreds of empty armchairs suggest that something is not quite right. Airlines are falling out of love with first class. And that is true even of Emirates, which sells far more first-class tickets than any other carrier (see chart 1). The time to launch new first-class offerings is at ITB Berlin, the world's largest trade show for the travel industry, which opened on March 6th. At this event in 2017 Emirates unveiled a new onboard bar and lounge for its highest-paying passengers. The same year its big rival in the Gulf, Qatar Airways, launched the world's first skyborne double-beds. But the mood has changed. Last year Emirates stopped attending the show at all.

The decline of first-class air travel seems at first glance surprising. Facilities onboard have never been so good. On its A380 superjumbos, Emirates first class provides in-flight showers. Moreover, the number of very rich people has risen sharply. *Forbes*, a magazine, estimates that the stock of billionaires has doubled to more than 2,100 over the past two decades. And the rest of the luxury-travel business is booming. Richard Clarke of Bernstein, a research firm, estimates that the number of luxury hotels in Asia could increase by as much as 168% over the next decade.

Even so, many analysts predict that first class will soon disappear. In America it is already almost extinct. Ten or so years ago almost all the many hundreds of long-haul aircraft based there offered first-class seating; now only about 20 do. Elsewhere in the world an increasing number of airlines, including Turkish Airlines and Air New Zealand, have already scrapped

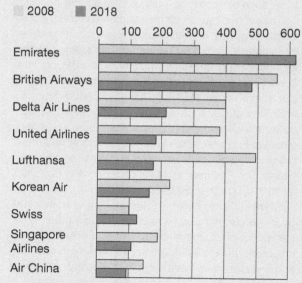

2008   2018

	0	100	200	300	400	500	600

Emirates
British Airways
Delta Air Lines
United Airlines
Lufthansa
Korean Air
Swiss
Singapore Airlines
Air China

Source: The Economist.

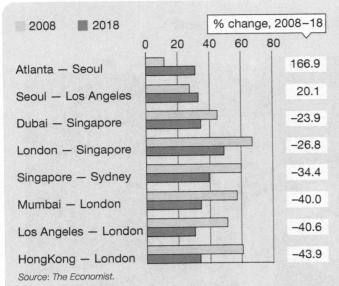

Source: *The Economist*.

it completely. On the majority of the most-travelled long-haul routes the number of first-class seats available has fallen sharply in the past decade (see chart 2). Even the airlines that sell the most first-class fares are curbing their enthusiasm. The number of first-class seats has been slashed from 14 to 11 on Emirates' superjumbos and from 12 to six on those flown by Singapore Airlines.

When commercial aviation got going after the Second World War there was only one class: first. Economy appeared in the 1950s. It was followed in the 1970s by business class and in the 1990s by premium economy, to fill the gap between business and cattle class.

Despite the proliferation of cheaper seats, airlines still make a lot of their money from the more expensive ones. Emirates claims that first- and business-class passengers are 12% of the total but generate about 40% of its turnover. High demand for flat beds on transatlantic flights is what has saved European flag-carriers such as British Airways (BA), Air France and Lufthansa from going out of business. Ross Harvey of Davy, a stockbroker, points out that transatlantic low-cost airlines that have tried to offer just economy or premium-economy seats, such as Norwegian and WOW, have struggled to make money.

Airline bosses are acutely worried about the decline in demand for first class. But they have themselves partly to blame. The industry has disrupted itself, points out Geoffrey Weston of Bain & Company, a consultancy. On short-haul flights, the low-cost model has won. Most 'first-class' passengers on these routes now sit in seats with the same legroom as economy passengers, albeit with an empty middle seat, and make do with extras such as lounge access, and food and drink.

On longer routes, new seats that turned into fully flat beds were a game-changer. These were originally introduced by BA in first class in 1995, and much sought after. If travellers can sleep comfortably in the sky, they can save the cost of a hotel or, more importantly for time-pressed corporate warriors, a day's working time. However, in 2000 BA launched a similar seat in business, and most carriers have followed suit. That has weakened the case for flying first class. Most companies think a flat bed in business class is good enough for their employees. Only a few honchos are allowed to enjoy first class on the company dime, says Greeley Koch of the Association of Corporate Travel Executives, a trade group.

Changing attitudes among the very rich are also sapping demand. Over the past decade the number of billionaires has grown fastest in China, India and the tech hubs of America. But many self-made tycoons want their children to have the 'normal' middle-class upbringings they themselves had, says Charlotte Vangsgaard of RedAssociates, a consultancy. So they book themselves and their families into business, or sometimes economy, rather than first.

Airlines that offer first class say they still do so for two main reasons. The first is to use upgrades from business class as an incentive for loyalty from both corporate and individual customers. But as the gap between business and first has narrowed, frequent flyers have begun to respond better to other incentives, such as access to lounges or to special hotlines.

The second reason for maintaining first class is also weakening. That is what Samuel Engel of ICF, another consultancy, calls the 'halo effect' an airline creates by advertising first-class facilities. In other words, flyers begin to think economy on Emirates, say, is fancier than on other airlines by association with features in its first class, such as in-flight showers. This can be an effective marketing tool. For instance, Etihad, a rival to Emirates in the Gulf, has probably had more press coverage for its onboard first-class apartments called 'The Residence', of which it has only ten, than all its 30,000 other seats combined.

Many airlines, however, are no longer convinced by this argument and have slimmed down their first-class offerings. One such is Air France-KLM, whose chief executive in 2014, Alexandre de Juniac, claimed that first class was "little more than a costly marketing gimmick" and that "no one makes money out of it".

Yet some still do, particularly Emirates. One advantage it has is that it can combine traffic from various destinations using its hub in Dubai. This helps it make first class viable on routes where it might otherwise struggle to attract first-class passengers. As a result, over 90% of its first-class bookings are paid for, rather than free upgrades.

Why do some passengers still want to fly first rather than business? Privacy is one reason, says Sir Tim Clark, the airline's president. Smaller cabins and walled-off seats make it easier for a celebrity to fly unnoticed by fellow passengers who might otherwise tweet unflattering pictures of them drooling in their sleep. Another is flexibility. First-class passengers want to sleep and eat when they choose, not on a timetable set by cabin crew, as often happens in business class, says Joost Heymeijer, head of Emirates Inflight Catering.

But even Emirates' first- and business-class sales are threatened by private jets. These let executives avoid the wait for a scheduled flight. It is also much quicker to pass through security in a private-jet terminal than an airport. And in America ten times as many airports are open to private jets as are available for the bigger aircraft airlines use. Moreover, executive jets are becoming cheaper in relative terms, says Adam Twidell of PrivateFly, a private-jet booking service. New shared-ownership and ride-hailing services allow the cost of a private jet to be spread over many users.

The rise of the private jet may be good news for bigwigs rushing to meetings. But it is bad news for the environment. The World Bank estimates that first- and business-class passengers on a narrow-body jet already generate between 2.5 and six times more carbon emissions per person than the poor saps crammed into the cheap seats. Private jets, obviously, are worse. A half-filled private jet is roughly five times dirtier than business class and 12 times dirtier than economy on short-haul routes.

A new breed of supersonic executive jets will be even more polluting. The International Council on Clean Transportation, a think-tank, estimates that their emissions will be five to seven times greater than for standard jets. Boom, one of the startups hoping to produce these jets, has forecast that up to 2,000 such supersonic aircraft will be built by 2035.

Another trend that could hasten the end of the arms race in first-class facilities is the shift towards smaller passenger jets. On February 14th Airbus, maker of the A380 superjumbo, announced that it will stop production of new ones from 2021. This aircraft's bulbous fuselage left space that could be devoted to fancy first-class features such as Emirates' showers and Etihad's apartment suites. The smaller and more efficient jets that have consigned the A380 to an early grave lack this extra space. It would be hard to fit showers, for instance, in the new long-haul narrow-body jets now available.

So Emirates will need another way to get its passengers to pay extra – perhaps by further upgrading those cavernous lounges. Its lounge manager in Dubai sounds perplexed: 'You need to do something different to make first class worth it.'

Source: this article appeared in the International section of the print edition of *The Economist*, under the headline 'The people in front' 09/03/19 (DUBAI).

Discussion questions

1 Why do analysts predict that first class will soon disappear?

2 How is air travel segmented? How could it be segmented?

3 Why is Emirates still offering first class? Is this sustainable?

CHAPTER 8
SEGMENTATION AND POSITIONING RESEARCH

'Researchers are anxious to find a magic formula that will profitably segment the market in all cases and under all circumstances. As with the medieval alchemist looking for the philosopher's stone, this search is bound to end in vain.'

Baumwoll (1974)

Sole woman: Nike embraces female footwear

By Carola Long

The brand is rethinking how it sells trainers to women – and that means unisex sizing and curated spaces

Many sneaker-loving women will know the frustration of spotting the perfect pair of trainers only to find out that, yet again, they only come in men's sizes. The women's sections of sports shops are often dominated by overtly girly details, from pink or gold trims to snakeskin inserts. Not everyone wants to do the tennis court or commute in sugary sneakers.

Now, Nike has taken this realisation and made it a central part of its new female-centric retail concept, Nike Unlaced. It will take the form of an online destination on the Nike website, launching March 27, as well as a physical, curated area in key Nike Stores from the summer. Amy Montagne, global vice-president and general manager of Nike Women, says: 'One of the most important things we will be doing is giving women access to and choice of product like never before. We are removing barriers with unisex sizing throughout the lines – and that

Source: Robert Stainforth / Alamy Stock Photo.

includes high-heat [the most covetable] products like the new Virgil Abloh x [Air] Jordan I – which is really important for women.'

Capitalising on women's increasing appetite for cutting-edge sportswear makes sense for the brand. Although at the end of the last financial year the women's sportswear business at Nike was worth less than the men's, at $6.6bn compared with $16bn, sales of women's shoes and apparel at Nike have been growing faster than men's for several years, and they expect that trend to continue. The Unlaced concept was initially trialled in Nike retail stores in London and the brand saw strong double-digit sales increases compared with the same period the previous year.

Julie Igarashi, vice-president and creative director of Nike Women, picks up on the appetite for unisex sizing: 'People are multidimensional today, especially the millennial generation; we want to express our style in a variety of different ways.' And she believes that a passion for sneakers isn't restricted to men, as is often the stereotype. She reports that when Nike hosted a pre-launch of the 1 Reimagined collection, footwear created by a 14-strong female design collective, at New York Fashion Week, 'we had women queuing up to buy it – there is definitely a rise in female sneakerheads.' As part of Unlaced, consumers will have access to personal stylists, and Nike has also enlisted global fashion experts and influencers to curate their women's products and inject a fashion sensibility that reflects their particular city.

The rise of athleisure-wearing sportswear-inspired garments as everyday clothing – and the boom in gym-going – has fuelled this growth. Montagne says: 'One of the things we have seen over the last few years is that women truly are the leaders of the sport and fitness lifestyle. We see a big shift in how women are living their lives, and fuelling the overall industry, and this has pushed us into some new zones.' Recent high-profile launches for women at Nike have included the campaign for their new 'Pro Hijab' modest headwear and a plus-size sportswear collection.

There will be a continued crossover between fashion and function. Montagne says: 'We have been listening to female consumers and athletes for 40 years and we have always been rooted in performance and innovation. We have also learned that it's really important to deliver on the fact that for women in particular there is no performance without style.'

And which styles are seeing the most demand? Igarashi cites the Cortez, which was Nike's first shoe for women, introduced in 1972 and recently reinvented. The Monarch is one of the top-selling styles ever at Nike, but it's not everyone's idea of a hip shoe. It's a clumpy white normcore running trainer of the kind American dads who wouldn't know their Balenciaga from their Balmain might wear to the mall, but over the past six months Igarashi reports that it has had a major revival as part of an ironic dad-fashion movement Nike is dubbing 'Mr Nike'. In a true rejection of preconceived ideas about what women like in their shoes, the stylist Julia Sarr-Jamois will be curating a whole Mr Nike selection for Nike Unlaced, available online. Igarashi says: 'This launch is really going to put some gas under sneaker culture.'

 Source: from 'Sole woman: Nike embraces female footwear', *Financial Times*, 28/02/18 (Long, C.).

Discussion questions

1 What are the issues here?

2 How can segmentation and positioning research help solve these issues?

Introduction

While the last chapter was concerned with the underlying concepts and principles for the key strategic issues of competitive positioning and market segmentation, the subject of this chapter is the research and modelling techniques that can be applied to evaluate these issues operationally.

The first section of the chapter focuses on *segmentation research* – in particular, the critical question of whether or not to pursue a segment-based approach, and if so whether this is based a priori on some predefined segmentation scheme, or developed post hoc on the basis of research. The second part of the chapter turns to positioning research, which may often be carried out in parallel to *segmentation research*, applying both qualitative techniques such as focus groups and depth interviews together with quantitative modelling methods such as perceptual mapping through multidimensional scaling.

The process of identifying potential market targets can be one of the most creative aspects of marketing. However, there is no single 'right way' to segment any market. Different competitors may adopt different approaches in the same market. All may be valid, but each may lead to a different view of the market, and subsequently a different marketing approach and a different strategy. The creative aspect of segmentation research lies in finding a new way to conceptualise your market, and a way that will offer some competitive advantage over the ways competitors choose.

Two broad approaches to segmentation research are typically pursued. First the a priori approach. This entails using an 'off-the-shelf' segmentation scheme, such as socio-economic or geodemographic classifications. Central to this approach is that the segmentation scheme is known in advance and the number of segments predetermined by the scheme chosen. By its very nature, **a priori segmentation** uses schemes that are in the public domain and hence also available to competitors.

The second approach is a **post-hoc** or **cluster-based** approach to segmentation. In this approach, the final segmentation scheme is not known in advance, nor is the appropriate number of segments. The criteria on which to segment are defined in advance, but may typically be multidimensional (for example, usage and attitude data). Data are then collected on these criteria (through the use of qualitative and/or quantitative marketing research) and analysed to identify underlying patterns or structure. The segmentation scheme emerges from the data analysis reflecting patterns identified in response. The data analysis itself is part science (using statistical techniques) and part art (employing judgement on which criteria to include and how to interpret the output). In this way, the segmentation scheme emerging is likely to be unique to the specific analysis. This offers potential for looking at the market afresh and identifying new opportunities not necessarily seen by competitors. It also, of course, requires that any segmentation scheme created be rigorously tested to ensure that it is not merely an artefact of the specific dataset or the analytical technique employed.

Following the discussion of segmentation approaches, the chapter goes on to examine alternative methods for researching and presenting positions in the marketplace. Two broad approaches are discussed. First the use of **qualitative** research methods to uncover brand, product and company images. These approaches are particularly popular in the development of advertising programmes. Second, **quantitative** approaches to modelling positions are explored, from simple profiling on semantic or similar scales, through to the more complex modelling available to multidimensional scaling and correspondence analysis techniques.

To segment or not to segment? That is the question

Although a central part of most marketing programmes, there are circumstances in which segmentation may be inappropriate. For example, the needs and wants of customers in a particular market could be essentially homogeneous, and therefore similar offerings can be made to appeal to the whole market, or the costs associated with pursuing individual market segments with tailored marketing programmes could outweigh their longer-term economic value.

A company following a segmented approach has either to choose a single market segment at which to aim, and therefore have a marketing mix that is inappropriate for other customers, or to develop a series of marketing mixes appropriate for customer segments with different needs.

Both these approaches have limitations, depending on the company's longer-term objectives. A single-focus company has limitations because the market segment itself is limited. If the company has expansion and growth objectives, these may be constrained by the size of its target market. This, of course, would be far less of a problem for a small or medium-sized company deliberately trying to stay small and focused. A company taking the multiple segment approach may face diseconomies in managing, supplying and promoting in a different way to each of the segments it has chosen. In some cases, an economic alternative is to use an undifferentiated mix designed to appeal to as many segments as possible. The company does not fine-tune offers to any one segment but hopes to attract a sufficient number of customers from all segments with one mix. The company can therefore benefit from economies of scale in a simple operation, but may be damaged by the 'sameness of the mix', by not appealing to the customers in each segment completely, or by better targeted competitors.

The appropriateness of segmenting or not segmenting depends on economies of scale, the cost of developing separate marketing mixes and the homogeneity of the needs of different markets (issues that are pursued further in Chapter 9). Such are the similarities in demand for petroleum, for example, that the products being supplied by competitors converge as they all seek to develop a mix with broad market appeal. Certainly segments do exist, but not of significant magnitude or difference to justify separate appeals. The aerospace industry and automobile industry have markets that are diverse but in which development and manufacturing costs are such that it is not feasible to develop products to fit all market needs exactly. Successful companies, therefore, focus on a relatively small product range with variations that appeal to individual customer preferences. More recently, car manufacturers have sought to expand their ranges and tap 'new' niches through advances in production techniques (for example, Lamborghini and Rolls Royce entering the 4×4 'off road' segment). However, broadly, the premise of relatively small range/variations to appeal to specific segments remains true.

Even in markets whose main body does not demand segmentation, there are often small-scale opportunities where companies can thrive by pursuing a focus strategy. There are many examples of manufacturers of sports cars that do this, but Pagani and Morgan would be two such companies. Therefore, even in markets where the major players are using a mass strategy, segmentation offers opportunities for some smaller participants. For small market share companies, in particular, the advice is 'Segment, Segment, Segment'! Indeed, Palmatier and Sridhar (2017) argue in their first-principle approach to marketing strategy that principle number one is that all customers differ and therefore organisations 'must make strategic decisions to manage this heterogeneity'. They identify five sources of customer heterogeneity:

- basic individual differences, for example personality;
- life experiences, such as where they are born and grow up;
- functional needs based on personal circumstances – for example, needing a waterproof camera to take underwater pictures;
- self-identity/image – for example, expressing their status through the car they drive;
- marketing activities – for example, by developing a brand identity that resonates with potential customers.

Whereas the previous chapter concentrated on the concept of segmentation and possible bases for segmentation, this chapter follows the process of identifying usable market segments. First, we discuss a priori approaches to segmentation. The chapter then goes on to discuss post-hoc, cluster-based approaches. For the latter we broadly follow a model originally developed by Maier and Saunders (1990), which takes segmentation research from initiation through to eventual tracking. Within this framework, the wide range of approaches and techniques for segmentation are discussed.

8.1 A priori segmentation approaches

8.1.1 Single variable segmentation

A priori, or off-the-shelf, methods are the easiest way of segmenting markets. In their original form this involved searching among demographic or socio-economic characteristics and identifying which of these form significant and useful splits within the marketplace. Usually the search for appropriate criteria would be guided by some expectation of how the market could be divided.

The major advantage of this approach is that it can be undertaken from secondary sources and can be related directly to advertising media and messages. Consumer markets studies such as the Target Group Index (TGI Survey Data, provided by Kantar Media – a leading research, data and insights company) enable managers to identify heavy users of a product group, and relate this directly to their media usage and advertising strategy.

There are some clear cases where a priori segmentation has proved a powerful tool. The successful toy company LEGO, for example, has carefully developed assembly toys to fit the development of children from birth to mid-teens and beyond; segmenting the market on the basis of age. Duplo, its pre-school product, starts with rattles and manipulative toys, which are not immediately intended for assembly but do have fixture mechanisms that allow the child to progress into Duplo proper (chunky and brightly coloured bricks and shapes that can be assembled into all manner of toys). Duplo overlaps with LEGO, a system of building bricks upon which the LEGO empire was formed. Almost identical to Duplo parts in every other way, the LEGO units are half the size, and therefore suitable for a child's enhanced manipulative ability, and to allow more detail in construction. They are also cleverly designed to link with the Duplo units and therefore allow relatively easy progression from one to the other. As the children get older, so they can progress to LEGO Technic, and other specialist variants, which again build on the manipulative, assembly and design skills inculcated with earlier sets.

Age is also used as a powerful segmentation variable in the package tour market – for example, Saga Holidays are aimed specifically at the over-50s.

Despite their ease of use and intuitive appeal, attempts to validate demographic and socio-economic bases in terms of product preferences have met with little success. One of the earliest reported attempts to validate this approach was by Evans (1959), who sought to use demographic variables to distinguish between Ford and Chevrolet owners in the United States. He concluded that:

> demographic variables are not a sufficiently powerful predictor to be of much practical use . . . [they] point more to the similarity of Ford and Chevrolet owners than to any means of discriminating between them. Analysis of several other objective factors also leads to the same conclusion.

In other markets, conclusions have been similar. Some relationships were found, but no more than could have been expected to occur by chance if the data were random. Unfortunately, study after study throws doubt on the direct usefulness of demographic characteristics as a predictor for product purchase as they fail to capture the nuances of human behaviour.

These findings do not dispute the certainty that some products with clearly defined target consumers depend heavily on demographic characteristics. For instance, nappies are purchased by families with babies and incontinence pads mostly by 'older' people. However, evidence seems to indicate that demographic characteristics alone are incapable of distinguishing between subtle differences in markets that are not explained by the physiological differences between human beings. Perhaps most limiting, they have been found to be poor differentiators of individual products within the broad categories identified (such as brand of nappy).

In business markets, perhaps the most often used segmentation variable is the Standard Industrial Classification, or SIC, code. In the United States, however, the North American Standard Industrial Classification System (NASICS) is being increasingly used. By selecting appropriate classification codes, business marketers can identify the other businesses that may be most receptive to its offerings. Again, however, for businesses selling products and services that can be used across industry classifications (such as stationery, machine tools or consultancy services), SIC may be of little practical value as a segmentation base. While giving the impression of detail, the codes do not offer many clues as to why specific products are purchased or what is likely to appeal to individual customers.

8.1.2 Multiple variable a priori methods

Recently, the traditional demographic and socio-economic means of off-the-shelf segmentation have been supplemented by more sophisticated methods being promoted, in consumer marketing at least, by advertising and market research agencies. These encompass the subjective methods and the marketing-specific objective measures discussed in Chapter 7. The distinction between these and the approaches discussed previously is that multiple criteria are considered simultaneously, and segments created on the basis of these multiple measures. A number of different consumer classification schemes have been suggested, such as ACORN (http://acorn.caci.co.uk), MOSAIC (http://www.experian.co.uk/business-strategies/mosaic-global.html) and VALS (http://www.strategicbusinessinsights.com/vals). These schemes have been created through analysis of large datasets (in the case of ACORN, two sets of official census data) using cluster analytical techniques. They are still considered a priori because, once formed, they are then available for any users off the peg from the agencies concerned.

Earliest of the multiple variable a priori techniques was the extensive use of personality inventories in the 1960s and 1970s. At that time, researchers were seeking to identify personality typologies that could be related, in much the same way as socio-economic factors were, to purchase decisions and consumption patterns. Techniques of personality measurement were borrowed by marketing from psychologists. Standard psychological tests such as the Jackson Personality Inventory and the Catell 16 PF Inventory were tested in a marketing context. Unfortunately, these tests proved to be of little more discriminating power than the less sophisticated demographic and socio-economic methods.

Compared with demographic and socio-economic off-the-peg methods, personality inventories have a slight but insubstantial advantage. They do appear to be able to discriminate to a small extent between some high-involvement products, but even in these cases they leave the majority of variance unexplained. As with demographic and socio-economic methods, they seem to have most power to discriminate in markets where their measurement has a clear role, such as smoking, which reflects a drug dependency, or deodorants, which suggest anxiety. However, the subtlety of personality measurement renders it less useful as an off-the-peg measure in most cases because the personality differences are less strong and obvious than the physiological differences that demographics can measure: introversion and dependency are well-defined personality traits, but they are nowhere near as easily measured or as linked to behaviour as gender or age.

At the same time that personality traits were being explored as potential bases for segmentation, marketers were also experimenting with combining demographic characteristics to create the idea of the consumer life cycle. Under this model, age, marital status and family size were combined to identify a life cycle stage. This approach has been used for the marketing of holidays, insurance, housing, baby products and consumer durables.

The introduction of CACI's ACORN geodemographic database once represented one of the biggest steps forward in segmentation and targeting techniques. Its basis was segments derived from published census information that provides a classification of neighbourhoods based on housing types. The great strength of the service depends on CACI's own research linking the neighbourhood groups to demographics and buyer behaviour, together with the ability to target households. The system, therefore, provides a direct link between off-the-shelf segmenting and individuals, unlike earlier methods that provided indirect means only of contacting the demographic or personality segments identified.

Like the other a priori techniques, the limitation of CACI's approach is the variability within neighbourhoods and the dissimilarity in their buying behaviour for many product classes. English (1989) provides an example of this where five enumeration districts (individual neighbourhood groups of 150 households) are ranked according to geodemographic techniques. Of the five, two were identified as being prime mailing prospects. However, when individual characteristics were investigated, the five groups were found to contain 31, 14, 10, 10 and 7 prospects respectively: the enumeration districts had been ranked according to the correct number of prospects, but neighbourhood classifications alone appeared to be a poor method of targeting. With only 31 prime target customers being in the most-favoured enumeration district, 119 out of 150 households would have been mistargeted. To be fair, as with other means of off-the-peg segmentation discussed, geodemographics are powerful when related to products linked directly to characteristics of the neighbourhood districts; for instance, the demand for double glazing, gardening equipment, etc. Even in the case provided, targeting the best enumeration districts increases the probability of hitting a target customer from less than 10 per cent to over 20 per cent, but misses are still more common than hits.

Lifestyle segmentation provides an opportunity to overlay geodemographic data with lifestyle characteristics. This has sometimes been used in conjunction with demographics and forms the second part of two-stage segmentation. Third Age Research has done this, after first identifying the over-65s as a target market and then breaking them up into lifestyle segments of apathetic, comfortable, explorer, fearful, organiser, poor me, social lion and status quo. To anyone who has contact with more than one older person, it is clear that these labels provide a far more powerful way of putting a face on the over-65 customer than does their age alone.

Stanford Research Institute in the United States developed a lifestyle segmentation scheme called Values and Lifestyles (VALS) that has seven categories: **belongers** (patriotic, stable traditionalists content with their lives); **achievers** (prosperous, self-assured, middle-aged materialists); **emulators** (ambitious young adults trying to break into the system); **I-am-me group** (impulsive, experimental and a bit narcissistic); **societally conscious** (mature, successful, mission-orientated people who like causes); **survivors** (the old and poor with little optimism for the future); and **sustainers** (resentful of their condition and trying to make ends meet). A similar scheme has been developed for use in pan-European marketing, including: **successful idealists; affluent materialists; comfortable belongers; disaffected survivors**; and **optimistic strivers** (Hindle and Thomas, 1994).

While the relative merit of demographic variables and lifestyle tends to vary from situation to situation overall, in the comparisons that have been conducted lifestyle comes out worst. It must therefore be concluded that, as with their less sophisticated demographic brethren, lifestyle segments are no panacea for marketing. Although, when added to databases, they provide a powerful means of shifting from target markets to individual customers, their low coverage renders them of limited value. On the other hand, lifestyle segments, where valid, do provide a more graphic portrayal of customers than do demographics, and hence can give suggestions for advertising copy platforms. As with single demographic variables, it is too much to hope that a single classification will work beyond markets for which it is particularly well suited.

All these approaches are in the public domain and hence, even where they do offer reliable segmentation schemes of a market, they may not offer the marketer any originality (or advantage) in viewing it. The essence of a competitively useful segmentation scheme is that it is fresh, new and (possibly) original, and provides insights into the market that competitors do not have. To achieve this originality requires primary research, where preconceptions about the market structure are put on one side and patterns sought from the original data.

8.2   Post hoc/cluster-based segmentation approaches

Unlike the methods discussed for segmenting markets, the post-hoc approach does not commence with a preconception of market structure. The analysis is undertaken with a view to uncovering naturally existing segments rather than shoehorning customers into predefined categories.

The remainder of this chapter discusses how firms can go about this more creative approach to segmentation. In doing so it follows a model developed by Maier and Saunders (1990) (see Figure 8.1). The process flows from initiation of the desire, to segmenting the market creatively, through to the tracking of continuing segment usefulness.

8.2.1 Setting the boundaries

Original and creative segmentation research needs both market and technical expertise. This often necessitates a dialogue between a manager commissioning a segmentation study and an agency or individual conducting the necessary research. The value of the final segmentation results will depend on the effort the individuals concerned have taken in bridging the gap between the technical requirements of segmentation methods and the practical knowledge of marketing and sales management. It is customary to see this bridge-building role as a responsibility of the researcher (who will typically be a modeller or marketing scientist) but, since marketing managers will depend on the results, and are likely to be responsible for implementing them, they have a clear interest in ensuring mutual understanding is achieved. While the modeller or marketing scientist faces rejection if the technical gap is not bridged, the marketing manager may face failure in the marketplace if the relationship fails. When employing an agency, the marketing manager will certainly need to know how to cross-examine the agency, to ensure its methods are appropriate and assumptions valid.

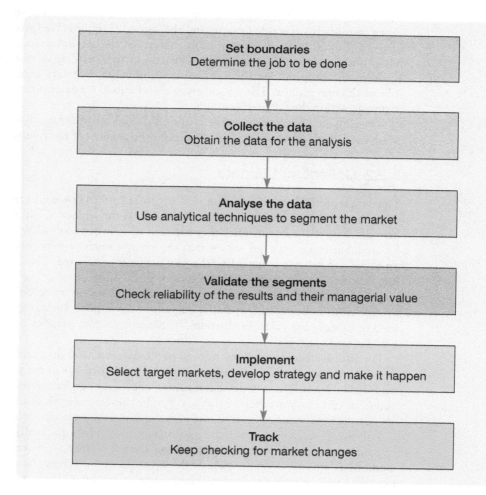

Figure 8.1
A model for segmentation research

Source: Based on Maier and Saunders (1990).

The entry of the marketing researcher or marketing modeller into the segmentation process is similar to opening a sale. If good initial relationships are not formed, the chance of further progress is slight. The researcher has to establish credibility by showing relevant expertise while fitting into the client's culture. As in selling, the prior gathering of information about the industry, the company and the personnel is beneficial. A grasp of terminology popular in the company is particularly useful. This preparation accelerates the formation of the mutual understanding necessary for successful model implementation.

The roles of the salesperson and the marketing researcher should be different because, although a salesperson usually has a limited set of products to sell, the marketing researcher should theoretically be able to choose without bias from a wide portfolio of appropriate techniques. Unfortunately this perspective is an ideal, for many marketing research agencies have a predisposition towards techniques with which they are familiar, or may even have developed in-house. So, in commissioning segmentation research, the marketing manager has to have sufficient knowledge to resist being supplied from a limited portfolio of solutions. Beware the researcher adopting the 'one size fits all' approach!

The major lessons for starting a segmentation project are that the first contact is critical and that successful segmentation depends on the marketing manager and the marketing researcher being sympathetic to each other's needs – not necessarily knowing each other's business perfectly, but certainly having the ability to ask the right questions.

At this initial stage, it is essential to agree the focus of the project, the product market to be investigated and the way in which the results are intended to be used. Multi-product companies may choose to start with one application and proceed to others if the trial is successful. There may also be market structures – such as the division between industrial and consumer markets – that suggest a two-stage approach: the first stage breaking the market down into easily definable groups, and the second being involved with the segmentation analysis proper. In their segmentation analysis of the general practitioner (GP) market, Maier and Saunders (1990) used such a process by first dividing doctors into general practitioners and hospital doctors – this distinction being necessary because of the different jobs of the two groups. The second stage then focused on determining the product usage segments within the GP markets.

Agreeing on a focus reduces the chance of initial misunderstandings leading to dissatisfaction with the final results and maximises the chances of the results being actionable.

8.2.2 Collecting the data

The data required for segmentation studies can be broken down into two parts: that which is used in conjunction with cluster analysis to form the segments, and that which is used to help describe the segments once they are formed. Cluster analysis will allow any basis to be used, but experience has shown that the most powerful criteria are those that relate to attitudes and behaviour regarding the product class concerned. These could include usage rate, benefits sought, shopping behaviour or media usage.

Before such data can be collected, however, it is necessary to be more specific about the questions to be asked. Typically, qualitative techniques, such as group discussions, are used to identify the relevant attitudes, or benefits sought, prior to their incorporation in representative surveys.

For effective benefit segmentation, in particular, it is vital that exhaustive prior qualitative research is undertaken to ensure that all possible benefits of the product or service are explored in depth. The benefits that the firm believes the product offers may not be the same as the ones the customers believe they get. For the subsequent analysis to be valid, the customers' perspective is essential, as is the use of the customers' own language in subsequent surveys.

Following qualitative research, a segmentation study will usually involve a quantitative survey to provide data representative of the population, or market, under study. The method of data collection depends on the usage situation. Where the aim is to define target markets based on attitudes or opinions, the data collection is usually via personal interviews using semantic scales that gauge strength of agreement with a number of attitude statements. The results then provide a proxy to the interval-scaled data, which is the usual basis for cluster analysis.

By contrast, where the segmentation in a study is to be used in conjunction with a database that can rely on direct mailing, the data sources are far more limited. For example, the lifestyle classifications mentioned earlier use simple checklists so that consumers can be classified according to their interests. In the database segmentation study conducted by Maier and Saunders (1990), the basis was product usage reports by general practitioners. It is clearly a limitation of database methods that their data collection is constrained by the quality of data that can be obtained from a guarantee card or self-administered questionnaire. There inevitably tends to be an inverse correlation between the coverage in segmentation databases and the quality of the data on which they are formed.

Where surveys are conducted to collect data for segmentation purposes, these data are usually of two main types. The primary focus is on the data that will be used to segment the market: the benefits sought, usage patterns, attitudes and so on. In addition, however, the survey will also collect information on traditional demographic and socio-economic factors. These can then be related back to the segments once formed (they are not used to form the segments) to enable a fuller picture of the segments to be painted. For example, a benefit segmentation study may find that a significant segment of car purchasers is looking for economical and environmentally friendly cars. To enable a marketing programme to be directed at them, however, requires a fuller picture of their purchasing power, media habits and other factors. Often, age and social class are used as intermediary variables; where these factors discriminate between segments they can be used to select media.

8.2.3 Analysing the data

Once the data on which the segments are to be based have been collected they need to be analysed to identify any naturally occurring groups or clusters. Generically, the techniques used to identify these groups are called **cluster analysis** (see Saunders, 1999 or Lee and Lings, 2008).

It should be realised that cluster analysis is not a single analytical technique but a whole class of techniques that, while sharing the same objective of identifying classifications with homogeneity internally but heterogeneity between them, use different methods to achieve this. This diversity of approach is both an opportunity and a problem from the practitioner's point of view. It means that the approach can be tailored to the specific needs of the analysis, but requires a degree of technical expertise to select and implement the most appropriate technique. Not surprisingly, it has been found that cluster analysis is relatively little used and understood among marketing practitioners, but is far more widely used by marketing research companies.

The most common approach to clustering is called hierarchical clustering. Under this approach, all the respondents are initially treated separately. They are then each joined with other respondents who have given identical or very similar answers to the questions on which the clustering is being performed. At the next stage, the groups of respondents are further amalgamated where differences are small. The analysis progresses in an interactive fashion until all respondents are grouped as one large cluster. The analyst then works backwards, using judgement as well as the available statistics, to determine at what point in the analysis the groups that were unacceptably different were combined.

Even within hierarchical clustering, however, there is a multiplicity of ways in which respondents can be measured for similarity and in which groups of respondents can be treated. Grouping can be made, for example, on the basis of comparing group averages, the nearest neighbours in two groups or the furthest neighbours in each group. Table 8.1 summarises the main alternatives.

Comparative studies consistently show two methods to be particularly suitable for marketing applications: Ward's (1963) method (one of the minimum-variance approaches listed in Table 8.1) and the K-means approach of interactive partitioning.

Table 8.1 Clustering methods

Favoured name	Method	Aliases
Hierarchical methods		
Single linkage	An observation is joined to another if it has the lowest level of similarity with at least one member of that cluster	Minimum method, linkage analysis, nearest neighbour cluster analysis, connectiveness method
Complete linkage	An observation is joined to a cluster if it has a certain level of similarity with all current members of that cluster	Maximum method, rank order typal analysis, furthest neighbour cluster analysis, diameter method
Average linkage	Four similar measures that differ in the way they measure the location of the centre of the cluster from which its cluster membership is measured	Simple average linkage analysis, weighted average, centroid method, median method
Minimum variance	Methods that seek to form clusters that have minimum within-cluster variance once a new observation has joined it	Minimum-variance method, Ward's method, error sum of squares method, H GROUP
Interactive partitioning		
K-means	Starts with observation partitioned into a predetermined number of groups and then reassigns observation to cluster whose centroid is nearest	Non-hierarchical methods
Hill-climbing methods	Cases are not reassigned to a cluster with the nearest centroid but moved between clusters dependent on the basis of a statistical criterion	

Source: Based on Punj and Stewart (1983).

In fact, an analyst does not have to choose between these two, because they can be used in combination, where Ward's method is used to form the initial number of clusters (say, seven), and the K-mean approach used to refine that seven-cluster solution by moving observations around. If desired, after finding the best seven-cluster solution, Ward's method can then be re-engaged to find a six-cluster solution that is again optimised using K-means. This may seem a computationally cumbersome approach, but fortunately packages are available to allow this process to be used. Arguably, Ward's method in conjunction with K-means is the best approach for forming cluster-based segments; the analyst has removed the necessity to sort among numerous cluster alternatives and is able to choose between the clustering programs that are available.

While there is plenty of advice available on which techniques to use, the determination of the most appropriate number of segments to select following analysis is very much more

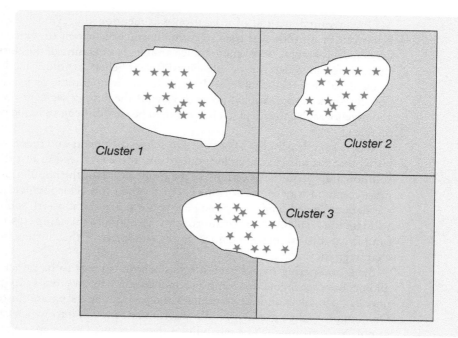

Figure 8.2
Clustering
of objects in
two-dimensional
space

judgemental. The statistics produced will offer a guide as to where amalgamation of groups results in two quite dissimilar groups being joined. The internal homogeneity of the group will suffer. This is a starting point, and in some circumstances, where segmentation is very clear-cut, will be the best choice.

Figure 8.2 shows an example where there are three fairly clearly defined segments on the basis of the two dimensions studied. In this case, 'eyeballing' a plot of the positions of each object (in segmentation studies the objects are usually individual respondents) shows three clusters of objects scoring similarly, but not identically, on each of the two dimensions.

In most situations, however, there will be several dimensions on which the clustering is being conducted, and several candidate solutions, possibly ranging from a three-group to a ten-group solution. After narrowing down through examination of the statistics, the analyst will then need to examine the marketing implications of each solution, basically addressing the question: 'If I treat these two groups separately rather than together, what differences will it make to my marketing to them?' If the answer is 'little difference' the groups should usually be amalgamated. This is the creative element of segmentation, where judgement is crucial!

Finally, it should also be noted that lifestyle and geodemographic databases depend on some form of cluster analysis to group customers who are alike. The results obtained for ACORN and MOSAIC, for example, are based on judgement as to how many clusters are needed to represent the population adequately, just as tailor-made approaches are.

Once the segments have been identified, and described across other criteria, there is a need to validate the segments found.

8.2.4 Validating the segments

One of the beauties and problems of cluster analysis is its ability to generate seemingly meaningful groups out of meaningless data. This, and the confusion of algorithms, has frequently led to the approach being treated with scepticism. These uncertainties make validation an important part of segmentation research.

One favoured method of validation was mentioned previously, where product class behaviour or attitude was used to form clusters; the extent to which those clusters also vary on demographic or psychographic variables is a measure of the cluster's validity. If the cluster is found to describe people with different beliefs, attitudes and behaviour, it would be expected that they could also have different demographic or psychographic profiles. Equally, from an operational point of view, if the market segments are demographically and psychographically identical it is going to be very difficult to implement any plan based on them.

Where sample data have been used to suggest segments and there is a hope of extrapolating those results to the fuller population, there is a need to test the reliability of the solution and to ask the question 'do the results hold for the population as a whole?'. The most common way to test for this is cross-validation. This involves randomly splitting the data collected, and using one part to form a set of clusters and the second part to validate the results. A simple approach is to conduct the same cluster analysis on both samples and to compare them to see the similarity of the clusters in terms of size and characteristics.

Since comparing two cluster analysis solutions tends to be rather subjective, several authors have recommended using discriminate analysis for cross-validation. This approach once again involves taking two samples and performing a separate cluster analysis on each. One sample is then used to build a discriminate model, into which cases from the other sample are substituted. The reliability is then measured by comparing the allocation using discriminate analysis with the allocation by cluster analysis. Integrated data analysis packages, such as SPSS (Statistical Package for the Social Sciences), enable such linked analyses to be conducted quickly and efficiently.

It is necessary to supplement this statistical validation with operational validation, to check if segments have managerial value. At a first level this means the segments having face validity and appearing to provide marketing opportunities. If further endorsement is needed, an experiment can be run to test if the segments respond differently or not. For example, Maier and Saunders (1990) used a direct mailing campaign to a sample of GPs to show that their segments captured major differences in the doctors' responses to certain self-reported activity.

8.2.5 Implementing the segmentation

Implementation is best not viewed as a stage in segmentation research, but seen as the aim of the whole research process. Implementation has become one of the central issues in market modelling. A successful (validated) model adequately represents the modelled phenomena, and implementation changes decision making, but a successful implementation improves decision making. In many cases it is worth going beyond the concept of implementation to implantation. By this we mean the results of the exercise not just being used once, but adopted and used repeatedly once the marketing scientist has withdrawn from the initial exercise. This again suggests that implementation not only begins at the start of the segmentation research process, but continues long after the results have been first used by the marketing manager. Microsoft's DPE unit is a business-to-business (B2B) example of successfully developing and implementing segmentation for the first time to better target its message: the company found it could use *Star Wars* characters to depict and appeal to different segments (*Marketing Week*, 2012).

Successful implementation, therefore, depends on more than the correct transfer of a model into action. The whole model-building process needs to be executed with implementation in mind. In particular, the segmentation researcher must be involved with the potential user in order to gain their commitment and ensure the results fit their needs and expectations. An unimplemented segmentation exercise is truly academic in its more cynical sense.

Segment selection and strategy development are two critical stages that follow the technical activity of segmentation research. These are managerial tasks that are central to marketing strategy and on which successful implementation depends. (Chapter 9 focuses upon these and links them to the broader issues of strategic positioning.)

8.2.6 Tracking

A segmentation exercise provides a snapshot of a market as it was at the point of data collection. Any time delays between data collection, analysis and management action could mean that the information is, in effect, out of date; it inevitably becomes an increasingly poor fit to 'reality'. Modelling myopia occurs when successful implementation leads to the conviction that market-specific 'laws' have been found that make further analysis unnecessary (Lilien and Kotler, 1983). The converse is of course true, as success means modelling should continue. What is clear is that customers and competition changes, and successful implementation itself may also change the market and competitors' behaviour.

Tracking of segmentation schemes for stability or change over time is essential in rapidly changing markets. As segmentation and positioning strategies are implemented they inevitably change the pattern of the market and customer perceptions, wants and needs. Through tracking the impact of various campaigns on segmentation, it may be possible to refine and detail the sort of promotional activity that is appropriate for them. If the segments do not prove to be stable, either showing gradual changes or a radical shift, that itself can create a major opportunity. It may indicate a new segment is emerging or that segment needs are adjusting, and so enable an active company to gain a competitive edge by being the first to respond.

Positioning research is often carried out in parallel with segmentation research. Indeed, the quantitative approaches discussed later in the chapter typically have as their aim the development of a multidimensional model representing both the positioning of objects (typically brands or companies) and customer segments.

| 8.3 | **Qualitative approaches to positioning research** |

The images of brands, products, companies and even countries have long been of interest to marketing researchers. Qualitative research approaches to this are semi-structured techniques aimed at gaining a more in-depth understanding of how respondents view aspects of the world (or more specifically markets) around them. These include focus groups and depth interviews (see Chapter 4).

Calder (1994) relates a qualitative research study into the image of a for-profit hospital in the United States. The hospital chain was opening a new 100-bed facility in a town with two existing and much larger hospitals. The problem was how to position the new hospital given its relatively small size and lack of established reputation. A number of focus group sessions were held, which showed that the relative size was known by respondents but not seen as necessarily negative. Indeed, the smaller size led to expectations of a friendlier, more personalised service. Comments during the discussions included:

> 'Very friendly and you get a lot of good care there. The others are a little big for that kind of care.'

> 'From what I hear it has a more personalised service. Mealwise and otherwise. You even get wine [with meals]. It's more of a personalised hospital.'

> 'I understand it has quite an excellent menu to choose from. Wine. They have the time to take care of you.'

The researchers concluded that the new hospital could be positioned very differently from the existing ones and it built on the friendly, caring image in subsequent marketing.

Through the use of projective techniques during qualitative research, images can be uncovered that serve to show how the brand product of the company is positioned in the mind of the respondent. Some of the most popular techniques include the following:

- **The brand or company as animal or person:** Under this approach, respondents are asked to name a person or an animal that embodies their view of the product or company under study. Calder (1994) cites the use of the technique to uncover the image of the US Army among potential recruits. Respondents were asked: 'If you were to think of the Army as an animal, which would it most be like?' The answers were, in order: tiger, lion, bull, wolf, bear. The Army was not seen as: mule, horse, dog, squirrel, elephant or cow! The researchers concluded that the Army was symbolised (positioned) as strong, tough, aggressive, powerful and dominating. This positioning had some negative effects on potential recruits, who feared failure in the training/induction period. It is interesting to note that more recent recruitment advertising in the UK has served to stress the 'team' nature of military service – an attempt at some repositioning and understanding of those they are trying to connect with.

- **Role-play:** In role-playing, the respondent is asked to assume the role or behaviour of another person, or of an object under research. Tull and Hawkins (1993) give an example of research for a premium brand of Canadian whisky marketed by Schenley, called O.F.C. During a group discussion, a member of the group was asked to role-play a bottle of O.F.C. and explain his feelings. The player explained that he didn't think anyone could like him as he didn't have a real name and hence no real identity. Further probing and discussion resulted in the name 'Old French Canadian' being suggested (using the letters of the original name, building on the origin of the liquor in the French-Canadian area of Quebec and on the favourable image of 'Canadian Club'). The brand was relaunched with the new name, a stronger personality and a clearer positioning in the market.

- **The friendly martian:** In this approach, the interviewer or group moderator assumes the role of an alien recently landed from space and asks members of the group to explain a particular product and how it is used. By acting as an alien, the moderator can ask basic questions to which the respondents would normally assume the moderator knew the answers. In a group discussion for the British Home Sewing and Needlecrafts Association, the researcher (a male in a female-dominated market) was able, through use of this technique, to discover that knitting was 'positioned' as a craft hobby that could be undertaken as a background activity while doing other sedentary activities such as watching television. Sewing, on the other hand, was 'positioned' as a thrift activity, undertaken primarily to save money, especially with children's garments, and required full attention to the exclusion of other activities.

A number of stimuli can be used to prompt respondents and aid them in articulating the images they hold of objects. These include the following:

- **Association techniques:** Here, respondents are asked for associations with a particular stimulus. They may, for example, be asked what words, or values, or lifestyles they associate with a BMW car. The words elicited can then be further explored through discussions and other techniques.

- **Concept boards:** These are boards with pictures of the brand or the brand logo on them, which are shown to respondents and their reactions sought through probing.

- **Animatics:** Drawings are shown of key frames from a commercial, with 'bubble' speech. Respondents are then asked for their reactions and helped to describe the feelings they have towards the items being advertised.

- **Cartoon and story completion:** These are cartoons of situations, such as the purchase of a specific brand, where the speech 'bubbles' are left blank for the respondent to fill in. Tull and Hawkins (1993) relate the use of story completion in researching changing drinking habits for Seagram. The unfinished scenario used was:

> Sarah hadn't seen Jane for a long time. She seemed very sophisticated and self-assured these days. At the bar she ordered . . .

Completion of the scenario by female drinkers most often had Jane ordering a glass of wine – reflecting, as the researchers interpreted it, her higher level of knowledge of drinks and general sophistication. Based on this and further qualitative research, the company developed a wine-based drink with a twist of citrus to liven it up – 'Taylor California Cellar's Chablis with a Twist'.

- **Visual product mapping:** This is a qualitative form of the perceptual mapping approaches discussed later in the text under quantitative techniques. Here, respondents are given a large piece of paper – the size of a flip-chart – with two dimensions drawn at right-angles to each other. Respondents are then given a number of objects (such as brands or companies) on small cards, or in the case of small-pack products such as shampoos they may even be given a number of real packages. They are then asked to position the cards or packs on the chart with similar brands close to each other but far apart from dissimilar brands. The dimensions that can be used to explain these differences are then discussed and written on to the maps. Alternatively, the identity of the dimensions may have been elicited from earlier parts of the interview (such as 'price', 'quality', etc.), and respondents are asked to 'position' the objects on the dimensions directly.

Qualitative approaches to uncovering the images and positions of objects in the minds of respondents have been particularly popular among advertising agencies, who value the in-depth, rich data that can be derived. The images and positions articulated are in the respondents' own language and hence offer insights for direct communication with them as customers.

However, the classic concern of qualitative research remains. That is, how representative of the population in their normal everyday shopping and consumption experiences are the responses of a relatively small number of respondents in often very artificial settings, completing strange and unfamiliar tasks? In most instances, positioning research needs to go beyond the qualitative to develop models of images and positions based on more representative samples in a quantitative study.

8.4 Quantitative approaches to positioning research

While qualitative approaches to image research often focus on the core object (brand, product, company, etc.) in isolation, the more quantitative approaches typically consider positioning relative to the positioning of major competitors and relative to the desires, wants and needs of target customer segments.

As a starting point, therefore, it is necessary to define the competitive set that will be analysed along with the focal brand, product or company. While positioning studies *can* focus at the level of the company or the product, most typically focus at the brand level.

For example, a company analysing the market for hover-mowers might be interested in how customers perceive competitors' brands (Flymo, Qualcast) and the products they sell. When buying such a product, a customer is likely to have a reasonable idea about the likely size and cost of the item they wish to buy and, therefore, give most attention to products within that price performance envelope. Among the competitors, the customer is likely to see various dimensions of importance, such as value for money, reliability, safety, convenience, etc., and it is the relationships between the direct competitors with which positioning is particularly involved. If the direct competitors have not been correctly identified, the researcher may include within the survey manufacturers of sit-on mowers (Mountfield or Honda). This would not only add to the burden of respondents whose perceptions are being sought, but could also change the perceptions since, when compared with sit-on mowers, conventional hand-mowers may all look similarly inexpensive, time-consuming and compact.

The mower market is relatively simple compared with some others. Consider the problem faced by a company wishing to launch a low-alcohol lager. Should the competitors be other low-alcohol lagers or should it include low-alcohol beers as well? Or maybe the study should be extended to include other low-alcohol drinks such as shandy, cider or wine? In the United Kingdom, the rapid increase in the consumption of soft drinks that has been associated with the concern for the health and safety of alcohol consumption may suggest that soft drinks, too, should be considered as an alternative to low-alcohol lagers, but should diet and caffeine-free versions also be considered? Maybe it is a matter of just taste, and it is more appropriate to low-alcohol drinks with variants with normal alcohol content. Production orientation is a danger when trying to reduce the number of product alternatives. A brewer may well consider low-alcohol lagers or other lagers as the direct competitors, but certain customer groups may easily associate low-alcohol drinks with colas or other beverages. It is clearly necessary to take a customer-orientated view of the direct competitors.

One way of defining direct competitors is to look at panel data, to see what customers have done in the past. By tracking the past purchases of customers it may be possible to identify product alternatives when switching takes place. The danger in this approach is the dissociation of the purchasers with the usage situation and the user. For instance, a buying pattern that shows the purchase of low-alcohol lagers, lemonade, beer and cola could represent products to be consumed by different people at different times, rather than switching between alternatives. Another approach is to determine which brands buyers consider. For consumer durables, customers might be asked what other brands they considered in their buying process. For low-involvement products it may be inappropriate to ask a buyer about a particular purchase decision, so instead they could be asked what brands they would consider if their favourite one was not available.

Day *et al.* (1979) proposed a more exhaustive process as a cost-effective way of mapping product markets. Termed 'Item by Use Analysis', the procedure starts by asking 20 or so respondents the use context of a product, say a low-alcohol lager. For each use context so identified, such as the lunchtime snack, with an evening meal, or at a country pub, respondents are then asked to identify all appropriate beverages. For each beverage so identified, the respondent has to identify an appropriate use context. Once again, the process is continued until an exhaustive list of contexts and beverages is produced. A second group of respondents would then be asked to make a judgement as to how appropriate each beverage would be for each usage situation, the beverages then being clustered on the basis of the similarity of their usage situation. For instance, if both low-alcohol lager and cola were regarded as appropriate for a company lunchtime snack but inappropriate for an evening meal, they would be considered as direct competitors.

Rather than using consumers, it can be tempting to use a panel of experts or retailers to guide the selection of direct competitors. This could be quicker than using customers, but is likely to lead to a technological definition of preference. There can be a vast difference between what is perceived by experts and what is perceived by customers. Since the focus of positioning is to gauge customers' images of offerings and their preferences for them it is difficult to justify using any other than customers to define competitors.

8.4.1 Attribute profiling methods

One of the simplest ways of collecting quantitative position data is through the use of attitude or attribute scaling. Under this approach, the dimensions that respondents use to differentiate and choose between alternative offerings are included in a survey (usually personally administered, though it is also possible to collect these data by mail, telephone, or 'e' surveys) and presented as semantic scales for respondents to give their views on.

An example from a survey of store images and positioning is given in Figure 8.3. Here respondents were asked to rate two competing stores on six attributes identified as important in prior qualitative research: quality, price, staff attitudes, range of goods, modernity

Figure 8.3
Modelling store images through the use of semantic scales

and ease of parking. Results are shown from one respondent only. Also shown is that respondent's ideal store profile – what he or she would ideally like in terms of the features listed. For most purposes, the responses from the sample would be averaged[1] and those averages used to show the differences in positioning and requirements. Where ideal requirements differ across the sample they could be first grouped together (using cluster analysis) to identify alternative segment requirements.

This approach examines each dimension separately, bringing them together in the diagram to enable a more complete image to be drawn. Some dimensions may, however, be more important to particular market segments than others. For instance, in the store positioning example it might well be that for one segment price considerations outweigh convenience, range and other factors. It is therefore essential to examine the relative importance of the dimensions, either through weighting them differently to reflect importance or through assessing the dimensions simultaneously, such that more important dimensions come to the fore.

8.4.2 Multidimensional positioning analysis

Increasingly, researchers and managers are seeking to create multidimensional models of the markets in which they are operating. The essence of these models is that they seek to look at a number of dimensions simultaneously, rather than separately, in an attempt to reflect more closely the way in which customers view the market.

To explain this approach, we shall follow a case involving the positioning of leisure facilities accessible from the east Midlands region of the UK. For the sake of simplicity, only the major attractions and segments are considered in this case. Interviews with respondents revealed six leisure centres that, although very different, were all seen as major attractions. These were:

- **The American Adventure theme park:** a modern facility, with a Wild West emphasis (the park has closed since the research work was undertaken).
- **Alton Towers:** since 1990 it has been acquired by a series of owners including The Tussaud's Group, Merlin Entertainments, Dubai International Capital and Prestbury. This is a large leisure facility based around a country house. It has inherited several natural

---

[1] Note that where there is wide variation in the evaluations from individual respondents it may be necessary first to group respondents by perceptual segments, i.e. those sharing a common view of the market, prior to analysing alternative segment requirements.

features, such as the house itself, the gardens and lakes, but particularly focuses on dramatic, white-knuckle rides.

- **Belton House:** one of many country houses owned by the National Trust and, as with most of these, has splendid gardens and furnished accommodation, which visitors may see. Atypical of National Trust properties, the house also has a large adventure playground in a nearby wood, this being a venture started by the family who owned the house prior to its being passed on to the National Trust.
- **Chatsworth House:** one of the largest stately homes in the United Kingdom and still the residence of the owning family. Its extensive grounds and the house itself make it a popular place for families to visit.
- **Warwick Castle:** one of the best-kept and most-visited medieval castles in the United Kingdom. As with many estates, it has been lived in from medieval times and the current owners have built a country house into the fabric of the building. Now owned by Prestbury Group and operated by Merlin Entertainments, the castle's attractions have been extended beyond the building and its gardens, to include contemporary waxworks within the furnished accommodation, medieval knights, jousting tournaments and medieval torture chambers.
- **Woburn Abbey and Safari Park:** like Chatsworth, still the residence of the family owning the estate. However, the family in this case have developed two distinct attractions, the house and the safari park, the latter also having a fairground.

Although the attractions are widely different in their appeals, ownership and background, the respondents' interviews clearly indicated that these were direct competitors and were alternatives they would choose between when deciding on an outing.

The positioning research process (see Figure 8.4) shows the determination of competitive dimensions, competitors' positions and the customers' positions as parallel phases. This is because there are certain techniques that can be used to extract all these simultaneously. In

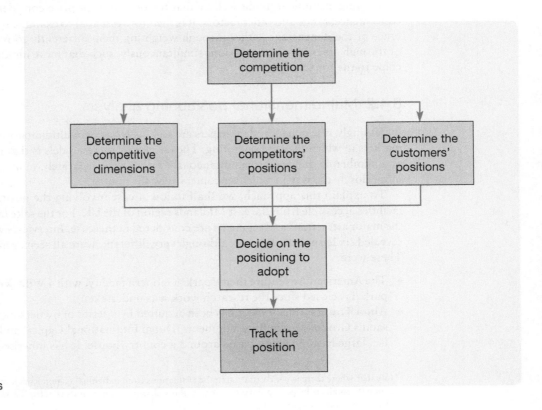

Figure 8.4
The positioning
research process

this case, the phases are taken in sequence. Details of other approaches that are available are given later.

Identifying product positions

It is an odd feature of many of the techniques used in positioning research that the competitors' positions can be determined before it is understood how the customer is differentiating between them. Such an approach was used to represent the leisure park market in the east Midlands. The approach is called similarities-based multidimensional scaling. In this, respondents were given a shuffled stack of cards that contained all possible combinations of the six leisure parks. There were 15 pairs in all, ranging from American Adventure linked to Alton Towers, to Warwick Castle linked with Woburn Safari Park. The respondents were then asked to rank the pairs in accordance with their similarity, the pair most alike being on the top and the pair least alike being on the bottom. Since this can be a rather cumbersome process, it is sometimes advisable first to ask respondents to stack the cards into three piles representing those pairs that are very similar, those pairs that are very unalike and a middling group. The respondent then has to rank the pairs within each group.

Figure 8.5 presents the ranking from one such process. It shows that this particular respondent (one of many) thought Belton House and Woburn Safari Park were the most similar. As the next most similar, the pair of Belton House and Chatsworth House were chosen, and so on, until the least similar pair of the American Adventure and Chatsworth House. An indication that the respondent is using different criteria to judge each pair is shown by the judgement that Belton is similar to Woburn and Chatsworth, but Woburn and Chatsworth are not alike. Such are the permutations and combinations of pairs each respondent can choose that it is almost inevitable that each individual's similarity matrix is different.

The objective from this point is to develop a plot of the stimuli (leisure parks) that shows those that respondents said were similar close together, and those that respondents said were dissimilar far apart. Although this is a difficult task to conduct manually, computers are particularly adept at finding such solutions, and researchers in the field of multidimensional scaling have produced many computer packages that can be used. The similarity matrix for our example, and the perceptual map produced from it, are presented in Figures 8.5 and 8.6 respectively. Chatsworth House, Alton Towers and Woburn Safari Park are some distance apart, while American Adventure, Alton Towers and Belton House are somewhat closer together on the map.

There are two reasons why the fit is not perfect:

1 The perceptual map presented in Figure 8.6 is in two dimensions, whereas the customers' actual perception of the market is rather more complex; and
2 the perceptual map is an aggregate of a number of customers' views, whereas the similarity matrix in Figure 8.5 represents the views of just one customer.

The software we used in this example can produce a perceptual map for a single customer, but it is more common to produce a map that aggregates either all customers or a segment's view.

	(A)	(T)	(B)	(C)	(W)	(S)
American Adventure (A)	—					
Alton Towers (T)	3	—				
Belton House (B)	4	11	—			
Chatsworth House (C)	15	13	2	—		
Warwick Castle (W)	5	12	7	8	—	
Woburn Safari Park (S)	6	10	1	14	9	—

Figure 8.5
Individual similarity matrix of leisure facilities

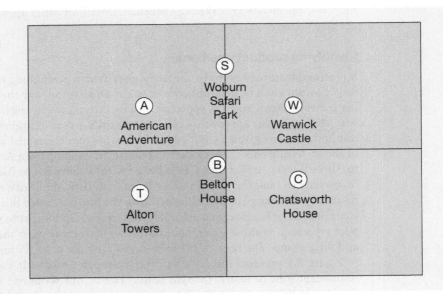

Figure 8.6
Perceptual map of
leisure centres

Uncovering the dimensions of perception

While the map shows a representation of the similarities between objects (leisure attractions), in itself it tells us little of why they are seen as similar or dissimilar. We need to go further to identify and understand the dimensions, or criteria, that were being used by respondents in giving their similarity judgements.

Two methods of determining the dimensions or criteria are not recommended. The first is using experts' judgements as, like their judgements of competitors, it is likely to be different from that of customers. The second is trying to eyeball the perceptual map to try to work out what the dimensions represent. Such maps are often ambiguous and there is a particular danger of researchers superimposing their own views of what is going on. A better, but still imperfect, technique is to ask customers directly how they differentiate the market. The problem here is that customers may give a relatively simplistic answer, which may not represent all the dimensions they may, sometimes subconsciously, use to differentiate product offerings.

More useful is a research-based approach where respondents are asked first to choose two or more similar products and say why they consider them to be alike, then to choose some products they consider quite dissimilar and say why they see them as unalike. An approach such as this was used to determine the dimensions of the perceptual space for the leisure facilities. The respondents were first asked why they chose the first pair (Woburn Safari Park and Belton House) as most alike. They were then asked what made Belton House and Chatsworth House alike, and so on, until the respondents had difficulty saying that pairs were alike at all. The opposite tack was then taken, where the respondents were asked to explain why they considered pairs to be unalike; first of all, the most dissimilar pair of Chatsworth House and American Adventure, then Chatsworth House and Woburn Safari Park, etc. The result was a long list of attributes, which was reduced to ten after some similar ones were combined and less frequently used ones were deleted. The ones remaining were:

- big rides;
- educational;
- fun and games;
- sophisticated;
- noisy;
- for teenagers;
- strong theme;

- for all the family;
- synthetic/artificial;
- good food.

Kelly grids are a popular marketing research technique that could also have been used to identify the dimensions underlying the perceptual map. For these grids a four-step approach is typically taken:

1 Respondents are presented with three stimuli (in our case, three leisure attractions) and asked to state one way in which two of them are alike and yet different from the third.
2 The criteria on which the two were said to be alike (say 'noisy') is labelled 'the emergent pole' and associated dissimilarity (say 'quiet') is labelled 'the implicit pole'.
3 The remaining stimuli (leisure attractions) are then sorted equally between the two poles.
4 Another three stimuli are selected and the process is repeated until the respondent can think of no new reasons why the triad are alike or dissimilar.

To find how the dimensions fit the perceptual map in Figure 8.6, respondents were asked to rank each of the leisure facilities on the basis of the attributes identified. Once again, the result is a series of matrices that are difficult to analyse manually but, once again, software comes to our aid. In this case a package called PREFMAP was used. This takes the perceptual map of product positions in Figure 8.6 and fits the dimensions as they best describe the respondents' perceptions. To identify the meaning of these vectors, each one can be traced back through the centre of the perceptual map (see Figure 8.7).

The score of each of the leisure centres (stimuli) on the dimension (vector) is measured by their relative position as the vector is traced back through the centre. For instance, the respondents saw Chatsworth House as being the most 'sophisticated' (on the east–west dimension), followed by Warwick Castle, Woburn Safari Park, Belton House, American Adventure and Alton Towers. In almost complete opposition to sophistication was the vector representing noisy and rowdy, on which Alton Towers and American Adventure scored highest. Projecting back the vector that represents a strong theme showed the highest-scoring leisure centre to be Woburn Safari Park, followed by the American Adventure and Warwick Castle with an almost equal rating, and finally Belton House, Alton Towers and Chatsworth House. Once again, it is likely that respondents' individual or aggregated scores are not perfectly represented by the

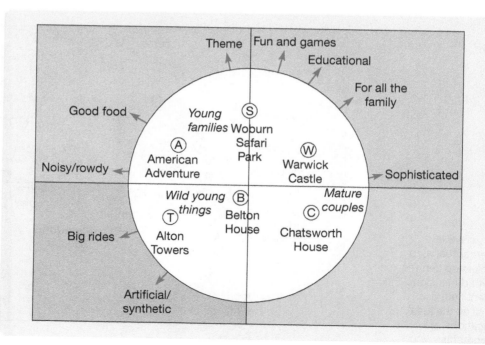

Figure 8.7
Perceptual map of leisure centres with dimensions identified

map that was generated. This is inevitable, considering that the picture is now trying to represent even more information in the same two dimensions. The magnitude of this problem can be reduced by resorting to portraying the picture using three or more dimensions, but usually the situation becomes less understandable rather than more understandable as the map goes beyond our normal experience. It may also be that segments of the market have distinctly different views and therefore it is more appropriate to produce maps that represent their different perceptions rather than aggregating the market, as has been done so far.

Identifying market segment locations

A two-stage process was used to add customer positions to the perceptual map of leisure centres. First, respondents were asked to rate the leisure centres in terms of their preference. Cluster analysis was then used to form segments with similar preferences; this indicated the presence of three main clusters. Analysis of their demographic characteristics revealed these to be mature couples or young sophisticates who found Chatsworth House and Belton House most attractive; young families who preferred American Adventure and Woburn Safari Park; and 'wild young things' who were most attracted by Alton Towers and American Adventure.

Once again, PREFMAP was used to locate these segments in relation to product position. However, in this case the segments were to be expressed as ideal points within the body of the map, rather than as vectors in the way that the dimensions were examined. Figure 8.8 gives the final map. This shows clearly the strategy of American Adventure, the latest of the leisure centres to enter the market. Aimed at the family market, it has big rides, good food and plenty of opportunity for fun and games, particularly for very young children. Although lacking sophistication and being perceived as artificial, it is well positioned for young families and for wild young things. Less successful appears to be Belton House, where the National Trust has found itself running a country estate, with which it is very familiar, and an adventure playground, with which it is unfamiliar. Although the house and gardens may provide the sophistication and tranquility desired by mature couples, the existence of the adventure playground would make it too rowdy for them. Equally, the direction of so many resources into maintaining the house and gardens to National Trust standards provides facilities that are unlikely to be attractive to the wild young things (which the National Trust probably thinks is good) or young families.

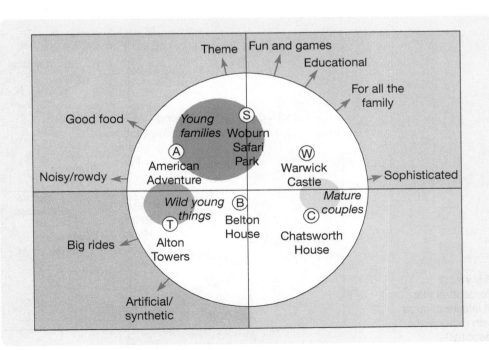

Figure 8.8
Perceptual map of leisure centres with dimensions identified, as well as the ideal locations of segments

The map also shows the dangers of product positioning without consideration of market segments. The positions of the leisure centres suggest there may be an opportunity to develop one that excels in the provision of an educational experience for the pre-teens, or for all the family. Vacant that position may be, but it is dangerously away from the needs of the three major segments that have been identified in this case. Maybe parents would have liked such a leisure centre, but the children would be happier with a less pretentious, synthetic attraction providing fun and games.

8.4.3 Alternative algorithms

In developing positioning maps, researchers are spoilt (and possibly confused) by the number of alternative approaches that can be used. For instance, PREFMAP allows the stage where segments were formed from individuals to be missed out and so produces a map representing the ideal point of each individual. Rather than the picture seen in Figure 8.8, which presents the ideal points of each segment, the map would then show the product positions, the market dimensions and the position of each individual relative to the product. From there it may be possible to eyeball the positions of individual respondents to identify a group that are worthy of being targeted.

A further approach is offered through correspondence analysis. Correspondence analysis is a multivariate method for analysing tables of categorical data in order simultaneously to identify relationships between the variables (both rows and columns). It can therefore operate with commonly collected data, such as usage and attitude data, to produce perceptual maps that simultaneously show the positions of objects (brands or segment ideals) and attributes (dimensions). Originally developed in France as an alternative approach to multidimensional scaling, correspondence analysis is now available in leading MDS packages.

Anyone who starts to use this diversity of approaches will find that the map produced depends on the approach used. This is because of the differences in the data-gathering techniques and the assumptions and methods used to optimise the results. In that way, the use of multidimensional scaling to produce perceptual maps is similar to cluster analysis, where the results depend on the clustering algorithm used. However, just as in cluster analysis, this should not be seen as a defect but the realisation that there are numerous ways of looking at a market. Life would be more convenient if there was just one map that represented a market, but any attempt to compress the richness of a market into so simple a perspective is likely to result in opportunities being lost, or never seen.

Only a few years ago, the access to the packages was difficult and the programs themselves were poorly documented and hard to use. Now the situation has changed completely, and there are a host of user-friendly and relatively inexpensive packages available – the ones previously cited and used as examples are a very small sample. Software is increasingly used by leading market research companies in order to increase levels of decision-making success and marketing effectiveness.

Summary

Considerable research has shown that the naive practitioner of segmentation and positioning research can be easily confused and disappointed. The traditional a priori, off-the-shelf methods of segmentation have proved to be a poor guide to segmenting markets, other than those that have a direct and immediate link to the markets concerned, such as gender-, age- or race-based products. Although more expensive, and providing a far more graphic view of the marketplace, the more modern psychographic methods appear to provide little advantage. As with demographic bases for segmentation, they do work in certain circumstances, but only when the product class or form and the segmentation criteria are very closely related. Within a product class or a product form, however, they rarely differentiate between brands.

The need to find segmentation bases that are closely associated with the product market in question means that successful implementation often involves a company developing product-specific bases. Here there is a potential barrier because of the perceived complexity of the approach and the confusion that researchers have created by their own misunderstandings. Although once a major block to implementation, sufficient case law on using cluster analysis in marketing has been accumulated to allow some of the confusion to be removed. Comparative studies come down firmly in favour of Ward's (1963) method in conjunction with iterative partitioning.

There is rightly much scepticism about the results from cluster analysis. This is justifiable, given the confusion of the algorithms used, the tendency of cluster analysis to produce results even if the data are meaningless and the lack of validation of those results. Being aware of these dangers, it is vital that validation, both statistical and operational, has a central role within segmentation research. In particular, tests should be done to see if the segments formed can be replicated using other data, that the segments are managerially meaningful and respond differently to elements of the marketing mix.

As with segmentation research, there is a wide variety of positioning research approaches and techniques available. Typically they require the collection of primary data relating to brand images and customer requirements. Multidimensional scaling techniques can be used to summarise the mass of data collected in visually appealing and easily communicable ways. They are perhaps best seen as visual models of the customer's mind. As such, they should be treated with caution, as any model is a simplification of reality and should be used with care. They can never replace the individual manager's insights, which are central to creative marketing decision making. At best they are an aid to that process.

Segmentation and positioning researchers have failed to find a single criterion that will fit all markets, despite the claims of those selling lifestyle segmentation. However, rather than finding a single criterion, researchers have found consistently reliable methods of using product market data to segment customers into groups that are of managerial significance and to represent their views and opinions in visually communicable ways. While Baumwoll (1974) was right in predicting that no philosopher's stone would be found, researchers have, however, perhaps discovered how to make philosophers' stones!

Case study

How millennials became the world's most powerful consumers

By John Gapper

They are the biggest global generation – and their choices are upending business from the US to China

When Scott Norton and Mark Ramadan were undergraduates at Brown University in Rhode Island a decade ago, they were horrified not by the 2008 financial crisis but by Heinz tomato ketchup. The bright red sauce was so common in shops and kitchens round the world that it seemed it would be there forever. 'At the centre of supermarkets were all these classic American brands that hadn't evolved in 70 years,' recalls Mr Norton.

As they talked to their student friends, they realised that none of them wanted bland, mass market products shipped from factories by huge corporations. So they started to mix their own organic ketchup in an off-campus apartment. On graduation, they founded a company and, having no origin story with resonance, invented a joke one. They named it after a mythical Victorian called Sir Kensington, a monocled adventurer who had 'advised the British East India company in the acquisition of spices'.

The pair are now 31, at the heart of a millennial generation that has come of age, transforming business not only in the US but round the world. In April, their company was acquired by Unilever, the British-Dutch group that had fended off a takeover by Kraft Heinz. Their ketchup, once a student jape, has just gone on shelves in Walmart and Target. 'Sir Kensington's is the playbook for reaching millennials,' says Richard Hartell, president of strategy and transformation at Publicis Media.

Millennials are 'core' business

This is the millennial moment, long expected and feared by companies that built their brands for baby boomers. They are ageing and their offspring, once called the 'echo boom', are no longer teenagers, or even students. Pew Research Center, the US research group, defines millennials as the 73m Americans aged between 22 and 37, who will next year overtake boomers in number. 'We don't think of them as special or different any more. They are the core of our business,' says Alan Jope, president of beauty and personal care at Unilever.

The coming of age of the world's 2bn millennials is not only a generational shift: it is one of ethnicity and nationality. Forty-three per cent of US millennials are non-white, and millennials in Asia vastly outnumber those in Europe and the US. Despite China's former one-child policy, it has 400m millennials, more than five times the US figure (and more than the entire US population) while Morgan Stanley estimates that India's 410m millennials will spend $330bn annually by 2020.

Millennials have reached what the bank calls 'the most important age range for economic activity', when households are formed, babies are born and money is spent not just on going out but on settling down. Simon Isaacs, co-founder of Fatherly, an information and ecommerce site for millennial parents, cites family camping as one of its most popular topics. 'That does extremely well for us. They like to buy cool family tents and share videos of their trips.'

This reflects the depth to which technology is integrated into millennials' lives and habits. The oldest were teenagers at the time of the Netscape initial public offering in 1995, as the internet became a mass medium, and the youngest were 11 when the Apple iPhone was launched in 2007. They are used not only to communicating online but buying most things there: $25bn was spent on Alibaba's Singles Day online shopping festival in China on November 11.

Big companies have scrambled to adjust to millennial tastes. 'Local, original, and what they can feel and trust are all good. Maybe there is a bit of a reaction to globalisation,' says Laurent Freixe, who heads Nestlé's US and Americas business. 'Organic, natural, and non-GMO are crystallising in the US very fast.' Nestlé last year bought the Blue Bottle chain of coffee shops and in May signed a $7.1bn licensing deal with Starbucks to refresh its Nescafé and Nespresso brands.

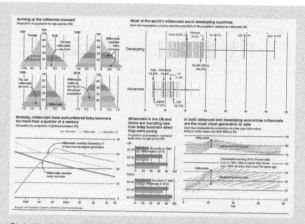

Globally, millennials have outnumbered baby boomers for more than a quarter of a century

Source: John Gapper (2018) How millennials became the world's most powerful consumers, The Financial Times.

But it is placing immense strain on institutions that once thrived on mass marketing of products through television advertising. Growth has slowed and investors are unhappy. 'They are only about global brands, one size fits all. That was great in the '80s and '90s but the world has changed. Millennials want these little brands, local brands,' Nelson Peltz, the 75-year-old activist investor, said last year as he attacked Procter & Gamble.

Some are being outflanked by young rivals with roots in internet and mobile. Google and Facebook have shaken marketing groups such as Publicis and WPP, and the streaming service Netflix last month overtook Walt Disney as the world's most valuable entertainment company. Often, revenues are simply nibbled away by upstarts: Boston Consulting Group estimates that between 2011 and 2016, large US consumer groups lost $22bn in sales to smaller brands.

'We cannot change things'

Ella Kieran, head of WPP's Stream conferences for its clients, is the epitome of the high-flying young global executive. At 31 years old, she and her entrepreneur husband have a one-year-old daughter, and she divides her time between London and New York. But the couple are still renting and she worries about her generation's future.

'The pessimism of my generation is the sense that you cannot change things,' she says. 'If you don't have a lot of money, it does not feel as if you are going to get it. Now, as I have a family, I'm happy that baby food is better, thanks to five years of people before me saying: "This brand does not speak to me." But you guys got houses and we got slightly nicer shampoo.'

In the US and Europe, many millennials are disenchanted with their lot as they attain maturity. A UK Resolution Foundation study found that pessimists outweighed optimists by two to one when they were asked about their chances of improving on their parents' fortunes. They are highly educated: 39 per cent of British 25 to 39-year-olds are graduates, compared with 23 per cent of those between 55 and 64. But their sophistication and ambition is not matched by security.

This is largely an accident of history. Older millennials entered the workforce in the mid-2000s, and many lost jobs after the 2008 crisis. They were also caught by rapid inflation in house prices as interest rates fell and remained low. The milestones of leaving home, getting a job, marrying and having children have been delayed — 45 per cent of 18 to 34-year-old Americans had done all four in 1975, but only 24 per cent had in 2015.

It has spawned widespread distrust, both in organisations and individuals. A Pew study in 2014 found that only 19 per cent of millennials believed that others could be trusted, compared with 40 per cent of boomers and 31 per cent of the generation Xers born between 1965 and 1980. Millennial faith in institutions is also low. 'This generation is incredibly sceptical of governments and big corporations,' says Keith Niedermeier, professor at the Wharton business school.

Malcolm Harris, author of *Kids These Days*, a book about 'why it sucks to have been born between 1980 and 2000', says distrust is only natural among a generation that has to struggle for security. 'If competition is the main feature of your world, you would be a fool to find people trustworthy,' he says. The preference for local, organic and craft products is also logical, in his view: 'You want to be part of a circle of production and consumption that is not centred on enriching the 1 per cent.'

Breaking traditional habits

The pattern of preferring smaller, independent brands and outlets extends to media consumption. Technology and social media have unleashed an extraordinary fragmentation in how they absorb information. In the US, they watch 19 hours a week of broadcast and cable television, compared with the average adult's 34 hours, according to Nielsen. Radio stations have lower reach among millennials but 37 per cent of them listen to at least one podcast a week.

New companies can reach millennials via social media, which further encourages fragmentation. Beauty is a prime example. Revenues of smaller brands grew 16 per cent a year between 2008 and 2016, according to the consultancy McKinsey. Millennials will often experiment with edgier brands such as Urban Decay, which was acquired by L'Oréal in 2012. Make-up artists, including Charlotte Tilbury and Trish McEvoy, have attracted large followings.

Beauty's expansion into a $250bn global industry has been fuelled by Instagram. Marla Beck, co-founder of Bluemercury, a US chain of cosmetics

Global millennial spending power is set to Permanently overtake generation X by 2020

Forecast annual aggregate income, by generation ($tn)

Source: World Data Lab

Global millennial spending power is set to overtake generation X by 2020 and will continue to rise

Source: John Gapper (2018) How millennials became the world's most powerful consumers, The Financial Times.

stores, cites the growth of face masks, including many Korean brands, as an example. Smaller companies are now selling black, silver and even rainbow masks. 'Masks used to be a teeny category but they are very visual,' she says. 'You can display your face [on Instagram] and show that you know about lifestyle, that you take care of yourself.'

Technology has not eliminated a millennial desire for community experience. Shared workspaces are expanding – the co-working company WeWork was valued at $20bn last year – members' clubs such as Soho House are growing and festivals have proliferated. Live music alone had global revenues of $26bn in 2016, according to PwC. 'I laugh about the terms community and experience, but they are exactly what we provide,' says Nick Jones, founder of Soho House.

Big spenders in Asia

Asia's millennials, the biggest generation of all, share many attributes with those in the West, but not their insecurity. They are confident of living better lives than their parents, particularly in China, where baby boomers lived through Maoism and the cultural revolution of the late 1960s and 1970s. Even in south-east Asian 'tiger' economies that achieved rapid growth, families often saved all that they could.

Millennials in China, many of whom are single children, behave quite differently. 'They are very optimistic about the future and they are willing to spend money,' says Jessie Qian, KPMG's head of consumer markets in China. McKinsey, the consultancy, describes young Chinese adults as 'confident, independent minded, and determined to display it through consumption.'

It is having a profound effect on global patterns of consumption, with more to come. Emerging and

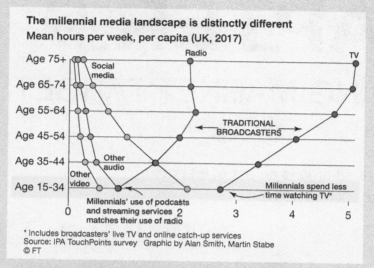

The millennial media landscape is distinctly different
Mean hours per week, per capita (UK, 2017)

The millennial media landscape is distinctly different

Source: John Gapper (2018) How millennials became the world's most powerful consumers, The Financial Times.

developing economies are home to 86 per cent of millennials, and the World Bank estimates that Chinese millennials' income will overtake that in the US by 2035. The luxury industry has tilted towards Asia, where prestige brands are seen as guarantees of quality. A third of Chinese millennials said in one survey that they were very likely to buy a Swiss watch.

Like others, the luxury industry is having to adjust to what these consumers want. It was once tightly controlled, with seasonal fashion shows to unveil designs that were then pushed through stores. Now, social media influencers such as Chiara Ferragni, an Italian fashion maven with 13m Instagram followers, set the trends and the pace has quickened. 'They need more regular product, more drops, something new on Instagram,' says Helen Brand, UBS European luxury analyst.

The surprise is the degree to which Asia's luxury consumers have been joined by a segment of millennials in the west. 'A few years ago, millennials were seen as young people who could not afford luxury,' says Ms Brand. The bank estimates that they account for 50 per cent of Gucci's sales and

65 per cent of Yves Saint Laurent's. It is a taste of millennials' buying power – their collective annual income will exceed $4tn by 2030, according to the World Bank.

This also reflects the divide in fortunes among millennials in the US and Europe, not just between high and low earners but between those born to asset-rich baby boomers and those lacking familial wealth. Accenture estimates there will be a transfer of at least $30tn in wealth from US baby boomers to millennials during the next three decades. The move has started with parental loans to young adults to buy homes, and will continue through death and inheritance.

Other millennials are out of luck, along with the institutions that flourished in the baby boom era and are being disrupted. Ms Kieran of WPP has little sympathy for the consumer giants. 'We can't win on anything else, so if we rattle the cage of corporations on sustainability, that's good.'

Hers is the voice of a generation that now wields greater power than even some of its members realise. The companies that cannot meet their demands are in trouble.

 Source: from 'How millennials became the world's most powerful consumers', *Financial Times*, 06/06/18 (Gapper, J.).

Discussion questions

1 How are millennials defined?

2 Why are companies keen to attract millennials?

3 How can segmentation and positioning research help these companies succeed?

CHAPTER 9
SELECTING MARKET TARGETS

> 'Attacking a fortified area is an act of last resort.'
> Sun Tzu, c.500 BC. Clavell (1981)

Rough ride

Harley-Davidson brought low by tariffs and demographics

A tour of the modernist building of the Harley-Davidson museum in Milwaukee helps to explain why the midwestern maker of motorcycles has iconic status, but also why it is struggling. Nearly all the visitors are white, middle-aged men, some clad in leather and heavily tattooed, others dressed conservatively. Harley is the quintessential baby-boomer brand but its customers are slowing down.

Sales keep plunging in the home market
Source: Digital-Fotofusion Gallery/Alamy Stock Photo.

Advertising

The firm has been losing sales at home for eight consecutive quarters with the latest being no exception. Sales in America plunged by a tenth in the three months ending at the end of December compared with the same period a year earlier, it said this week. The total cost of tariffs (those imposed specifically on its bikes by the European Union and China, and also those levied by America on imports of steel and aluminium, its main materials), together with restructuring costs, wiped out its profits.

Latest stories

The 116-year-old business has been through tough times before. It almost went under in 1981 when America was in recession and Japanese makers of motorcycles dumped unsold inventory onto the American market at extremely low prices. Then a group of employees bought the company, persuaded the government to impose tariffs on Japanese bikes, improved the quality of its wares and returned to the heavy retro look of the 1940s. That did the trick for baby boomers who flocked in droves to the expensive toys cleverly marketed as a symbol of freedom, individualism and adventure on America's scenic roads.

Now tariffs are the enemy: the company expects their cost to rise to $120m this year. Matt Levatich, Harley's boss, stoked President Donald Trump's ire when he announced in June his plans to move production of motorcycles destined for the European

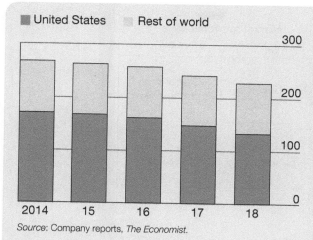

■ United States   Rest of world

2014   15   16   17   18

Source: Company reports, *The Economist*.

market out of America to avoid new EU duties. Some attribute recent poor sales to Mr Trump's Tweet in August supporting a boycott of the firm. But, 'most Harley enthusiasts don't care,' says Steven Levin, a surgeon from Chicago who has owned a succession of Harleys since college.

Harley's other challenge is to win over millennials, women and non-white buyers. Last year Mr Levatich unveiled a five-year plan centred on the introduction of 16 new motorcycle models such as Livewire electric bikes, and increasing Harley's appeal in international markets.

Dealers are counting on the new models to be more affordable, and attractive to a wider audience. Harley may suffer from the quality of its older wares. Sales of used bikes are outpacing those of new ones by three to one (a decade ago it was the other way around). But while old bikes, and Harley accessories and clothing sold in specialist shops and on Amazon, are selling well, they won't compensate for the damage done to the hogs by tariffs and youthful disinterest.

Source: from 'Rough ride', *The Economist*, print edition | Business (02/02/19).

Discussion questions

1 Discuss Harley's recent choice of target market(s).

2 What is behind Harley Davidson's attempt to appeal to a wider audience?

Introduction

One of the key decisions a company faces is its choice of market, or markets, to serve. However, many firms enter markets with little thought as to their suitability in the longer term. They are entered primarily because they appear superficially attractive for the firm's products or services. As we shall see in this chapter, a strong case can be made for choosing markets and industries where the prospects are attractive, but also where the firm can establish a strong, defensible, position. Figure 9.1 suggests that if we compare, in general terms, the attractiveness of markets and the strength of the competitive position we can take, then there are several traps to be avoided:

- **Peripheral business:** areas where the firm can take a strong and secure competitive position, but where the market simply does not deliver the benefits that the company needs. It is easy for those with great enthusiasm for a product or service in which they specialise to drive into these areas, but they will never deliver the margin and growth that is needed and will absorb resources and management time.
- **Illusion business:** areas where the market appears very attractive, because it is large, dynamic, expanding and so on. However, these are areas where the firm can only ever hold a weak position – perhaps because these are typically the markets defended most fiercely by entrenched competitors. It is easy for managers to be seduced into entering these markets because of the potential they offer, without acknowledging that they can never reach that potential.
- **Dead-end business:** markets that are not attractive and where the firm can only take an 'also-ran' position. Few managers will deliberately enter these markets, but this may describe markets from which the firm should exit – they may have been attractive in the past, but have declined, or the firm's competitive position may have been undermined by new competitors and technologies.

Figure 9.1 Market attractiveness and competitive position

Source: Adapted from Piercy (2016a).

Ideally the firm is seeking to position its offerings in:

- **Core business:** markets offering the benefits and returns needed, where the firm can take a strong, defensible, position. Clearly these are the highest priority for investment of time and resources. The major issue here is how well we understand what makes a market attractive for a particular company, and what makes a market position strong (Piercy, 2016).

While the strategic traps are easily described, the importance of the issue is underlined by the fact that market choices are just that – choice, which may mean ignoring some markets and some customers and some ways of business, to focus on the areas where superior performance and results can be achieved. Making such choices may be difficult. Michael Porter has suggested the heart of the problem:

> To put it simply, managers don't like to choose. There are tremendous organizational pressures towards imitation and matching what the competitor does. Over time this slowly but surely undermines the uniqueness of the competitive position.
> *(Porter, quoted in Jackson, 1997)*

Porter's argument is that a key challenge is to make clear trade-offs and strategic choices. The alternative is that a company risks destroying its own strategy:

> They start off with a clear position, and over time they're drawn into a competitive convergence where they and their rivals are all basically doing the same thing. Those kinds of competitions become stalemates.
> *(Porter, quoted in Jackson, 1997)*

However, the importance of market and segment choices must be put in the context of the potential complexity of markets and the consequent uncertainty surrounding the ideal choices to make. Indeed, as we shall see, defining markets and segments is not simply an exercise in statistical analysis, it is also a subjective and highly creative process (for example, see Aaker and Moorman, 2017). Considering alternative perspectives on markets and segments is a way to enrich our understanding of the customer, and to establish competitive differentiation in the way we go to market.

The purpose of this chapter can be described as follows. Chapter 7 was concerned with the different ways in which markets could be segmented. Alternative bases for segmentation were examined and the benefits of adopting a segmentation approach discussed. Chapter 8 then looked at the research techniques available to help segment markets. In this chapter, market definition and market targeting are discussed in more detail. In particular, the process of identifying the market segments where the company's capabilities can be used to the best advantage is considered, together with the selection of the appropriate marketing strategy.

In deciding on the markets and segment(s) to target, four basic questions need to be asked:

1 How do we define the market – what is its scope and constitution?
2 How is the market segmented into different customer groups?
3 How attractive are the alternative market segments?
4 How strong a competitive position could we take – where do our current or potential strengths lie?

9.1   The process of market definition

The definition of the markets a company serves, or those it is evaluating as possible targets, is partly a question of measurement and conventional competitive comparisons. It is also in part a creative process concerned with customer needs. Stanley Marcus of Neimann Marcus is frequently cited on this point: 'Consumers are statistics. Customers are people.'

A number of points are worth bearing in mind in approaching market definition:

- **Markets change.** The development of marketing strategy takes place in the context of a constant process of change. From this perspective it is unreasonable to assume that a company's definition of markets should remain static.
- **Markets and industries.** We have made the point before that markets are not the same as industries or products. Industries are groups of companies that share technologies and produce similar products. Markets are groups of customers with similar needs and problems to solve. Defining markets around industries and products exposes a company to its competitive position being overturned by competition from outside the conventional industry. Developing robust marketing strategies and strong competitive positions requires not only understanding the existing industry (see Chapter 3), but also the market from the customer's perspective (see Chapter 4).
- **Different definitions for different purposes.** Day (1992) makes the point that we may need different market definitions for different types of marketing decision: tactical decisions such as budgeting and salesforce allocation are likely to require narrow and easily understood market definitions (existing customers, similar products, existing channels), while strategic decisions require broader market definitions (including new market opportunities, changes in technology and substitute products, and potentially new types of competitive entrant).

9.1.1 Defining markets based on customers or competitors

Day (1992) suggests that markets can be defined in two ways: on the basis of customers, or on the basis of competitors:

- **Customer-defined markets.** This approach takes us beyond products that are 'substitutes in kind' (that is, the same technology), to 'substitutes in use' (that is, all the products and services that may meet the same customer needs and problems). This is what disruptors focus on – for example, Airbnb competing with AccorHotels.
- **Competitor-defined markets.** This approach focuses on all the competitors that could possibly serve the needs of a group of customers, and reflects technological similarity, relative production costs and distribution methods – for example, AccorHotels competing with Hilton Hotels.

In general, competitor-based definition will be important for allocating marketing resources and managing the marketing programme – responding to price cuts, salesforce coverage and so on. On the other hand, customer-defined approaches are likely to be more insightful in understanding the dynamics of the market, the attractiveness of alternative markets and in developing strong competitive positions.

One practical approach to evaluating the characteristics of markets is the product–customer matrix.

9.1.2 Product–customer matrix

Figure 9.2 suggests that the underlying structure of a market can be understood as a simple grouping of customers and products/services. The challenge is to examine a market using this matrix to identify no more than five or six groups of products and services and five or six groups of customers, that constitute the market. If this is impossible then this is probably not a single market but several, and the exercise should be subdivided.

The important perspective that can be built using this approach is one that recognises:

- **products/services** – in terms of what they do for customers, not in terms of how they are produced, or by whom;
- **customers** – in terms of important differences between groups in needs, preferences, priorities or ways of buying.

For example, vast arrays of retail financial services products provided by banks and their competitors can be reduced to six categories of products by considering what customer benefits they provide. Rather than hundreds of products, the market consists of only six groups of products and services to: provide access to cash; provide security of savings; buy now, pay later; make cashless payments; get a return on assets such as savings; and acquire a range of specialist services. The same process of reduction can be applied to products/services. For example, do not describe the market as 'computers', but as what different mixes of computer hardware, software and services actually deliver to customers in a particular market, such as accounting systems, internal communications, management information and so on.

This approach provides a start in defining markets in such a way that we move past the core market of similar products to find the extended market. This analysis can be used for a variety of purposes, but one advantage of this type of initial approach is that it starts to identify the way a market divides into distinctly different segments.

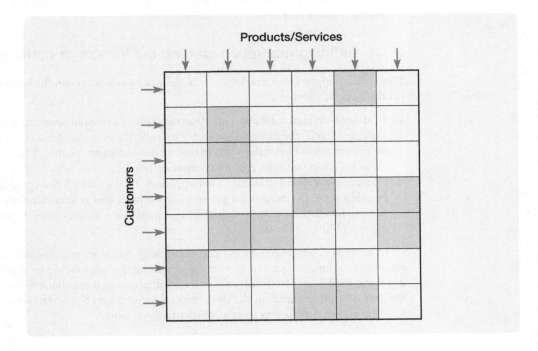

Figure 9.2
The product–customer matrix

9.1.3 Other ways of defining markets

Ecosystem marketing

More recently, Kotler and Sarkar (2019) have examined the concept of ecosystems in marketing. In ecosystem marketing the market is understood as a network of participants within 'four distinct yet interrelated ecosystems' (company, competitor, category and customer), and 'companies must understand the dynamics of competition in their ecosystems' (Kotler and Sarkar, 2019).

Jobs-to-be-done theory

Tony Ulwick, pioneer of the jobs-to-be-done theory, advocates defining markets around customers' jobs to be done. A market is defined as 'a group of people and the job they are trying to get done'. He further suggests to move away from the buyer and focus on the executor, with the job executor and the job as the focus for analysis. He cautions marketers to be careful when defining the job to be done. The job their product gets done may or may not be different from the job customers are trying to get done. For example, farmers might use herbicides to kill weeds. However, killing weeds may not be the job that users of herbicides want to be done, but, rather, to enable a crop to grow. Such an approach forces marketers to focus on the entire job to be done (value chain) and/or customer journey, rather than a partial contribution to it (Ulwick, 2016).

9.2   Defining how the market is segmented

As discussed in Chapter 7, there are many ways in which markets can be segmented. Often, a useful starting point is to ask how management views the market, on the basis of their experience in the marketplace. Management definition of market segments may typically be on the basis of products/services offered or markets served.

9.2.1 Products or services offered

Describing segments on the basis of products or services offered can lead to broad-based segmentation of the market. John Deere, for example, competing against the much larger Caterpillar company in the US crawler tractor (bulldozer) market initially segmented the market into 'large' and 'small' bulldozers. On the basis of its marketing assets (defined in terms of better service support through local dealer networks and lower system price), Deere decided to concentrate its efforts in the small bulldozer market, thus avoiding head-on competition with Caterpillar, which was stronger in the large bulldozer market (where market requirements centred around spare parts availability).

Many market research companies operating in the service sector define their market segments in terms of the services they offer – for example, the market for retail audits, the market for telephone surveys, the market for qualitative group discussions or the market for professional (industrial) interviewing.

Underlying this product- or service-based approach to identifying markets is a belief that segments defined in this way will exhibit the differences in behaviour essential to an effective segmentation scheme. The strategy adopted by Deere made sense, for example, only because the requirements of purchasers and users of large and small bulldozers were different. Where the requirements of customers are essentially the same, but satisfied by different products or services, this segmentation approach can lead to a myopic view of the market.

9.2.2 Market or markets served

Many companies now adopt a customer-based or markets-served approach to segmenting their markets. Segments are defined in terms of the customers themselves, rather than the particular products they buy. In consumer markets, management may talk in terms of demographic and socio-economic segments, while in industrial markets definitions may be based on SIC or order quantity. A particularly useful approach in many markets is to segment on the basis of the benefits the customer is seeking in consuming the product or service, and/or the uses to which the product or service is put. This can lead to new opportunities and even redefining business models. For example, Ikea is trialling leasing furniture – tapping into the changing concept of 'ownership' and the growing rental market. 'We will work together with partners so you can actually lease your furniture. When that leasing period is over, you hand it back and you might lease something else', Torbjorn Loof, chief executive of Inter Ikea, which owns the Ikea brand, told the *Financial Times* (Milne, 2019). This concept could be the start of a 'scalable subscription service'. This also helps with the company's drive towards increased sustainability and prolonging the life of products through refurbishing and recycling.

Central to the success of creative marketers is an unwillingness merely to accept the segmentation of the market adopted by others. In many consumer products/services markets, there has been a tendency to over-segment on the basis of background customer characteristics or volume usage. By looking beyond these factors to the underlying motivations and reasons to buy, companies can often create an edge over their competitors.

9.2.3 Marketing to communities

Kotler, Kartajaya and Setiawan (2017) affirm that, in a digital world, communities are the new segments and that marketing is moving from '"segmentation and targeting" to "customer community confirmation"' (Kotler *et al.*, 2017). They argue that, in traditional marketing, segmentation and targeting are symptomatic of a vertical relationship with customers and without their input. Through digital media, connected customers form communities (horizontal relationships) of their own accord. Brands need 'to fit in naturally – acting as friends, showing care and genuine concern to address customers' needs and wants. In essence, the process of segmentation, targeting and positioning is made more transparent' (Kotler *et al.*, 2017). They do nevertheless maintain the relevance of traditional segmentation and targeting, but urge transparency.

Once the segments have been identified, the alternatives need to be evaluated on the basis of market attractiveness and company strength, or potential strength, in that particular market segment. This evaluation is carried out across a number of factors.

| 9.3 | **Determining market segment attractiveness** |

It is clear that many factors may be considered in evaluating market, or specific segment, attractiveness. In Chapter 2 we discussed multi-factor approaches to evaluation in the context of assessing the portfolio of product offerings, while here they are discussed as strategic tools for deciding which markets to enter in the first place. There have been many checklists of such factors, but one way of grouping the issues is as follows:

- market factors;
- economic and technological factors;
- competitive factors;
- environmental factors.

However, it should be noted at the outset that a general checklist of this kind is only a starting point – the factors important to making a market attractive or unattractive to a specific company are likely to reflect the specific characteristics of that company and the priorities of its management. For example, one company may see a market segment that is growing as highly attractive, while in the same industry another company may look for slower rates of growth to avoid stretching its financial and other capacities. Similarly, a company that has cost advantages over its rivals may see a price-sensitive segment as highly attractive, while its competitors do not. In fact, there is a group of factors that impact on judgements of market attractiveness that are wholly subjective.

9.3.1 Market factors

Among the market characteristics that influence the assessment of market attractiveness are the following (see Figure 9.3).

Size of the segment

Clearly, one of the factors that makes a potential target attractive is its size. High-volume markets offer greater potential for sales expansion (a major strategic goal of many companies). They also offer potential for achieving economies of scale in production and marketing and hence a route to more efficient operations.

Segment growth rate

In addition to seeking scale of operation, many companies are actively pursuing growth objectives. Often it is believed that company sales growth is more easily achieved in growing markets.

As the global unit sales of smartwatches grew by 56 per cent in 2018, some analogue watch makers decided to build connected or 'hybrid' watches in an attempt to tap into that growth segment. This comes from research showing that fans of analogue watches will never completely give them up. Hybrid watches combine the aesthetics of traditional watches with some of the functions of smartwatches via a bluetooth-enabled chip. Adopters are happy to sacrifice the full functionality of a smartwatch for a classic design. As technology improves, so will the capability of these hybrid watches. Although the jury is still out as to the future successes of these watches, a Juniper's research conducted early 2019 'concluded that hybrid watches would account for more than half of the smartwatch market by 2022' (de Burton 2019).

Stage of industry evolution

We looked earlier (see Chapter 3) at the characteristics of markets at different stages of evolution. Depending on the company's objectives (cash generation or growth), different stages may be more attractive. For initial targeting, markets in the early stages of evolution are generally

Market factors Size; growth rate; life cycle stage; predictability; price elasticity; bargaining power of buyers; cyclicality of demand	**Economic and technological factors** Barriers to entry and exit; bargaining power of suppliers; technology utilisation; investment required; margins
Competitive factors Intensity; quality; threat of substitution; degree of differentiation	**Business environment factors** Economic fluctuations; political and legal; regulation; social; physical environment

Figure 9.3
Factors affecting market segment attractiveness

more attractive as they offer more future potential and are less likely to be crowded by current competitors (see competitive intensity later in the chapter). Typically, however, growth requires marketing investment (promotion, distribution, etc.) to fuel it, so that the short-term returns may be modest. Where more immediate cash and profit contribution is sought, a mature market may be a more attractive proposition, requiring as it does a lower level of investment.

Predictability

Earlier we stressed the predictability of markets as a factor influencing their attractiveness to marketers. Clearly the more predictable the market, the less prone it is to discontinuity and turbulence, the easier it is to predict accurately the potential value of the segment. The more certain, too, is the longer-term viability of the target.

Price elasticity and sensitivity

Unless the company has a major cost advantage over its main rivals, markets that are less price sensitive, where the price elasticity of demand is low, are more attractive than those that are more sensitive. In the more price-sensitive markets there are greater chances of price wars (especially in the mature stage of industry evolution) and the shake-out of the less efficient suppliers.

Bargaining power of customers

Those markets where buyers (ultimate customers or distribution chain intermediaries) have the strongest negotiating hand are often less attractive than those where the supplier can dominate and dictate to the market.

In the UK grocery market, the buying power of the major supermarket chains is considerable. Together the top five chains supply around 78 per cent of the nation's food shopping needs. Food manufacturers and processors compete vigorously for shelf space to make their products available to their ultimate consumers. Indeed, some supermarket chains are now moving towards charging food manufacturers for the shelf space they occupy.

Similarly, in the market for military apparel a concentration of buying power (by the governments) dictates to potential entrants on what basis they will compete.

Seasonality and cyclicality of demand

The extent to which demand fluctuates by season or cycle also affects the attractiveness of a potential segment. For a company already serving a highly seasonal market, a new opportunity in a counter-seasonal market might be particularly attractive, enabling the company to utilise capacity all year round.

9.3.2 Economic and technological factors

Issues reflecting the broader economic characteristics of the market and the technology used include the following.

Barriers to entry

Markets where there are substantial barriers to entry (such as protected technology or high switching costs for customers) are attractive markets for incumbents but unattractive markets for aspirants. While few markets have absolute barriers to entry in the long term, for many companies the costs of overcoming those barriers may make the venture prohibitively expensive and uneconomic.

Barriers to exit

Conversely, markets with high exit barriers, where companies can become locked into untenable or uneconomic positions, are intrinsically unattractive. Some new target opportunities, for example, may have substantial investment hurdles (barriers to entry) that, once undertaken, lock the company into continuing to use the facilities created. In other markets, powerful customers may demand a full range of products/services as the cost of maintaining their business in more lucrative sectors. When moving into high-risk new target markets, a major consideration should be exit strategy in the event that the position becomes untenable.

Bargaining power of suppliers

The supply of raw materials and other factor inputs to enable the creation of suitable products and services must also be considered. Markets where the suppliers have monopoly or near-monopoly power are less attractive than those served by many competing suppliers (see Porter, 1980).

Level of technology utilisation

Use and level of technology affects attractiveness of targets differently for different competitors. The more technologically advanced will be attracted to markets that utilise their expertise more fully and where that can be used as a barrier to other company entry. For the less technologically advanced, with skills and strengths in other areas such as people, markets with a lower use of technology may be more appropriate.

Investment required

Size of investment required, financial and other commitments, will also affect attractiveness of market and could dictate that many market targets are practically unattainable for some companies. Investment requirements can form a barrier to entry that protects incumbents while deterring entrants.

Margins available

Finally, margins will vary from market to market, partly as a result of price sensitivity and partly as a result of competitive rivalry. In grocery retailing, margins are notoriously low (around 2–4 per cent), whereas in other markets they can be nearer 50 per cent or even higher.

9.3.3 Competitive factors

The third set of factors in assessing the attractiveness of potential market targets relates to the competition to be faced in those markets.

Competitive intensity

The number of serious competitors in the market is important. Markets may be dominated by one (monopoly), two (duopoly), a few (oligopoly) or none ('perfect competition') of the players in that market. Entry into markets dominated by one or a few key players requires some form of competitive edge over them that can be used to secure a beachhead. In some circumstances it may be that the existing players in the market have failed to move with changes in their markets and hence create opportunities for more innovative rivals.

Under conditions of perfect, or near-perfect, competition, price competitiveness is particularly rife. The many small players in the market offer competitively similar products so that differentiation is rarely achieved (the stalemate environment – see Chapter 3), and it is usually on the basis of price rather than performance or quality. To compete here requires either a cost advantage (created through superior technology, sourcing or scale of operations) or the ability to create a valued uniqueness in the market. In segments where there are few, or weak, competitors there may again be better opportunities to exploit.

Quality of competition

Chapter 5 discussed what constitutes 'good' competitors – those that can stabilise their markets, do not have over-ambitious goals and who are committed to the market. Good competitors are also characterised by their desire to serve the market better and hence will keep the company on its toes competitively rather than allow it to lag behind changes in the environment. Markets that are dominated by less predictable, more volatile competitors are intrinsically more difficult to operate in and control and hence less attractive as potential targets.

Threat of substitution

In all markets there is a threat that new solutions to the customers' original problems will be found that will make the company's offerings obsolete. The often-quoted example is substitution of the pocket calculator in place of the slide rule, though other less dramatic examples abound. With the increasing rate of technological change experienced in the twenty-first century, it is probable that more products will become substituted at an accelerating rate.

In such situations, two strategies make sense. First, for the less technologically innovative, seek market targets where substitution is less likely (but beware being lulled into believing substitution will never occur!). Second, identify those targets where your own company can achieve the next level of substitution. Under this strategy, companies actively seek market targets that are using an inferior level of technology and are hence vulnerable to attack by a substitute product. Hewlett-Packard's success with laser printers, followed by inkjet printers in the PC peripherals market (attacking dot matrix printers), is a classic example.

Degree of differentiation

Markets where there is little differentiation between product offerings offer significant opportunities to companies that can achieve differentiation. Where differentiation is not possible, often a stalemate will exist and competition will degenerate into price conflicts, which are generally to be avoided.

9.3.4 The general business environment

Lastly, there is the issue of more general factors surrounding the market or segment in question.

Exposure to economic fluctuations

Some markets are more vulnerable to economic fluctuations than others. Commodity markets, in particular, are often subject to wider economic change, meaning less direct control of the market by the players in it. For example, the New Zealand wool export industry was badly affected in the mid-1990s by an Australian decision, in the face of declining world demand and increasing domestic stockpiles, to lower the floor price on wool by 20 per cent. Australia is such a dominant player in the essential commodity world market that New Zealand exporters were forced to follow suit.

Exposure to political and legal factors

As with exposure to economic uncertainty, markets that are vulnerable to political or legal factors are generally less attractive than those that are not. The exception, of course, is where these factors can be used positively as a means of entering the markets against entrenched but less aware competitors (for example, when protection is removed from once government-owned monopolies).

Degree of regulation

The extent of regulation of the markets under consideration will affect the degree of freedom of action the company has in its operations. Typically, a less regulated market offers more opportunities for the innovative operator than one that is closely controlled.

Again there is an exception, however. Regulated markets might afford more protection once the company has entered. This might be protection from international competition (for example, protection of European car manufacturers from Japanese car imports by quotas), which effectively creates a barrier to (or a ceiling on) entry. The warning should be sounded, however, that experience around the world has generally shown that protection breeds inefficiencies and when that protection is removed, as is the current trend in world trade, the industries thrown into the cold realities of international competition face major difficulties in adjusting.

Social acceptability and physical environment impact

Increasingly, with concern for the environment and the growth of 'green' politics, companies are looking at the broader social implications of the market targets they choose to go after. When a company is widely diversified, the impact of entering one market on the other activities of the company must be considered.

With increasing concern for the natural world, its fauna and flora, some cosmetics companies are now looking to non-animal ingredients as bases for their products, and manufacturers of aerosols are increasingly using non-ozone-depleting propellants in place of CFCs. The Body Shop, a cosmetics and toiletries manufacturer and retailer, has built its highly successful position in the market through a clear commitment to the use of non-animal ingredients, just as Innocent trades on 'natural' values with its fruit (and nothing but fruit) drinks. The late 2010s saw the beginning of a 'clean beauty' boom, with small, millennial-friendly labels taking on the giants. Brands such as Haeckels, Austin Austin Organic and Kahina Giving Beauty, based on sustainable, natural beauty, are carving a niche for themselves. This trend could become big business as, according to Mintel, clean beauty is a big market – the percentage of shoppers who would buy or boycott a brand based on its ethical values has grown from 20 per cent in 2017 to 57 per cent in 2018. However, for these small businesses it is not about growing big, it is about focusing on quality and purity and about sustainability from cutting down waste and protecting the environment (Cook, 2019).

Source: Sofiaworld/Shutterstock.

The disastrous oil spill in the Gulf of Mexico in the spring of 2010 had major implications for the reputation of the oil giant BP, which was responsible for the Deepwater Horizon oil well. Repeated failed attempts to stem the leak led to a loss of confidence in the technical competence of the firm, and indeed the whole oil industry, such that permission for new well drilling in the USA was suspended for a six-month period while safety procedures were re-examined and revised.

Summary

The quality of a market is dependent on a number of factors. Other factors being equal, segments that are big and growing offer the best prospects for the future. Other factors rarely are equal, however, and size and growth are not the only criteria that should be taken into consideration. Of prime importance is the scope for building a valuable and defensible position for the company in that segment. This will also require a clear identification of the company's strengths with regard to the proposed segment.

9.3.5 Making the criteria clear and explicit

We made the point earlier that the factors making a market or segment attractive to a particular company are likely to be unique to that company, rather than simply reflecting a general checklist of the type discussed previously. We also made the point that it is likely that the direction of a decision criterion will also vary – high-growth markets are attractive to some companies and unattractive to others in the same industry.

It is also the case that some of the real criteria for evaluating market/segment attractiveness may be highly subjective and qualitative. For example, a brewery evaluating alternative markets for its by-products identified the criteria of market attractiveness as:

- **Market size:** it defined a minimum market value to be of interest.
- **Market growth rate:** moderate growth was preferred (it did not want to invest large amounts in keeping up with a by-products market).
- **Low competitive intensity:** it wanted to avoid head-on competition with others.
- **Stability:** it wanted a stable income flow.
- **Low profile:** it did not want to invest in any area that would attract media criticism, or regulatory activity by the government.

What we see is a mix of the qualitative and the quantitative, the objective and subjective. None the less, these are the issues that matter to that management group. There is much advantage in making the real criteria as explicit as possible, notwithstanding that some reflect corporate culture and management preferences rather than economic market analysis.

Indeed, the Virgin Group typically makes explicit the criteria that make further markets attractive to Virgin. The head of corporate development, Brad Rosser, states that Virgin will invest in a market only if it meets at least four out of the following criteria:

1 The products must be innovative.
2 They must challenge established authority.
3 They must offer customers good value for money.
4 The products must be of high quality.
5 The market must be growing.

This describes Virgin's original mission of offering 'first class at business-class prices' and then applying the brand to new market opportunities.

9.3.6 The impact of change

It should also be remembered that nothing is static – things change, and sometimes they change rapidly in a number of ways:

- **Company change.** As companies evolve, their views about market attractiveness may develop. In the Virgin example given, these criteria may describe the company's view of how it is developing; they do not describe how it has invested in markets in the past.
- **Markets change.** The attractiveness of a market can alter dramatically. Matthew Clark, the UK drinks group, reported at the end of 1996 that sales of Diamond White and K Ciders had dropped 40 per cent, with declining profits following. The reason was a switch by young drinkers to alcopops such as Bass's 'Hooch' brand of alcoholic lemonade. Disparaged by the industry experts, a year after launch alcopops were selling 100 million litres a year. Nevertheless, ten years later and the cider market was experiencing another boom with a 23 per cent increase in sales in 2006 alone (growth that is continuing to date, albeit at a slower pace). Dubbed the 'Magners Effect' (the brand grew by 225 per cent in 2006), this was attributed to a 'step change in consumer attitudes' (National

Association of Cider Makers). The boom in cider sales became global partly due to the absence of gluten in the drink and increased awareness of gluten-intolerance. The growth of cider sales has now flattened, while gin has replaced it in experiencing a boom as drinking habits change again, this time driven by millennials. At the end of 2017, Britain alone could count 315 gin distilleries (up from 116 in 2010).

- **Competitors change.** The UK market for household vacuum cleaners had been dominated by Hoover and Electrolux since the 1950s, with very conventional technology. James Dyson offered his new product, 'the world's first bag-less vacuum cleaner', to the existing players and was laughed at. After many difficulties he launched his own product – with unknown technology and a high price. He sold £3 million worth of vacuum cleaners in the first year and has tripled sales every 12 months. Hoover's share of the upright vacuum cleaner market halved, and in 1995 in the high-margin market for cleaners priced over £180 Dyson took 58 per cent of the market, compared with Hoover's 14 per cent. The attractiveness of markets, and segments within them, can change dramatically: in 2015 Dyson launched its first cordless handheld vacuum cleaner, and as soon as late 2018 announced it had stopped developing its corded vacuum cleaners as the new technology had supplanted the traditional one. Dyson has also developed a robotic vacuum cleaner to tap into this fastest growing vacuum cleaner category. This segment was forecast to grow by 14 per cent between 2016 and 2021.
- **Reinventing the market.** Market attractiveness can also change dramatically as a result of those who 'reinvent the business', by establishing new ways of doing business. Daewoo took 1 per cent of the British car market (and a much higher share of its segment) in the fastest time ever, by establishing a new direct distribution channel and a brand proposition of high value and 'hassle-free' car buying. Amazon.com made significant inroads into book retailing through offering sales over the Internet, where additional services (such as online searches, book reviews, etc.) could be offered quickly and cheaply. And Apple iTunes took 80 per cent of the UK digital music market in 2006. In 2015, Apple launched Apple Music, a streaming service, which occupies second place after Spotify (a Swedish streaming service launched in 2008), with Amazon in third (respectively a 17 per cent, 36 per cent and 10 per cent share in subscriber numbers in 2017). See Figure 9.4.

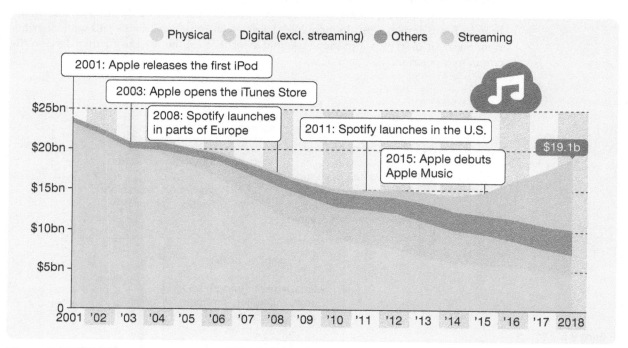

Figure 9.4 Streaming drives global music industry resurgence
Source: IFPI.

- **Market boundaries change.** The issue of market definition we considered earlier cannot be separated from the question of market attractiveness – attractiveness always refers to a specific market. As we saw earlier, a characteristic of many markets is that traditional boundaries and definitions are in flux. Avoiding the investment traps we described at the outset may involve constant awareness of how boundaries are changing as a result of new technologies and new types of customer demand.

9.4	Determining current and potential strengths

The importance of the resource-based theory of the firm, and the practicalities of assessing a company's strengths (and weaknesses) were considered in Chapter 6. The issue to consider now is how those resources, capabilities and competencies can be deployed in a specific market or segment (see Figure 9.5). One approach to this evaluation divides the issue as follows:

- the firm's current market position;
- the firm's economic and technological position;
- the firm's capability profile.

9.4.1 Current market position

A start in evaluating strengths in a particular market or segment can be made with consideration of the following issues.

Relative market share

In markets that the company already targets, market share serves two main functions. First, it acts as a barometer of how well the company is currently serving the target: a higher share will indicate better performance in serving the needs of the customers. Second, market share can, of itself, confer an advantage in further penetrating the market: high-share brands, for example, typically have high levels of customer awareness and wide distribution. Share of market is a prime marketing asset that can be used to further develop the company's position.

Current position

Relative share; change in share; exploitable resources; unique and valued market offerings

Economic and technological position

Relative cost; capacity utilisation; technology

Capability profile

Management strength and depth; marketing strength; forward and backward integration

Figure 9.5 Factors affecting business strength

Rate of change of market share

Absolute market share in itself can confer a strength to the company; so too can rapidly increasing share. Growing share demonstrates an ability to serve the market better than those competitors currently losing share. A company with a low but increasing share of the market can demonstrate to distributors the need for increased shelf space and availability.

Exploitable marketing resources (assets and capabilities)

Central to this text has been the identification and exploitation of the company's marketing resources. In target markets where marketing assets and capabilities have potential for further exploitation (a favourable image, brand name, distribution network, customer relationships, etc.), the company has potential strength from which to build. Identifying marketing assets and capabilities was discussed at length in Chapter 6. Of interest here is how these affect the strength of the company in serving particular market segments. What may be a strength with one target segment may be a weakness with another.

Unique and valued products and services

In potential markets where the company has superior products and services that are different in a way that is valued by the customers, there is potential for creating a stronger competitive position. Similarly, a competitive advantage based on low price relative to the competition is likely to be attractive to price-sensitive segments, but may actually deter segments more motivated by quality.

9.4.2 Economic and technological position

The evaluation should also address the company's relative economic and technological characteristics and resources.

Relative cost position

The company's cost structure relative to competitors was listed as a potential marketing asset in Chapter 6. Low relative production and marketing costs – through technological leadership, exploitation of linkages or experience and scale effects – give a financial edge to the company in the particular market.

Capacity utilisation

For most companies, the level of capacity utilisation is a critical factor in its cost structure. Indeed, the PIMS study has shown that capacity utilisation is most crucial to small and medium-sized companies. Few companies can hope to achieve 100 per cent utilisation (there will inevitably be downtime in manufacturing, and slack periods for service companies), and indeed running at 'full' capacity may produce strains on both systems and structures. But what is clearly important in any operation is to identify the optimum level of utilisation and seek to achieve and maintain that.

Technological position

Having an exploitable edge in technology again creates a greater strength for the company in serving a market. That may or may not be leading-edge technology. In some markets a lower technology solution to customer requirements may be more suitable than state-of-the-art applications. Again, the key is matching the technology to the customers' problems or requirements.

9.4.3 Capability profile

The third set of factors affecting competitive strength centres on the resources that can be brought to bear in the market.

Management strength and depth

A major asset, and hence potential strength, of any company is its human resources – and particularly its management strength and depth. The skills and competencies of the staff working in an organisation are the tacit strengths on which it can exploit opportunities in the marketplace. In service organisations (such as consultancy companies, health services, etc.) in particular, the strength of the supplier often comes down to the individual skills of the managers who deal directly with the customers.

Marketing strength

Marketing strength stems from experience and synergy with other product areas. Companies operating primarily in consumer markets often believe they have superior marketing skills to those operating in slower-moving industrial markets. They then see these markets as areas where they can use the fast-moving consumer goods skills they have learned elsewhere to good effect. Experience of transferring skills from one business sector to another, however, has not been universally successful.

Forward and backward integration

The extent of control of the supply of raw materials (backward integration) and distribution channels (forward integration) can also affect the strength, or potential strength, of a company in serving a specific target. Where integration is high, especially in markets where supplier and buyer power are high, the firm could be in a much stronger position than its rivals.

Summary

The important point to consider when assessing company or business strength is that strength is relative to competitors also serving the segment and to the requirements of customers in that segment.

| 9.5 | Making market and segment choices |

Conventional approaches suggest the use of portfolio matrices as a useful way of summarising the alternative business investment opportunities open to a multi-product company, and for making explicit choices between markets and segments. While such matrices have been used to assess the balance of the portfolio of businesses the company operates (see Chapter 3), the same techniques can usefully be adapted to help with the selection of market targets.

Classic portfolio techniques include the Directional Policy Matrix (DPM) developed by the UK Chemical Division of Royal Dutch Shell (Robinson *et al.*, 1978) or the McKinsey/GE Business Screen (Wind and Mahajan, 1981). These are generally considered as methods for modelling existing portfolios, but they are actually, in many instances, better suited to deciding which markets to target in the first place. An adapted model is presented in Figure 9.6; this is the operational version of the conceptual model we saw in Figure 9.1 at the start of our evaluation of market targets.

Using this approach, the factors deemed relevant in a particular market are identified (typically from the factors listed previously) and are each assigned weights depending on their perceived importance (using hard data wherever possible). The subjective choice and weighting of the factors to be used in the analysis ensure that the model is customised to the needs of the specific company. The process of selecting and weighting the factors can, in itself, prove a valuable experience in familiarising managers with the realities of the company's markets. Where appropriate, factors can be more objectively assessed through the use of marketing research or economic analysis.

		Market segment attractiveness		
		Unattractive	Average	Attractive
Current and potential company strengths in serving the segment	Weak	Strongly avoid	Avoid	Possibilities
	Average	Avoid	Possibilities	Secondary targets
	Strong	Possibilities	Secondary targets	Prime targets

Figure 9.6 Target market selection

Once the factors have been determined and weighted, each potential market segment is evaluated on a scale from 'excellent = 5' to 'poor = 1', and a summary score on the two main dimensions of 'market segment attractiveness' and 'company business strength in serving that segment' computed using the weightings. Sensitivity analyses can then be conducted to gauge the impact of different assumptions on the weight to attach to individual factors and the assessments of targets on each scale.

The resulting model, such as that shown in Figure 9.7 for a hypothetical company, enables the alternatives to be assessed and discussed objectively.

Ideally, companies are looking for market targets in the bottom right-hand corner of Figure 9.7. These opportunities rarely exist, and the trade-off then becomes between going into segments where the company is, or can become, strong, but that are less attractive (such as target opportunity 1), or alternatively tackling more attractive markets but where the company is only average in strength (target 2).

To develop defensible positions in the marketplace, the former (sticking to areas of current or potential strength) often makes the most sense. Indeed, many would argue (see Ohmae, 1982) that most companies are better advised to consolidate in apparently less attractive markets where they have considerable exploitable strengths than to 'chase the rainbows' of seemingly attractive markets where they are only average or weak players.

Where business strength is weak, investment should be avoided in average or unattractive markets (target 7), unless in very attractive market segments where some strengths could be built or bought in through merger/acquisition (target 3). Similarly, investment in unattractive segments should be avoided unless particular company strengths can

Figure 9.7 Evaluating market targets for a hypothetical company

lead to a profitable exploitation of the market (target 4). Market segments of medium attractiveness where the company has medium strength should be invested in selectively (targets 5 and 6).

A further factor in selecting target markets for the overall business is how those individual targets add up – the overall portfolio of businesses or markets the company is operating in (see Chapter 3). Companies are typically seeking to build a balanced portfolio of activities – balanced in terms of cash use and generation, risk and return, and focus on the future as well as on the present.

9.6 Alternative targeting strategies

The classic approach to segmentation or targeting strategies is provided by Kotler, most recently in Kotler and Keller (2016). Kotler's model suggests that there are three broad approaches a company can take to a market, having identified and evaluated the various segments that make up the total (see Figure 9.8). In addition to Kotler's three approaches, a fourth category of customised marketing is emerging in all sectors of business:

- **undifferentiated marketing:** essentially, producing a single product designed to appeal across the board to all segments;
- **differentiated marketing:** offering a different product to each of the different segments;
- **concentrated marketing:** focusing attention on one, or a few, segments; or
- **customised marketing:** co-creating products with customers.

9.6.1 Undifferentiated marketing

An undifferentiated marketing approach entails treating the market as one whole, rather than as segmented, and supplying one standard product or service to satisfy all customers. It is the approach carried out in Porter's (1980) cost leadership strategy. This approach was particularly prevalent in the mass marketing era in the days before the emergence (or recognition!) of strongly identified market segments. More recently, however, as the existence of market segments has become more widely accepted, the wisdom of such an approach in all but markets where preferences are strongly concentrated has been called into doubt.

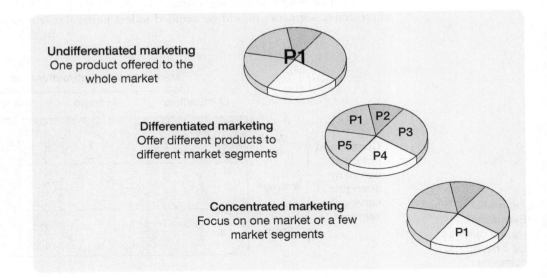

Figure 9.8
Alternative
marketing
strategies

9.6.2 Differentiated marketing

Differentiated marketing is adopted by companies seeking to offer a distinct product or service to each chosen segment of the market. Thus, a shampoo manufacturer will offer different types of shampoo depending on the condition of the hair of the customer. The major danger of differentiated marketing is that it can lead to high costs, both in manufacturing and in marketing a wide product line.

Depending on the company's resources, however, differentiated marketing can help in achieving overall market domination, as AccorHotels has achieved in its main global market through its brand portfolio.

9.6.3 Concentrated marketing

For the organisation with limited resources, however, attacking all or even most of the potential segments in a market may not be a viable proposition. In this instance, concentrated or focused marketing may make more sense. Under this strategy, the organisation focuses attention on one, or a few, market segments and leaves the wider market to its competitors. In this way it builds a strong position in a few selected markets, rather than attempting to compete across the board (either with undifferentiated or differentiated products).

The success of this approach depends on clear, in-depth knowledge of the customers served. The major danger of this strategy, however, is that, over time, the segment focused on may become less attractive and limiting on the organisation.

The Lucozade brand of soft drink was first marketed in the 1920s. It was originally developed by a Newcastle chemist as an energy drink for his daughter, who was recovering from jaundice. The brand was bought by Beechams in 1938 and marketed in a distinctive yellow cellophane wrapper, with the slogan 'Lucozade Aids Recovery'. During the 1950s and 1960s it was Beechams' biggest selling brand. By the 1970s, however, lower levels of sickness, less frequent flu epidemics and price increases had contributed to a decline in sales. From 1974 to 1978 sales fell by 30 per cent. The company decided that the brand needed to be repositioned.

The first repositioning was as an in-house 'pick-me-up' for housewives in the late 1970s. Sales initially increased by 11 per cent, but growth was not maintained and by the end of 1979 sales had levelled out. In 1980 a new 250 ml bottle was launched and the new slogan 'Lucozade Replaces Lost Energy' was developed. But by 1982 a usage and attitude survey showed that the brand character had not changed significantly – it was still used primarily for illness recovery.

More radical repositioning was considered. In the carbonated soft drinks market, Lucozade was competing head-on with well-established brands such as Coca-Cola and Pepsi. Lucozade also suffered from a poor image at the younger end of the market – it had been given to them by their mums when they were ill! A new positioning was developed around the theme: 'Lucozade is not only delicious and refreshing but can quickly replace lost energy.' The potential of the sports market became apparent, and in July 1982 the advertising started to use Daley Thompson, an Olympic decathlete. Initially, however, although the target customers liked Daley, they did not connect him with the brand. Lucozade has since maintained this positioning, but with a different advertising strategy.

The next phase of repositioning was the 'traffic lights' TV commercial, using Daley and the heavy metal music of Iron Maiden to 'portray' rather than 'explain' the message. The advertisements graphically conveyed the energy replacement message in a way that younger users immediately identified with. In the first year of the new campaign, sales volume increased by 40 per cent. Qualitative research showed the message getting across to existing users and, crucially, to the younger target market.

Since then Lucozade has enjoyed continued success, and new flavour variants have been launched. The year 1988 saw the launch of the Lucozade Sport isotonic drink and 1995 the launch of the NRG teen drink. The same positioning strategy has been pursued successfully in Ireland, Asia and Australasia. From 1985 to 1995, worldwide sales grew from £12 million to £125 million (Salmon, 1997). In 2002, the brand was promoted through the Lara Croft/ Tomb Raider association. At the time of writing, Lucozade remains number one in the UK sports and energy drink market, with a share of over 40 per cent.

Similarly, Red Bull started as a 'tonic' called 'Krating Daeng' – basically, Thai for 'Red Bull' – and was originally developed to keep factory workers and truckers awake and productive by the late Chaleo Yoovidhya, founder of TC Pharmaceuticals in Thailand. Austrian entrepreneur Dietrich Mateschitz discovered Krating Daeng accidentally, rebranded it Red Bull and made it global by 1997. In fact, the creation of the energy drinks segment is attributed to him. The brand is lifestyle orientated with a strong social media input, and the product is made part of that lifestyle, which appeals to millennials (to the value of $7.2 billion dollars and 40 million Facebook fans).

In its early days, Red Bull was taken to the streets by youth 'guerilla marketing' teams. Then, careful systematic associations with extreme sports helped boost credibility – for example with the company's ownership of NASCAR and Formula 1 teams, and its sponsoring of famous athletes. It has now also entered the alcoholic mixer sector (Bell, 2015).

9.6.4 Customised marketing

When Harrods' new chief marketing and customer officer, Amanda Hill, says she does not believe in segmentation that is because she believes in a customer-centric approach – each potentially worthy of a bespoke service. Indeed, consumers increasingly look for something specific to them and technology is the great enabler of mass customisation (that is, meeting each customer's requirements, Wind and Rangaswamy, 2001). Although prevalent in the service sectors, one-to-one marketing (as it is also known) is growing in other sectors such as consumer apparel, where co-creation of products with customers is feasible. Nike, for example, is offering NIKE BY YOU (which it qualifies as 'Just you, us and a million possibilities') – a customisation service that allows customers to choose from different materials, sole designs, colours and more. 3D printing empowers mass customisation by offering customers the possibility to create personalised products, from 3D printed jewellery or plastic items to hip replacements!

The most effective strategy to adopt with regard to target market selection will vary from market to market. Certain characteristics of both the market and the company, however, will serve to suggest the type of strategy that makes most sense in a given situation.

The classic statement on how to approach the segmentation strategy choice comes from Frank et al. (1972). They propose that the choice of strategy should be based on:

- segment size – to determine its value and prospects;
- the incremental costs faced in differentiating between segments – which may be small, or may be high enough to undermine a full segmentation strategy;
- the extent and durability of segment differences – if segments are only marginally differentiated they may not be worth taking as separate targets, and if the differences are transitory then the viability of a segmentation strategy may be questionable;
- the stability and mutual compatibility of segment targets;
- the 'fit' between segment characteristics and company strengths (see Chapter 7); and
- the level and type of competition in the prospective segment targets.

Summary

The selection of which potential market segment or segments to serve is the crucial step in developing a robust and comprehensive marketing strategy. Until the targets have been clearly identified, their requirements and motivations fully explored, it is not possible to develop a robust competitive positioning.

No-frills Ryanair faces test with Business Plus

By Vincent Boland in Dublin and Jane Wild in London

There are no flat bed seats, no free champagne and no left turn. But Ryanair still claims it is offering a business service.

On Wednesday the low-cost Irish airline unveiled Business Plus, a service designed to lure the famously bare-bones airline passengers who usually fly business class on other carriers and are used to curtain dividers, hot towels, free meals and other perks.

None of those frills will be part of the Ryanair package. Instead, according to Kenny Jacobs, the airline's chief marketing officer, what potential business class travellers want are flexible tickets, multiple same-day return flights, fast-track security, priority boarding and seats near the exits and over the wings, which have more legroom.

In other words, Business Plus will be business-class flying – Ryanair style.

'There was no demand for some of the traditional trappings of the business class product – the bad sandwiches, the bad coffee,' says Mr Jacobs. 'What [passengers] wanted us to do was to tweak the schedules to make them more business-friendly. This is a big segment for us, and we want to tailor that service to the needs of business passengers. The numbers stack up from our point of view.'

Ryanair is playing catch-up after admitting that rival easyJet has taken the lead in attracting business passengers. The Irish airline is trying to make inroads into the lucrative market as part of an overhaul to increase its appeal and soften its image for poor service and peremptory treatment of passengers.

The 'caring, cuddly, sharing' Ryanair includes offering allocated seating and mobile boarding passes, revamping its website, as well as giving families some incentives such as discounts and warming babies' bottles.

Enticing business class passengers from their cosseted ways is tough, as easyJet has found. It has lifted the proportion of business travellers it carries from 18 per cent to 20 per cent over the past few years.

Stephen Furlong, an analyst at Davy, the Dublin brokerage, says that for low-fares airlines, winning business passengers 'is a slow, incremental grind'. Moreover, some airlines are moving in the opposite direction. Aer Lingus and SAS no longer offer the full business class service on short-haul flights.

Sales keep plunging in the home market
Source: Ian G Dagnall/Alamy Stock Photo.

Mr Jacobs says a quarter of the 86m passengers Ryanair has carried over the past year are 'business travellers', but they are paying standard fares, which start at €19.99.

Ryanair will have to convince more of them to pay the higher fare – the cheapest Business Plus ticket will cost €69.99. That is less than the business ticket on traditional carriers, but it does not include incentives such as loyalty programmes.

'It will be tough to get business class passengers on the flag carriers to come across to Ryanair,' says David Holohan, who follows the company for Merrion Capital in Dublin. He says that if the Ryanair offering succeeds in luring more higher-paying passengers, the rewards could be significant given the gap between Business Plus and regular fares.

But he says the airline would be doing well to get 5 per cent of its passengers to pay the higher business product fare regularly.

One factor that may count against Ryanair is that it often flies to out-of-the-way airports. EasyJet has been building positions at primary airports for years; they now account for 70 per cent of its destinations. Ryanair is trying to increase its share of primary airports, and says it will move from 35 per cent to 45 per cent within two years.

But Michael O'Leary, chief executive, says Ryanair will not fly to Europe's three main business hub airports – London Heathrow, Paris Charles de Gaulle and Frankfurt. The toughest challenge then for Ryanair may be to make its business product work even if it does not serve Europe's main business airports.

Oliver Sleath, airlines analyst at Barclays, says: 'Ryanair is coming at this with a brand that will take some time to improve, and a network/frequency offering that is fundamentally less attractive, although evolving quickly.'

'Wait and see if easyJet can materially drive up their share of business passengers before assuming Ryanair will be successful.'

Mr O'Leary does not sound entirely convinced that being nice will make Ryanair more money, but he is willing to give it a try. In Dublin last week to announce new routes, he said his staff had assured him that if he kept up his efforts to be 'caring, cuddly and sharing', Ryanair would win more business passengers from Aer Lingus, its local rival.

'So I am doing my level best, and funnily enough it's working,' he said.

That boast is about to be put to the test.

Ride of private equity heavyweight Bonderman

David Bonderman, the 71-year-old chairman of Ryanair, has been an ever-present figure at the Irish low-cost airline.

The co-founder of Texas-based buyout group TPG Capital, who has chaired the company for 18 years, personally invested £1m for a 20 per cent stake in the low-cost airline in 1996, when the founding Ryan family was looking for a partner to boost the company's expansion internationally.

Airlines have always been the sweet spot of the private equity financier. The former lawyer rose to prominence in the US with the turnround of Continental Airlines in 1993, making almost 12 times his original investment.

Back in 1996, Ryanair's founders managed to get Mr Bonderman to drop a planned venture he was negotiating with Richard Branson to back their company instead, writes Siobhan Creaton in her book, 'Ryanair: How a small Irish airline conquered the world'. The financier participated in a refinancing of the company and bought a stake alongside the family and the management.

A year later, Ryanair became a public company and Mr Bonderman's stake was worth £60m. Since then the company's share price has surged from €0.4 to €7.1, bringing its market capitalisation to €9.6bn. The US financier, whose private equity firm is now seeking $10bn for a new leveraged buyout fund, has since sold down his stake to 0.55 per cent, which is worth €54m.

However, addressing the International Air Transport Association in 2006, Mr Bonderman said: 'It's time to sell, ladies and gentlemen,' he told his audience in Paris. 'This is as good as it gets in the airline industry. It's only going to get worse.'

 Source: from 'No-frills Ryanair faces test with Business Plus', *Financial Times*, 27/08/14 (Boland, V. and Wild, J.).

Discussion questions

1　What is the rationale behind Ryanair's decision to compete in the business segment?

2　How attractive do you assess the business segment to be to Ryanair and why?

3　What targeting strategy is Ryanair trying to pursue? What difficulties do you anticipate Ryanair will face in following such a strategy?

PART 4

COMPETITIVE POSITIONING STRATEGIES

Part 4 looks at the main ways in which firms strive to create a competitive advantage.

Chapter 10 discusses ways of creating sustainable competitive advantage once the target market has been decided. Routes to achieving cost leadership and differentiation are examined, both as alternative and as complementary strategies. The dangers of falling between these strategies, and not executing either effectively, are also addressed. The chapter then goes on to discuss how competitive positions can be communicated effectively to customers, as well as the characteristics of sustainable competitive advantage through positioning. It concludes by examining strategies for building position, holding position, harvesting, niching and divesting.

Chapter 11 considers the new marketing mix, including recent developments in e-business and e-marketing and their impact on marketing strategies. Following the early hype of the **dot.com** boom, and the equally spectacular **dot.com** bust (or **dot.bomb** as it is being referred to), the chapter takes a more measured view of the opportunities and threats Internet-based technologies have to offer organisations, and looks at how they integrate with the more traditional elements of the marketing mix.

Chapter 12 assesses the role of innovation and new product/service development in creating competitive positions. The critical factors for success in new product development are identified, together with common reasons for failure. The processes of new product development are discussed along with suggestions for speeding up and enhancing the likelihood of success. The chapter concludes by considering organisational issues in new product development and innovation.

Chapter 13 looks at the role of service and relationship marketing in building stronger competitive positions. The goods and services spectrum is introduced to show the increasing importance of the service element in the marketing implementation mix, even for goods marketers. Relationship marketing is discussed in the context of building and maintaining long-term relationships with key customers and customer groups. Techniques for monitoring and measuring customer satisfaction are presented, with particular emphasis on the use of gap analysis to track problems in customer satisfaction back to their root causes.

CHAPTER 10

CREATING SUSTAINABLE COMPETITIVE ADVANTAGE

'Competitive Strategy is the search for a favourable competitive position in an industry. Competitive Strategy aims to establish a profitable and sustainable position against the forces that determine industry competition.'

Michael Porter (1985)

Samsung to launch new mobile payment service in the US

By Song Jung-a in Seoul

Samsung Pay, the mobile payment service of Samsung Electronics, is to debut in the US on Monday, as the South Korean group looks to diversify its features to revive slowing phone sales.

The world's largest smartphone maker hopes its platform will have an edge of rival services from Apple and Google in the annual $67bn mobile payment market, as Samsung's technology is designed to work with existing credit card readers.

Samsung rolled out the payment service in its home market last month and the South Korean company said its adoption was 'beyond our expectations' with about $30m transactions in its first month.

Source: REUTERS/Alamy Stock Photo.

Samsung plans to expand the service to the UK, Spain and China, and is expected to adopt the payment feature to enhance its new low-to-mid-end smartphones next year.

However, analysts remain doubtful of the prospects of Samsung Pay abroad, given the company's relatively late entry market and weaker software ecosystem. Apple is leading the field but even the US company is still struggling to turn the mobile phone into a mainstream method of payment, with Apple phone users complaining that the service gets rejected at many merchants.

'In the US, Samsung is facing stiff competition by coming late to the mobile payments scene,' said Siyun Zeng, analyst at IHS. 'Apple Pay has established a lead in the US and Google is revamping Google Wallet to Android Pay.'

While Apple has accumulated 800m payment card accounts associated with iTunes, Ms Zeng said Samsung lacks a critical element for its payment service to gain traction. She also cautioned that Samsung Pay's co-existence with Android Pay, which was launched in the US earlier this month and works with a broader range of Android devices, could create friction as Android users could get confused by the two payment options.

Still, Samsung is hopeful its payment system will become a popular choice, given its compatibility with existing magnetic-strip card readers – Apple Pay and Android Pay require retailers to install new equipment compatible with their near-field communication technology.

However, such advantage is poised to disappear as a new US standard requires merchants and banks to switch from a card system using magnetic strips towards chips until next month to prevent fraud.

Analysts said that the diversification of services is a meaningful step for Samsung – one that could set its Galaxy smartphones apart from rival devices in the crowded handset market, although the new service will not generate direct revenues for the company.

'Samsung's handset revenue has been declining [since] 2014; investment into software is a step for Samsung to offset [such] loss,' said Ms Zeng. 'Samsung doesn't have to rely on Samsung Pay as its core revenues [maker] but [it is] a means to tie users into the ecosystem.'

The company has been struggling to defend its market share, squeezed between premium maker Apple and lower-cost Chinese rivals such as Huawei and Xiaomi. Samsung's global market share fell from 26.2 per cent a year earlier to 21.9 per cent in the second quarter, according to research group Gartner.

 Source: from 'Samsung to launch new mobile payment service in the US', *Financial Times*, 25/09/15 (Jung-a, S.).

Discussion questions

1 What issues is Samsung trying to address?

2 Why is Samsung launching Samsung Pay in the USA?

Introduction

Chapter 9 discussed the choice of target market suited to the strengths and capabilities of the firm. This chapter focuses on methods for creating a competitive advantage in that chosen target market. While few advantages are likely to last forever, some bases of advantage are more readily protected than others. A key task for the strategist is to identify those bases that offer the most potential for defensible positioning.

 Using organisational resources to create sustainable competitive advantage

In Chapter 6 we assessed organisational resources. These we classed as three main types: organisational culture; marketing assets; and marketing capabilities. Any organisation will be able to create a long list of its resources, but some of these will be more useful than others in creating competitive advantage. Fortunately, research under the resource-based view of the firm suggests that there are three main characteristics of resources that, when they coincide, help create a sustainable competitive advantage (SCA): that the resource contributes to creating value for customers; that the resource is rare, or unique to the organisation; and that the resource is hard for competitors to imitate or copy (see Figure 10.1) (Collis and Montgomery, 1997).

10.1.1 Contribution to creating customer value

The prime consideration of the value of any resource to an organisation lies in the answer to the following question: does this resource contribute to creating value for customers that can be leveraged to create value for the organisation? Value creation may be direct, such as through the benefits conveyed by superior technology, better service, meaningful brand

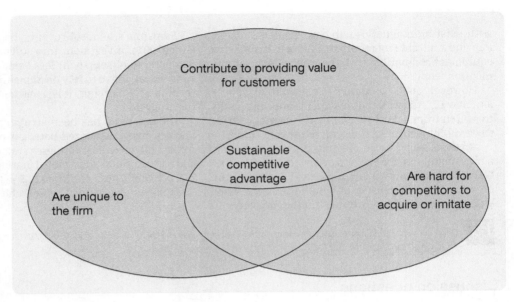

Figure 10.1
Advantage-creating
resources

differentiation and ready availability. The resources that contribute to these benefits (such as the technology deployed, skilled and motivated personnel, brand name and reputation, and distribution coverage) create value for customers directly they are employed. Other resources may, however, have an indirect impact on value for customers. Effective cost control systems, for example, are not valuable to customers in and of themselves. They only add value for customers when they translate into lower prices charged, or by the ability of the organisation to offer additional customer benefits through the cost savings achieved.

The value of a resource in creating customer value must be assessed relative to the resources of competitors (see Chapter 5). For example, a strong brand name such as Nike on sports clothing may convey more value than a less well-known brand. In other words, for the resource to contribute to sustainable competitive advantage it must serve to distinguish the organisation's offerings from those of its competitors.

10.1.2 Uniqueness or scarcity

Where resources do contribute to customer value, their uniqueness to the organisation also needs to be assessed. Some resources, such as distribution outlets used, may offer little differentiation from those available to competitors. In the grocery business, for example, distribution through the major multiple grocery stores is essential for companies such as Unilever and Procter & Gamble, but the outlets are not unique to either company and hence do not create sustainable competitive advantage for either. Those competence resources that are unique to the organisation have been termed **distinctive competencies**, in contrast to **core competencies** by some commentators (Collis and Montgomery, 1997). For an advantage to be sustainable, the rarity of the resources used to create it must be sustained over time.

10.1.3 Inimitability

Even resources that are unique to the organisation run the risk in the longer term of imitation or substitution by competitors (see Figure 10.2). In addition, competitors may find ways of acquiring or appropriating critical resources. In service organisations, for example, key staff may be 'poached' from a competitor with offers of enhanced salaries, better working conditions and so on. In the advertising industry, the danger of losing clients when key staff move to competing agencies has been long recognised, and agreed codes of practice have been drawn up, including 'golden handcuffs', to minimise the damage caused by lost resources.

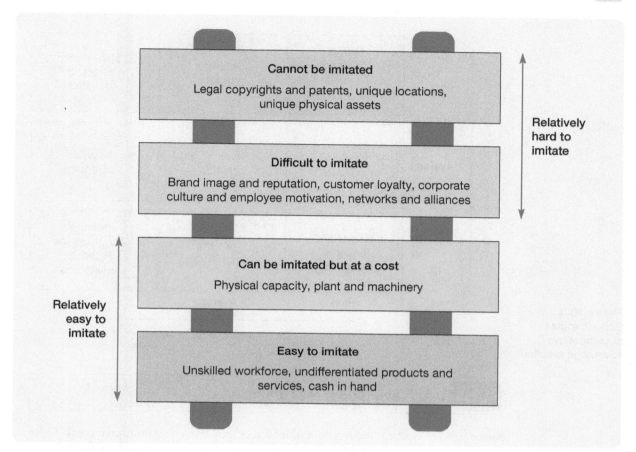

Figure 10.2 Resource imitability ladder

Source: Adapted from Collis and Montgomery (1997).

In Chapter 6, the ways of protecting resources from competitor copy, or isolating mechanisms, were discussed. These include enhancing causal ambiguity (making it hard for competitors to identify the underlying value-creating resources in the first place), building economic deterrence (making resource acquisition uneconomic), establishing legal protection (through patents and copyrights) and creating path dependency (the need to devote time and effort to the establishment and/or appropriation of resources). In the longer term, however, few resources can be effectively protected against all competitor attempts to imitate.

10.2 Generic routes to competitive advantage

As noted in Chapter 2, Porter (1980) identified two main routes to creating a competitive advantage. These he termed cost leadership and differentiation. In examining how each can be achieved, Porter (1985) takes a systems approach, likening the operations of a company to a 'value chain' from the input of raw materials and other resources through to the final delivery to, and after-sales servicing of, the customer. (The value chain was discussed in the context of competitor analysis in Chapter 5 and was presented in Figure 5.5.)

Each of the activities within the value chain – the primary activities and the support functions – can be used to add value to the ultimate product or service. That added value, however, is typically in the form of lower cost or valued uniqueness. These options are shown in Figure 10.3.

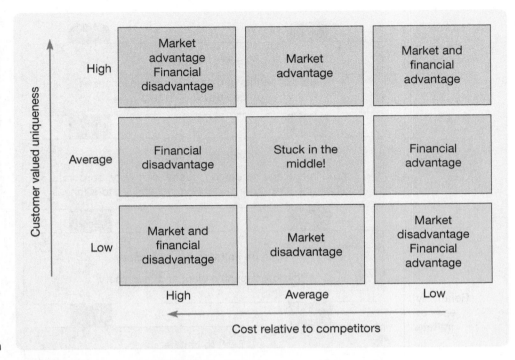

Figure 10.3
Generic routes
to competitive
advantage creation

10.3   Achieving cost leadership

Porter (1985) has identified several major factors that affect organisational costs. These he terms 'cost drivers'; they are shown in Figure 10.4 and each is reviewed briefly.

10.3.1 Economies of scale

Economies of scale are perhaps the single most effective cost driver in many industries. Scale economies stem from doing things more efficiently or differently in volume. In addition, sheer size can help in creating purchasing leverage to secure cheaper and/or better-quality (less waste) raw materials and securing them in times of limited availability.

There are, however, limits to scale economies. Size can bring with it added complexity that itself can lead to diseconomies. For most operations there is an optimum size, above or below which inefficiencies occur.

The effects of economies of scale are often more pronounced in the manufacturing sector than in services. While manufacturing operations such as assembly lines can benefit through scale, the advantages to service firms such as advertising agencies are less obvious. They may continue to lie in enhanced purchasing muscle (for the ad agency in media purchasing, for example) and spread training costs.

10.3.2 Experience and learning effects

Further cost reductions may be achieved through learning and experience effects. Learning refers to increases in efficiency that are possible at a given level of scale through an employee having performed the necessary tasks many times before.

The Boston Consulting Group (BCG) extended the recognised production learning curve beyond manufacturing and looked at the increased efficiency that was possible in all aspects of the business (such as in marketing, advertising and selling) through experience. BCG estimated empirically that, in many industries, costs reduced by approximately 15–20 per cent each time cumulative production (a measure of experience) doubled. This finding suggests

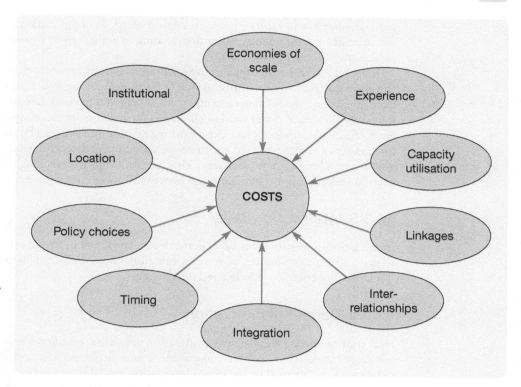

Figure 10.4
Cost drivers

Source: adapted from
*Competitive Advantage:
Creating and Sustaining
Superior Performance* (by
Michael E. Porter, 1985)
with the permission of
Free Press, a Division of
Simon & Schuster, Inc.,
Copyright © 1985, 1998
by Michael E. Porter. All
rights reserved.

that companies with larger market share will, by definition, have a cost advantage through experience, assuming all companies are operating on the same experience curve.

Experience can be brought into the company by hiring experienced staff, and be enhanced through training. Conversely, competitors may poach experience by attracting away skilled staff.

The experience curve as an explanation of costs has come under increasing scrutiny. Gluck (1986) argued that when the world changed from a high-growth 'big is beautiful' mentality to a low-growth 'big is bust' realisation, the experience curve fell into disfavour. He concluded that in today's business environments, competitive advantages that rely too heavily on economies of scale in manufacturing or distribution are often no longer sustainable. In addition, a shift in the level or type of technology employed may result in an inexperienced newcomer reducing costs to below those of a more experienced incumbent, essentially moving on to a lower experience curve. Finally, the concept was derived in manufacturing industries and it is not at all clear how far it is applicable to the service sector.

10.3.3 Capacity utilisation

Capacity utilisation has been shown to have a major impact on unit costs. The PIMS study (see Farris and Moore, 2004) has demonstrated a clear positive association between utilisation and return on investment. Significantly, the relationship is stronger for smaller companies than for larger ones. Major discontinuities or changes in utilisation can add significantly to costs, hence the need to plan production and inventory to minimise seasonal fluctuations. Many companies also avoid segments of the market where demand fluctuates wildly for this very reason (see Chapter 9 on factors influencing market attractiveness).

10.3.4 Linkages

A further set of cost drivers is linkages. These concern the other activities of the firm in producing and marketing the product that have an effect on the costs. Quality control and inspection procedures, for example, can have a significant impact on servicing costs and costs attributable to faulty product returns. Indeed, in many markets it has been demonstrated that superior quality, rather than leading to higher costs of production, can actually reduce costs (Johnson *et al.*, 2017).

External linkages with suppliers of factor inputs or distributors of the firm's final products can also result in lower costs. Just in time (JIT) manufacturing and delivery can have a significant impact on stockholding costs and work in progress. Beyond the cost equation, however, the establishment of closer working links has far wider marketing implications. For JIT to work effectively requires a very close working relationship between buyer and supplier. This often means an interchange of information, a meshing of forecasting and scheduling and the building of a long-term relationship. This, in turn, helps to create high switching costs (the costs of seeking supply elsewhere) and hence barriers to competitive entry.

10.3.5 Interrelationships

Interrelationships with other SBUs in the overall corporate portfolio can help to share experience and gain economies of scale in functional activities (such as marketing research, R&D, quality control, ordering and purchasing).

10.3.6 Degree of integration

Decisions on integration, such as contracting out delivery and/or service, also affect costs. Similarly, the decision to either make or buy components can have major cost implications. (The extent of forward or backward integration extant or possible in a particular market was discussed as one of the factors considered in assessing target market attractiveness to the company in Chapter 9.)

10.3.7 Timing

Timing, though not always controllable, can lead to cost advantages. Often, the first mover in an industry can gain cost advantages by securing prime locations, cheap or good-quality raw materials and/or technological leadership (see Chapter 12). Second movers can often benefit from exploiting newer technology in order to leapfrog first mover positions.

As with other factors already discussed, however, the value of timing goes far beyond its impact on costs. Abell (1978) has argued that a crucial element of any marketing strategy is timing – that at certain times 'strategic windows' are open (there are opportunities in the market that can be exploited), while at other times they are shut. Successful strategies are timely strategies.

10.3.8 Policy choices

Policy choices, the prime areas for differentiating, have implications for costs. Decisions on the product line, the product itself, quality levels, service, features, credit facilities etc. all affect costs. They also affect the actual and perceived uniqueness of the product to the consumer and hence a genuine dilemma can arise if the thrust of the generic strategy is not clear. The general rules are to reduce costs on factors that will not significantly affect valued uniqueness, to avoid frills if they do not serve to differentiate significantly and to invest in technology to achieve low-cost process automation and low-cost product design (fewer parts can make for easier and cheaper assembly). The policy choices pursued by Ryanair, for example, of reducing service levels and charging for all extras, enable the company to offer consistently low air fares. In 2013, following growing customer discontent, the company embarked on a customer experience improvement programme ('Always Getting Better') and introduced a business service in 2014. Nevertheless, its unrelenting commitment to lower costs and to keep fares low remains, when its competitors are putting their prices up.

10.3.9 Location and institutional factors

The final set of cost drivers identified by Porter (1985) are location (geographic location, to take advantage of lower distribution, assembly, raw materials or energy costs), and institutional factors such as government regulations (for example, larger lorries on the roads can reduce distribution costs but at other environmental and social costs). The sensitivity of governments to lobbyists and pressure groups will dictate the ability of the company to exercise institutional cost drivers.

10.3.10 Summary of cost drivers

There are many ways in which a company can seek to reduce costs. In attempting to become a cost leader in an industry, a firm should be aware, first, that there can only be one cost leader and, second, that there are potentially many ways in which this position can be attacked (through using other cost drivers). Cost advantages can be among the most difficult to sustain and defend in the face of heavy and determined competition.

Cost leadership in itself does not give the customer a reason to buy unless translated into low prices in the marketplace. It is essentially an internally focused strategy based on efficiency rather than effectiveness.

That said, however, it should be a constant objective of management to reduce costs that do not add significantly to ultimate customer satisfaction.

10.4 Achieving differentiation

Most of the factors that have been listed as cost drivers could also be used as 'uniqueness drivers' if the firm is seeking to differentiate itself from its competitors. Of most immediate concern here, however, are the policy choices open to the company. These are summarised in Figure 10.5.

10.4.1 Product differentiation

Product differentiation seeks to increase the value of the product or service on offer to the customer. Levitt (1986) has suggested that products and services can be seen on at least four main levels. These are: the core product, the expected product, the augmented product and the potential product. Figure 10.6 shows these levels diagrammatically. Differentiation is possible in all these respects.

Figure 10.5
Uniqueness drivers

Figure 10.6 Levels of product/service offering

At the centre of the model is the core, or generic, product. This is the central product or service offered. It is the petrol, steel, banking facility, mortgage or information, etc. Beyond the generic product, however, is what customers expect in addition – the expected product. When buying petrol, for example, customers expect easy access to the forecourt, the possibility of paying by credit card, the availability of screen-wash facilities, air for tyres, radiator top-up and so on. Since most petrol forecourts meet these expectations, they do not serve to differentiate one supplier from another.

At the next level, Levitt identifies the augmented product. This constitutes all the extra features and services that go above and beyond what the customer expects, in order to convey added value and hence serve to differentiate the offer from that of competitors. The petrol station where, in the self-serve world of today, one attendant fills the car with petrol while another cleans the windscreen, headlamps and mirrors, is going beyond what is expected. Over time, however, these means of distinguishing can become copied, routine, and ultimately merely part of what is expected.

Finally, Levitt describes the potential product as all those further additional features and benefits that *could* be offered. At the petrol station these may include a free car wash with every fill-up, gifts unrelated to petrol and a car valeting service. While the model shows the potential product as bounded, in reality it is only bounded by the limitations of the imagination and ingenuity of the supplier.

While in the past suppliers have concentrated on attempts to differentiate their offerings on the basis of the generic and expected product, convergence is occurring at this level in many markets. As quality control, assurance and management methods become more widely understood and practised, delivering a performing, reliable, durable, conforming offer (a 'quality' product in the classic sense of the word) will no longer be adequate. Levitt predicts that in the future there will be greater emphasis on the augmented and potential product as ways of adding value, creating customer delight and hence creating competitive advantage.

Differentiating the core and expected product

Differentiation of the core product or benefit offers a different way of satisfying the same basic want or need (see Figure 10.7). It is typically created by a step-change in technology, the

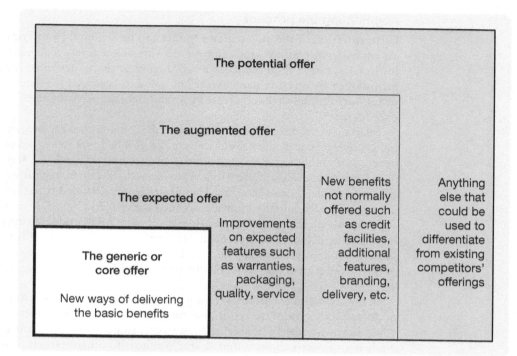

Figure 10.7
Product/service
differentiation

application of innovation. Calculators, for example, offered a different method of solving the basic 'calculating' need from the slide rules they replaced. Similarly, the deep freeze offers a different way of storing food from the earlier cold stores, pantries and cellars. A new strain of grass that only grows to 1 inch in height but never wears out could replace the need for a lawnmower.

However, it is at the core product level that the most radical differentiation is now occurring, often at the hands of disruptors making full use of significant breakthroughs in technology. Examples include downloadable and streamed music (Apple, Spotify), driverless cars (Tesla) and smart watches (Apple). Such differentiation can also be the result of applying different strategic thinking. The advent of the sharing economy has led to new business models, such as those followed by Uber ('getting a ride'), Deliveroo (take-away delivery), Airbnb (a room for the night) and many more.

Source: BAS CZERWINSKI/EPA-EFE/Shutterstock, as featured in 'Deliveroo delivers back-up police in long-time missing persons cases', Amsterdam, Netherlands (30 Apr 2019).

Augmenting the product

Differentiation of the augmented product can be achieved by offering more to customers on existing features (for example, by offering a seven-year guarantee as Kia does for its cars, rather than the more usual three-year guarantee most other manufacturers provide), or by offering new features of value to customers. There are two main types of product feature that can create customer benefit: performance features and appearance features.

Analysis of product features must relate those features to the benefits they offer to customers. For example, the introduction of the golf ball typewriter did not change the core benefit (the ability to create a typewritten page of text or numbers). It did, however, allow different typefaces and different spacing to be used, thus extending the value to the customer who wanted these extra benefits. The inkjet printer extended those benefits even further, offering virtually unlimited fonts, sizes and other effects.

In estimating the value to the consumers of additional product features and their resulting benefits, conjoint measurement can be particularly useful. This technique has been successfully applied, for example, to decisions on product features by companies operating in the audio market and to service features offered by building societies in high-interest accounts.

In the lawnmower market, Flymo introduced the rotary blade hover mower as a means of differentiating from the traditional rotating cylinder blade. In some markets, especially where lawns were awkwardly shaped or steeply sloping, the ease of use of the hover mower made it a very attractive, differentiated product. In other markets, however, the market leader, Qualcast, was able to retaliate by showing the advantage of the conventional mower in having a hopper in which to catch the grass cuttings. Under the Flymo system, the cuttings were left on the lawn. More recent developments have seen the introduction of rotary hover mowers with hoppers.

Quality

A prime factor in differentiating the product or service from that of competitors is quality. Quality concerns the fitness for purpose of a product or service. For manufactured products that can include the durability, appearance or grade of the product, while in services it often comes down to the tangible elements of the service, the reliability and responsiveness of the service provider, the assurance provided of the value of the service and the empathy, or caring attention, received (see Parasuraman *et al.*, 1988). Quality can reflect heavily, both on raw materials used and the degree of quality control exercised during manufacture and delivery.

Of central importance is consumer perception of quality, which may not be the same as the manufacturer's perception. For example, Johnson & Johnson in the mid-2010s suffered a downturn in its sales of baby products as millennial mothers switched to organic, natural products. However, natural ingredients are not necessarily safe on babies' skins and may cause irritations. So the company, as well as updating its baby range to ensure it offered the gentlest care possible, stressed its 'clinically proven, pure ingredients' in social media and advertising campaign. J&J also hosted educational events around the world focused on providing millennial mums with an understanding of how delicate babies' skin is.

Quality has been demonstrated by the PIMS project to be a major determinant of commercial success. Indeed, Buzzell and Gale (1987) concluded that relative perceived quality (customers' judgements of the quality of the supplier's offer relative to its competitors) was the single most important factor in affecting the long-run performance of a business. Quality was shown to have a greater impact on ROI level and be more effective at gaining market share than lower pricing.

Closely related to perceptions of quality are perceptions of style, particularly for products with a high emotional appeal (such as cosmetics). In fashion-conscious markets such as clothes, design can be a very powerful way of differentiating. Jain (1990) notes that Du Pont successfully rejuvenated its market for ladies' stockings by offering different-coloured tints and hence repositioned the stockings as fashion accessories – a different tint for each outfit.

Design

Design can be a differentiator. It is the one consistently used by Sir James Dyson across his whole product range, from bagless and cordless vacuum cleaners, hairdryers and fans to, in the future, electric cars. Bang & Olufsen and later Apple have competed with Dyson on design. Steve Jobs is famed for saying that 'most people make the mistake of thinking design is what it looks like. People think it's this veneer – that the designers are handed this box and told, "Make it look good!" That's not what we think design is. It's not just what it looks like and feels like. Design is how it works' (https://www.youtube.com/watch?v=sPfJQmpg5zk).

Packaging

Packaging, too, can be used to differentiate the product. Packaging has five main functions, each of which can be used as a basis for differentiation:

1 Packaging **stores** the product, and hence can be used to extend shelf life, or facilitate physical storage (such as Tetra Paks for fruit juice and other beverages).
2 Packaging **protects** the product during transit and prior to consumption to ensure consistent quality (such as the use of film packs for potato crisps to ensure freshness).
3 Packaging **facilitates use** of the product (for example, applicator packs for floor cleaners, wine boxes, domestic liquid soap dispensers).
4 Packaging helps **create an image** for the product through its visual impact, quality of design, illustration of uses, sustainability and caring for the planet. There are currently some strong ethical issues around the use of plastic in packaging, in particular single-use plastic.
5 Packaging helps **promote** the product through eye-catching, unusual colours and shapes. Examples of the latter are the sales of wine in carafes rather than bottles (Paul Masson California Wines) and the sale of ladies' tights in egg-shaped packages (L'eggs).

Branding

A particularly effective way of differentiating at the tangible product level is to create a unique brand with a favourable image and reputation. As discussed in Chapter 6, brand and company reputation can be powerful marketing assets for a company.

Brand name or symbol is an indication of pedigree and a guarantee of what to expect from the product – a quality statement of a value-for-money signal. Heinz baked beans, for example, can command a premium price because of the assurance of quality the consumer gets in choosing the brand. Similarly, grocery retailers such as Waitrose and Sainsbury's are able to differentiate their own branded products from other brands because of their reputation for quality that extends across their product ranges. Witness the yearly excitement when Interbrand, among others, announces which of Apple, Google or Samsung is the world's best brand, and who makes the top 100. Branding is also a highly defensible competitive advantage. Once registered, competitors cannot use the same branding (name or symbol).

Service

Service can be a major differentiating factor in the purchase of many products, especially durables (both consumer and industrial). Certainly, enhanced service was a major factor in the success of Wilhelm Becker, a Swedish industrial paints company. Becker developed

'Colour Studios' as a service to its customers and potential customers to enable them to experiment with different colours and combinations. Volvo, the Swedish auto manufacturer, used the service in researching alternative colours to use on farm tractors and found that red (the colour used to date) was a poor colour choice as it jarred, for many farmers, with the colours of the landscape. Changing the colour scheme resulted in increased sales.

In domestic paints, too, there has been an attempt to add service, this time provided by the customers themselves. Matchpots were introduced by a leading domestic paint supplier to allow customers, for a small outlay, to try different colours at home before selecting the final colour to use. In this case, however, unlike Becker's Colour Studios, copy by competitors was relatively easy and the advantage quickly eroded.

Service need not always be an addition to the product – in some circumstances a reduction can add value. The growth in home meal kits, where all the ingredients are provided together with a recipe, allows the customer to gain satisfaction through self-completion of the cooking process and in serving their families fresh, home-cooked food. Thus, the customer provides the service and becomes part of the production process (co-creation).

Providing superior service as a way of creating a stronger link between supplier and customer can have wide-reaching consequences. In particular, it makes it less likely that the customer will look for alternative supply sources and hence acts as a barrier to competitor entry.

To ensure and enhance customer service, it is recommended that each company regularly conducts customer satisfaction studies to gauge how well it is meeting customers' expectations and to seek ways in which it can improve on customer service.

Further elements of the augmented product that can be used to differentiate the product include installation, credit availability, delivery (speedy and on time, when promised) and warranty. All can add to the differentiation of the product from that of competitors.

Deciding on the bases for product differentiation

Each of the elements of the product can be used as a way of differentiating the product from competitive offerings. In deciding which of the possible elements to use in differentiating the product, three considerations are paramount.

First, what do the customers expect in addition to the core, generic product? In the automobile market, for example, customers in all market segments expect a minimum level of reliability in the cars they buy. In the purchase of consumer white goods (fridges, freezers, washing machines, etc.), minimum periods of warranty are expected. In the choice of toothpaste, minimum levels of protection from tooth decay and gum disease are required. These expectations, over and above the core product offering, are akin to 'hygiene factors' in Hertzberg's Theory of Motivation. They must be offered for the product or service to be considered by potential purchasers. Their presence does not enhance the probability of consumers choosing products with them, but their absence will certainly deter purchase.

The second consideration is what the customers would value over and above what is expected. In identifying potential 'motivators', the marketer seeks to offer more than the competition in order to attract purchasers. These additions to the product beyond what is normally expected by the customers often form the most effective way of differentiating the company's offerings. Crucial, however, is the cost of offering these additions. The cost of the additions should be less than the extra benefit (value) to the customers and hence be reflected in a willingness to pay a premium price. Where possible, an economic value should be placed on the differentiation to allow pricing to take full account of value to the customer (see Gallo, 2015).

The third consideration in choosing a way of differentiating the product from the competition is the ease with which that differentiation can be copied. Changes in the interest rates charged by one bank, for example, can easily be copied in a matter of days or even hours. However, the type of engagement it has with its customers and their purchasing journeys is more difficult to copy.

Figure 10.8 Alternative emphases for differentiation

Ideally, differentiation is sought where there is some (at least temporary) barrier precluding competitors following. The most successful differentiations are those that use a core skill, competence or marketing asset of the company that competitors do not possess and will find hard to develop. In the car hire business, for example, the extensive network of pick-up and drop-off points offered by Enterprise, the market leader, enables them to offer a more convenient service to the one-way customer than the competition. Emulating that network is costly, if not impossible, for smaller followers in the market.

Many companies overemphasise the core product in their overall marketing thinking and strategy. As it becomes increasingly difficult to differentiate on the basis of core product, greater emphasis will need to be put on how to 'add service' through the augmented (and potential) product. This change in emphasis is shown in Figure 10.8, which contrasts a product focus (core product emphasis) with a service-added focus (extending the augmented and potential products in ways of value and interest to the customer).

A focus away from the core product towards the 'outer rings' is particularly useful in 'commodity' markets, where competitive strategy has traditionally been based on price. Differentiation through added service offers an opportunity for breaking out of an over-reliance on price in securing business.

In summary, there are a great many ways in which products and services can be differentiated from their competitors. In deciding on the type of differentiation to adopt, several factors should be borne in mind: the added value to the customer of the differentiation; the cost of differentiation in relation to the added value; the probability and speed of competitor copy; and the extent to which the differentiation exploits the marketing assets of the company.

10.4.2 Distribution differentiation

Distribution differentiation comes from using different routes to market, having a different network or a different coverage of the market.

Nespresso differentiates itself through all the elements of the marketing mix, but more specifically in the way it distributes its products. It emphasises its aspirational luxury positioning with its exclusive Nespresso boutiques and concessions in top department stores, as well as its online club. This has the added advantage of allowing Nespresso full control of its customers' experience.

The growth of the Internet has made significant changes to the distribution strategies of many firms. Particularly for firms offering bit-based products such as information, or music, direct delivery to customers through their Internet connections is instant (see Chapter 11). Again, first mover advantages afforded short-term differentiation, but competitor copy has been rapid. Protecting an advantage in e-marketing, be it a distribution advantage or a communications advantage, is proving particularly difficult, and innovative companies such as Amazon.com are having constantly to find new ways to add value for their customers in an attempt to remain differentiated.

10.4.3 Price differentiation

Lower price as a means of differentiation can be a successful basis for strategy only where the company enjoys a cost advantage, or where there are barriers to competing firms with a lower cost structure competing at a lower price. Without a cost advantage, starting a price war can be a disastrous course to follow.

Premium pricing is generally only possible where the product or service has actual or perceived advantages to the customer and therefore it is often used in conjunction with, and to reinforce, a differentiated product.

In general, the greater the degree of product or services differentiation, the more scope there is for premium pricing. Where there is little other ground for differentiation, price competition becomes stronger and cost advantages assume greater importance.

10.4.4 Promotional differentiation

Promotional differentiation involves using different types of promotions (such as a wider communications mix employing advertising, public relations, direct mail, personal selling, and social media and permission marketing via emails), promotions of a different intensity (particularly heavy promotions during launch and relaunch of products) or different content (that is, with a clearly different advertising message).

Many companies today make poor use of the potential of public relations. Public relations essentially consist of creating relationships with the media and using those relationships to gain positive exposure. Press releases and interviews with key executives on important topical issues can help to promote the company in a more credible way than media advertising.

A small, UK-based electronics company brilliantly exploited a visit by Japanese scientists to its plant. The company gained wide coverage of the event, presenting it as an attempt by the Japanese to learn from this small but innovative firm. The coverage was in relevant trade journals and even the national media. The result was a major increase in enquiries to the company and increasing domestic sales of its products. The PR had two major advantages over media advertising. First, it was very cheap in relation to the exposure it achieved (the company could never have afforded to buy the exposure at normal media rates). Second, the reports appearing in the press attracted credibility because they had been written by independent journalists and were seen as 'news' rather than advertising (*The Marketing Mix*, television series by Yorkshire TV). Similarly, when Kodak sponsored a *Celebrity Apprentice* TV show in the USA, the company benefited from free publicity in all the countries the show was released in.

Using a different message within normal media advertising can also have a differentiating effect. When most advertisers are pursuing essentially the same market with the same message an innovative twist is called for. Most beers are promoted by showing gregarious groups of males in public houses having an enjoyable night out. Heineken managed to differentiate its beer by using a series of advertisements employing humour and the caption 'Heineken refreshes the parts other beers cannot reach'. Similarly an innovative campaign for Boddington's Bitter, emphasising the down-to-earth value of the beer and its creamy, frothy head, served to mark it out from the crowd.

Nike stands out from the crowd here too. In 2018 the company celebrated the 30th anniversary of its 'Just do it' campaign, claiming 'a record engagement' with the brand following the campaign and a real uptake in traffic and engagement, both socially and commercially (Vizard, 2018). Nike's CEO, Mark Parker, said they are all 'very inspiring athletes' who have helped Nike deliver a message that really connects with its consumers. 'We're motivated to inspire our consumers to connect and engage. We feel actually very good and very proud of the work we're doing with Just Do It, introducing Just Do It to the new generation of consumers on the 30th anniversary of the campaign', explained Parker. 'We know it's resonated quite strongly with consumers obviously here, in North America, but also around the world. It's really transcended the North American market to touch people around the world.'

Nike has been both praised and criticised for the campaign, with Kaepernick in particular proving a divisive choice. Kaepernick, a former NFL quarterback for the San Francisco 49ers, is known for 'taking the knee' – a reference to his refusal to stand during the national anthem at the start of games as a protest over racism and police brutality. That move has prompted heated debate from those both for and against his protest (Vizard, 2018).

Social media can be used to great effect to create differentiation. Starbucks has taken its established offline brand and replicated its vibrant coffee culture online. This success is attributed to the fact that drinking coffee is a social activity. In 2014, Starbucks had:

- 37.32 million Facebook likes;
- 6.56 million Twitter followers;
- 2.98 million Instagram fans;
- 2.86 million Google+ followers;
- 160 thousand Pinterest followers;
- 32 thousand YouTube subscribers.

For example, looking at Twitter alone:

> Starbucks has a fascinating and unique approach to Twitter updates – they don't do them all the time rather strategically! Fans who connect to the company on Twitter to catch the latest news and updates are in for a surprise. The team does post unique content but also uses the Twitter as a service to reach out to customers talking about their in-store or product experiences.
>
> All Tweets are directed at specific Twitter users who've 'spoken' to Starbucks in their own timeline, sometimes with a complaint or negative feedback. The Starbucks team checks in several times a day and encourages dissatisfied customers to get in touch with the company for follow-up using a Twitter-specific email address. It's an unorthodox but smart approach to deal with customer complaints before they have a chance to get out of hand (*Huff, 2014*).

10.4.5 Brand differentiation

Brand positioning places the customer at the centre of building a maintainable hold on the marketplace. It shifts from the classic idea of companies developing a 'unique selling proposition' (USP) to establishing a 'unique emotional proposition'.

Competing products may look similar to the hapless parent buying a pair of Nike trainers, but not to their children. They want Nike trainers, and the parent is pressured to pay the extra to get them. Nike's success at brand differentiation flowed from its Air Jordan range, which built upon the USP of air cells in the heels and their unique emotional proposition of being associated with top athletes. So powerful did this combination become that even in relatively crime-free Japan people paid huge price premiums for their Air Jordans, but would not jog in them for fear of being mugged (called jugging) for their Nikes. Adidas and Reebok promote their products using athletes and air in their heels, but Nike has won the battle for the minds of teenagers and their parents' pockets.

Nike is an exemplary case of gaining market strength by using Ries and Trout's (2001) ladder of awareness. Even though there may be numerous products on the market, consumers are rarely able to name more than a few. This was the problem faced by Audi when they realised that people mentioned Mercedes, BMW and Volkswagen as German cars, with all the connotations of quality and reliability that entails, but often omitted Audi (now owned by VW). The result was the 'Vorsprung Durch Technik' campaign, which concentrated on the German pedigree of the product and, through rallying and the Quatro, on its technical excellence.

Ries and Trout noted that the second firm in markets usually enjoys half the business of the first firm, and the third firm enjoys half the business of the second, etc. This flows through into profitability and return on investments where, in the long term, profitability follows the market share ranking of companies. Leading companies can also achieve major economies in advertising and promotion. Part of the reason for this is the tendency for people to remember the number one. When asked who was the first person to successfully fly alone across the Atlantic most people would correctly answer Charles Lindbergh, but how many people can name the second person? Similarly with the first and second people to set foot on the moon, or climb Mount Everest.

The importance of being number one is fine for market leaders such as Nike in sports shoes, Mercedes in luxury cars, Coca-Cola in soft drinks and Nescafé in coffee, but it leaves lesser brands with an unresolved problem. Positioning points to a way for these brands to establish a strong place in the mind of the consumer, despite the incessant call for attention from competing products. This involves consistency of message and the association of a brand with ideas that are already held strongly within the consumer's mind.

10.4.6 Summary of differentiation drivers

Where the route to competitive advantage selected is differentiation, the key differentiating variables (those that offer the most leverage for differentiation using the company's skills to the full) should be identified. Where possible, differentiation should be pursued on multiple fronts for its enhancement. In addition, value signals should be employed to enhance perceived differentiation (such as building on reputation, image, presence, appearance and pricing of the product). Barriers to copying should be erected, through patenting, holding key executives and creating switching costs in order to retain customers.

| **10.5** | **Sustaining competitive advantage** |

It will be clear from the previous text that there are a variety of ways companies can attempt to create a competitive advantage for themselves. Some of these will be easier for competitors to copy than others. The most useful ways of creating defensible positions lie in exploiting the following.

10.5.1 Unique and valued products

Fundamental to creating a superior and defensible position in the marketplace is to have unique and valued products and services crafted through the use of scarce and valuable organisational resources to offer to customers.

Dow Jones maintains high margins from unique products. *The Wall Street Journal* is a product that customers want and are willing to pay for. Central to offering unique and valued products and services is the identification of the key differentiating variables – those with the greatest potential leverage.

Uniqueness may stem from employing superior, proprietary technology, utilising superior raw materials, or from differentiating the tangible and augmented elements of the product.

Unique products do not, however, stay unique forever. Successful products will be imitated sooner or later, so that the company that wishes to retain its unique position must be willing, and indeed even eager, to innovate continually and look for new ways of differentiating (see Chapter 12). This may mean a willingness to cannibalise its own existing products before the competition attacks them.

10.5.2 Clear, tight definition of market targets

To enable a company to keep its products and services both unique and valued by the customers requires constant monitoring of, and dialogue with, those customers. This in turn requires a clear understanding of who they are and how to access them. The clearer the focus of the firm's activities on one or a few market targets, the more likely it is to serve those targets successfully. In the increasingly segmented and fragmented markets of the 2020s, the companies that fail to focus their activities are less likely to respond to changing opportunities and threats. As Sarah Mansfield, Unilever vice-president of global media for Europe and the Americas, puts it: 'What we say is it's a journey from mass reach to mass customisation to mass personalisation. It's about reaching large audiences but doing it in a really smart way.' To achieve this requires 'understanding consumers, their traits and behaviours, to identify actionable targeting segments for which we can develop different messages' (Barnett, 2018).

10.5.3 Enhanced customer linkages

Creating closer bonds with customers through enhanced service can help establish a more defensible position in the market (see Chapter 13). As suggested previously, a major advantage of JIT manufacturing systems is that they require closer links between supplier and buyer. As buyers and suppliers become more enmeshed, so it becomes more difficult for newcomers to enter.

Creating switching costs, the costs associated with moving from one supplier to another, is a further way in which customer linkages can be enhanced. Hagel, co-chairman for Deloitte LLP's Center for the Edge, in an interview with *The Marketing Journal* (2016), argues that technological advances such as Big Data and cloud computing enable what he calls a 'trusted advisor' business model:

> Companies that master the techniques of collaboration marketing will start to build more trust with customers based on their increasing helpfulness in addressing the customer's needs. Companies traveling this path will ultimately need to make a very difficult choice if they are truly going to win the deep trust that they will need from the customer. They will eventually need to shed their own product businesses to reinforce with customers that they are truly impartial in terms of evaluating the full array of products and services that might be relevant to their needs.

> Rather than staying wedded to traditional push-based marketing approaches that focus on intercepting, isolating and insulating the 'target' customer, collaboration marketing harnesses the power of pull to attract customers, motivating them to seek you out because you are becoming more and more helpful, assisting them to get more value from the products you're selling. One of the most effective ways to be helpful to customers is by mobilizing a large number of third parties who have complementary products and services that can help the customer get more value from your own products and services (Hagel, 2016).

10.5.4 Established brand and company credibility

Brand and company reputation are among the most defensible assets a company has, provided they are managed well and protected:

> Nike have an enviable reputation for superior quality workmanship over the world. Nike is emphasizing its digital transformation, rolling out its Nike app in stores and launched a new concept, called Nike Live that makes use of its Nike+ membership scheme to offer

a 'differentiated' experience in-store. 'We see growth in the physical environment being driven by smarter retail experiences that leverage digital technology to better serve consumers', said Nike CFO Andy Campion (Vizard, 2018).

The rate of technological and market change is now so fast, and products so transient, that customers find security and continuity in the least tangible of a company's assets: the reputation of its brands and company name. Brand, styles and products change year on year, but people the world over desire Apple, Nike, Sony, Mercedes, Levi's and Rolex. Indeed, the role of brand (that is, the pull of the brand over other factors such as price) and brand strength (its sustainability) are two of the three components used by Interbrand in its 'Best Brands' yearly ranking (visit **https://www.interbrand.com/best-brands/best-global-brands/ methodology/**).

10.6 Offensive and defensive competitive strategies

Successful competitive strategy amounts to combining attacking and defensive moves to build a stronger position in the chosen marketplace. A number of writers, most notably Kotler and Singh (1981), James (1984) and Ries and Trout (1986), have drawn an analogy between military warfare and competitive battles in the marketplace. Their basic contention is that lessons for the conduct of business strategy can be learned by a study of warfare and the principles developed by military strategists. Indeed, the bookshelves of corporate strategists around the world now often contain the works of Sun Tzu (Trai, 1991; Khoo, 1992) and von Clausewitz (1908).

Similarly, much can be learned from the approaches used in competitive sports, pastimes and team games, where brains as well as (or instead of) brawn are important for success. Successful sportsmen and women, such as Olympian rower Sir Steve Redgrave and coach Sir Clive Woodward, have made successful second careers through speaking about strategy and motivation at corporate development seminars.

There are five basic competitive strategies pursued by organisations. These include build (or growth) strategies, hold (or maintenance) strategies, niche (or focus) strategies, harvest (or reaping) strategies and deletion (divestment) strategies. The structure of the discussion draws from both Kotler and Keller (2016) and James (1984).

10.6.1 Build strategies

A build strategy seeks to improve on organisational performance through expansion of activities. This expansion may come through expanding the market for the organisation's offerings or through winning market share from competitors.

Build strategies are most suited to growth markets. In such markets it is generally considered easier to expand, as this need not be at the expense of the competition and does not necessarily provoke strong competitive retaliation. During the growth phase of markets, companies should aim to grow at least as fast as the market itself.

Build strategies can also make sense in non-growth markets, where there are exploitable competitor weaknesses or where there are marketing assets that can be usefully deployed.

Build strategies are often costly, particularly where they involve a direct confrontation with a major competitor. Before embarking on such strategies, the potential costs must be weighed against the expected gains.

Market expansion

Build strategies are achieved through market expansion or taking sales and customers from competitors (confrontation). Market expansion, in turn, comes through three main routes: **new users** (attracted as products progress through their life cycles from innovators

Figure 10.9
Market challenger
strategies

- Frontal attack
- Flanking attack
- Encirclement attack
- Bypass strategy
- Guerrilla tactics

to laggards via a trickle-down effect), **new uses** (introduced to existing or new users) and/or **increased frequency of use** (by encouraging existing users to use more of the product).

For products that have reached the mature phase of the life cycle, a major task is to find new markets for the product. This could involve geographic expansion of the companies' activities, domestically and/or internationally. Companies seeking growth but believing their established market to be incapable of providing it roll out into new markets.

Market share gain through competitor confrontation

When a build objective is pursued in a market that cannot, for one reason or another, be expanded, success must, by definition, be at the expense of competitors. This will inevitably lead to some degree of confrontation between the protagonists for customers. Kotler and Singh (1981) have identified five main confrontation strategies (see Figure 10.9).

Frontal attack

The frontal attack is characterised by an all-out attack on the opponent's territory. It is often countered by a fortification, or position defence. The outcome of the confrontation will depend on strength and endurance (see Figure 10.10).

The requirement of a similar 3 to 1 advantage to ensure success in a commercial frontal attack has been suggested (Kotler and Singh, 1981), further calibrated (Cook, 1983) and questioned (Chattopadhyay *et al.*, 1985). All agree, however, that to defeat a well-entrenched competitor who has built a solid market position requires substantial superiority in at least one key area of the marketing programme. For a frontal attack to succeed requires sufficient resources, a strength advantage over the competitors being attacked, and that losses can be both predicted and sustained.

Flanking attack

In contrast to the frontal attack, the flanking attack seeks to concentrate the aggressor's strengths against the competitor's weaknesses (see Figure 10.11).

A flanking attack is achieved either through attacking geographic regions where the defender is under-represented or through attacking underserved competitor segments. The principle is to direct the attack at competitors' weaknesses, not their strengths.

Attack where the competition is strong
and rely on outweighing them for victory

Figure 10.10
Frontal attack

Figure 10.11
Flanking attack

Identify less obvious lines of attack. Attack the
weak points in the competitor's defence

Segmental flanking involves serving distinct segments that have not been adequately served by existing companies. Crucial to a successful flanking strategy can be timing. The Japanese entry into the US sub-compact car market was timed to take advantage of the economic recession and concerns over energy supply. The strategy requires the identification of competitor weaknesses, and inability or unwillingness to serve particular sectors of the market. In turn, identification of market gaps often requires a fresh look at the market and a more creative approach to segmenting it.

Encirclement attack

The encirclement attack, or siege, consists of enveloping the enemy and cutting them off from routes of supply to force capitulation (see Figure 10.12).

There are two approaches to the encirclement attack. The first is to attempt to isolate the competitor from the supply of raw materials on which they depend and/or the customers they seek to serve. The second approach is to seek to offer an all-round better product or service than the competitor.

Figure 10.12
Encirclement
attack

Cut off the competitor from critical resources and
support, access to supply and access to market

Figure 10.13
Bypass strategy

Avoid competing where the competition is strong.
Go around to new positions

Bypass strategy

The bypass strategy is characterised by changing the battleground to avoid competitor strongholds (see Figure 10.13).

Bypass is often achieved through technological leapfrogging.

Guerrilla tactics

Where conventional attacks fail or are not feasible, guerrilla tactics may be employed. In chess, a player in an apparently hopeless situation may sacrifice a piece unexpectedly if it disrupts the opponent's line of attack (see Figure 10.14). In boxing, it has been known for a contender on the ropes to bite the ear of his opponent to disrupt the onslaught!

Unconventional or guerrilla tactics in business are employed primarily as 'spoiling' activities to weaken the competition. They are often used by a weaker attacker on a stronger defender. Selective price cuts, especially during a competitor's new product testing or launch, depositioning advertising (as attempted by Nokia with its product Lumia in the Galaxy S5-branded Terminal 5 at Heathrow), alliances, executive raids and legal manoeuvres can all be used in this regard. Guerrilla tactics are used by companies of all sizes in attempts to soften up their competitors, often before moving in for the kill. Their effectiveness lies in the difficulty the attacked has in adequately defending against the tactics due to their unpredictability.

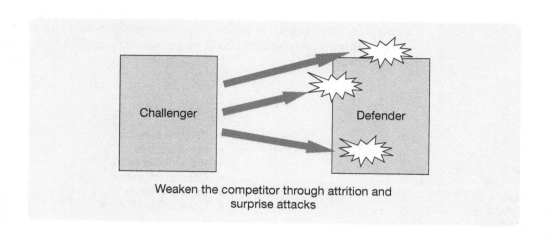

Weaken the competitor through attrition and
surprise attacks

Figure 10.14
Guerrilla tactics

10.6.2 Holding and defensive strategies

In contrast to build strategies, firms already in strong positions in their markets may pursue essentially defensive strategies to enable them to hold the ground they have already won.

For market leaders, for example, especially those operating in mature or declining markets, the major objective may not be to build but to maintain the current position against potential attackers. It could also be that, even in growing markets, the potential rewards judged to be possible from a build strategy are outweighed by the expected costs – due, for example, to the strength and nature of the competition (Treacy and Wiersema, 1995).

A hold strategy may be particularly suitable for a business or product group designated as a cash generator for the company, where that cash is needed for investment elsewhere.

Market maintenance

The amount and type of effort required to hold position will vary depending on the degree and nature of competition encountered. When the business dominates its market it may have cost advantages through economies of scale or experience effects that can be used as a basis for defending through selective price cutting. Alternatively, barriers to entry can be erected by the guarding of technological expertise, where possible, and the retention of key executive skills.

Defensive strategies

While in some markets competitor aggression may be low, making a holding strategy relatively easy to execute, in most, especially where the potential gains for an aggressor are high, more constructive defensive strategies must be explicitly pursued. Kotler and Singh (1981) suggest six basic holding strategies (see Figure 10.15).

Fortification strategies and position defence

Market fortification involves erecting barriers around the company and its market offerings to shut out competition (see Figure 10.16).

In business, a position defence is created through erecting barriers to copy and/or entry. This is most effectively achieved through differentiating the company's offerings from those of competitors and potential competitors. Where differentiation can be created on non-copyable grounds (for example, by using the company's distinctive skills, competencies and marketing assets) that are of value to the customers, aggressors will find it more difficult to overrun the position defended.

For established market leaders, brand name and reputation are often used as the principal way of holding position. In addition, maintaining higher quality, better delivery and service, better (more appealing or heavier) promotions or lower prices based on a cost advantage can all be used to fortify the position held against a frontal attack.

A fortification defence may also involve plugging the gaps in provision to shut out competitor attacks.

- Position defence
- Flanking defence
- Pre-emptive strike
- Counter-offensive
- Mobile defence
- Contraction defence

Figure 10.15
Defensive
strategies

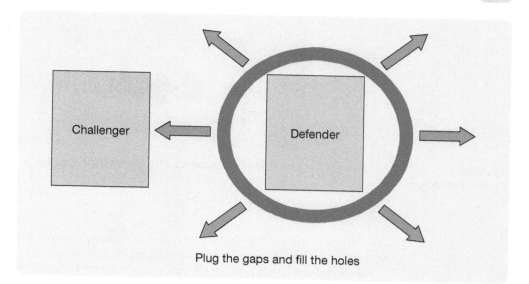

Figure 10.16
Position defence

Plug the gaps and fill the holes

Flanking defence

The flanking defence is a suitable rejoinder to a flanking attack. Under the attack strategy, the aggressor seeks to concentrate strength against the weaknesses of the defender, often using the element of surprise to gain the upper hand.

A flanking defence requires the company to strengthen the flanks, without providing a weaker and more vulnerable target elsewhere (see Figure 10.17). It requires the prediction of competitor strategy and likely strike positions. In food marketing, for example, several leading manufacturers of branded goods, seeing the increasing threat posed by retailer own-label and generic brands, have entered into contracts to provide own-label products themselves rather than let their competitors get into their markets.

The major concerns in adopting a flanking strategy are, first, whether the new positions adopted for defensive reasons significantly weaken the main, core positions. In the case of retailer own labels, for example, actively cooperating could increase the trend towards own label and lead to the eventual death of the brand. As a consequence, many leading brand

Figure 10.17
Flanking defence

Defend the flanks against attack by extending the
defences to cover peripheral weaknesses

Figure 10.18
Pre-emptive strike

Attack the competition before they attack you

manufacturers will not supply own label and rely on the strength of their brands to see off competition (effectively a position, or fortification, defence).

The second concern is whether the new position is actually tenable. Where it is not based on corporate strengths or marketing assets it may be less defensible than the previously held positions.

Pre-emptive defence

A pre-emptive defence involves striking at the potential aggressor before they can mount their attack (see Figure 10.18).

The pre-emptive defensive can involve an actual attack on the competition (as occurs in the disruption of competitor test marketing activity) or merely signal an intention to fight on a particular front and a willingness to commit the necessary resources to defend against aggression.

Sun Tzu (Khoo, 1992) summed up the philosophy behind the pre-emptive defence: 'The supreme art of war is to subdue the enemy without fighting.' Unfortunately, it is not always possible to deter aggression. The second-best option is to strike back quickly before the attack gains momentum, through a counter-offensive.

Counter-offensive

Where deterrence of a potential attack before it occurs may be the ideal defence, a rapid counter-attack to 'stifle at birth' the aggression can be equally effective. The essence of a counter-offensive is to identify the aggressor's vulnerable spots and to strike hard.

When Xerox attempted to break into the mainframe computer market head-on against the established market leader, IBM launched a classic counter-offensive in Xerox's bread-and-butter business (copiers). The middle-range copiers were the major cash generators of Xerox operations and were, indeed, creating the funds to allow Xerox to attack in the mainframe computer market. The IBM counter was a limited range of low-priced copiers directly competing with Xerox's middle-range products, with leasing options that were particularly attractive to smaller customers. The counter-offensive had the effect of causing Xerox to abandon the attack on the computer market (it sold its interests to Honeywell) to concentrate on defending its copiers (James, 1984).

The counter-offensive defence is most effective where the aggressor is vulnerable through overstretching resources. The result is a weak underbelly that can be exploited for defensive purposes.

Mobile defence

The mobile defence was much in vogue as a military strategy in the 1980s and 1990s. It involves creating a 'flexible response capability' to enable the defender to shift the ground

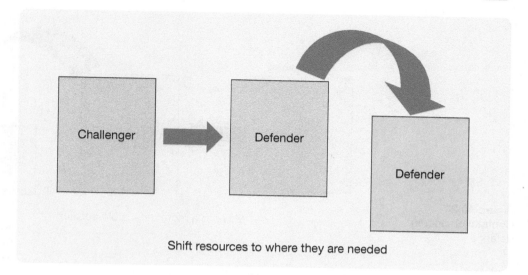

Figure 10.19
Mobile defence

that is being defended in response to environmental or competitive threats and opportunities (see Figure 10.19).

A mobile defence is achieved through a willingness to update and improve the company's offerings to the marketplace continuously. Much of the success of Persil in the UK soap powder market has been due to the constant attempts to keep the product in line with changing customer requirements. The brand, a market leader for nearly half a century, has gone through many reformulations as washing habits have changed and evolved. Reformulations for top-loading washing machines, front loaders, automatics and more recently colder washes, have ensured that the brand has stayed well placed compared with its rivals.

Interestingly, however, Persil went too far twice in recent years: first, when it was modified to a 'biological' formula. Most other washing powders had taken this route to improve the washing ability of the powder. For a substantial segment of the population, however, a biological product was a disadvantage (these powders can cause skin irritation to some sensitive skins). The customer outcry resulted in an 'Original Persil' being reintroduced. A few years later Persil came back again with the even more disastrous Persil Power with its magnesium accelerator. Initially Unilever denied its competitor Procter & Gamble's claim that Persil Power damaged clothes in many washing conditions. However, within months 'Original Persil' was back again.

The mobile defence is an essential strategic weapon in markets where technology and/or customer wants and needs are changing rapidly. Failure to move with these changes can result in opening the company to a flanking or bypass attack.

Contraction defence

A contraction defence, or strategic withdrawal, requires giving up untenable ground to reduce overstretching and allow concentration on the core business that can be defended against attack (see Figure 10.20).

For example, in response to both competitive pressures and an adverse economic environment, Tunnel Cement rationalised its operations. Capacity was halved and the workforce substantially reduced. Operations were then concentrated in two core activities where the company had specialised and defensible capabilities: chemicals and waste disposal.

Figure 10.20
Contraction (focus)
defence

Move to a more defensible position

Strategic withdrawal is usually necessary where the company has diversified too far away from the core skills and distinctive competencies that gave it a competitive edge.

10.6.3 Market niche strategies

Market niche strategies, focusing on a limited sector of the total market, make particular sense for small and medium-sized companies operating in markets that are dominated by larger operators. The strategies are especially suitable where there are distinct, profitable, but underserved pockets within the total market, and where the company has an existing, or can create a new, differential advantage in serving that pocket.

The two main aspects to the niche strategy are, first, choosing the pockets, segments or markets on which to concentrate and, second, focusing effort exclusively on serving those targets (see Figure 10.21).

Choosing the niche

An important characteristic of the successful nicher is an ability to segment the market creatively to identify new and potential niches not yet exploited by major competitors. The battleground, or niches, on which to concentrate should be chosen by consideration of both

Choose your target market carefully and focus all
efforts on serving it

Figure 10.21 Niche
strategies

market (or niche) attractiveness and current or potential strength of the company in serving that market.

For the nicher, the second of these two considerations is often more important than the first. The major automobile manufacturers, for example, have concentrated their attentions on the large-scale segments of the car market in attempts to keep costs down, through volume production of standardised parts and components and assembly-line economies of scale.

This has left many smaller, customised segments of the market open to nichers where the major manufacturers are not prepared to compete. In terms of the overall car market, these segments (such as for small sports cars) would be rated as relatively unattractive, but to a small operator such as Morgan Cars, with modest growth and return objectives, they offer an ideal niche where its skills can be exploited to the full. The Morgan order book is full, there is a high level of job security and a high degree of job satisfaction in manufacturing a high-quality, hand-crafted car.

Focusing effort

The essence of the niche strategy is to focus activity on the selected targets and not allow the company blindly to pursue any potential customer. Pursuing a niche strategy requires discipline to concentrate effort on the selected targets.

Hammermesh *et al.* (1978) examined a number of companies that had successfully adopted a niche strategy and concluded that they showed three main characteristics:

1 **An ability to segment the market creatively,** focusing their activities only in areas where they had particular strengths that were especially valued. In the metal container industry (which faces competition from glass, aluminium, fibrefoil and plastic containers), Crown Cork and Seal has focused on two segments: metal cans for hard-to-hold products such as beer and soft drinks, and aerosol cans. In both these segments the company has built considerable marketing assets through its specialised use of technology and its superior customer service.

2 **Efficient use of R&D resources.** Where R&D resources are necessarily more limited than among major competitors, they should be used where they can be most effective. This often means concentrating not on pioneering work but on improvements to existing technologies that are seen to provide more immediate customer benefits.

3 **Thinking small.** Adopting a 'small is beautiful' approach to business increases the emphasis on operating more efficiently, rather than chasing growth at all costs. Concentration of effort on the markets the company has chosen to compete in leads to specialisation and a stronger, more defensible position.

Over four decades on, these three guidelines for nichers remain as relevant as they have ever been.

10.6.4 Harvesting strategies

Building, holding and niche strategies are all applicable to the products and services of the company that offer some future potential, either for growth or revenue generation.

At some stage in the life of most products and services it can become clear that there is no long-term future for them. This may be because of major changes in customer requirements, with which the offering as currently designed cannot keep pace, or it may be due to technological changes that are making the offer obsolete. In these circumstances, a harvesting (or 'milking') strategy may be pursued to obtain maximum returns from the product before its eventual death or withdrawal from the market (see Figure 10.22).

Kotler and Keller (2016) define harvesting as:

a strategy that calls for gradually reducing a market offering or business's cost while trying to reap profitable sales.

Figure 10.22
Harvesting
strategies

Candidate businesses or individual products for harvesting may be those that are losing money despite managerial and financial resources being invested in them, or they may be those that are about to be made obsolete due to company or competitor innovation.

Implementing a harvesting strategy calls for a reduction in marketing support to a minimum, to cut expenditure on advertising, sales support and further R&D. There will typically be a rationalisation of the product line to reduce production and other direct costs. In addition, prices may be increased somewhat to improve margins while anticipating a reduction in volume.

10.6.5 Divestment/deletion

Where the company decides that a policy of harvesting is not possible – for example, when, despite every effort, the business or product continues to lose money – attention may turn to divestment, or deletion, from the corporate portfolio (see Figure 10.23).

Divestment – the decision to get out of a particular market or business – is never taken lightly by a company. It is crucial, when considering a particular business or product for deletion, to question the role of the business in the company's overall portfolio.

One company, operating both in consumer and industrial markets, examined its business portfolio and found that its industrial operations were at best breaking even, depending on how costs were allocated. Further analysis, however, showed that the industrial operation was a crucial spur to technological developments within the company that were exploited in the consumer markets in which it operated. The greater immediate technical demands of the company's industrial customers acted as the impetus for the R&D department to

Figure 10.23
Divestment
strategies

improve on the basic technologies used by the company. These had fed through to the consumer side of the business and resulted in the current strength in those markets. Without the industrial operations it is doubtful whether the company would have been so successful in its consumer markets. Clearly, in this case, the industrial operations had a non-economic role to play, and divestment on economic grounds could have been disastrous.

Once a divestment decision has been taken, and all the ramifications on the company's other businesses have been carefully assessed, implementation involves getting out as quickly and cheaply as possible.

10.6.6 Matching managerial skills to strategic tasks

These various strategies require quite different managerial skills to bring them to fruition. It should be apparent that a manager well suited to building a stronger position for a new product is likely to have different strengths from those of a manager suited to harvesting an ageing product. Wissema *et al.* (1980) have suggested the following types of manager for each of the jobs outlined previously.

Pioneers and conquerors for build strategies

The pioneer is particularly suited to the truly innovative new product that is attempting to revolutionise the markets in which it operates. A pioneer is a divergent thinker who is flexible, creative and probably hyperactive. Many entrepreneurs, such as Jeff Bezos at Amazon.com and James Dyson of vacuum cleaner fame, would fall into this category.

A conqueror, on the other hand, would be most suited to building in an established market. The conqueror's main characteristics are a creative but structured approach, someone who is a systematic team builder who can develop a coherent and rational strategy in the face of potentially stiff competition.

Administrators to hold position

The administrator is stable, good at routine work, probably an introverted conformist. These traits are particularly suited to holding/maintaining position. The administrator keeps a steady hand on the helm.

Focused creators to niche

This manager is in many ways similar to the conqueror but in need, especially initially, of more creative flair in identifying the area for focus. Once that area has been defined, however, a highly focused approach is necessary at the expense of all other distractions.

Economisers for divestment

The diplomatic negotiator (receiver, or hatchet man!) is required to divest the company of unprofitable businesses, often in the face of internal opposition.

Summary

While two basic approaches to creating a competitive position have been discussed, it should be clear that the first priority in marketing will be to decide on the focus of operations: industry-wide or specific target market segments. Creating a competitive advantage in the selected area of focus can be achieved through either cost leadership or differentiation. To build a strong, defensible position in the market, the initial concern should be to differentiate the company's offerings from those of its competitors on some basis of value to the customer. The second concern should then be to achieve this at the lowest possible delivered cost.

A variety of strategies might be pursued once the overall objectives have been set. The strategies can be summarised under five main types: build; hold; harvest; niche; divest. To implement each type of strategy different managerial skills are required. An important task of senior management is to ensure that the managers assigned to each task have the necessary skills and characteristics.

Case study

Volvo's heart will 'remain in Sweden'

By John Reed

Volvo's safe, trusted cars – a mainstay of affluent suburban enclaves in the US and Europe – have been called many things.

However, the Swedish brand has rarely been compared with a predator of the forest – at least until now.

Li Shufu, the colourful chairman of Chinese car maker Geely, Volvo's new owner, on Sunday likened Volvo to a tiger penned in a zoo that needed to be let loose to run free in the broader world. 'I think we need to liberate this tiger,' Mr Li declared.

At a ceremony in Volvo's hometown of Gothenburg, Mr Li's company signed a deal to buy Volvo for $1.8bn from Ford Motor, marking the US carmaker's last disposal of an overseas brand and China's first purchase of a premium western car marque.

Mr Li told reporters that the Volvo tiger's 'heart' would remain in Sweden, where it has two plants, and in Belgium, where it has one.

Geely's boss vowed to keep Volvo's manufacturing footprint in Europe, but said that the tiger's 'power should be projected across the world,' giving new life to its operations in mature markets.

Volvo sits in the 'near-luxury' or 'only-just-upscale' part of the car market, alongside rival Swedish brand Saab and Fiat's loss-making Alfa Romeo – a subsection of the premium market under attack from luxury leaders BMW, Mercedes-Benz, and Audi since the car industry's crisis began in 2008.

The German brands' superior sales and higher prices have allowed them to outspend Volvo on research and development, and ride out the crisis in fitter shape.

Volvo's signature contribution to car industry history is the three-point seatbelt, which it claims

Source: Oleksiy Maksymenko Photography/Alamy Stock Photo.

has saved more than 1m lives since it pioneered it in 1959, prompting other car makers to follow suit.

The Swedish brand celebrated the belt's 50th birthday last year – a fitting event for a car maker with a solid reputation for safety, but a dull and worthy image among some consumers and an urgent need to raise its game.

The brand is still seen as an industry leader in safety technology, though rival German brands and Toyota's Lexus have recently matched or outdone it in pioneering some safety features.

However, Volvo's reputation for building safe cars could help its business in China as safety becomes an increasing priority in the world's largest car market.

In design, Volvo is moving away from making boxy, square cars into more edgily fashioned, smaller and alternative fuel models – an area where Geely, which is developing electric cars, can help it.

 Source: from 'Volvo's heart will "remain in Sweden"', *Financial Times*, 29/03/10 (Reed, J.).

Discussion questions

1 How has Volvo achieved differentiation over the years?

2 Why did Geely acquire Volvo?

3 Suggest strategies for Volvo to build upon its unique strengths.

CHAPTER 11
COMPETING THROUGH THE EVOLVING MARKETING MIX

'[An executive is] a mixer of ingredients, who sometimes follows a recipe as he goes along, sometimes adapts a recipe to the ingredients immediately available, and sometimes experiments with or invents ingredients no one else has tried.'

(Culliton, 1948)

'When building a marketing program to fit the needs of his firm, the marketing manager has to weigh the behavioural forces and then juggle marketing elements in his mix with a keen eye on the resources with which he has to work.'

(Borden, 1964)

McDonald's to buy AI company Dynamic Yield

By Alistair Gray in New York

Acquisition will help burger group customise its menu displays based on differing variables

McDonald's is spending about $300m to buy an artificial intelligence company in the fast-food chain's latest technology investment.

In a rare move for the burger group, which has for years avoided acquisitions, McDonald's announced a deal on Monday to buy Dynamic Yield, a machine learning specialist founded seven years ago.

The technology will allow McDonald's to customise its menu displays based on variables such as the weather and the time of day – McFlurry ice creams in the heat or Sausage McMuffins at breakfast, for instance – as well as previous customer choices.

It will also assess restaurant footfall to suggest food that is faster to prepare when the kitchen is busy, or more elaborate items in quieter stretches.

McDonald's, which serves about 68m customers each day from almost 38,000 outlets, plans to roll out the technology at its drive-through locations in the US this year before expanding it overseas. The Chicago-based company also plans to introduce it inside restaurants and on mobile phones.

Steve Easterbrook, McDonald's chief executive, said: 'This technology has the capability and the flexibility to work on all of our digital platforms.'

Deal terms were not disclosed but people familiar with the matter said the consideration was about $300m.

Dynamic Yield, based in Tel Aviv and New York, employs 200 people. Clients include furniture retail group IKEA, football club Tottenham Hotspur and

McDonald's serves about 68m customers each day from almost 38,000 outlets

Source: Bloomberg/Getty Images.

online supermarket Ocado. Following the acquisition it will continue to be run as an standalone business by Liad Agmon, co-founder. 'We're thrilled to be joining an iconic global brand,' he said.

While small in the context of McDonald's, which has a market capitalisation of about $142bn, the purchase is its biggest in 20 years. It is also strategically significant as the company turns to big data to gain an edge over rivals in the highly competitive fast food business.

Self-order kiosks, mobile order and payment, and delivery via UberEats are among the tech initiatives introduced by Mr Easterbrook, a Briton who took charge in 2015.

The company has also been smartening up its outlets, rolling out new decor, kiosks, free-to-use tablets and phone chargers.

McDonald's said it would be Dynamic Yield's sole owner and would 'continue to invest' in the business following the deal. It would continue to serve its other clients, which also include beauty chain group Sephora, retail company Urban Outfitters and betting and gambling group Ladbrokes.

 Source: from 'McDonald's to buy AI company Dynamic Yield', *Financial Times*, 25/03/19 (Gray, A.).

Discussion questions

1 What are the issues facing McDonald's here?
2 How do they relate to the marketing mix?

Introduction

In the early 1960s, one of the leading US marketing writers, Neil Borden (1964), coined the term 'marketing mix' to cover the main activities of firms that were then thought to contribute to the marketability of their products and services. These were classified under the famous '4Ps' of marketing: product, price, promotion and place.

Recent thinking, spurred on through the development of relationship marketing (see Chapter 13), has extended the four Ps to include people, processes and physical evidence. In addition, as the service sector has grown in many developed economies, a new 'dominant logic' has emerged in marketing (see Vargo and Lusch, 2004; Lusch *et al.*, 2006), in which service provision rather than the exchange of goods has centre stage. This has further encouraged a rethink of the traditional elements of the marketing mix and their relevance to twenty-first century marketing.

Particularly significant has been the increasing use of the Internet for marketing purposes. The advent of the Internet as a major marketing medium has had impacts right across the spectrum of activities of the marketing mix. Initially seen primarily as a communications tool for reaching prospective customers, it is clear that the impact of the Internet has been far more pervasive, affecting the ways in which customers shop, how they gather and use information and also their expectations of the type and level of service they should receive. Not least, the Internet has resulted in new forms of product. Streaming and digital downloads have long overtaken physical CDs. New 'bit-based' products, immediately and cheaply downloadable, are affecting many markets.

In this chapter we summarise the main ingredients of the marketing mix and examine the opportunities brought about by technology.

11.1   The market offer

Most market offers are combinations of physical, tangible product and intangible service (see Chapter 13). For ease of presentation, here we refer to 'product' as the mix of physical, emotional, tangible and intangible elements that go to make up the overall market offer. It is important to always bear in mind that the product is what it does for the customer. Customers do not buy products; they buy what the product can do for them.

11.1.1 Key product/service concepts

Products are best viewed as solutions to customers' problems, or ways of satisfying customer needs. American marketing guru Philip Kotler (1997) put this neatly when he said that customers do not buy a quarter-inch drill bit – they buy the hole that the drill bit can create. In other words, customers buy the benefits a product can bring to them, rather than the product itself.

That has two particularly important implications for marketing. First, it follows that customer perceptions of the product – what they believe about it – can be as, or even more, important to them than objective reality. If customers believe that a product gives them a particular benefit (for example, enhanced attractiveness from using a particular cosmetic), that is what is likely to motivate them to purchase. Second, most if not all products are likely to have limited lives; they will only exist as solutions to customer problems until a better solution comes along. There is some evidence that product life cycles are shortening, with new offers coming to market more rapidly than in the past, and existing products becoming obsolete more quickly. That has implications for new product development (see Chapter 12).

11.1.2 Product/service choice criteria

The reasons why customers choose one product over another can be simple ('it's cheaper') or far more complex ('it feels right for me'). In seeking to understand choice criteria it is useful to distinguish two main sets: the rational and overt; and the emotional and covert (see Figure 11.1).

When questioned about their purchase decisions in market research surveys, most customers will rationalise their choices. They will articulate objective reasons for their actions that they feel can be logically justified. These might include the practical benefits of the product, belief about value for money, the availability of the product and perhaps habit. These are reasons customers can give without loss of self-esteem, demonstrating that they are in control of the buying situation.

For many products, however, emotional reasons may play as big, or even bigger, a role. The purchase of branded goods, for example, may be prompted by the reassurance that a well-known and respected brand can bring. The physical product may be no better, a

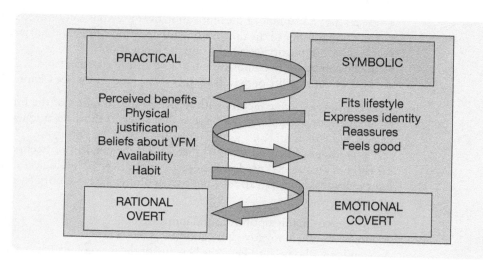

Figure 11.1
Product choice
criteria

'rational' comparison may show no differences, but customers will pay more to have the reassurance of the brand. Similarly, products may be chosen because they are believed to fit the lifestyle of the customer more closely, or to make a statement about the purchaser (why else would someone pay thousands of pounds for a watch, such as a Rolex, when a cheap alternative can be as accurate in delivering the overt, rational benefit of telling the time?).

While conventional quantitative market research may uncover the rational and overt motivations of customers, more in-depth, qualitative and often projective research is needed to uncover emotional and covert motivations. Famously, researchers in the USA trying to understand why more people did not fly between major cities rather than driving found through direct questions that reasons given were rational (cost of flying, greater convenience of driving), but when projective techniques were used (asking respondents why others did not fly more) fears of flying and concerns for safety began to emerge.

Most purchases are a combination of the rational and the emotional. The balance between the two, however, will vary significantly across products and it is an important task for marketers to understand the balance for their particular market offering.

11.1.3 Product/service differentiation

Central to successful marketing is product differentiation – ensuring that the total market offer is different and distinct from competitor offerings in ways that are of value to the target customer. (This was discussed in more detail in Chapter 10.)

With the convergence of manufacturing technology, and the widespread application of total quality management (TQM) methods, it is increasingly difficult for firms to differentiate on their core products. Differentiation in most markets now focuses on the augmented product (see Chapter 10), and in particular on ways of tailoring to individual customer requirements. In automobiles, for example, using basic building blocks of sub-frames, engines, body panels and interior options, there is now the opportunity for new car buyers to create near-unique cars, matching their requirements or tastes very closely. Indeed, the industry's quest in the 3DayCar Programme is to find ways to customise the vehicle to the buyer's exact preferences and to deliver it three or four days after it is specified and ordered.

11.1.4 Diffusion of innovation

New products (those new to the market) require careful management as they enter the product life cycle. A theory of the diffusion of innovations (of which new products are one type) was proposed by Rogers (1962) (see Chapter 3). He suggested that the rate of diffusion of any innovation depends on a number of factors, including:

- the relative advantage of the innovation over previous solutions to the customer's needs;
- the compatibility of the innovation with existing values and norms;
- a lack of complexity (ease) of using the innovation;
- the divisibility of the innovation facilitating low-risk trial; and
- the communicability of the advantages of the innovation (see Chapter 12 and Figure 12.3).

In considering these factors with regard to the adoption of the Internet and e-business techniques, for example, it can be seen that some of those techniques are likely to diffuse more rapidly than others.

Parasuraman and Colby (2001) introduced the concept of 'technology readiness' as a measure of customers' predispositions to adopt new technologies – based on their fears, hopes, desires and frustrations about technology. They identify five types of technology customers:

1 Explorers – highly optimistic and innovative.
2 Pioneers – the innovative but cautious.
3 Sceptics – who need to have the benefits of the technology proven to them.

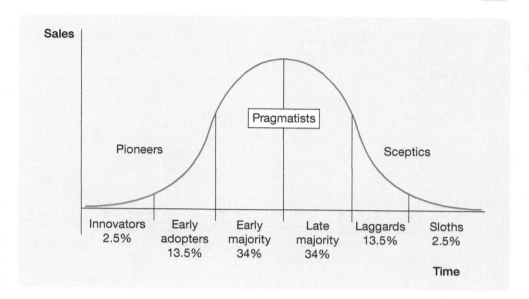

Figure 11.2 The diffusion of innovation

4 Paranoids – those who are insecure about the technology.
5 Laggards – those who resist the technology.

Rogers (2003) identified five adopter groups – innovators, early adopters, early majority, late majority and laggards – which were further developed by Moore (2004, 2006, 2014) in his discussion of the adoption of high-technology products and services. We add a sixth and final adopter group – the sloths (see Figure 11.2):

• Innovators are the first to adopt a new technology or product. Often, they are technology enthusiasts and adopt because the technology is new and they wish to be (and be seen to be) up to date. Initial demand for Apple's iPad, launched in the UK in May 2010, and the iPhone 4, launched in June 2010, was in large part driven by the desire to be seen as an innovator and first user of the new technologies. It is often the novelty value of the technology that drives their adoption. Many innovations fail because they are technology-driven rather than meeting the real needs of customers. Once the novelty value has worn off, and newer technologies have been substituted by the innovators, the product dies a natural death.

• Early adopters are similar to the innovators, but often demonstrate a more visionary reason for adopting the new technology. In business markets, for example, early adopters often see significant advantages from adoption, and ways in which the new technology can enable them to change the way a market works, to the benefit both of themselves and of customers. Early adopters of e-business approaches, for example, include Jeff Bezos at **Amazon.com** who saw in the use of the Internet a whole new way of retailing books and other products that could add value for customers. Vision such as this can lead to spectacular success, as well as spectacular failure.

• Early majority adopters are even more pragmatic than the early adopters. Typically they are less likely to see ways of revolutionising their markets and more likely to see incremental possibilities for improvement. They may, for example, take a particular aspect of the supply chain, such as purchasing, and use Internet technologies to improve the efficiency of this activity. Early majority adopters are often efficiency driven, while the early adopters had seen opportunities to improve effectiveness.

• Late majority adopters have been described as 'conservatives' (Moore, 2014) who often enter a market or adopt a technology largely because others in the market have done so and they fear being left behind. More reluctant in their adoption than the early majority, and in greater need of support and direction in use of the new technology, these adopters

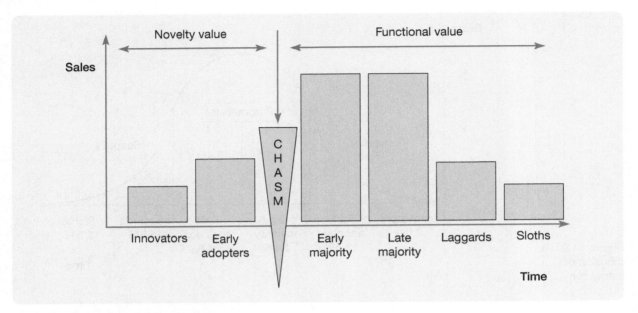

Figure 11.3 The new product chasm
Source: Based on Moore (1991), p. 17.

are often confused about how the technology can be beneficial to them and will wait until the technology has been tried and tested before adopting it. But they are sure that they need to embrace it or be overtaken by competitors.

- The laggards have been described as 'sceptics' who do not really see the potential for the new technology, will resist its adoption as long as possible, but may eventually be forced into adoption because all around them, including their suppliers, distributors and customers, have adopted.

- Finally, the sloths are the very last adopters of new technologies, often going to great lengths to avoid adoption. In some instances they change the way they operate to isolate themselves from the innovations taking place around them, and may even make a virtue of non-adoption. Some accountants still use the quill pen in preference to the spread-sheet! Some firms will never adopt e-business technologies, and may actually carve viable niches for themselves in serving similarly minded customers.

Moore (2014) argued that in the adoption of new high-technology products, a gulf existed between the early adopters and the early majority that he referred to as the new product chasm, into which many fall (see Figure 11.3). This is essentially the transition from a technology for enthusiasts and visionaries to a technology for the pragmatists. While the enthusiasm of the innovators and early adopters is often sufficient to carry an innovation forward, its ultimate success depends on its ability to convince the pragmatists of the productivity and process enhancements it can deliver. Apple seems to have pulled off the enviable trick of both attracting innovators and early adopters to its new products, but also providing value beyond novelty that bridges the chasm and delivers adoption beyond the technology geeks.

11.1.5 Managing the product over its life cycle

The concept of the product life cycle was introduced in Chapter 3 (see Figure 11.4). With changing market conditions over the life cycle, it is important that product and service strategies are designed to match. It will also be apparent that different adopter groups are likely to form key target markets at different stages of the product life cycle.

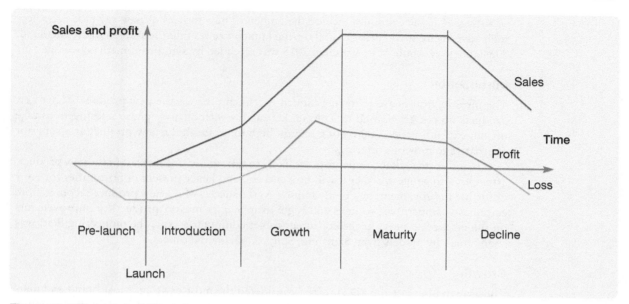

Figure 11.4 The product life cycle

Pre-launch

In the pre-launch phase, before the product has appeared on the market, the main emphasis of the organisation will be on research and development, as well as gearing up production capacity for launch. The development costs for the Airbus A380, for example, have been put at around €11bn. High levels of expenditure may be incurred before any returns are seen through sales receipts. Also important at this stage is market research to identify likely early adopters of the product (see Chapter 12) and to develop key sales messages demonstrating the benefits of the new offering relative to the current solutions to customers' problems.

Market research into wholly new products can be notoriously inaccurate. Sony's formal market research into the Walkman concept showed that there was little potential demand for a mobile music player, but the chairman, Akio Morita, went ahead anyway and created a whole new market that itself evolved into the advent of quality streaming and is now dominated by a totally different product: the smartphone. The lesson is that customers may not know what they want, or what they could find useful, before they see it. We refer to these as 'latent markets' – waiting for creative marketers to discover and exploit them.

In the advent of co-creation, firms turn more and more to social media tools at the idea-generation and screening stage to engage with their potential customers and to screen ideas (Roch and Mosconi, 2016).

Launch

The launch phase of the life cycle is the major opportunity for the organisation to shout loudly about the benefits the new product can offer. This will often take the form of explaining to customers the new benefits over and above those enjoyed from the products they currently use to satisfy their needs.

At this stage, by definition, there is one product in the market and the real task is one of convincing the best prospect customers (the innovators identified through research during pre-launch) of the value of the new offering. The launch period offers significant opportunities for creative communication with prospective customers while the product is novel and newsworthy. Public relations (PR) can be particularly effective at this stage, as can the use of exhibitions and conventions.

Expenditures can be very high during launch, with returns in the form of sales not yet realised. Significant budgets may need to be assigned to give the launch the best prospects of success. Classic examples include the launch of new movies or new car models, where high advertising spend prior to and during launch excites interest and stimulates demand. The launch by Apple of its watch in 2015 was attended by significant media coverage.

Introduction

The introduction phase following launch is crunch time for the new product. Many new products do not get beyond this phase. During the introductory phase sales begin to take off but expenditures on marketing remain high to establish the new product as a superior alternative to previous offerings.

It is at this stage that competitors are likely to take increasing interest in the new product, attempting to gauge whether it will be a success, and hence present opportunities for copy or further improvement, or a costly failure. As the success of the new product becomes more certain, so competitive products will begin to appear as 'me too' products or improvements on the market pioneer. In the consumer tablet computer sector, the pioneering iPad was soon joined by models from Samsung, Sony, Amazon and others.

Growth

The growth phase of the PLC is often considered the most exciting. Most brand and marketing managers prefer to operate in growth markets. At this stage the product is becoming readily accepted on the market, sales are growing rapidly and returns begin to outstrip expenditures. Other things also happen during this phase that significantly affect marketing strategies. First, the success and growth are likely to attract more competitors into the market – especially those that have adopted a 'wait and see' attitude during launch and introduction. Now that the market is proven, risks are lowered and potential returns beckon.

With further competitor entry comes greater product differentiation among offerings, and typically greater segmentation of the market. The early majority, the new macro-target, are likely to be diverse in their exact wants and needs, offering greater opportunities for micro-targeting. Expenditures continue to be high in researching market opportunities and product improvements, second generation and so on. In the MP3 player market, for example, by Christmas 2006 there were several different versions of the iPod available (from Shuffle to Nano to Video). For Apple, a problem began to emerge as the innovators, primarily younger and more fashion-conscious purchasers, saw their parents' generation buying the bigger, 60GB iPod Videos. In response, Apple launched coloured versions of the iPod Nano, with additional add-on features and skins, to retain the younger market. It is relevant to stress that iPod's sales peaked in 2008 after which it was replaced by the iPhone and other smartphones as the platform of choice.

It is at this stage that returns peak and surplus cash can be diverted into developing and launching the new generation of new products (see portfolio theory section).

Maturity

The mature phase is reached when growth slows and the bulk of the market (late majority) have entered. This phase can be characterised by particularly fierce competition, as those who entered the market during the growth phase fight for market share rather than market expansion to improve performance. Price wars are common, profit margins are squeezed and expenditures on marketing and research and development are scrutinised more critically.

Decline

The decline, and eventual death, phase sees profits squeezed even more as the next generation of products takes over the market. Figure 11.5 shows the sales of cameras in the USA. The sales of traditional, film-based cameras peaked around the year 2000, but since then have been in steep decline due to the growth of digital versions. Surprisingly, the market downturn for film-based cameras has been even more dramatic in countries such as China. This switch in market has been fuelled by technological advances (see Figure 11.6), where

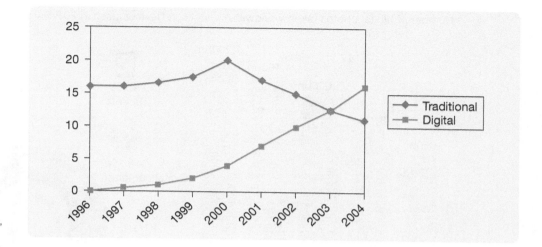

Figure 11.5 US amateur camera sales

Source: New Scientist, 2004, October 16.

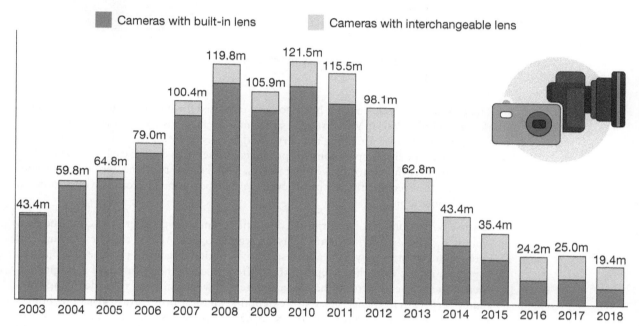

Figure 11.6 Digital camera sales dropped 84 per cent since 2010

Source: CIPA: StatistaCharts.

the cost of sharper definition in digital pictures (as measured by the number of megapixels) has plummeted, allowing the quality of digital pictures to rapidly challenge that of film.

Turning points

The phases of the product life cycle are notoriously difficult to predict, and especially difficult to identify are transitions between stages (see Figure 11.7). First, the transition from introductory phase to growth. Here the danger is being left behind as the market takes off. Second, the transition from growth to maturity. The clear danger here is being left with over-capacity, or high stock levels, of difficult-to-move products (as happened with the over-supply of mobile phones when the market became mature in the early 2000s). This is another reason why the mature phase is so competitive – firms often have excess capacity and stock available that they need to move. Finally, transition from steady state maturity to decline can leave some firms wedded to old technology and unable to embrace the new.

Figure 11.7 Smartphones overtake cameras as the device of choice
Source: InfoTrends via Bitkom: StatisticaCharts.

The product life cycle concept has also been criticised for encouraging tunnel vision in marketers (Moon, 2005). Moon suggests that managers slavishly following the PLC see only an inexorable advance along the curve, and because they all see the cycle in the same way they all adopt similar positions for products and services during each of the life cycle stages. To counter this convergence of strategies, Moon suggests three alternative positioning strategies for breaking free of the life cycle: reverse positioning; breakaway positioning; and stealth positioning.

- Reverse positioning involves stripping down the augmented product to its core, and then seeking new ways to differentiate. This strategy recognises that in the quest to augment core products, firms may have added so many additional features that they become the expected, rather than the exception that differentiates. The example of toothpaste is cited, where the core product has been augmented with whitener, fluoride, plaque preventative, breath freshener, etc. to the extent that all these now feature in leading brands and no longer serve to differentiate. IKEA has adopted this approach in its successful self-assembly furniture stores. Rather than adopt the strategy of other furniture retailers of carrying enormous product lines, varied inventories, high-pressure sales operations and seemingly permanent 'sales' and 'special offers', IKEA offers stores with play areas for children, Scandinavian restaurants, no high-pressure sales staff, very little in-store support or service, self-collection (rather than delivery weeks or months after order), self-assembly and now home delivery.
- Breakaway positioning is where a product is deliberately moved from one product category to another. The category a product occupies is determined by the way customers perceive that product – the competing products they associate it with, the messages that are employed to promote it, the price charged, the channels through which it is distributed – in short, the entire marketing mix employed. By switching categories, products can gain a new lease of life beyond the existing PLC. Swatch, for example, is an example of breakaway positioning. Before its launch in 1983, Swiss watches were sold as jewellery and most customers rarely bought more than one model. Swatch changed that by defining its watches as playful fashion accessories – fun, ephemeral, inexpensive and showy. Impulse buying was encouraged, and customers typically bought several watches for different outfits.

Table 11.1 Smartphones are taking over the global games market

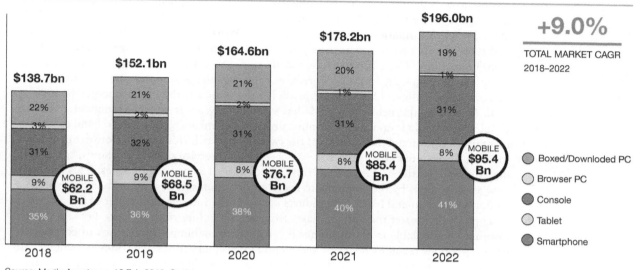

Source: Martin Armstrong, 16 Feb 2018, Statista.

- Stealth positioning involves shifting to a different product category in a covert way, rather than overtly as practised through breakaway positioning. This may be appropriate where there is prejudice about a product or the company that needs to be overcome. Moon stresses this is not the same as deceit, and can backfire if customers believe they are being cheated or exploited. Sony has been highly successful in the games console market with its PlayStation product, but its market penetration has been limited to a narrow customer base – primarily males in their late teens and early twenties. The company wished to broaden its platform for home entertainment and communications but found that the PlayStation format did not appeal beyond the narrow customer focus. In response, in July 2003 it launched a PlayStation product in Europe called EyeToy: Play. This included a video camera (EyeToy) and game software (Play) that plugged into the PlayStation 2 console but allowed the user to become part of the game, appearing inside the television where they interact with objects on the screen by moving their bodies, rather than using hand-held controllers. The product sold 2.5 million units in the first seven months, crucially engaging a much wider target market, including parents and even grandparents (Moon, 2005). It is worth noting that in the rapidly changing industry that is gaming, product life cycles are short. Indeed, since 2017 smartphones have taken over consoles as the gaming platform of choice (see Table 11.1).

11.1.6 The impact of the Internet on market offerings

With the advent of marketing over the Internet, two types of market offering became apparent: the so-called 'atom-based' and 'bit-based' products.

Atom-based products are physical offerings that have a separate presence and form for the customer. While they may be promoted over the Internet, they need to be physically shipped to the customer, are subject to returns where they are not satisfactory and can be resold by customers. Typical examples include books and videos (Amazon.com), clothes and appliances. For the customer, the product at the end of the day is the same as that purchased through a bricks-and-mortar retailer, but the experience may be enhanced through the additional services, convenience and low price available through Internet purchase. For the retailer, the logistics of delivery represent significant challenges.

Bit-based products, on the other hand, do not have a physical presence. They can be represented as digital data in electronic form. They are typically non-returnable but do not require separate shipping and can be transferred online. Bit-based products include music, news, information services, movies and TV programmes. Similarly, online lessons and tutorials are proving increasingly popular (such as **http://www.onlinelessonvideos.com/home.php**). These products are ideally suited to marketing over the Internet, as the complete supply chain (from procurement through sales and marketing to delivery) can be conducted online. This synergy provided the logic for the global merger in 2000 of AOL (a leading Internet service provider) with Time Warner (an entertainment and news conglomerate) as a foundation for online provision of enhanced information and entertainment products (though integration of the two business cultures proved more problematic). In 2019, Apple launched Apple TV + – a streaming service of its own shows, competing directly with Netflix and Amazon Prime video, as well as news and games. This has been seen as an attempt by the company to focus on premium services rather than hardware.

For both atom- and bit-based products sold over the Internet, the power of the customer is significantly greater than in purchases from bricks-and-mortar suppliers. Put simply, the information available to the customer is far greater, enabling wider search of competitor offerings, online recommendations and greater price comparisons. The online customer can decide at the click of a mouse to buy or bypass a firm's offerings, whereas in a face-to-face situation a vendor may rely more on personal selling and persuasion. For offerings to be consistently chosen over competing offerings they need to offer greater value to customers, through lower prices, greater convenience, additional valued features, speed, or whatever. Hence, the driver of web-based marketing is increasingly to look to the augmented product for differentiation (see Chapter 13).

The Internet has also facilitated integrated marketing of bit-based and atom-based products. In December 2001, New Line Cinema launched its epic movie *The Lord of the Rings: The Fellowship of the Ring* (LOTR), based on the bestselling books by J.R.R. Tolkien. More than 100 million copies of the books had been sold in 45 languages prior to the movie launch. To heighten interest in the movie, New Line created a website in May 1999 (now defunct). A trailer for the movie became available on the website in April 2000 and was downloaded more than 1.7 million times. The site was updated three to four times per week as part of a four-year editorial schedule spanning the life of the three films in the trilogy (the second was released in December 2002, the third in December 2003). The aim was to create an online community as a hub for the 400 fan sites devoted to LOTR. This type of integrated marketing started a trend now regularly followed: for example, for the *Star Wars* franchise (**www.starwars.com**), or the Marvel Studios productions including the *Avengers* franchise (**www.marvel.com/movies/avengers-endgame**), on which websites fans can find teasers of the latest release, access to news, games and apps and more.

Merchandising associated with the LOTR movie was extensive, with toys and 'collectibles' based on the film sculpted by WETA, the New Zealand-based firm that created the creatures and special effects of the film. There were also marketing partnerships with restaurants (Burger King), consumer products manufacturers (JVC, General Mills), booksellers (Barnes and Noble, Amazon – sales of the books went up 500 per cent after the launch of the film), theatre shows in London, which attracted over 700,000 people by the end of 2008, and even the New Zealand Post Office (in December 2001 a set of New Zealand stamps was issued with images from LOTR on them – see **http://www.newzeal.com/Stamps/NZ/LOTR/Rings.htm**). In addition, AOL Time Warner launched a new version of AOL (version 7) with an LOTR sweepstake, which generated 800,000 entries in its first two weeks.

Customer service and support

Potentially, the Internet offers many opportunities for customising and tailoring the service offered to the needs and requirements of individual customers. Jeff Bezos, CEO and founder of Amazon.com, is reported as saying that if Amazon has 4.5 million customers it should have 4.5 million stores, each one customised for the person who visits (Janal, 2000). When customers make initial purchases from Amazon, they are invited to give information, such as billing details and address shipping address, which will be stored and used for future transactions. On logging into Amazon, the customer is greeted by a 'personalised' greeting, recommendations for books based on previous purchases and one-click ordering for new books. The system is automated for efficiency, but from the perspective of the customer is tailored to their individual needs and requirements.

The interactivity of the Internet makes it possible to establish two-way relationships with customers, so that feedback on product performance or operational problems can be received, as well as advice for solving problems provided. Firms offering bit-based products, such as software, often use the Internet as a way of providing product upgrades and patches. Norton Antivirus, for example, updates subscribers' software automatically. Similarly, popular personal navigation systems, such as TomTom, offer map upgrades and safety camera locations over the Internet to subscribers (**https://www.tomtom.com/en_gb?sat-nav/maps-services/shop/travel-map/**).

Some firms offer added-value services by encouraging chat rooms and online communities through their sites. Reebok, for example, established an online community where potential customers could 'chat' with famous sports personalities. It regularly posts articles and news items of interest to its target customers. All these activities are designed to help build the brand and establish its credentials with the target market (Janal, 2000).

Deise *et al.* (2000) identify five types of website that allow or encourage customers to interact with the company. Content sites provide customers with basic information about the company, its products and its services. FAQ sites answer frequently asked questions and can help customers with common queries. Knowledge-based sites have knowledge bases, or databases, that can be searched by customers. These require a greater degree of involvement from the customer but may be more convenient than making a service call. Trouble ticket sites allow customers to post queries or problems and then receive personalised feedback or problem solving (often from other users). Interactive sites facilitate interaction between the firm and its customers. Often these are part of an extranet where customers are given access to proprietary information.

Again, however, it should be noted that the power lies with the customer. Online, as in the physical world, customers are only likely to be attracted by services that provide value for them. The key to successful service online will remain identifying what gives customers value, and what can be uniquely offered through the Internet. Because of the ease of competitor copying, however, service benefits need to be constantly upgraded.

There is also a broader concern for issues such as customer privacy, even with the introduction of GDPR (General Data Protection Regulation) in the EU, which may hold some back from Internet relationships with companies, and the enormous potential for dissatisfied customers to quickly spread news of their dissatisfaction through social media.

The Internet of Things

The Internet of Things (IoT) is 'the concept of basically connecting any device with an on and off switch to the Internet (and/or to each other). This includes everything from cellphones, coffee makers, washing machines, headphones, lamps, wearable devices and almost anything else you can think of' (Morgan, 2014). With an estimated 75.44 billion connected devices worldwide by 2025 (up from 26.66 billion in 2019), it is not difficult to imagine that the impact of the IoT on marketing will equal that of the Internet. Among these devices, smart speakers have already appeared in homes: their sales are forecast to overtake tablets by 2021 (see Figure 11.8).

Google Assistant, accessed chiefly through Google Home cylinders and Pixel phones, is now available on 400 million devices. In 2019, Apple launched a Siri-enabled HomePod, and Samsung has acquired Viv, an intelligent assistant company founded by Siri's creators, to bolster its Bixby AI assistant platform. Microsoft and Tencent have platforms for their own AI assistants (Cortana and Xiaowei), and virtual assistants Chumenwenwen and Xiaoice (of which the latter is capable of uncannily human conversations and reportedly has 40 million registered users) are already popular in China.

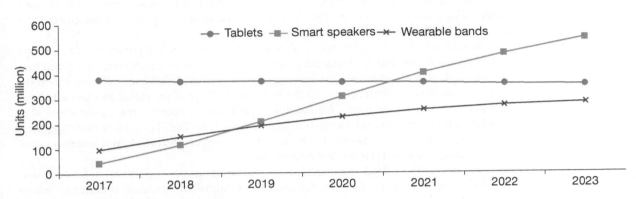

Figure 11.8 Sales and trends of smart speakers
Source: Canalys forecasts, Mobility Services, April 2019.

Connected kitchen
Source: Ross D Franklin/AP/Shutterstock.

Over the next decade, as these firms and others fight to establish the preferred consumer AI platform, AI assistants will transform how companies connect with their customers. They'll become the primary channel through which people get information, goods and services, and marketing will turn into a battle for their attention (Dawar, 2018).

11.2 Pricing strategies

Setting prices can be one of the most difficult decisions in marketing. Price too high and customers may not buy, price too low and the organisation may not achieve the profit levels necessary to continue trading or invest in its future.

11.2.1 Pricing considerations

A number of factors need to be taken into account when setting price levels (see Figure 11.9):

- **Production costs:** The simplest, and most often used, pricing method is to set price at cost plus a percentage mark-up (for example, cost plus 20 per cent). Provided the product sells in sufficient quantities at this price, this strategy ensures a given level of profitability and a good degree of predictability. It also ensures that products are not sold at below cost – a strategy that is not sustainable in the long term without subsidy. In practice, costs should be seen as a floor below which prices should not be allowed to fall.

- **Economic value to the customer (EVC):** The value of the product to the customer over its lifetime gives a ceiling above which prices would be unacceptable to customers. Doyle and Stern (2006) explain how EVC can be calculated with an example from B2B marketing (see later in text).
- **Competitor price levels:** Also important to consider are the prices set by competitors. Where two or more product offerings are similar on other characteristics, price can become the final determinant of choice. Firms may decide to price higher than competitors (as a signal of superior quality), at similar prices (and compete on other features), or lower prices (and compete primarily on price). In the UK market for petrol (gasoline), there is very little price differentiation between competitors. This is in part due to the high level of taxation (VAT and duty) on petrol, leaving little margin for price differences.
- **Desired competitive positioning:** The price charged can be a powerful signal to the market of the quality and reliability of the product. Too low a price may suggest poor quality rather than good value for money. In the hi-fi market, Bose has deliberately priced its offerings significantly higher than competitors as a signal of superior product quality. Other brands, such as LG, price below competition to attract the more price-sensitive consumer. In between these extremes, brands such as Sony, JVC and Samsung compete at similar prices but offering different features, styles and other customer benefits.
- **Corporate objectives:** A company must consider whether its objective is to grow the market rapidly (which might argue for a relatively low price), to harvest (which might argue for prices at the high end), or to maximise profit (which would indicate marginal cost pricing).
- **Price elasticity of demand:** A further consideration in setting prices is the extent to which demand will vary at different price levels. Some products, such as luxury goods, are highly price elastic – changes in price affect quantity demanded to a great extent. Others, such as essentials, are relatively price inelastic, with price having little effect on demand.

Figure 11.9 Pricing considerations

11.2.2 Price elasticity of demand

The price elasticity of demand is the effect of changes in price on demand for the product. Most demand curves slope downwards from top left to bottom right (see Figure 11.10). In other words, the lower the price, the more of a product is purchased, and conversely, as prices rise, less is demanded. Price elasticity is defined as:

Price elasticity = (% change in demand) ÷ (% change in price)

Where price elasticity >1 we term this 'elastic demand' (a change in price generates a greater change in quantity demanded); where price elasticity <1 we term this 'inelastic demand' (a change in price generates a smaller change in quantity demanded).

The extent to which quantity demanded is affected by differences in price varies from market to market. Where there is a steep slope to the demand curve (see 'a' in Figure 11.10), a change in price has relatively little effect on quantity demanded; demand is 'inelastic'. A price rise from P1 to P2 results in a reduction in quantity demanded from Q1 to Q2. By multiplying price by quantity we can see that revenue changes from P1 × Q1 to P2 × Q2. The loss of quantity demanded is offset by the higher prices, and revenues will increase. Markets that enjoy inelastic demand are often monopoly or near-monopoly supply, where customers have little or no choice about how much of a product they use, and where switching costs are high.

A shallow demand curve (see 'b' in Figure 11.10) occurs where a relatively small change in price stimulates a more significant change in demand; demand is 'elastic'. An increase of price from P1 to P2 results in a far more significant reduction of demand from Q1 to Q2. Similarly, price reductions are likely to have a more significant effect on stimulating demand. Markets where demand is more price elastic are generally characterised by greater levels of competition, more customer choice and the easy ability of customers to switch from one supplier to another.

11.2.3 Assessing value to the customer

Economic value to the customer (Forbis and Mehta, 1981) and customer value propositions (Anderson *et al.*, 2006) are central concepts in pricing of industrial products such as plant and equipment. This approach entails attempting to identify the lifetime value to the customer of the purchase, taking into account all costs (purchase price, running costs, maintenance, etc.) and all benefits.

Doyle and Stern (2006) show the example of a market-leading machine tool selling at €30,000. In addition to the purchase price, the customer will incur €20,000 start-up costs

Figure 11.10 Price elasticity of demand

(including installation, training of operatives, etc.), and post-purchase running costs over the life of the machine of €50,000. In total, the lifetime cost is €100,000. Of this, the initial purchase price is less than one-third. A new competitor coming into the market might be tempted to charge less for the product, but the effect of that lower price over the life will be considerably less. For example, a 20 per cent reduction of €6,000 from the initial price is, in effect, only a 6 per cent reduction in lifetime costs.

A more productive approach might be to estimate the total output value to the customer over the life of the machine. This could be done by estimating the number of outputs from the machine tool over its life, together with an assessment of likely defects. If the new machine is an improvement on the existing one, with say 20 per cent greater efficiency, it can be expected to save 20 per cent of total costs or produce 20 per cent more output (both equivalent to €20,000 added value for the customer). Hence, there is scope to actually increase the initial purchase price to, say, €40,000, while still offering an overall saving of €10,000 to the customer. In this case, a higher price might also be needed to signal a higher-quality product that can deliver the 20 per cent savings claimed. A lower price might raise doubts on ability to deliver the savings.

In markets where lifetime value may be less easy to demonstrate (such as consumer markets for appliances), the perceived value of the product can be used as an alternative to EVC. Using techniques such as Vickrey auctions, value to the customer can be estimated. In normal auctions the item will go to the highest bidder. There can be times, however, where bidders will bid below the perceived value of the item in an attempt to get a bargain (this happens regularly on eBay!). Vickrey auctions are a technique to get to the true value the bidder places on the item. They use sealed bids to purchase, where bidders submit written bids without knowledge of who else is bidding for the same item. While the highest bidder wins, they pay the price bid by the second highest, not the price they bid. This creates a powerful incentive for bidders to bid the real value they place on an item, rather than gamble on getting it for a bargain lower price.

Trade-off analysis (also called conjoint analysis) can also be used to estimate the 'utility' of different price levels, and how customers will trade off between alternative configurations of benefits (features) at different prices (see Green *et al.*, 1981; Orme, 2005).

11.2.4 Pricing methods

A number of alternative pricing methods are used by organisations, sometimes in combination:

- **Cost plus pricing:** This is the simplest approach to setting prices and requires little understanding of customers and their needs. Prices are set at cost plus a percentage mark-up. Prices therefore reflect directly the costs of creating and delivering the product. The disadvantage of this method, of course, is that it takes no account of the value of the product to the customer. If the value to the customer is greater than cost plus mark-up, the product will be attractive, but if the value to the customer is lower, sales are likely to suffer.
- **Going rate pricing:** In some markets, such as petrol and diesel, prices are typically set on a 'going rate' basis – at what others set – and there is little price competition between suppliers. Competition takes place on other factors such as availability, location and convenience.
- **Perceived value pricing:** Pricing products at their perceived value to customers requires sophisticated research methods to identify value. When customers are asked direct questions about value (such as 'how much would you pay for . . . ?'), few would vote for high prices! Projective techniques and other approaches such as trade-off, or conjoint, analysis (mentioned previously) can be more useful. Under these approaches, customers are put into simulated purchasing situations and their behaviour is observed to gauge the value they perceive in the market offer.

- **Sealed bids:** In many industrial purchasing situations, especially in capital projects, a number of potential suppliers may be invited to bid to supply. Normally at least two stages will be employed. First, a specification stage where suppliers need to demonstrate their ability to supply to specification and on time. This stage will reduce the number of potential suppliers to a manageable number. Second, a sealed bid that indicates the price each selected supplier would charge. Deciding how to bid under competitive situations can be highly sophisticated. Typically, firms will take into account not only their own costs but also their predictions of the prices competitors will bid at (based on their costs and expectations of competitors). Game theory may be useful in this context. Game theory refers to a set of techniques and approaches that studies situations where players choose different actions in an attempt to maximise their returns. It provides a formal modelling approach to situations in which decisions are not made in isolation, and where the decisions of one party can be influenced by the decisions of others. Hence, the need to model and predict the intentions of others (see **http://www.gametheory.net**). The growing use of Internet auctions, which ask suppliers to bid prices online to a purchaser's product specification, is the newest approach to this situation.

11.2.5 Promotional pricing

- **Loss leaders:** Used extensively by retailers and other suppliers as a means of attracting customers into their stores, or on to their websites, loss leaders are products sold below cost for promotional purposes. Once customers have been attracted in by the loss leader the retailer will attempt to sell other market offerings at a profit. Manufacturers also use this tactic where the lifetime cost of a product is considerably greater than the initial purchase price. Home photograph printers, for example, are sold at very low prices with little margin because the manufacturers and retailers can make their profits through selling ink cartridges, photo-quality paper and other consumables.
- **Special events:** Seasonal sales, special price promotions and 'once in a lifetime' deals are ways in which price is used to gain customers. Discount sales originated as a means of moving old stock to make way for new-season offerings, but some organisations now appear to have near-permanent sales, suggesting that really they are offering products at prices lower than the 'ticket price' but, because they do not want the product to appear low quality, justify this through discount.
- **Cash rebates:** Money-back offers and coupons are popular among marketers of fast-moving consumer goods. Coupons can be most cost effective as not all are cashed in, and only when another purchase is made. Money back can be more expensive as claims are more likely to be made.
- **Low-interest finance:** For the purchase of significant goods such as furniture and automobiles, some suppliers will offer low, or 'zero' interest on hire purchase deals. In effect, this gives a discount on price when net present values are calculated and can be a powerful inducement to customers to move to higher price points.
- **Psychological pricing:** Pricing just beneath psychological barriers (for example, €2.99 rather than €3 or €9,995 rather than €10,000) is common practice. The assumption (rarely tested) is that customers have a psychological price threshold and will group prices in broad bands for comparison purposes. A car priced at €19,995 is seen in a lower price band than one priced at €20,000. Increasingly, with Internet searches set to look for products at 'prices up to . . . ', psychological pricing is likely to be employed.

11.2.6 The effects of the Internet on pricing decisions

The Internet makes it far easier for customers to compare prices than in the past. Not only can prices be compared between manufacturers (for example, the price of a BMW compared with the price of an equivalent-model Mercedes), but also the prices of alternative suppliers of the same product or model. And the latter is no longer confined to the immediate geographic vicinity – comparisons can be made nationwide and even globally. The advent of a single currency in some parts of the EU has made price comparisons across the euro-zone even easier.

Kerrigan *et al.* (2001) report that in B2B markets, customers experience price savings of around 10 per cent for commodity products and up to 25 per cent for custom purchases. These result from the increased choice customers enjoy, coupled with increased price competition between suppliers. P&G, for example, is reducing its supply costs by conducting 'reverse auctions' with suppliers, and estimates annual savings in the order of 20 per cent on supplies of around $700 million.

In addition, customer-to-customer (C2C) communications or chat lines between customers help to spread information about competitive prices, as well as product and service recommendations or warnings. Through customer-to-business (C2B) communications, reverse auctions are now taking place where buyers post what they are looking for and invite suppliers to bid to supply them.

Overall, the Internet has made customers more, rather than less, price sensitive as they have access to greater amounts of information, easily searched and not controlled by the sellers. 'Ultimately the customer is only willing to pay for the value he or she gets. The challenge for any seller is to find out what this perceived value is and then price the product or service accordingly. The customer stays loyal only if the exchanges with the seller cultivate a lasting sense of fairness. Customer satisfaction is the only way to maximize long-term profits' (Simon, 2015).

11.3   Communications strategies

For many people, advertising is synonymous with marketing. In practice, advertising is just one (albeit an important one) of the ways in which firms communicate with their customers and prospective customers. The range of communications tools available is increasing as new technologies present new opportunities. Online communications (such as podcasting) have become standard tools in the communications toolbox, and other approaches will be developed.

11.3.1 The communications process

Communications are about two-way exchanges between sender and recipient (see Figure 11.11).

All marketing communications take place under 'noisy' conditions. Other communicators, both direct competitors and others with different market offerings to communicate, are also bombarding the same audience with messages. It has been estimated, for example, that US consumers are subjected to some 5,000 advertising messages each day. It is therefore important to ensure that the message is clear as well as effectively communicated. A starting point is to be clear about what the communications objectives are. These are best viewed using a simple model of marketing communications.

Figure 11.11 The communications process

Source: Developed from Doyle and Stern, 2006.

11.3.2 A basic communications model

A number of models of how communications work has been developed. Most, however, come back to a basic model called AIDA – Awareness → Interest → Desire → Action:

- **Awareness:** At a very basic level, marketing communications set out to create or raise awareness of the market offering among the selected target market. If customers are not aware of the existence of the offer, they are very unlikely to purchase! Awareness raising is particularly important at the launch and introductory stages of the product life cycle. In the early stages of the smart speaker market, for example, the communications task was to explain to the market what a smart speaker was and what it did.
- **Interest:** Once awareness has been created, the communication goal changes to creating interest in the market offer. Customers are bombarded by many messages every hour of every day and may have an awareness of many products and services. Relatively few will interest them, however. Key to creating interest is demonstrating how the offer is relevant to the wants and needs of the customer. In the case of the smart speakers, aside form the ability to stream music they can be connected to other smart devices in a home, meaning owners can use their voice to switch the lights on and off, call a family member, ask for the weather forecast and more.
- **Desire:** Once interest has been stimulated, communications seek to create desire for the offer, ahead of other offers in the market. Rather than demonstrating the benefits of the generic product group, the emphasis is now on creating a desire for this particular brand or offering. Much of Amazon's promotion of its Echo smart speakers and Alexa voice-control system centres on the practical and 'human' aspect of connectivity. Worldwide sales were 5.2m units in 2016, up from 2.4m in 2015.
- **Action:** Awareness, interest and desire are of little value to a supplier unless they result in purchases or other forms of support. Communications aimed at taking the customer to the next stage (creating action), include offers, promotions and deals to stimulate purchase, as well as the use of personal selling.

11.3.3 Communications decisions

A number of decisions need to be made regarding communications:

- **What message to convey:** First and foremost, the message to be conveyed needs to be clearly understood and accepted by those responsible for sending it. Confused messages create confusing signals in the minds of customers. The most effective communications have a single but clear message they are trying to get across. This has been referred to as the USP (unique selling proposition) of the market offer. Communications centering on conveying the key benefits of the product in a novel and attractive way (see later in the text) help not only to raise awareness, but also to create a powerful position for the product in the mind of the customer.
- **What communications tools to use:** There are many different communications tools available. These include advertising, public relations, sales promotions, personal selling (see Chapter 14), direct marketing and sponsorship. Each has advantages and disadvantages. Some are better at creating awareness (such as advertising), while others focus more on creating desired actions (personal selling, for example). The various tools are used in combination at different stages in the communications process.
- **How to translate the message in copy:** Not only is it important for the communicator to know what message they are trying to convey, they must also translate it into effective words and symbols that the recipient of the message can understand and decode. Too subtle, or complicated, translations can result in a confused message being received, or even the wrong message being received. Early anti-drug use advertisements in the UK

were criticised for actually making drug taking look glamorous, rather than getting across the message that drugs can seriously damage your health.

- **Which media to use:** The media available for marketing communications vary across different countries, as do their effectiveness. Relevant media include press, television, cinema, posters, Internet, radio, post box (email inbox as well as the physical letterbox still used for direct mail), point of sale, fax machines and mobile phones.
- **How much to spend on communications:** Setting a communications budget is notoriously difficult. Years ago a marketing executive said, 'Half my advertising budget is wasted – the trouble is, I don't know which half!' Advertising effectiveness modelling by leading firms such as Millward Brown can assess the levels of awareness created through promotional campaigns (see Maunder *et al.*, 2005) by surveying the target audience regularly and modelling the relationship with advertising activity.

11.3.4 Communications tools

- **Advertising:** Advertising is particularly effective at creating awareness. It can have high visual impact, wide reach and is easily repeated to reinforce messages. Its disadvantages are that it is impersonal, lacks flexibility, is generally not interactive with the customer (questions cannot be answered, objections cannot be overcome) and has a limited ability to close the sale on its own. Total media ad spending worldwide rose 7.4 per cent to $628.63 billion in 2018, 44 per cent of which was via digital media due to rising global ecommerce spending and shifting viewership from traditional TV to digital channels. It is expected that, by 2020, digital's share of total global advertising will be 50 per cent.
- **Public relations:** PR can be more credible than advertising as it uses a third party, the reporter and the medium used, to convey the message – the final message to the customer does not come directly from the marketer. As such it can have a higher impact than advertising for a fraction of the cost, and may also reach audiences that would be difficult or impossible to reach otherwise. The major disadvantage, however, is the loss of control. Once a press release has been issued there is no guarantee that it will be taken up and acted on by the media, and it is quite possible that the message will be distorted so that it does not get across as intended. It may also reach the wrong audience.
- **Sales promotions:** Sales promotions include money off, bonus packs, three for the price of two, free samples, coupons, loyalty cards, prizes, bulk discounts, competitions, allowances and any other creative 'deal' that firms can dream up. Their advantages are that they can have a very direct effect on behaviour, and those effects can generally be directly monitored and evaluated. The disadvantages are that their effects may be short-lived and hence they could be a costly way of achieving sales. Excessive use of promotions may also weaken the image of a brand ('it can't be very good if they are always giving it away!').
- **Personal selling:** One of the most effective tools for closing a sale is personal selling (see Chapter 13). It is flexible, can be adjusted to individual situations, can be used to build relationships with customers and can be used to understand, address and overcome barriers and objections to purchase. It can, however, be costly, is highly dependent on the skills of individual salespeople and, in some markets, may incur customer resistance.
- **Direct marketing:** At its best, direct marketing can offer a highly personalised service, tightly targeted to those customers who are prime targets for the offers made. Thus there is less wastage of the promotional budget. At its worst, however, direct mail can be indiscriminate, can generate high levels of scepticism among customers and result in message and material overload. As with all communications tools, effective

targeting is the key to ensuring the messages are directed effectively to the target market.

- **Sponsorship:** Sponsorship of sporting, social, cultural and other events, or of teams, causes or facilities, can be an effective way of targeting potential customer groups through their wider interests and concerns. This can also help with credibility building and reputation enhancement. However, it is perhaps the most difficult communications tool to measure the impact of. It can be expensive, and may not be particularly effective in achieving awareness goals – sponsorship of the London Olympics achieved very low levels of recall among target audiences. It can also be subject to 'ambush' – competitor products achieving placement in sponsored events.

Communications tools effectiveness

Figure 11.12 shows the effectiveness of each of these tools across the four stages of the communications model. In general, advertising, PR and sponsorship are better at raising levels of awareness and interest than creating desire or action. Personal selling, direct marketing and sales promotions are more effective at inducing action. An effective communications campaign will determine first what the objectives are, then select an appropriate mix of tools to achieve that objective.

11.3.5 The use of the Internet for marketing communications

Globally, most of the advertising budget is going online, and primarily on mobile devices.

As noted previously, a significant feature of the Internet is the shift in power away from manufacturers and retailers towards customers. While the period to the middle of the twentieth century saw power concentrated in the hands of manufacturers and suppliers (due to demand typically outstripping supply in many industries), a major feature of the last quarter of that century was the shift in power to retailers. It was the retailers who controlled the connection between manufacturers and customers, and crucially managed the information flows to customers. Customers who wanted

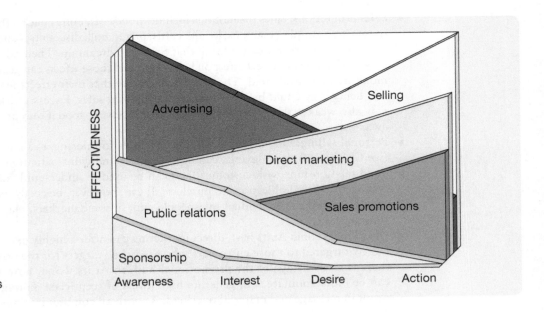

Figure 11.12
Communications
effectiveness

to gather information about competing products could do so, but the process was often time-consuming and cumbersome, resulting in choices being made with limited, imperfect information. A major characteristic of the Internet-based marketplace of the twenty-first century is the 'information superhighway' that makes comparative information far more easily available to customers. Indeed, the customer now typically initiates information search, whereas in the past the manufacturer or the retailer initiated and controlled this.

For example, powerful retailers such as Tesco and Walmart participate in global online exchanges based on the Web. They can source products from the cheapest suppliers anywhere in the world. They can also pressure their suppliers to switch sources for raw materials and components to cheaper alternatives located on the exchange; though not obliged to adopt such suggestions, suppliers find that their prices are adjusted down as though they had. This represents a significant change in the marketing communications process, and a shift in power from seller to buyer. Information search is more likely to be triggered by customers than by marketers, despite the large sums being spent on online advertising.

Customers are becoming information seekers rather than passive recipients, as evidenced by the extensive use of search engines such as Google and Yahoo. Coupled with this are changes in media viewing habits brought about by the explosion in channel availability through cable satellite and mobile, and media merging as the boundaries between phones, television and Internet technologies become blurred.

One of the potential benefits of communicating online is the possibility of relating sales to promotions more accurately. This is reflected in a number of new marketing communication methods emerging to take advantage of the particular characteristics of the Internet. Among these are display advertising and social media marketing.

Display advertising

Display advertising can take one of a number of forms.

Banner advertising is the use of advertisements on web pages that have click-through options to take browsers through to company websites. They are currently the main form of advertising on the Internet. Advertisers bid on key words they believe potential customers will use in their searches (using Google, Yahoo or other Internet search engines). The search engines then display advertisements next to the results of the Internet search. While irritating to some customers, they have proven very successful when linked to the page content being viewed. For example, search engines such as Yahoo and Lycos will flash links to commercial sites offering goods and services related to the items that are the subject of searches. Much of the early success of Amazon was attributed to the banner advertising it enjoyed on the AOL website, which directed purchasers to books on the topics of interest. The effectiveness of banner advertisements in general, however, is questionable, with Timmers (1999) reporting that click-throughs (visitors clicking on banner ads to link through to the corresponding website) can be as low as 0.5 per cent (one in two hundred). As users of the Internet become more sophisticated and experienced, it is likely that the click-through rate will fall rather than increase. To be effective, a banner advertisement must make an immediate impact on an often-crowded computer screen, as well as conveying in a few words the reasons to click through.

Pop-up advertising is another form of display advertising that is losing popularity due to the growth of ad-blocking software (by around 30 per cent in 2016).

Rich-media advertising, including video (often containing live information), is gaining in popularity because it involves interaction and engages consumers.

However, it is worth stressing that, as presented in, mobile advertising represents the largest share, with the fastest growth of all forms of online display advertising.

Social media marketing

Kotler *et al.* (2017) propose that the world we operate in has seen a major power shift from the vertical to the horizontal:

> In a world where the horizontal, inclusive and social forces trump the vertical, exclusive and individual forces, customer communities have become ever more powerful. They are now more vocal. They are not afraid of big companies and big brands. They love to share stories, good and bad, about brands.

Social media marketing 1.0: viral marketing

Viral marketing involves creating a marketing message with the intention that people will forward it to friends. This has a significant advantage over 'spam' messaging in that the friend will have some level of credibility, which may cause the message to be viewed more sympathetically. While not unique to the Web, Internet-based technologies have greatly facilitated easy use of this type of marketing.

The paint maker Dulux, for example, wanted to sell more paint to British women. Rather than indiscriminately bombarding women with email messages to 'buy more paint', the company created a website featuring a 'belly fluff' game and emailed 10,000 women invitations to play. In the event, 13,000 did play. The company estimates that one-third of the people entering the competition received the email forwarded from a friend (*The Guardian*, February 2002).

Viral marketing can also be 'led' by customer-driven interaction. For example, in December 2018, Iceland, the British frozen-food supermarket, struck a partnership with Greenpeace, the environmental organisation, to run its 90-second animated film *Rang-tan* as its Christmas 2018 advert. The actress Emma Thompson, a Greenpeace ambassador, narrated in the commercial the story of an orangutan called Rang-tan whose habitat is being destroyed by the growth of palm oil plantations. The body that approves ads for TV banned the Iceland commercial on the basis that it was political, as it was originally created by Greenpeace. This triggered a massive response on social media: within a week, the ad went viral and was viewed by more that 15 million people who shared it on Twitter. The video, posted on Iceland's YouTube channel, received nearly four million views and was shared over 615,000 times on its Facebook page. A pinned Tweet on the Iceland Foods account received over 90,000 re-Tweets and more than 8,000 likes were clicked on the official Iceland Foods Instagram account. A petition to get the ad released on TV attracted more than 670,000 signatures (Rogers, 2018).

Forrester Research (**www.forrester.com**) estimates that a high-quality email distribution list should generate a response rate (purchase) of around 6 per cent. A list created through panning will generate just 1 per cent. Viral marketing, on the other hand, has achieved response rates of between 25 and 50 per cent (Forrester Research, quoted in *The Guardian*, February 2002).

Nestlé uses viral marketing for its Nescafé products, including Blend 37. In one campaign, 20,000 Nescafé drinkers were emailed invitations to click onto a weblink to enter a prize draw for tickets to the Silver Historic Festival in August 2001. The top 36 scores won VIP passes to an event at the Silverstone racing circuit (*Precision Marketing*, 29 June 2001).

Social media marketing 2.0

Social media marketing can be considered as the second generation of social media marketing, when viral marketing was the first one. The main difference is the 'extensive feedback to the company itself (double arrows back to the company)' (Opresnik *et al.*, 2017). Social media (that is, Facebook, Twitter, LinkedIn, Snapchat, Tumblr) are vehicles for carrying content (either company-created or user-created content) and can be used to create further value for current or potential customers. The Internet essentially supports a pull strategy.

Opresnik *et al.* follow the '6-C model of social media marketing' to explain the creation and maintenance of consumer engagement:

> The **company** and **content** it originally creates. The **control** that it eventually hands over to to online **communities** of interest (including influencers) and **customers** (a subset of a community) and **conversations** that ensue.

With 57 per cent of the world's population using the Internet, 45 per cent active on social media, 67 per cent unique mobile users and 42 per cent active social mobile users (see **www.smartinsights.com**) in 2018, and growing, social media marketing is no longer optional. However, still in its infancy it is experiencing an unparalleled level of change and fluidity that makes developing social media marketing strategies difficult (Ford, 2018). Nevertheless, companies such as Airbnb, Uber and Yelp have succeeded in developing business models based around social commerce.

Airbnb, in particular, has mixed the right balance of global strategy and local implementation. Critical to the company's success is the use of local influencers (individuals who can influence the actions/decisions of a loyal group of local online followers with regard to their particular level of expertise) to drive brand awareness through a series of cleverly designed campaigns (Backaler and Shankman, 2018).

Pre-launch promotion

The Internet can be an ideal vehicle for 'teaser' ads prior to new product launches (see, for example, the *Avengers: Endgame* film). Before launching its new Crest Whitener toothpaste into the US market, P&G set up a pre-retail launch website that attracted 1.2 million visitors and actually sold 140,000 units (worth over $6 million retail). The company estimated that the initiative created around 500,000 buyers before the launch advertising and retail distribution had begun (*Marketing Business*, July/August 2001).

Advertising audience measurement

In order to standardise the ways in which measurements of advertising reach and effectiveness are made, the UK advertising industry has established a Joint Industry Committee for Web Standards (JICWEBS). The committee has now agreed definitions of 'users', 'page impressions', 'visits' and 'sessions'.

11.4   Distribution strategies

Distribution strategy focuses on how products and services will be physically delivered to the customer. The distribution network used or created will depend on a number of factors, including whether the final customers are consumers or other businesses.

11.4.1 Channels of distribution

The main choice facing most marketers is whether to sell through intermediaries or direct to customers. Intermediaries, such as wholesalers and retailers, can have a number of advantages. The most significant advantage is that they have direct relationships with customers that may be helpful.

In consumer grocery markets, for example, retailers such as Waitrose, Sainsbury's, Aldi, Leclerc, Walmart, etc. have loyal customers who regularly shop in their stores. Products sold through the stores gain credibility in the eyes of the customer because of where they are sold. The disadvantage, however, is that the retailer has many competing products on its shelves, and has little incentive to promote one brand over another. Suppliers attempt to counter this through either a 'push' or a 'pull' strategy. A push strategy is one where the retailer is given incentives to stock the product (for example, bulk discounts or additional promotional offers that might encourage additional shoppers into the store). A pull strategy, on the other hand, is where the supplier encourages customers to go into the store demanding the product. In this way the product is 'pulled' through the distribution channel, rather than being 'pushed'.

In business markets, intermediaries may also be used (usually trade wholesalers), but it is more common to find direct sales through the firm's salesforce. The advantages of direct selling through a salesforce have already been discussed. The obvious disadvantage is the cost incurred, though this is generally offset by the higher prices that can be charged. In addition, many firms may hire a contract salesforce to help with special activities, such as the launch of a new product, or in peak demand periods.

11.4.2 Effects of the Internet on distribution strategies

The Internet has greatly facilitated the distribution of bit-based products such as information, music and video. Indeed, in the recorded music industry, many now suggest that physical products such as the CD are on the point of obsolescence because of the attractiveness of downloading music from the Web. The challenge for the music companies is to find ways of generating income from music downloads in the face of competition from pirate sites providing the music free.

With atom-based products the key to success has often rested with efficient and effective distribution systems and logistics. Every book sold by Amazon online must be delivered to the customer, and customers increasingly accustomed to rapid access via the Internet also expect rapid physical delivery once they have made purchases. The traditional '28-day delivery' period is no longer acceptable to many customers. Failures in distribution destroyed many of the dot.coms – eToys found, for example, that the 'virtual business' is an illusion when you have to operate warehouses full of toys. The fulfilment strength of Amazon.com is proving a core competence, driving many of its alliances.

The past few years have seen an explosion of direct-to-consumer (DTC) brands, disrupting established industries and reshaping relationships with consumers. Among these, successful brands include Dollar Shave Club (a subscription shaving brand, now owned by Unilever), or Away (a luggage lifestyle brand founded in 2016). The focus of Away's conversations with consumers is away from product features and towards the overall travel concept. For these brands, just as for Amazon, supply chain is crucial – particularly as the main aim is to serve the customer better than traditional brands (Rogers, 2018).

Even established brands such as Nike take DTC seriously: it grew its direct-to-consumer channel eight times faster than its wholesale business in 2017. While this channel only generated $9.1 billion of revenue, or 28 per cent of Nike brand sales for the company, it accounted for 70 per cent of the growth.

Increasingly, the distribution issue becomes one of multi-channels – numerous ways in which the same products and services reach the customer. Multi-channel customer management refers to 'the design, deployment, and evaluation of channels to enhance customer value through effective customer acquisition, retention and development' (Neslin *et al.*, 2006). For example, one major strength of the Tesco.com Internet grocery offering was that it recognised that Internet grocery purchasing is not a substitute for store visits; it is a supplement. Managing complex multi-channel systems will be a substantial challenge for many companies. The critical tension will be between what companies want from multi-channel strategies and how customers react to them.

For example, PC market leader Dell Computers aimed to get the majority of sales onto the Web because of the huge economies this achieves. However, the company also has internal and external salesforces to promote new products with corporate customers and to win business from the competition. Dell's view is that, if you want to buy a few PCs, then you buy on the Web or go elsewhere. If you want to buy for a whole company, then you buy through the direct salesforce. If you are another Boeing with a potential installed base of 100,000 PCs, then the founder Michael Dell will come and see you. To make this multi-channel work, Dell has grasped the nettle of paying salespeople commission for sales through the Web, and even offering salespeople additional bonuses for moving smaller buyers onto the Web.

However logical multi-channel models may be, they can be reinterpreted by customers in other ways. One leading financial services company in the UK designed its channel system with three main options: the Internet, the branch network and postal/telephone banking. It saw its customers as either Internet customers or branch customers. Customers, on the other hand, tended to redefine the model in their own terms: why not go to the branch to open a deposit account and get a passbook, then do all the transactions through the post or on the telephone, and then operate the current account on the Internet? The company's multi-channel strategy was wrong-footed (along with all the cross-selling and promotional plans in each channel), but it is learning to cope with the fact that this is how its customers want to use different channels.

As on and offline intertwine, the concept of omnichannel has surfaced, principally in B2C but it is also relevant to B2B. Omnichannel initially refers to the cross-channel content strategy that companies use to improve their customer experience. Rather than working in parallel, communication channels and their supporting resources are designed to work in unison and integrate. The term is now more often applied to retailing. The concept is about ensuring a smooth and seamless customer journey throughout the buying process across media and for all touchpoints (see Figure 11.13). It is the 'synergetic management of the numerous available channels and customer touchpoints, in such a way that the customer experience across channels and the performance of channels is optimized' (Verhoef *et al.*, 2015).

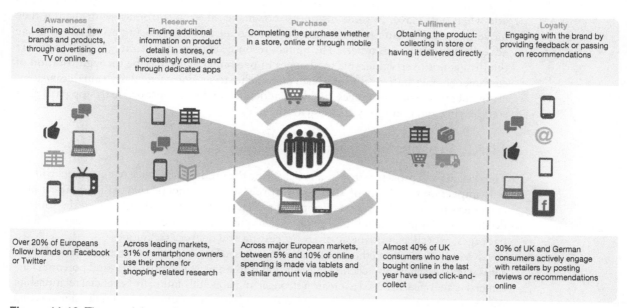

Figure 11.13 The omnichannel purchase journey

Source: The omnichannel opportunity: Unlocking the power of the connected consumer, Deloitte 2014.

| 11.5 | **The extended marketing mix – people, processes and physical evidence** |

11.5.1 People

While important in any business, the quality, training and enthusiasm of the people employed in the organisation are absolutely critical to service businesses. Happy, skilled and motivated staff are far more likely to serve customers well and effectively, and establish an ongoing relationship that can be mutually beneficial. A number of factors are important in designing the staffing strategy:

- **Job design and description:** The starting point is to have a clear idea of the job roles and tasks that staff will be required to carry out. This will include identifying the level of technical competence required, as well as the softer skills for dealing with people in a manner that will leave them satisfied (or better still, delighted). In service firms, however, jobs rarely conform to exact specifications. There is a need for flexibility to adapt the job as conditions change and as customer requirements also change.
- **Selection:** Choice of which staff to employ is largely driven by the job specification. If a 'bouncer' is being hired for a nightclub, the job specification will include an ability to physically defend himself and others. In hiring an accountant, however, other technical qualifications will be more important.
- **Training:** While staff may be highly skilled on appointment, ongoing training is essential to ensure that skills are maintained and enhanced in the light of changing circumstances. Much training may occur on the job, but it can also be important to allow time out for reflection and to sharpen specific skills.
- **Appraisal:** Also important is regular appraisal and feedback to staff on their performance. Provided this is done in a constructive manner, most staff welcome feedback on their performance and suggestions as to how it can be improved. Also part of the appraisal process is revisiting the job description and updating it in the light of experience.

Because the people employed have the direct contact with customers, it can be problematic when staff leave. In some instances they make take the customers with them if they move to a rival organisation (for example, account executives being poached from one advertising agency to another). The human resource management strategy needs to ensure the firm is not over-vulnerable to changes in personnel. This may be through rotation of customer contact staff, or through team approaches to serving particularly valuable customers or clients. In some instances, 'golden handcuffs' might be appropriate to stop particular staff leaving and taking key clients with them.

11.5.2 Processes

The systems and processes involved in delivering the product or service to customers will not only impact on the ability of staff to effectively serve customers, they will also affect how customers judge the level of service they have received. Staff need to be given the tools to do the job. This may include ICT tools such as customer relationship management (CRM) packages, as well as more basic order processing and delivery techniques.

CRM covers all the methods and technologies used by companies to manage their relationships with customers and clients. Information held on existing customers (and potential customers) is analysed and used to create a stronger and hopefully mutually beneficial relationship. Amazon.com uses automated CRM processes to generate automatic personalised marketing (such as book and CD suggestions or recommendations) based on the customer information, including recent purchases, stored in the system. Using this technology advantage, Amazon is becoming a general trading platform for diverse products and services beyond books and music (for example, it recently launched Amazon Pantry – a version of a supermarket).

An effective CRM system helps organisations to acquire customers, build closer relationships with them, provide better customer services and hence retain valued customers. By tracking customer contacts through the CRM, the organisation is able to ensure appropriate levels of contact are maintained, and to monitor the effectiveness of specific interactions.

In the public sector, universities are increasingly using CRM packages to track contacts with students through initial enquiry, decision to study, course performance and progress, on to graduation, career progress and alumni status. In this way, additional opportunities can be pursued for improving the overall student experience through a complete life cycle, as well as maximising the return to the university by way of repeat business, donations and endowments from the student.

CRM applications often track customer interests and requirements, as well as their buying habits. This information can be used to target customers more selectively. In addition, the products a customer has purchased can be tracked throughout the product's life cycle, allowing customers to receive information concerning a product or to target customers with information on alternative products once a product begins to be phased out. Baby products companies now have sophisticated CRM packages that alert them to stages in the baby's development when, for example, there is a need to change from one type of nappy to another, or from baby food to toddler food. In some cases they even trigger automatic birthday cards.

11.5.3 Physical evidence

As discussed in Chapter 13, a key aspect of service delivery evaluation is tangibles, or the physical evidence that accompanies the offer. In the marketing of physical, atom-based products the appearance of the product itself and its packaging, together with the surroundings in which it is marketed, can have an impact on the overall attractiveness to customers. For example, sophisticated retail facility design pays detailed attention to the smells and sounds that comprise part of the retail experience, as well as the sound and feel of the floor underfoot, and the space allowed to avoid the 'butt brush' (when one shopper brushes against another and disturbs their purchase consideration), and the effect of lighting on mood and ambience. In service encounters, the appearance and demeanour of staff can be equally important.

Customers take many cues as to the quality of the product or service they are purchasing from the physical evidence that surrounds it. When lecturing to MBA students or executives on management development programmes, most faculty members will dress in a more 'business-like' fashion than when teaching undergraduates. The formalities of dress code are used to establish rapport with the audience and are varied depending on the particular audience. Packaging for products may also vary to give cues as to quality. For example, the Sunday Times Wine Club distributes to members some of its fine wines in wooden crates, while more everyday wines are dispatched in cardboard boxes.

11.6 New businesses and business models

In the wake of the uncertainty and undoubted opportunities generated by the Internet, three distinct types of firms are emerging: Internet pioneers, Internet pragmatists and unicorn companies.

11.6.1 Internet pioneers

The Internet pioneers have set up radically new types of business to exploit the benefits of the new technology to do business in very different ways. Straub and Klein (2001) refer to these as 'omega'-level firms and note that the successful ones have harnessed the power of the new technology to gather information about customer preferences and to tailor products and services specifically to the needs of individual customers. These firms are relatively rare, but do include the likes of Amazon.com in consumer goods retailing, eBay in online auctions and Monster.com in the jobs market.

eBay is a prime example of an Internet pioneer. In the late 1990s it became the preferred place on the Web to trade collectibles, building its position largely through word of mouth rather than media advertising, and creating a virtuous circle whereby more buyers attracted more sellers, who in turn attracted more buyers. In 2016, eBay had 162 million users worldwide. In 2018, eBay sold $95 billion worth of goods, 60 per cent of which was outside the USA, and had more than 1.2 billion listings.

11.6.2 Internet pragmatists

The second type of firm to emerge has been termed 'Internet pragmatists' (Fahy and Hooley, 2002). These firms have embraced the opportunities of the Internet to enhance their existing business models. Dell, for example, uses online ordering to enhance its direct marketing operations, FedEx uses the technology to enable personalised tracking of customer packages during transit (3.1 million packages per day with 99 per cent on time, accurate delivery) and Cisco saves US$700 million annually through offering customer support over the Web. These pragmatists have used the Internet to enhance the services they already offered to their customers, and also to reduce costs, but have not completely thrown out their existing business models. Rather, these have been adapted to the new environment.

The national roll-out of Tesco's Internet grocery service in 2000 followed almost five years of preparation and piloting, and that preparation means Tesco.com leads the Internet quality measurements published by the Chicago-based Gomez company, and is regarded by many US companies in this field as a world leader. Certainly, Tesco.com was the world's largest e-grocery business, with over $1 billion in online sales in the UK alone by September 2008. The formulation of Tesco Direct's value proposition and business model was based on close study of what customers wanted from Internet grocery shopping. Contrary to expectations that online shoppers would want to abandon traditional stores, they found customers liked to visit stores to examine fresh produce personally and to see what new products were available, and trusted their local stores to provide quality goods at fair prices. Most customers did not see online shopping as a substitute for traditional shopping, but as a complement. For this reason the online shopper uses the same store that they visit in person, choosing from the same regional product selection and buying at the same prices. The proposition was to 'shop online from my store'. The Tesco model integrates online and offline business – online sales are part of branch sales and feed into store-based replenishment. The value proposition is convenience and time-saving, but also greater personalisation – the software remembers previous purchasing and gives 'reminders', and can also warn those vulnerable about things such as nut allergies and food choices. The relatively low start-up costs (£35 million) and fast national coverage reflect use of the conventional stores as 'mini-depots', where pickers can make-up six online orders a time using a special trolley. Company estimates are that the average online shopping order is 2 or 3 per cent more profitable than the average in-store order, because Internet shoppers tend to select the higher-margin products on offer.

The difference between the pioneers and the pragmatists can clearly be seen by the stage of diffusion at which they adopted the newer technologies. It seems that we are now firmly in the majority phase of diffusion of the Internet as an enabling technology (possibly even late majority stage) where the majority of adopters are pragmatists, using the new technology to enhance and improve existing business models, rather than to revolutionise them.

Many of the pragmatists represent the much-maligned 'old economy'. These are companies that, in some instances, were slow to join the information technology revolution, and also includes those firms that are selective in their use of the Internet. For example, firms such as IBM and Cisco Systems have moved most of their customer service online and customers now serve themselves from the menus of options available on their websites. These companies claim cost savings of the order of $500–700 million per annum through providing service online. Some of the kinds of online customer service currently available include customised web pages, targeted information, customer service provider interaction, customer-to-customer interaction, customised products and rewards and incentives (Walsh and Godfrey, 2000).

Similarly, right through the business system, pragmatists are using the Internet to enhance what they are currently doing (Porter, 2001). For example, Compaq Computer Corporation is increasingly distributing software online rather than on CD and floppy disk. It has pioneered a 'try it and buy it' distribution system, where customers use the software for a trial period and then the licence is extended should a customer wish to purchase. Sales conversion rates have increased significantly using this system. Many of the basic organisational activities are now being outsourced electronically. Mobile phone companies such as Vodafone offer fleet management services for corporate clients, while corporate health plans can be managed off-site by companies such as BUPA. Corporate training services can be managed remotely by e-learning companies such as Smartforce, and even basic corporate R&D activity is enhanced by vast stores of information now available electronically. In summary, Internet pragmatists are those that have adopted the Internet to enhance existing products and processes. These are frequently labelled 'bricks and clicks' operations, meaning that the company sees the Internet as an additional channel that complements existing activities. Dell Computer Corporation found that its make-to-order model was very well suited to the Internet and consequently more than 50 per cent of its business is now being conducted through this medium. Allied Irish Banks examined the option of setting up an Internet-only bank to compete with the likes of First-e, but dropped the idea in favour of improving its Internet banking facilities for existing customers. While the Internet pioneers have grabbed the headlines, it is likely to be Internet pragmatists who eventually dominate the use of the Internet as a business channel.

11.6.3 Unicorn companies

A unicorn company is a start-up company founded after 2003 that has a 'current' valuation (in 2018) of more than \$1billion or more. The term has been coined because a \$1billion technology start-up wold have once been the stuff of myth. *Fortune* produces its own list that includes Uber (transportation services), Xiaomi (consumer electronics), Airbnb (lodging services), Didi Kuadi (transportation services), Flipkart (e-commerce) and others. These companies built their business models around social commerce (Opresnik *et al.*, 2017). The question is whether this large number of start-ups with high valuations are a sustainable reflection of a new wave of technologically driven productivity. Only the future will tell.

11.7	The connected marketing mix

Kotler *et al.* suggest that we are moving 'from selling the four Ps to commercializing the 4 Cs: co-creation, currency, communal activation and conversation' (Kotler *et al.*, 2017). Co-creation relates to the fact that in the digital economy we are in, customers are involved in new product development and mass-customisation. The term 'currency' reflects the dynamic aspect of pricing – that is, setting price in line with demand fluctuation and capacity. The concept of channel is also evolving, with customers often playing an active part in it (for example, when setting a delivery time or choosing a click-and-collect service), plus the advent of the sharing economy. 'In a connected world, customers demand access to products and services almost instantly, which can only be served with their peers in close proximity. This is the essence of communal activation' (Kotler *et al.*, 2017). Finally, the proliferation of social media facilitates customer engagement and conversations: customers actively talk to each other about companies' products and their experiences of them.

Summary

The marketing mix is constantly changing. New ingredients are being added all the time by creative marketers. The most significant development over the last decade, however, has been the coming of age and greater exploitation as a marketing tool of the Internet. This has significantly impacted on all aspects of the marketing mix, from product and price through to promotions and distribution. A number of conclusions (and possible warnings) emerge:

1 Don't assume that the Internet will cure all your marketing ills. Firms that are poor at marketing in the bricks-and-mortar world are unlikely to suddenly succeed in the virtual world of the Internet. For creative, Internet-savvy firms, however, the new technologies may offer ways of leapfrogging more conventional competitors and adding value for customers in innovative ways.

2 Remember that atom-based products will still need efficient and effective distribution systems to physically get them to customers. Indeed, the logistics and distribution systems of online retailers may need to be even more effective than those of bricks-and-mortar firms, as expectations of speed are greater for Internet-based firms.

3 Beware of assuming that today's atom-based products will be tomorrow's atom-based products. Increasingly, physical products (such as music CDs, videos, newspapers, magazines) are being turned into bit-based products. Because of the Internet, the market for TVs and PC monitors is blurring; tablet computers and mobile telephones can now access broadcast material.

4 Continue to base your competitive advantage on the marketing resources you possess that can be protected from competitor imitation. Actively develop the new resources, skills and competencies necessary to take advantage of the new technologies and the digital age.

Case study

How ABB FIA Formula E championship built a fan base from scratch

By Simon Gray and Kate Walker

The all-electric motorsport tapped into e-gaming and social media to attract young supporters

Traditional motorsport fans were not particularly captivated when Formula E, an all-electric racing series, launched in 2014. Even its chief marketing officer Jérôme Hiquet acknowledges that diehard fans were dismissive of the new series, especially when it was compared with Formula One.

Now in its fifth series, the ABB FIA Formula E championship has succeeded in mobilising an audience and public profile that has delighted sponsors and backers, not least in connecting with a younger, urban audience.

Nearly half (49 per cent) of engagement on the series' Facebook page is from people in the 13–17 and 18–24 age brackets, according to figures from Formula E. The company says that the 18–24 category is their second largest 'follower group' on the social network, after the 25–34-year-olds.

The electric series gives its F1 elders a lesson in how to mobilise social media, e-gaming and a range of communication platforms to build a young fan base from scratch.

Interaction is key, says Mr Hiquet. 'It is a younger audience than for other motorsport series, and they consume content not only through traditional channels, but through social media and short-format content.'

Racing line: Formula E driver Edoardo Mortara makes his way through the crowd towards the podium in Hong Kong
Source: Handout/Getty Images.

The Formula E team invests in providing fans with just that. 'We have a full team of community managers at the track commenting on almost everything that is happening before and during the race on social media, capturing content that is interesting in real time.' This includes live tweeting races and sharing images on social media channels for fans to use as background pictures on their mobile phones.

Formula E has also developed a number of ways to enable fans to interact with the sport. 'Ghost racing' will place fans in the middle of the action in real time, while with 'Fanboost' supporters can directly affect the outcome of a race. 'Attack Mode' – a new addition this series – increases the element of surprise and makes for even more unpredictable racing.

That racing style provides a spectacle for even the most traditional motorsport fans, according to Mr Hiquet. He acknowledges that the introduction of the second-generation car has been critical to the popularity of the sport.

The new car is more powerful than its predecessor, with a top speed of around 280kph, and improved battery life. Before its introduction, drivers had to switch vehicles mid-race, which interrupted the momentum and served as an uncomfortable reminder of the limitations of electric technology.

It is this showcasing of green technology that sets Formula E apart among its younger fans, according to Mr Hiquet. The sport is more than a racing series, he says, as it embodies a serious social purpose by showing how technology can tackle global problems such as climate change and air pollution.

'Studies tell us that the younger demographic want to be connected with brands that convey an authentic purpose and mission,' he says. 'Formula E has done a good job of putting that at its core from the very beginning.'

It is also a message that resonates with commercial backers. Marco Parroni, head of global sponsorship at wealth manager Julius Baer, official global partner to the championship, says: 'Formula E is not just a car race, it is a race with a purpose: to create enthusiasm for electric mobility, to promote research and development.'

The series has a final trick up its sleeve for attracting fans: its city-centre locations. 'It enables us to get potentially closer to people who may be attracted to come to a race in a way that they would attend an NBA or a football game,' says Mr Hiquet. Fans can get to events on foot or by public transport, unlike F1, for example, where many races are in more remote locations.

The city-centre tracks make the races and surrounding events more accessible, introducing the sport to people who may not have considered buying tickets, but might do so in the future.

This urban focus is popular with partners including title sponsor ABB, the Swiss engineering group, a leader in electric vehicle charging infrastructure. Nicolas Ziegler, head of markets, brand and events, says the championship is a good fit because 'e-mobility is at the core of what we are doing'. His company is 'highly engaged' with smart city and smart infrastructure development, he adds.

This mix of new technology, social media and gaming is capturing the affection of the next generation of motorsport fans — and taking significant commercial interest with it.

Sponsors: Social aspect has commercial appeal

Alongside the challenge of building its young fan base, Formula E also needs to attract big-name sponsors: Virgin, Panasonic and Shell, for example, are all supporting teams this season.

Argo Group, a global underwriter of speciality insurance, has been involved in Formula E since 2016, first sponsoring the now-defunct Team Aguri and now with Dragon Racing.

'The . . . appeal, first and foremost, is the association with the innovation, teamwork and sustainability,' says Gary Grose, Argo Group's global marketing and communications leader. 'Those are the pillars that we want our brand associated with, so we've tagged to those sports that we feel are cutting edge in those areas.'

If branding is important, it is the business opportunities that are crucial – and the access sponsors gain attracts Argo.

The championship's VIP area, the Emotion Club, is an open space that allows teams and sponsors to network among themselves and with each other. This contrasts with Formula One's teams' hospitality suites, which are run as private units, separate from their garage and the other teams.

This access does not just make for good client entertainment, it also gives Argo regular contact with Dragon's founder and principal, Jay Penske, of the renowned American racing family.

As well as his racing interests, Penske is chairman and chief executive of the Penske Media Corporation, the parent company of more than 20 print and digital brands including Variety, *Rolling Stone*, IndieWire and *WWD (Women's Wear Daily)*.

Access to Mr Penske and his 'brand power' is one aspect that pulls in sponsors. 'You're dealing with Jay Penske's media empire which really helps push our brand out as part of the deal,' says Mr Grose.

 Source: from 'How ABB FIA Formula E championship built a fan base from scratch', *Financial Times*, 10/04/19 (Gray, S. and Walker, K.).

Discussion questions

1 Which target markets is Formula E aiming at?

2 How is Formula E competing in the world of motorsport?

3 How does Formula E use digital media in its marketing mix?

CHAPTER 12
COMPETING THROUGH INNOVATION

'Self-driving cars. . . 3-D printing. . . the Internet of Things. . . the Apple Watch. . . legal marijuana. . . plants that glow in the dark to replace street lights. . . up-market office supplies for addicts. . . printable make-up. . . mobile light switches for the home. . . a vegan condom. . . a vacuum cleaner that uses ultraviolet rays to kill bacteria in carpets. . . light-producing walls to replace light bulbs. . . sensors in floors to measure gait and diagnose health problems. . . health spas for 5-year-olds. . . printable electronics to produce Harry Potter-style live newspapers. . . the world is full of novelties and new products.'

Fitness trackers enter the pet insurance market

By Alexandra Howlett

Regularly exercised dogs can collar premium discounts for their owners

Taking your dog for a walk could cut the cost of future pet insurance premiums, with the launch of a new product powered by a collar-mounted doggy fitness tracker.

In the latest development in the world of 'insurtech', insurer MoreThan has launched a partnership with PitPat – the dog world's equivalent of the FitBit – offering cash rewards of up to £100 for owners who regularly exercise their pet.

From next month, customers receiving a new MoreThan pet insurance quotation for a dog will be given the option of signing up to PitPat Life.

At £4 a month, the subscription service includes the collar-mounted PitPat activity monitor which tracks the pet's exercise levels via a linked smartphone app. This will devise a personalised daily exercise goal based on your dog's age, weight and breed.

Users accumulate points for achieving these goals and completing tasks such as weighing their dog regularly. PitPat said that if dogs and their owners accomplished the exercise goal every day for a year, the maximum reward of £100 could be unlocked.

Points can be exchanged for perks, including money off dog food, a caricature of your pet, or put towards renewing their MoreThan insurance policy.

Points are not rewarded for exceeding the goal and doing more exercise than necessary, as this can be detrimental to a dog's health.

The latest innovation to hit the UK's £1.2bn pet insurance market, MoreThan hopes the venture could cut the numbers of podgy pooches.

Source: Petr David Josek/AP/Shutterstock.

'Happy and healthy dogs lead longer and richer lives,' said Andrew Moore, director of pet claims at MoreThan. A qualified vet, Mr Moore added: 'The love we have for our canine friends means it can be easy to overfeed them, with our research showing 50 per cent of dogs are overweight due to being overindulged by their owner.'

PitPat's brand ambassador Rory the Vet – who stars in CBBC's The Pet Factor with more than 30,000 Instagram followers – said he saw more pets suffering from obesity, which can affect everything from a dog's heart to their spine, than anything else within his work.

Thought to be the first pet insurance product of its kind, dog owners – and people without a pet – can already take out policies linked to health-tracking apps from providers including Vitality to receive discounts on life and health insurance.

PitPat's founder Andy Nowell described the new product as 'a bit like Vitality, but for dogs'.

While the link up with MoreThan is new, the PitPat activity monitor has been on the market for three years and has evolved considerably, Mr Nowell said.

'We realised that dogs roll in poo. The monitor is now waterproof, has a battery life of a year and the Velcro is replaceable,' he added.

By the end of next year, PitPat Life hopes to have 50,000 members and has already expanded to Denmark. However, until Mr Nowell has put a PitPat activity monitor on all 8.9m dogs in the UK, he won't think of branching out into the cat insurance market.

However, he said he was aware of some particularly enthusiastic cat owners who had purchased a monitor and selected a small breed of dog.

Source: from 'Fitness trackers enter the pet insurance market', *Financial Times*, 27/03/19 (Howlett, A.).

Discussion questions

1 What innovations are discussed here?

2 What could be sources of innovation for an insurance company such as MoreThan?

Introduction

A recent report by McKinsey predicts that after decades of expansion, global economic growth will slow dramatically as the world's population ages. The data suggest that the rate of gross domestic product will decline by 40 per cent over the next 50 years, and it is feared that today's feeble growth rates, collapsed oil prices and low interest rates may mark the start of a new era of austerity and low growth. However, the bright spot in the McKinsey work is that it concludes that with pro-market reforms and radical technological innovation, growth may accelerate again. Economic growth can be driven by creativity and, above all else, by innovation (cited in Tett, 2015). The priority for companies to compete through innovation has probably never been higher.

Certainly, many companies are experiencing the squeeze between investor demands for sustained earnings growth and shrinking and fiercely contested post-recessionary markets. It is a problem that, in the past, marketing has tended to fixate on serving and retaining current customers, which has been reinforced by company rewards and incentives that emphasise short-term market share and profitability. Marketing should be central to corporate growth, but it is in danger of being marginalised in important decisions about growth strategy – some see marketing and sales only as the people responsible for selling what is produced and hitting volume targets. Instead, marketing's real role is to contribute to a firm's growth through better anticipation of market opportunities and evaluation of risks, tighter linking of technological possibilities with market concepts and faster adjustment to shifting market needs and competitive moves (Day, 2003). The key has become **competing through innovation**.

There are many factors that encourage a company to innovate. These factors include internal pressures to exploit existing and new technologies to the full, together with the desire to use the organisation's resources, its assets and capabilities, as effectively as possible.

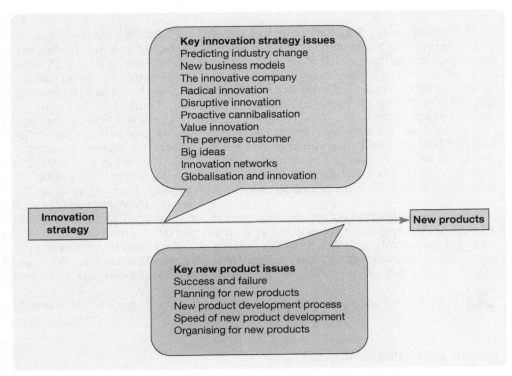

Figure 12.1
Innovation strategy
and new products

External pressures include the push from intense competition, increasingly demanding customers whose priorities have changed through the recession, and the technological drive of shortening product life cycles (see Chapter 3).

We examine the mandate to compete through innovation at two levels in this chapter (see Figure 12.1). First, we examine key issues in innovation strategy, industry change driven by innovation and the impact of disruptive innovation initiatives, leading to an emphasis on value innovation achieved through new business models and global innovation networks. Second, we turn our attention to the operational aspects of new product development, which are driven by a company's innovation strategy.

Certainly, new systematic product planning is a vital activity for every company, and it applies as much to services as it does to physical products. Generally, companies that are successful with new products follow a step-by-step process of new product planning combined with effective organisation structures and processes for managing new products. Experience and learning help these firms to improve product planning over time. Importantly, however the process is organised, the corporate cultures of companies such as Apple, IBM, Facebook and Google actively encourage and reward innovation. It is imperative for executives to understand the reasons for new product failure and to avoid these pitfalls. By understanding the drivers of new product success, managers can check if their firm has the requirements for effective product innovation. If it does not, they should develop means by which the essentials of successful innovation are acquired to minimise the likelihood of market failure.

12.1   Innovation strategy

One of the most critical issues facing executives is the need for radical innovation in the value they provide to their customers. In many practical situations, while true innovation addresses superior customer value, many of the existing bureaucratic processes in corporate marketing are geared towards making only marginal changes in products and brands, and in avoiding mistakes rather than taking risks (Vence, 2007). Real innovation means more than producing new products that are marginally different to their predecessors. It is about the quest for delivering superior value to customers. Accordingly, before turning to the tactical and operational aspects of managing new product development, as part of marketing strategy and enhanced competitive positioning it is worth considering some of the broader arguments supporting innovation as an essential key point of focus for executives.

12.1.1 Innovation predicting industry change

A powerful argument developed by Clayton Christensen and his colleagues is that understanding innovation patterns and emergent events is key to predicting the direction and extent of change in an industry – simply 'seeing what's next' (Christensen *et al.*, 2004). They suggest that major recurring questions for managers include issues such as: whether a new start-up will succeed or fail; which emerging technologies will be accepted by consumers; whether a new entrant is a serious threat to existing competitors; whether government regulation will affect competition significantly; whether company managers are making good or short-sighted decisions; and which firms are likely to come out on top. Answering such questions correctly is fundamentally important to making effective strategic decisions. Christensen's work suggests that theories of radical and disruptive innovation provide a basis for addressing these questions (see the following sections).

For example, in the IT sector, Google is reshaping the industry based on the strength of its search capabilities, but particularly through the impact of cloud computing. The 'cloud' refers to the idea of software and services running on remote computers, connected via the Internet, rather than on your personal computer. For most people, their first awareness of the cloud began with a file storage service, although today a huge amount of commercial and consumer-level services use the cloud. Google provides a cloud system, and was one of the first to do so. However, by 2019 many other providers had entered the market. Unlike its predecessor, the supercomputer, Google's system never ages – as individual computers die, they are replaced individually with newer, faster boxes. This means the cloud regenerates as it grows, almost like a living thing. As the concept of computing clouds spreads, it expands Google's footprint way beyond search, media and advertising, and Google could become, in effect, the world's primary computer. IBM's head of research operations notes that 'compared to this, the Web is tiny'. No individual corporate computing system can match the efficiency, speed and flexibility of resources like Google's cloud. It is estimated that Google can carry out a computing task for one-tenth of what it costs a typical company. The move to cloud computing represents a fundamental change in how we handle information. It is almost the computing equivalent of the evolution in electricity supply from a hundred years ago, when farms and businesses closed down their own power generators and bought power instead from efficient industrial utilities (this illustration is based on 'The clouds raining on the computer business', in Piercy, 2009a, pp. 162–167). Of course, given this potential, cloud computing is an area of fierce competition between providers such as Google, Amazon.com, IBM and others to dominate cloud computing.

By contrast, in the pharmaceuticals sector, the new product pipelines of the major pharmaceutical companies have largely run dry – there are few new blockbuster drugs in prospect from conventional R&D, and current blockbusters are losing out to generic drugs as patents expire. Instead, the drug treatment innovation is being driven by small biotechnology start-ups based on less conventional science and technology in which big pharma has been slow to invest. Small biotechnology firms are commanding massive premiums as they sell out to big pharma (who have belatedly recognised that this new technology will shape the future of their industry) (Cookson, 2006).

An interesting and growing area of speculation at present is whether Silicon Valley companies (Google, Apple) will challenge Detroit (Ford, General Motors) for control of the automotive industry. As Google and Apple are pioneering self-driving cars, they are in partnership with companies such as Bosch, Continental and Delphi – leading suppliers to the industry. The growing technology content of the vehicle – about 40 per cent of the cost of the average vehicle already – creates a potential shift in power away from traditional brands and manufacturers to technology-led groups. While speculative for the moment, executives need to be constantly aware that innovation may reshape their industries in dramatic and unexpected ways (Gapper, 2015).

Increasingly, the challenge facing executives is not simply to launch new and better products and services, but to grasp how fundamental change is reshaping the industry and how to respond to this challenge.

12.1.2 Developing new business models

The business model, or business design, describes how a company makes money – how it generates revenue and profit by delivering value to customers – including the infrastructure and processes needed to achieve this goal. One of the hardest decisions for executives to confront is when the established business model has become obsolete, and how to change it. Tackling inefficiencies and developing better internal organisational processes is an important part of a manager's role, but coping with inefficiencies is ineffective if the business model has been displaced by something better.

The displacement of the recorded music CD by digital music downloads and now music streaming; the unbeatable challenge of the low-cost budget airlines to the established full-service flyers; the superiority of agile fast-fashion companies such as H&M and Zara in speed and cost over established fashion clothes retailers; Google's attempts to make the value chain in wireless mobile like that in the broadband Internet market (where applications are developed independently of device manufacturers and network operators) may relegate operators to a minor and unprofitable role; the impact of open-source (free) computer software from Linux and Sun on conventional software producers such as Microsoft – all are examples of new business models displacing the old by offering better value to customers. Further, it's worth noting that many (if not all) of these innovative models may seem obvious now, but most certainly did not at the time of their introduction.

A prime example of the power of a new business model is provided by the Uber taxi service business model. Uber has proved to be an incredibly disruptive business model in many cities and countries across the globe, and at the time of writing is poised to go public in just a few days, targeting a value of $90 billion, all without ever having made a single cent in profit. While Uber has expanded its initial ride-hailing offering into food delivery, freight and other services, it's worth reflecting on Uber's initial offering in more depth. Uber's 'big idea' was to see that an online platform could allow individual customers to contact individual drivers to arrange rides ('ride-hailing'), without the transaction costs and aggregation inefficiencies inherent to prior business models (traditional taxi companies). This allows a lower cost to the customer, and greater convenience. Further, costs to Uber are lower because it does not need to own any vehicles, or technically employ the drivers themselves, who are classed as independent contractors. Of course, this arrangement has proved popular with customers, but less so with regulators or conventional taxi firms. Indeed, Uber is at this point facing a strike by many of its drivers in protest at their share offering, because they feel exploited by the firm. Local and national regulators also take a strong interest in the employment model Uber and companies like it operate. This model has been termed the 'gig economy', and has come in for significant criticism for marginalising workers and avoiding protections such as unionisation and employment benefits. On the other hand, many Uber drivers praise the flexibility that the model offers them. Either way, the genie is out of the bottle, and the basic Uber concept has spread far and wide, so that online platforms don't just coordinate hundreds of thousands of freelancers to drive taxis (Uber), but also rent rooms (Airbnb), clean laundry (Laundrapp) and perform other services. These are all businesses that create a platform by combining the characteristics of companies and markets in which the supply chain operates as a marketplace. The Uber phenomenon is about the creation of new business forms that replace the tired, unresponsive, clumsy, slow structures of conventional companies as a better way of delivering value to customers. Traditional organisations are increasingly unable to support the innovation and radical change demanded by the marketplace.

It is increasingly the case that competition is between business models rather than products and companies. It follows that companies require a capacity for continuous reconstruction or resilience to overcome forces that do no more than perpetuate the past, and to seek out innovation for the future (Hamel and Välikangas, 2003). This explains the swapping of workers between Google and Procter & Gamble – the goal is to stimulate innovation in taking consumer products into online value chains.

The organisational changes at successful companies such as Procter & Gamble and IBM in their search for valuable innovations that benefit customers, underline the fact that real innovation, which taps into new value creation opportunities, is likely to be disruptive and challenging, not incremental and predictable. Indeed, although innovation in marketing often refers to technology and products, the most important innovations may actually be in how we think about management and implement organisational change – management innovation changes how we work and is directly linked to sustainable competitive advantage. The constant search for better ways of managing underpins outstanding successful innovation at companies such as Toyota and Procter & Gamble (Mol and Birkinshaw, 2007). In many ways, the 'innovative company' has become the critical aspiration for management.

For example, several car makers are looking at 'pay-as-you-go' plans for younger consumers, as well as participating in new car-sharing schemes, which aim to free urban dwellers from the need for car ownership in any form. Daimler, for instance, is working on a new 'pay-as-you-drive' business model that makes car use more like using a mobile phone than owning a vehicle in the conventional way. In the cosmetics sector, L'Oréal is pursuing a new business model based on 'accessible innovation' to expand its base into new and emerging markets. In the retail sector, new value chain models include 'pop-up shops' – temporary retail outlets operated by firms such as Prada and Harvey Nichols, or by Internet fashion houses, to provide a new offer to their online communities. Marmite, for example, had a novel temporary store on London's Regent Street. These are innovations in business models, not simply in products.

These broad strategic issues should be addressed operationally in considering the link between effective marketing strategy and positioning and innovation. In several important ways, the most appropriate words to describe modern markets are revolution, reinvention and renewal:

- **revolution** – in the ways industries and markets operate and the sources of competition that become important, and consequently in the strategies that successful organisations pursue;
- **reinvention** – in the creation of new business models that make traditional ways of doing business obsolete as routes to delivering and sustaining superior customer value; and,
- **renewal** – in the strategies of change and repositioning by companies whose business models have become outdated, as they rebuild and respond to change. Increasingly, the priority is not just short-term performance but building the robustness to bounce back, to change, to survive, to turn things around (Cravens *et al.*, 1998).

In using the structure in Figure 12.2 to analyse a company situation, we accept that the changes in the market amount to a **revolution**. It is inevitable that radical market and customer change provides disruptive pressures for the established players in the market. The challenge for them is to understand the specific changes unfolding and where they are going, and to respond with coping and adaptation mechanisms – **renewal**. The same market changes identify the new opportunities to create superior value for customers by designing new business models – that is, to develop new ways of doing business that are aligned with market change – **reinvention**. Tracking the specifics of fundamental market changes and

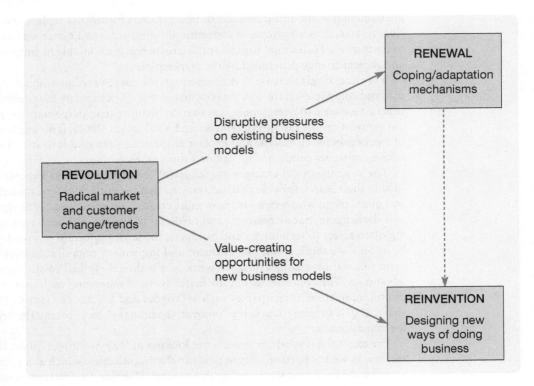

Figure 12.2
Innovation drives
strategy renewal
and reinvention

Source: Adapted from
Nigel F. Piercy (2017).

the disruptions created is the basis for developing effective responses and evolving new business models.

One interesting question when using this approach is whether the existing competitors in a market are capable of reinvention, or whether emerging value-creating opportunities will instead be exploited by new entrants to the market. It is quite possible that the new entrant, unencumbered by existing ways of doing things, will take the strongest position. When the laptop computer market became obsessed with the size and weight of the machines, the first sub-three-pound laptop did not come from Dell, IBM or Hewlett-Packard – it came from Sony. Sony had no real track record or capabilities in the computer business, but is just very good at making things smaller. In the move to develop electric and hydrogen-powered vehicles as an alternative to high-pollution petrol fuels, it is small start-ups, notably in Silicon Valley, that are driving innovation, not the big car makers who have been reluctant to invest and slow to respond (Reed, 2008). While today almost all car makers have electric vehicles on the road, and are committed to developing them, it is Tesla that led the way in making the electric car a desirable reality for customers.

Increasingly, it looks like success goes to the company that can invent a whole new category of products: brewing coffee at home from expensive pods in expensive coffee makers has taken the market away from traditional but cheaper ways of making coffee; Microsoft's Xbox live gaming system combines a traditional video game with a subscription-based online service; the creation of Spanx has revolutionised the underwear business by the creative use of a new fabric type. Companies that create new categories show high performance compared to their competitors.

12.1.3 The innovative company

Increasingly, and in most industrial sectors, one key survival factor is the ability to build creative, innovative companies. A new corporate model is taking shape in successful organisations, that focuses on creativity and innovation to provide new pathways to growth. As technology and information become commoditised and globalised, so the advantage of making things cheaper, faster and better diminishes and profits decline. Design strategy begins to play a key role in product differentiation, decision making and understanding the consumer experience. Creative innovation becomes the key driver of growth, because companies create products that address consumers' unmet and often unarticulated needs. The successful creative corporation emerges with a new 'innovation DNA' and a fast-moving culture that routinely beats the competition because of a high success rate in innovation (Nussmaum, 2005). The transformation of software company Intuit came from the creation of the company as 'a design-driven innovation machine' and its 'Design for Delight' initiative to produce the most user-friendly software in the world. Today, Intuit has leveraged the cloud to move beyond software provision towards service – a fundamental shift in business model that, like many others already mentioned, seems obvious in hindsight.

Companies such as Apple, Google, Toyota and General Electric are regularly rated as the most innovative in the world, ahead of their competitors (McGregor, 2007). The move by Apple from computers to the music and movie business; the evolution of Google from Internet search to advertising, to data organisation, to online software, to mobile phones; the dominance of Toyota in hybrids; GE's search for 'imagination breakthroughs', which has led into emerging market initiatives and green technology – all represent the power of ideas in changing markets and achieving step-changes in performance. Breakthrough ideas represent new market power. Steve Jobs at Apple achieved a step-change in the music business because of the iPod – not even a new product to the world, but one that was a better-conceived and better-designed version of an existing product – because Jobs had the power to attract customers with his superior ideas (Colvin, 2007).

The challenge for marketing is to drive creative and powerful innovations that make a difference and reshape markets. Innovation that creates superior value provides a route to above-average earnings, even in turbulent markets (Henry, 2006).

12.1.4 Radical innovation

Importantly, the strategic imperative for effective innovation is not incremental change to products and services, but deep-seated change in the way we approach the market, and a deep focus on customer value – everything else is just variation on a theme (Vence, 2007). By contrast, it should be noted that it is estimated that minor innovations make up 85–90 per cent of most companies' development portfolios, but rarely generate the growth that companies seek – in effect, at a time when companies should be taking bigger, but smarter, risks, their bias is in the other direction (Day, 2007). The failure to innovate at this level has been tracked to: (1) paying too much attention to the company's currently most profitable customers; (2) creating products and services that do not do the jobs customers want done; and (3) the misguided application of financial analysis as an accomplice in the conspiracy against innovation (Christensen *et al.*, 2008).

In fact, authors such as Daniel Pink argue that the very basis of value creation is shifting from the disciplines of logic, science and linear thinking to the intuitive, non-linear processes of creativity and imagination (Pink, 2006). Terms like the 'imagination economy' describe the move from technology and services to create value, to creativity and imagination (Colvin, 2006). The focus is on innovation so radical it may even frighten customers – for example, a major concern at companies such as Samsung and LG, is that the growing sophistication of their products will put off buyers (Gowers *et al.*, 2005).

When you identify the world's most innovative companies, the top five usually include Apple, Google, Microsoft, IBM and Amazon, but in fact when you look more closely at the list, 15 of the top 50 are Asian companies and the majority of the top 25 are based outside the USA. *BusinessWeek* concludes: '. . . we're starting to see the beginning of a new world order. The developed world's hammerlock on innovation leadership is starting to break' (Arndt and Einhorn, 2010).

1 Alphabet/Google
2 Amazon
3 Apple
4 Microsoft
5 Samsung
6 Netflix
7 IBM
8 Facebook
9 Tesla
10 Adidas

Source: BCG (2019)

These companies are managing deep-seated change, not just in products but in their business models.

Examining the issue of radical change in value offered to a market highlights issues such as: **disruptive innovation** – innovation that changes the way an industry operates; **cannibalisation** – the resulting forces that drive successful companies to compete with themselves; **value innovation** – the companies that pioneer change with increasingly **perverse customers**; **big ideas** – nurturing the big ideas that will change an industry; and **innovation networks** – the shift in managing innovation to open business models and cross-boundary collaboration. Importantly, **globalisation** may be one of the most important sources of radical innovation. We consider each of these issues.

12.1.5 Disruptive innovation

The failure of many major organisations to innovate and change is in some important ways explained not because managers are complacent, but because they follow conventional wisdom in their industries. Clayton Christensen described what he calls the 'innovator's dilemma' (Christensen, 1997). His research question concerned why major companies get left behind. Why, he asked, when the computer market moved from mainframes to mini-computers, was IBM left behind, and then when the market moved again from mini-computers to personal computers, were the makers of mini-computers (Digital, Wang, Nixdorf and the rest) left behind in their turn? Could it be that these companies were too short-sighted to see how the market was changing, or was there something else at work?

Christensen argues that the PC was an example of a 'disruptive technology'. Generally, new technologies tend to do things better from the customer's viewpoint – these are 'sustaining technologies', because they allow us to sell similar things to current customers, but better, cheaper and faster. But, the distinguishing characteristic of the disruptive technology is that it does the job **worse** than the existing technology – although it is cheaper. However, as disruptive technologies improve over time, and get to do the job adequately, then their lower prices drive the existing technology out of the market. Disruptive technologies are fundamentally different to conventional or 'sustaining' technologies.

For example, until the 1920s, the established technology for excavators was the steam shovel. This was followed by the machines powered by the internal combustion engine, which did the job better, and which was a sustaining technology. Most large steam shovel excavator manufacturers made the transition successfully. In 1947, J.C. Bamford developed the hydraulic shovel, or backhoe. This did a poor job – it could only handle small bucketsful of earth, far smaller than was demanded by the big contractors in mining and sewage construction. The JCB was, however, cheap, because it worked off the back of a tractor. Initially its market was restricted to digging narrow trenches in the street. As its technology became more robust, backhoes attacked the main excavator market. Few of the traditional manufacturers survived.

Established manufacturers are bad at coping with these breakthroughs *because* they are so good at serving their customers. These companies knew about the innovations in question; the reason they did not adopt them was that their customers did not want them. The new technology appeals to less sophisticated, lower-margin customers. The product is not as good as what went before. It is not what our (currently) most profitable customers want.

In other words, sticking to tried-and-tested strategies with major customers may blind a company to changing market needs and to those competitors with new technologies. The risk faced is that established firms, excelling in the core competencies that keep their biggest customers happy, fail to see the threat of disruptive innovation in time because their customers do not see it, need it, want it, or ask for it (Donath, 2000). It is also the case that while the disruptive innovation undermines some business models, it may at the same time be a sustaining technology for others. The Internet, for example, disrupted Compaq's distributor-based approach to computer marketing, but was an important sustaining technology for the direct marketers Dell and Gateway – the Web allowed them to serve customers in the same way they always had, but faster and cheaper.

Christensen also tells us that few established firms succeed in adapting to disruptive innovation. The best hope is to create an independent business with a completely new business model designed to attack the competition, including its own parent company. It also has to ignore the wishes of existing major customers – he calls this 'agnostic marketing', or the 'innovator's solution' (Christensen and Raynor, 2003).

More recently, Downes and Nunes (2013) have coined the term 'big-bang disruptors' to describe innovations that do not start at the bottom of the market with a lower-priced and inferior alternative to existing products. Big-bang disruptors can come out of nowhere and instantly be everywhere, and once launched they are hard to fight. Navigation-product makers such as TomTom, Garmin and Magellan were completely wrong-footed by the free navigation apps now pre-loaded on every smartphone, which are cheaper and far better than stand-alone devices. Consumers in every segment defected in a matter of weeks.

Faced with existing or potential disruptors in your market, the advice is to (1) identify the strengths of the disruptor's business model, (2) identify your own relative advantage, and (3) evaluate the conditions that would help or hinder the disruptor from beating your current advantages in the future. The goal is to develop a disruption of your own before it is too late – to participate in new, high-growth markets while you still can.

It may be that responding to such radical, game-changing market shifts requires an equally radical change in a company. One view, for example, is that resilience to these market shifts comes from two different efforts: first, repositioning the core business by adapting its current business model to the changed marketplace; and second, creating a separate, disruptive business to develop the innovations that will become the source of your future growth. Apple and IBM both took this twofold approach to adapting to changed markets. IBM rethought its mainframe business, shifting from proprietary systems to servers running open standard software, while creating a Global Services organisation that became the source of future growth. Apple repositioned its struggling computer business, trimmed the offering and focused on design; it was then ready to launch the iPod, open the iTunes store and proceed with the 'i-revolution'.

Executives should constantly bear in mind that the evidence is that, in the volatile markets we now deal with, disruption can occur anywhere – and likely will.

An interesting example of large-scale disruptive innovation is the television business. The once-dominant cable companies face new online and digital competition to which the existing providers find it difficult to respond. Cable and satellite operators compete to gain viewers, while services such as Netflix try to draw them away. The likely response is mega-mergers to create giant media companies providing all services, from conventional television to video-on-demand and streaming of programmes and movies (Gapper, 2014).

Even in a more traditional area, utilities companies in countries such as the United States fear a 'death spiral' as more businesses and homeowners produce their own electricity with solar and wind power. They fear that the power company will go the same way as the telephone landline. DIY electricity is spurred by falling costs for solar panels and government incentives, so US homes and companies are producing more of their own power. Utilities fear this will squeeze their revenues while leaving them to bear the costs of maintaining the electricity grid. European utilities, notably in Germany, have already been battered by weaker demand and the EU's support for renewable energy. Responding effectively to disruption on this scale is challenging (Crooks, 2015).

Responding effectively to disruptive innovation also identifies the challenge of innovations that compete with what we already do – cannibalisation.

12.1.6 Proactive cannibalisation

(This section draws from Cravens *et al.*, 2002.) One of the strongest conventional arguments against radical innovation is that we end up simply competing with ourselves – we cannibalise our own sales to our existing customer base. Executives often believe that it is unproductive for a company to compete with its own products and services, rather than targeting those of competitors – it risks under-exploiting existing investments for no gain in sales (or probably profits). However, the idea of 'proactive cannibalisation' has taken grip of many strategists' minds. At its simplest the logic is compelling – someone is going to compete with you and attack the sales of your products and services, so you might as well do it yourself and retain the customer. More elegantly expressed:

> What causes some firms to be radically innovative over long periods of time, whereas many others ossify and perish? We suggest that the answer lies in the extent to which firms are prepared to give up the old and embrace the new. Firms must break out of the natural human trait that propels them to use yesterday's bag of tools to solve tomorrow's problems. They must do so today, while they still have options, not tomorrow, when they will have nothing left but a useless bag of tools. They must be willing to cannibalise before there is nothing left of value to cannibalise. (Chandy and Tellis, 1998a)

These researchers conclude that, although it is counter-intuitive for many managers and organisations, willingness to cannibalise is one of the most powerful drivers of radical product innovation (Chandy and Tellis, 1998b).

For example, Volkswagen's multi-brand strategy (VW, Audi, Seat and Skoda) leads to some competition between its brands in the middle of the market (all the brands have similar hatchbacks built on a similar engineering platform), but had enabled VW to break Fiat's control of the European car market and achieve leadership, until the emissions test scandal of 2015 weakened the company's position.

Nonetheless, considerable care is required. Faced with the invasion of the British and European internal flight market by 'no frills', low-price operators such as easyJet and Ryanair, BA needed to respond to stop the decline in market share. Having looked at buying its new competitors or putting them out of business, and being prevented by the European regulators from doing either, BA's response was to establish its own 'no frills' airline – Go. However, from the start, Go was priced substantially higher than the existing 'no frills' operators but offered less service and convenience than BA's regular flights. Predictably, the major effect of Go was to cannibalise sales of BA flights but with little impact on the 'no frills' operators, who continued to expand. By 2001, BA was ready to sell Go (for much less than the original asking price). Go was sold to venture capitalists 3i for £110 million, who promptly resold the business to easyJet, the rival low-cost airline. It seems a conventional full-cost airline lacked the will or the ability to operate a genuine 'no frills' operation, and BA had simply established a stronger competitor for itself. A similar result was achieved by Buzz, launched by KLM as its low-cost brand, which was bought by Ryanair in 2003 for £15 million (based on O'Connell, 2003).

Less extreme is defensive cannibalisation – or at least cannibalisation resulting from defensive strategies – which is different to proactive cannibalisation, when the price of innovation is to compete with your own products. For example, Intel's continuous improvement of computer chips and Gillette's continuing introduction of improved shaving technology show cannibalisation that has positive benefits at relatively low risk.

12.1.7 Value innovation

The growing challenge for companies is to focus innovation thinking on customer value. Broad-based innovation is increasingly critical – extending far beyond new products and services to include ideas, processes, business practices and designs (Shervani and Zerrillo, 1997) – and is not just concerned with conventional new product development, and minor brand extensions. Gary Hamel is critical, for example, of the type of product-led, incremental change led by marketing departments in the past – his challenge is that we should be creating radical new products, concepts and business models or face the alternative of 'crash and burn'. He says, 'Radical, non-linear innovation is the only way to escape the ruthless hyper-competition that has been hammering down margins in industry after industry' (Hamel, 2000). For example, in one major research programme, the study of 100 major new business launches found that 86 per cent were 'me-too' launches, or incremental improvements, but these generated only 62 per cent of launch revenues and 39 per cent of profits. By contrast, the other 14 per cent of launches – those radical enough to create or re-create markets – generated 38 per cent of revenues and a massive 61 per cent of profits (Kim and Mauborgne, 1998).

The reality is that as products tend to converge and become more similar, it is no longer possible to beat the competition by making incremental improvements and changes because they will be instantly copied, and in modern markets you quickly reach the point of diminishing returns (Jones, 2000).

An important insight comes from the work of W. Chan Kim and Renee Mauborgne at INSEAD. Their observation is that between 1975 and 1995, 60 per cent of the *Fortune 500* companies disappeared. The reason was that in industry after industry, companies building innovative businesses raced ahead by replacing established firms who were focused on improving existing businesses. Their research suggests that the really high-performing companies in every sector are those who achieve 'value innovation' – they do not just imitate competitors, or invest for competitiveness against established rivals, they innovate in new value for customers. They suggest that one useful exercise is to assess portfolios of products and services on their 'Pioneer-Migrator-Settler' map, because innovation linked to value determines the real growth prospects. They argue that managers should examine and predict the competitive offerings and entries in terms of those three categories (Kim and Mauborgne, 2014):

- **Settlers** – these offer 'me-too' value, based on equalling what competitors do, usually in the same way that they do it, but often cheaper.
- **Migrators** – these offer conventional value improvements over competitors – for example, in product function improvements or design.
- **Pioneers** – these are the businesses that represent real value innovations, such as the Sony Walkman, the Dyson bagless, cyclone carpet cleaner, the Swatch watch, and so on. Apple's iPhone is a pioneer, because by introducing the App Store and linking app developers and app users, Apple created an entire platform, not just another phone product (Van Alstyne *et al.*, 2016).

A portfolio that is heavy with settlers leads to a company's decline. One dominated by migrators offers some growth potential, but is vulnerable to the strength of a value innovator. The issue is whether we are gearing our planning towards pioneers, or merely settling for the *status quo*. The challenge is to continuously shift the portfolio away from settlers. This may produce very different conclusions to those based on just looking at current numbers such as market share, sales revenue, customer satisfaction and profitability – because these numbers all represent the past, not the future (Kim and Mauborgne, 1997, 1998).

The underlying principle is that 'understanding the needs of customers is what distinguishes innovation from novelty . . . pioneers are routinely pushed aside by rivals whose skills are in the marketplace rather than the laboratory' (Kay, 2009). For example, Apple's achievements are less about its new technology and more about deploying existing technology in ways that meet consumer needs and attracting buyers through beautifully designed devices that are user friendly. The issue is creating superior customer value through innovation and this is the critical challenge for marketing strategy.

12.1.8 The perverse customer

One further driver of value innovation is the truculent or perverse post-recessionary customer. A weakness of much of the literature of marketing and management, and perhaps even more of economics, is the assumption of the compliant and acquiescent customer who responds predictably to price and other marketing stimuli, and is a willing partner in the consumption process. In reality, we face the sophisticated consumer who often rejects (or at least claims to reject) traditional marketing messages. One overarching impact of economic downturn and recession is a wholesale loss of confidence in institutions, both public and commercial, and in particular a loss of trust in business and the professions, which takes consumer sophistication much further. Hence, we have the perverse customer.

It is not so much that we have to deal with the sophisticated customer who is more demanding in relatively conventional ways, but rather a customer who is actually perverse and maven-like in their dealings with business and with authority in general. The perverse customer is the one who takes a positive delight in confounding the attempts by their political masters, lobbyists, or by business to change their behaviour. In other words, the customer who delights in being awkward and who changes the rules. Consider the pressure placed on consumers to adopt electric/hybrid cars promising environmental benefits. In spite of all the hoopla and policy pressure, it took Toyota a decade to sell the first million Prius vehicles, in a world with more than a billion vehicles on the road. The evidence is that the customer decisions on vehicles regarding size and fuel-efficiency have more to do with oil prices than environmental conscience. With the plunge in oil prices, companies such as Tesla in the electric car market suffered badly, because car buyers returned to fast sports saloons and 4×4s. One might say that Tesla's key insight was to make electric cars 'cool', rather than virtuous, purchases. Indeed, it is probably more due to recent governmental policy drivers that mainstream manufacturers now are looking to move wholesale into electric vehicles.

The real point is that in the tough, cynical post-recession markets in which we have to survive, we have to identify new value-creating and profit-generating opportunities and innovate in the areas that customers value. Consider the following examples of the perverse customer, but importantly, what comes out in business opportunities:

● **Train fares:** The confusion pricing policies adopted by some railway companies create anomalies – buying two single tickets may be cheaper than a return; splitting journeys into segments and buying a separate ticket for each segment can often produce a cheaper total fare. Confusion pricing only works if customers cannot be bothered to untangle the confusion, and most times they cannot or will not. However, that untangling is really easy for a computer algorithm. The opportunity is underlined by **Trainsplit.com**, which already offers the online service of splitting journeys into legs to minimise fares, even though it requires a whole set of tickets for a single journey. Most consumers will not bother with this and will go on paying higher fares. The perverse customer is the one who will go for the ticket splitting, and moreover will take pleasure in beating the train company. Similar opportunities abound in international air travel, taken advantage of by numerous app platforms.

● **Medicine:** Writing prescriptions for medicines and diagnostic tests has long been a monopoly of doctors and a few other clinicians. But doctors often do not do what they are told by patients and generally make the process of getting things you want difficult – including waits of up to a month to get to see a GP, forcing people to sit in a waiting room full of ill people and making them wait weeks for test results. Most consumers put up with this 'rationing by inconvenience'. Some do not. Companies such as Direct Laboratory Services and WellnessFX in the United States have already leapt on the opportunity provided by perverse customers – they sell diagnostic tests direct to consumers, cutting out the barrier of the doctor. You want a battery of blood tests or a thyroid function measurement – there you go, all yours, no doctor interfering. Rapid and at-home diagnostics are a very attractive and growing niche in the global health care business. Similarly, 23andMe provides the consumer direct with genetic testing based on DNA analysis (Piercy, 2017). And that is before you even consider the potential for self-prescription and the growing purchase of pharmaceuticals on the Internet. This will grow even faster when quality assurance is more advanced. Consumers are cutting the doctor out. It may not be wise, but it seems to be what is happening.

- **Privacy:** It is clear that privacy and the rights of the individual provide one of the hottest issues in the twenty-first century. The state has given itself unprecedented rights to observe and track citizens and monitor their behaviour, all the way from intense coverage of public areas by cameras through to checking phone calls and emails and exploiting health and bank data. Similarly, there are a growing number of business models that rely on using personal and individual data for commercial advantage. For example, Facebook and Google are advertising-supported businesses that use members' social interactions and search behaviour to sell behaviour-directed advertising – that is how they make money. For others it is a lucrative by-product: retailers track consumers through their mobile phones; gaming machines and smart TVs observe and monitor users in their homes; the NHS sells patient data; and so on (Piercy, 2017). Some consumers simply do not care. Others are really quite miffed, and definitely interested in products and services that make it difficult or impossible for others to invade their privacy. We are already seeing the launch of encryption software to prevent email monitoring; secure mobile phones that cannot be monitored; walled-garden social networks to avoid Facebook; people refusing to supply their personal data when they do not have to, or submitting false data; and growing pressure to assert the right to anonymity. There is even a resurgence in sales of manual typewriters in some areas where privacy is paramount – try hacking a typewriter! In fact, privacy will become one of the biggest products in the twenty-first century, as people become prepared to pay to avoid being observed, monitored and targeted.

Governments and powerful lobby groups cannot resist tinkering with markets in their desire to change other peoples' behaviour. Often, they get it wrong. Decades of persuading people not to eat butter because it is 'bad' for them turns out to have been based on bad science and possibly even harmful to people's health, as well as severely damaging to the dairy industry. Nonetheless, even after tinkering and intervention, markets adjust and identify dissatisfied customers who will be responsive to new offers. Markets always adjust in the end. As mature markets become more fragmented or granular, the perverse customer is becoming an interesting target in a growing number of situations. Observing the diverse ways in which perverse customers get their own way, and smart companies make more money as a result, is an interesting exercise for any manager. Learning to deal with a defiant, awkward, yet sophisticated customer, who does not plan to be cooperative and docile any time soon, is a major challenge for suppliers of all kinds, but that is where opportunities reside. The search for value innovation opportunities may lead in surprising directions.

12.1.9 Big ideas

The heart of radical innovation is the search for 'big ideas', rather than settling for 'small ideas'. To stay relevant and to succeed, companies need bold, innovative strategies. But this relies on the ability to create and resource big ideas, and to overcome inertia, narrow-mindedness and risk aversion that provide barriers to true innovation – what Bernd Schmitt calls 'big think strategy' (Schmitt, 2007). For example, the launch of the iPhone by Apple – an attractive mobile phone, though based on out-of-date technology – achieved mixed sales results. On the face of things, the iPhone was a straightforward extension of the iPod and iTunes music business, with the prospect of competing against the BlackBerry in the business market. In fact, as the underlying iPhone strategy unfolded, a very big idea became apparent. By allowing software manufacturers to create applications, or 'apps', custom-built for the iPhone – freed by the iPhone's breakthrough touch screen from the constraints of fixed buttons and small screens – the goal was to allow the iPhone to develop into the 'third great platform' for software makers, after the personal computer and the Internet. This was now a 'big idea', not just another mobile phone (Allison, 2008).

In another example, after a history of missing out on some of the most important big ideas when they arrived, IBM is putting some of its brightest and best talent behind new ventures that break free of the existing business. Because new ideas fall between organisational boundaries and sometimes conflict with existing business units, they are managed differently. 'Horizon Three' businesses, as opposed to Horizon One businesses (mature businesses such as mainframe computers) or Horizon Two businesses (current growth businesses), are protected from the rest of the organisation. They are put in separate organisational units with dedicated teams, providing visibility and management sponsorship. The young Horizon Three business units are insulated from traditional management methods and performance yardsticks – efficiency measures can squeeze the life out of a promising new idea. There is a clear understanding that Horizon Three businesses benefit from personal sponsorship by senior managers, to prevent middle managers using their power to block new developments that might not fit their personal agendas (Waters, 2001).

There is also a compelling argument that sustainability is, and should be, a key driver of innovation. For example, Nidumolu and colleagues argue that sustainability is linked to lowering costs and increasing revenues and should be part of all thinking about innovation. They believe that only companies that make sustainability a goal will achieve competitive advantage (Nidumolu *et al.*, 2009). Certainly, sustainability is one of the 'big ideas' that executives should consider when planning and making innovation choices.

Generally, growing emphasis is being placed on developing an 'ideas culture' in companies (Overell, 2005). However, in IBM as in many other companies, the search for big ideas as the basis for radical innovation increasingly relies on collaboration with others and open source approaches, rather than relying on in-house development.

12.1.10 Innovation networks

The growing emphasis on collaboration and cooperation (see Chapter 15) in radical innovation strategies is underlined by Lynda Gratton's research into 'hot spots' of energy and innovation in companies (Gratton, 2007). Gratton sees hot spots as points where people work together in exceptionally creative and collaborative ways. For hot spots to emerge, they need: (1) a cooperative mind-set; (2) an ability to span boundaries; and (3) a successful igniting of purpose – followed by making productive capacity available to create real value. The old, protective barriers set up by businesses around themselves are increasingly a barrier to the new open business models that underpin radical innovation (Chesbrough, 2006).

For example, Procter & Gamble sets high targets for the proportion of its new products developed with external partners, and there are many other examples of effective innovation partnerships demonstrating how open innovation can power growth:

- **Nike+** – Nike worked with Apple to develop a sensor that can transmit data from the heel of its running shoes to the wearer's iPod or iPhone, launched in 2006.
- **Little Swimmers Sun Care** – Kimberly-Clark created adhesive plasters for children that use ultraviolet sensitive material to warn parents of the risk of sunburn, developed and marketed in partnership with Sunhealth Solutions in the USA and launched in 2007.

- **Aquafresh White Trays** – GlaxoSmithKlein's Consumer Healthcare's entry into the tooth whitening strip market in 2007 came through a partnership with Oratech, a private manufacturer supplying dental products (Birchall, 2010).

Further insight into new forms of collaboration and open source innovation comes from Don Tapscott's *Wikinomics* (Tapscott and Williams, 2007). A 'wiki' is a piece of software that allows thousands of people to edit the same website. Tapscott's view is that if people from all over the world can get together to create an encyclopaedia – Wikipedia – there are no limits to what they can create. Wikinomics brings people together on the Web to create a giant new brain. Companies are exploiting this in the form of 'crowd-sourcing'. When Procter & Gamble needed a new chemical to remove red wine stains from clothing, instead of turning to their own R&D department, they created a website called InnoCentive, where anyone could come up with a solution and be paid. The logic is that 1.5 million people on the Web are more likely to come up with the solution than 9,000 chemists in the company.

Many companies have realised that going 'open source' or collaborating and sharing ideas means many innovations can be created and developed outside the company. At Procter & Gamble, in a massive turnaround of a business that had stalled, under A.G. Lafley the company abandoned its reliance on in-house R&D. The classic corporate drive to research and develop was replaced by a 'connect and develop' strategy of working with outside partners. By 2007, 35 per cent of P&G's new products came from outside the company. Under Mr Lafley, P&G's performance saw a step-change improvement, and rival Unilever was left behind. This is an 'era of open innovation' (Ancona and Bresman, 2007).

Indeed, for many major organisations, reduced spending on traditional R&D activities has encouraged a broad global search for new ideas from any source. Companies such as Intel are locating satellite research facilities close to leading research universities to tap into academic expertise. In some cases, the breakthrough ideas come from research-based collaboration. For example, Xerox has broken with tradition to look to outsiders to help develop optical-network technology. One result is the inclusion of Xerox's imaging technology expertise in a joint project with Intel, to produce a new microprocessor tailored to document imaging. In complex and rapidly changing markets, many companies are exploring new and faster ways to capture new ideas from diverse sources as the basis for developing new products and services (Greene *et al.*, 2003).

Worldwide innovation networks are increasingly central to maintaining and enhancing competitiveness. This may involve a worldwide research and development organisation. Microsoft is tapping into a new talent pool with its advanced technology centre outside Beijing. IBM has major labs in China, Israel, Switzerland, Japan and India. For smaller companies, global innovation networks involve loose structures of in-house engineers, contract designers and manufacturers, university scientists and technology suppliers brought together around a single project. At a time when technology crosses borders faster than ever – because of the Internet, cheap telecoms and advances in interactive design software – the location of R&D matters less than who controls the networks (Engardio, 2004).

12.1.11 Globalisation and innovation

The examples given emphasise the global perspective needed to understand how innovation is changing.

For example, Indian company Mahindra & Mahindra opted to design and manufacture one of its motor scooters in the United States, turning conventional wisdom on its head. The company aimed for an 'all American product' generated by its 'global new-product manufacturing set-up'. In 2017 it announced it was doubling its $1 billion investment, encouraged by the potential of electric scooters. Emerging-market companies are rapidly evolving their traditional business models (Mallett and Crabtree, 2015).

The broader implications are interesting. A number of influential global companies, such as General Electric and Procter & Gamble, are adopting strategies of 'reverse innovation' – that is, turning products created for the emerging markets into low-cost products for developed world customers (Govindarajan and Trimble, 2012). The new approach is also known as 'trickle-up innovation'. GE, for example, has created a portable ultrasound business, stemming from products originally designed for China, which has achieved growth rates of 50–60 per cent a year in its early stages (*BusinessWeek*, 2009).

In another example, consumer goods company Nestlé is bringing sales and packaging techniques pioneered in emerging markets to improve its position in problematic markets in Europe. Marketing innovations developed in countries such as Thailand and Russia are being applied in stressed European markets including Greece, Spain and Ireland, to familiarise less affluent consumers with Nestlé brands. Innovations include smaller packs of Nescafé instant coffee and 'refill' coffee packs, and Maggi soup powders sold in individual units (Simonian, 2010).

It is clear that emerging markets are not only providing multinationals with faster growth prospects, but also new products, services, manufacturing methods and business processes. For example, Pulpy is a drink developed by Coca-Cola's Chinese offshoot, which is being launched in eastern Europe after a successful entry to Latin American markets. Similarly, Levi Strauss, makers of Levi's jeans, has brought its Denizen brand of jeans, nurtured in China, back to its home US market. A mobile payment system that has revolutionised business and banking in sub-Saharan Africa is being brought to Europe by Vodafone. These are examples of emerging markets spawning new products with global potential. While once business solutions flowed only from the West to the East, they are now flowing from East to West as well (Wagstyl, 2011).

The underlying point is that the model that companies such as GE have followed in the past – developing high-end products for the home market and adapting them for export – does not work as growth slows in the developed markets. The goal is to develop products in markets such as China and India, and then distribute them globally to tap into value-based segments across the world (Immelt *et al.*, 2009).

Indeed, some argue that the real revolution in business is doing more with less. For example, Radjou and Prabhu make a compelling case for 'frugal innovation', learning from the emerging markets where engineers move away from plentiful resources in a rich market to constrained resources and value-hungry customers (Radjou and Prabhu, 2015). When Renault found its expensive cars were outsold in India by the $6,000 locally produced Lada, they created the no-frills $6,000 Logan. Designed for India but now selling well in Europe, Renault developed a line of low-cost vehicles that today constitutes nearly half its global sales. A similar view is adopted by Charles Leadbeater in his work on 'shoestring innovation', emphasising reuse and recycling in low-cost innovation (Leadbeater, 2014). Frugal innovation has produced ultra-cheap laptops, mobile phones, refrigerators and even ECG machines (Coy, 2015).

Radjou and his co-authors use the Hindi word *jugaad* to describe the approach of entrepreneurs in India and other emerging markets, where innovation is driven by finding opportunities in scarcity and developing smart ways to make more from less. They argue that businesses in the richer Western world have lost their innovation edge and executives should study and learn from *jugaad* innovation. The focus should be on simplicity, not endless new product features (Radjou *et al.*, 2012).

The globalisation of innovation suggests new approaches and models from which to learn. Certainly, it is likely that radical innovation will lie at the heart of strategic thinking in many companies, and the new context is global. Indeed, as we noted earlier, the most important innovations may be in how we change the ways in which we work, organise and manage (Mol and Birkinshaw, 2007) – the issue is not just a new product, but a new business model.

We turn attention now to the innovation process – or new product development – within a company.

12.2 New products

Studies that compare new product successes with failures are consistent in their observations of the key factors that influence a new product's success in the marketplace. Getting to grips with these factors helps executives to understand successful product innovation. For example, one interesting method of categorising the new products that firms produce is as follows:

- **Dinosaurs** are products that have missed their niche, the market has moved on and the demand for them has passed. Where product development times are overly long, there is a danger that even well-researched products take too long to come to market. By the time they are launched the market has moved on, customer requirements have changed and/or competitors have more successfully met those needs.
- **Flamingos** are products that are beautiful but unsaleable. The development process has resulted in products with well-designed features and a multitude of characteristics – but unfortunately the costs of producing are too high, due to over-specification, such that customers cannot afford to buy. Unless there are enough potential customers willing and able to buy, the flamingo runs the risk of early extinction.
- **Ostrich** products are blind to the future. They may meet today's market needs but take no account of future changes in the market, and are not well placed to adapt and change as customer requirements and competitive pressures evolve. An example is the Iomega PocketZip drive, which saved on a disk and was launched just when self-sufficient flash memory cards came on the market.
- **Pearls** are the constant quest of effective new product development. A pearl will always be of value, and even if its popularity wanes it can be modified into a jewel or traded for other resources required. The pearl offers the source of a profitable future for a foreseeable period.

12.2.1 Successful new products

Successful new products provide better performance than existing products and often they succeed despite being offered at higher prices than competitors. In fact, most failures offer price parity or inferior value. Successful products offer advantages that matter to customers (see Figure 12.3). Failures, too, have performance advantages, but in fringe areas where customers see little benefit.

As well as price and performance advantage, successful new products often provide benefits that are dramatically different from current offerings. For example, Innocent fruit smoothies (which contain nothing else but fruit) provided a uniquely healthy snack/drink. New products need to have a significant advantage over existing products.

Conventional thinking also suggests it is almost always better to be first to market.

Figure 12.3
Accelerated diffusion of innovations

Despite the inevitable risk of being a pioneer, first to market is often best for several reasons. The news value of an innovation peaks in the early stages, and this offers maximum communication impact and a chance for widespread consumer trial. The innovator catches consumers first; this means that competitors who follow must improve their market positioning and produce better and/or cheaper products to make consumers switch. This may not be easy to achieve once the pioneer has secured strong consumer loyalty and a reputation for innovation in the marketplace.

For example, Richard Branson explains: 'A good idea for a new business tends not to occur in isolation, and often the window of opportunity is very small. So speed is of the essence' (Hamm, 2006). In many companies, the time to bring new products to market has halved in recent years: at Nissan, the development time for new cars used to be 21 months, now it is 10½ months; Nokia and Motorola used to take 12 to 18 months to develop new mobile phone models, now it is six to nine months; H&M can get fashion clothes from sketch pad to the racks in its stores in just three weeks; Samsung partnered with XM Satellite Radio to bring the first portable satellite radio combined with music player to store shelves in nine months from the partners shaking hands on the deal. Similarly, by closely aligning design, R&D and marketing, appliance maker Electrolux cuts product launch times by a third compared to competitors (Matlack, 2013). At the other end, it also follows that fast innovators such as Virgin and Google are also fast to get out of a venture when things underperform (Hamm, 2006).

Nonetheless, it should be noted that first mover advantage is not always the best goal. In some situations, strategy may be more about 'active waiting', rather than speed and trying to establish a first-mover advantage. Donald Sull argues, for example, that really attractive business opportunities are quite rare, and their timing is almost never under the control of an individual company, suggesting that we should be ready when the big opportunities emerge and protect resources during the long periods of 'business as usual'. He argues that successful businesses often falter because managers experienced in stable, familiar markets stumble when they enter less certain, volatile markets – they fail to create a long-term strategy that will produce sustainable advantage. Active waiting involves anticipating and making preparations, ready to seize opportunities and deal with threats when they arise (Sull, 2005).

Making a reasoned decision on how quickly to move and the type of business model appropriate to deliver the speed required has become a key part of strategic thinking. The most obvious answers are not necessarily the most useful ones. The strategic issue is not just what to do, but when and how quickly.

12.2.2 The case of business products

Studies of new business-to-business product successes and failures make the following distinctions between successes and failures: product uniqueness (innovativeness) or superiority; management's possession of market knowledge and marketing proficiency; and presence of technical and production synergies and proficiency.

The first dimension – industrial product uniqueness/superiority – is very close to that for consumer products. In this respect, industrial and consumer products are similar. It is likely that industrial and consumer products are similar in other ways too. Successful industrial innovators study their customers and market well. They carry out market research to gain knowledge of customers' requirements/needs; they are sensitive to price as well as to the intricacies of buyer behaviour.

Successful innovators acquire as much of the required information as possible to enable them to forecast market size and determine potential demand for their new product. They test the market prior to product launch. There is strong and often well-targeted sales support, which recognises the need for forceful communications to stimulate primary demand and to prise open new markets.

Successful industrial innovations are clearly not the result of sophisticated technology alone. Mismanagement of technical and technological resources can have a detrimental effect on new product performance. Successful industrial innovators ensure there is synergy between the firm's engineering and production capabilities and the new product project. They also undertake a range of technical activities and do these proficiently – preliminary technical assessment, product development, prototype testing with customers, production start-up, with facilities well geared for launch. Their technical staff know the product technology well. They are familiar with the product design.

12.2.3 New product failures

One question central to manager interests in innovation strategy is, in what ways do new products fail? Answering this question helps us appreciate what actions the firm should take to avoid different types of product failure. One way of classifying new product failures is shown in Figure 12.4.

1 **The better mousetrap no one wanted** is the classic 'technology-push' type innovation for which little or insufficient market demand exists. Customers do not perceive they have a real need for the technology and, consequently, are not prepared to buy the innovation. Sinclair's C5 electric car falls firmly into this category – an innovation without an obvious market.

2 **The me-too meeting a competitive brick wall** is the result of followers failing to reconcile with the market leader's or established competitors' strengths. Nokia's (and by extension Microsoft's) attempts to gain position in the smartphone market may be in this category.

3 **Competitors** can spring surprises and come up with a better product that is preferred by customers. 'Competitive one-upmanship' is not easy to predict but can be seen in the case of Apple's iPhone upstaging Nokia, Samsung and the others in the mobile phone business, or Google wrong-footing the automotive industry with its advances in autonomous vehicles (self-driving cars). Innovations may achieve great short-term advantage, but if competitors can easily and simply imitate the innovation (and have other advantages as well), then the innovator is likely to achieve little long-term value.

4 **Environmental or market ignorance** occurs when the innovating firm fails to study market or customer requirements or to monitor and scan its external environment for signals of change. Socio-economic, technological, political and/or legislative conditions and/or changes are ignored, overlooked or misunderstood, resulting in poor sales after launch.

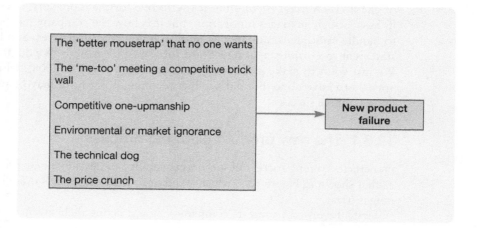

Figure 12.4
Some reasons for new product failures

5 **The technical dog** product does not work or users are dogged by technical problems (such as Jaguar Land Rover vehicles, which were frequently seen in this way until the take-over by Tata and a major investment in quality improvement).

6 **The price crunch** comes when the innovating firm sets too high a price for a new product whose value is not perceived by target customers to be better or greater than existing products. Often, if competition offers a lower-cost product the innovating firm has to cut its price so fails to obtain the required return on investment from the innovation. Even Apple's innovative iPhone was priced too high at launch and disappointing sales led to an early price reduction and refunds to early purchasers.

12.3 Planning for new products

The fact that innovation is so uncertain raises the question whether innovation can be managed? Certainly it seems that using formalised new product development processes achieves greater new product success in some situations than does an *ad hoc* approach to product innovation. There is, however, a distinction between invention and innovation. The former is the discovery of a new device or a new process. It is fair to say that managers cannot specify deadlines for the discovery of new ideas or predict when a particular invention will occur or, indeed, when exactly a scientific discovery will be made. Invention cannot be planned. Often it is left to chance, or the perseverance and ingenuity of the scientist/inventor. Innovation is different. Once the new scientific or technical discovery is made, or a novel product idea has been conceived, its chances of being successfully commercialised rest predominantly on the astuteness of the firm's management in new product planning and strategy determination, as well as the proficiency with which certain new product developments and launch activities are undertaken. From discovery/conception of the idea to marketplace, management and employees of the firm have direct control and influence over the fate of the discovery/idea.

Businesses can reduce the risk of product innovation while improving the likelihood of success by adopting a planning orientation and sophisticated new product development process. There was nothing accidental or *ad hoc* about the results achieved by Glaxo for Zantac in the anti-ulcer drugs market, or McDonald's in fast foods – they succeeded through careful preparation of the strategies for product development and market entry.

Nonetheless, one important caveat is that some of the most innovative companies in the world achieve their success through far less organised behaviours. The bureaucracy of conventional product planning plays little role in creating and managing innovation at Google. Indeed, innovation at Google appears to the outsider to be almost anarchic – disordered, in disarray and embroiled in uncomfortable uncertainty, living on the edge of chaos (Lashinsky, 2006) – but it is effective for that company. There are many risks in how Google manages innovation, but it is how the company has built the capability to handle multiple, simultaneous, radical innovation initiatives. Similarly, in a famous statement to *Fortune* magazine, Steve Jobs of Apple stated: 'We do no market research. We just want to make great products' (quoted in *Fortune*, 2008), which is what Apple appears to have done. Formal product planning procedures may be useful, but they do not guarantee success.

12.3.1 The new product planning process

Nonetheless, many successful innovating companies develop a new product process, such as that shown in Figure 12.5, which is linked to their company's overall longer-term planning process.

First, the process suggests companies should define their business mission by asking: what business are we in? And what business do we want to be in? By considering the

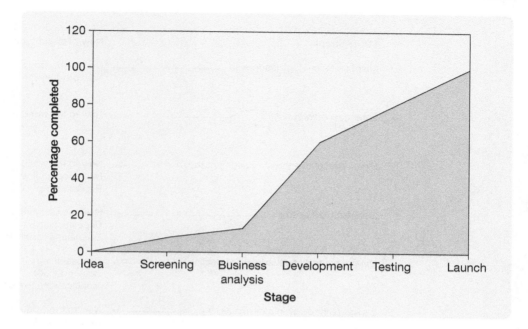

Figure 12.5
New product
development
stages and time
lapse

Source: Adapted from
Booz et al. (1982).

growth potential of the sales and market share and profitability of the company's current range of products, and the extent to which growth objectives will be fulfilled, management can begin to identify gaps in achievable and desired growth. The role of new products and how the firm's portfolio of businesses might be changed to achieve planned growth can be determined.

Firms also have to decide on the types of new product that are to be developed. It is usual to classify new products according to the degree of newness to the company and to the customers (see Figure 12.6).

Six categories of new products emerge, each one taking the company further and further away from its current activities and being, therefore, progressively more risky:

1 **Cost reductions,** which provide similar performance at lower cost.
2 **Repositionings,** which are current products targeted at new customer segments or new markets. For example, Lucozade, a soft drink, traditionally aimed at the 'convalescent', then targeted the youth and sports user segment as an energy drink.
3 **Modifications,** in the form of improvements or revisions to existing products, which enhance performance or perceived value and replace existing products. For example, car

Figure 12.6
New product
innovation

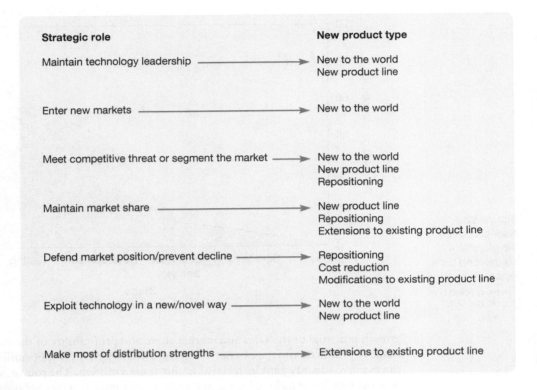

Figure 12.7
Strategic role of
new products

manufacturers tend to upgrade existing models, supplying 'new products' with improved performance and/or more features, as opposed to developing radically new models from scratch.

4 **Extensions** to existing product lines that supplement a firm's established product lines.
5 **New product lines**, which enable a company to enter an established market for the first time, such as Virgin's financial services products.
6 **New-to-the-world products**, which create an entirely new market.

Depending on the sales, market share and financial objectives set by the firm, and the overall strength of its current range of products, management has to select the appropriate type, or combination of types, of new product to develop. Usually a firm would have to invest in various types of new product development to maintain a healthy and balanced portfolio of products. The firm's functional capabilities and available resources have to be considered when deciding the strategic direction to be taken. Figure 12.7 shows the various strategic roles for new products and the types of new product that are likely to fulfil each of these roles. The magnitude of the risk attached to innovation alters with the type of new product being developed. Planning can help; failure to do so increases the risks, while decreasing the chances of new product success.

12.4   The new product development process

12.4.1 Idea generation

For new products, a firm has to find novel ideas, do new things and do things differently. This is the essence of product innovation. New ideas trigger the innovation process and the development of new products. Ideas are where all new products start. Both the creativity of individuals and the methods of idea generation can be employed to obtain novel ideas.

Creativity and productive ideation – really innovative ideas come out of inspiration and use appropriate techniques. Because of the high mortality rate of new ideas, it is desirable to generate and consider a large number of them. The use of appropriate methods to generate new product ideas can improve the productivity of in-house ideas generation. A company can also facilitate the generation of innovative new product ideas by creating an environment that will induce and facilitate creativity. How can the creative potential of individuals be harnessed, and what techniques aid the creative ideas generation process?

Defining creativity – creativity is the combining of previously unrelated parts into a useful whole so that one can get more out of the emergent whole than one has put in (Miller, 1996). This explanation of creativity suggests that one condition has to be satisfied for really novel ideas to emerge, which is that many widely disparate ideas must coexist long enough in the individual's mind to combine, to yield a 'useful whole'.

The creative process is not easily implemented, and many managers would assert that creativity cannot be supervised, unlike the pursuit of quality or other functional operations. It is not possible to predict when a creative person will generate a novel idea. It is almost as if management should leave outbursts of creative thinking to nature and chance. However, contrary to conventional wisdom, creativity *can* be managed. Rather than spotting creative individuals within the firm and encouraging them to tap their creative potential, the manager would do better to ask if barriers to creative thinking exist and, if so, how these barriers might be overcome.

Nonetheless, there may also something in the view that fresh thinking about important issues should not be the preserve of conventional executives skilled in running the existing business. Companies need to think about attracting unconventional people with unconventional ideas – possibly 'weird' people – to become in-house mavericks. However, managing mavericks is usually far from easy, and they need a 'maverick-friendly' environment in which to operate. At the same time, one must take care not to alienate other employees by giving overtly 'special treatment' to these mavericks. Google is a high performer that employs such people, but this is not just about the new economy – companies such as IBM and Procter & Gamble are also exploring ways of capturing maverick creativity and innovation to channel it into mainstream business (Taylor and LaBarre, 2008). Dan Cable argues that if your goal is to create something that is valuable, rare and hard to imitate, then, compared to your competitors, your people need to be downright strange (Cable, 2007). He argues that far from benchmarking against competitors, we should aim to accentuate differences in our thinking, even to the point of becoming a little strange. That way you can focus on an obsession with commitment to doing things differently (and better) than anyone else. Strange is weird but good in thinking strategically about innovation.

For example, some product designers are turning to 'extreme users', from obsessive cleaners to dominatrices, to get new ideas: a cocktail expert shares tips on the quality and complexity of ice with a home appliance maker; dominatrices share the secret of how to avoid blisters from wearing uncomfortable high-heeled shoes; and skateboards were developed and branded after sports equipment manufacturers spotted teenagers improvising their own. Designers are finding that mavericks, outliers and obsessives can provide ideas for new products and valuable improvements (Clegg, 2014).

Aids to idea generation – some of the many techniques that can help creative thinking – are shown in Table 12.1. The best way is to use a variety of approaches. Leeway is essential so it's important to try out, adapt and fit approaches to the problem at hand. There are many possible approaches: suggestion boxes; competitive products analysis or negative engineering; patents searches; customer need assessment; and problem-detection studies. There are almost as many techniques as there are creative people.

Table 12.1 Aids to thinking

Thinking aid	Process	Blocks confronted
Question the problem (ask a lot of questions about the problem at hand)	Inculcate a questioning attitude; ask questions about the problem to gain familiarity with it rather than hiding ignorance	• Perceptual (overcomes problem of having narrow viewpoints, clarifies problem) • Emotional (addresses fear of looking like a fool, betraying ignorance – individual is forced to ask questions instead of hiding ignorance by not questioning) • Intellectual (questions about the problem stimulate generation of information/ideas that later help conception of solution to problem)
Listing (force individual to make a list of ideas to facilitate generation of many ideas)	Encourage problem solvers/idea generators to make a list of the ideas, whatever comes to mind; once the individual's thoughts are flowing, this simple but disciplined ideas-listing exercise can facilitate 'fluency' of thought (i.e., aid individual to generate many ideas)	• Emotional (attacks inflexibility of thinking and triggers creation of a large volume of ideas)
Attribute listing	Break a product into its main components. For each component, list all the physical attributes or functions and then examine possible alternatives for fulfilling each of these in isolation	• Perceptual (helps individual examine the problem from a variety of angles/see it more clearly)
Applied imagination checklist	Use an explicit checklist to identify new product opportunities. Questions act as triggers: Can the product be used in any new way? What else is like it and what/whom could we copy? Can the product be changed in meaning, function, form, usage pattern? What can be added to the product? To make it bigger, stronger, longer, thicker, etc.? What can be deleted from it? How to make it smaller, lighter, etc.? What can be substituted? Other materials, processes, ingredients, etc.? Can we rearrange its components? Can it be combined with other things?	• Perceptual (by encouraging problem solver to extend thinking/ look at problem from a variety of perspectives) • Emotional (pushes the imagination)

12.4.2 Screening

If you take ten new product ideas, the chances are that two will pay, seven will fail, and only one will be a big winner. New product idea screening and selection is not about dropping bad ideas but identifying the winner. Picking a potential winner is not an easy task. What should managers take into account when evaluating new product ideas? What are the critical screening criteria? How do managers choose the best from among a pool of apparently viable ideas?

Systematic screening

If resources are committed to the development of a new product idea, management should assess the commercial potential and technical (including production) feasibility of the idea. If there are alternative ideas or projects competing for development funds and management time, these have to be screened and the more viable and attractive ideas selected.

Ideas screening is, therefore, an important component of the product innovation process. Screening can take up management's time. It is often tempting for the management team to devote a minimum amount of time and effort to it, and even to skip the exercise, in the rush to get idea development started and new products out to market quickly. An idea coming from a senior manager in the firm may sometimes also escape thorough screening and evaluation because of the assumed credibility of the source – which could turn out to be a costly error of misplaced confidence. Or ideas may not be systematically evaluated because management regards screening as a superfluous exercise given the lack of concrete data, in the early stages, on what are still apparently vague and ill-formed ideas.

Whatever the barriers, it pays to give serious attention to screening. There are good reasons for doing this. Screening helps avoid potentially heavy losses by reducing the possibility of bad ideas being accepted, and raises the chances of good ideas being developed. It encourages more efficient resource allocation by directing the firm's attention to the 'best' ideas and encourages firms to pursue those ideas that build on its core strengths. Also, as screening experience accumulates, it improves the managers' precision in ideas selection, so increasing the chances of success.

Initial screen

Screening can be conducted at different levels of detail. The preliminary screening may be treated as a coarse filter, enabling managers quickly to separate out useful ideas for further investigation. Figure 12.8 shows the key screening questions. Remember that the initial screen is only a crude filtering device. Sometimes a new product idea might hit a legal, technical or marketing barrier that might not be particularly insurmountable. It is therefore important for the management team to use the tool cautiously, taking on board internal company, as well as market and technological, developments that could be exploited to avoid premature closure of new product opportunities.

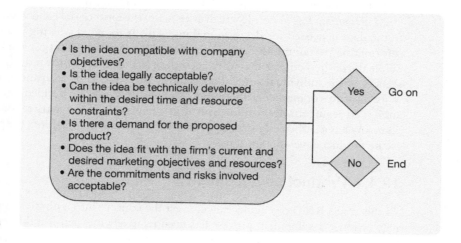

Figure 12.8 Initial screening of ideas

Formalised screening system

Potentially viable ideas should be evaluated more thoroughly for selection purposes. It is important for management to appreciate that full screening requires identification of specific information and the investment of resources to obtain these data. Formalised screening means that new product ideas are evaluated logically and within a systematic structure. It is less impressionistic than initial screening and attempts to increase the objectivity of idea selection.

When actual data are unobtainable, the management team doing the screening must exercise subjective, qualitative judgements. It is important to record all major assumptions and quantitative estimates so that they can be used as control standards for future reference.

The screening devices are not a panacea for a poor innovation record. The analyses rely on the ability of the firm's management team to combine high-quality subjective judgements with good objective data. The tools do not absolve the management team using them from exercising creativity, nor are these techniques a substitute for management vision.

The analyses are time- and resource-consuming. The many uncertainties at the early stage of ideas selection make detailed and sophisticated evaluation somewhat meaningless. This encourages rejection of screening. But it is certainly misguided to make no attempt to consider the determinants of project success and failure, or the attendant risk and uncertainty when committing resources to major product innovation programmes.

The output of screening and evaluation is only as good as the input data. This means that, to benefit from utilising screening systems, management must commit time and resources to building an information system geared to supporting ideas screening, evaluation and selection decisions. As with building any management information system, this takes time but, if implemented properly, yields a lasting and positive effect.

Screening based on the opinions and judgements of staff within the firm can be highly biased. Judgements can be distorted because of undue pressure applied on individuals, information sparseness/inaccuracy, psychological pressures, personal influences, etc. The market viability of an idea should always be tested against criteria judged important by the customer/potential customer.

12.4.3 Business analysis

Business analysis considers the attractiveness of the market for the proposed new product idea and the company's capabilities, and whether it has the business skills required to cater to the needs of the market in a way that gives it a distinct edge over the competition.

Sales, costs and profit projections for a new product show whether they satisfy the company's objectives. To estimate sales, the company looks at the sales history of similar products and surveys market opinion. Estimates of minimum and maximum sales give the range of risk. Starting with a sales forecast, the expected costs and profits for the product, including marketing, R&D, manufacturing, accounting and finance costs, are calculated.

Management has to decide which criteria are the most critical and what level of accuracy in the data is needed for decision making. This is to avoid wasting resources on refining information pertaining to factors to which the project's viability is relatively insensitive. While the desired criteria may vary according to the nature of the industry and the circumstances of the individual firm, some criteria are likely to be relevant to most companies. With measures of market attractiveness and business position decided, the process becomes similar to segment selection (described in Chapter 9). If the market is attractive and the company has a sufficiently strong position relative to the competition, the product can move to the product development stage.

12.4.4 Product development

At this stage, R&D or engineering convert the concept into a physical product. So far, the new product development process has been relatively inexpensive; the product has existed only as a word description, a drawing or perhaps a crude mock-up. In contrast, product development calls for a large jump in investment. It will show whether the product idea can be turned into a working product.

The R&D department will develop physical versions of the product concept: a prototype that will satisfy and excite consumers and that can be produced quickly and at budgeted costs. Depending on the product class, developing a successful prototype can take days, weeks, months or even years. Nonetheless, new technologies such as 3-D printing are drastically reducing the prototyping time for some products.

Prototypes must have the required functional features and convey the intended psychological characteristics. When the prototypes are ready they must be tested. Functional tests are then conducted under laboratory and field conditions to make sure that the product performs safely and effectively. A new car, for example, must start easily; it must be comfortable; it must be able to corner without overturning. Consumer tests are also needed, in which consumers test the prototype and rate its attributes.

When designing products, the company needs to look beyond simply creating products that satisfy consumer needs and wants. Too often companies design their new products without enough concern for how the designs will be produced – their main goal is to create customer-satisfying products. The designs are then passed along to manufacturing, where engineers must try to find the best ways to produce the product.

Increasingly, businesses use Design for Manufacturing and Assembly (DFMA) to fashion products that are both satisfying *and* easy to manufacture. This often results in lower costs while achieving higher quality and more reliable products. For example, using DFMA analysis Texas Instruments redesigned an infrared gun-sighting mechanism it supplies to the Pentagon. The redesigned product required 75 fewer parts, 78 per cent fewer assembly steps and 85 per cent less assembly time. The new design did more than reduce production time and costs; it also worked better than the previous, more complex version. Thus DFMA can be a potent weapon in helping companies to get products to market sooner, while offering higher quality at lower prices.

12.4.5 Market testing

By this point in the product innovation process there is a physical product, or complete specifications for a new service. The product has passed a use test that has suggested that the product works and fulfils the need as originally expressed in the concept. The next phase is market testing or trial sell. Test marketing is not one, but a range of techniques, from a simulated sale using carefully selected customers to a full test market in one or more regions of a country.

Up to this stage in the overall new product development process, testing has not been conducted under realistic market conditions. It is dangerous to trust any customer judgement completely until it is made under typical market conditions. This is where market testing plays a role in helping the firm to gauge whether its marketing plan for the new product will work and to confirm that the product, with its attendant claims, does, in fact, motivate customers to buy it and that they keep on doing so, if repeat purchase is an important factor. Market testing could be regarded as a form of 'dress rehearsal' that enables management to gather information to forecast new product sales and test effectiveness of the marketing plan (that is, pricing, advertising and promotion and distribution). It checks that all key operations fit with each other and are adequately geared up for launch, and provides diagnostic information to help managers revise/refine the marketing plan. Full test markets can test competitive response and gauge if their efforts affect the judgements of customers. This is a mixed blessing, since full test markets can be deliberately spoilt by competitors as well as give them an early warning of intended activities.

12.4.6 Commercialisation

Commercialisation is often the 'graveyard' of product innovation, not because new products die here but because real innovation often stumbles at this point of the process. By this we mean that things are going wrong and the product concept that seemed so feasible in the beginning is now tarnished and facing considerable pressure of compromise because of time, cost and other resources. Managers who are impatient to get the product to market fail to allocate sufficient time and resources to developing an effective launch campaign. Surprisingly, after all that has gone into development, products often fail because they are launched with insufficient marketing support. Most new products fail, not because of any inherent deficiency, but because the market launch strategy and tasks were poorly conceived and executed.

The launch managers should work closely with sales and other operating staff to achieve good coordination of the timing and scheduling of all these activities. Every effort must be made to ensure that critical activities (such as salesforce training, sales and promotions materials) are completed proficiently to secure launch success. In conjunction with key operating personnel, the launch manager has also to put together a launch plan, which consists of a programme outlining the sequence of tasks to be performed, a schedule that relates the programme to a time sequence and budgets for the programme and schedule.

Launch programmes easily turn into a complicated and unwieldy task. There is little point in turning out project control or milestone events charts hundreds of pages long because this is bound to break down, providing hardly any basis for effective project control. Except for the most complex technological developments, as found in car, aerospace and defence projects, complex, computer-based systems for project control are usually not necessary. For the small to medium-sized company, simple checklists may suffice. Remember, there is also 'eyeball control', which relies on managers being constantly on the go, visiting every area of the firm (daily, if possible), gathering their own information and becoming 'expert' enough to exercise sound judgement and keep launch tasks under control.

12.5 Speeding new product development

Managers must appreciate the value of being fast at innovation. A company that takes less time to develop and commercialise a new product can be expected to be more competitive than a slower competitor. The firm would be able to launch more new products in a given period of time, therefore building a strong innovation leadership image. Speedy companies are also able to respond faster to changing customer requirements, thereby securing sales and building customer loyalty. Also, by increasing the frequency with which it introduces new products into the market, the firm could pre-empt competition, thereby creating and maintaining a market leadership position.

At the same time, fast efficient processes also allow an earlier decision on which new product projects to kill. There are advantages in culling weak projects at the earliest reasonable opportunity to contain costs and avoid 'organisational creep' leading to growing commitment to continue with weak ventures simply on the basis of the time and resource invested to date.

The cost of new product development could be reduced by undertaking innovation of an incremental, as opposed to radical, nature, with substantial reduction in the risks of innovation. Companies should, however, ascertain if they have the capabilities for accelerating new product development. Also, management should ensure that the firm supports a balanced innovation programme, such that opportunities are not forgone because of failure to fund more radical (and longer-term) product innovation programmes in view of the obsession with speed.

Speeding the new product development process needs action at all stages of the process. At the start, avoid delays in approving budget for developing product ideas and pay early attention to 'snagging' at the end of the process. Overlapping product and process design and development phases has two benefits. It means that processes take place in parallel and forces the formation of multifunctional project teams (design, engineering, production, sales, marketing, etc.). Big technological breakthroughs are not necessary to make big commercial gains, so take an incremental approach to product improvement and development, making many small steps rather than attempting giant leaps forward. New product innovation often clashes with the systems and controls designed to make firms 'well managed'. To overcome this, successful businesses adapt operational and organisational procedures to give the flexibility and freedom that new product innovation needs.

12.6 Organising for new product development

There may be a variety of roadblocks and barriers to innovation in a company. The nature and intensity of these blocks vary from individual to individual, but organisations that innovate effectively recognise and avoid them (see Figure 12.9).

12.6.1 Blocks and bugs

- **Perceptual blocks** prevent the person from perceiving clearly either the problem itself or the information needed to solve the problem (problem isolation difficulty, narrow definition of problem, limited viewpoints examined).
- **Cultural blocks** are acquired as a result of exposure to a given set of cultural values or patterns (such as tradition is preferable to change, intolerance of subjectivity, fantasy/reflection/playfulness is a waste of time, humour is 'out of place' where problem solving is concerned).
- **Environmental blocks** are imposed by our immediate social and physical environment and are, therefore, closely linked to cultural barriers (for example, an autocratic boss, lack of trust/cooperation among colleagues, distractions, unsupportive organization, lack of financial support to implement ideas).
- **Emotional blocks** interfere with the freedom with which we explore and play with ideas and prevent us from communicating them effectively to others (such as fear of failing or looking like a fool, intolerance of ambiguity, preference for judging ideas rather than generating them, inability to incubate and 'sleep on it').
- **Intellectual and expressive blocks** arise because intellectual capabilities are limited and verbal/writing skills needed to communicate ideas, not only to others but to yourself, are deficient (for example, lack of information, incorrect information, poor language skill, failure to apply appropriate mental problem-solving tactics).

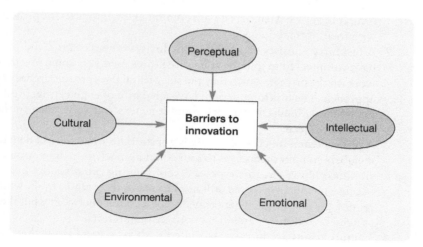

Figure 12.9
Barriers to
innovation

12.6.2 Organisational support for innovation

It is people, not plans or committees, who create ideas and achieve innovation. It is their efforts that truly determine whether businesses succeed or fail. If managers have grand visions for their business, the surest way of bringing these to fruition is to have their staff on their side, to encourage, enthuse and motivate them and, above all, to reward them for their achievements.

Three conditions are required for a firm to innovate successfully:

1 **closeness to customers:** managers must know their customers and understand their needs and requirements well;
2 **cross-functional communications:** innovation in most companies (except the 'one-man-band', which is not stereotypical of the average established small/medium-sized firm anyway) is about the flow of information between key functions;
3 **multifunctional teamwork:** successful product innovations are almost invariably the result of people in the firm working together in teams, rather than independently.

These are three deceptively simple criteria for innovation success. In practice, they are often very difficult for a firm to achieve. Large, bureaucratic firms face this problem most of all. Small companies that can still maintain a cohesive unit may find criteria 2 and 3 easy to achieve, but, if led by excessively product-orientated technocrats, will frequently drift away from 1. The manager of a small company must, however, take note of the 'fast-forgetting' syndrome: as the business grows and the organisation expands, the three principal requirements for innovation become increasingly difficult to preserve – frequently resulting in management losing sight of the very factors that brought success to the business in the first place. Entrepreneurship, although highly desirable, is, on its own, insufficient for successful innovation, especially continual innovation. To remain successful innovators, business managers must continually review their firm's ability to meet these three conditions for effective innovation.

12.6.3 Organisational alternatives

Although marginal product changes can be managed within conventional organisations, radical innovations need suitably radical organisations. Six broad approaches are suggested that differ in their isolation from day-to-day business activities. All help small groups escape from entrenched departments and attitudes:

1 **The functional approach** utilises people from different business areas (such as finance or marketing). Tasks are carried out by the various departments. Individuals meet to make the necessary decisions. Usually a new products or product planning committee reviews project progress. Members do not commit all their time to the project, which must mesh with their normal duties.
2 **A taskforce** consists of several individuals who either are hand-picked by the boss or have volunteered to join the team. Taskforce members come together more regularly to work on the project, which they pursue with slightly greater urgency than in the previous approach. The taskforce should have a balance of engineering, production and marketing talents. Members' primary commitment is still very much to their function rather than the project.
3 **A project team–functional matrix** is appropriate when project demands are high. Team members commit themselves to the project as much as to their normal functional responsibilities. However, this type of 50:50 thinking often results in indecision and delay because members involved still need to see to their regular job, while the project needs require greater 'push'. There may also be a conflict between what the project team needs to achieve and their parent functions' main interests.
4 **Venture teams** are mostly associated with very small firms that have few people and no entrenched departments. The venture group should contain a mix of people with

different functional skills, not just specialists. For bigger companies, the venture option is used to free people from current functional pressures so that they can focus their entire effort on the project. The group is given complete autonomy and power to forge ahead, and incentive compensation for taking the risks.

5 **Spin-outs** are completely detached from the parent company. Big companies use this option to support very risky product innovation projects that do not currently fit the corporation's core business. Outside capital could be sought. The venture is sold off for an equity stake in the new start-up firm. For small firms, spin-offs are not a logical route for nurturing innovation, but they could consider another type of venture approach – the joint venture.

6 **Inside–outside venture** approaches fit both big and small/medium-sized firms. Smaller firms with the advantages of advanced technology, flexibility, vigour and/or entrepreneurial flair could team up with larger firms with the capital, distribution network and marketing muscle to gain market entry. The big firm gains through achieving entry into promising technologies that were too risky and ill-fitted to their mainstream business (the alliances between pharmaceuticals and biotechnology firms are a case in point).

The more radical the new product project (which means higher risk), the greater the need for project focus and its protection from current departmental and operational influences and constraints. The functional and taskforce options are therefore appropriate for low-risk, incremental product innovations (such as improvements, repositionings, new sizes, etc., involving present product lines). A project team–functional matrix is most suitable for marginally riskier projects, involving expansion in the number of product lines. Venture teams, spin-outs and inside–outside venture options are for radical, high-risk projects where internal constraints and opposition are expected to be very high.

The proposed radical structures help large firms capture the benefits of a small firm. Ironically, the idea that 'small is good' stems from the observation that large, innovative firms work in non-bureaucratic, smaller settings. They try to gain the advantages of being small. But, of course, size is not a determinant of innovation success. Many new products introduced by small firms fail because they should never have come about – it may be that they were badly conceived, they failed to meet market needs, or that the company lacked the marketing skills required to prise open new markets.

Summary

In this chapter we approach innovation at two levels: strategic innovation issues and the mechanics of new product development processes.

Innovation strategy is driven by the goal of creating the innovative company and achieving real value innovation that drives effective strategy and positioning in a market. Issues examined include: the link between innovation patterns and fundamental change in an industry; the creation of new business models to drive effective value innovation; the impact of radical and disruptive innovation on competitive patterns; the possibilities for proactive cannibalisation strategies; and the creation of innovation networks, often on a global basis, to encompass collaborative and open source innovation.

We then turned attention to the product development process in companies. Importantly, we saw that product innovation is not a one-off activity. A successful, profitable innovation can see a firm through for a while, but long-run survival depends on new products to balance its future portfolio (Chapter 2), replace declining products and cater for new customer needs.

Many businesses are caught out because management has failed to use the profits from current innovations to develop more innovations for future markets. Today's breadwinners will eventually dry up as competitive forces intensify over the product's life cycle. New products – tomorrow's breadwinners – are necessary to maintain the firm's position in the marketplace. One win is insufficient; multiple wins are necessary for corporate longevity.

The more the firm innovates, the greater the experience accumulated; the greater the experience gained, the better it gets at innovation; the better the firm becomes at this daunting activity, the greater its chances of competitive survival. A virtuous cycle of innovation is established.

Increasingly, a multidisciplinary, team-based approach to product innovation is required. Team work is important and has been one of the most significant organisational factors behind companies' ability to accelerate new product development in the drive to achieve lasting competitive advantage – as observed, for example, in the consumer electronics, computer and motor vehicle markets.

There are many factors that affect new product performance. Neglect of one factor alone can bring about failure. Management should check that their firm is pursuing a balanced and realistic new product development strategy, that customer/market needs are clearly identified and well understood, and that requisite technical and technological skills are married with a market orientation to ensure success.

Case study

Apple moves into fashion business with Watch launch

By Tim Bradshaw and Richard Waters in San Francisco

Apple launches new products

Google is investing hundreds of millions of dollars in self-driving cars and prolonging life. Amazon is testing deliveries by drone. Facebook is toying with virtual reality and flying internet access into far-flung places in solar powered planes.

Apple, meanwhile, is going into the fashion business.

In spite of the seemingly different scales of ambition and complexity, all have something in common: they are long-term bets that will take many years to make a significant dent in these vast companies' bottom lines.

After years of speculation, Apple's new Watch was launched by Tim Cook, chief executive, in Cupertino on Tuesday. As the unusual group of

Source: James Copeland/Alamy Stock Photo.

Vogue editors and other fashion journalists invited to the event attests, Apple sees the device as more than just technology: 'It's something functional yet incredibly beautiful,' Mr Cook said.

While others in Silicon Valley may try to bring forward a science-fiction vision of the future, Mr Cook says that Apple wants to create products that help people's everyday lives, such as through the smartwatch's health-tracking apps, and solve more personal technological challenges.

'We wanted to create something that was very personal. We felt that the wrist was the best place to do that,' Mr Cook told the *Financial Times*.

'We can help people live a better day with this. But we love innovating around things that require seamless innovation of hardware, software and services. You can see all those together in the watch.'

As well as these technological achievements, Apple stands to profit handsomely from its Watch if it proves anywhere near as popular as the iPod, iPad and iPhone.

The device will cost upwards of $350 when it goes on sale early next year – a price that is higher than many analysts had predicted, and one that will jump for the gold version with a leather strap.

That cost may limit how many customers can afford Apple's Watch, but of the 200m people who already own compatible iPhones, many affluent consumers may shell out for Apple's latest gadget purely for early-adopter kudos.

'Tim Cook has been under a lot of pressure the past 12 months,' said Geoff Blaber of CCS Insights. 'They needed to get a toe in the water.'

After seeing the Watch, Citi predicts that Apple will sell 14m in its first year and 15m in its second. That overshoots its forecast for Samsung to sell 4m smartwatches and fitness bands this year, and will add $12bn to Apple's revenues over the next two years.

But given the vast scale of Apple's existing iPhone business, which has sold more than 550m devices to date, Citi sees the Watch making up just 3 per cent of its annual sales.

With pent-up demand from Apple customers with older models, analysts see the iPhone 6 kick-starting a huge upgrade cycle. Many see the jumbo-sized 5.5-inch iPhone 6 Plus, which costs $100 more than previous models, as driving higher margins, although that may be offset by Apple increasing the memory it provides for the same price in more expensive models.

Concerns linger about Apple's ability to meet consumer demand for the iPhone 6 Plus in the run-up to Christmas. Nonetheless, IHS, a researcher, predicts that the new iPhone will propel Apple ahead of Microsoft's Nokia as the world's second-largest maker of mobile phones after Samsung – including all phones, not just smartphones.

'The introduction of larger-screen iPhones eliminates a key differentiator that has insulated Samsung, Sony, HTC and LG large-screen flagship smartphones from iPhone competition,' IHS said.

For the Watch to move the financial needle – and impress Wall Street, which left Apple shares broadly flat after Tuesday's announcements – the tech group will need to convince more than just early adopters that its pricey bracelet belongs on their wrists.

That is something Apple's competitors have failed to do, analysts say. Some have chastised Apple for being slow to catch up with arch-rival Samsung, which launched its first smartwatch more than a year ago, but Mr Cook is unruffled by such complaints.

'We ship things when we believe they are ready,' he said. 'For us, it's much more important to be the best than to be the first.'

Apple did not have the first MP3 player, smartphone or tablet, either, he continued. 'You could say we had the first modern one of all of those, and I think you can make the same point today that we have the first modern smartwatch.'

Some analysts watching Apple's event on Tuesday seemed to agree.

'They got the design right,' said Carolina Milanesi of Kantar Worldpanel, a market research unit of WPP. 'They've taken the technology out of it, which is not what everyone else is doing. They made it much more appealing to a wider audience.'

Many noted that Apple packed a lot more ideas in to its smartwatch than the first version of the iPhone, which lacked seemingly key features such as 3G wireless and an app store.

'I've seen a lot of smart watches – this one was really polished,' said Richard Doherty of Envisioneering.

But some complained that Apple had lost its famous focus by trying to sell consumers on something that is part jewellery, part sports device, part communicator, part wallet and even, according to Mr Cook, a remote control for the Apple TV box.

'I'm underwhelmed,' said Om Malik, a tech blogger turned investor with True Ventures, a San Francisco group that counts fitness band maker Fitbit among its portfolio.

'I feel that they should have tried to do a few things well. Apple is missing its editor,' Mr Malik added, in a reference to Apple co-founder Steve Jobs' capacity to axe features and products even at late stages of development.

Many are looking to the app developer community to come up with something to convince consumers to buy the Watch. Here, Apple retains an advantage over rival app stores such as Android's Google Play.

Mr Cook said that part of the reason for launching the Watch months in advance of its release to consumers was to get developers working.

If they do not come up with the substance, Apple will have to fall back on the Watch's style until they do, analysts say.

'Every wearable device we've seen to date has been in search of a reason to use it,' said Mr Blaber. 'This is a step in a long journey.'

 Source: from 'Apple moves into fashion business with Watch launch', *Financial Times*, 10/09/14 (Bradshaw, T. and Waters, R.).

Discussion questions

1 Why would Apple want to move into the fashion business?

2 What type of innovation is Apple's new watch?

3 What role does innovation play for a company such as Apple?

CHAPTER 13
COMPETING THROUGH SUPERIOR SERVICE AND CUSTOMER RELATIONSHIPS

'Companies still have much to learn about the true meaning of service. . . If the two characters on my doorstep really had come to instal my broadband connection, why did they have the appearance and demeanour of a pair of burglars? I asked them to identify themselves. One fished in his sweatshirt and produced a plastic card on a silver necklace. The other chortled that he had lost his identification. . . Those first impressions can be so misleading, can't they? Not really. . . '

Michael Skapinker, *Financial Times* (2003)

Halfords boosted by fall in new car sales

By Colm Fulton

Growing demand for car maintenance products a boon for the group

The motoring and cycling retailer Halfords has reported rising sales and said it will deliver on its full-year profit expectations, despite a challenging market.

The group said total revenue was up 2.8 per cent for the 20-week period until August 17, with retail sales up 2.6 per cent and revenues in its autocentres up 4 per cent, compared to the same time last year.

AJ Bell, the investment advisers, said, 'While the robust trading is encouraging, it is important not to get carried away given Halfords served up a profit warning as recently as May.'

At the time, the group reported a fall in underlying pre-tax profit because of a weaker pound and increased investment in staff training and customer service.

Source: British Retail Photography/Alamy Stock Photo.

AJ Bell added that the latest results provided 'some evidence' that 'spending on customer service, staff training and marketing, while initially undermining profitability, may be beginning to have some impact on the performance of [Halfords] stores'.

According to Amy Higginbotham, a Retail Analyst at GlobalData, improved customer service and staff expertise is key to the group's strategy for competing with online retailers.

She said: 'ensuring that customers purchase the right product for them is very important. Doing so helps maintain customer trust. . . and provides a key point of difference from emerging online players.'

The results come at a time of difficult trading conditions for bricks-and-mortar retailers. Last week DIY chain Homebase was forced to shut 42 stores in order to remain solvent.

According to Ms Higginbotham, robust growth in the group's autocentres business was also helped by 'stricter MOT regulations introduced earlier on this year'.

Falling sales of new cars also worked in the group's favour: demand for car maintenance products increased by 4.5 per cent and motoring retail sales in total were up 3.8 per cent.

Laith Khalaf, an analyst at Hargreaves Lansdown, said, 'Declining car sales are actually a tailwind for Halfords, as more older models on the road means a greater need for parts and servicing.'

Source: from 'Halfords boosted by fall in new car sales', *Financial Times*, 04/09/18 (Fulton, C.).

Discussion questions

1 What are the issues here?
2 How can Halfords' spending more on customer service improve the performance of stores?

Introduction

The pressure on companies to compete through superior service and effective customer relationships has never been higher. But achieving appropriate competitive positioning based on service and relationship investments has never been harder. Certainly, the post-2008 financial crisis consumer is more demanding than has ever been the case before. Equally, the case for 'lean consumption' built by leading operations experts is compelling:

> The concepts underlying lean consumption boil down to six simple principles:
>
> 1 Solve the customer's problem completely by insuring that all the goods and services work, and work together.
> 2 Don't waste the customer's time.
> 3 Provide exactly what the customer wants.
> 4 Provide what's wanted exactly where it's wanted.
> 5 Provide what's wanted where it's wanted exactly when it's wanted.
> 6 Continually aggregate solutions to reduce the customer's time and hassle.
>
> (Womack and Jones, 2005)

Similarly, from a marketing perspective, Barwise and Meehan (2004) put the central competitive strategy issue nicely when they underline the fact that as products have become more difficult to differentiate (largely because there are few real differences between them), companies have resorted to excessive branding and marketing, leaving customers less satisfied now than they were a decade ago. Their appealing logic is that customers do not want bells and whistles and trivial brand differences – they just want quality products, reliable services and fair value for money (Barwise and Meehan, 2004). It may even be that 'consumer decadence' is dead and that marketing must focus on the basics of value, practicality and durability – even luxury car brand Lexus in the USA has run ads with the tagline 'lowest cost of ownership' to emphasise fuel economy and resale value rather than extravagance (Helm, 2008). Indeed, Price and Jaffe (ex-Amazon executives) argue in their book, *The*

Best Service Is No Service (2008), that most customers do not want a relationship with a company, they just want things to work.

For example, a recent multinational survey concludes that many consumers find the rising volume of marketing messages on the Internet and in the mobile-enabled world to be simply overwhelming. It seems that rather than attracting customers and building loyalty and effective relationships, marketers are pushing them away with relentless and ill-conceived efforts to engage with them. It seems that what customers want most is 'decision simplicity' – ease in gathering trustworthy information about a product so they can confidently and efficiently weigh their purchase options and choose. It seems what customers want from marketers is actually simplicity, not more complexity and confusion (Spenner and Freeman, 2012).

Similarly, it has been argued that companies should stop trying to 'delight' their customers and just focus on solving their problems. While the rewards for over-the-top service are small (if they exist at all), the loss of customers because you do not solve their problems is likely to be large. Customers punish bad service but may not reward exceptionally good service. The link between service and loyalty is not straightforward. So, telling staff to exceed customers' expectations is liable to produce confusion, wasted time and effort, and expensive give-aways (Dixon *et al.*, 2010).

Indeed, while customer loyalty has long been a central tenet of marketing, it is increasingly being called into question. The modern customer may increasingly be a 'serial adulterer' rather than conventionally loyal (Hill, 2014). Perhaps customer loyalty does not really matter anymore? Loyal customers may not actually be cheaper to serve as conventionally suggested. For example, one study that goes against the conventional marketing grain divides customers into: **true friends** (long term and highly profitable), **butterflies** (transient but profitable), **strangers** (with the lowest potential for profit) and **barnacles** (who create 'additional drag' and need to be removed or converted into better customers). Conventional loyalty programmes may just attract butterflies – less than a third of Tesco shoppers are 'highly loyal' (that is, spend 50 per cent of their grocery budget there), while for Sainsbury's the figure is only 9 per cent, and for M&S Food less than 3 per cent. Grocery customers appear to be overwhelmingly disloyal, in spite of all attempts to gain their affections.

Far from customers providing a devoted, monogamous relationship, Simonson and Rosen (2014) suggest the customer relationship has become an 'open marriage', where customers evaluate each new model of the camera, car or computer on merit rather than on marketing messages or prior preference. This opens the way for upstarts to challenge with better products – as Asus laptops did successfully when it took on Dell and Hewlett-Packard. Traditional measures of customer loyalty become meaningless, as do attempts to measure customer lifetime value, if consumers spend their lifetime flitting between brands. The key issues become not loyalty, but quality, service and consistency (Simonson and Rosen, 2014).

It is important that executives should rigorously evaluate the controversies surrounding issues such as customer loyalty, satisfaction and service/relationship investments with a critical perspective. Many conventional assumptions may be misleading.

Nonetheless, more conventionally, one of the most significant changes in contemporary marketing thinking and practice was the shift in focus from achieving single transactions to establishing longer-term relationships with customers (see, for example, Vargo and Lusch, 2004). While transactional marketing is concerned with making a single sale, relationship marketing is more concerned with establishing a rapport with the customer aimed at achieving higher customer satisfaction, more repeat business, greater word-of-mouth referral, more opportunities for further business development and enhanced revenues and profitability for the supplier.

Certainly, in the contemporary environment, many markets in developed countries can be regarded as mature, or at best growing only slowly, suggesting that there are fewer new customers for which to compete. Demographics emphasise this condition – an ageing population coupled with high youth unemployment in the West constrains market growth in many markets. Competition is increasingly intense, particularly in the new competitive landscapes that are the legacy of economic downturn, and the costs of attracting new customers are high. It has been estimated that the costs of attracting new customers can be up to five times as much as the costs of adequately serving existing ones to ensure that they stay with you.

Ideas such as lean, waste-free consumption and fair value for money resonate with the demands of the post-recession consumer. Appropriate service and relationship strategies are critical issues for executives to address in developing robust marketing strategies for the environment we all now face.

Note that conventional logic suggests that customer retention is a key predictor of profitability. Support for this view dates back to Reichheld and Sasser (1990), who claimed to show the value to companies, operating in a variety of markets, of cutting customer defections (lost customers) by as little as 5 per cent: for an automobile service chain a 5 per cent cut in customer defections resulted in a 30 per cent increase in profits; for an industrial laundry a 47 per cent increase in profits; for an insurance brokerage a 51 per cent increase; and for a bank branch a staggering 84 per cent increase. Customers that have been with a company longer tended, on average, to spend more on each transaction, offer more opportunities for cross-selling (selling them other products and services) and give better recommendations to their friends and colleagues. In the bank, customer relationships of ten years or more accounted for 29 per cent of the account base but 71 per cent of the profits. Nonetheless, while the logic appears compelling, there are some suggestions that there are limits to its universal applicability. Some companies are placing more emphasis on making choices between customers based on profitability and future prospects rather than simply longevity of relationship. Maintaining some customer relationships may become expensive compared to the value of the customer in question to the company.

Indeed, in all this, it is important that we distinguish between customer *retention* and customer *loyalty*, together with the relationship each of these has with customer satisfaction. There is a danger, in practice, that these concepts become confused. Customer retention is essentially a measure of repeat purchase behaviour, and there are many reasons why customers may come back, even if we have failed to provide them with a high level of satisfaction – they may have no choice or they may not know any better. Fraser (2007), for example, warns of 'conflicted consumers' who buy your product and appear highly satisfied, but in fact are a stealth segment ready to defect as soon as a viable alternative appears. Customer loyalty, at least as most managers and customers would understand the term, goes beyond simple repeat behaviour and habit, and is more to do with how customers feel about us: do they trust us? Do they actively want to do business with us? Will they recommend us to others?

To confuse retention and loyalty can be dangerous. Retention may be achieved through a 'bribe' – discounts for repeat purchase, additional exclusive value-added services and so on. Achieving high customer loyalty is likely to be far more difficult (perhaps in some cases impossible) and requires greater long-term investment. The practical difference is great. That said, marketers should always think carefully about whether they really *need* loyalty, or whether repeat purchase is their goal. Certainly, many commentators and authors assume loyalty leads to more predictable and consistent repeat business, but this relationship is by no means proven in practice.

For example, 'customer loyalty' card schemes offered by many retailers are more about customer retention than loyalty and satisfaction, and it is likely that their effects will last only until there is a better offer available. On the other hand, the John Lewis Partnership achieves high customer loyalty through satisfaction building above and beyond such 'loyalty cards'. This is expressed in their Partnership Business Model: 'We work to build brand trust and loyalty and provide customers with increasingly personalised, unique and exclusive products and services that are authentic and inspiring. And because we're Partners, we're invested to build that trust and loyalty.' (**www.johnlewispartnership.co.uk/annualreport Page 12**). John Lewis has been rated as the most admired British company for honesty and trust, and wins many awards for customer satisfaction. Indeed, as airlines have discovered, for example, if all competitors offer the same thing, then customer 'loyalty' programmes such as frequent flyer awards become a cost of being in business rather than a differentiator. Many frequent fliers will have loyalty cards with several airlines or alliances.

To build customer retention, anticipating the major financial benefits it brings, let alone longer-term customer loyalty, requires companies to invest in strategies focused on these goals, not just on sales volume. But it is suggested that retention is not enough as an absolute concept and that these strategies should also be about correcting any downward migration in customers' spending habits long before they defect. A two-year study of attitudes of US households about companies in 16 diverse industries showed that 'improving the management of migration as a whole by focusing not only on defections, but also on smaller changes in customer spending can have as much as ten times more value than preventing defections alone' (Coyles and Gokey, 2005).

This may involve brand building (of the type practised at Virgin), or specific programmes (such as 'loyalty' schemes or product innovation), but increasingly it involves emphasis on achieving excellence in the service activities that augment the basic product offering. Nonetheless, for the reasons given previously, a company faces an important strategic decision about the level of service and relational investment it should make in a given market or customer group, compared to the value of that market and its service delivery capabilities. Low-service strategies are a viable option where non-service benefits such as low price are key value drivers for some customer groups.

This chapter explores the concept of 'service' and examines methods for competing through service as an important element of marketing strategy and competitive positioning, in which executives face some challenging choices. Figure 13.1 sets out the structure we are following to provide systematic appraisal of the key issues in competing through superior service and customer relationships.

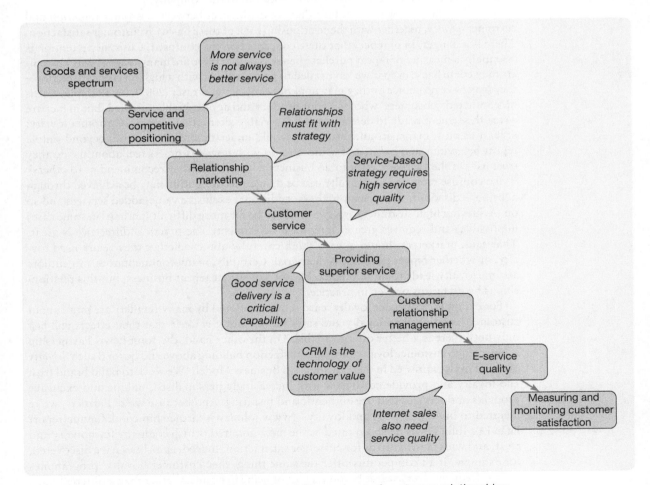

Figure 13.1 Key issues in competing through superior service and customer relationships

13.1 The goods and services spectrum

It is important to recognise that most offerings in a marketplace represent some combination of tangible and intangible elements, as illustrated in Figure 13.2.

The tangible elements of what people buy can be seen, touched, smelled, heard or tasted. They constitute the physical aspects of the offer, such as the product itself and the surroundings in which it is bought or consumed. The intangible elements are often more elusive. They comprise the level of service offered in support of the tangible elements, and the image, associations or beliefs that surround the product.

At the left-hand end of the spectrum, the offer to customers is primarily physical and hence tangible. Examples include packaged goods such as baked beans and batteries, and consumer durables such as stereos and tablets. From the customers' perspective, however, the benefits derived from purchase and consumption may well be less tangible – baked beans defeat hunger, batteries provide portable light, stereos provide entertainment and tablets provide access to online media. The distinguishing factor is that these benefits are primarily delivered by the physical features and characteristics of the product. There are also, of course, even less tangible elements to these purchases. Physical products are sold through retail outlets where sales staff may provide advice and demonstrations. Individual brands, through their media advertising and other promotional activities, may have established images and reputations in the minds of customers that will enhance value to them.

At the right-hand end of the spectrum, the relative importance of intangibles and tangibles is reversed. In medical services, for example, the essence of the 'offer' is intangible. It is concerned with the service provided to the patient and the way in which the patient interacts with doctors, nurses and technology. There are some tangible, physical elements involved, such as medicines, prosthetics, written instructions and the physical surroundings. The essence of medical services, however, is the intangible process that takes place in the diagnosis and treatment of the medical problem. Ultimately, the success of the medical

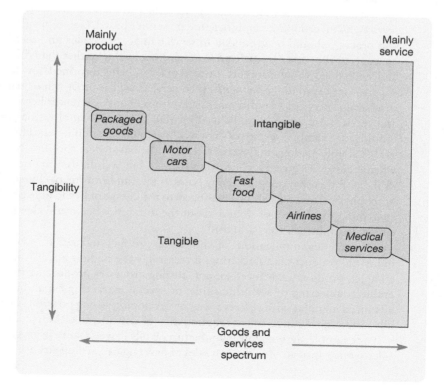

Figure 13.2
Goods and services

services process is determined by the way the patient responds to, and interacts with, the services provided.

It is also worth bearing in mind that the services sector now accounts for some three-quarters of the gross domestic product of the EU countries and over three-quarters of EU jobs (see **http://ec.europa.eu/trade/creating-opportunities/economic-sectors/services/**, accessed 2019). Services are growing quickly in the world economy, making up almost 64 per cent of gross world product, suggesting huge potential in emerging markets (see The World Factbook, **https://www.cia.gov/library/publications/the-world-factbook/geos/xx.html**).

Between these two extremes lie offers that combine tangible and intangible elements in more equal proportions. In fast-food outlets, for example, the offer is a combination of the physical food (tangible) together with the ambience of the restaurant and the speed of the service provided (intangibles).

As more companies have embraced quality control and assurance techniques in the production of their physical products, so the scope for differentiation between one supplier and another on the tangible elements of offer has diminished. Total quality management has been increasingly applied to the physical element of products, reducing variability, tightening tolerances and ensuring fewer defects (or even approaching the cherished goal of zero). Increasingly, companies operating at the left-hand end of the spectrum are looking to enhance differentiation through focusing on the intangible elements of the offer. These efforts include branding the offer and the delivery of service to augment the physical product offer. At the right-hand end of the spectrum, companies and other service providers are recognising that the type and quality of the service they offer is their major means of differentiation. The line between tangible and intangible elements is becoming blurred and moving downwards, so that the intangible elements such as service are becoming increasingly important across the whole spectrum.

For example, Vargo and Lusch (2004) have pioneered a 'service-dominant logic' (SDL) that has attracted huge attention globally. SDL proposes that organisations, markets and society are fundamentally concerned with exchange of service – the applications of competences (knowledge and skills) for the benefit of another party. That is, 'service is exchanged for service', such that all firms are service firms; all markets are centred on the exchange of service and all economies and societies are service based. Consequently, marketing thought and practice should be grounded in service logic, principles and theories. SDL embraces concepts of the 'value-in-use' and 'co-creation of value' rather than the 'value-in-exchange' and 'embedded-value' concepts. Instead of firms being informed how to *market to* customers, they are urged to *market with* customers, as well as other value-creation partners in the firm's value network. Traditional assumptions about differences between marketing goods and services are severely challenged by SDL. The fuller implications of SDL continue to unfold (for example, see **http://www.sdlogic.net/** for updates and further insights). That said, a simple analogy may serve to clarify the basic idea: specifically, it is often said that when a customer goes to a hardware store to buy a drill, they are not actually buying the drill, but rather they are purchasing holes. It's a simplification of course (and there are many other physical and psychological aspects to the choice of brand at least), but it does express something reasonably profound about the difference between value in use (the hole) and embedded value (the physical drill).

The practical implications of choices on product and service mix are considerable. In industrial product manufacturing, increasingly the highest added-value lies in technically complex products. Advanced manufacturing processes produce items that require considerable engineering or scientific skills, or special marketing capabilities. Shifting towards advanced manufacturing offers a way of developing strong positions in niche markets globally, although the investment required may be considerable (Marsh, 2009).

For example, aero-engine manufacturer Rolls Royce's strategy has been to expand after-sales service, instead of relying on sales of new engines, selling airlines outsourcing packages in which it takes responsibility for maintaining its engines. As new generations of complex 'low-carbon' engines become available, it is likely the outsourcing business will expand further – currently around half Rolls-Royce's income is from servicing engines (O'Connell, 2009). In this sense, Rolls-Royce claims it does not sell engines any more, it sells thrust. Of course, every good idea generates competition, and in more recent years other manufacturers have caught up with Rolls Royce. For example, General Electric's equivalent offering is sold as 'power by the hour' – a phrase that really sums up the concept well.

13.2 Service and competitive positioning

A critical starting point in building a strategy is the issue of what level of service provision is to be offered and how this defines a company's positioning in the market or market segment in question. Of course, into this choice must also be factored the capabilities of the company to deliver the service level being offered, but a first question is how we want to be perceived in terms of service level and quality compared to the alternatives in this market.

In many modern markets the base-level requirement for service is higher than ever before. Without meeting this minimum level of service provision, it is unlikely we can be a significant player in this market – this is the cost of being in this business. But importantly, beyond this point significant choices exist. It is competitively risky and very expensive to assume that all service is good service, so the more we provide the better, forever. In fact, important strategic choices should be addressed by executives in this regard.

Figure 13.3 suggests some important positioning choices as they relate to service provision. The attractions of a high service strategy are in enhancing customer retention and satisfaction through hard-to-imitate added-value in the form of intangibles. Much conventional wisdom supports this as an attractive option. However, it is important to recognise that there are choices. In many situations, a low service strategy may be an effective alternative that defines a distinct space in the market and delivers high customer value through lower prices or other factors. In many ways, it is easy to come to the conclusion that this line of thinking is diametrically opposed to the 'service-dominant logic' concepts discussed earlier. However, this is not entirely correct. Specifically, one could think about such ideas as trying to focus on the 'core' service the consumer is interested in getting when they purchase, rather than the extraneous add-ons that have

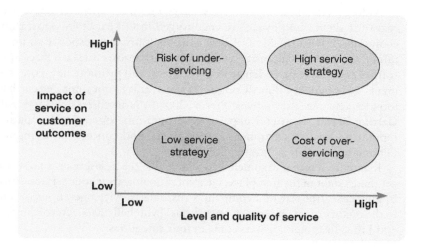

Figure 13.3
Service and competitive positioning

often come to dominate companies' thinking about what makes 'service' provision. For example, when buying an air ticket, is the customer primarily interested in the travel service, or something else? If the former, are they willing to pay more for 'other' aspects of the service, and can this provide a competitive differentiation to the firm? Keep these ideas in mind as you read on.

13.2.1 Low service strategy

Low service strategy is a component of the positioning of budget hotels such as Accor's Formula 1. By stripping out the services typically provided by a two-star hotel and focusing on a better sleeping environment, Accor found a successful way to deliver a two-star hotel level of comfort for a one-star hotel price. The model is based on the observation that people trade up from one star to two star for the better sleeping environment, not for the other services provided by conventional two-star hotels, and trade down from two star to one star just for the lower price.

Low service strategies have been particularly successful in some sectors during the economic downturn and recession of the 2010s and what has followed since. For example, low-cost retailers Aldi and Lidl have made significant inroads into Tesco's market leadership during the toughest of economic conditions. While high service strategies at Sainsbury's and Waitrose have, to a degree, protected their competitive position, low service and very low-price strategies at Aldi and Lidl have also been incredibly effective. Market leader Tesco has been left looking increasingly 'stuck in the middle' of the UK grocery market (Piercy *et al.*, 2010a).

A prime example of an effective low-service strategy is the European no-frills airline Ryanair. It is the most successful of the European 'no-frills' airlines, based on the model of Southwestern Airlines in the USA – offering very low fares but stripping out many of the expensive services provided by conventional airlines. The chief executive of Ryanair, Michael O'Leary, even at one point mooted plans to go from being a 'low-cost airline' to a 'no-cost airline', by making tickets free, while earning more from additions such as food and luggage charges. In some promotions, Ryanair has offered to pay people £1 to sit in a seat on the aircraft (that is, deduct £1 from the airport taxes and charge no fare). Ryanair has given new meaning to the 'art of cheap': a quarter of seats are already 'free' except for airport charges and taxes; the planes are stripped down with seats that don't recline (you can fit in more passengers instead and, worse, reclining seats break and have to be fixed, which slows things down); no seat-back pockets (less cleaning costs); no entertainment; advertising on seat-back trays; tickets sold online (along with insurance, hotels and car rentals); flight attendants selling food and cosmetics; and, soon, flights providing a cell-phone service. Passengers who want ancillary services are required to pay extra for them. Employees are encouraged in O'Leary's low-cost thinking. Faced with economic downturn, Mr O'Leary said his 'only one response to any consumer uncertainty' would be to intensify a price war, with moves 'to slash fares and yields, stimulate traffic, encourage price-sensitive consumers, and promote new routes and base developments'. He believes that during recessions, travel does not get cut back but people do look for cheaper alternatives (Piercy, 2009d). Nonetheless, 2015 saw Ryanair's 'Always Getting Better' customer experience programme operating to counter the company's reputation for low customer services levels, and concessions being made to customers (Thomas *et al.*, 2015).

Relatedly, a recent argument is that actually 'the best service is no service', because if you get things right in the first place, customers do not want your service (Price and Jaffe, 2008). In this sense, 'the size of a company's customer service operations is in inverse proportion to the quality of its underlying operations' (Mitchell, 2008). According to research by Price and Jaffe, customer contacts come in **four categories**:

About 1 in 7 customer contacts:	Are triggered by basic quality defects – 'it doesn't work'	Which have to be addressed by quality improvements
Another 25% or so:	Take the form of 'How do I?' questions	Which means the company has failed to communicate properly or its processes are confusing, and these are the issues to address
About 40%:	Are 'Where can I get?' queries	If the web page or other self-service options are done properly customers should be able to answer these for themselves
The last 20%:	Are people who want to buy stuff	The more the first 80% can be reduced, the more the company can invest in helping customers when they actually need and value it.

Making assumptions is dangerous, even though sometimes the evidence is highly counter-intuitive. A Canadian study of shop assistants found that in luxury shops, the 'snooty' attitude of assistants may actually boost sales – consumers may react in a positive way to rude and rejecting behaviour. It seems those who value designer labels crave the acceptance of the retail assistants in expensive shops. In an experiment, the researchers found that consumers who felt rejected when shopping liked the brand and were willing to pay more for it than those who were treated well. The researchers reason that social rejection drives people to conform and work harder in an attempt to be accepted – though in the context of shopping for luxuries, not routine shopping (Ward and Dahl, 2014).

13.2.2 Under- and over-servicing traps

Examining links between service level and quality and customer impacts also highlights the potential problems of under- and over-servicing. Over-servicing occurs when services are provided to an extent and at a quality level that exceeds customer needs and has little impact on outcomes such as customer retention or satisfaction. The same effect can occur when service efforts are concentrated in activities that matter little to the customers in question and do not create value. The low-cost operations already described exploit the over-servicing and wrong-servicing of conventional competitors.

To understand the idea of 'wrong-servicing', consider, for example, US retail giant Walmart's experiences in the European market. Walmart is the world's biggest supermarket retailer. Its US value proposition of lowest price and highest service has been incredibly successful domestically. As part of its global expansion, in January 1998 Walmart arrived in Germany. However, this is a country where the rules of retailing seem to be 'the grumpier the better', the 'customer comes last', and 'shopping is boring', and the emphasis is on efficiency. Walmart arrived determined to pamper every customer in sight. Walmart's 'ten-foot rule' states that if a customer comes within ten feet of an employee, the latter must smile and offer to help. Complaints/requests must be dealt with 'by sundown'. In fact, the result was a major culture clash. The Walmart tactics infuriated consumers and aroused their suspicions – if someone takes hold of their purchases at the checkout (to pack them in a bag), they think someone is trying to steal from them. Locally employed shop-workers have been found hiding in the lavatories to avoid the embarrassing but mandatory morning Walmart chant. By late-2000 Walmart's losses were running in excess of £150 million a year in Germany from its 95 stores, and the company was ranked bottom of all retailers in Germany in an annual customer satisfaction survey. Analysts blamed Walmart's reluctance to adjust its retail model to the demands of German customers. In April 2001, the company announced it was scrapping its expansion plans in Germany and would not be launching the planned 50 new stores by the end of 2002. In 2006, after eight years of losses, Walmart beat a retreat from Germany, selling its stores to Metro, Germany's leading retailer, losing $1 billion in the process. Walmart admitted it had completely misjudged German shopping tastes and habits. Being excellent at the wrong service is very expensive (Piercy, 2009d).

Correspondingly, offering a low level of service to a customer group where service has a high impact on the outcomes desired (sales, retention, satisfaction) is also risky, unless a new market position can be defined and defended around a low-service offer. In many situations, an under-serviced position indicates the need to invest more in service level and quality.

Increasingly, in harsh economic conditions and with more demanding customers, the conclusion is that we should think in terms of *appropriate* service and quality strategies, that match the most important needs of our target customers but also our ability to deliver. The diagram in Figure 13.3 may assist in looking at our competitors and their service-based positioning and how well they are doing, and comparing their performance to our own. Before reaching conclusions about what works and what does not, it is useful to examine the distribution and spread of service-based competition – is high customer satisfaction achieved through service and quality or other issues (and if so, which dimensions of service and quality or other issues); is low customer satisfaction associated with high or low service provision, or is there no clear relationship? Indeed, we might then look at which types of firms are doing best in market share and profitability terms.

There is a danger that executives confuse customer satisfaction, customer loyalty and the goals of customer service. Unsurprisingly, the result is many unsatisfied customers, disloyal customers and criticisms of customer service delivery. What is worse is a failure to identify what levels of customer satisfaction, loyalty and service are needed to implement our marketing strategy with these customers. In some cases, the obvious conclusion from a company's performance is that its strategy has failed because poor customer service is linked to low customer satisfaction and loyalty and a poor reputation, with adverse effects on its performance (sales, growth profitability). But in other cases, high performance may be driven by low service levels (typically coupled with lower prices and other benefits).

Dealing effectively with the service/competitive positioning issue rests on understanding what aspects of customer service are important to the customers who are important to us, and aligning service capabilities with these priorities. This relates to where a company wants to be in the market compared to competitors and the type of value to be offered to different customers. The risk is that not challenging assumptions about service and value means we provide services to customers who do not value them, or deny services to our target customers because we spread our efforts over all customers. The critical issue is alignment between service capabilities and delivery and marketing strategy.

13.3   Relationship marketing

In conventional efforts to improve the probability of retaining customers, many organisations have turned to the techniques and philosophy of relationship marketing. The focus of relationship marketing is on building bonds and ties between the organisation and its customers to improve feedback and ultimately enhance the prospects of customer loyalty.

Figure 13.4 shows the classic 'relationship marketing ladder', originally developed by Payne et al. (1995). The ladder shows a number of identifiable stages in relationship building. At the bottom of the ladder is the prospect, or the target customer. The initial emphasis

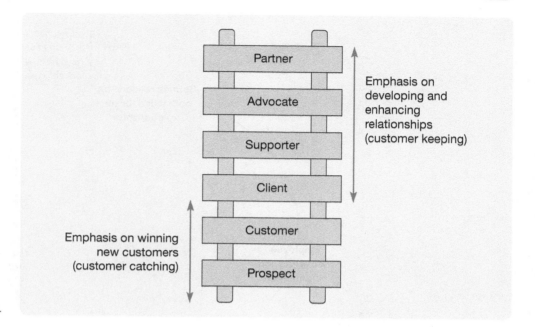

Figure 13.4
The relationship
marketing ladder

Source: Payne, C.,
Clark, M. and Peck,
H. (1995) *Relationship
Marketing for Competitive Advantage*, Oxford,
Butterworth-Heinemann.

will be to secure the prospect as a customer. To achieve this, marketing effort is concentrated on customer catching. Once the customer has been caught, however, the emphasis shifts to securing a longer-term, ongoing relationship. While a customer may be essentially nameless and have done business with the company once or only occasionally, a client is more individual and does business on a repeat basis. Clients may, however, be ambivalent or neutral towards the supplier company. Relationship marketing seeks to convert clients into becoming supporters – those who have positive feelings towards the supplier, and even advocates – those who may actively recommend the supplier to others. The top rung of the ladder is partner. At this level, the supplier and the customer are working together for mutual benefit. The focus of relationship marketing is moving customers up the ladder, finding ways of enhancing the value both parties get from the relationship.

Clearly, not all prospective customers will be equally worth the effort needed to move them up the ladder. Critical to a successful relationship marketing strategy is targeting customers of sufficient value (current or potential) to warrant the investment in creating a relationship with them. IBM, for example, has identified its top 1,000 customers and puts great effort into identifying their current and future needs. The firm has combined its customer relationship management processes with its opportunity management system and ranked these customers according to their estimated lifetime value to IBM. When a high-ranking customer launches a big project with opportunities for IBM to tender, it is given highest priority across the organisation (Eisenstat *et al.*, 2001).

Nonetheless, effective relationship marketing requires sound reasons for the relationship on both sides (see Figure 13.5). In some markets, such as rail travel, customers may not see advantages in becoming 'partners' and may prefer to stay at arm's length from the supplier. One respondent filling in a customer satisfaction questionnaire on a train was overheard to say: 'I wish I could go back to being just a passenger rather than a customer!'

Indeed, in some cases there may be an element of spuriousness about the relationship offering made by some companies. From the customers' perspective, the British Airways relationship does not offer more seat room (unless, of course, one qualifies for an increasingly rare upgrade), and the Sainsbury's relationship does not offer much more than a bribe to come back next time. The only tangible aspect of the customers' relationship with these companies seems to be becoming the target of large quantities of direct mail (Piercy, 2009a). These inappropriate and often ineffective approaches to relationship marketing can be the

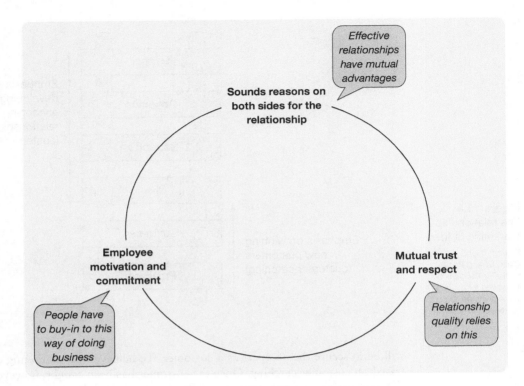

Figure 13.5
Foundations
of relationship
marketing

result of poorly designed programmes based on weak value propositions (see Capizzi and Ferguson, 2005). In fact, a survey conducted by IBM of about 1,000 customers of 10 major retailers discovered that factors relating to overall customer experience were far more relevant to customer satisfaction than price and value (Chu, 2002).

In other markets, firms may misjudge the value customers put on relationships. In financial services, for example, attempts to create closer relationships with individual clients may have been naive in assuming the client will automatically see a value in having a 'personal banking manager'. Fundamental to establishing a relationship is to determine what each party gets, or could get, from that relationship, as well as what they value in such a relationship. Too many organisations still look primarily from their own perspective, recognising the value to them of customer retention or loyalty, but not thinking through clearly what value the customer will get from the deal that would motivate them to participate.

In contrast, other firms are now coming to realise that the type of relationship customers want with a supplier can in itself be an effective way of segmenting markets around fundamental customer needs. This can lead to focusing relationship-building resources on those customer groups where this is mutually advantageous, and significantly cut the cost and the ill will created through more scatter-gun approaches. In business markets, for example, Narayanda (2005) suggests four types of customers depending on their location on the loyalty ladder and the sellers' costs of serving them:

- **Commodity buyers** are only interested in obtaining the lowest price and are unlikely to be worth investments to move them up the relationship ladder.
- **Under-performers** should not be allowed to remain in that position as they have low loyalty and are expensive to service.
- **Partners** are expensive to run but high on the ladder and normally rewarding financially. Their management requires ongoing care to prevent them from becoming underperformers.
- **Most valuable customers** (normally accounting for less than 10 per cent of revenues) are as loyal as partners but cheaper to service.

Essential for more advanced relationships such as partnering, or awarding most valuable customer status, is the establishment of mutual trust and respect between the parties. This involves being prepared to share sometimes commercially sensitive information.

The core message is that effective relationship marketing focuses on choosing the 'right' customer as the target for service and relational investments – this may not be those who currently generate most revenue, but those who unlock the most value in the company. So, for example, Amazon has four very different types of customer: consumers, sellers, enterprises and content providers. But Amazon devotes maximum resources to pleasing consumers – even if it means sellers or content providers sometimes feel short-changed. The unwavering focus on consumers has resulted in unparalleled consumer loyalty and incredibly high stock valuations (Simons, 2014).

Indeed, research in the United States suggests that the challenge to companies in business-to-business markets is no longer simply to sell, but to become the 'outsource of preference', through a collaborative relationship between vendor and customer. The customer expects the vendor to know the customer's business well enough to create products and services that the customer could not have designed and created, and to give proof in hard evidence that the supplier has added value in excess of price. The excellent suppliers are those that add value to the customer's business by being close enough to measure the customer's needs, develop added-value services to improve the customer's business performance and prove to the customer that this has been done. This is a long way removed from simple, transaction-based business (Chally, 2006). We consider this particular issue in more detail in the chapter on strategic customer management (Chapter 14).

The third cornerstone of relationship marketing stems from employee involvement and commitment to the relationship building and maintaining process. While companies may set strategies in the boardroom for relationship marketing, the success of those strategies ultimately rests with the employees who are charged with putting them into practice. Employees, from front-line sales staff through accounts personnel to car park attendants, need to understand their role in relationship building, be committed to it and be motivated to achieve it. In many situations, as far as the customer is concerned, the employee they meet at the point of sale or service delivery *is* the company and its brand. (We will consider the importance of this relationship when examining the growing importance of internal marketing in Chapter 16.)

13.3.1 Building relationships with customers

Various approaches have been suggested for building closer links with customers, and hence moving them higher up the relationship marketing ladder. These approaches can be grouped into three main categories: building enhanced benefits of loyalty; creating structural ties; and creating delighted customers.

Building enhanced benefits of loyalty

One basic approach to building relationships is through the development of enhanced benefits of loyalty for customers. These might be financial or social benefits.

Financial benefits give the customer a financial reason to enter into a longer-term relationship and remain loyal to the supplier. These might include discounts for bulk or repeat purchases or other rewards for loyalty. Typical examples include store loyalty cards, where shoppers build credits towards free purchases, or the collection of air miles through the use of credit cards.

Social benefits might include the establishment of regular social groupings, and increasingly companies now use Internet-based blog sites and specialised social networks to create such benefits. Sermo is a US online social networking site for doctors, with no advertising and open unedited interactions between members. Pfizer works in collaboration with Sermo's Internet-based social network to establish how drug makers can best communicate with doctors online. Mothercare launched Gurgle.com, a social networking site for parents of babies. Unilever's Dove brand operates an online community around its natural beauty concept and products.

On the other hand, social benefits might include corporate hospitality or social events sponsored by a firm, where its clients can meet other clients with a view to developing their mutual business interests or technical knowledge (for example, through seminars and workshops on product technology and industry change).

Creating structural ties and bonds

Through offering enhanced benefits, companies may create structural ties with their clients, which then make it difficult, or costly, for their clients to defect. Professional medical equipment supply companies, for example, provide hospital surgeons with the equipment needed to help perform knee and hip implants with their own make of implant. The equipment works poorly with competitors' implants and is hence a major incentive for the surgeons to remain loyal. Sponsorship of the surgeons at symposia and conferences to enable them to stay up to date with medical advances also helps to strengthen their relationship with the supplier and build corporate goodwill, although there are important ethical constraints on some such actions.

In some industries, the structural ties might be based on legal agreements and commitments, particularly where the use of protected patents is concerned. Ties are also created through the sharing of knowledge and expertise to which the client would otherwise not have access.

When structural ties are strong, even dissatisfied clients may stay loyal due to the high switching costs involved. Some experts discuss 'strategic bundling', whereby companies build barriers to customer defections through offering groups of interrelated products. Banks, for example, may offer several different types of accounts, together with mortgage and loan facilities. Despite dissatisfaction with one or more of these services, the costs to the customer of switching to a competitor may be substantial when all the services are taken into account. (The growing significance of collaborative relationships with customers and the formation of networks of collaborative organisations is discussed in more detail in Chapter 15 on strategic alliances and networks.)

Creating delighted customers

One view is that the most fundamental basis for establishing a lasting relationship with clients, and moving them up the ladder to become supporters, advocates or even partners, is by ensuring that customers get more from the relationship than they were originally looking for. However, we expressed some reservations about this view earlier.

Historically, research has suggested that merely satisfying customers is rarely enough to give them a reason for staying loyal and becoming advocates rather than merely clients (Jones and Sasser, 1995; Reichheld, 1993). Depending on the level of competition in the market, and hence the level of choice available to the customer, and the degree of involvement the customer feels with the product or service, customer retention rates among 'satisfied' customers may vary dramatically. For example, some time ago, British Airways found that its retention rate was exactly the same among satisfied and dissatisfied customers. As noted earlier, customer retention is not the same thing as customer satisfaction and loyalty. Reichheld (1993) reports that 65–85 per cent of customers who defect say they were satisfied with their former supplier. Among dissatisfied customers (with freedom of choice), retention rates rarely exceed 20 per cent, and among the seriously dissatisfied, 'terrorists' or 'well poisoners' can pose a significant threat to the business as they tell others about their poor experiences.

The concept of customer delight receives some support, though. For example, Guy Kawasaki, an Internet entrepreneur who worked on the marketing of Apple Macs in the 1980s, uses the word 'enchantment' to describe the 'process of delighting people with a product, service, organisation or idea'. He claims that the outcome of enchantment and delighted customers is 'voluntary and long-lasting support that is mutually beneficial' (Kawasaki, 2012).

It appears to follow that to improve the probability of customer retention, it may be necessary to go beyond what is expected and deliver even greater value to customers. Among very satisfied or delighted customers, retention rates are significantly higher, and they are more likely to become 'apostles', or advocates, telling others of their good experiences. Creating delighted customers demands that a high priority be given to customer service, both in the strategies the organisation designs and the actions it takes in the marketplace.

Nonetheless, there remains controversy in this area, and some authorities would suggest that delighting customers is a fast route to losing money, since many customers will happily receive and demand benefits that are not justified by their value to the seller:

> The idea that companies must 'delight' their customers has become so entrenched that managers rarely examine it. . . loyalty has a lot more to do with how well companies deliver on their basic, even plain-vanilla promises than on how dazzling the service experience might be. Yet most companies have failed to realise this and pay dearly in terms of wasted investments and lost customers.
> *(Dixon et al., 2010)*

Recall the views of Barwise and Meehan, considered at the beginning of the chapter, on the power of providing customers with good value for money rather than gimmicks.

It is clear that some considerable care is needed in assessing the investment required to retain a customer compared to the actual benefits achieved by retaining them. (We consider this further in a business-to-business context in Chapter 14.)

13.4   Customer service

Where customer service is seen as key to competing effectively, conventional wisdom is that there are three critical ingredients to successful service provision. These have been called the 'three Ss of service': strategy, systems and staff.

First, there is a need to have a clear service strategy that is communicated throughout the organisation, so that everyone knows their role in providing service to customers and clients. The strategy needs to demonstrate the company's commitment to service and its role in overall corporate strategy. Increasingly, companies are using customer satisfaction measures alongside financial and other criteria for measuring overall performance, signalling the higher priority they now give to creating customer satisfaction. Indeed, some of these companies now promote and reward staff on the basis of customer satisfaction ratings achieved.

Second, not only do firms need to be committed to superior service in their strategies, but they need to put in place the systems to enable their staff to deliver service to their clients.

Third, and perhaps most important of all, the staff must recognise the importance of customer service and be committed to providing it. That means recruiting, training and empowering employees to provide the levels of service that will create customer delight and then rewarding them appropriately. Central is the provision of information, both on what customers require and how well the organisation is doing in providing that level of service. Also important is the power for employees to make decisions that will affect the level of service provided. One analyst advises executives: 'Remember there are two groups of people who know the business better than you do. They are customers and the people who deal with them. You need to talk to them both, often' (Skapinker, 2003).

13.5   Providing superior service

If superior service is an important element of competitive positioning (accepting this is not always the case), then understanding the requirements for providing better service becomes an important management concern. In fact, there is long-standing research literature published in the United States (Berry and Parasuraman, 1991) and in Europe (Gummesson, 1987; Grönroos, 1994; Payne *et al.*, 1995) that looks at the nature of 'service' and what constitutes excellent or superior service in the eyes of customers.

Much of the literature on customer satisfaction measurement (such as Berry and Parasuraman, 1991) concludes that customers measure their experiences against a benchmark of the service they expect to receive. The quality of service provision, and subsequently the level of satisfaction of the customer, is directly related to the difference (or 'gap') between expectations and experiences (see Figure 13.6). This has become the conventional wisdom in assessing service quality, though it should be noted that some recent research challenges the notion that buyers have pre-formed expectations of this kind, and looks for other approaches to measuring service quality, such as comparing the importance of a service attribute to its performance, or simply the measurement of performance alone (for example, see Caruana *et al.*, 2000).

13.5.1 Expectations

In the conventional approach to service quality measurement, Berry and Parasuraman (1991) discuss two different ways in which expectations may be used as comparison standards. First, there are expectations of what customers believe will occur in a service encounter. These they call predictive expectations. Second, there are what customers want from the service encounter – their desires. These two levels indicate adequate and desired levels of service. Between these two levels, Berry and Parasuraman (1991) suggest there is a 'zone of tolerance'. A performance level above the zone of tolerance will pleasantly surprise the customer and strengthen loyalty, while performance below the zone of tolerance will create customer dissatisfaction, frustration and may ultimately lead to decreased customer loyalty (see Figure 13.7). Their research showed that both types of expectations are dynamic – over time, expectations generally increase. There was some suggestion, however, that desired levels change more slowly than adequate levels.

Several factors have been found to influence expectations, ranging from the personal needs of the customer through to the alternative services considered, and to the specific promises made by service providers in their bid to win business in the first place.

Figure 13.6
Assessing
customer
satisfaction

Source: Adapted from
Parasuraman, Zeithaml
and Berry (1985).

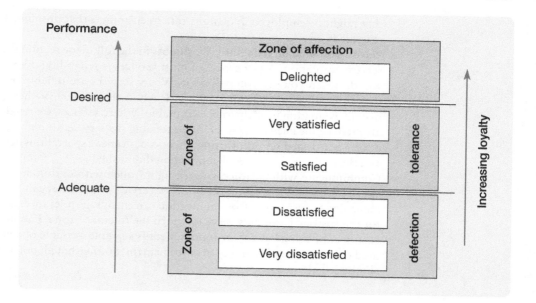

Figure 13.7
Performance, satisfaction and customer loyalty

Word-of-mouth communications with influencers and the customers' past experiences also affect service level expectations.

Prior experiences with the service provider, or with similar providers, are often the starting point in creating expectations. When customers step into a restaurant they are often judging the experience based on other restaurants they have visited. They typically make verbal comparisons: 'It was more relaxed than. . . '; 'The food was better than it was at. . . '. In addition to the customer's own prior experiences, expectations are also often affected by the opinions of friends, relatives or colleagues, who have related their experiences. Depending on the standing of these opinion makers in the customer's esteem, they can have a significant influence on what is expected, and even deter trial of a particular service.

A third major determinant of expectations is the promises the company itself makes prior to customers using it. These promises, by way of advertising messages, sales pitches and general image created through pricing strategies and so on, set up standards to which the company is expected to live. Pitching them can be difficult: promising too little may result in failing to attract the customers in the first place (they may be seduced by more attractive competitor promises); promising more than can be delivered may result in dissatisfied customers. The smarter companies manage their customers' expectations at each step of the service encounter, so that expectations align with what the firm can actually deliver (Coye, 2004).

Managing and exceeding customer expectations

From Figure 13.7 it can be seen that, in order to create delighted customers, organisations need to exceed customer expectations. There are two main ways to achieve this: provide an excellent service or manage customer expectations downwards so that they *can* be exceeded. These methods are not, of course, mutually exclusive, but should be used together. Berry and Parasuraman (1991) offer a number of suggestions for managing customer expectations:

- **Ensure promises reflect reality:** Explicit and implicit promises are directly within the control of the organisation, yet many promise what they can never deliver in the desire to win business. Promises should be checked beforehand with the personnel responsible for delivering them, to ensure they are achievable, and attention paid to methods that might be employed to demonstrate to customers that promises have been kept (or exceeded).

- **Place a premium on reliability:** We discuss in the following section the main elements of service evaluation. A key aspect of most services is reliability: doing what you say you will do when you say you will do it. Where services are reliably performed, although they may fall down on other criteria (such as the manner of their performance), the overall evaluation is likely to be acceptable. Where services are reliably performed they also reduce the need for reworking or redoing the service – a highly visible indicator of poorly performed service. During rework, customer expectations are likely to be raised and the chances of successful completion diminished.

- **Communicate with customers:** Keeping in touch with customers to understand their expectations and to explain the limits of service possibilities can be a powerful way of managing expectations. Communication can encourage tolerance, demonstrate concern for the customer and may serve to widen the tolerance zone. Phoning ahead to warn a customer of being late for an appointment is a simple example of communication being used to reduce the probability of customer frustration (though not a guarantee it will be eliminated altogether).

13.5.2 Evaluation

Customers evaluate the performance of a service provider against expectations. Again, there are a number of factors that customers typically take into account when evaluating the service they have received. The most enduring classification is the five-dimensional model proposed by Parasuraman *et al.* (1988) and easily remembered by the acronym RATER: reliability, assurance, tangibles, empathy and responsiveness:

- **Reliability** is the ability of the provider to perform the promised service dependably and accurately. In other words, it is conformance to specification – doing what you said you would do when you said you would do it. In many service situations, reliability has been shown to be the single most important aspect to many customers. Besides contributing to customer satisfaction, reliable service reduces the costs of redoing the service and can contribute to higher employee morale and enthusiasm (Berry and Parasuraman, 1991).

- **Assurance** stems from the knowledge and courtesy of employees and their facility to convey trust and confidence in their technical abilities. Customers want to be assured that the chef in the restaurant can cook without giving them food poisoning, that the garage mechanic can fix the car and that their accountant will not have them convicted for tax evasion. Assurance stems from professional competence. It is not enough, however, merely to have a high level of competence. It must also be demonstrated to the customers, often through the use of tangible cues.

- **Tangibles** are the appearance of physical features: equipment, personnel, reports, communications materials and so on. Chartered accountants, for example, are critically aware of the impression their physical appearance creates with their clients. Care and attention is exercised when choosing company cars for partners and managers. Too expensive or luxurious a car might signal to clients that they are paying too high a fee for the services they are getting, while too cheap a car might signal that the firm is not particularly successful. Tangibles can be used in this way as indicators of professional competence.

- **Empathy** is the provision of caring, individualised attention to customers. It is the quality that good doctors have of being able to convince patients that they really care about their welfare beyond addressing the current ailment. Empathy implies treating customers as individual clients and being concerned with their longer-term interests.

- **Responsiveness** is the ability of the organisation to react positively and in time to customer requests and requirements. Some businesses (such as Richardson Sheffield Ltd, which makes kitchen knives under the Laser brand), have built their positions on being more responsive to the customer than their competitors. Richardson Sheffield claims to respond to written enquiries within the day, electronic enquiries within minutes and telephone enquiries instantly. They can also provide samples of products the next working day, even to new specifications. In some markets, instantaneous (or near-instantaneous) responsiveness is critical. In Japan, for example, a key factor for success in the elevator business is the speed with which faults are fixed. Responsiveness typically requires flexibility. Customer requests can often be offbeat, unexpected. The highly responsive organisation will need to predict where possible, but build into its systems and operations the capacity to respond to the unpredictable.

These five main dimensions of service quality have been found in many different service situations, from banking to restaurants, construction to professional services (Parasuraman *et al.*, 1988). The relative importance of each might vary, and the way in which each is manifested in any situation will be different, but time and again these factors have been shown to be relevant to customers in their evaluation of the services they receive.

13.6   Customer relationship management

The importance of enhanced customer relationships has led to large investments by many companies in formalised customer relationship management (CRM) systems – most commonly manifested in call centres, customer service/loyalty programmes and data warehousing. In fact, CRM is better understood as a cross-functional core business process concerned with achieving improved shareholder value through the development of effective relationships with key customers and customer segments (Payne and Frow, 2005).

For example, the French hotel group Accor links CRM data to its guest survey information in its Sofitel and Novatel hotels, to anticipate the preferences of frequent users. The vice president for sales and marketing for Accor North America notes:

> It takes us back to the time when there were small inns and the owner knew every customer and treated them as an individual. It should help streamline check-in and accommodate preferences for guests who, for example, request the same room every time. The group will be able to market with a microscope instead of a telescope.
> *(Edmunds, 2000)*

The goal of CRM systems is to form and sustain valuable customer relationships (Kale, 2004). CRM encourages a focus on customer loyalty and retention, with the goal of winning a large share of the total lifetime value of each profitable customer. However, one of the primary conclusions of research concerning CRM performance is that achieving desired customer outcomes requires alignment with the entire organisation – avoiding the narrow and incomplete perspective of viewing CRM just as the technology of call centres and data warehousing.

It is clear that successful CRM initiatives are guided by a carefully formulated and implemented organisational strategy. CRM offers sellers the opportunity to gather customer information rapidly, identify the most valuable customers over the relevant time period and increase customer loyalty by providing customised products and services (Cravens and Piercy, 2012). This has been described as 'tying in an asset', when the asset is the customer and CRM supports a customer-responsive strategy. The logic is that CRM expertise gains competitive advantage for a company when it:

- delivers superior customer value by personalising the interaction between the customer and the company;
- demonstrates the company's trustworthiness and reliability to the customer;
- tightens connections with the customer;
- achieves the coordination of complex organisational capabilities around the customer (Day, 2000).

Nonetheless, there have been many criticisms of the operation of CRM systems in practice, and questions raised about their real impact. Call centres are frequently disliked by customers. The recent case of a call centre in the UK making 6 million cold calls in a single day – selling debt consolidation and legal claims against financial institutions – illustrates the source of some consumer annoyance (Davies *et al.*, 2015).

Moreover, the reputational damage from crude culling of apparently less-valuable customers may be substantial. Barclays Bank has attracted negative publicity and lost customers by shifting customers from one account to another because they did not meet an income threshold – effectively suggesting they were too poor to merit a paid-for account (Black, 2015). Similarly, private banks such as Deutsche Bank Private Wealth Management have been 'managing out' lower-margin customers, even those with portfolios worth hundreds of thousands of pounds – they are rich, just not rich enough (Cumbo, 2012). Similar approaches have led to good payers on credit cards having their cards withdrawn because the card operator makes low margins from such customers (Ashton and Watts, 2008). The gain from tactical customer culling should be weighed carefully against the threat to the company's reputation, image and competitive position, and its ability to deliver its marketing strategy.

Generally, the successful implementation of CRM is linked to the following factors:

- a front office that integrates sales, marketing and service functions across all media (call centres, people, retail outlets, value chain members, Internet);
- a data warehouse that stores customer information and the appropriate analytical tools with which to analyse those data and learn about customer behaviour;
- business rules developed from the data analysis to ensure the front office benefits from the firm's learning about its customers;
- measures of performance that enable customer relationships to continually improve;
- integration into the firm's operational support (or 'back office' systems), ensuring the front office's promises are delivered (Knox *et al.*, 2003).

However, research by consultants Bain & Co. suggests that there are four significant pitfalls to avoid in CRM initiatives:

1 Implementing CRM before creating a customer strategy – success relies on making astute strategic customer and positioning choices, and this outweighs the importance of the computer systems, software, call centres and other technologies.
2 Putting CRM in place before changing the organisation to match – CRM affects more than customer-facing processes; it also impacts internal structures and systems that may have to change.
3 Assuming that more CRM technology is necessarily better, rather than matching the technology to the customer strategy.
4 Investing in building relationships with disinterested customers, instead of those who value the business (Rigby *et al.*, 2002).

From the perspective of marketing strategy and competitive positioning, it is important to consider the CRM interface as a key element of the capability of a company to manage customer relationships effectively. CRM capabilities and investments need to be examined when formulating and implementing effective customer strategies.

13.7   E-service quality[*]

The rapid and pervasive growth in online trading by both consumers and businesses underlines the need to include online service and relational issues in executive thinking. This is relevant in both the pure-play or Internet-only operations (such as Amazon.com) and for companies combining 'bricks and mortar' and online channels in their value chains (for example, Tesco stores and Tesco Direct).

13.7.1 Online versus offline

In fact, Internet retailing is a multi-billion-pound industry that continues to experience double-digit growth rates. Intense competition and increasingly demanding customers make the delivery of high-quality services vital for success in this marketplace.

There has been wide-ranging research into online services quality. The first wave of early research focused on simple measures such as website usage statistics. From this, researchers moved on to look specifically at the website as the key aspect of online service. In the past several years, focus has shifted again to consider measuring the online service experience as a whole. There remains little consensus on the exact dimensions of online service quality, with many studies providing different results (see, for instance, Parasuraman et al., 2005 or Wolfinbarger and Gilly, 2003). However, it is possible to identify several broad themes in online research. First, the core delivery of products and services is the foundation of quality service in any context, be it online or offline. This said, two major differences emerge in comparing online to offline service: the company–customer interface becomes technologically mediated, and the role of trust is accentuated as the service provider is more separated from the customer.

The continuing importance of service fulfilment

Some important differences do exist in the customer service experience when shopping online – for example, those buyers with the technological competence to shop online are attracted to a wider range of products and the opportunity to shop at any time from home, as well as lower prices than traditional retail. Nonetheless, despite these unique characteristics of online purchasing, service fulfilment and delivery reliability remain the most important aspects of service quality and the strongest predictor of customer satisfaction online. Offering better-quality service can enable online and offline retailers to achieve significant competitive advantage, charge higher prices and benefit from customer recommendations.

Service fulfilment covers a range of customer service issues. For instance, Parasuraman et al. (1988) emphasise reliability, responsiveness and willingness to help customers as the critical elements in customer service. On the other hand, Warrington and Eastlick (2003) highlight product range and pricing as vital when dealing with physical products, while Dabholkar et al. (1996) propose product quality and availability as the most important issues. Pragmatically, these issues concern the delivery of the core product or service of the nature described and at the time promised to the customer. In Internet commerce, this basic mission remains the foundation for service delivery. This includes accurately displaying and describing products, the required items being in stock, delivery of what is ordered when promised and accurate billing. When problems occur, responding to customer issues effectively is also increasingly important.

Change at the customer–company interface

The clearest difference in online versus offline service is the technology mediated nature of the customer–company interface. Traditional service quality issues related to human-to-human

---

[*] The section of this chapter concerning e-service has been contributed by Dr Niall C. Piercy, University of Bath, UK, from unpublished sources.

interactions (such as responsiveness or empathy), as well as the context of service delivery (tangible elements), are replaced with customer experiences via the website. Offline, the design, quality and surroundings of the physical retail store and the knowledge, nature and actions of sales staff all send signals to customers about the quality of products and services on offer. These important sensory cues about the reliability of the product and store are absent online. The website therefore takes on a dual role as substitute for both physical context and human interaction in signalling the potential credibility and quality of the business prior to purchase. Such signals become more important online, where the customer is dislocated from the business and requires greater reassurance.

Online customers also place greater importance on information about products and companies prior to purchase online. The Internet makes information location easier but the computer screen provides a smaller viewing window, with different characteristics, than a traditional retail store, so information must be concisely and usefully conveyed in a customer-friendly format.

The website also takes on a role in providing personal service. Internet purchasing often lacks the feedback of face-to-face or telephone interactions, making it harder for Internet sellers to customise service offerings. Technology does allow for customised service by remembering customers' previous purchases in order to make recommendations of potential products to buy, which can drive sales. Nonetheless, the website plays a crucial role in online service, but remains only one part of the broader service bundle.

An increased role for trust and assurance

Interestingly, offline evaluations of service quality have paid relatively little attention to customer trust issues. Major offline service studies, such as the SERVQUAL measure of Parasuraman *et al.* (1988) or the retail adaptation by Dabholkar *et al.* (1996), include no specific dimension on trust or security. However, the separation of the customer from the company in Internet buying suggests a significantly greater importance for trust in effective online strategies.

Trust in the online environment is multifaceted and complex. Three key trust issues appear in online retail: that the company will deliver products as promised; that the company will respect customer privacy, not disclosing personal details to third parties; and that the company will securely handle financial information. These issues affect both new and long-term Internet users. Some research has found that trust in the company can be a major driver of customer loyalty, far more than is the case with offline selling (Harris and Goode, 2004).

As Internet commerce has continued to grow, and online company brand names have become as recognised, or more, as those in offline operations, many thinkers have suggested that trust issues may decline in importance. Research in the early part of the 2000s started to back this up, identifying a role for trust that is reduced from the early pivotal role suggested by some analysts (Wolfinbarger and Gilly, 2003). However, by 2019 the role of Internet companies and social media in various scandals and social harms appears to have rolled back any progress made by online companies in generating trust in consumers and the public. Certainly, most customers now expect to get what they bought online, but trust issues now centre on the use of personal information and behavioural data, as well as the prevalence of untrustworthy information ('fake news', etc.) online. Such global issues affect perceptions of all online businesses. Thus, online service quality cannot be evaluated without major attention being placed on trust issues.

It is important that management thinking about customer service quality perceptions and relationships with sellers should recognise important differences in their growing online channels compared to more conventional offline operations. Not least among the reasons is that customers who become disaffected because of online experiences with a company may easily transfer their negative perceptions to the company's offline business.

13.8 Measuring and monitoring customer satisfaction

One start to measuring customer satisfaction can be made through complaint and suggestion systems. These catch those highly dissatisfied customers who bother to complain. The problem, of course, is that it may be too late to retrieve the situation, though swift attention to customer problems has actually been shown to help bond closer relationships – what Berry and Parasuraman (1991) refer to as 'doing the service *very* right the second time'.

For every dissatisfied customer who complains, however, it is estimated that around 12 others will be equally dissatisfied but not bother to complain. They will simply take their business elsewhere and may even tell others about their bad experiences (the 'well poisoners'). There is, therefore, a need for a more systematic assessment of customer satisfaction rather than sitting back and waiting for problems to emerge.

A more systematic approach is the use of regular customer satisfaction surveys, as now used by many service providers from railway companies to the leading international accounting firms. A four-step approach is typically adopted (see Figure 13.8):

1 **Identify the factors that are important to customers:** These are not necessarily the same as the factors that managers think are important. Qualitative research techniques such as group discussions and depth interviews can be useful here. Depth interviews with the clients of a large accountancy firm showed that partners demonstrating that they really cared about the development of the client's business (showing empathy) was critical to building a long-term relationship.

2 **Assess the relative importance of the factors identified and measure customer expectations on those factors:** While some clients may expect their problems to be dealt with immediately, others may have more relaxed expectations. While for some reliability may be paramount, for others cost could be more critical.

3 **Assess performance of the service provider on the factors important to the clients:** Here it can be useful to assess directly performance relative to expectations (Parasuraman *et al.*, 1994). Did performance live up to, fall short of, or exceed expectations? At this stage, a useful summary can be made of the factors under consideration in a performance–importance comparison (see Figure 13.9). Here the factors are plotted in terms of their importance to customers and the performance of the firm on them.

A typical example is shown in Figure 13.10 for a firm of chartered accountants (disguised data). The evaluations were made by a client – a finance director of a large national company. The factors were identified through depth interviews and the evaluations of performance made against 'what would be expected of a leading firm of accountants'. The matrix can be used to focus attention on those aspects of the service of particular importance ('essential') to the client, but where performance is judged to be below par.

In the example, five elements of service were identified as being 'essential' to this client. On three of the factors, performance exceeded expectations, while on two it fell below. Technical competence ('assurance' of technical ability to perform the audits), efficient use of the client's time ('reliability' in taking the time originally specified) and

Figure 13.8
Monitoring customer satisfaction

Figure 13.9
Performance and importance

discussing charges in advance (and 'reliably' keeping to them) all constitute differentiators for this firm with their client. Where they fall down, however, is in showing little interest in the client's business (a lack of 'empathy') and some problems in the punctuality of staff or reports ('unreliable' delivery). Clearly, these factors need to be addressed as a priority.

At the next level of importance, the firm is poor at demonstrating flexibility ('responsiveness' to client requirements, especially when they change) and in being readily available to help when needed (again, a lack of 'responsiveness' to the client). On the other hand, they are well organised and have a good standard of written documents ('tangibles'). Again, areas for action are suggested.

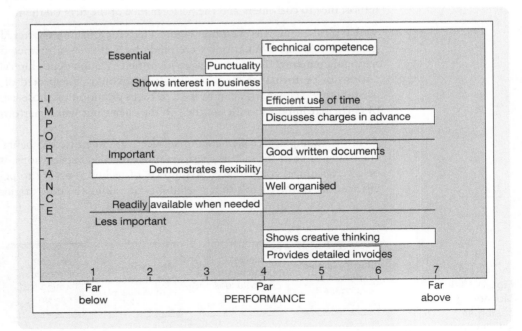

Figure 13.10
Performance summary (chartered accountant)

Finally, the chart also shows that the firm excels in areas less important to the client. They rate highly on showing creative thinking and in providing detailed invoices. It may be that providing these less important aspects of service is distracting attention from getting the basics right on the more important factors, and hence might be candidates for rationalisation. As a warning, however, we should note that sometimes factors are not important to customers until they start to go wrong. If the detailed invoices were not provided, for example, it could be that they start to become essential!

4 **Analyse the differences between expectations and performance through gap analysis:** For important factors, where there is a significant gap, there is a need to identify the reasons behind it and identify suitable remedial action.

13.8.1 Gap analysis

Figure 13.11 shows the ways in which a satisfaction gap could have arisen. By working systematically through the framework, the root causes of dissatisfaction can be identified and dealt with.

A starting point is to determine whether the provider really understood the expectations and needs of the client in the first place. The market intelligence gap is the difference between customer expectations and supplier understanding, or perception, of those expectations. This could be brought about through inadequate research of customer wants and needs, or through arrogance on the part of the supplier in assuming knowledge of the customer. It could also be brought about through poor internal communications, such that customer requirements are not passed on from the marketing researchers through to those responsible for designing the service that will be provided.

Where customer expectations are understood, they may still not be adequately catered to in the service specification. The design gap is the difference between what the supplier

Figure 13.11 Quality gap analysis

Source: Adapted from Parasuraman, Zeithaml and Berry (1985).

believes the customers expect and the service specification. This could typically be caused by resource constraints, where a service provider is too stretched to provide the service he or she knows the customer expects. Rather than increase the resource, or admit that the expected service cannot be provided, the service provider attempts to get as close as possible to customer expectations.

Even where the service specification is closely aligned to customer expectations, there is a possibility that the actual service delivered falls short. The production gap is the difference between the service specification and the service that is actually delivered to the customer. There are a number of reasons why there may be a gap here. First, the service design might be so complex as to make accurate delivery unlikely. Service promises may be unrealistic given the resources put into them. Response times planned for telephone enquiries, for example, may be unrealistic given the number of staff available to answer the phone or the number of lines available to take the calls. Second, staff may not have the skills or the systems back-up to deliver the service as specified. Poor employee training, poor technology provision or even inadequate internal communications can result in frustrated employees unable to deliver the service as specified to the customer. Third, a major problem in service provision is the very heterogeneity of services. The quality of service can vary from employee to employee, and from time to time for the same employee. Quality control systems are more difficult to implement in services than in manufacturing; they can be no less important, however.

The final gap that can lead to a satisfaction gap is the perceptual gap. Here it may be that the service has been delivered to specification and that the specification was in tune with customer expectations, but that the client, for one reason or another, does not believe the service has been delivered as expected. This could be brought about through poor use of tangible cues, lack of reinforcement of delivery, poor delivery manner or through the intercession of external influencers. In many ways, a perceptual gap is the easiest to rectify. It requires the service provider to demonstrate to the client that the service really has been delivered to original expectations.

Summary

There is growing controversy surrounding conventional prescriptions of high customer service and relationship-building investments that executives should consider. Nonetheless, this chapter focuses on the idea that, for many companies, successful competitive positioning is about creating ongoing relationships with selected target customers, rather than relying on more sporadic transactions. However, an important strategic choice exists regarding the appropriate or 'right service' level and quantity for a specific firm. In general terms, relationship marketing seeks to build longer-term relationships with selected customers, moving them up the relationship marketing ladder from customers to clients to supporters to advocates and ultimately, where applicable, to partners. A major factor in creating longer-term relationships is often the provision of superior service, beyond original customer expectations.

Customer satisfaction monitoring is a means of assessing the quality of the service offered. Where there is a gap between expectations and customer evaluations of the service provided, a systematic gap analysis can be used to identify and eliminate the causes. Renewed attention is being given to service quality and customer satisfaction issues in the context of online trading and the mix between 'bricks-and-mortar' and online offers in new types of value chain.

Case study

Property portals hand control to homeowners

By Kate Allen

Source: Sjscreens/Alamy Stock Photo.

One of Britain's least popular professions, the high street estate agent, is facing a shake-up as the digital revolution finally reaches the business of selling and renting bricks and mortar.

The growing popularity of property portals Rightmove and Zoopla has made it possible for homeowners to take control out of estate agents' hands.

It has enabled the rise of online estate agencies, which offer sellers and landlords a way of advertising on the portals without having to pay the high fees that traditional high street agents charge. Portals do not allow individual sellers to list properties directly but they do permit them to list through online agencies.

A recent survey by analysts Jefferies found that 79 per cent of consumers would list their homes directly if they were allowed to. Three-quarters said estate agents' fees were too high.

Most high street estate agents charge between 1 and 2 per cent of the property's sale value, plus value added tax at 20 per cent of the fee. With the average British home now worth £265,000, that could cost the seller more than £6,000.

Online agents such as emoov, Hatched and Housenetwork charge roughly £300–£600 for their main packages and have a sliding scale of fees, depending on which optional services a seller chooses. Options include photography, floor plans, and help with appointments and negotiations.

Yet to date they have only claimed a tiny slice of the market – just 2 per cent of home sales. By contrast they make up more than 10 per cent in the US, France, Canada and Germany.

Even the most established sites have sold only a few thousand homes so far; in total there are 1m properties for sale or rent every day on Rightmove.

But in recent months there has been a flurry of activity in the online agency sector – spurred in part by rising house prices and transaction volumes – that is creating more business for all parts of the estate agency industry.

This week veteran fund manager Neil Woodford backed start-up Purplebricks with a £7m investment. And next month entrepreneur Stelios Haji-Ioannou will launch his new site, easyProperty.

'Traditional agents have got to wake up to the modern world – it's adapt or die,' says Robert Ellice, chief executive of easyProperty.

'The portals have enabled people to know as much about a property as the owner does, before they even view it. Sellers are better-educated than ever before and they want flexibility but the existing agents don't allow that. The industry is absolutely ripe for disruption, it's a model that hasn't changed in 30 years.'

Traditional estate agents argue that the new brand of online disrupters do not offer the same levels of customer service. Ed Mead, a director of London chain Douglas & Gordon, says 'selling a property is not like selling a car'.

'Eighty per cent of the work done in selling is after an offer is agreed, and involves a lot of hand-holding and time,' he says. 'The internet provides many things, a personal service is not one of them.'

More than a third of all deals fall through before completion and it takes agents three months on average to close a sale, Mr Mead adds.

In an important test case last year, Country Properties, a high street agent, complained to the Advertising Standards Authority about Hatched. co.uk, alleging that it was misleading advertising for Hatched to claim to offer 'a complete estate agency service at a fraction of the cost'.

Hatched won that case, with the ASA ruling that the online agent did provide a complete service that was comparable to high street agents.

Adam Day, director of Hatched, says its model fuses the best of the old with technology to customise services.

'We offer everything a high street agent does, if the client wants it,' he says. 'But it is a waste of a client's money to advertise in a newspaper or having a window display or paying the rent on a prime high street office.'

This, however, makes online agents very dependent on portals – something which not all businesses are keen on. Other start-ups are bypassing Rightmove and Zoopla to create standalone sites.

Aidan Rushby and Logan Hall launched Movebubble in June, using travel website Airbnb as an inspiration.

'Yes Rightmove and Zoopla are great channels but from a business perspective it makes you quite vulnerable,' Mr Rushby says. 'It's then a race to the bottom, who can be cheapest. That kind of business model isn't a fun one to be in – low margins, high risk and ultimately you're not the one who is finding your customers.'

Instead, Movebubble matches landlords directly with potential tenants. It is free for landlords and charges tenants a flat £50 fee if they take up a rental through the site.

'This is the age of the collaborative customer,' Mr Rushby says. 'There is a very big shift in all areas of consumer business towards openness and transparency. People love the fact that they can deal directly with each other [on the Internet].'

While Movebubble focuses on the rental market, the Little House Company helps homeowners to find buyers directly. One of Britain's oldest portals, first set up in 2000, it will relaunch with a new name and ambitious growth plans later this year.

Miles Shipside, Rightmove's commercial director, said the emergence of online agents was still only a small part of the total market: 'Consumers now have more choice than ever before with a record number of agents in the market, and ultimately they will decide what level of service they want or need.'

The disrupter: Stelios Haji-Ioannou, easyProperty

Now that budget airlines have become industry stalwarts, it is hard to remember how disruptive the arrival of easyJet was.

Founded almost two decades ago, the airline aimed to 'make flying as affordable as a pair of jeans' and made direct booking popular, cutting travel agents out of the equation.

Since then, easyGroup has brought this corporate insurrectionism to other industries including hotel rooms, car rental, bus services, office rental and gyms.

Now it aims to take its tried-and-tested formula to the real estate market.

Easily the biggest brand name yet to enter the online business, easyProperty will launch in September as a rentals site, with a sales site planned for next year.

Having raised an initial £5m from friends and family in February, easyGroup founder Stelios Haji-Ioannou and easyProperty chief executive Rob Ellice have just launched a second funding round targeting ultra-high net worth individuals and individual private City figures.

With 10,000 properties already pre-registered, the site aims to be letting around 4,000–5,000 homes a month by the end of this year and is considering expanding across Europe within three years.

'We have very aggressive targets, we are going into the market in a very big way,' Mr Ellice said. 'The main problem with high street estate agents is wastage – only around 25 per cent of the deals that agents pitch for actually generate cash for their bottom line. It's a very inefficient model.'

By contrast easyProperty plans to avoid upfront fees but users will pay for optional extras. Services such as hosting viewings, drawing up floor plans and advising on pricing will be carried out by its network of 400 freelancers.

The big spender: Neil Woodford, Purplebricks

The face of Invesco Perpetual for more than a quarter of a century, Mr Woodford's new £2.3bn fund invests in small, rapidly growing companies.

His latest – taking a £7m stake in newly launched online estate agency Purplebricks – marks the biggest investment to date by a major investor into the emerging digital home sales market.

Launched in April, Purplebricks only operates in parts of southern England, and has sold fewer than 500 homes. But it has plans to roll out to the Midlands this autumn and aims to build to national scale and a £100m turnover within two years.

Chief executive Michael Bruce previously ran a traditional high street estate agency chain. Seeing the scope for 'a more cost-effective, convenient and transparent means of selling property', he sold his business in 2011 and invested an initial £1.5m in creating a software platform and website.

Since then he has put together a staff of 80 people, which will rise to 500 by the time the site is fully national. Four-fifths of these are 'boots on the ground' workers whose job it is to present a friendly and experienced face to potential clients.

'People aren't yet ready to go entirely online,' Mr Bruce says. 'They still want guidance from an expert on pricing and some local presence [in the property market].'

Purplebricks represents a fusion of old and new; its key goal is to make property selling into a 24-hour business. 'You can book a restaurant or a hairdresser 24 hours a day, but you can't currently do that with an estate agent,' Mr Bruce said.

The veteran: Sarah Beeny, Tepilo

Television personality and veteran property developer Sarah Beeny was one of the first on the digital home-selling scene, launching Tepilo.com in 2009.

Initially set up to cut estate agents out of the sales process completely, letting sellers and buyers interact directly with each other, it relaunched last autumn taking on a more traditional intermediary role.

That move, says Ms Beeny, was entirely driven by the need to get properties on to online property portals Rightmove and Zoopla.

'Our customers wanted to be there, the vast majority of people buying a house will be looking on those sites,' she said.

But expanding into estate agency does not necessarily mean taking on all the trappings. 'The old model of having a high street shop with branded cars and an in-house coffee shop and all those costs is part of the reason why estate agents have had to charge so much for so long,' cautions Ms Beeny. 'We felt there should be an option for people not to have to pay £6,000–10,000 just to get their home seen by buyers.'

Tepilo is selling around 50 homes a month and aims to reach £1m in turnover in its first year as an agent. It has about 25 employees, with a register of freelance local surveyors who visit advertised properties.

Ms Beeny is a serial digital entrepreneur, having also set up dating website Mysinglefriend. She first got the idea for a property-selling website while working as a developer.

'All my businesses have started from a sense of irritation that nobody else has done something that I've wanted,' she says. 'Tepilo was born when I thought that I don't understand why I'm having to pay up to 2.5 per cent plus VAT to sell a house.'

The experience is now feeding back into her day job – this autumn she will host a Channel 4 show called *Clicks And Mortar*, in which families try to sell their homes online.

 Source: from 'Property portals hand control to homeowners', *Financial Times*, 22/08/14 (Allen, K.).

Discussion questions

1   How can 'customer service' be a differentiator in the service industry?

2   How can a company such as easyProperty ensure 'e-service quality'?

3   Do you agree with Ed Mead when he said 'the internet provides many things, a personal service is not one of them'? Explain your reasons.

4   The information in this case dates from 2014, when online real estate was in its infancy. Explore the current state of the market in the UK. Who continues to be successful of the companies mentioned? Why, in your view? How has the industry evolved?

PART 5
IMPLEMENTING THE STRATEGY

Part 5 examines a number of the most topical and relevant issues emerging in marketing practice, which have a profound influence on a company's decisions about marketing strategy and competitive positioning. These topics are linked by a focus on the challenges of implementing or executing marketing strategies.

We feature here two areas not extensively covered in traditional approaches to marketing strategy: the management of strategic customer relationships through sales and account management processes (Chapter 14), and the topical question of corporate social responsibility and ethical standards and their links to competitive positioning and advantage (Chapter 17). The logic for these additional points of focus is that these are topics proving of substantial and growing significance to the shaping and implementation of marketing strategy, particularly in the post-recession environment we now face.

In the earlier parts of the text, we have provided extensive coverage of the analytical and theoretical underpinning of marketing strategy: planning market-led strategy; analysis of the competitive marketplace and organisational capabilities; and market segmentation and competitive positioning. However, the focus now changes from the content of strategy to the context – the organisational and environmental realities in which marketing strategy must be put into effect. Nonetheless, the conventional dichotomising of strategy and implementation is largely unproductive. Both issues are interdependent parts of the same process of strategic development and market performance. It is also intriguing that in each area of strategy context that we examine, there are both challenges and obstacles for executives to meet, but also importantly new opportunities to compete more effectively and develop new types of competitive advantage.

Chapter 14 is concerned with strategic customer management. The focus here is the strategic role of the sales organisation and the development of strategic account management approaches to handle relationships with large, powerful, dominant business-to-business customers. We examine the role of strategic sales capabilities in managing business-to-business customer relationships and the evolution of the strategic sales organisation to enhance and apply these new types of capabilities. Strategic customer management is concerned both with the strategic management of investment of resources in different parts of the customer portfolio, but relatedly also with the management of relationships with strategic customers. Very large (or more strictly, very important) customers provide the domain of strategic account management – moving from transactional and relationship marketing approaches to major accounts, toward the partnering with a small number of key accounts. This strategy has potential gains in locking-in relationships with the most dominant customers in the portfolio, but also carries substantial risks from dependence and customer opportunism, which should be carefully weighed. Nonetheless, strategic account management approaches are highly topical, and a balanced case should be established prior to making decisions and commitments.

Our concern with key external dependencies continues in Chapter 15, which examines the role of alliances and networks in marketing strategy as the organisational forms developed by many organisations to take their strategies to market. Environment change and complexity has heralded for many organisations an era of strategic collaboration. We examine the drivers of collaboration strategies and the types of networks, alliances and partnerships that result. Our emphasis is in the emergence in many sectors of alliances as the way in which we compete, but we also underline the risks in strategic alliances. Competing through strategic alliances offers many potential benefits, but requires attention to the underlying rationale and priorities for collaboration and investment of effort in managing and appraising alliances, which pose quite different challenges to conventional organisational structures.

Chapter 16 turns explicit attention to strategy implementation and internal marketing, where our focus is more on key internal dependencies than external ones. We review the sources of the continuing implementation or execution challenges in marketing, and examine internal marketing as a set of tools, or a template, for structuring and managing the implementation process. The development and scope of internal marketing has been associated with enhancing service quality, improving internal communications, innovation management and internal markets, but our focus is on strategic internal marketing as a parallel to external marketing, which focuses on the organisational and behavioural changes required to effectively implement strategy. A particularly vital purpose of strategic internal marketing is achieving cross-functional collaboration and seamlessness in delivering value to customers.

The last chapter in Part 5 – Chapter 17 – focuses on the rapidly emerging area of corporate social responsibility and ethics, and its impact on the ways organisations must adapt to new societal demands, but also how it is creating new areas to consider in developing different kinds of competitive strength. Corporate social responsibility and ethical issues are linked in their relationship with corporate reputation. This chapter is concerned with an important relationship between external and internal dependencies. At one level, attention to corporate social responsibility concerns is mandated by customer pressures, both in consumer and business-to-business markets. However, a fuller consideration of the scope of corporate citizenship suggests that the drivers of social responsibility go much further than moral obligation and are linked to the ability of companies to compete effectively. We look at defensive social responsibility initiatives in responding to competitor and customer pressures. However, what emerges is a view of corporate social responsibility as a route to competitive advantage. This view emphasises a strategic perspective on social responsibilities, where a social dimension becomes part of the company's value proposition to its customers. The goal becomes not altruism for its own importance, but the combination of business and social benefits. It is clear that this challenge will be extremely important to management thinking in the current business environment.

CHAPTER 14

STRATEGIC CUSTOMER MANAGEMENT AND THE STRATEGIC SALES ORGANISATION

'Selling is changing fast and in such a way that sales teams have become strategic resources. When corporations strive to become customer focused, salespeople move to the foreground; engineers recede. As companies go to market with increasingly complex bundles of products and services, their representatives cease to be mere order takers (most orders are placed online, anyway) and become relationship managers.'

Thomas Stewart, *Harvard Business Review* (2006)

Hacker-for-hire company Synack raises $21m

By Hannah Kuchler in San Francisco

Microsoft Ventures and HP Enterprise invest in group started by ex-NSA workers

Synack, a start-up that offers hackers for hire to companies from finance to healthcare as well as the US government, has raised $21m from Microsoft Ventures, Hewlett Packard Enterprise and telecoms group Singtel.

The new investors join GV, formerly known as Google Ventures, and Silicon Valley venture capitalists Kleiner Perkins in backing the start-up, founded by two former employees of the US National Security Agency. The company has raised $55m in total.

Jay Kaplan, Synack co-founder and chief executive, said the company had experienced 'explosive growth' in the past 18 months as customers signed up to rent their 'red team', expert security researchers who hack into networks to highlight vulnerabilities.

Synack selects the top 10 per cent of security researchers who apply to be part of their platform. Companies then pay the researchers to find flaws before hackers do.

The start-up hopes to help solve the problem of a shortage of cyber security professionals, which the

Source: DragonImages/iStock/Getty Images Plus.

Global Information Security Workforce Study estimates will rise to 1.8m vacancies by 2020. Customers can access experts who they may not have been able to pay full time or who may be based in other parts of the world.

Mr Kaplan said it was particularly exciting that government agencies including the US Department of Defense and the IRS have signed up, given they are traditionally conservative and usually only employ US nationals.

'They are starting to get more and more comfortable with the notion of engaging with researchers outside of the confines of the US,' he said, adding that for now, they were only employing people from allied countries.

'The reality is they are getting attacked every single day by sophisticated adversaries all over the world. Just because you're in another country doesn't necessarily mean you are a bad person.'

Synack is also winning new clients in Europe as companies fear being fined up to 4 per cent of global revenue under the new general data protection regulations coming in next year. Mark Kuhr, co-founder and chief technology officer, said companies were rushing to improve their cyber security because the regulations will 'drastically raise the prices for a breach'.

The start-up will now work with Microsoft, Hewlett-Packard and Singtel's sales organisations to sell the platform to their customers. Nagraj Kashyap, corporate vice-president at Microsoft Ventures, said the company admired the start-up's 'innovative, crowd-focused approach'.

 Source: from 'Hacker-for-hire company Synack raises $21m', *Financial Times*, 11/04/17 (Kuchler, H.).

Discussion questions

1 What are the issues here?

2 Why has Synack linked up with Microsoft, Hewlett-Packard and Singtel?

Introduction

Many of those concerned with marketing strategy or competitive positioning pay relatively little attention to issues concerning the salesforce or strategic account management structures. The view has generally been that marketing executives and business planners make strategic decisions, create value through product and brand innovation and make strategic choices, while sales and account managers are really concerned only with the implementation of the plans created by the strategic decision makers. However, this over-simplified view of the world does not stand up to the scrutiny of managers who have to develop and implement strategy in the complex and highly competitive conditions that characterise most business-to-business situations. It is illustrative that a growing number of companies are making appointments such as 'director of strategic customer management' or 'strategic customer manager', or making other organisational changes to reflect new realities. Indeed, some firms have created a new senior executive position – 'chief revenue officer' or 'chief customer officer' – who oversees both sales and marketing functions.

For example, Proctor & Gamble, under A.G. Lafley's leadership, was transformed from the stodgy, slow-moving, inward-looking bureaucracy of the 1990s into a nimble, innovative and aggressive competitor, beating the rest in the 2000s. A significant and enduring part of that transformation was the creation of customer business development (CBD) organisations at the front of the business. The goal of CBD was to transform the old, narrow idea of buyer–seller relationships with customers, into a multifunctional, collaborative approach designed to achieve mutual volume, profit and market share objectives. CBD teams work with customers to develop the customer's plans and strategies to the advantage of both customer and P&G. CBD team members work collaboratively with experts from finance, management systems, customer service and brand management to develop and implement business strategies that deliver sustainable competitive advantage for P&G brands (Piercy and Lane, 2009a).

The ability of organisations to achieve superiority in how they manage customer relationships to create value and to sustain profitable relationships is increasingly recognised as a core capability – but a capability that has often been ignored in the literature of marketing strategy (Piercy and Lane, 2009a). This chapter seeks to explain why the sales organisation and related strategic account management activities should form an important element for executives considering the development of marketing strategy – and how they define important implementation capabilities (see Chapter 16).

Indeed, many marketing strategy implementation failures can be explained by the poor alignment of strategy with sales capabilities. One problem is that many traditional marketing and sales approaches were not designed for complex, consultative and collaborative technology-based customer relationships where, for example, the 'product' is just as much being created jointly by buyer and seller as it is being 'sold'. Sales capabilities provide a critical resource that differentiates suppliers from each other in the eyes of professional purchasers. There have been calls to recognise sales as the key to business success and worthy of a 'corner office' (Delves Broughton, 2012).

For example, it is apparent that in many sectors, traditional sales models are obsolete as a result of growing customer sophistication. Indeed, in the pharmaceuticals business, high sales pressure placed on doctors to prescribe new drugs has resulted in formal training courses in medical schools to teach future doctors how to resist sales pitches (Weintraub, 2008). This is symptomatic of the search by the pharmaceutical industry for new and better ways to get to market. Companies such as Pfizer, Wyeth, Novartis and GlaxoSmithKlein recognise that the era of 'hard sell' is over in their sector and are working to develop new, more appropriate, business models. Fundamental changes in the requirements of business customers mandate a strategic response from sellers that is more robust than simple acquiescence to demands for lower prices and higher service levels. The challenge is to reposition sales as a core part of a company's competitiveness, where the sales organisation is closely integrated into a company's business and marketing strategy (Stephens, 2003).

The pressure is on to achieve a better alignment between marketing strategy and sales and customer management capabilities. The idea of 'marketing and sales fusion' is gaining traction in many situations as a way of overcoming organisational separation and problems of coordination (Chartered Institute of Marketing, 2011). Certainly, better alignment between marketing and sales has become a priority for many companies (Act-On Software, 2015). According to a study by Aberdeen Group in 2011, highly aligned organisations achieved a 32 per cent year-on-year revenue growth, while less aligned competitors saw a 7 per cent decline in revenue (Aberdeen Group, 2011).

Of particular importance to strategic decision makers, the financial and reputational costs of some sales-related behaviours may be enormous, acting to undermine a company's market positioning and destroy its strategic credibility. In 2014, leading drugs company GlaxoSmithKlein was fined £297 million by the Chinese authorities for paying incentives to doctors to prescribe the company's drugs. The company quickly moved to stop paying its sales representatives volume-based commission and to stop paying doctors to speak on its behalf at medical conferences (Griffiths, 2014). The company was accused of systemic bribery over a sustained period of time (Anderlini *et al.*, 2014). In some ways, the company was a scapegoat for a traditional sales approach in this market – a former salesman comments, 'I never met a doctor who refused a handout unless it was too little' (Ward and Waldmeir, 2014). Nonetheless, GSK saw a 60 per cent collapse in sales in China resulting from the corruption probe (Griffiths, 2014).

The crisis in China follows fines for pharmaceutical companies in the United States related to their sales and marketing policies: GSK paid $3 billion to the Department of Justice to settle claims including 'cash payments disguised as consulting fees, expensive meals, weekend boon-doggles and lavish entertainment'; Abbott paid $1.6 billion for illegal marketing of a bipolar disorder drug; Johnson & Johnson paid $181 million to settle claims over marketing of an anti-psychotic drug, and the final bill could reach $2.2 billion (Andrew and Waldmeir, 2013). US estimates are that payments and gifts by pharmaceutical companies to physicians add up to $19 billion a year (Weintraub, 2007). Pharmaceutical

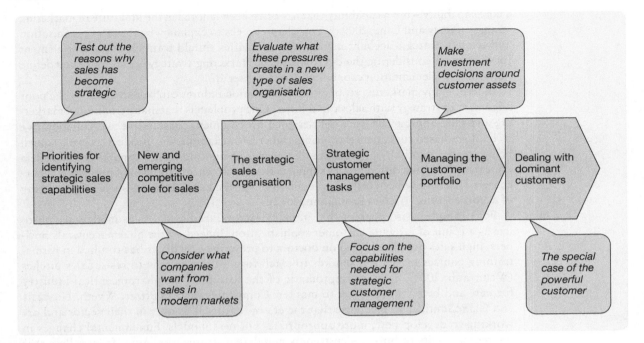

Figure 14.1 Key issues in strategic customer management

companies are not alone in being criticised for their sales and marketing approaches – financial services, public utilities and social media are very much in the firing line. Banks in the UK were warned that they were failing to shed their aggressive, bonus-led sales culture, and the regulators continue to take a close interest (Arnold, 2014).

Sales and marketing activities are under intense scrutiny on a global basis. Aside from simple damage to corporate reputation and brand equity, the danger is that crises of these kinds reduce a company's ability to implement its marketing strategy and undermine its competitive position. This underlines the strategic significance of the front-line of the business.

In this chapter, we first examine the factors that should encourage executives to re-examine the salesforce as a strategic capability, and the marketplace demands that are reinforcing these efforts. Then, we examine the strategic sales organisation – the new forms of organising the front-line resources that impact on customer relationships and deliver superiority in customer value.

This brings us to the issue of 'strategic customer management'. In the same way that companies have come to recognise the strategic aspects of operations management (for example, in total quality deployment, and business process reengineering initiatives), and in supply chain management (supplier relationship management approaches rather than simpler notions of transportation and warehousing), there is now an increasing priority for a strategic perspective on the management of customer relationships.

There are two aspects of strategic customer management. The first relates to the strategic management of the customer portfolio – making investment choices between different types of customer to deliver the goals of marketing strategy, but also to shape that strategy. The second aspect relates to the management of strategic customers – building relationships with the dominant customers in the company's portfolio, some of which may be classified as strategic accounts and handled differently in a new type of partnership-based business model. These are important strategic decisions that impact directly on the profitability and risk profile of the company's business. The structure we have adopted to cover these issues is illustrated in Figure 14.1.

14.1   Priorities for identifying strategic sales capabilities

To begin, consider the factors encouraging executives in many major organisations to re-examine the role of salesforce capabilities in the context of developing and implementing marketing strategy. This is an important starting point in understanding the potential role of strategic customer management approaches to enhancing the development and implementation of marketing strategy.

Traditional views suggest that marketing and sales should be considered separate entities in the organisation because, according to Levitt, 'Selling focuses on the needs of the seller; marketing on the needs of the buyer' (Levitt, 1960). The conventional subordination of sales (tactical) to marketing (strategic) was elaborated in statements such as Drucker's view that 'the aim of marketing is to make selling superfluous' (Drucker, 1973). However, it should be noted that Levitt was writing 60 years ago, and Drucker more than 45 years ago, underlining the risk that their views may have dated somewhat. Consider the following issues when reaching a view about the strategic significance of sales capabilities in a particular company situation. Figure 14.2 summarises the approach we are taking.

Customer relationships

Clearly, in many companies, channel development has included the establishment of direct channels, such as those based around Internet websites – in consumer marketing by 2014 almost a third of British household purchases apart from groceries were made online (Poulter, 2014b). Indeed, by 2014 Internet shopping was blamed for the closure of 16 high-street stores a day (Poulter, 2014a), and in 2019 *The Guardian* predicted that by 2029 more than half of all retail sales in the UK will be online (Butler, 2019). The proportion of spending going online is much higher for many business-to-business sellers. At the same time, there is a growing trend towards outsourcing routine sales operations to third parties (Anderson and Trinkle, 2005). In the USA, Proctor & Gamble has a 200-person team wholly dedicated to Walmart (the single customer that constitutes 20 per cent of P&G's business); it is relatively straightforward for P&G to outsource routine sales visits to stores to a third-party sales organisation. For example, Acosta in the USA provides the third-party sales team for Kellogg's, P&G and Nestlé in American supermarkets, and their clients include the number one and number two brands in most grocery categories (Boyle, 2011). Similarly, global corporate expenditure on customer relationship management (CRM) technology is measured each year in billions of dollars, and individual spends by companies can be in tens of millions of dollars. CRM explicitly aims to automate many of the functions traditionally associated with the salesforce.

However, this leaves the vital issue of whether a company's most important business-to-business customer relationships can really be managed to full advantage through a website, a third-party seller, or a call centre? Answering this question is important to understanding the strategic role of sales for a company, rather than considering only the routine activities involved in taking and processing orders, For instance, Dell Computers is an Internet-based company – the majority of sales and service provisions are on the Web. Nonetheless, Dell

Figure 14.2 Pressures on sales capabilities

maintains both account executives in the field as well as internal salespeople in branches, because the view is that the technology exists to free salespeople to sell and develop customer relationships, not to process orders (which the technology generally does better and cheaper). As Dell struggles to rebuild its weakened market position, its multichannel sales capabilities are critical to success.

There is a substantial business and competitive risk in underestimating the role of the salesforce in defending and sustaining a competitive position. Consider the case of a $210-million manufacturer of speciality industrial lubricants, based in Atlanta. Expecting, in an Internet-enabled world, that the 400-person salesforce would be increasingly irrelevant, the company spent $16 million on its website, e-portals, call centres and an integrated CRM system. When the new sales model went live, the anticipated 35 per cent sales increase in sales turned out to be an 18 per cent decline, with falling margins (largely because of the cost of the new Internet infrastructure). In addition, nearly a third of the salesforce resigned in just over a year (including 17 of the top 20 salespeople), because there was a general feeling that there was no point in staying to compete with the new website, after spending years developing personal relationships with their customers. There had been no customer involvement in developing the new sales model – the company had not bothered to ask customers how they wanted to do business. When asked, customers identified this company's only real competitive advantage as the expertise of its salesforce and their ability to design solutions to solve technical problems for customers. A new sales model now deploys salesperson expertise in the specification and design phases, and in negotiating prices and terms, and uses the Web for routine repeat purchases and order tracking; the competitive situation is being retrieved (Friedman, 2002).

Understanding and enhancing the ways in which sales resources add value and protect customer relationships is becoming of strategic importance in markets being driven towards commoditisation. To the extent that a marketing strategy depends upon strong and sustained customer relationships, there is an implicit reliance on sales capabilities. To the extent that a salesforce has built and sustains strong customer relationships by creating value for customers, this provides a strategic resource for the company, which should impact on its strategic choices.

Customer sophistication and complexity

The growing sophistication and aggressiveness of purchasers in business-to-business markets has also escalated the strategic importance of effectively managing buyer–seller relationships (Jones et al., 2005). For a company such as IBM, for example, how can traditional marketing cope with consultative selling, when the product is being designed as it is being sold? The challenge to the seller is to implement effective marketing strategy in a dramatically changed world of sophisticated buyers (Shapiro et al., 1998). This change is underlined by the shift in the traditional role played by purchasing functions in customer organisations.

Increasingly, purchasing has become a strategic function linked to the customer's strategic plans, with a major level of responsibility for profitability, cost control and enhanced shareholder value (Janda and Seshandri, 2001). Professional purchasing managers use complex sourcing metrics to select the 'right' suppliers, and to dictate terms on how they will be supplied, so more than ever supplier profitability is determined at the point of sale, where the sales organisation interacts with the customer (De Boer et al., 2001; Talluri and Narasimhan, 2004). Correspondingly, the sales task has become far more complex and the stakes much higher.

Sellers in business-to-business markets increasingly face more complex decisions about their marketing and sales investments in customer relationships. Historically, seller profits were generally in line with account size, because prices tended to be cost-based, sales costs were relatively low and the size of accounts did not vary dramatically. However, consolidation by merger and acquisition and attrition through recession has changed this situation in many markets. In industrial markets, sales situations are increasingly characterised by fewer, larger and more complex purchasing organisations, and in consumer markets there has been a massive shift in power to retailers (Shapiro *et al.*, 1998). Unsurprisingly, very large customers are powerful and demand customised sales and account management, and are challenging in terms of profitability for the supplier. Other customers also demand special treatment, but it is likely to be different. Small and medium-sized accounts require yet more different approaches, mainly because of the cost of serving them. The strategic challenge is to match sales efforts and approaches to different parts of a complex portfolio of customers, to balance revenue and profitability with business risk. These choices impact substantially on corporate performance.

Market trends of this kind have elevated the importance of the effective deployment of sales capabilities to a strategic issue. In particular, we will explore the themes of the customer portfolio and the impact of dominant customers as the chapter develops.

Commoditisation

One impact of the revolutions that have taken place in operations management and supply chain design has been to reduce product and service differentiation in many sectors. Competing products are frequently built on near-identical modularised platforms, and supply chains are designed for maximum speed and lowest cost. Benchmarking systems encourage suppliers to achieve similar performance against the same metrics. It is unsurprising that the result is growth in product similarity rather than differentiation.

In parallel, customer organisations increasingly pursue aggressive commoditisation strategies with their suppliers – if all competitive offerings are essentially similar, then differentiation can only be achieved through price, because that is how commodities are sold. This may be the preferred situation for the purchaser, but not usually for the seller. The chief purchasing officer's modern armoury includes: RFPs (Request for Proposal, or an invitation to suppliers to bid for business on a specific product or service); Internet auctions; purchasing consultants; and buying consortiums. These mechanisms all seek to reduce purchasing to a comparison of prices and product technical specifications. The challenge to sellers is to constantly expand the scope and value of the offering to the customer, and the impact of the offering on the customer's business performance. Achieving differentiation with strategic customers requires new types of buyer–seller relationships that assist customers in implementing their own strategies. This underlines the need for the sales organisation to take a more strategic and less tactical role in developing and implementing business and marketing strategy.

Indeed, it may be that the sales/customer interface is the place where competitive differentiation is actually achieved. Research by the US consultancy H.R. Chally, suggests that salesperson effectiveness accounts for as much as 40 per cent of business-to-business customer choice of supplier, because technology has made products increasingly substitutable (Stephens, 2003).

For example, SKF is the world's largest maker of industrial bearings – a business highly susceptible to commoditisation. SKF's fight to overcome commoditisation threats relies on the company's 5,000 sales engineers developing close relationships with customers and liaising with technical experts deep inside their own businesses. The goal for sales is to align customer needs with complex technical solutions, often involving customised products. In several important ways, the sales engineer stands between the company and commoditisation (Marsh, 2007).

Corporate expenditure

Corporate expenditure on sales operations is estimated to greatly exceed that on higher-profile advertising and sales promotion activities. Indeed, it is also clear that sales activities are frequently among the most expensive in the marketing budget. Research in the USA finds that while in some sectors companies spend as little as 1 per cent of revenue on their salesforce (for example, in banking or hotels), the average company spends 10 per cent of sales revenue on the salesforce, and some spend as much as 22 per cent (such as in printing and publishing) (Dartnell Corporation, 1999). Indeed, it is not uncommon for sustained salesforce costs to be as high as 50 per cent of sales in some cases (Zoltners *et al.*, 2004).

In addition, the sales function employs more people than marketing and in many companies is a much larger function. Interestingly, estimates in both the UK and the USA suggest that sales employment is expected to continue to increase. Indeed, the economic recession saw aggressive companies such as Hewlett-Packard, Southwest Airlines and FedEx actually adding to their sales resources to attack competitors weakened by the economic downturn (Piercy *et al.*, 2010a). The 'death of the salesperson' that was forecast as a result of the expansion in Internet marketing and other direct channels may actually be greatly exaggerated.

Expenditure levels and the growth in employment suggest that managers are likely to continue asking questions about the full utilisation of these resources to add value to the company. Indeed, evidence in the USA suggests that many senior managers are dissatisfied with the productivity of their sales organisations, and many see salesforce costs poorly aligned with strategic goals (Deloitte Touche, 2005). These indications support the view that the sales organisation is becoming a substantially higher-priority issue for strategic decision makers. However, notwithstanding the cost of the salesforce, the changing role of the sales organisation is driven by more than cost, and reflects the power of salesforce capabilities to change a company's competitive position for better or worse.

14.2   The new and emerging competitive role for sales[*]

Understanding the evolution of the sales organisation and the strategic capability it represents, as well as the forces shaping this capability, has become an important issue for strategic decision makers in marketing.

14.2.1 The evolution of the sales organisation to strategic importance

There is little doubt that the role of the sales organisation has gone through major changes in many companies in recent years, and it is likely that this change process will continue and escalate. However, what should not be underestimated is the extent to which such changes are increasingly radical and disruptive to traditional business models and theories (Shapiro *et al.*, 1998).

For example, in identifying priorities for sales, Thomas Leigh and Greg Marshall wrote that 'the sales function is undergoing an unparalleled metamorphosis, driven by the plethora of changing conditions' (Leigh and Marshall, 2001). They suggested that this metamorphosis was seeing the selling function shift its role from that of selling products and services to one emphasising 'increased customer productivity', through enhanced revenues or cost advantage. They support the transformation of the traditional sales function to a pan-company activity or process, driven by market pressures: 'customers indicate that the seller's organisation must embrace a customer-driven culture that wholeheartedly supports the salesforce' (Leigh and Marshall, 2001). Interestingly, they also underline the parallel between the transformation of the sales organisation and other company-wide marketing developments, such as market orientation (Jaworski and Kohli, 1993), market-oriented organisational culture (Homburg and Pflesser, 2000) and marketing as a cross-functional process rather than a functional department (Workman *et al.*, 1998).

---

[*] This section of the chapter draws on Piercy and Lane, *Strategic Customer Management: Strategizing the Sales Organization*, Oxford: Oxford University Press, 2009.

Another analysis suggested that:

the sales function is in the midst of a renaissance – a genuine rebirth and revival. Progressive firms are becoming more strategic in their approaches to the sales function. . . Enlightened firms view their customers as assets, and are entrusting their salespeople to management of these assets.
(Ingram et al., 2002)

These authors call for joint action by sales managers, educators, trainers, consultants and professional organisations to improve the conceptualisation and practice of sales management. Certainly, there appears growing consensus that traditional approaches will fail, and that 'the shaping of the selling function has become a strategic corporate issue', requiring clarity about the new sales role, new structures and new management approaches (Shapiro *et al.*, 1998).

Many suggest that this revolution has already arrived, even if marketing executives (and educators) have yet to notice. One British commentator has suggested that: 'sales functions are in the early stages of a transformation comparable to that which reshaped manufacturing 20 years ago' (Mazur, 2000). The evolution of the sales organisation is already becoming apparent in studies of marketing organisations, and there is growing evidence of the expanding influence of sales over strategic decisions. For example, research findings suggest that the sales department has more influence than the marketing department on many so-called 'marketing' decisions (Krohmer *et al.*, 2002), and that 'primary marketing coordinators increasingly reside in sales rather than the marketing organisation' (Homburg *et al.*, 2000), while sales plays a growing role in formulating as well as executing marketing strategies (Cross *et al.*, 2001). In fact, even the success of marketing initiatives such as market orientation may depend in large part on the sales organisation – for example, one study shows the impact of market orientation on performance to be fully mediated by the adoption of customer-orientated selling by the salesforce (Langerak, 2001). Similarly, the sales organisation may have a decisive influence on shaping the direction of new product innovation through the intelligence collected and how it is interpreted (Lambert *et al.*, 1990), and in assessing and accessing targeted key market segments (Maier and Saunders, 1990).

A more strategy-orientated salesforce has to cope with a range of interfaces with internal functions and departments, and increasingly partner organisations, to deliver value seamlessly to customers. For example, when Sam Palmisano took over as CEO at IBM, he conducted a painful overhaul of the 38,000-person salesforce (see Hamm, 2005, 2008). In the 1990s, salespeople representing the various IBM business units were essentially on their own – looking for good opportunities to sell individual products or services. Palmisano 'reintegrated' IBM in front of customers by bringing together specialists from computers, software, consulting and even research into teams that meet with customers to help solve their business problems and develop new business strategies. Collaborating with customers, suppliers and even rivals was part of his plan to invent new technologies and to create new markets. IBM's new sales capabilities underpinned a strong performance during the economic recession by focusing on technical services rather than selling hardware.

These arguments suggest an urgent need in many companies to consider the transformation of the traditional sales organisation, and its more strategic role as a focus for strategic customer management (Piercy and Lane, 2009a).

14.2.2 Shaping forces for the new sales organisation

Clearly, the sales organisation has for some time been subject to powerful company and customer forces that have reshaped its role and operation (Jones *et al.*, 2005). The forces acting to reshape the sales function in organisations are summarised in Figure 14.3. As we have already seen, the implementation of new types of marketing strategy requires the realignment of sales processes with the strategy. At the same time, multi-channelling and the growth in Internet-based direct channels are substituting for many traditional sales activities.

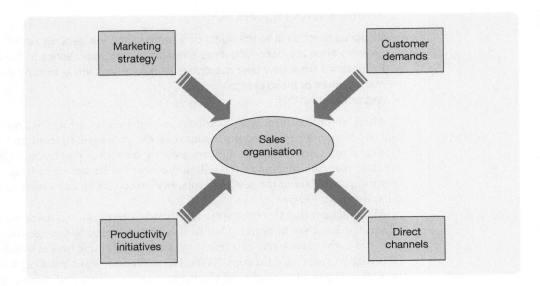

Figure 14.3
Forces acting
on the sales
organisation

Perhaps most telling in business-to-business marketing has been the dramatic escalation in the demands for enhanced service and added value by customers. As a consequence, one study calls on management to abandon their fixation of process compliance in sales (scorecards, activity metrics and so on) and adopt a more flexible approach to selling driven by salespeople's reliance on insight and judgement – 'insight selling' is one response to customers demanding new and better engagement with their suppliers (Adamson *et al.*, 2013). Put this in the context of the Chally Group finding that nearly 40 per cent of business-to-business buyers say that they select a supplier because of the skills of the salesperson rather than price, quality or service features, to understand the importance of selling quality (Fogel *et al.*, 2012).

Further, the H.R. Challey Group consultancy's *World Class Sales Excellence Research Report* (2006) lists the views of corporate purchasers and their expectations for the relationship with the salesperson from a supplier:

1 *Be personally accountable for our desired results* – the sales contact with the supplier is expected to be committed to the customer and accountable for achievement.
2 *Understand our business* – to be able to add value, the supplier must understand the customer's competencies, strategies, challenges and organisational culture.
3 *Be on our side* – the salesperson must be the customer's advocate in their own organisation, and operate through the policies and politics to focus on the customer's needs.
4 *Design the right applications* – the salesperson is expected to think beyond technical features and functions to the implementation of the product or service in the customer's environment, thinking beyond the transaction to the customer's end state.
5 *Be easily accessible* – customers expect salespeople to be constantly connected and within reach.
6 *Solve our problems* – customers no longer buy products or services, they buy solutions to their business problems, and expect salespeople to diagnose, prescribe and resolve their issues, not just sell them products.
7 *Be creative in responding to our needs* – buyers expect salespeople to be innovators, who bring them new ideas to solve problems, so creativity is a major source of added value.

These qualities characterise how world-class salesforces are distinguished in the eyes of their customers. They describe a customer environment that is radically different from the transactional approaches of the past, and that poses substantially different management challenges in managing business-to-business customer relationships. However, at the same time, business constraints in seller organisations suggest that in most companies there is considerable pressure to reduce costs and enhance productivity in the salesforce.

One example of changing customer demands is the development of 'social selling' – the coming together of online, mobile and social media with personal selling in how customers make purchase decisions and how sellers are engaging customers and building stronger customer relationships. Customers have far more control over the sales process than in the past. The emergence of new technologies to create a new digital and social media age places emphasis on a strong, multi-skilled sales team able to integrate technology with selling. The requirement in a new digital buying environment is for sellers to build their sales processes around the new customer buying process. Effective salesforces are escalating their use of social media to engage customers throughout the buying process (Giamanco and Gregoire, 2012; Green, 2013).

While the ways in which traditional sales organisations are likely to transform to meet these contrasting forces to reshape will vary considerably between different industrial and commercial sectors, one way of integrating the outcomes in general terms is in a model of the strategic sales organisation.

14.3 The strategic sales organisation

The importance of strategic customer relationships mandates a strategic response from sales and account management. The strategic sales organisation is an attempt to capture the range of changes that may transform the traditional sales organisation into a strategic force, impacting on the ability to implement marketing strategy, but also providing leadership in the shaping of that strategy.

Most attention given to the sales and account management area in the past has been largely concerned with tactical and operational issues, and has failed to adopt a strategic perspective on the management of customer relationships. Interestingly, similar comments would have applied in the operations and supply chain strategies prior to the revolutions in thinking and practice experienced by those disciplines in the 1990s and early 2000s. The sales and account management field is in the early stage of a similar and related revolution, characterised by a shift in approach from tactical to strategic. There can be little further doubt that, as Shapiro and his colleagues at Harvard asserted some time ago, once again: 'Sales is a board room topic' (Shapiro *et al.*, 1998), and that the strategic sales organisation is positioned on the top management agenda in many organisations.

However, the new processes and structures needed to enhance and sustain value delivery to customers through the sales organisation are likely to require careful evaluation and appraisal that extends to domains far beyond those traditionally associated with selling activities (Ogbuchi and Sharma, 1999). To support this analysis and to provide a framework for management action, we propose the framework shown in Figure 14.4 and identify several tools for practical application (Piercy and Lane, 2009a).

The framework suggests the following imperatives for management focus:

- *Involvement* – placing the sales organisation in the centre of the business and marketing strategy debate in companies and aligning sales operations with strategic direction.
- *Intelligence* – building customer knowledge as a strategic resource critical both to strategy formulation and to building added-value strategies with major customers.
- *Integration* – establishing cross-functional relationships necessary to lead the processes that define, develop and deliver superior value propositions to customers, and managing the interfaces between functions and business units impacting on service and value as they are perceived by customers.
- *Internal marketing* – using sales resources to 'sell' the customer across functional and divisional boundaries within the company and across organisational boundaries with partner companies, to achieve seamless value delivery.

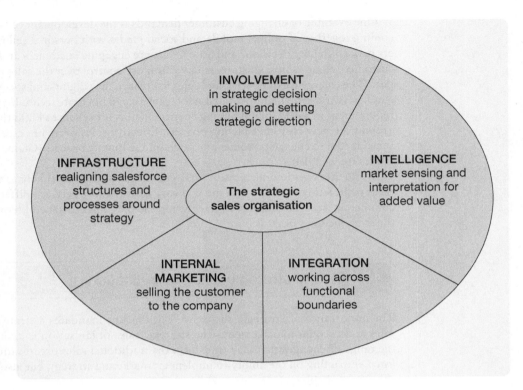

Figure 14.4
The strategic sales
organisation

- *Infrastructure* – developing the structure and processes needed to manage sales and account management organisations to match customer relationship requirements and to build competitive advantage.

14.3.1 Involvement in strategic decision making

As customer demands for superior seller relationships continue to evolve and escalate, then a distinct new role is becoming critical in selling organisations – the strategic management of the relationship with the customer. While harsh economic conditions and the search for a competitive edge mandate cost reductions to increase margins, sales revenues and profits are derived not only from finding new customers and sales channels, but from growing relationships with existing customers and sales channels. However, conventionally, sales organisations manage customers for short-term revenues, which in highly competitive markets often results in declining margins and commoditisation (Lombardi, 2005). Underpinning a strategic response to radical market change is the challenge of repositioning sales as a core part of the company's competitiveness, where the sales organisation is closely integrated into marketing strategy (Stephens, 2003).

In calling on companies to put sales at the centre of strategy, Frank Cespedes (2014) suggests that too often management embarks on a strategy without considering the realities facing the people who must execute the strategy with paying customers, and notes that 'strategists, years removed from customer contact, often have an obsolete vision of the company–customer interface' (p. 24). He concludes that, logically, the sales organisation should be part of every conversation about strategy.

Involvement of the sales organisation in strategy has two aspects. The *first* strategic sales issue is concerned with developing a perspective on the sales organisation that does not focus simply on the tactical management of transactional sales processes, but examines the relationships formed with different types of customers as the basis for long-term business development (Olson *et al.*, 2001). This implies a new appraisal of the activities and processes required to enhance and sustain value delivery to customers through the sales organisation. It is also increasingly the case that major customers require a highly specific value proposition built around 'unique value' for the customer.

The *second* strategic sales issue is concerned with the role of sales and account management in interpreting the customer environment as a basis for strategic decisions. As the costs of dealing with major customers continue to increase, companies face important choices in where they choose to invest resources in developing a customer relationship, and where they choose not to invest. With large customers, in particular, the risks in investment or disinvestment are high, and it is likely that the intelligence-gathering and market-sensing capabilities of the sales and account organisation will play a growing role in influencing strategic decisions about resource allocation in the customer portfolio. The shift in thinking required is from the tactical management of sales transactions to focus instead on the relationships formed in different ways with different types of customer as the basis for long-term business development (Olson *et al.*, 2001). We will consider the customer portfolio as a tool for surfacing these issues.

14.3.2 Intelligence to add value

One clear and repeated demand by corporate buyers is that salespeople should demonstrate deep knowledge of the customer's business, such that they can identify needs and opportunities before the buyer does (Chally, 2006). The deployment of such superior knowledge and expertise is a defining characteristic of the world-class sales organisation in the buyer's eyes. The buyer logic is straightforward: if the seller cannot bring added value to the relationship by identifying new opportunities for the buyer to gain competitive advantage in the end-use marketplace, then the seller is no more than a commodity supplier, and can be treated as such (the product will be purchased on price and technical specification).

This represents a challenging change in focus in the way sales organisations interact with major customers. While traditional selling activities focus primarily on the need to convert product and service into cash flow, conventional marketing shifts the focus from seller need to buyer need and developing the customer relationship. However, in many situations now faced by suppliers, strategic customers demand that the seller displays not simply a superior understanding of the customer's own organisation, but detailed and insightful knowledge of the customer's end-use markets. The strategic sales role is becoming one of deploying end-use market knowledge to enhance the customer's competitive position and cost efficiency. This is summarised in Figure 14.5, which provides a framework for evaluating where a company's salesforce is currently focusing efforts and how this compares to customer demands.

Even in the consumer goods sector, retailers continue to report that their suppliers perform inadequately in key areas that might help differentiate them to the consumer, such as consumer insight development. Major retailers emphasise that trade relationships are no longer based on buyer–seller roles, and characterise the best-in-class supplier as one that has a firm understanding of the retailer's position, strategy and ambitions in the marketplace – they require consumer insight from their suppliers (IBM, 2005).

Successful business models, such as those at companies as diverse as Dell Inc. in computers, Johnsons Controls in automotive controls and Kraft in groceries, display this type of end-use market perspective in strategic sales relationships. Major customers evaluate their suppliers on the seller's success in enhancing the customer's competitive position, and increasingly expect proof of this achievement.

The challenge to suppliers from an increasing proportion of their major customers is to understand the customer's business and the customer's end-use markets, to leverage that knowledge to create competitive advantage for the customer. The alternative is to face growing commoditisation and declining margins. Meeting this challenge with major accounts and strategic accounts is a central element of strategic sales choices. The corresponding

Figure 14.5 Changing focus in buyer–seller relationships

challenge for the reformed sales organisation is to develop, deploy and sustain new skills and capabilities in market sensing.

14.3.3 Integration across functional boundaries

Turbulent and demanding markets create new challenges for managers in supplier organisations. Powerful customers increasingly demand problem solving and creative thinking about their business, requiring the commitment of, and access to, the supplier's total operation. One European executive describes this as 'the convergence of strategic management, change management and process management, all critical elements of transforming the sales function to meet today's customer requirements' (Seidenschwartz, 2005). Certainly, in some cases, programmes of value creation around major customers have been plagued by problems of 'organisational drag' – where the seller's organisational functions are not aligned around processes of creating and delivering customer value (Koerner, 2005). Similarly, retailers emphasise supplier organisational structure and culture as key obstacles to improving customer management effectiveness (IBM, 2005).

Success in the new marketplace increasingly demands the integration of a company's entire set of capabilities into a seamless system that delivers superior customer value – what has been called elsewhere 'total integrated marketing' (Hulbert *et al.*, 2003). This logic is based on the observation that superior-performing companies share a simple characteristic: they get their act together around the things that matter most to their customers, and they make a totally integrated offer of superior value in customer terms. Management attention must focus on the actual and potential contributions of functional units and departments, and third-party suppliers in alliances and networks, in delivering superior value to customers, and how to improve the integration of these activities.

One of the developing roles of the sales organisation will be in managing processes of value definition, development and delivery that cut across functional interfaces to build real customer focus. Many of the barriers to developing and delivering superior customer value come from the characteristics of supplier organisations. One challenge of strategic customer management is that it demands effective approaches to cross-functional integration around value processes. Rather than managing only the interface with the customer, the reformed salesforce must cope with a range of interfaces with internal functions and departments, and increasingly partner organisations, to deliver value seamlessly to customers. (We discuss the issue of cross-functional partnership further in Chapter 16.)

14.3.4 Internal marketing of the customer

It seems inevitable that a strategic approach to the role of sales in managing customer value will simultaneously impose the problem of positioning and 'selling' the customer value strategy inside the organisation.

For example, consider the issue of service quality, which has proved to be a decisive competitive weapon in many industries (see Chapter 13). Service quality is normally evaluated in the customer marketplace in terms of the perceived delivery of the product or service confirming or disconfirming customer expectations to create satisfaction or dissatisfaction (Berry and Parasuraman, 1991). However, those same dimensions of attitudes and beliefs are mirrored in the internal marketplace of company employees and managers.

In the internal marketplace, expectations are concerned with anticipations by people inside the company of external customer preferences and behaviour, and perceived delivery is about differences between internal and external criteria of what 'matters' – priorities of people in the 'back office' or the factory may conflict with those of the external customer. Confirmation/disconfirmation relates not to consumption of the product, but to judgements people inside the company make about the external customer. When external customers 'disappoint' employees by their adverse reaction or complaints, this may easily have a negative effect on the future behaviour of employees in dealing with customers (Piercy and Lane, 2009a).

The risk of undermining the competitive position with a major customer as a result of such internal market factors is too serious to be ignored. One role of the reformed sales organisation is likely to be 'selling' the customer to employees and managers, as a basis for understanding customer priorities and the importance of meeting them and as an activity that parallels conventional sales and marketing efforts, as suggested in Figure 14.6. (Internal marketing is discussed further in Chapter 16.)

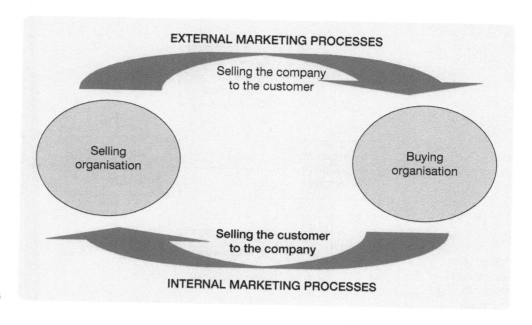

Figure 14.6 The internal marketing challenge for sales

14.3.5 Infrastructure for the new sales organisation

The role of the transforming sales organisation is unlikely to be implemented effectively through traditional salesforce structures and processes. Shapiro and his colleagues suggest that 'most established salesforces are in deep trouble. They were designed for a much simpler, more pleasant era. . . The old salesforce must be redesigned to meet the new needs' (Shapiro *et al.*, 1998). New definitions of the sales task will require substantial shifts in the way that the sales organisation is managed. Turbulent markets mandate constant attention to alignment between sales processes and the goals of market and business strategy (Strelsin and Mlot, 1992). Certainly, research suggests that the move from transactional relationships with customers (selling on the basis of price and product advantages) to value-added relationships is proving extremely challenging for many organisations striving to pursue this strategy (*American Salesman*, 2002).

Change in the infrastructure supporting the strategic sales organisation is likely to span organisation structure, performance measurement systems, competency creation systems and motivation systems – all driven by the definition of the new task and role of the sales operation (Shapiro *et al.*, 1998).

Figure 14.7 suggests some of the areas where particular attention is required, and where new research into sales organisation effectiveness indicates some of the productive approaches to be explored. The Figure 14.7 logic is that the overall result on which attention should focus is the effectiveness of the sales organisation in implementing business strategy and meeting organisational goals. Traditionally, management attention has focused on outcome performance as the main indicator of effectiveness (that is, meeting sales volume and revenue targets). However, if strategy requires the development of closer customer relationships and the implementation of a value-based strategy, then salesperson behaviour performance may be a more productive point of focus (not simply what salespeople sell, but the behaviours they undertake to achieve their goals and to build customer relationships).

If salesperson behaviour performance is key to delivering the outcomes and overall effectiveness required as marketing strategy moves towards a relationship focus, then this has several important implications for the competencies and behaviours to be developed in salespeople, and against which to evaluate their performance. This in turn, has major implications for the type of people to be recruited to sales and account management roles, as well as for the way in which they are managed (Baldauf *et al.*, 2001a, b). Particular controversy is reserved for the move from outcome-based control (primarily in the form of compensation-based incentives such as sales commission and bonuses) towards behaviour-based control

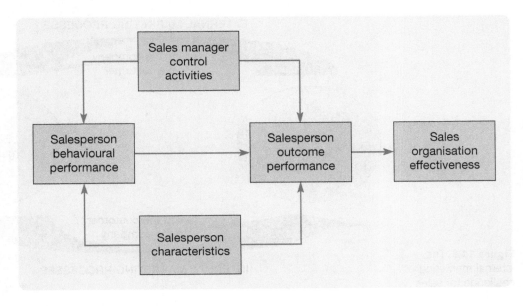

Figure 14.7
Realigning sales
structures and
processes

(direct manager intervention in how salespeople do their jobs, and greater reliance on fixed-salary compensation packages) (Piercy *et al.*, 2004a, b).

The process of 'reinventing' the salesforce to meet the challenges of new markets and new strategies is likely to require attention to several critical issues:

- Focus on long-term customer relationships, but also assessing customer value and prioritising the most attractive prospects.
- Creating sales organisation structures that are nimble and adaptable to the needs of different customer groups.
- Gaining greater ownership and commitment from salespeople by removing functional barriers within the organisation and leveraging team-based working.
- Shifting sales management from 'command and control' to coaching and facilitation.
- Applying new technologies appropriately.
- Designing salesperson evaluation to incorporate the full range of activities and outcomes relevant to new types of sales and account management jobs (Cravens, 1995).

For example, when the then-new CEO of Hewlett-Packard began that company's remarkable performance improvement, he found that there were as many as 11 layers between him and a customer. Correspondingly, H-P was slower to respond to customers than its competitors, and of the 17,000 people working in corporate sales, only 10,000 directly sold to customers – the rest were support staff or managers. His overhaul of H-P's vast corporate salesforce involved: closing a large sales group that sold a broad portfolio of products and reallocating salespeople to product-specific groups, so they could master the products they sold; cutting hundreds of under-performing salespeople; removing three levels of sales management; and paring back internal meetings so salespeople could spend more time with customers. H-P's salesforce therefore spent more time in front of customers, responded faster to their needs and won more corporate sales deals (Tam, 2006).

Although beyond the scope of this present review, a study of the antecedents and consequences of sales management control strategy reveals several issues, which are commonly neglected in leveraging change and superior performance in the salesforce as part of aligning sales efforts with strategic direction (Baldauf *et al.*, 2005). It should be quite apparent, however, that new business and marketing strategies and an evolving role for the sales organisation in leading strategic customer management will inevitably require considerable re-evaluation of the management of the sales organisation.

While this agenda provides a framework for examining the operational characteristics of the strategic sales organisation, and evaluating organisational needs by defining the new domain for the strategic sales organisation, it is important to note that research also suggests the need to place developments into a broader context of shaping factors as well. This logic is summarised in Figure 14.8. The context for the strategic sales organisation includes factors such as:

- **Inspiration** – part of the outcome of reinventing the traditional sales organisation should be to renew the ability of those who manage key external relationships with customers to inspire and provide broader leadership within the business.
- **Influence** – a test of whether the strategic sales organisation is taken seriously is the degree to which it exerts influence over the company's strategic agenda and the key strategic decisions that are made.
- **Integrity** – there has never been a time when scrutiny of the ethical and responsible behaviour of companies was greater, and when the cost of being judged unethical or irresponsible was higher. Managing relationships with customers, partners and suppliers with integrity is a huge challenge, but not one that can be ignored. Increasingly, major customers cannot do business with people whom they cannot trust, or whose poor corporate reputations carry a danger of contamination by association. This may be among the highest priorities in new types of buyer–seller relationship (Galea, 2006).

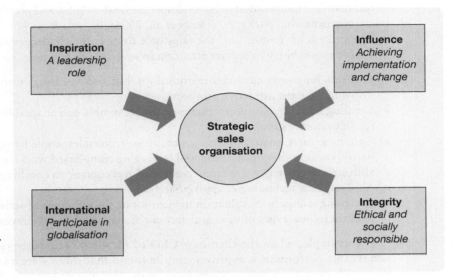

Figure 14.8
Shaping factors for
the strategic sales
organisation

- **International** – the globalisation of markets, the emergence of global customers and the spread of international competition mandates an international perspective on how we manage customer relationships in domestic and overseas markets. We expand on this fuller agenda in more detail and with operational tools elsewhere (Piercy and Lane, 2009a).

14.4 Strategic customer management tasks

The transformation of the traditional sales organisation into a strategic force that should feature centrally in the analysis that underpins strategic choices by marketing executives, may be achieved by moves towards at least some of the characteristics of the strategic sales organisation. However, the larger goal we pursue is a strategic customer management perspective, which may be achieved through the strategising of sales processes and structures. The key distinguishing features of a strategic customer management (SCM) approach are summarised and developed further in the sections that follow. The domain for strategic customer management is described in Figure 14.9.

14.4.1 Alignment of sales processes with strategy

At one level, the SCM mandate is concerned with the issue of marketing strategy implementation. To many business-to-business customers, the salesperson who visits *is* the supplier company, and has far more impact on customer perceptions of the supplier than promotional and other communications approaches. The interface between the customer and the supplier managed by the salesforce has long been recognised as a major source of implementation failures. We consider implementation issues in Chapter 16, but particular problems relating to the sales/marketing strategy interface that are frequently encountered include:

- Marketing strategies that aim to build strong competitive positions through superior customer relationships fall foul of sales organisations where salespeople are rewarded by volume-based commission paid for sales transactions – traditional evaluation-and-reward

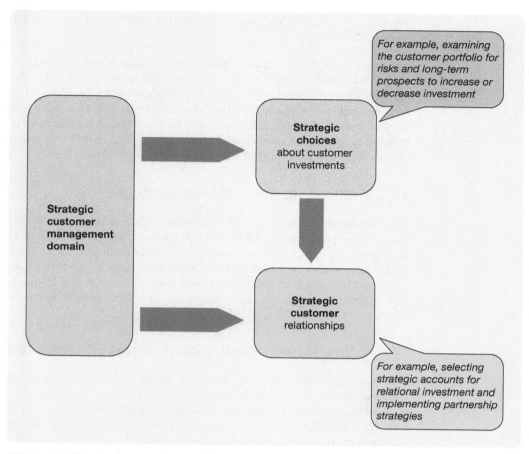

Figure 14.9 The domain of strategic customer management

systems often value highest sales activities that run counter to strategic goals of customer orientation and relationship building and favour short-term volume.

- Strategies are built around vertical markets and customer focus, but salespeople struggle to implement these approaches because they are organised into geographical areas or product divisions.
- Sales managers do not 'buy in' to marketing strategies, and cling to traditional leadership behaviours and performance management in controlling sales operations.
- Traditional conflicts of interests between marketing and sales executives (they are frequently rewarded for different achievements and evaluated against different measures) spill over into lack of cooperation and coordination.
- Marketing strategies are developed in isolation from the customer and competitor insights provided by salespeople and account managers, and without any understanding of the company's sales capabilities compared to competitors.
- Salespeople and sales executives experience job ambiguity and conflict in attempting to implement strategies that fit poorly with the systems and structures in the sales organisation, experiencing lower motivation and job satisfaction and perhaps higher levels of stress and burn-out (Hulbert *et al.*, 2009).

Poor alignment of the realities of existing sales processes and structures and the intent of marketing strategy is likely to make effective implementation difficult to achieve. Nonetheless, it must be recognised that changing issues such as evaluation-and-reward systems, leadership and control strategies and organisational structures in the salesforce is usually not a minor undertaking.

14.4.2 Providing the real customer perspective in marketing strategy

The importance of understanding the sales/customer interface is vital to strategy analysts and decision makers for another reason as well. In most business-to-business situations, the salesforce represents a key market-sensing capability, or source of intelligence. However, research evidence suggests that this resource is generally poorly used or applied by marketing decision makers (Fitzhugh and Piercy, 2006). A high priority is emerging for the better management of market-sensing processes, which involve the salesforce and account management teams as some of the primary sources of intelligence.

14.4.3 Managing the customer portfolio

Our earlier comments on changing customer relationship requirements and demands for service enhancement suggest that different customer groups should be evaluated very differently in terms of their potential attractiveness and the supplier's cost to serve them. Choices regarding in which customers to make investments of selling efforts of different types, and where not to make such investments, will shape the future of a business and merit senior management attention. We will consider the customer portfolio in the next section of this chapter.

14.4.4 Developing effective positioning with dominant customers

Currently, one of the most troublesome issues for developing effective strategy in business-to-business companies is the impact of powerful customers and the demands that they can make on their suppliers – whether the consumer goods manufacturer dealing with very large retailers such as Tesco and Walmart, or the components manufacturer dealing with automotive companies. One response to this has been the growth in strategic (or key) account management approaches, to 'partner' with the most important customers. However, it is clear that some customers do not provide good partnership prospects – while they may be large, they are transactional customers, not collaborators. The last section of the chapter turns to the issue of dominant customers.

| 14.5 | Managing the customer portfolio |

In much the same way that we can examine a portfolio of products or brands, the importance of customers as assets and investment centres mandates a similar portfolio analysis. Figure 14.10 shows an approach to mapping the number of customer accounts held by a company or business unit, by their sales level and potential, and their service and relationship requirements from the supplier. This categorisation initially can be made simply by the number of accounts, but can be subsequently enhanced by examining the profitability and stability of business in the different account categories. Identifying the categories is the important first step.

The *direct channel* is typically the route to market for smaller accounts with low relationship/service requirements, such as the Internet or telemarketing. Importantly, customer development strategy may also involve moving some accounts towards the direct channel, because they are consuming more service/relationship resources than they merit, but also moving some out of the direct channel, based on changing prospects and the costs of serving the account. Such considerations illustrate the potential importance of shifting some salesforce resources from a short-term transactional focus, to longer-term business development issues in line with business and marketing strategy.

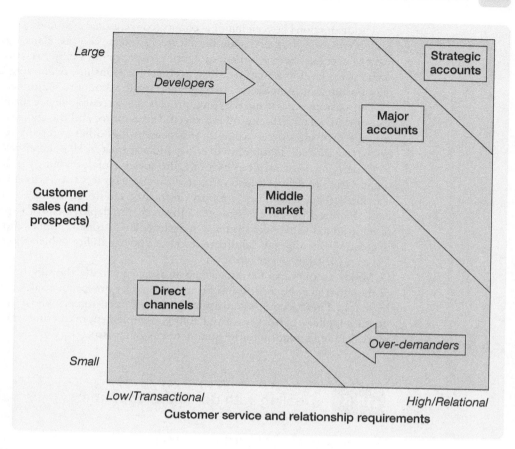

Figure 14.10 The customer portfolio

The *middle market* contains customers with varying prospects, but generally with moderate relationship/service requirements. These are the most conventional buyer–seller relationships. Those with promising potential may be moved into the major account area over time, while those with relationship/service requirements that are excessive compared to their potential may be moved towards the direct channel.

Major accounts are usually large in the supplier's terms and have high relationship/service requirements, but they are customers in a conventional buyer–seller relationship. While major accounts are important to the supplier, it is quite possible that the supplier is of far less importance to the customer (if accounting for a relatively small part of the customer's expenditure, or capable of being replaced reasonably easily). However, major account size and prospects identifies the need to develop appropriate salesforce approaches to deliver added value to these customers. Nonetheless, it is likely that appropriate salesforce strategies will be, and should be, substantially different between major accounts and strategic accounts.

Strategic accounts are those where collaborative and joint problem-solving approaches are appropriate to win status as a strategic supplier. Strategic account management strategies and structures have developed in many companies as a way of establishing close, long-term and collaborative relationships with the most important customers and meeting their needs in ways that the traditional salesforce did not (Homburg *et al.*, 2002). Important questions surround the selection and management of relationships with strategic accounts – who may be the most expensive customers to serve? Growing buyer concentration in many markets mandates collaborative relationships with these accounts as strategic suppliers, but the costs of partnership and the growing dependence involved underlines the need for careful choices and evaluation of performance.

The distinction between major accounts (conventional customers) and strategic accounts (collaborators or partners) underlines several strategic choices. Plans may include the movement of accounts between these categories – developing a closer relationship with a major account to develop a new strategic account relationship, or moving away from a close relationship that is ineffective to move a strategic account to major account status.

This customer portfolio mapping process is a screening device for identifying the most appropriate relationship to offer a specific account to, and the choices to be made in allocating scarce salesforce, account management and other company resources, as well as evaluating the risks involved in over-dependence on a small number of very large accounts.

Underlying the strategic sales issue is the question of developing the capability of the sales organisation to deliver added value in different ways to various categories of customers. It is unlikely that a traditional, transaction-focused salesforce will be able to deliver the added value required by some customers. However, the deployment of expensive resources to develop added-value sales strategies for particular customers implies choices and investment in creating new types of salesforce resource and capability, which should be confronted at a strategy level in an organisation.

Major accounts and strategic accounts are normally the supplier's largest customers (although it may be more appropriate to consider prospective sales rather than just existing sales). These accounts constitute the dominant customers whose impact can be massive on the supplier's performance and ability to implement marketing strategies. We now turn more detailed attention to the dominant customer issue.

14.6 Dealing with dominant customers[*]

One important insight from the customer portfolio analysis is the recognition of the different types of customer in the company's portfolio, and their differing demands for value and relationship. Particular questions are raised about the largest and most influential customers – perhaps the 20 per cent of customers who may account for 80 per cent (or more) of the supplier's business.

It is important for strategic decision makers in marketing to understand the basis for the different types of customer relationship that exist in the portfolio, and particularly the idea of a transition from traditional transactional relationships to much closer links between the seller and the most dominant buyers. Figure 14.11 summarises some of the most common business-to-business buyer–seller relationships, and the critical differences between them.

The *conventional buyer–seller relationship* is the most familiar – it typifies the middle market. Links are between salespeople and purchasers, and the relationship may be purely transactional (depending largely on the importance of the purchase to the customer, or the way in which the customer chooses to do business), or it may involve a higher-level or closer relationship being built between buyer and seller. This is the type of relationship that most traditional salesforces were created to manage.

However, the existence of larger, more dominant customers requires different approaches. The *major account orientation* case is where the size and impact of a customer requires that sales and management efforts should be refocused to provide a dedicated approach to a particular customer. This may involve the appointment of an account manager, or a national account specialist, and the development of plans around this customer's specific needs. Nonetheless, the relationship remains largely a conventional buyer–seller format.

The *major account resource commitment* situation takes things substantially further in terms of dedicated efforts around the major account. Substantial teams of people may

---

[*] This section draws on Piercy and Lane, 2006a, b, 2007, 2009a.

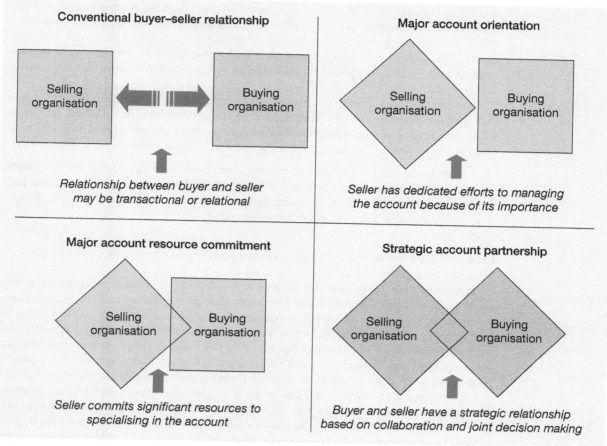

Figure 14.11 The transition from customer to strategic partner

now work around the single account and offerings may be substantially different for this customer. Nonetheless, the resource commitment remains essentially one-sided. Proctor & Gamble's 200-person team for the Walmart account is P&G's investment in that customer. Correspondingly, while Dell Computers has a dedicated team for its major customer, Boeing, this does not suggest that Boeing makes decisions about Dell's business. At the end of the day, these relationships remain buyer–seller transactions. The investment is essentially one-sided – it is made by the seller.

The big difference is with the *strategic account partnership*. This type of account relationship is based on collaboration and joint decision making between the buyer and seller. It is a two-sided relationship – both buyer and seller invest time and resources in the relationship. (This relationship has much in common with the strategic alliances discussed in Chapter 15.) The impact of strategic account relationships and management merits more detailed attention.

14.6.1 Strategic account management

Growth in management attention given to strategic account management (SAM)[*] as a way of developing and nurturing relationships with a company's most important customers is unprecedented. While currently given relatively little attention in the mainstream strategy

[*] For purposes of discussion we regard the terms 'strategic account management' and 'key account management' as interchangeable, and our commentary generally applies to what some designate as 'national account management' and 'global account management'.

literature, a Google search reveals hundreds of Web pages detailing managerial books about SAM, countless consultants eager to offer advice, numerous training courses for executives and a growing number of business school programmes in SAM in universities across the world. The underlying concept is the shift from adversarial buyer–seller relationships towards collaborative or partnership-based relationships, with the company's most important customers.

Many major international companies have made SAM an important element of how they manage relationships with their largest customers. For example, IMI plc is a major UK engineering group, whose published strategy statement identifies SAM as a key theme in achieving its goal of 'leading global niche markets'. The company is investing heavily:

> to enhance our ability to create and manage close customer relationships with our clients [and] provide IMI business managers with the skills to create and develop close and successful relationships with major customers. . . which places key account management among the central elements of IMI's business approach.
> *(IMI, 2010)*

For a growing number of companies, SAM is a deep-seated strategy for customer partnering, often on a global basis.

At the same time, many major buyers have adopted radical strategic supplier strategies. For example, Ford Motor Company has spent considerable time and effort in recent years consolidating its supply base for its $90 billion components purchases from 2,000 suppliers down to 1,000 globally. Moreover, the first seven 'key suppliers' constitute some 50 per cent of Ford's parts purchases, and will enjoy superior access to Ford's engineering resources and product planning. Ford will work closely with its key suppliers, giving them access to key business plans for new vehicles and committing to give them business (Mackintosh and Simon, 2005).

On one hand, a compelling case can be made for the attractiveness of SAM as a strategy of collaboration and partnership with major customers. However, there are several assumptions and propositions underpinning the case for SAM, which appear to have been largely ignored by its adopters and advocates. As suggested in Figure 14.12, balancing these issues is an important challenge for strategic decision makers in marketing.

14.6.2 The case for strategic account management

One study suggests that strategic/key account management is one of the most fundamental changes in marketing organisation (Homburg *et al.*, 2000), and yet one in which a sound research foundation to guide management's strategic decisions remains almost completely lacking (Homburg *et al.*, 2002). Indeed, while there is a long stream of research in the areas of national and key account selling, starting in the 1960s, this research has not addressed the long-term impact of SAM on buyer–seller performance (Workman *et al.*, 2003).

Figure 14.12
The case for and against strategic account management

The rationale for SAM is that demands from large customers have caused suppliers to respond with dedicated organisational resources to concentrate on these 'key' or 'strategic' accounts and to incorporate special value-adding activities (such as joint product development, business planning, consulting services) into their offering to the customer (Dorsch *et al.*, 1998). Fundamental to the logic of SAM is the suggestion of an inevitable concentration effect, whereby a small number of customers provide a disproportionately large share of a seller's sales and profits (the so-called '20:80 rule'). Almost as a natural consequence, suppliers frequently dedicate most of their resources to the core portfolio of buyers who represent the highest stakes and are identified as 'strategic accounts' or 'key accounts' (Pardo, 1997).

SAM is a strategic development that has become increasingly widespread in response to a variety of customer and market pressures, which may be summarised as:

- escalating levels of competition in most markets and consequently higher selling costs for suppliers;
- increased customer concentration resulting from merger and acquisition activity, as well as competitive attrition in many markets during the recession;
- growing customer emphasis on centralised strategic purchasing as a major contributor to enhancing the buyer's cost structure and building competitive success in their end-user markets;
- active strategies of supplier base reduction by larger buyers to reduce purchasing costs;
- increasing exploitation by large customers of their position of strategic importance to their suppliers to gain lower prices and enhanced terms of trade (Capon, 2001).

Importantly, however, SAM is not seen simply as an organisational response that focuses on meeting growing demands from dominant customers; it is seen as progression towards a form of 'partnership' with those customers, characterised by joint decision making and problem solving, integrated business processes and collaborative working across buyer–seller boundaries, described as a process of 'relational development' (Millman and Wilson, 1989). However, while we have discussed the strengths in effective strategic account relationships, decision makers should also recognise the growing evidence that ineffective strategic account relationships may create a range of strategic vulnerabilities for sellers.

14.6.3 Vulnerabilities in strategic account relationships

There are a number of potential flaws in the underlying logic for SAM, which may make it unattractive for sellers in some situations, and which should be made explicit in strategic choices.

Investing in strategic weakness

There is a case that SAM involves the seller investing in strategic weakness, in the sense that it may be unattractive to institutionalise dependency on major customers as a way of doing business. The SAM approach rests on the notion that the '20:80 rule' produces a situation for the seller that is attractive, or at least inevitable. Conversely, it can be argued that any company that has reached a situation where a '20:80' position exists – that is, 80 per cent or more of profits and/or revenue come from 20 per cent or less of the customer base – has already witnessed the failure of its business model. The business model has failed because it has led to such a high degree of dependence on a small number of customers that the company's strategic freedom of manoeuvre has been undermined, and much control of the supplier's business has effectively been ceded to its major customers. The eventual outcome for selling companies in this situation is likely to be falling prices, commoditisation of their products and progressively lower profits as major customers exert their market power.

Clearly, many practitioners would argue that in businesses such as grocery there is no choice other than to deal with the major retailers who dominate the consumer marketplace, because there is no other route to market and little choice other than to accept the terms they offer. Similarly, suppliers of automotive components would point to the limited number of automobile manufacturers in the world, and producers of computer components would argue that if you want Dell's business, then you do business on Dell's terms, robust though those terms may be. Such responses at least clarify that in many 'strategic account' situations, the real issue is less partnership and more about one party dictating terms to the other, which is not the concept of 'collaboration' normally advanced to justify SAM investments by suppliers.

If it is conceded that powerful customers will ultimately exploit that power to their own advantage, then their business carries a disproportionately higher risk than that of less powerful, less dominant customers, and it is less attractive as a result. If it is inevitable that major customers will demand more concessions and pay less, then it is likely they will also be substantially less profitable than other customers. There is little consistent empirical evidence, but there are suggestions that, for many sellers, strategic or key accounts are the least profitable part of their business.

The importance of understanding the balance of power

Notwithstanding the importance of strategic buyer–seller relationships, there seems a strong case that the party in the supply chain enjoying the balance of power will use that to their advantage. For example, in spite of surging raw material costs, the pricing power of suppliers has continued to deteriorate in many markets. Producers may have to absorb most cost increases because they are unable to pass them fully through the supply chain, simply because powerful buyers will not permit it (Cave, 2005). It is illustrative that in the automotive components market, notwithstanding escalating steel and raw material prices faced by producers, Volkswagen told its parts suppliers in 2005 it wanted 10 per cent cost savings over the following two years. At Chrysler, the CEO demanded an immediate 5 per cent price cut by suppliers, with a further 10 per over the following three years (Mackintosh, 2005).

Another example is a study of Tesco that suggested that at one point it had some 2,600 suppliers providing £9 billion worth of goods. The largest supplier had less than 3 per cent of Tesco's total sales and the median supplier less than one-hundredth of a per cent. If a contract is lost, the absolute maximum impact on Tesco's sales would be 1–3 per cent, and normally far less. For the supplier, it could mean a loss of sales of 10–30 per cent of total revenue, without an alternative sales outlet (Giles and Tricks, 2005). Consider the negative impact on Premier Foods' profitability and share price, when Tesco elected to de-list 11 out of 18 bread product lines that Premier produces, rather than accept a price rise (Kavanagh, 2011). This neatly defines the relative power of buyer and seller.

For such reasons, in sectors such as automotive components, suppliers are actively seeking to diversify their customer bases and to change product portfolios to reduce dependence on a small number of powerful accounts (Simon, 2005). The issue is becoming one of staying close to key customers, but reaching out to other customer groups as a route to reduced dependency on a few enhanced profits (Witzel, 2005b). Indeed, this shift in dependency may be one of the highest strategic priorities impacting on survival.

The real buyer–seller relationship

The critical issue is interdependence between buyer and seller, or perhaps more aptly the balance of dependence, since it is rarely symmetrical. The question is 'who is dependent on whom' in the buyer–seller relationship? Failure to grasp the simple issue of the direction of dependency is likely to blind the seller to a critical vulnerability of SAM, while simultaneously souring relationships with the account in question – professional purchasers find it difficult to work with suppliers who misunderstand the nature of the relationship they really have with the buyer. Sellers with an exaggerated view of their strategic importance to a buyer have unrealistic expectations of the customer, with the potential for growing frustration because the customer does not behave in the way expected, and ultimately leading to conflict between buyer and seller.

Figure 14.13 illustrates a buyer perspective on supplier types – the professional purchaser distinguishes on the basis of risk (substitutability) and impact (reduced costs or improved

Figure 14.13
Customer
purchasing strategy

competitive advantage in the end-use marketplace). From a purchaser perspective, suppliers with significant impact on the buyer's business, but who can easily be replaced, are mainly targets for pressure on price and terms, while those with low impact, who can be easily substituted, are likely to be treated as commodities, where the goal is to routinise transactions to reduce supply chain costs. With suppliers who cannot easily be replaced, but have limited impact, the goal is to reduce the customer's risk exposure (perhaps by negotiating guaranteed supplies). Only where a supplier cannot easily be substituted by a competitor, *and* has a major impact on the customer's business, is the customer likely to work towards a strategic supplier relationship. At any time, for most buyers it is likely that very few suppliers will have strategic importance. It is important to understand the relationship defined by the customer, before assuming that the buyer should be treated as a strategic account.

The risks of dependence

A related point is that SAM exposes the seller to another type of risk, which is derived from the strategic account's own end-use markets. The closer the relationship becomes to strategic account/strategic supplier status, the higher this risk becomes for the supplier.

Quite simply, if the key account's performance declines, or if its business fails, its strategic suppliers will suffer business losses that are likely to be substantial, and over which they have little control.

For instance, consider the dilemma faced by tyre manufacturer Dunlop, and many other smaller suppliers, created by the 2005 collapse of MG Rover – it is believed some 15–20 per cent of Dunlop's UK business was lost with Rover's demise. Further, the value of Dunlop's investment in a long-term collaborative relationship based on new product development for Rover was also lost. The impact was equally serious for some 1,500 small car parts manufacturers who supplied Rover, both in lost business and bad debts (Quinn, 2005a). Focus on a strategic account creates a shared business risk for suppliers, which may be uncontrollable, unrecompensed and unattractively high.

The paradox of customer attractiveness and competitive intensity

Advocates of SAM strategy argue that this model should only be applied to the customers who are most 'attractive' to a particular supplier (Capon, 2001). Setting aside the issue of how a company defines its criteria of attractiveness, the paradox is that the customers who are most attractive to one supplier will probably at the same time be the most attractive to competitors. While there will be situations of 'fit' that make a customer attractive to one supplier and unattractive to others, this is likely to be the exception rather than the rule. Accordingly, the most 'attractive' customers for a SAM strategy are also likely to be those where competitive intensity is highest and consequently where the ability of the customer to substitute one supplier for another is highest. The likelihood seems that competitive intensity will deny strategic supplier status for any seller and place all in the routinised, commodity supplier category. The most 'attractive' customers become the least 'attractive' through processes of competitive convergence of suppliers on the same customers as strategic accounts (Saunders *et al.*, 2000).

The case for strategic account investment

This brings us to a critical question – if strategic accounts may be less profitable for a supplier and impose higher levels of risk on the supplier's business, then how is it possible to make a case for increasing dependence on such accounts, and to invest in SAM systems to further reinforce the dependence of the company on low-profit, high-risk business? There may be no choice, certainly in the short term, other than to meet the requirements of dominant customers for special treatment, but to regard this element of the business as the highest investment priority for the longer term may be questionable. Indeed, the more rational course might be to find ways of ring-fencing such customers and diverting resources to develop other, more profitable, parts of the customer portfolio.

SAM strategy also carries the substantial opportunity cost that heavy management focus on key accounts reduces the attention given to other customers, who in reality offer higher margins and lower risk. Indeed, there is a significant danger that having invested in SAM with a customer, even as the account becomes progressively less profitable because of excess demands, inertia and reluctance to admit failure may easily cause the supplier to cling to the key account relationship regardless of disappearing margins.

There is a strong, and for some companies urgent, argument that investment priorities should be reconsidered in many customer relationships, with an emphasis on long-term profitability and balanced risk exposure, and less on the short-term characteristics of existing markets. The logic is that if the business model has failed, then the issue becomes one of searching for and developing a new business model, not persisting with the old model until commercial failure ensues. The goal is to invest in strength and enhanced future earnings, not to invest in positions of weakness and to maintain the status quo, only to enjoy progressively reduced earnings.

Understanding customer relationship requirements

The European purchasing manager with a leading engineering company observes that:

> I love it when a supplier tells me I am a key account – I make a lot of fuss of them. However, most times all I really do is to get concessions on price and terms. I almost feel guilty, it is so easy, but it's my job.
> *(Piercy and Lane, 2006a)*

Underpinning the weakness of SAM strategy in potentially mismanaging critical interorganisational dependencies is the observation that suppliers frequently tend to have exaggerated views about the relationship that major customers want to have with their suppliers.

It is likely that SAM can only be an effective strategy from a supplier perspective where there is a close match between seller and buyer relationship requirements. Consider the scenario in Figure 14.14. Frustration results for the supplier attempting to build closer relationships with customers who mainly want efficient transactions – from the buyer perspective the supplier is not important enough to justify strategic supplier status, or this may simply not be how this company does business with its suppliers. On the other hand, conflict arises when a customer looks for a close relationship with a supplier prepared only to offer more limited engagement – this customer does not warrant a larger relationship investment by the supplier. Only where there is continuous alignment between buyer and seller relationship

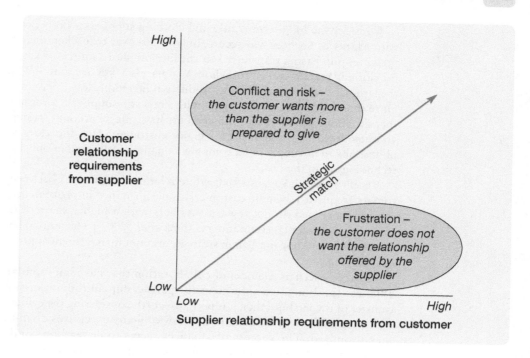

Figure 14.14
Buyer and seller
relationship
strategies

requirements is there potential for effective SAM. The problem facing suppliers seems to be recognising how rare alignment may be in practice, as well as how transitory.

Distinguishing large (major) customers from strategic accounts

The tendency among sellers is to equate large customers with strategic accounts. We commented earlier on the importance of distinguishing major accounts from strategic accounts in the customer portfolio. The danger of not distinguishing these types of customer is three-fold: first, confusing the major account with the real strategic account prospect, leading to unproductive investments in the relationship; second, diverting attention from developing new and profitable major accounts growing out of the traditional middle market; and, third, neglecting the productivity enhancements available by moving over-demanding customers from the traditional middle market to the direct channel. Identifying major customers wrongly as strategic accounts is capable of undermining the management of the whole portfolio of accounts being serviced by the seller, with likely further negative effects on overall performance and profitability.

Furthermore, some major customers may be relatively unattractive because they offer little profit or future growth. The fact that such customers may presently be large buyers does not alter this fact. On these grounds, simply being a large customer does not justify supplier relationship investments such as SAM. There is no logic in building stronger relationships with unattractive customers, particularly if this reduces opportunities to invest more productively elsewhere. As noted earlier, in many ways, the large low-profit customer should encourage ring-fencing to minimise additional investment to the lowest level that retains the business, and the diversion of resources to more profitable applications elsewhere in the business.

Understanding the reality of customer loyalty

Much of the attraction of SAM lies in the promise that collaborative relationships with key customers will enhance the retention of that business – that is, strategic accounts will reciprocate by offering loyalty to their long-term strategic suppliers. This promise is intuitively attractive, but in reality may not always be fulfilled.

Consider the long-term textile and clothing suppliers who believed their relationship with Marks & Spencer was secure, only to discover that when their customer was under pressure, purchasing transferred to cheaper off-shore sources. Examine the US situation for clothing manufacturers for whom Walmart is a 'key account' – Walmart is now among the largest purchasers of Chinese products at incredibly low prices, which matters to them more than long-term relationships with domestic suppliers. Alternatively, view the Dell Inc. situation – a company renowned for its strategic account strategy, acting almost as an outsourced IT department for major customers. Dell Inc. does not extend the same philosophy to its suppliers – a company remains a Dell supplier only as long as it has better technology than the rest.

Recent research suggests that while relational exchanges between suppliers and customers frequently benefit customers in performance improvements, generally the customers concerned do not reward suppliers with a higher share of their expenditure or long-term contractual commitments (Fink *et al.*, 2007). The mutual benefit and long-term relationship building implicit in strategic account management approaches may have been exaggerated.

If SAM is seen as a model of collaboration that has many similarities with strategic alliances (both involve agreement for partnership and joint decision making, with no transfer of ownership), then it is perhaps worth considering the evidence that the majority of strategic alliances fail, and in the view of many executives do not deliver the benefits they promised. The success of alliances seems to depend on conditions of mutuality and symmetry between partners. Those conditions do not appear to exist in many SAM situations.

Underestimating the rate of change

Even if a customer is willing and eager to offer a seller the status of a strategic supplier and is treated as a strategic account, with all the additional investment that this is likely to require, some sellers mistakenly believe that strategic relationships with these accounts will be stable and long term.

The more likely truth is that as a seller's own strategy changes, the importance of a particular supplier will change – possibly dramatically and quickly. As the recorded music business transformed to one based on Internet downloads instead of physical products, strategic suppliers became those with expertise in the new technology, not those offering CDs and support for the old technology. Indeed, supplier switching may increasingly be an explicit element of a company's business strategy. In 2005, Apple announced it was teaming up with Intel to provide the components suitable for new generations of Apple products, effectively bringing an unexpected end to long-term supplier relationships with IBM and Freescale (formerly Motorola) (Morrison and Waters, 2005; Witzel, 2005a). Apple's goal was to build on the momentum created by its iPod digital music player and to meet the lower prices demanded in the mass consumer market. Supplier switching may be an inevitable consequence of strategic change.

The reality is that the strategic supplier relationship for many suppliers will be temporary and transitory, as customers develop their own market strategies and adopt new technologies. This leaves the supplier investing heavily in the strategic account relationship, only to see that relationship disappear as the customer moves on. Customers rarely offer recompense to a supplier to cover the costs of dismantling a redundant SAM system.

Even more traumatic is the sudden collapse of a key account/strategic supplier relationship. Changes in customer businesses may end relationships that had taken years to build: the key account is taken over and the acquiring company imposes its own supplier arrangements on the acquired business; there is a change in supply strategy from the top of the customer organisation – for example, the move from single sourcing to multiple sourcing; the customer learns technology and process from its strategic supplier, enabling it to undertake production of the product in-house; or customer personnel move on and their replacements do not have a close relationship with the supplier and maybe do not want one. The collapse of a strategic account relationship will have a major negative impact on sales volume, which may not have been predicted. The end of a SAM relationship may impose additional and substantial costs – adjusting operations capacity to allow for short-term volume reduction, disentangling integrated systems, rebuilding processes previously shared with the key account, reallocating or removing personnel previously dedicated to the key account, or putting in place new arrangements to retain whatever residual business there may be in the account.

The failure of a strategic account relationship may be very public and create additional vulnerability. If a company's shares are written down because of the collapse of business with a strategic account, then the supplier becomes vulnerable to a predator – perhaps even the customer in question, who has the opportunity to in-source the product by buying the supplier, or possibly a competitor, or possibly a stalker from outside the sector. The point is that the cost of a failed key account relationship may not simply be losing the customer, it may be losing the company as well.

Consider the experiences of Marconi in its strategic relationship with British Telecom. Marconi was the rump of the former GEC and through the 1990s focused heavily on investment with dominant customers in the telecommunications sector. Marconi was one of British Telecom's largest suppliers of network equipment for several decades. By 2004, BT represented a quarter of Marconi's total sales – as much as the next nine customers put together. Notwithstanding being described as a 'terrific partner' by the chief executive of BT Wholesale, in 2005 Marconi was shut out of BT's £10-billion '21st Century Network' project. BT's decision was based on price, not technology or relationships, and Marconi could not equal the prices of overseas competitors from eight countries, ranging from France to China. Under BT pressure, Marconi had even lowered prices to a level that would have represented substantial losses in its UK operation, but not enough to satisfy BT. With the loss of a quarter of its sales base, shares falling 60 per cent in value and substantial job losses in prospect, Marconi's experience underlines the risks of over-reliance on one customer, and the critical error of believing that a customer would be a loyal partner. The loss of the BT business fundamentally weakened Marconi's ability to compete globally in new areas such as Internet Protocol networks. Within months of the BT decision, it was clear that investors were looking for Marconi to sell the business or merge to survive. Marconi's Chinese joint venture partner, Huawei, gained two parts of the BT contract, and BT even hoped it would get access to Marconi's technology through this lower-price channel. In 2006, the main Marconi business was sold to Ericsson, leaving Marconi only a smaller services business working on maintenance of legacy systems (Ashton, 2005; Brummer, 2005; Durman and Box, 2005; Grande, 2005).

Challenging the regulator

True SAM strategy is akin to a full-blown merger between buying and selling organisations – in that buyer and seller make joint investment decisions, exchange proprietary information, exclude third parties and so on. SAM strategy creates a potential for anti-trust violation. Competition regulators are increasingly taking the view that such close collaboration between buyer and seller is potentially anti-competitive.

Believing that SAM is easily implemented

Lastly, there appears inadequate recognition of the implementation barriers and organisational issues faced in SAM strategy. To assume that this is a strategy that can be made effective easily underestimates the degree to which this is a quite radical new business model. Even if a SAM strategy is appropriate for a supplier to manage strategic relationships with certain critical customers, there remains the issue of whether the supplier has the capabilities and resources to make the strategy real, in ways that matter to the customer.

14.6.4 Balancing the case for strategic account management

We have attempted to contrast the apparently compelling case for strategic account management (SAM) models that develop collaborative and integrative relationships with major or dominant customers, with the serious flaws in the underlying assumptions of those models and the potentially damaging traps for the unwary. In many situations, it appears that the adoption of SAM models is based on the suspect logic that the best use of a company's resources is to invest heavily in that part of the business (the largest, most dominant customers) that has the lowest margins and the highest business risk.

Defenders of the SAM model argue that this scenario reflects not the weakness of the model, but poor choice of key accounts by companies. There is some merit in such a response. However, since the apparent reality is that companies choose as strategic accounts those customers to which they sell most, or respond to the demands of large customers for special treatment, then suggesting that the weaknesses inherent in the SAM model can be overcome by better choice of strategic accounts seems somewhat unrealistic.

One logic is that the search should be for alternative strategies that avoid the trap of high dependence on a small number of powerful dominant accounts. Some would probably suggest that this is a search doomed to failure – the most powerful customers control markets and are unlikely to surrender this control willingly. Yet, on the other hand, consider the potential disruption of the status quo in a market by the introduction of a new business model. For example, consumer and business computer users have voiced numerous complaints over the years about the product functionality of Microsoft offerings, and struggled in vain against the massive Microsoft market share in areas such as operating systems and server software. In 2005, we saw the dramatic impact of Linux software – available free or cheaply – developed through a peer-to-peer network, in a business model that appears uninvolved with concerns such as profitability. Microsoft struggled for a long time to respond to challenges such as this, as well as finding effective responses to competitors such as Google, Amazon and Sony, and open-source software suppliers. However, more interesting yet is the fact that much of the Linux revolution has been driven and facilitated by IBM, Sun Microsystems and Dell, who are dramatically reducing their dependence on the old adversaries at Microsoft. Actively managing dependence between buyer and seller may be one way out of the trap.

Another example concerns Heinz, which attempted to reduce its heavy dependence on traditional retailers (Tesco, Sainsbury's) by making products available in petrol stations, convenience store chains, Mothercare stores (for baby foods) and garden centres (Wiggins, 2009). The same logic explains the involvement of Amazon.com in the grocery business in the UK – supported by big brands who are tired of poor treatment and low returns from the dominant supermarkets (Felsted, 2010). That said, such a strategy does have the makings of a 'from frying pan to fire' idea. Similarly, the strategic relationship between Google and Procter & Gamble involving the exchange of knowledge on how to develop P&G online is illustrative (Byron, 2008).

It is noteworthy that 2006 saw the Proctor & Gamble/Gillette merger to create the world's largest consumer brands group. The combined portfolio of brands provides a much stronger hand in dealing with major retailers (Quinn, 2005b). However, the merger also represents a fundamental change to P&G's business model. The goal is to serve not only the world's most affluent one billion consumers in developed countries, but to serve the world's other six billion consumers, with a new focus on lower-income consumers in such markets as China and India. In developing these emerging markets, P&G was deliberately not partnering with global retailers such as Walmart and Carrefour. Instead, in China P&G offers Gillette access to a huge distribution system staffed by an army of individual Chinese entrepreneurs – what P&G calls a 'down the trade' system ending up with a one-person kiosk in a small village selling shampoo and toothpaste. The intention is that stable growth in Asian markets will reduce the combined company's dependence on mature markets dominated by powerful retailers (Grant, 2005).

New business models that will be effective in avoiding the dominant-customer trap will probably share some of the following characteristics:

- reducing critical dependencies and risks by developing alternative routes to market – consider the example of the automotive manufacturers developing direct channel strategies to take back control of the value chain and reduce dependencies on independent distributors;
- developing alternative product offerings to rebuild brand strength as a counter to the power of the largest;
- emphasising the need for high returns to justify taking on high-risk business, not the other way around;
- reducing strategic vulnerabilities created by excessive levels of dependence on a small number of customers or distributors;
- clarifying the difference between major accounts and key accounts and developing appropriate ways of managing these different types of relationship profitably;
- actively rejecting business from some sources because the customer is unattractive in terms of profitability and risk, even if the business on offer is large;
- managing customer accounts as a portfolio using criteria of attractiveness and prospective performance, not simply customer size.

There are situations when SAM is an effective strategy to manage relationships with major buyers and to develop collaboration and partnership rather than adversarial transactions. However, what requires careful management consideration is under what conditions this is true, and whether these are truly the conditions being faced. There is potential insight in evaluating the customer portfolio and its changing composition, and to consider not simply the quantity of business offered by the largest accounts, but also the quality of that business. The quality of business with major accounts includes the profitability of the business, but also the business risk involved, the impact of increased dependence on a small number of customers, and the opportunities given up. A balanced evaluation of this kind provides the basis for a more informed decision, but may also be the trigger for the search for strategic alternatives that may avoid the downside of dependence on powerful key accounts. This balanced evaluation and search for new business models appears urgently needed in many organisations.

Importantly, strategic sales capabilities define in a number of important ways the strategic options available to a company and its ability to implement them. The realities of buyer–seller relationships cannot be underestimated when understanding strategic strengths and weaknesses, and the ability to exploit market opportunities.

Summary

Strategic sales capabilities are an increasingly vital resource in adding value and sustaining effective customer relationships, which executives need to consider when formulating marketing strategy. Better alignment between marketing and sales is a high priority for many companies, as well as recognition of a more strategic role for sales and account management. This new relationship is important to the development and effective implementation of marketing strategy.

Strategic customer management is a broad term describing the sales and account management relationships that link buyers and sellers in business-to-business markets. In particular, it focuses on the choices companies face in how they allocate selling and marketing resources between different customer types and the approaches taken to implementing effective relationships with powerful, dominant customers. The growing attention given to these issues reflects the internal company pressures to reform and reshape the traditional sales organisation so that it can deliver the value and the customer relationship upon which marketing strategy implementation rests. However, the strategic sales organisation elevates attention from the salesforce as the route to implementing strategy, to a force that participates in shaping strategy around the realities of the marketplace.

Analysis of the customer portfolio provides the basis for distinguishing between customers in a direct channel and in the traditional middle market, but also importantly between major accounts and strategic accounts. Strategic account management represents a new business model based on collaboration and joint decision making between buyer and seller. It provides a mechanism for managing some dominant customer relationships. Nonetheless, while there is a compelling case for strategic account management, there is a balancing case of the vulnerabilities and risks in this model. Managers need to balance these factors carefully in deciding whether to implement strategic account management models. The analysis of choices in marketing is closely related to strategic sales capabilities in the business-to-business marketing company.

Case study

Power of the 'mummies' key to Nestlé's strategy in DR Congo

By Katrina Manson in Kinshasa

The global consumer group adapts to local tastes and targets micro-entrepreneurs

Hervé Barrère is an amiable Tahitian with an easy smile and a flair for Congolese dance. He also has an eye for the 'mummies on the table tops'. These are the women traders at markets across the Democratic Republic of the Congo, and Mr Barrère, the country director for Nestlé, the Swiss consumer group, believes these women are key to understanding local tastes and purchasing decisions.

At 'Petit Pont', Kinshasa's main spice market, one of the 29 open-air markets in the capital, a sprawling array of wooden tables are topped with loose garlic, onions and red chillies, near to a rickety bridge that gives the market its name. Mummies are pitching cartons of Maggi's red and yellow-wrapped stock cubes – the Swiss company's flagship brand – against cheaper competitors from Spain's Jumbo and China's Top.

Mr Barrère believes Maggi is now winning thanks to four strategic aspects – taste, margins, marketing and trade organisation. 'We had to work on trade and consumer insight; you need to immerse yourself in this understanding,' says Mr Barrère, who regularly visits the markets to talk to the mummies.

As attempts to cash in on the 'Africa rising' phenomenon go, picking DR Congo must be among the bravest. For all the allure posed by untapped African markets and consistently impressive growth

Source: Kumar Sriskandan/Alamy Stock Photo.

rates, few multinationals set their sights on the vast sprawling country at the heart of the continent. It might have a population of 70m with growth rates close to 9 per cent a year, but poor roads, poor legal frameworks and poorer customers – 60 per cent exist on less than $2 a day – make it a tough market to crack.

Since Nestlé took the plunge, investing $43m in a new factory in Kinshasa that started producing in 2011, the company has set about overcoming the hurdles in a fashion reminiscent of a smaller, more nimble business. But it is far from plain trading. The Swiss corporate is already in court over tax issues there and sales have been disappointing. It sells the same number of its Maggi stock cubes in neighbouring oil-producer Republic of Congo, a country of 5m people, as it does in DR Congo, a country of 70m albeit with a per-capita income 15 times as small.

The Kinshasa factory site remains spacey: only a few machines fill the void. Mr Barrère, however, is confident that the factory will be furnished with more equipment in the future. 'I am waiting for the [growth] wave to come; we need to be ready before the others,' he says. 'Consumption will come if the country is growing, if the people [have] money. Since we got a better understanding of the market we are growing very fast.'

Senior executives credit Mr Barrère with turning around prospects in DR Congo. The company is now selling 100 tonnes of Maggi a month, up from 30 tonnes when he arrived two years ago, and sales in the country are growing at 30 per cent a year. It is this expansion that gives Nestlé – which also sells dairy products in the country – the confidence to bill Maggi as the market leader.

Mr Barrère says it is all down to a better understanding of how DR Congo's markets work, with ragtag stalls and profit-seeking micro-entrepreneurs, and structuring sales to match.

To this end he goes into people's homes to see how women cook and what families like to eat, in an attempt to develop the right product as well as encourage higher usage. While Kenyans like their stock cubes filled with salt and coriander, and Nigerians go for a more fermented soya taste, DR Congo has a more eclectic palate, based on spices Nestlé has tried to replicate in its products. Even its 'standard' flavour is adapted to the market, with extra doses of nutmeg and garlic, and in others, extra aubergine and dried fish. Five years ago, Nestlé even developed the green 'pondu' tablet, a flavour made specifically from cassava leaves to match the beloved Congolese stew made from the same.

'In Lubumbashi they cook with tomatoes and in Kisangani they cook with pondus,' says Mr Barrère, keenly aware that tastes vary throughout this forested country the size of western Europe.

Developing a successful sales chain to sell the stock cubes, which start at 50 francs (three pence) for two individually wrapped 4-gram portions, has been the hardest task. Although open-air markets take only a quarter of sales, he believes their role in the trading chain and their potential reach into the population makes them critical to Nestlé's expansion in DR Congo.

'The mummies are really at the heart of what we are doing in terms of our business. I have been married so many times with them!' he jokes, saying social interactions in DR Congo must be 'super energetic' and 'extremely positive' if they are to succeed. He refused to cut his hair this year until he made his first-half sales target, prompting laughter from women traders in a country where long hair on men is more commonly a sign of madness than market determination.

'For the mummies on the table top, if you don't have the right margin you're out of the market; they have to be clear how much they will earn and be clear what the demand is,' says Mr Barrère.

That is why, under their new director, Nestlé overhauled its sales approach. Previously, it sold to both retailers and wholesalers, which made pricing chaotic. In order to impose order and discipline on prices and the distribution chain, Mr Barrère now sells only to wholesalers. The company sends agents to oversee the chain, ensuring the mummies secure daily credit to buy fast-selling stock, meaning they can repay the loan by lunchtime. They even oversee such minutiae as the arrangements of merchandise on the table tops.

The company puts on regular Maggi neighbourhood promotions – Mr Barrère frequently jumps up on stage and dances at such events. It also holds cookery demonstrations, encouraging women to use three stock cubes, which Mr Barrère says is more healthy than the women's typical method – using two plus extra salt.

Following Nestlé's market reorganisation, Beatrice Betuma is now one of only two wholesalers in the whole of Kinshasa. In the past two years, sales at her shop at a crossroads where women cook stews in huge vats on the ground have gone from $30,000 a month to $170,000. 'I have a lot more customers; now my name is famous,' says Ms Betuma, once a 'mummy on a table top' herself. Loyalty programmes, targets and incentive schemes – Nestlé took Ms Betuma on a holiday to South Africa as a reward for increased sales – are key. 'Now I want to go to Canada,' says the 51-year-old mother-of-three, whose husband lives in neighbouring Angola.

Penetrating DR Congo beyond Kinshasa is a further feat. Due to hazards such as theft, damage and red tape, sending cargo by train to Lubumbashi takes two months. But Mr Barrère insists it is worth doing, claiming to have tripled sales in Lubumbashi in the past year and a half. In the east, access was so prohibitive, and the road over-run by rebels at the time, that he took to airfreighting the goods to Goma until only two months ago, making them 'the most expensive stock cubes in the world'. Last month, he managed to deliver a consignment by the huge, bending Congo River for the first time. 'It is so amazing,' says Mr Barrère. 'It is like, how do we conquer the full Congo.'

Further reading: Emotional appeal

Supporting the local economy appeals to market-women, and Nestlé draws on this, says Hervé Barrère, the company's Congo director. Unlike Nestlé's products, competitors' stock cubes are made and imported entirely from abroad.

However, some of Mr Barrère's toughest competition, he discovered, came from Nestlé itself: its stock cubes had been smuggled from Nigeria and Kenya. In both cases the taste and the packaging – in English – were not adapted to a French-speaking market with a more eclectic palate. Several tours to the factory, which employs 60 people, convinced the women to switch. 'It was very emotional: one of the mummies cried because . . . she realised she has a role to play to develop the country.'

 Source: from 'Power of the "mummies" key to Nestlé's strategy in DR Congo', *Financial Times*, 01/10/14 (Manson, K.).

Discussion questions

1 How does strategic customer management differ from selling? How is it strategic?

2 How is Nestlé using strategic customer management in the Democratic Republic of the Congo? What are the benefits of such an infrastructure?

3 How is such an approach also helping with the rest of the marketing mix?

CHAPTER 15
STRATEGIC ALLIANCES AND NETWORKS

'Good relationships between companies are of crucial importance. They represent the effective teamwork that allows partners to create value for customers and shareholders that could not possibly be created by individual firms.'

(Gibbs and Humphries, 2009)

'But, on the other hand . . . We have no permanent allies, we have no permanent enemies, we only have permanent interests.'

(Attributed to Henry John Temple, Viscount Lord Palmerston 1784–1865, Foreign Secretary and Prime Minister of Great Britain during Queen Victoria's reign)

MasterCard cashes in on smart transit

By Andrew Edgecliffe-Johnson in New York

Credit card company promotes seamless ticketing in cash-dominated market

MasterCard is building a network of partnerships to realise the potential of contactless and mobile payments to make urban transit systems work more efficiently, as it looks to the trend for 'smart cities' as a means of expanding the market for its cards.

In tests from Philadelphia to Gujarat, MasterCard has begun to integrate payment systems for train, metro, bus and road toll systems.

'85 per cent of the world's payments are still in cash. To me that's our largest opportunity,' Ajay Banga, MasterCard's chief executive, told the *Financial Times*.

Mastercard analysis found that transit systems – along with coffee and newspapers – were one of the largest markets in which cash dominates payment cards. 'It's $200bn a year in different cities around the world, which has the opportunity to be transformative for our business,' he said.

The company announced a partnership in March with Cubic Transportation Systems, which uses traffic data to advise network operators from London to Chicago whether they need to change routes or pricing to cope with rush hour demand, and to alert

Source: Maurice Savage / Alamy Stock Photo.

commuters through their smartphones of the best options.

Other new partners include Masabi, which allows users to buy tickets through their mobile devices, and Parkeon, a parking company with which MasterCard this week announced a plan to turn parking meters into kiosks that offer coupons for local businesses.

Mr Banga said MasterCard's aim in cities such as Philadelphia, where a pilot programme is due to expand into a full consumer launch later this year, was to cut the time train passengers spend buying a separate bus ticket, and 'intelligent personal routeing', using data to advise users of their best routes home.

'All transit systems are built for the peak of the peak. If you could find a way to take 5–7 per cent of the peak of the peak traffic off to less used routes you could reduce the cost of how you build and plan transit systems enormously,' he said, estimating that large urban transit systems could save $150m–$200m by being able to delay upgrades to their infrastructure.

Citing the example of Transport for London, which has opened up its ticketing systems from depending on its Oyster Card contactless payment system to accepting ordinary bank cards, Mr Banga said MasterCard could save transit system operators the cost of maintaining their own systems. 'It's actually cheaper for them' than maintaining their own systems and handling cash, he said. 'It takes out the friction.'

Mr Banga said that getting transit systems to accept payment cards could be a 'critical factor' in expanding MasterCard's market. It processed more than 11bn transactions in the first quarter from the 2.2bn MasterCard and Maestro cards in issue.

Mr Banga added that most MasterCard users are in cities, which are home to more than half of the world's population and about half of the world's 'financially excluded' – a group MasterCard has been targeting through separate initiatives with the UN, the World Bank and others.

The company is among several, including IBM and Google, to have identified the business potential in the rise of 'smart cities' – increasingly automated and connected urban areas whose authorities use data to inform the provision of public services.

More public–private partnerships would be needed as urbanisation puts a strain on cities' networks, Mr Banga added, saying the challenges transit systems face were 'too vast, too deep' to tackle alone.

 Source: from 'MasterCard cashes in on smart transit', *Financial Times*, 02/07/15 (Edgecliffe-Johnson, A.).

Discussion questions

1 What are the issues facing MasterCard?

2 How is the company attempting to address these issues?

Introduction

In developing marketing strategy, it is important for executives to consider the new organisational forms and routes to market that are developing, and in particular the impact of strategic alliances and networks as a way of competing. However, from the outset, two points are important: first, what matters are your strategic objectives – alliances and networks are a means to an end, not an end in themselves; and second, if partnership and alliance is your way forward, then you need to take a strategic approach to managing these new types of business relationships, or they will fail – one estimate is that between 60 and 70 per cent of alliances fail (Hughes and Weiss, 2007).

Thus, this chapter adopts a critical perspective that examines the following issues as a framework for competing through strategic alliances and networks:

- the implications of an era of strategic collaboration for our strategic choices;
- the types of partnership, collaboration and strategic alliance that are emerging in the marketplace, as important ways of building networks;
- the forms that networks of collaborating organisations take, and the development of new organisational forms for marketing based on networks;
- the importance of strategic alliances as a competitive force in global markets;
- the risks involved in strategies of collaboration and alliance.

A clear management agenda is needed that details the issues that should be addressed in evaluating alliance-based strategies as a way for us to go to market. Figure 15.1 shows the structure of our coverage of this topic.

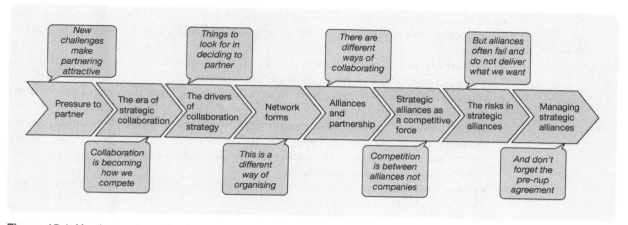

Figure 15.1 Key issues in evaluating strategic alliances and network organisations

It is important from the outset to recognise that alliances and networked organisations may be the basis for driving new business models and new marketing strategies in markets everywhere. For example, Chinese e-commerce phenomenon Alibaba became the world's largest stock market flotation in 2014, with a $22 billion valuation on the New York stock exchange, which some see as heralding the end of US dominance in e-commerce. Alibaba is the world's largest online marketplace for trade between companies and has built an unrivalled online retail platform in China. It ships around £90 billion worth of goods a year, and handles more packages annually than Amazon and eBay combined. Its Taobao website has been the engine of growth by linking consumers together on a peer-to-peer model. More recent emphasis is on the Tmall website that hosts large retailers selling to consumers. Alibaba operates on a net margin of 50 per cent because its model is to connect buyers and sellers and leave others with the costly business of moving goods around. Helping merchants to market their goods in China accounts for half of Alibaba's sales; sellers' commissions account for a quarter; and most of the rest comes from the wholesale business and international commerce. Cost of sales is incredibly low. The wall around Alibaba's business is the network effect – the company has the most buyers and sellers, giving current users an excellent reason to stay and new users reasons to come. Alibaba has created multiple sites – each tailored for a different style of transaction, and each with the potential for massive global reach. Alibaba is a global channel in a way that Amazon is not, because it facilitates so much business into and out of China (Collack and Armstrong, 2014). Alibaba is a compelling example of the strength of a networked competitive model.

15.1 Pressures to partner

The topicality of alliance and network concerns reflects the fact that the environment in which businesses go to market has changed radically in most sectors and continues to be turbulent and higher risk than ever before. We will consider the nature of this revolution and its profound implications further in Chapter 18. For the moment we note that the new environment for business is increasingly characterised by:

- **scarcer resources** – both in the physical environment, but also in terms of downsized, leaner, strategically focused corporations;
- **increased competition**, frequently from new sources, new types of competitor and new technologies, at home and overseas;

- **escalating customer expectations** for higher service and quality from more sophisticated and better-informed customers, which demands higher levels of expertise at the market level;
- **pressures from strong distributors**, such as retailers in consumer goods marketing, to achieve ever-greater economies in supply-chain costs;
- **high levels of customer concentration** in many business-to-business markets, shifting power from seller to buyer;
- the pervasive onslaught of the **internationalisation of markets and competition**, driven by technology such as the Internet;
- **faster rates of change in markets and technologies**, demanding higher levels and more rapid responsiveness in organisations;
- **a post-recession environment** characterised by a lack of trust in business and an unprecedented emphasis on customer value; and,
- **more turbulent, unpredictable markets**, where change is greater in magnitude and very difficult to anticipate with any degree of certainty.

Importantly, business environment changes of this kind, and the new business models they demand, continue to be associated with the evolution and growth of new organisational forms. This process sees the displacement of traditional, hierarchical, free-standing monoliths by flexible, agile, responsive organisational forms. Over a substantial period, it is clear that many of these new forms will depend on inter-organisational collaborations or alliances and hollow organisations with a virtual Internet-based form. Importantly, often these new types of organisational arrangements completely reverse historical trends of aggregation and integration in large conventional structures, in favour of disaggregation and devolution of functions:

> Organisations of the future are likely to be vertically disaggregated: functions typically encompassed within a single organisation will instead be performed in independent organisations. The functions of product design and development, manufacturing, and distribution . . . will be brought together and held in temporary alignment by a variety of market mechanisms.
> *(Miles and Snow, 1984)*

The realignment of company resources with the demands of new and more challenging business environments – characterised by the post-recession era – has seen the widespread emergence of strategies of collaboration and partnership with other organisations as a key element of the process of going to market. While precise terminology does not exist, these new organisational forms and network arrangements have been variously termed 'marketing partnerships', 'strategic alliances' and 'marketing networks' (Cravens and Piercy, 2012).

For example, Prahalad and Krishnan (2008) have described a fundamental transformation of business structure taking place in numerous industries. Their argument is that this fundamental transformation is being driven by two main factors. First, they argue that the age of mass production is over and customers demand unique value: 'value is shifting from products to solutions and experiences', in such a way that relationships are taking over as the central element of exchange. Second, they argue the consequence is that, increasingly, no single business is likely to be big enough to cope with the complexity and diversity of customer demands that are emerging. In turn, this underlines the importance of alliances and networks to deliver customer value – constellations of suppliers that can be configured in different ways to meet different customer needs. Success will increasingly rely on abandoning the business models of the past and managing through new collaborative networks.

The effects may be dramatic. For instance, already more than a third of Proctor & Gamble's new products come from external alliances, and more broadly P&G is a prototype of a multinational corporation that has transformed itself through collaboration. For example, P&G has a strategic relationship with Google, whereby P&G aims to enhance its Web capabilities and Google looks to gain a higher share of P&G's advertising. P&G has also taken a stake in Ocado in the UK, as a testing ground for new online concepts. With insights gained from its partners, P&G has already started selling its brands direct to the US consumer from its 'eStore' site (Birchall, 2010).

Some partnerships may be surprising. Apple and IBM were once fierce rivals, but have struck a deal to sell iPads, iPhones and apps deeper into the corporate marketplace. In collaboration they are developing more than 100 apps for a range of industries. Apple hopes that IBM's vast network of corporate clients will win it business customers, while IBM will use Apple devices to sell more of its software and services (Stock, 2014). New strategies built around attractive business opportunities outweigh traditional rivalries.

Indeed, IBM itself has been transformed into a borderless organisation working globally with numerous partners to enhance the value of its offerings to customers on a worldwide basis. IBM is a highly internationalised business. It has over 50,000 employees in India – IBM's second biggest operation outside the US. Interestingly, the company has moved its head of procurement from New York to Shenzhen in China (*The Economist*, 2007; Palmisano, 2007). In fact, IBM's former chairman and CEO, Samuel Palmisano, defined a vision for the globally integrated enterprise (GIE), as the twenty-first century successor to the multinational corporation. Palmisano argued that businesses are changing in fundamental ways – structurally, operationally and culturally – in response to imperatives for globalisation and the impact of new technology. The emerging GIE is a company that shapes its strategy, management and operations in pursuit of a new goal: the integration of production and value delivery worldwide. Shared business practices and connected business activities make it possible for companies to transfer work from in-house operations to outside specialists. Global integration forces companies to choose where they want work performed geographically, and whether they want it performed in-house or by an external partner. The centre of the GIE is global collaboration, both with commercial partners and governments.

Along similar lines, Hagel and Seely-Brown (2005) suggest that lowered barriers to international trade and technological developments mean companies have no choice but to concentrate on their areas of expertise, while collaborating globally with others specialising in different activities. The goal is to find ways of working with suppliers not simply to cut costs but to collaborate on product innovation. Li & Fung is a Hong Kong-based clothing supplier that Hagel and Seely-Brown describe as a 'process orchestrator'. The company produces goods for Western companies drawing on a network of 7,500 partners – yarn from Korea, dyed in Thailand, woven in Taiwan, cut in Bangladesh, assembled in Mexico, with a zip from Japan. Importantly, these companies are partners to Li & Fung, rather than simply suppliers. By operating as a network, the partners help each other innovate in both design and manufacture (Hagel and Seely-Brown, 2005). Nonetheless, Li & Fung's reliance on alliances has unnerved investors, and what is now the world's largest sourcing company is subject to drastic overhaul (Hughes and Kirk, 2013; Sevastopulo, 2014).

Working with partners to create enhanced customer value creates a need for flexible yet effective integration of inputs to deliver seamless value to customers. While building effective customer relationships has always depended on understanding and predicting customer needs, the additional role is to work with a set of providers of different parts of the value offering – some internal and some external to the company – to construct and deliver a coherent value offering to the customer.

Nonetheless, by way of balance, it should be recognised that the challenges in working effectively with external partners mean that this is not always the best route to superior customer value. Rolls-Royce runs a global service network, providing a real-time support and maintenance service to airlines operating planes with Rolls-Royce engines – there are more than 50,000 Rolls-Royce engines flying, and the support extends decades after the original purchase. Conventional wisdom was for aero-engine makers to license out much support and maintenance – that is, to collaborate with third-party suppliers – and their after-market business was restricted to spare parts and distress repairs. To align the interests of airlines with its own, Rolls-Royce runs its own operations centres, in a move that has revolutionised the industry. Support and maintenance grew to generate 55 per cent of Rolls

Royce's revenues by the late 2000s (Pfeifer, 2008). Partnership strategies are not always the best, or only, response to complex customer and market situations. Similarly, many European producers are moving outsourced production back closer to home because of disappointing results in working with overseas partners in emerging markets. One reason is that managing across organisational and national boundaries is frequently not straightforward (Milne, 2008).

In a growing number of markets, however, it is clear that complex networks of partnerships will be the way in which business is done. The transition to working across traditional organisational boundaries identifies a new and possibly complex integration challenge. Responding effectively to that challenge is a growing part of the marketing strategy and implementation problem (see Chapter 16).

Certainly, it is likely that the strategic internal relationships, which will be vital to achieving effective integration in networked companies, will be between the organisational units and processes that manage key external relationships. As customer demands for more complex value offerings grow, the ability to work collaboratively to create solutions will emphasise the need for close coordination between suppliers, partners and sellers. The management of that coordination will require the effective management of relationships between those responsible for strategic marketing and sales, those who manage relationships with suppliers and those who are tasked with the management of alliance and joint-venture relationships with external organisations. In many companies, these strategic internal relationships may be one of the core value-creating processes (see Chapter 14). Furthermore, these strategic internal relationships will often have to cope with complex markets where there are also links between our suppliers and our partners and between them and our customers, in the way suggested by Figure 15.2.

Indeed, in some interesting ways, the trend towards inter-organisational collaboration in the route to market provides the other face of relationship marketing. While the priority of managing better customer relationship remains, for a growing number of companies this is accompanied by the need for efforts to be made in managing the relationship with the

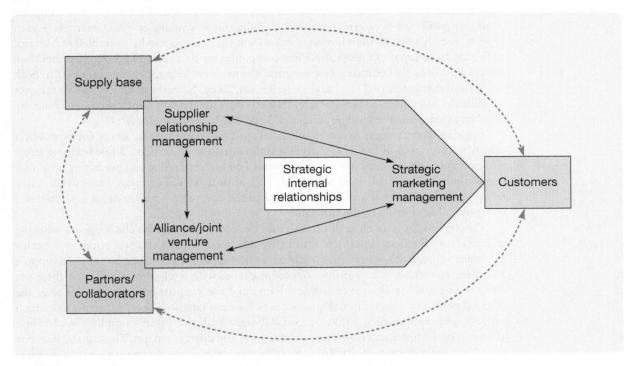

Figure 15.2 Strategic internal relationships and value chain collaboration

collaborator as well. Importantly, these new collaborative and networked organisations are distinctive and different to conventional structures. They are, for example:

> characterised by flexibility, specialisation, and an emphasis on relationship management instead of market transactions . . . to respond quickly and flexibly to accelerating change in technology, competition and customer preferences.
> *(Webster, 1992)*

Correspondingly, it is important to recognise that in many industries the emergence of networks of collaborating organisations, linked by various forms of alliance, has become a dominant platform for strategic development.

The growing importance of alliance and inter-organisational collaborative forms means it is important that our thinking about the implementation of our own strategies, and also our understanding of the emerging forms of competition we face in the market, should embrace the strategic alliance and the resulting growth of networks of organisations linked by various forms of partnering relationship. It is also important to emphasise that some of the strategic issues faced in alliances and networks go far beyond simple inter-organisational cooperation, and are leading to new ways of doing business with the customer, as shown by the Alibaba example mentioned previously (see also Chapter 14).

15.2 The era of strategic collaboration

Executives should be aware that collaborative forms characterise competitive behaviour in many sectors, with major implications for strategic choices. For example, Cravens and Piercy (2012) argue that factors such as the emergence of new value-enhancing opportunities, rapidly changing markets, a complex array of technologies, shortages of important skills and resources and more demanding customers, present organisations with an unprecedented set of challenges. Importantly, one central feature of developing an effective response to these challenges has been the recognition by many business executives that building relationships with other companies is essential to compete effectively in the turbulent and rapidly changing post-recession era confronting the developed world economies, and in working with the rapidly growing opportunities in the Asian and Chinese markets. Indeed, in some sectors such as the automotive industry, conventional acquisition strategy has largely been dropped in favour of alliance-based ventures. In effect, we are experiencing an important change from an era of competition to an era of strategic collaboration.

There are a variety of inter-organisational relationships that we have to consider in building effective marketing strategies: vertical channel relationships and supplier/manufacturer collaborations (see Chapter 14), and horizontal relationships in the form of strategic alliances and joint ventures all share a growing emphasis on collaboration and partnership rather than simple contractual obligations.

These new collaboration-based relationships with customers, suppliers, distributors and even competitors are resulting in a variety of new organisational forms, which are commonly grouped together and classified as 'networks', where members may constitute 'virtual corporations' (for example, existing only on the Internet). Many of the pioneers have been in the services sector, but networks spanning complexes of supply chains are becoming more usual. In fact, the network paradigm may become the dominant organisational form of the twenty-first century, but the reality we face may be a complex mix of collaborative organisational forms with conventional structures.

We shall examine a variety of examples of network organisations, but the characteristics of network organisations can be discussed in the following terms. A defining characteristic of the network organisation is the performance of marketing and other business functions by different independent organisations and individuals – the process of 'vertical disaggregation'. The network is a flat organisational form, involving interaction between network partners rather than the multi-layered functions of the traditional hierarchical organisation. In fact, dramatic changes have taken place in the traditional hierarchical forms of organisations as a result of alliance and network strategies. Although in some ways similar to channel of distribution networks (such as suppliers/producers, marketing intermediaries and end-users), network organisations may display both horizontal and vertical structures (for example, collaborations between suppliers as well as supply-chain linkages). Moreover, networks are frequently complex and liable to change more frequently than traditional distribution channels.

Typically, network operations are guided by sophisticated information and decision support systems, often global in their scope, which perform many of the command and control functions of the traditional hierarchical organisation. The resulting network is flexible and adaptable to change, and the more successful network designs are customer driven – guided by the needs and preferences of buyers – but may be complex and unfamiliar to executives.

The inter-organisational ties in a network may span organisations from suppliers to end-users, and/or actual or potential competitors. The network may also include service agencies, such as advertising, research, consulting services and distribution specialists. The relationships among the firms in a network may include: simple transactional contracts of the conventional buyer–seller type; supplier–producer collaborative agreements; strategic alliances or partnerships; consortia; franchising and distribution linkages; joint ventures; or vertical integration. We shall examine these relationships in more depth.

Starting from these general points about alliances and networks, this chapter builds a framework for evaluating, designing and managing alliance and network-based organisations as part of the implementation of marketing strategy and as a fundamental change in the competitive scenario. Nonetheless, it should be remembered that limited knowledge and often the absence of effective management capabilities for managing in these new organisational forms are illustrated by the continued high failure rates of strategic alliances.

15.3 The drivers of collaboration strategies

A starting point is to identify the potential drivers, or motivating factors, that lead organisations towards collaboration in delivering their strategies to market. Such driving forces include those outlined in Figure 15.3 and discussed in the following sections.

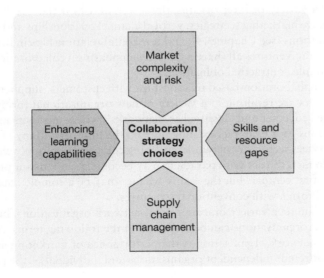

Figure 15.3
Drivers of
collaboration
strategy

15.3.1 Market complexity and risk

Modern markets are frequently characterised by complexity and high degrees of risk. One way of coping with that complexity and reducing (or sharing) risk is through collaboration. Complexity and risk may be exhibited in various situations:

- **Blurring of market boundaries:** Conventional market definitions may become outdated and expose a company to new types of customer demand and new types of competition. The information industry is a prime example, where we see the convergence of Internet companies, telecommunications, consumer electronics, entertainment media, publishing and office equipment industries. A converging industry greatly increases the complexity for a single firm trying to compete in the face of a widening range of customer requirements and technologies to satisfy customer needs. Many of the products required are likely to be beyond the design, manufacturing and marketing capabilities of a single company, thus driving companies to pool their skills. This pooling of capabilities may be very effective. Technological convergence in making the mobile telephone both a camera and a music player has had severe disruptive effects for the traditional photography and music businesses. High-technology businesses of this kind have seen many alliances formed, though often lasting only a short period of time as competitive priorities change.

- **Escalating customer demands:** In many markets, buyers are demanding increasing value but also uniqueness in their purchases: one-to-one marketing, or micro-segmentation, is becoming a reality. To respond positively to this demand may be beyond the scope of a single company in terms of expertise and economy, and may require new ways of doing business. For example, the taxi firm Uber, and other firms growing in the 'sharing economy', have revolutionised their sectors. Uber's car-sharing model provides an online, pre-paid, online-tracked taxi ride, but by using freelance drivers with their own cars, Uber avoids owning vehicles or taxi depots and yet provides a greatly superior model – at least to the consumer and the company itself (see Figure 15.4). Its 'product' is

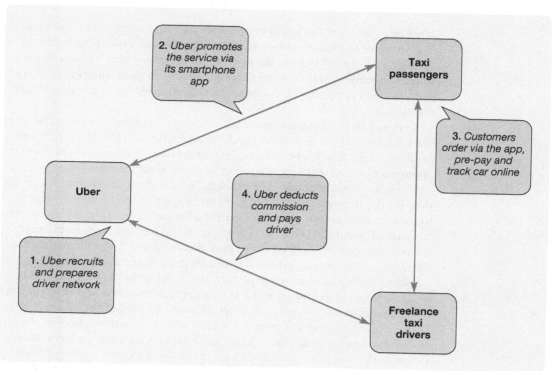

Figure 15.4 Uber's network organisation

to connect passengers to pre-existing fleet and car owners through its smartphone app. Uber started with $307 million from a group of backers including Google Ventures and Jeff Bezos, founder of Amazon. The Uber concept is to make booking a taxi as easy as making an online dinner reservation or checking a price on Amazon. By 2014, Uber was operational in 246 cities in 46 countries, and was valued at $40 billion. Models like Uber are springing up in many sectors – people can rent out spare rooms or holiday homes on Airbnb or HomeAway, and get Gesty or UrbanBellhop to welcome the guests and clean up after them. There are Uber-type models for laundry (Washio), massages (Zeel), alcohol (Minibar) and many more – the network concept is a powerful response to escalating customer demands. That said, concerns are growing that the model, while great for consumers, has negative effects on workers. It is likely that what is now known as 'the gig economy' will be a central battleground of the next decade in terms of employment policy, workers' rights, and the like. It's worth bearing this in mind, particularly as the world (or at least large parts of it) appears to be moving more towards a 'sustainability' and 'purpose-driven' model.

- **A borderless world:** It is three decades since Ohmae (1990) wrote about the interlinked economy of *The Borderless World*. Companies are increasingly driven to compete globally, and collaboration offers an attractive alternative to competing alone in a new environment. We mentioned earlier the global networks being developed at IBM to reflect changing international connectedness. Another global initiative is the long-standing partnership between competitors General Mills from the USA and Nestlé from Switzerland. They created a joint venture – Cereal Partners Worldwide – to market General Mills' cereal brands in 130 countries outside North America. General Mills contributes its high-quality cereal brands and Nestlé provides its extensive international distribution channels and local market knowledge, for an effective and enduring global collaboration (see **https://www.nestle.com/aboutus/overview/businesses/cereal-partners-worldwide**).

15.3.2 Skills and resource gaps

It follows that there are growing pressures on firms to collaborate to compete effectively in globalised, technology-driven markets. The costs of developing internally the full range of skills and capabilities needed to compete effectively may be beyond the resources of a single company, or simply more cheaply available through alliances with specialised partners – where each partner can concentrate on applying its own core competencies, what it does best.

This may be of most importance with strategic accounts – the powerful major customers upon whom we have greatest dependence as a seller (see Chapter 14). Strategic customers generally seek 'solutions-orientated' packages that relate to their business problems and opportunities, and will accept nothing less from their strategic suppliers. Selling products or services is not acceptable. The problem faced is that constructing the appropriate 'solution' for the strategic customer may involve expertise and technology that forces the seller to partner with others. Johnson Controls, for example, is the highly successful seller of automotive seating and electrical switching. While Johnson manufactures seat and switches, it has had to partner with others to provide the simple 'bolt-on', modularised seating and electronics components systems required by modern car assembly plants.

Filling skills and resource gaps may also involve the creation of new brands and new business forms in surprising ways. For example, some years ago Honda Motor and Hong Kong Disneyworld formed a strategic alliance. As part of the alliance, Honda sponsors Disneyworld's 'Autopia' attraction, which allows visitors to 'drive to the future' in electric cars and experience 'outer space', and supports the park's safety features. Honda gets exclusive rights to use Disneyland images to promote its cars, motorcycles and power equipment products in Hong Kong and China. The partners are looking for further opportunities for both brands to collaborate, and interestingly appear have to found ways to merge automotive and entertainment industry interests. Disney has similar corporate alliances with Siemens, Coca-Cola, Hewlett-Packard and others to share the Disney brand.

In other cases, an alliance may provide enhanced market access and open new ways of trading. For example, the fast-food chain McDonald's has an alliance with Sinopec, the state-owned oil company in China that operates 30,000 petrol stations (and adds around 500 more every year). The alliance is to support McDonald's strategy of expanding drive-through restaurants in China. The strategy is based on changing eating habits in heavily populated Chinese cities, which are becoming more Westernised, with more widespread car ownership and mobile lifestyles among the young, who favour purchases directly from vehicles. McDonald's believes that Sinopec will provide a platform to build its China business around drive-through restaurants.

Much of the growth strategy at Alliance Boots is based on partnering – Boots and Waitrose sell each other's products in the UK and the company has merged with Walgreens in the USA to achieve global expansion. Alliance Boots' goal of expanding sales of its emerging skincare brands is supported by a deal with P&G, which markets and distributes Alliance Boots' Laboratories Serum 7 skincare range to pharmacies in Italy, Spain, Germany, Austria and Switzerland (Felsted, 2011). The partnership puts the power of P&G's distribution network and marketing expertise behind Alliance Boots' products, while giving P&G (the maker of Olay) a more exclusive brand to expand the skincare product portfolio it sells in these markets (Rigby and Felsted, 2010a, b).

15.3.3 Supply-chain management

One recent manifestation of the pressure to collaborate is the proposal for the 'lean enterprise' (Womack and Jones, 1996), which involves partnering between companies at different stages of the supply chain. The Efficient Consumer Response (ECR) programme of 'cooperative partnerships' between retailers and manufacturers who have committed to reducing costs in markets such as grocery, is illustrative of this.

When Google launched Android as a key part of its mobile phone strategy, the package of open-source software was designed to make it easier and cheaper to build the next generations of smartphone services. However, on a broader front, Google also launched its Open Handset Alliance to attack Nokia and Microsoft. The alliance had 34 mobile and technology company members at the outset, including handset makers Samsung and Motorola and mobile operators NTT, DoCoMo and T-Mobile. Importantly, open handsets running any applications desired by the user weakens the existing mobile phone companies' business model. Google was trying to make the value chain for wireless mobile like that in the broadband Internet market – where applications are developed independently of the device manufacturer and network operators, thus relegating operators to a minor role (Waters and Taylor, 2007). Google's gamble was that redesigning the value chain would reshape the mobile phone business to its advantage (Taylor *et al.*, 2007). Certainly, it appears to have paid off, in that Microsoft and Nokia are no longer serious players in the smartphone space. That said, Apple's huge share of the smartphone market remains, operating with a completely different 'walled garden' framework.

Sometimes supply-chain collaborations may be problematic, as discovered when the French train operator Société Nationale des Chemins de Fer and network operator Réseau Ferré de France acquired a fleet of trains too wide to fit French railway station platforms – 1,300 platforms have to be trimmed to fit the new trains at a cost of almost $70 million (Horobin, 2014). On a broader scale, Boeing's 787 'Dreamliner' relied on a key strategy of outsourced manufacturing. Only 10 per cent of manufacturing is done by Boeing, the rest is supplied by 40 partners – wings built in Japan, the carbon composite fuselage in Italy and the United States, and the landing gear from France. The Dreamliner has 367,000 parts sourced from a global network of 900 suppliers. Managing a collaborative supply chain this complex has severely stretched Boeing's capabilities, and there have been major problems with poorly fitting components and delays leading to cancelled orders (Weitzman, 2011).

15.3.4 Enhancing learning capabilities

One reason for alliance may be to learn and acquire new capabilities. For example, as mentioned previously, consumer products giant Procter & Gamble has recently taken a shareholding in Internet retailer Ocado, seen as a testing ground for P&G to evaluate its ability to sell direct to the consumer and challenge the power of major 'bricks-and-mortar' retailers. Other P&G projects include swapping executives with Google to learn more about search behaviour and Internet use, in developing a new business model in the conventional value chain (Piercy *et al.*, 2010b).

With the promise of biotechnology to provide new generations of drugs at a time when many pharmaceutical companies have clung to more traditional areas of R&D, big pharma companies such as Novartis and Merck are rapidly forming alliances with small biotechnology companies to strengthen their position in the race to develop new cancer immunotherapies. This category is expected to be worth $40 billion a year within a decade, and the large companies cannot afford to miss out but must tap into the knowledge of others (Ward, 2015).

These developments cannot be ignored, as they provide powerful pressures towards collaboration between companies conventionally viewed as having only a buyer–seller relationship, or who were traditionally competitors. It is important that in evaluating our markets and our strategies for the future, we should carefully and systematically consider the emergence of these factors, which may drive our competitors' and our own strategies into collaborative network forms.

The next questions to consider relate to the types of networks that can be identified and the nature of the links that hold them together. As strategic alliances have become one of the most important organisational forms in modern business, managers are frequently faced with decision choices in terms of which type and form of alliance to adopt (Pansiri, 2005).

15.4 Network forms

There is no broadly accepted typology of network organisational forms. However, the approach discussed here is useful in clarifying our ideas about the types of network that exist and may emerge in our markets. Cravens and Piercy (2012) report the integration of the perspectives offered by Achrol (1991), Powell (1990), Quinn (1992) and Webster (1992) to propose the model of network organisation types shown in Figure 15.5. They argue that there are different kinds of networks that can be classified in two important respects:

1 **The type of network relationship**, which can vary from the highly collaborative (involving various forms of inter-organisational cooperation and partnership), to the mainly transactional (the traditional buyer–seller transaction, for example).

2 **The volatility of environmental change** – the argument that in highly volatile environments, external relationships with other organisations must be flexible enough to allow

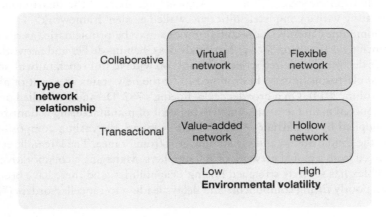

Figure 15.5
Types of network organisation

for alteration – and possibly termination – in a short time period. On the other hand, when the environment is more stable, more enduring forms of collaboration are more attractive.

Using these dimensions to classify networks produces the model in Figure 15.5, which suggests that there are at least four types of network prototype:

1 **The hollow network**: a transaction-based organisational form, associated with highly volatile environments. The term 'hollow' emphasises that the core organisation draws heavily on other organisations to satisfy customer needs. For example, organisations that compete in this way are often specialists that coordinate an extensive network of suppliers and buyers. One example of this type of network is Monster.com, the online recruitment and careers company. Monster connects job seekers with employers, as well as providing them with careers advice online. Some 75 million individuals have established personalised accounts with Monster, which operates in 36 countries with 4,200 employees. A hollow organisation offers a buffer against the risks in a frequently changing environment.

2 **The flexible network**: associated with conditions of high environmental volatility but characterised by inter-organisational links that tend to be collaborative and long term in duration, where the network coordinator manages an internal team that identifies customer needs and establishes sources of supply to satisfy customer requirements. For example, as noted earlier, many of the multinational pharmaceutical firms are tied to core competencies in organic and inorganic chemistry and are seeking to establish alliances with entrepreneurial biotechnology firms. The larger firms have too much invested in their current technology to switch completely to biotechnology, but want to exploit partnerships to ensure they have a source of biotechnology-based products. The Uber example discussed earlier also provides a model of a flexible network, where Uber acts as a hub promoting and defending the service and providing the smartphone software, but using a network of external partners (drivers) to provide the taxi ride to the customer.

3 **The value-added network**: associated with less volatile environments and based mainly on transactional relationships between network members. For example, the network coordinator may use a global network of suppliers, but still maintain substantial internal operations – the core organisation may contract out for many added-value functions such as production, but retain responsibility for innovation and product design. Industries using this type of network are clothing manufacture, furniture, eye-glasses and some services – the link is that the value-added network fits situations where complex technologies and customised product offerings are not required.

4 **The virtual network**: associated with situations where environmental volatility is relatively low, and the core organisation seeks to establish collaborative relationships with other organisations. This is similar to what has been called the 'virtual corporation', which seeks to achieve adaptability to meet the needs of segmented markets through long-term partnerships rather than internal investment. In these cases, market access and technology access are the key drivers and, as with the flexible network, formal strategic alliances are the most common method for collaborating. The virtual network provides a buffer against market risks and allows access to new technology.

A broader and more complex view of network types was provided by Achrol (1997), who attempted to reflect three important characteristics that may differentiate different types of network: whether they are single-firm or multi-firm, whether they are single-industry or multi-industry; and, whether they are stable or temporary. Achrol's (1997) view of networks identifies the following types:

- **Internal market networks**: this describes the reformation of major companies to break free of the restrictions of traditional hierarchies and multi-divisional forms, by organising into internal enterprise units that operate as independent profit centres. For example, at one stage General Motors reorganised rigid and inefficient component manufacturing units into eight internal market units, each specialised in an automotive system area and able to sell its products on the open market as well as to GM, including sales to GM's competitors in automotive manufacture.

- **Vertical market networks,** or **marketing channel networks**: reflect the traditional view of vertical channel relationships, but go further to recognise the focal firm that coordinates upstream supplier firms and downstream distributor firms. Often the integrator specialises in marketing functions and uses specialists for manufacture and distribution. Early forms included the 'hollow corporation' – for example, Casio, Nike and Liz Claiborne. In such networks, the typical pattern is that the integrator is the firm that owns the brand and specialises in the marketing function, while alliance partners are specialised resource centres providing some aspect of product or production technology. An example is provided by IKEA, the retailer of Swedish furniture, which successfully operates a global sourcing network of 2,300 suppliers in 67 countries, to get 10,000 products on the shelf at prices up to 30 per cent cheaper than traditional rivals.

- **Intermarket or concentric networks**: this is largely the province of the Japanese and Korean economies – the well-known *keiretsu* and *chaebol* 'enterprise groups' representing alliances among firms operating in a variety of unrelated industries. The intermarket network involves institutionalised affiliations among firms operating in different industries and the firms linked in vertical exchange relationships with them. They are characterised by dense interconnections in resource sharing, strategic decision making and culture and identity. The centre may be a trading company – possibly functioning as the marketing arm of the network – associated with manufacturing affiliates, which in turn have large vertical clusters of subcontractors, distributors and satellite companies, and are often involved in technology alliances with competitors. For example, Toshiba has around 200 companies in a direct exchange relationship, and another 600 'grandchild companies' below them.

- **Opportunity networks**: this is represented as a set of firms specialising in various products, technologies or services that form temporary alignments around specific projects or problems. Characteristically, the hub of the network is a marketing organisation specialising in collecting and disseminating market information, negotiating, coordinating projects for customers and suppliers, and regulating the network. Achrol (1991) has described this as the 'marketing exchange company'. One prototype is the direct marketing company using media such as the Internet to market a wide variety of consumer products and novelties.

This review illustrates the diversity and potential complexity of network organisational forms as they are emerging and as we are trying to classify and understand them. However, even with 20 years' experience with these innovations, it remains true that our general understanding is not well developed: 'network and virtual organisations have been here for a long time, although our ability to define them and communicate their true content is still limited' (Gummesson, 1994).

We may be able to improve that understanding in practical terms by turning attention next to the nature of the links that tie organisations together in these various forms of collaboration.

15.5 Alliances and partnerships

It is useful to think about networks in terms of relationship marketing, where the relationships between network partners go beyond those that would be defined by contract or written agreement, or buyer–seller exchanges in the channel of distribution. Achrol argues that 'the mere presence of a network of ties is not the distinguishing feature of the network organisation', but that 'the quality of the relationships and the shared values that govern them differentiate and define the boundaries of the network organisation' (Achrol, 1997).

Figure 15.6 Forms of collaboration and inter-organisational commitment

This said, one starting point in understanding the dynamics of the network organisation, and its attractiveness or otherwise in developing a specific marketing strategy, lies in analysing partnership. It is important that we do not see strategic alliances and network formation as ends in their own right, but as a means to an end – the implementation and regeneration of our marketing strategy and the enhancement of our process of going to market – to be used selectively and appropriately based on our objectives and our capabilities for managing collaborations with other organisations.

One way of categorising collaborative relationships is shown in Figure 15.6. These relationships form a spectrum running from a largely traditional, transactional relationship to full-scale vertical integration. The relationships shown in Figure 15.6 have the following characteristics.

15.5.1 Outsourcing

At one extreme is an 'arm's length' relationship, where we may simply buy-in goods and services from outside, as the alternative to producing them internally. This might involve outsourcing for services such as advertising, market research, the salesforce and direct marketing expertise. It may also describe how we buy-in goods for resale, or handle relationships with our distributors. However, increasingly, even at this end of the spectrum, people may see suppliers and distributors as partners and use terms such as 'strategic alliance' to describe what appear to be no more than conventional, though close, buyer–seller relationships. This may be inaccurate, but underlines the point that networks are about more than the nature of the legal ties between partners. Transactional relationships of this kind also characterise what Cravens *et al.* (1996) described as value-added and hollow networks. It is also true that in many situations, arm's length relationships are reshaping into closer collaborative relationships. What starts as outsourcing may acquire many of the collaborative characteristics of a formal strategic alliance.

However, it is worth noting that the general growth of outsourcing may have peaked because of several factors. For example, many German companies that outsourced work to countries such as Poland and Romania struggled with lack of loyalty and broken contracts in outsourced markets (Woodhead, 2007). Similarly, while in 2007 NCR Corporation decided to outsource the production of its bank ATMs to cut costs, by 2009 it was bringing production back in-house and describing outsourcing as 'an enormous and costly exercise' that led to product delays and upset customers (Engardio, 2009). Certainly, the economics have changed in many situations – outsourcing IT functions to India and China has to be placed in the context of higher wage costs, making Vietnam, China and Brazil more attractive locations (Leahy, 2007). Indeed, India's Wipro Technologies began reverse offshoring by sending work from its Indian clients to offices in Egypt (Leahy, 2009).

Companies make different choices where the outsource/insource decision is a key strategic choice. For example, Jeff Immelt, CEO of General Electric, has declared that outsourcing is 'mostly outdated as a business tool' (Mallaby, 2013). Certainly, Lenovo has decided to keep production in-house as a competitive strength, while competitors in smartphones, tablets and Internet televisions outsource manufacturing (Chao, 2012).

Nonetheless, outsourcing models remain central to the strategic choices faced in going to market and achieving an effective competitive position. For example, a crucial strategic difference between rivals Sony and Samsung in the 3D television business is that Sony has gambled on outsourcing its television production, while Samsung is dedicating its resources to its own manufacturing capacity (Ihlwan, 2010). Certainly, the use of outsourcing strategies by government has greatly expanded in the UK, and outsource firms look forward to continued good earnings (Plimmer, 2015).

In supply chain management, the use of third-party logistics providers (3PLs) is illustrative of successful long-term outsourcing. A growing number of firms outsource some or all of their logistics to 3PLs, such as FedEx Logistics or DHL Logistics. In fact, a group of 3PLs dominate logistics outsourcing around the world. Manufacturers need absolutely reliable sources of supply. Retailers need flexible links to suppliers with low-cost production, but these suppliers are often in remote regions. At the same time, retailers need rapid delivery channels for an ever-expanding distribution network of consumers. These global 3PLs provide transportation, consolidation, forwarding and customs brokerage, warehousing, fulfilment, distribution and virtually any logistics and trade-related services that their international customers need. In a global 3PL market worth $270 billion a year, the top three companies turn over around $42 billion a year. The global market leaders are Excel (UK), Kuehne + Nagel (Switzerland) and Schenkler (Germany). Unsurprisingly, the top seven global 3PL providers are European, since 3PL use is more widespread in Europe than the USA. Companies use 3PL providers for several reasons. First, because getting the product to market is their main focus, these providers can often do it more efficiently and at lower cost. Outsourcing typically results in 15–30 per cent in cost savings. Second, outsourcing logistics frees a company to focus more intensely on its core business. Finally, integrated logistics companies understand increasingly complex logistics environments.

15.5.2 Partnerships

These are collaborations that involve a closer relationship between organisations, but stop short of a formal strategic alliance agreement, shared ownership in a joint venture or vertical integration. Lambert *et al.* (1996) suggest that partnerships vary in the degree and type of integration. They suggest that: (1) some partnerships are short term in focus and involve limited coordination; (2) other partnerships have a longer-term focus and move beyond coordination to integration of activities; and (3) the closest partnerships are viewed as 'permanent', and each party views the other as an extension of its own firm.

For example, in one strategic alliance, Dell Inc. and EMC had a partnership relationship in the data storage business, providing advanced networked storage solutions for organisations of all sizes. The partnership made Dell the fastest-growing disk storage systems seller, and EMC the mid-tier market share leader in revenue. The combined capabilities of Dell and EMC made a major impact on the data storage business. Dell and EMC leveraged a unique model of sales, marketing, engineering and manufacturing collaboration to exploit each other's strengths and deliver superior value to customers, but the relationship had a fixed term (*Al Bawaba*, 2006). In the end, Dell purchased EMC in 2016, taking the relationship-building process to its extreme.

A different form of marketing alliance was shown by the Jigsaw Consortium formed by Cadbury Trebor Bassett, Unilever and Kimberly-Clark. The consortium was managed for the members by direct marketing agency OgilvyOne. The members of the consortium owned brands including Persil, Flora, Lynx, Huggies, Cadbury Creme Egg and Flake. The alliance created a consumer database covering the purchasing behaviour and brand attitudes of nine million consumers. Importantly, while retailers such as Tesco and Sainsbury's have a strength of consumer purchase data through point-of-sale scanning, the consortium database included attitudinal data for additional insight and predictive power.

In the same sector, excess capacity in British supermarkets is driving them to collaboration in the form of placing concession stores within major supermarkets. With rapid expansion now a thing of the past, supermarkets are looking to high-street retailers and leisure operators to take up their unproductive floor space. The first two Argos stores opened in Sainsbury's in 2015, with more to follow. Sainsbury's has also signed agreements with Jessops, the photographic retailer, and Western Union to begin global money transfer services to its stores. Asda has partnered with French sports retailer Decathlon, while Tesco strongly considered bringing Sports Direct into its stores. Deals between supermarkets and dentists, opticians and hairdressers have also been considered, although remain rare. These horizontal collaborations have not always been successful in the past, but it looks like they will expand, driven by the excess selling space in large supermarkets, which face tough competition from discounters and convenience stores (Shubber, 2015).

15.5.3 Strategic alliances

Strategic alliances are more formal arrangements, sometimes under contract, for companies to collaborate and act jointly. The defining characteristics of strategic alliances are that: (1) two or more companies unite to pursue a set of agreed goals, but remain independent even though in an alliance; (2) the alliance members share the benefits of the alliance and control over the assigned tasks; and (3) the firms in the alliance contribute on a continuing basis to one or more strategic areas (such as technology sharing, product development or marketing) (Taylor, 2005; Todeva and Knoke, 2005).

In some sectors, such as airlines, strategic alliances have become the dominant way of doing business. Most of the world's big airlines are members of one of the alliances. The three major airline alliances are Star Alliance (United Airlines, Lufthansa and 25 others); SkyTeam (Delta, Air France/KLM and 17 others); and Oneworld (American Airlines, British Airways, Cathay Pacific and 12 others). Between them, the big three alliances carry almost two-thirds of all passengers flying in the world and control more than half the global fleet of commercial passenger aircraft. While these alliances offer airlines advantages in code-sharing, loyalty programmes and marketing, they are also fragile as members move allegiance. It is also noteworthy that many of the world's rapidly growing airlines (Emirates, Etihad) are not alliance members, and most of the successful no-frills fliers are unaligned (easyJet, Ryanair, Southwest). Some analysts predict a fracturing of the existing alliances and a fresh wave of consolidation in the airline industry. While alliance-based competition brings strengths, alliances may not last (Tovey, 2015).

15.5.4 Joint ventures

These are relationships where the ownership of a project or operation is shared between the parties concerned. For example, Mercedes, the German car company, and Swatch, the Swiss watch company, entered into a short-lived joint venture to produce the Smart mini-car, supported by partnership sourcing from its ten key suppliers, which relocated their operations to a 'smart ville' in France. This relationship focused on partners from different industries sharing innovative design abilities, technological expertise and marketing capabilities to innovate. The concept was that the partners were selling 'mobility' as a total product, not just a car – the overall market offer included the ability to borrow larger cars when needed for particular mobility needs. The joint venture became a wholly-owned subsidiary of Daimler Chrysler and is now owned by Daimler AG.

Joint venture collaborations have proved highly problematic in some cases. BP's growth strategy of partnering with companies in resource-rich countries such as Russia is illustrative. The relationship between BP and its Russian partners in TNK-BP was plagued with problems and conflicts of interest, culminating in the Russian security services raiding the joint venture offices, withdrawing visas for BP executives and chasing the TNK-BP CEO out of the country, from where he continued to run the business in hiding (White and Chazan, 2008). TNK-BP accounts for around a quarter of BP's total global oil production and reserves. Eventually, BP had no choice but to concede to the demands of its Russian partners and accept it was no longer the 'senior partner'. As such, what appeared a strategic triumph for BP had turned into a costly trap, and in 2013 TNK-BP was taken over by the Russian oil company Rosneft.

15.5.5 Vertical integration

Here, an activity in another part of the value chain is fully owned by the core organisation, although the relationship may still be seen as a strategic alliance, even though strictly one company owns another. Apple Inc. provides an interesting example of a company that is vertically integrated using both outsourcing and direct financial ownership. Apple designs the computer hardware, accessories, operating system and much of the software itself, but does not manufacture. Production is outsourced to specialist suppliers such as Foxconn. Apple established a chain of high-profile, up-market retail outlets to protect its consumer market position, using forward vertical integration to retain control over its product presentation in the marketplace.

In another sector, Italian company Luxottica is the world's largest eyewear business. The company produces many famous eyewear brands – including its own Ray-Ban and Oakley brands and licensed brands such as Burberry, Chanel, Polo Ralph Lauren, Dolce & Gabbana, Donna Karan, Prada, Versace and Bulgari. It then sells these brands through some of the world's largest optical chains – LensCrafters, Pearle Vision and Sunglass Hut – that it also owns. In another example, integrating the entire distribution chain, from its own design and manufacturing operations to distribution through its own managed stores, has turned Spanish clothing chain Zara into the world's fastest-growing fast-fashion retailer (*The Economist*, 2012; Berfield, 2013).

It is important that executives consider carefully the strengths and weaknesses of these different degrees and types of partnership in developing appropriate alliance strategies, and that we recognise that, in reality, networks may contain a mix of different partnership styles. It should also not be assumed that inter-organisational relationships are static – collaborative forms may change or be removed during the course of a project if, for example, one partner is gaining benefits while the other(s) is/are not. For instance, BMW and Rolls-Royce operated an alliance in the form of a joint venture – BMW Rolls-Royce GmbH – for some ten years in the aerospace industry, focused on advanced aero-engine development. The partners succeeded in producing a commercially successful family of advanced engines. The alliance provided Rolls-Royce with a stronger product strategy, but after ten years BMW withdrew to concentrate on automotive and the business became wholly owned by Rolls-Royce as Rolls-Royce Deutschland (Smith, 2003).

| 15.6 | Strategic alliances as a competitive force |

It is important that we recognise in our marketing strategy development that in some markets, competition is increasingly based on the relationship between alliances and the networks they create and no longer simply between individual companies or brands. We saw this in the airline industry example mentioned previously. This is particularly true in global businesses. Consider the following examples:

- Increasingly, the global automotive business is characterised by global networks, rather than free-standing manufacturers. This sector is characterised by a fast-moving and flexible array of alliances: 2012 saw Nissan and Daimler partnering to build engines together in the USA (Reed, 2012); GM and Peugeot have a broad alliance for European car operations as GM seeks to improve its European performance (*Wall Street Journal*, 2012); Ford and Toyota have teamed up on hybrid car and truck development in response to higher emissions standards in the United States (Bennett and Ramsey, 2011); and the highly successful entry of Western carmakers into China has been mainly through joint ventures with local firms (Mitchell, 2014).

- In the aerospace industry, a strategic alliance between Boeing and Lockheed Martin means that, by working together, the companies can leverage their expertise in air traffic management and aircraft-focused solutions to transform air traffic control system products. Lockheed-Martin brings air traffic route management experience, while Boeing contributes expertise in aircraft systems, avionics and airspace simulation and modelling (*Airline Industry Information*, 2007).

- In the rapidly evolving biotechnology industry, companies such as Novartis and Merck are forging alliances with biotechnology firms to stake a claim for part of the $40 billion market for new breakthrough cancer treatment drugs. Partnerships around immunotherapy developments offer traditional pharmaceutical companies access to new areas of growth. This is only one example of numerous technology-based alliances between traditional pharmacists and biotechnology ventures. Competition is increasingly between alliances rather than individual companies (Ward, 2015).

- In a completely different business, Coke and Pepsi are fighting over the growing 'ready-to-drink' coffee market. But this is a battle between partnerships – Pepsi has partnered with Starbucks, and Coke with Illycaffe from Italy to respond and counter Pepsi's initiative.

- Meantime, the media and communications sector shows a constant flurry of alliances and networks – many of which are short-lived. For example, Apple's strength is integration of hardware and software and its network of apps developers. In response, Google teamed up with Motorola, and Microsoft with Nokia, to emulate Apple's integrated hardware and software strategy – although neither alliance was really effective or sustainable. More generally, we saw the Web worlds of Internet search and social networks collide in a war for followers, with an alliance between Facebook and Microsoft's Bing as the first salvo, along with a Google and Yahoo partnership replacing an earlier Microsoft and Yahoo alliance. Of course, time has shown that many inter-organisational relationships in this sector are transitory, with little to be seen of these alliances today, given Facebook and Google's hegemony. Indeed, Apple and Google were once allies (with cross-board memberships) but now they are rivals. Apple and IBM were once rivals, but later developed a collaboration to push Apple's digital devices into IBM's corporate heartland.

- Similarly, the 'Internet of Things' is bringing together search, software, apps and hardware manufacturers in novel ways as the fight is on to dominate this new category of products – no one can move fast enough alone, which encourages acquisitions, partnerships and alliances. The battle to shape the 'Internet of Things' is rapidly hotting up, as technology and telecoms companies race to build the infrastructure to connect billions of devices in homes and offices. For example, in 2014 Google bought Nest Laboratories for $3.2 billion – twice what it paid for YouTube. Nest makes smart thermostats and smoke alarms, but has redesigned these appliances as connected, digital devices for the smartphone age. Google intends to provide the resources for Nest's technology to run peoples' smart homes, which is a huge market. Underpinning this move is the battle for whose service – Google, Amazon, Apple, Microsoft, or others – will coordinate the new 'smart home'.

Nonetheless, alliances and networks are a means to an end – that of delivering a strategy to the market and achieving the companies' goals. The strategy matters more than the specific structures used to implement it. But, at the very least, our analysis of competitive structures would possibly be misleading if we did not account for the potential impact of strategic alliances – both existing and potential – on our ability to successfully implement a strategy.

15.7   The risks in strategic alliances

We stressed earlier that strategic alliances are no panacea. They may be an important way to achieve the things we need, but there are significant risks also. To begin with, we should be aware that, for one reason or another, strategic alliances sometimes simply do not work, and they may crash spectacularly. Consider the airline alliances and information technology examples examined previously. Strategic alliances may be transitory. For example, an early study by Cravens *et al.* (1993) found that in 82 large multinational corporations, fewer than half the companies operating strategic alliances were satisfied with the effectiveness of those alliances, and other evidence concurs with this finding of a dismal failure rate for strategic alliances (Hughes and Weiss, 2007). The underlying concern is that the greater the reliance of a company and its strategy on alliance and network, the greater is the associated risk.

It has never been wise to overestimate the strength and durability of strategic alliances. Quinn noted some time ago:

> Like earlier decentralisation and SBU concepts, some of these newer organisational modes have been touted as cures for almost any managerial ill. They are not. Each form is useful in certain situations, and not in others. But more importantly, each requires a carefully developed infrastructure of culture, measurements, style and rewards to support it. When properly installed, these disaggregated organisations can be awesomely effective in harnessing intellectual resources for certain purposes. When improperly supported or adapted, they can be less effective than old-fashioned hierarchies.
> *(Quinn, 1992)*

Indeed, as well as the outright failure of an alliance and the crash of the network involved, there are a number of other important issues to bear in mind as potential limitations to the application of strategies of collaboration.

Achrol (1997) argued that we should consider the following factors as key elements of designing and operating network organisations:

- **Power:** we need to take a careful look at the relative dependence and power within a network, both in terms of whether the relative position we take is acceptable to us and if we are going to be able to cope with the way power is likely to be exercised in the network, and how vulnerable this may make us.
- **Commitment and interdependence:** at its simplest, are the people in the partnering companies going to be behind the alliance, and what mechanisms may be needed such as interlocking directorships and exchange of personnel or other liaison mechanisms? In a *keiretsu* (business group in Japan), the Japanese refer to what is necessary to 'keep each other warm' – their example suggests we should not underestimate the importance of people's commitment, or lack of it, in an effective network organisation.
- **Trust:** the network organisation requires that each partner gives up some influence or control over important issues and becomes vulnerable to ineffective or hostile actions by other network members. This is a key aspect of relationship management in a network. The cases of network failure discussed earlier illustrate the vulnerability involved. Compare this to the risk of lack of commitment to a collaboration through an unjustified lack of trust in the partner organisation, and the significance of the issue becomes clearer.
- **Social norms:** it is suggested that network organisations should be considered in terms of behavioural issues, such as: (a) solidarity – the unity of action among network members; (b) mutuality – network partners acting for the common good and receiving a payoff in terms of benefits from the collaboration; (c) flexibility – the willingness of partners to change the joint arrangements as conditions change; (d) role integrity – clarity in what each partner organisation is to do; and (e) conflict handling – agreement on how conflicts will be handled in the network. The important point to bear in mind is that, while organisations are familiar with how to handle these questions in conventional,

independent, hierarchical structures, we are still learning how best to manage them in the very different setting of the collaborative network of organisations.

In a transparent, brand-orientated world, we can add to this list concerns about **damage by association**: the performance of an organisation in terms of its competitive behaviour and social responsibility stance may make it a more or less attractive partner because of the association. For example, one surprising consequence of BP's disastrous oil spill in the Gulf of Mexico in 2010 was that its partner company – Anadarko – found its existence and future plans in jeopardy because it was tainted by its relationship with BP (Klump and Reed, 2010).

The stability or instability of an alliance may also reflect **changing strategic priorities**: when an ally becomes a rival because its strategies change over time, then alliance may no longer work. For example, while Apple and Google had maintained a cooperative relationship for a number of years (primarily against the common enemy, Microsoft), 2009 saw Eric Schmidt, CEO of Google, resigning from Apple's board. As the two companies' products began to overlap, cooperation gave way to competition, and Google membership of Apple's board was no longer appropriate (Menn, 2009).

Moreover, we need to consider the attractiveness of a collaborative or alliance-based strategy in terms not simply of the pressures of factors such as resource gaps and market access, but also in the light of whether we can design and implement an effective network, and whether we have the skills and capabilities to manage through a network of relationships with other companies.

We shall consider these points in more detail in the managerial agenda discussed in the next section. Issues such as trust, commitment and power may hold the key to identifying the large business risks involved in reliance on strategic alliances. As situations change, so may the commitment of a partner to an alliance. The risk of opportunistic behaviour by a partner is an important issue to be monitored (Kale *et al.*, 2000).

15.8   Managing strategic alliances

The previous discussion and the examples examined in this chapter suggest that the managerial issues that should be addressed carefully and systematically in evaluating the strategy of collaboration and alliance as a route to market are those summarised in Figure 15.7 and discussed in the following text.

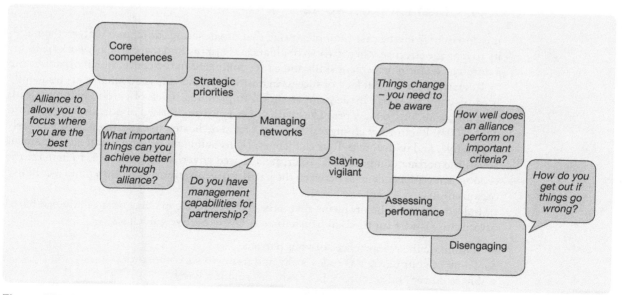

Figure 15.7 Issues to consider in managing strategic alliances

15.8.1 Core competences

One of the fundamental attractions of collaboration and partnership with other organisations is that it allows each organisation to focus on its own core competences and to benefit from the specialisation of other organisations in their own areas of expertise (Achrol, 1991; Webster, 1992). Quinn (1992) noted: 'If one is not "best in world" at a critical activity, the company is sacrificing competitive advantage by performing that activity internally or with its existing techniques.' Certainly, research by Buffington and Frabelli (1991) in the telecommunications industry suggests that when partners in a collaboration do not contribute their core competences, then the probability of success for the alliance is substantially reduced. This suggests that clarity in defining those core competences may be critical to negotiating and sustaining effective inter-organisational relationships of this type.

However, there are two problems. First, it is clear that the identification of core competences may be far from straightforward within an organisation or between partners (see Cravens and Piercy, 2012). Second, we have to factor in not just existing and recognised core competences, but issues of complementarity and 'fit' between potential partners, and the potential for synergy through collaboration. This is a complex and largely subjective evaluation that executives must make.

15.8.2 Strategic priorities

The issue of core competences also raises important questions about competitive strategy and the choices faced in when, where and how to compete (Prahalad and Hamel, 1990). While networking offers a company the opportunity to focus on and exploit its core competences, only rarely will it create such capabilities for a company.

However, this focus and concentration may create vulnerabilities. For example, some years ago the British Airways alliance with USAir collapsed before the new alliance with American Airlines was approved. This left BA with no US-based collaborator and highly exposed to competitive attack by other alliances. While there is much current favour in corporate thinking for strategic focus and concentration, using collaborations as a vehicle, we should be aware of the risks involved in this prioritising. Reliance on partners to perform critical activities involves risks if the partnership fails or underperforms, and may leave us without the capacity to develop new competences.

15.8.3 Managing networks

It is apparent from the case examples given, that organisations differ markedly in their ability to manage effectively in networks or alliances. Forming and managing networks calls for a different set of management skills and issues compared to the conventional organisation.

Research suggests that lack of success in business partnerships and alliances is frequently because companies pay inadequate attention to planning. Lack of careful planning leads to conflicts about strategy, problems with governance and missed opportunities (Bamford et al., 2004). Bamford et al. suggest forming a team dedicated to exposing tensions as early as possible, and to deal with four challenges: (1) to build and maintain strategic alignment across the partner companies; (2) to create a shared governance system; (3) to manage the economic interdependencies between the partner organisations; and (4) to build a cohesive organisation.

Indeed, many of the problems that have emerged in the management of alliance-based organisations were captured in Bensimon's (1999) executive guidelines:

- Assimilate the competences of your partner.
- Think of your partner as today's ally and tomorrow's competitor.
- Share power and resources, but share information wisely.
- Structure your alliance carefully.

Before making the commitment to enter an alliance, we should consider the following factors:

- **Drivers**: which of the drivers of collaboration strategies apply in this case? What does a collaboration strategy offer us in terms of asset/cost efficiencies, customer service improvements, marketplace advantage over the competition and profit stability/growth?
- **Choice of partners**: which potential partners are available, and what basis do we have for believing that we could create an environment of trust, commitment and cooperation between the members of the alliance (Cravens *et al.*, 1997)?
- **Facilitators**: are the circumstances and environment favourable for a partnership? Lambert *et al.* (1996) suggest that partnerships are more likely to be successful if the following conditions prevail:
  - *corporate compatibility*: the cultures and business objectives of the partners must mesh;
  - *managerial philosophy and techniques*: are the partners' organisational structures, attitudes towards employees and methods of working compatible?
  - *mutuality*: are there equally important benefits for both partners?
  - *symmetry*: are the partners similar types of company who understand each other?
  - *exclusivity*: are the partner organisations willing to shut out others who are not part of the network?
  - *shared competitors*: partnerships work best as an alliance against a common foe;
  - *prior history*: experience in successful collaboration is a plus;
  - *shared end-user*: when partners serve the same customer, collaboration is likely to be more successful.
- **Components**: these are the activities and processes that management establishes and controls throughout the life of the partnership, and effective partnerships understand these from the outset. This includes arrangements for joint planning, joint operating controls, communications between partners, equitable risk/reward sharing, facilitating trust and commitment between partner organisations, a contract acceptable to both sides, the definition of the scope of the partnership and clarity about the financial investments to be made by partners.
- **Network effectiveness**: we saw earlier that it has been found that many companies pursuing alliance-based strategies are dissatisfied with the results. Defining realistic expectations at the outset and evaluating progress against them is required. We may have to think in terms of somewhat different measures to the conventional evaluation of effectiveness – network stability and sustainability, relationship strength, network synergy and the like. If we cannot find convincing evidence that the network provides a superior way of going to market, it is unlikely to endure. (We consider the evaluation and appraisal process in more detail in a later section.)
- **Organisational change**: it is highly likely that the formation of network organisations will be stimulated by, and in turn lead to further, changes in alliance companies' internal organisational structures and processes. The requirements for effectiveness here may be complex and currently outside the experience of many senior managers in traditional organisations. The complexity of this issue was underlined early on by Gummesson (1994): 'organising a network business requires continuous creation, transformation and maintenance of amoeba-like, dynamic processes and organisational structures.'
- **Market orientation and customer service**: a particular point of concern for the marketing strategist is the impact of networked operations on the market orientation of the new type of organisation, and its ability to deliver the required levels of customer service and superior customer value. Where the primary motivation for collaboration is technological or supply-chain efficiency, this may be a particularly significant concern. For example, some companies in the airline business are moving towards the concept of the 'virtual airline', which owns no aircraft or facilities and exists primarily as a brand and information system with a small core staff. Some executives suggest that while the core organisation is highly market-orientated and committed to high service quality, in a networked organisation they lack the means to share these imperatives with their

partners. Quite simply, we may believe in service quality at the core airline, but is this shared by the people who run the operation that the customer experiences at check-in (Cravens and Piercy, 2012)? This suggests that one of the major questions we need to consider is what mechanisms we may need to create to drive goals such as service and quality through a network to the end-user.

- **The role of marketing in network organisations**: there is some lack of clarity about how marketing is located and operated in a network organisation. Some suggest that the critical role for marketing in the alliance-based network is applying relationship marketing skills to managing the links between partners in the network (see Chapter 16 and our discussion of internal marketing as an implementation approach in partnerships). Certainly, there is a compelling argument that the concepts and processes of relationship marketing are pivotal to the management of networks. Relationship marketing involves the creation and distribution of value through mutual cooperation and interdependence, and we have seen that cooperation and interdependence are central features of network organisations. It is too early to reach conclusions about the role that marketing can and will take generally in these new organisational forms, although it is highly likely that there will be some redefinition of its role, which may be radical.

15.8.4 Staying vigilant

As experience grows in the advantages and pitfalls of going to market or operating key processes through strategic alliances, it is apparent that there may be temptations to persist with alliance relationships way past the point where this makes sense. The benefits of some inter-organisational relationships may be transitory, and the relationship may need to be reconsidered on a regular basis. Indeed, one of the attractions of networked organisations is that they may be designed to be temporary and to exploit a given opportunity, and then be dissolved. However, there is evidence that recognising the point when the alliance should end and managing the dissolution or disengagement process may pose some problems.

For example, there is some evidence that managers may be reluctant to end alliance relationships, even though they have evidence that the alliance is failing to meet its purposes and there is little chance that things will improve. This appears to be most likely with large joint ventures, when closing costs may be high, sunk costs may have escalated and where the alliance has high visibility – terminating large, expensive partnerships may impact negatively on management careers and prospects (Delios *et al.*, 2004).

While an early concern about strategic alliances was that they could be unstable and unreliable because of the nature of inter-organisational, non-ownership relationships, it has been suggested, for example, that alliances may be *too* stable. Companies are urged now to routinely review and re-think their alliance arrangements. Rather than waiting for a crisis to emerge, a company should scan its major alliances to see which need restructuring, to understand the root causes of the venture's problems and to estimate how much each problem is costing the company (Ernst and Bamford, 2005).

Indeed, there may be greater risks, which emerge in some situations, which are even more threatening than inertia allowing underperforming alliances to stay in place. The outsourcing or contract manufacturing area provides an illustrative example of the risks to be considered. Contract manufacturing is attractive to an original equipment manufacturer (OEM), the traditional brand owner, because it reduces labour costs and frees up capital to outsource manufacturing, leaving the OEM free to focus on product research, design and marketing. This practice started in the computer business, and has spread to areas as diverse as toys, clothing, footwear, beer and pharmaceuticals. Even in the automotive sector, Finland's Valmet Automotive assembles the Porsche Boxer, and Austria's Magna Steyr assembles cars for Mercedes, BMW and Saab. However, research suggests that the outsource relationship may develop in threatening ways, where the contract manufacturer (CM) displays:

- **promiscuity** – the CM seeks business with the OEM's competitors;
- **infidelity** – the CM becomes a competitor by selling to the OEM's retailers and distributors;

- **betrayal** – the CM shares the OEM's intellectual property with competitors or retains it for its own exploitation.

Meanwhile, the OEM cannot terminate the outsourcing because there are no alternative sources of product. Considerable care is required in making outsourcing decisions and deciding when they should end (Arruñada and Vázquez, 2006).

It is likely that as reliance on strategic alliances continues to increase, but as situations change, companies will need to consider what is involved in effective disengagement from an alliance.

15.8.5 Assessing the performance of strategic alliances

It is perhaps symptomatic of the relative lack of maturity of the strategic alliance organisational model that it is claimed that a major reason for the high failure rate of alliances is that relatively few have developed and implemented formal performance measures. Appropriate control mechanisms will depend upon the underlying rationale for the alliance relationship – that is, the strategic intent of the partners, the form of the alliance relationship and the strategic objectives of the relationship. This context provides the basis for selecting evaluation criteria and methods of evaluation, and implementing an alliance evaluation plan. For example, the evaluation criteria for a global airline alliance, reflecting the 'balanced scorecard' approach (Kaplan and Norton, 1996), and the several stages of management control activity, are shown in Table 15.1.

Table 15.1 Selecting the evaluation criteria for a global airline alliance

Management control activities	Balanced scorecard dimensions			
	Financial	*Customer focus*	*Internal business process*	*Learning and growth*
Planning	Profit by route and coverage of destinations	Identify potential customer groups not served by existing routes	Identify partner responsibilities	New ideas for the extension of the collaboration
Coordinating	Potential income from network	Use of airline lounges by partners' passengers	Savings from shared services	Increase in market share from collaborative routes
Communicating	Detailed financial reports by segment for passengers using alliance network	Potential increase in load factors from partners' customers	Process improvements initiated by partners relative to the alliance	Employee satisfaction regarding alliance
Evaluating	Revenue per seat mile from collaboration relative to potential	Repeat and new customer passenger miles by customer type and route	Provision of comparable service for customers on collaborative routes	Employee productivity by function and general service activity for collaborative routes
Deciding	Operating profit per seat mile from collaboration	Market share on collaborative routes	On-time performance on collaborative routes	Demand information by segment on collaborative routes
Implementing	Percentage contribution of collaboration load factor	Customer complaints from collaborative routes	Performance improvement and complaints reduction on collaborative routes	Staff turnover relative to collaborative routes

Source: Adapted from Cravens et al., 2000.

This provides a generic template, but one that should be adapted and refined for specific application. The goal of establishing and clarifying the performance criteria for an alliance and evaluating performance against those criteria is, however, a general requirement.

15.8.6 Disengaging from alliances and networks

Vigilance and more thorough appraisal are likely to identify situations where it is desirable to end an alliance relationship. Research suggests that companies face important challenges in withdrawing or disengaging from alliances that are underperforming or have outlived their usefulness. For a start, companies may not recognise the life cycle underlying the alliance relationship, and may treat alliances as though they were permanent organisational arrangements (Taylor, 2005). The problem is compounded because, typically, disengagement is not agreed at the outset of the alliance. It is highly desirable to negotiate exit options while still at the alliance formation stage, with clarity about the events or contingencies that will trigger the termination of the alliance.

It appears that part of the problem is that, without clear agreement on how to withdraw from an alliance relationship, when tensions arise between partners managers may be reluctant to report problems, fearing they will be blamed for the alliance's failure. Instead, they tend to blame their alliance counterparts. The typical outcome is likely to be a dysfunctional strategic alliance characterised by deep animosity between alliance managers, making negotiation of alliance termination highly problematic. It may be more effective to handle alliance disengagement with a core team of senior managers, chosen in part because they were not involved in the original alliance. A strong communications plan also assists in avoiding damage to the company's reputation during the break-up (Gulati *et al.*, 2007).

Summary

We have argued in this chapter that there are many factors compelling organisations to collaborate and form alliances with others, rather than to compete independently – we may be in an era of collaboration rather than competition. The network paradigm is impossible to ignore for two reasons: it may be how we take our strategy to market; and it may be how our competitors build their market power. The factors driving this process include market complexity and risk, skills and resource gaps, supply chain management imperatives and the strategic priority of focusing on core competences and outsourcing to partners for other activities and resources.

We attempted to identify the types of networks that are emerging in the modern marketplace. One approach looks at the type of relationship on which alliance is based and market volatility in order to identify the hollow network, the flexible network, the value-added and the virtual network. A broader view suggests that there are internal market networks, vertical market networks, intermarket or concentric networks and opportunity networks (Achrol, 1997). Related issues concerned the type of relationship ties between network members, ranging from outsourcing, through partnership, to joint venture and vertical integration.

The conclusion we reached at this point was that strategic alliances are a major competitive force, which in some industries such as airlines, computing and telecommunications are replacing conventional competition between individual companies. However, the cases and studies available to date suggest that while the potential gains may be great, strategic alliances and networks carry major risks.

This led us to an important management agenda to be considered in evaluating the importance of strategic alliances and networks as part of marketing strategy. We suggest that in considering a strategy of alliance, managers should focus on the issue of core competences brought to the alliance by each partner, and the benefits and vulnerabilities associated with focus and outsourcing, and the capabilities that a company has to manage its strategy through a very different organisational environment. Questions to raise regarding those managerial capabilities include: understanding the underlying drivers favouring collaboration strategies, the choice of partners, the facilitators and components important to effective collaboration, the ability to define and evaluate network effectiveness in achieving marketing goals and the capacity of a network to deliver the customer value on which our marketing strategy is based. The redefinition of the role of marketing also falls into this area. Maintaining vigilance regarding changing circumstances and an effective alliance appraisal approach are priorities for managing in networked strategies. Managing disengagement or withdrawal from ineffective or damaging alliances may be a necessary consequence of improved appraisal and control.

Strategic alliances and networks are not a panacea for strategic problems. They are an important development with many potential benefits. They also carry major strategic risks and vulnerabilities, and demand new managerial skills. This is an issue requiring particularly careful and detailed analysis.

Case study

UPS and FedEx turn focus to consumer behaviour

By Robert Wright

On the ground floor of United Parcel Service's $2.2bn Worldport Hub, workers are stuffing into huge airfreight containers some of the roughly 1.1m packages that the centre in Louisville, Kentucky, handles every night.

Most of the containers have sped through Worldport's maze of whirring conveyor belts and been reloaded in less than four hours. At 2.30am, some of the 100 or so flights that will carry the packages around the US and the world are starting to leave.

Amid the dazzling efficiency, however, is evidence of the significant challenge that UPS and FedEx, its main US rival, are facing. Many of the boxes bear the logo of Zappos.com, the internet footwear retailer. Another box contains frozen artificial skin for use in surgery, while one bears the simple legend, 'Live Tropical Fish'.

Online retailing and business-to-business ordering are driving up traffic volumes for both UPS and FedEx but also making flows harder to predict.

The question for both companies is whether management changes and technology investments can help them to avoid a repeat of the chaos that engulfed UPS last Christmas, when demand surged more than anticipated. Volumes on its busiest day, December 23, were 13 per cent up on 2012's peak and the network was clogged. Many packages were delivered after December 25.

The problems reflect the behaviour of the individual consumers who increasingly drive big operators' deliveries worldwide, according to Alan Braithwaite,

Source: JOHAN NILSSON/epa european pressphoto agency b.v./Alamy Stock Photo.

a UK-based logistics consultant. They are more likely than logistics operators' corporate customers to order at the last minute.

'The peaks are getting even peakier,' he says.

Fewer goods are being delivered in bulk via single stops on vehicles' routes to retail outlets, according to Henry Maier, chief executive of FedEx Ground, the company's road-delivery division.

'Now those individual items get boxed up and sent to somebody's house, so that creates a stop,' Mr Maier says. 'The challenge across the industry is managing the stops.'

UPS is improving its management systems and investing $500m in extra capital spending this year to boost capacity, according to Kurt Kuehn, the group's chief financial officer.

'We're very focused on expanding capabilities and capacity to meet the current growth, not to mention the peak season,' Mr Kuehn says. 'We have what is in many ways an enviable problem.'

One of UPS's efficiency-boosting investments is on display at the Louisville Centennial Hub, a base for UPS's ground operations near Worldport. Jerry Durham, a driver, each morning consults a bank of computers running Orion, a new computer system, to work out the most efficient route between his scheduled drop-offs.

The technology has raised the average number of drop-offs per mile from 1.9 when drivers devised their own routes to 2.2 now, says Roger Hicks, UPS's business manager for Louisville East.

The system has overcome his initial scepticism, according to Mr Durham.

'I've gotten to like it a lot more,' he says.

Mr Maier praises new hand-held scanners for boosting FedEx's efficiency. The scanners know the GPS co-ordinates of every address in the US and will alert drivers if they appear to be delivering in the wrong place. Such technology helps to cut down worker errors, especially among temporary staff taken on for the peak season.

'It makes our temporary resources much more effective,' Mr Maier says.

An innovation at Centennial typifies UPS's approach. In the past year, sorters have been given technology that scans package labels and tells them into which delivery bag they should post them. The technology has cut down on wasteful 'mis-sorts'.

Mr Kuehn says most investments are focused on such local hubs, rather than the efficient Worldport, and predominantly into computer systems.

Yet, for UPS, last Christmas's biggest failing may have been in communication rather than in technology. UPS failed to spot its customers' higher than expected order volumes in time. Much of the short-term effort has focused on ensuring future volume forecasts and communications with customers are better than last year's. FedEx says that such forecasting also plays a key role in its peak-season planning.

'We're working with some large customers to get enhanced visibility,' Mr Kuehn says.

In the long run, meanwhile, both companies expect to overcome the challenges partly through making more of their facilities operate like Worldport.

FedEx already operates all 33 of its ground network's hubs in the US on Worldport's highly automated model, with minimal handling by humans. Mr Maier says it expects to start introducing such advanced technology in still more, smaller facilities.

For UPS, meanwhile, Worldport, the world's biggest fully automated package-handling facility, remains noticeably more advanced than smaller hubs such as Centennial, where much sorting is still by hand.

As the company adapts to the challenges of handling more shoes, medical supplies and fish, that will have to change, Mr Kuehn says.

'[Worldport is] a highly automated, incredible asset, driven by technology,' he says. 'There are several other generations of buildings around the country that we're going to be renovating to look more like Louisville.'

Customised needs

In the middle of a warehouse near the end of Louisville Airport's runway stands a line of heavy-duty freezers, an electronic stopwatch sitting on the lid of one. The stopwatch is intended to protect the delicate sheets of artificially-grown skin inside the freezers, used to treat diabetics' foot ulcers. Supervisors time how long each freezer is open when stocks are being retrieved, to ensure the temperature stays low enough.

The business in the warehouse illustrates how thoroughly UPS and other logistics companies have involved themselves in some customers' operations. Next to the skin freezers, workers are preparing to ship batches of influenza vaccine. In another section of the building, workers are putting together packages of mobile telephones for Sprint, the mobile telecoms company. They customise devices for customers with special requirements, including government departments that want employees' phone cameras disabled.

Such supply chain business is separate from the flagship express parcel operations of UPS, FedEx and other logistics operators but adds a vital extra dimension to the services they can offer companies. According to Rich Shaver, division manager for healthcare in UPS's Americas Central District, the growing popularity of outsourcing reflects the increasing pressure on healthcare companies to save money and compete more effectively.

'The customers have to have a competitive advantage,' he says. 'The only way they can have a competitive advantage is if they have a very nimble, flexible supply chain that at the same time is looking for what regulations and changes are coming.'

The healthcare business, unlike high technology, remains relatively conservative and goods are shipped mostly to retail outlets, hospitals and other corporate customers.

However, the Louisville warehouse already employs pharmacists to handle prescriptions for some goods heading direct to customers. The company is receiving increasing numbers of requests to suggest ways that customers can deliver more healthcare products direct to consumers, according to Mr Shaver.

'Most times, it's going to be a progressive, step-by-step process,' he says.

 Source: from 'UPS and FedEx turn focus to consumer behaviour', *Financial Times*, 12/08/14 (Wright, R.).

Discussion questions

1   What issues are UPS and FedEx facing here?

2   How do UPS and FedEx contribute to their clients achieving a competitive advantage?

3   What are the drivers for collaboration in the examples given?

CHAPTER 16
STRATEGY IMPLEMENTATION AND INTERNAL MARKETING

'Drawing a line between strategy and execution almost guarantees failure. . . It's a commonly held idea that strategy is distinct from execution, but this is a flawed assumption. The idea that a strategy can be brilliant and its execution poor is simply wrong.'

(Martin, 2010)

'Where is the value zone?. . . In the interface between employee and customer. . . So what business should the management of the company be in? Enthusing, enabling, encouraging and creating an environment so employees can create value.'

(Nayar, 2010 – CEO of HCL Technologies and author of *Employees First, Customers Second* quoted in Davidson, 2010)

Ryanair cancels flights after strike by pilots and cabin crew

By Arthur Beesley in Dublin and Naomi Rovnick in London

Chief executive under pressure to settle disputes by Christmas

Ryanair customers suffered more disruption on Friday after the European low-cost airline was forced to cancel flights due to a 24-hour walkout by pilots and cabin crew in Belgium, the Netherlands, Portugal, Italy and Germany.

One year after a rostering crisis that led Ryanair to recognise trade unions for the first time in its 30-year history, the budget carrier is still struggling to overcome a long and bitter campaign by its staff for better pay and conditions in large parts of its network.

This has hit investor confidence in the company's leadership. A growing investor protest led almost 30 per cent of Ryanair shareholders to reject the re-election last week of David Bonderman, the US

Travellers at the Charleroi Airport in Belgium on Friday
Source: John Thys/AFP/Getty Images.

private equity tycoon who has been chairman of the airline for 22 years.

About 250 flights were cancelled on Friday as a result of the strike action, ramping up pressure on Michael O'Leary, chief executive, to make good on his promise to settle the disputes by Christmas.

The airline and its passengers also suffered a wave of strikes during the summer, among them a walkout in five countries that led to the cancellation of 400 flights on August 10.

Customers whose flights were affected on Friday received text messages and emails from Ryanair. Those affected can either apply for a refund or change to another flight free of charge. But the company said it was not required to pay compensation under EU rules because the strikes were beyond its control.

The Dublin-based airline has entered into agreements with crew in Ireland, Italy and Britain and it has a recognition deal with one German union.

But Mr O'Leary, who has long had fractious relations with cabin crew representatives, insists Ryanair will not 'roll over' in the face of industrial action by crew. He also said pay increases would add €200m to the airline's annual costs.

Some unions have sought the right to be hired under local law, seeking a change to Ryanair's practice of recruiting under Irish law. Mr O'Leary has said the company has lobbied the Irish government to change the country's tax law to facilitate such a move.

Ireland's double taxation treaties require Ryanair to employ crew under Irish law in line with the company's registration of aircraft in the country.

At the same time, Ryanair has blamed workers at rival airlines for stoking the disputes.

In a complaint this week to the European Commission, Ryanair claimed its talks with staff in some countries were being impeded by a 'collective campaign' involving the European Cockpit Association and the International Transport Workers' Federation.

On Friday, Peter Bellew, Ryanair's chief operations officer, claimed Germany's VC union, which had urged the German pilot walkout, was 'controlled' by its competitor Lufthansa.

Mr Bellew also said it had already agreed to arbitration with the VC union over pay and conditions for its German pilots, who are seeking higher wages and improved contracts.

'This is another example of a strike being organised in Ryanair by association by a union controlled by competitor airline employees, despite the fact that Ryanair has agreed to arbitration,' he said.

The UK's Local Authority Pension Fund Forum, whose members own about 1 per cent of Ryanair, said the airline had made 'encouraging comments' about the treatment of staff at its annual meeting last week.

'It's up to the company to negotiate the details but we hope Ryanair will repair its troubled relationship with employees as soon as possible to end disruption for the company and its customers,' said Paul Doughty, an executive member of the forum who spoke at the annual meeting.

Source: from 'Ryanair cancels flights after strike by pilots and cabin crew', *Financial Times*, 28/09/18 (Beesley, A. and Rovnick, N.).

Discussion questions

1 What are the potential issues here?
2 What could be the link between relationships with employees and relationships with customers?

Introduction

This chapter takes marketing strategy further by considering strategy implementation, and particularly the role of internal marketing in enhancing and sustaining a company's ability to compete. There are several different models of internal marketing that overlap to a degree and require clarification (since as a consequence there are a number of different roles that internal marketing can play in a company's strategic development in different situations). There are important linkages to consider between internal marketing and certain of the issues we have examined earlier. Our focus in this chapter is on a company's implementation capabilities and the essential fit between strategic choices and the ability to execute those choices. The ability to execute is perhaps the most critical capability of all.

In an interesting example, in 2011 Google set out to build a value chain in mobile phones to challenge Apple's business model, integrating software and hardware businesses. Google acquired Motorola's mobile phone business for $12.5 billion – its largest ever acquisition. As creator of the fast-growing Android operating system, Google wanted to be able to make its own smartphones and tablet computers. Motorola's 17,000 patents were also important – for example, getting Google into the consumer living room via Motorola's TV set-top boxes. However, as a software company, Google now faced the challenge of running manufacturing plants, controlling inventory and managing relationships between carriers and retailers. The move also took Google into competition with existing Google partners already licensing its Android operating system. Google had earlier attempted to manufacture laptops running its Chrome software to rival Microsoft's Windows, but the execution problems forced it to work instead with brand-name hardware manufacturers such as Acer and Samsung. With Motorola, the companies were separated by half a continent, a different legacy (Google is a software company and Motorola is an 80-year-old hardware operation) and very different corporate cultures. By 2012, Google was looking to reduce Motorola staffing by 20 per cent to regain profitability in the business, and its intentions for the business had become unclear. Early in 2014, Google sold Motorola's mobile phone operations to Lenovo for $2.91 billion, getting the world's dominant mobile operating systems company out of the business of making mobile phones. The implementation risks in the Google strategy had always been high, and they ended up at that point walking away (Fitzgerald, 2012; Berman, 2012). Google still, of course, *sells* phones under the Google brand, but they're manufactured by another firm, even if Google does not formally say that anymore. So, we can see that implementation capabilities are a critical consideration in making strategic choices. Indeed, as of 2018, Google has changed course and gone *back* into making phone hardware, much like Apple does, using a contract manufacturer.

Much thinking and practice in strategic marketing is concerned with *managing relationships*: with the customer (see Chapter 13) and with partners in strategic alliances (see Chapter 15). However, a further aspect of relationship management and relationship marketing is the relationship with the employees and managers, upon whose skills, commitment and performance the success of a marketing strategy unavoidably relies. This is the *internal market* inside the company. The thinking in an increasing number of companies is that building effective relationships with customers and alliance partners will depend in part (and possibly in large part) on the strengths and types of relationships built with employees and managers inside the organisation. The goal may be for all employees to become 'brand ambassadors'. Brand owners such as Unilever, SABMiller, and BT are among those with established internal marketing excellence programmes to pursue this goal (*Marketing Week*, 2006). At Honda, for example, all new staff receive the *Book of Everything* containing the normal employee handbook information but also extensive explanation of the Honda brand philosophy – 'spreading "Honda-ness" and turning people into brand ambassadors' (Croft, 2007). In some companies, the emphasis has turned from internal communications to internal branding to build employee understanding and buy-in to corporate brand values (Dowdy, 2001). For instance, faced with a drain of key employees to Google, Microsoft appointed a Chief Happiness Officer, to focus on retention of key people and to improve morale (Conlin and Greene, 2007).

While some of these approaches may seem extreme, employee buy-in becomes particularly significant in times of change and repositioning, as well as in recovery from the economic downturn and adjusting to more demanding customers whose priorities fundamentally changed in recession. For example, fast-food giant McDonald's pursued a 'balanced lifestyles' positioning to counter links between its products and obesity (MacArthur, 2005). Cynics parodied the McDonald's campaign for trying to suggest to employees that 'It's not a McJob, it's a McCalling' (Helm and Arndt, 2007). Nonetheless, with a stronger employee buy-in, clearer competitive positioning, competitive prices and new menus, as well as challenges to Starbucks as a coffee shop, McDonald's performed strongly through the economic downturn after 2008, although is doing less well in recovery.

Similarly, recovery of market position for Heinz's UK division was based not simply on launching new products but also on reinvigorating employee and manager morale and engagement with the business: Monday morning product tasting sessions; monthly meetings with all employees to obtain their views on issues; managers expected to work in the factories and watch how food is produced; and a *Dragons' Den*-style programme for staff to pitch their ideas for new products (Waples, 2008).

Importantly, it should be noted that there are various indications that employees in companies worldwide show evidence of detachment from their work – they simply do not care very much about their job (Stern, 2008). Conversely, the characteristics of organisations that display high levels of employee engagement are that they: have high ethical standards; show clear core values; have employees who respect management and are treated with respect; and have a management team that seeks the opinions of employees (MacLeod and Brady, 2007). For example, it has been suggested that one of the worst outcomes for Nike of the criticism it received for its use of Asian 'sweatshops' to produce its sports shoes was not the negative impact on brand image, but the negative impact on employee morale. It is therefore perhaps surprising that many organisations fail to meet these basic criteria and consequently suffer in their ability to deliver their strategies to the marketplace.

Further, it is worth recalling from the commentary in Chapter 15, concerning strategic relationships and the increasing dependence of companies on cross-boundary collaboration, that building and sustaining effective ties with allies is a major challenge. We saw that the field of strategic alliances and partnerships is full of failed relationships. The reliance on third parties brings significant political, reputational and logistical risks for a company (Beattie, 2005). Yet, as we have seen, networked organisations based on collaboration are core to the success of companies such as IBM and Procter & Gamble. While internal marketing is normally framed in terms of winning the support of managers and employees inside the company for strategic change, increasingly that internal marketplace will extend to partner organisations, whose buy-in is also needed to make strategy implementation effective.

We have also emphasised the importance of *competitive differentiation* to build market position. Yet truly exploiting a company's potential competitiveness and its capabilities in reality is often in the hands of what Evert Gummesson (1990) called the 'part-time marketers' – that is, the people who actually run the business and provide the real scope for competitive differentiation. Indeed, in some situations, the employees of a company may be the most important resource that provides differentiation. Certainly, research has found internal marketing to be one of the top three determinants of a company's financial performance – companies with better integration of internal and external marketing report better financial results (Chang, 2005).

In a similar way, the growing emphasis on competing through superior *service quality* relies ultimately on the behaviour and effectiveness of the people who deliver the service, rather than the people who design the strategy. For example, when the Hampton Inn hotel chain in the USA was ready to roll out 122 changes to its products and services, its new marketing campaign was 'Make It Hampton', but it was aimed at hotel managers and employees, not guests. Building internal brand enthusiasm and employee motivation involved creating a giant model of a hotel to showcase the improvements and allow employees to experience them, motivational conference calls, focus groups, targeted newsletters and training materials. The end of the first phase of 'Make It Hampton' saw a five per cent increase in market share, and a similar growth in the percentage of highly satisfied customers (Drake *et al.*, 2005).

Increasingly, it is recognised that one of the greatest barriers to effectiveness in strategic marketing lies not just in a company's ability to conceive and design innovative marketing strategies or to produce sophisticated marketing plans, but in its ability to gain the effective and enduring *implementation* of those strategies. One route to planning and operationalising implementation in strategic marketing is 'strategic internal marketing' (Piercy, 2009a).

Practical applications suggest that, depending on the particular circumstances, the internal marketing process might include the following types of activity and programmes:

- Gaining the *support* of key decision makers for our plans – but also all that those plans imply in terms of the need to acquire personnel and financial resources, possibly in conflict with established company 'policies', and to get what is needed from other functions such as operations and finance departments to implement a marketing strategy effectively.
- Changing some of the *attitudes and behaviour* of employees and managers, who are working at the key interfaces with customers and distributors, to those required to make plans work effectively (but also reinforcing effective attitudes and behaviour as well).
- Winning *commitment* to making the plan work and 'ownership' of the key problem-solving tasks from those units and individuals in the firm whose working support is needed.
- Ultimately, managing incremental *changes in the culture*, from 'the way we always do things' to 'the way we *need* to do things to be successful', and to make the marketing strategy work.

The potential importance of internal marketing to relationship marketing strategies, to strategic alliances, to competitive differentiation, to delivering superior service quality and above all to effective marketing implementation is underlined by the growing emphasis placed by companies on this issue. Nonetheless, studies suggest that many organisations reveal an inadequate state of internal marketing – they cannot deliver their brand propositions, for example, because of lack of investment in the internal company marketplace (*Marketing Week*, 2003).

Certainly, it remains true that internal marketing means very different things in different companies and different situations. If we are to evaluate the potential contribution of internal marketing to building and implementing our (external) marketing strategy and achieving our chosen position in the market, then we need to consider such issues as the following:

- the types of internal marketing practice in companies;
- how internal marketing can be planned as part of a competitive strategy;
- the implication for other significant relationships, such as the potential partnership between marketing and human resource management within organisations to achieve the effective implementation of marketing strategies; and
- building implementation capabilities as a long-term marketing resource.

However, first we place internal marketing in the context of strategy implementation, and the challenge that execution poses for marketing managers. Our view of internal marketing is that it provides a model to facilitate a company's effective execution of marketing strategies.

Attention to marketing strategy and competitive positioning decisions by executives needs to be placed in the context of implementation capabilities and the need for effective change management in execution. The structure of our approach to these issues and the key questions to be raised are summarised in Figure 16.1.

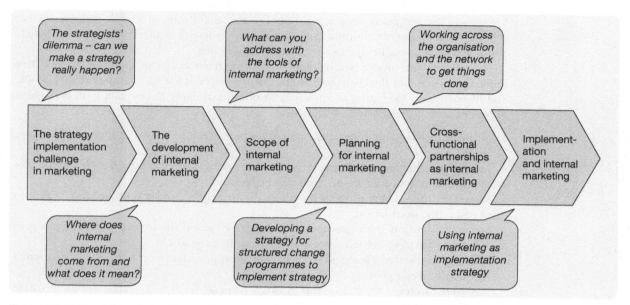

Figure 16.1 Key issues in looking at strategy implementation and internal marketing

16.1   The strategy implementation challenge in marketing

Achieving more effective implementation or execution of marketing strategies remains a high priority for many organisations, because of the long history of strategy implementation failures experienced by many. For example, on the general strategy front, Miller (2002) suggests that organisations fail to implement more than 70 per cent of their new strategic initiatives.

It is apparent that implementation is not generally well understood, as compared to the issues in strategy generation, and one large-scale international study suggests that the problem is compounded by the myths surrounding strategy implementation:

- **Myth 1 – Execution equals alignment**: actually, companies seem pretty good at cascading goals down the organisation but less so at managing coordination across the units and functions in the company.
- **Myth 2 – Execution means sticking to the plan**: companies invest heavily in formal planning and budgeting, but are less skilled at real-time adjustment to changed circumstances or the agility to achieve effective implementation.
- **Myth 3 – Communication equals understanding**: managers are shocked at how poorly their strategy is understood throughout the organisation, in spite of large investments in 'communicating', which results in messages that are unclear and change too often.
- **Myth 4 – A performance culture drives execution**: in reality, execution is not just about performance-orientation; a culture that supports execution must recognise and reward other things as well, such as agility, teamwork and ambition.
- **Myth 5 – Execution should be driven from the top**: in fact, in complex organisations, execution lives and dies with 'distributed leaders' – the middle managers and technical experts who run critical parts of the business. They are the ones who represent management to most employees, partners and customers. Execution should be driven from the middle, but guided from the top (Sull *et al.*, 2015).

The authors of this study suggest we should think carefully about what is really needed to achieve strategy implementation and consider the worry that several widely-held beliefs about how to implement strategy are actually misleading.

In fact, there are many pitfalls faced in moving from strategies and plans to effective implementation, and the changes that are usually involved for an organisation, its people and its partners. One listing of implementation pitfalls likely to resonate with managers' experiences identifies the following issues:

- **Strategic inertia** – things never get started because executives resist change, or fail to give it priority.
- **Lack of stakeholder commitment** – not having everyone on board, particularly at middle-management levels, where progress can be blocked.
- **Strategic drift** – a lack of focus on where the strategy should end up, leading to failure to reach that destination.
- **Strategic 'dilution'** – an absence of strong drive behind the strategy as managers give more priority to operational decisions than strategic goals.
- **Failure to understand progress** – not having the appropriate metrics to monitor progress towards strategic goals.
- **Initiative fatigue** – too many 'top priority' projects leads to cynicism and inadequate emphasis on the strategy.
- **Impatience** – expecting results too quickly, and giving up when the reality is slower.
- **No celebrating success** – failing to recognise and reward milestones that lead towards the strategic goal (Freedman, 2003).

Indeed, there is a strong argument that much of the implementation problem comes from the fact that, generally, managers are trained to plan, not to execute, and frequently are judged on their capabilities for managing day-to-day operations rather than strategic initiatives. The problem is likely to be worse when execution is seen as a low-level responsibility in the organisation (Hrebiniak, 2006). In fact, the reality is that strategy and implementation are interdependent – strategic choices should be linked to implementation capabilities, and implementation capabilities should be developed in line with strategic imperatives, and the dichotomy between strategy and implementation is false and unproductive (Cespedes and Piercy, 1996). Martin (2010) describes this as the 'execution trap', and argues that drawing a line between strategy and execution almost guarantees failure. Nonetheless, the tendency to separate strategy from implementation remains in organisations and creates obstacles and challenges in executing strategic initiatives.

Hrebiniak (2006) draws on a range of research studies and discussions with managers to identify the following factors as the top obstacles to effective strategy execution:

- **Inability to manage change effectively and overcome resistance to change** – managing change well is vital to effective strategy implementation. Nonetheless, where change impacts on corporate culture, then moving too fast may be dangerous.
- **Poor or vague strategy** – good implementation capabilities cannot compensate for a strategy that is weak or ambiguous. Strategy drives execution, and if strategy is unclear or weak, then implementation is irrelevant.
- **Not having guidelines or a model to guide strategy implementation efforts** – managers want a logical model to guide implementation efforts and actions, particularly in translating strategic imperatives into practical actions.
- **Poor or inadequate information sharing among individuals/units responsible for strategy execution** – poor sharing of information or poor knowledge transfer and unclear responsibility and accountability make it unlikely strategy implementation will be effective.
- **Trying to execute a strategy that conflicts with the existing power structure** – working against the power structure presents a major obstacle to implementation effectiveness, and underlines the importance of gaining the support of those influential in the organisation, and of forming coalitions to share implementation responsibility.

- **Unclear responsibility or accountability for implementation decisions or actions** – lack of clarity in responsibility for implementation and the achievement of measurable progress presents another obstacle to effective implementation (Hrebiniak, 2006).

Similarly, Alexander's (1991) contention remains just as apposite today as when it was first raised in the early 1990s:

> One key reason why implementation fails is that practicing executives, managers and supervisors do not have practical, yet theoretically sound, models to guide their actions during implementation. Without adequate models, they try to implement strategies without a good understanding of the multiple factors that must be addressed, often simultaneously, to make implementation work.
> *(Alexander, 1991)*

Implementation capabilities

It emerges from the debate about execution that there is a corporate resource that we can label as 'implementation capabilities'. Certainly, the capability of people and organisations that allows them to get things done is not neatly defined by academics, but is instantly recognisable by executives. However, it is also apparent that a company's implementation capabilities may be:

- **time-specific** – things change, sometimes radically;
- **culture-specific** – what works in one organisation may not work elsewhere;
- **partial** – being good at doing one type of thing does not necessarily transfer to others;
- **latent** – we may not have learned how to do things;
- **internally inconsistent** – some parts of the organisation are better at execution than are others;
- **strategy-specific** – we are good at doing one type of business; and,
- **person-specific** – some individual managers may be the ones who are best at getting things done (Piercy, 1998).

Careful thought is needed when identifying the location of implementation capabilities in the organisation, and particularly the people most likely to drive change effectively. It is interesting that one of the first management matrices was produced by Helmuth von Moltke, head of the Prussian army, a century-and-a-half ago. He divided his officers on two criteria: clever versus dim, and lazy versus energetic, to identify the following categories:

- **Dim and lazy** – good at executing orders.
- **Dim and energetic** – very dangerous because they take the wrong decisions and drive them forward.
- **Clever and energetic** – excellent staff officers.
- **Clever and lazy** – top field commanders who get results (Kellaway, 2015).

Evaluating and assessing executives for implementation capabilities is an important stage in preparing for effective execution.

The important point is that implementation capabilities are not a given that should be taken for granted, but something to be evaluated carefully and enhanced where possible. One implication is that trying to create and execute a strategy for which a company lacks implementation capabilities carries a high risk of failure and loss – consider the Google–Motorola example discussed earlier. Further, enhancing and sustaining implementation capabilities may be one of the most important elements of managing strategic change in a company.

While it is not a complete answer to overcoming implementation obstacles, internal marketing provides us with a set of tools to address some of the major barriers faced in the effective implementation of marketing strategies, and to manage the associated organisational changes. It provides us with a model for structuring and managing the implementation process, defining responsibilities, evaluating progress and managing the cross-functional relationships important to strategy execution. It provides a way of enhancing and applying implementation capabilities.

16.2 The development of internal marketing

Conventional training and development of marketing executives, quite reasonably, focuses primarily on the *external* environment of customers, competitors and markets, and the matching of corporate resources to marketplace targets. The internal marketing logic is that while analysing markets and developing strategies to exploit the external marketplace is quite appropriately the central focus, it is frequently not enough on its own to achieve the effective implementation of marketing strategies. In addition to developing marketing programmes and strategies aimed at the external marketplace, in order to achieve the organisational change that is needed to make those strategies work, there is a need to carry out essentially the same process for the *internal marketplace* within companies.

However, because it is still relatively new, the term 'internal marketing' is difficult to pin down to a specific definition, which suggests a dilemma:

> What to call this emerging area of internal alignment, engagement or whatever. Clearly, the new discipline is holistic. It must be inclusive. It is cross-functional and not just involve selling, service and operations. Most importantly, it must focus on delivery of corporate promises, both internally and externally.
> (Schultz, 2006)

In essence, the internal marketplace is made up of the people, the culture, the systems, the procedures, the structures and developments inside the company, where skills, resources, participation, support and commitment are needed to implement marketing strategies. The internal marketplace extends to include our partners in alliances and network organisations (see Chapter 15).

It seems that the reality in many organisations is that an assumption is made by executives that marketing plans and strategies will 'sell' themselves to those in the company whose support and commitment are needed. When made explicit in this way, it is apparent that this is just as naive as making similar assumptions that, if they are good enough, products will 'sell themselves' to external customers. It is often surprising that those same executives who have been trained and developed to cope with behavioural problems – such as 'irrational' behaviour by consumers and buyers, or the problems of managing power and conflict in the distribution channel, or the need to communicate to buyers through a mix of communications vehicles and media, or the problems of trying to outguess competitors – have taken so long to arrive at the conclusion that these same issues have to be coped with *inside* the company. Real commitment to strategic marketing must involve a managerial role of creating the conditions necessary to permit strategic change to happen.

What we are calling strategic internal marketing here has the goal of developing a marketing programme aimed at the internal marketplace in the company that *parallels* and *matches* the marketing programme aimed at the external marketplace of customers and competitors. This model comes from the simple observation that the implementation of external marketing strategies implies changes of various kinds within organisations – in the allocation of resources, in the culture of 'how we do things here', and even in the organisational structure needed to deliver marketing strategies to customer segments. In practical terms, those same techniques of analysis and communication, which are used for the external marketplace, can be adapted and used to market our plans and strategies to important targets within the company and to alliance partners. The goals of the internal marketing plan are taken directly from the implementation requirements for the external marketing plan, and the objectives to be pursued.

There is certainly well-established historical precedent for use of the terms 'internal marketing' and the 'internal customer' in the marketing and services literature. We see these developments as important for two main reasons. First, the internal marketing paradigm provides an easily accessible mechanism for executives to analyse the organisational issues that may need to be addressed in implementing marketing strategies. Quite simply, concepts of marketing programmes and targets are familiar to marketing executives and they are 'comfortable' with them. And second, the internal marketing model provides a language that actually legitimises focusing attention on issues such as power, culture and political behaviour, which appear quite often to be avoided by executives as somehow 'improper'.

16.3 The scope of internal marketing

It follows from the emergence of the internal marketing paradigm from diverse conceptual sources that the practice of internal marketing and its potential contribution to marketing strategy are similarly varied. It is possible to consider the following 'types' of internal marketing, although they are probably not equal in importance:

- internal marketing that focuses on the development and delivery of high standards of *service quality* and customer satisfaction;
- internal marketing that is concerned primarily with development of *internal communications programmes* to provide employees with information and to win their support;
- internal marketing that is used as a systematic approach to managing the *adoption of innovations* within an organisation;
- internal marketing concerned with providing products and services to users *inside the organisation*; and
- internal marketing as the *implementation strategy* for our marketing plans.

16.3.1 Internal marketing and service quality

The original and most extensive use of internal marketing was in efforts to improve the quality of service at the point-of-sale in services businesses, such as banking, leisure, retailing and so on – the so-called 'moment of truth' for the services marketer. Some call this 'selling the staff', because the 'product' promoted is the person's job as a creator of customer service and value. This tends to impact on customer care training programmes and similar initiatives. These types of internal marketing programme are, in practice, essentially tactical and often restricted to the operational level of the organisation.

The logic is that marketplace success is frequently largely dependent on employees who are far removed from the excitement of creating marketing strategies – service engineers, customer services departments, production and finance personnel dealing with customers, field sales personnel and so on. As we noted earlier, these are all people whom Evert Gummesson (1990) called 'part-time marketers' – they impact directly and significantly on customer relationships, but are normally not part of any formal marketing organisation, nor are they typically within the marketing department's direct control.

Indeed, US research suggests we should think more carefully, for example, about the impact of the organisation's external marketing communications on employees – as 'advertising's second audience' (Gilly and Wolfinbarger, 1996). Actually, the chances are that employees are aware and influenced by our advertising as much as our external customers, so the suggestion is that we should use that awareness productively to deliver messages to employees.

There are a growing number of cases of companies whose service quality excellence has been driven by explicit attention to internal marketing. Southwest Airlines is the much-admired originator of the 'no frills' airline model, and has achieved not only outstanding profit performance in a difficult sector, but has also regularly won industry awards for service quality and low levels of customer complaints. From the outset, Southwest's mission statement said, 'Above all, employees will be provided the same concern, respect and caring attitude within the organisation that they are expected to share externally with every Southwest customer'. The company uses high employee morale and service quality to achieve excellent profitability. Tactics include offering employees a vision that provides purpose and meaning to the workplace, competing aggressively for the best people, providing skills and knowledge, but also emphasising teamwork and motivation, and ensuring that organisational management understands the internal customer. The effect is an integrated internal marketing approach that drives service quality. Southwest shows the positive impact of internal marketing on employees, external customers and performance. Southwest's success has been based in large part on its employees' positive attitudes, high productivity and customer orientation (Czaplewski *et al.*, 2001), and this continues today, with Southwest so far being profitable for 44 years in a row (as of 2018).

Similarly, Marriott is a company that stands out in the luxury hotel business for the way it treats its employees to bolster its higher service strategy. Its approach includes pre-shift dance sessions for housekeepers, Oscar-style award nights, free travel for some and clear career development opportunities, and consequently employee retention is high. The company believes that a seasoned workforce does a better job and costs less money (Gallagher, 2015).

It can be argued that there is no one 'right' strategy in any given product market situation, but there are certainly good and bad ways of *delivering* market strategies, which determine if they succeed or fail. The critical issue is becoming the consistency between strategies, tactics and implementation actions. This suggests that real culture change is a central part of the process of going to market effectively. At its simplest, the disgruntled employee produces the disgruntled customer. Bonoma (1990) summarised this point succinctly: 'treat your employees like customers, or your customers will get treated like employees'.

However, it is apparent that successfully exploiting the linkage between employee and customer satisfaction may not always be straightforward. Research into the way in which customer satisfaction is measured and managed in British companies is revealing (Piercy, 1995). Studies suggest that:

1 There is a need to create *clarity* for all employees regarding customer service quality policies and customer satisfaction targets. It is not enough to pay lip-service to these ideals and to expect success in attaining them. The starting point must be to identify what has to be achieved in customer satisfaction to implement specific market strategies, and to position the company against the competition in a specific market. It is unlikely that achieving what is needed will be free from cost. We need to take a realistic view of the time needed and the real costs of implementation in aligning the internal market with the external market.

2 *Internal processes and barriers* suggest the need to consider both the internal and external markets faced in implementing customer satisfaction measurement and management systems. To ignore the internal market is to risk actually damaging the company's capacity to achieve and improve customer satisfaction in the external market. If, for example, management uses customer feedback in a negative and coercive way, then it may reduce employee enthusiasm for customer service, or create 'game-playing' behaviour where people compete for 'Brownie points' in the system at the expense of both the company and the customer. This said, we have also to recognise not just the complementarity between internal and external markets, but the potential for conflict of interest. Achieving target levels of customer service and satisfaction may require managers and employees to change the way they do things and to make sacrifices they do not want to make. This may take more than simple advocacy or management threat.

3 Related to this argument, recognising the internal market suggests that there may be a need for a structured and planned *internal marketing programme* to achieve the effective

implementation of customer satisfaction measurement and management. This has been described elsewhere as 'marketing our customers to our employees' (Piercy, 2009a), and can be built into the implementation process to address the needs of the internal customer and to confront the types of internal processual barrier we have encountered.

4 Also related to the recognition of the internal market is the need to question the *relationship* between internal and external customer satisfaction. This can be discussed with executives using the structure shown in Figure 16.2. This suggests four possible scenarios that result when internal and external customer satisfaction are compared:

(a) **Synergy**, which is what we hope for – when internal and external customer satisfaction are high and we see them as sustainable and self-regenerating. As one hotel manager explained it: 'I know that we are winning on customer service when my operational staff come to me and complain about how I am getting in their way in providing customer service, and tell me to get my act together!' This is the 'happy customers and happy employees' situation, assumed by many to be obvious and easily achieved.

(b) **Coercion** is where we achieve high levels of external customer satisfaction by changing the behaviour of employees through management direction and control systems. In the short term this may be the only option, but it may be very difficult and expensive to sustain this position in the longer term, and we give up flexibility for control.

(c) **Alienation** is where we have low levels of satisfaction internally and externally, and we are likely to be highly vulnerable to competitive attack on service quality and to the instability in our competitive capabilities produced by low staff morale and high staff turnover.

(d) **Internal euphoria** is where we have high levels of satisfaction in the internal market, but this does not translate into external customer satisfaction – for example, if internal socialisation and group cohesiveness actually shut out the paying customer in the external market. These scenarios are exaggerated, but have provided a useful way of confronting these issues with executives.

5 A critical mistake is to ignore the real *costs and challenges* in sustaining high service quality levels and the limitation that may exist in a company's capabilities for improving customer satisfaction levels. While advocacy is widespread and the appeal is obvious, achieving the potential benefits requires more planning and attention to implementation realities than is suggested by the existing conventional literature.

Figure 16.2
Customer satisfaction in the internal market and external market

16.3.2 Internal marketing as internal communications

As well as customer care training and a focus on service quality, internal marketing may also be seen as internal communications. In fact, the largest growth in this area has been investment by companies in broader internal communications programmes of various kinds – where 'communications' is understood as providing employees with information and delivering messages that support the business strategy. The goal of internal communications normally is to build both understanding and commitment. Often, these activities tend to be a responsibility of the human resource department. One industry study (Pounsford, 1994) suggested that managers saw the role of internal communications in the terms (and with the advantages) shown in Table 16.1.

The manifestations of this form of internal marketing include company newsletters, employee conferences and training, video-conferencing, satellite TV transmissions, interactive video, corporate social media platforms, email and so on. Increasingly, creating dialogue within an organisation and encouraging employee involvement can involve approaches such as Web-based internal blogs (Hathi, 2007). These delivery mechanisms are important, but are in danger of obscuring an important point: instructing and informing people about strategic developments is not the same as winning their real involvement and participation. Real communication is a two-way process – listening as well as informing. This may be why internal communications appear ineffective in some companies. There is a risk that internal communications programmes become about telling and persuading, not listening. This may be said to be internal *selling* not internal *marketing*.

Indeed, large companies such as Microsoft and Germany's SAP have an organisational role for a 'chief storyteller' to promote storytelling as internal communication related to management, innovation and change to staff and investors, although some commentators are sceptical about their value (Hill, 2014).

Table 16.1 The role of internal communications

Perceived role	Illustrative comments
Team building	Educate employees about breadth and diversity of the organisation
	Assist cooperation between divisions
Damage control	Prevent managers getting communications wrong
	Suppress bad news
	Counter pessimism
Morale builders	Build confidence
	Increase motivation
Involvement	Represent employee opinions upwards
	Create channel to share problems/values
	Increase people recognition
Change management	Increase understanding of the need for change
	Test new ideas
	Help people relate to rapidly changing environment
Goal setting	Help steer organisation in a coordinated direction
	Provide focus on corporate goals
	Generate support for policies

An interesting illustration of the gains from two-way communications comes from Dana Corp, the US car parts manufacturer. At that company, the 'suggestions box' is described by the CEO as 'a core part of our value system'. Employees contribute ideas to improve operations and service, and 70 per cent are actually used. Dana is an example of an organisation where employees have taken a share of the responsibility for keeping the company competitive. This underlines the important practical difference between producing company newsletters and taking internal communications seriously.

Indeed, some major companies, such as Procter & Gamble and Cisco Systems, are actively seeking out the employees who are most influential inside the organisation because of their social links and social media communications. The logic is to harness the clout of these influencers to identify new product opportunities, get other employees on board with big changes and spread information throughout the organisation. The twenty-first century is very much the era of the network (Feintzeig, 2014; Mattu, 2011). Others use 'reverse mentoring' and have employees mentor managers – for example, informing them about the reality of social media or bridging the 'generation gap' so that managers understand younger consumers and employees better – an established practice at Tesco, Deloitte's and GE (Jacobs, 2013).

16.3.3 Internal marketing and innovation management

Somewhat different is the use of the internal marketing framework to place and gain use of innovations, such as computers and electronic communications in the IT field. These applications use tools of market analysis and planning to cope with and avoid resistance and to manage the process of change. This may be particularly important where the effectiveness of a marketing strategy relies on the adoption of new technologies and ways of working. The argument here is that people in an organisation are 'customers' for the company's ideas and innovations. This view encourages us to consider:

- **looking at customer needs** – even in hierarchical companies, people are not robots waiting to be told what to do, so making the effort to understand their needs increases the likely effectiveness of innovation;
- **delivering the goods** – the needs of customers tell us what matters most to them;
- **raising unrealistic expectations** – which is as dangerous with internal customers as it is with external customers (Divita, 1996).

For example, the use of technology by a geographically dispersed salesforce in one company was guided by the analysis of the 'internal market' using the classic 'diffusion of innovation' model to identify opinion leaders as key influencers in the adoption process. Similarly, the BT problem of marketing its information systems and services to its internal customers was addressed through the same principles used to market solutions to the organisation's external customers: segmentation, targeting and positioning IS solutions to the internal customer base (Morgan, 2004).

16.3.4 Internal markets instead of external markets for products and services

The terms 'internal market' and 'internal marketing' have been applied to internal relationships between different parts of the same organisation – making them suppliers and customers as a way of improving the focus on efficiency and value. This is common in total quality management programmes, and in wider applications such as the attempted reforms of the UK National Health Service.

This can lead to some interesting issues. For example, work with the R&D division of a major brewery suggested that the internal customer issues were really about the type and degree of dependence between the internal supplier (in this case the provider of R&D solutions to process problems in the brewery) and the internal customer (here the production and sales units of the brewery), which in turn reflects the freedom of either internal supplier or customer to deal with third parties outside the company.

16.3.5 Strategic internal marketing

Strategic internal marketing (SIM) is an approach to the structured planning of marketing strategy implementation, and analysis of underlying implementation problems in an organisation. This form of internal marketing is a direct parallel to the conventional external marketing strategy and marketing programme, which aims at winning the support, cooperation and commitment we need inside the company, if our external market strategies are to work. This is a somewhat different view of internal marketing compared to those discussed previously, although it is informed by the other types of internal marketing that have a longer history. The key underlying issue here is the organisational and cultural change needed to make marketing strategies happen.

A structure for an internal marketing programme is shown in Figure 16.3. The underlying rationale is that the easiest way to make practical progress with this type of internal marketing, and to establish what it may achieve, is to use exactly the same structures that we use for planning *external* marketing. This suggests that we should think in terms of integrating the elements needed for an internal marketing mix or programme, based on our analysis of the opportunities and threats in the internal marketplace represented by the company with which we are working. This is shown in Figure 16.3 as a formal and legitimate part of the planning process.

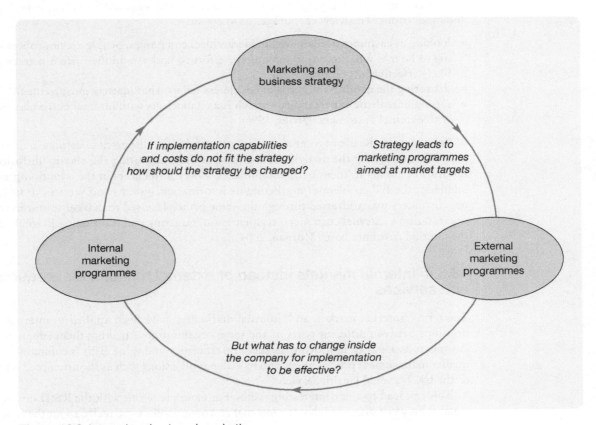

Figure 16.3 Internal and external marketing

In this model, we take the internal marketing programme not only as an *output* of the planning process and the external marketing programme, but also as an *input* – that is, constraints and barriers in the internal marketplace should be considered and analysed as a part of the planning at both strategic and tactical levels. For the proposals to make sense in practice, we rely on this iterative relationship.

The starting point for this approach is that the marketing strategy and the planning process may define an external marketing programme in the conventional way, and less conventionally the internal barriers suggest that some external strategies are not capable of being implemented in the time-scale concerned, and we have to feed back into the planning process the message that some adjustments are needed while there is still time to make those adjustments to plans.

More positively, however, it is equally true that our analysis of the internal market may suggest new opportunities and neglected company resources that should be exploited, which in turn impact on our external marketing plan and thus on the planning process. What we are trying to make explicit for executives is the need to balance the impact of both internal and external market attributes on the strategic assumptions that they make in planning.

The structure of such an internal marketing programme is suggested in Figure 16.4 and can be presented in the following terms:

- **The product:** At the simplest level, the 'product' consists of the marketing strategies and the marketing plan. Implied, however, is that the product to be 'sold' is those values, attitudes and behaviours that are needed to make the marketing plan work effectively. These hidden dimensions of the product may range from increased budgets and different resource allocations, to changed control systems and criteria used to evaluate performance, to changed ways of handling customers at the point of sale. At the extreme, the product is the person's job – as it is redefined and reshaped by the market strategy to make people's working lives more enjoyable. There may also be negatives – changes people will not like, which brings us to price.
- **The price:** The price element of the internal marketing mix is not *our* costs, it is concerned with what we are asking our internal customers to 'pay', when they buy-in to the product and the marketing plan. This may include the sacrifice of other projects that

Programme	Contents	Examples
Product	The strategy and the plan, including the values, attitudes and behaviours needed to make them work	For example, the written plan, the new company initiative
Price	What we are asking internal customers to 'pay' – other projects abandoned, personal and psychological adjustment to change	For example, stepping out of comfort zones for new types of operations
Communications	Media and messages to inform and persuade	For example, reports, plans, presentations, videos, roadshows
Distribution	Physical and social venues for delivering the product and communications	For example, meetings, workgroups, training sessions and workshops, informal meetings, social occasions

Figure 16.4
Content and structure of internal marketing programmes

Source: Adapted from Piercy (2009a).

compete for resources with our plan, but more fundamentally the personal psychological cost of adopting different key values and changing the way jobs are done, and asking managers to step outside their 'comfort zones' with new methods of operation. The price to be paid by different parts of the internal marketplace, if the marketing plan is to be implemented successfully, should not be ignored as a major source of barriers and obstacles of varying degrees of difficulty.

- **Communications:** The most tangible aspect of the internal marketing programme is the communications media and the messages used to inform and persuade, and to work on the attitudes of the key personnel in the internal marketplace. This includes not only written communications, such as plan summaries and reports, but also face-to-face presentations to individuals and groups who are important to the success of the plan. Broadly, we should remember that to assume that simply 'telling' people will get them on our side is likely to be as naive inside the company as it is outside. We suggest it is important to consider the full range of communications possibilities and associated goals, as we would with external customers, and we should not forget to budget the time and financial costs that may be associated with these activities. At the simplest level, the purpose of our internal marketing communication may be served by a video presentation explaining things, or a roadshow taking the message out to the regions and the distributors. But real communication is two-way – we listen, we adapt, we focus on our audience's problems and needs.

- **Distribution:** The distribution channels element of the mix is concerned with the physical and socio-technical venues at which we have to deliver our product and its communications: meetings, committees, training sessions for managers and staff, seminars, workshops, written reports, informal communications, social occasions and so on. Ultimately, however, the real distribution channel is human resource management, and in the lining up of recruitment training, evaluation and reward systems behind marketing strategies, so that the culture of the company becomes the real distribution channel for internal marketing strategies. In fact, as long ago as the 1990s, Ulrich (1992) made some radical points about this, which are worth confronting. He said that if we really want complete customer commitment from our external customers, through independent, shared values and shared strategies, then we should give our customers a major role in our:

  - staff recruitment and selection decisions;
  - staff promotion and development decisions;
  - staff appraisal, from setting the standards to measuring the performance;
  - staff reward systems, both financial and non-financial;
  - organisational design strategies; and
  - internal communications programmes.

In effect, this means using our human resource management systems as the internal marketing channel, thus taking the internal and external customer issue to its logical conclusion. Companies developing such approaches include General Electric, Marriott, Borg-Warner, DEC, Ford Motor Company, Hewlett Packard and Honeywell.

In many important ways, the revitalisation or transformation of a company, as well as the implementation of a new strategy, may be in large part dependent on incorporating employees fully in the challenge to change the ways they deal with conflict and learning, leading differently in order to maintain employee involvement and instilling the disciplines that will help people learn new ways of behaving and sustain that new behaviour (Pascale et al., 1997). Managers who fail to get employees to understand what they are doing and why, and to build their enthusiasm, should not be surprised when strategy execution fails. Indeed, one argument is that the real role of management should be to connect employees better with end-users of the product or service, because they can energise the workforce far better than can managers (Grant, 2011).

For example, a simple internal marketing analysis for two companies is illustrated in Tables 16.2 and 16.3. These examples concern a key customer account strategy in a financial services organisation and a vertical marketing strategy in a computer company. In both cases we can see a 'formal' level of internal marketing that concerns the marketing plan or strategy, but also levels of internal marketing concerned with the informal organisation and the processes of decision making and change inside the company. In the computer company, vertical marketing is not a simple strategy because it is linked to changing resource allocation and departmental responsibilities, and also to a change of management culture. In the financial services company, a key account strategy involves not simply a new marketing direction, but a change in line management freedom and ways of doing business. These cases are indicative of the types of implementation and change problem that can be addressed by internal marketing.

Table 16.2 Internal marketing in a computer company

Internal market targets	(1) Business unit management (2) Product group management (3) Salesforce		
Internal marketing programme	Internal marketing levels		
	Formal	Informal	Processual
Product	Marketing plan to attack a small industry as a special vertical market, rather than grouping it with many other industries as at present, with specialised products and advertising	Separation of resources and control of this market from the existing business unit	Change from technology-orientated management to recognition of differences in buyer needs in different industries – the clash between technology and customer orientation
Price	Costs of developing specialised 'badged' or branded products for this industry	Loss of control for existing business units	Fear of 'fragmentation' of markets leading to internal structural and status changes
Communications	Written plan Presentations to key groups	Support for plan by key board members gained by pre-presentation 'softening up' by planners	Action planning team formed, including original planners, but also key players from business unit and product group – rediscovering the wheel to gain 'ownership' Advertising the new strategy in trade press read by company technologists and managers
Distribution	Business unit board meeting Product group board meeting Main board meeting Salesforce conference	Informal meetings	Joint seminars in applying IT to this industry, involving business unit managers and key customers Joint charity events for the industry's benevolent fund

Table 16.3 Internal marketing in a financial services organisation

Internal market targets *(1) Branch managers of retail banks and finance company offices*
(2) Divisional chief executives for the banks and the finance

Internal marketing programme	Internal marketing levels		
	Formal	Informal	Processual
Product	Integration of selling efforts around key customers, as a key marketing strategy	Head office group-based planning and resource allocation with greater central control	Change in the individual manager's role from independent branch entrepreneur to group-based collaborator
Price	Branch profit/commission from independent selling to smaller customers, to be sacrificed to build long-term relationships with key accounts	Loss of freedom/independence of action in the marketplace Potential loss of commission-earning power	Time, effort and psychological 'pain' of collaborating with former 'competitors' with different ethnic/educational/professional backgrounds – the 'banker versus the hire purchase salesman' Fear that the other side would damage existing customer relationships
Distribution	Written strategic marketing plans Sales conferences	Written communications Informal discussion of chief executive's 'attitude' Redesign of commission and incentives systems in both companies	Joint planning/problem-solving teams for each region – built around central definition of target market segments Combining/integrating management information systems, and changing structure to reflect new segments
Communications	Formal presentation by chief executive at conferences Written support from chief executive Redesign market information systems to be more up to date	Sponsorship by chief executive – 'the train is now leaving the station, you are either on it or. . . ' (written memo sent to all branches)	Social events Joint training course Redefinition of markets and target segments

It also follows that we can use conventional market research techniques inside the company to get to grips with who has to change, in what way, how much and what the patterns are in our internal marketplace.

Finally, as with the external marketing programme, we should not neglect the importance of measuring results wherever possible. This may be in terms of such criteria as people's attitudes towards the market strategy and their commitment to putting it into practice, or customer perceptions of our success in delivering our promises to them – or, perhaps more appositely, our lack of success as presented by complaints, and so on.

Again, in exact parallel with the conventional external marketing plan, our internal marketing programmes should be directed at chosen targets or segments within the market. The choice of key targets for the internal marketing programme should be derived directly from the goals of the external marketing programme, and the types of organisational and human changes needed to implement marketing strategies. The internal marketplace may be segmented at the simplest level by the job roles and functions played by groups of people, such as top management, other departments and marketing and sales staff.

Alternatively, we might look beyond job characteristics to the key sources of support and resistance to the external marketing plan that is anticipated, to identify targets for reinforcement, or for persuasion and negotiation. Perhaps at the deepest level we might choose our targets on the basis of the individual's attitudes towards the external market and customers, and the key values that we need communicated to external customers, together with people's career goals.

It can be seen, therefore, that internal marketing can be used in different ways, and that the role may vary from developing customer care and service quality programmes to improving and maintaining service standards and customer satisfaction at the point-of-sale, through to internal communication programmes, to providing a structured approach to planning the full implementation of marketing strategy. We noted also that internal marketing may be of particular importance in the alliance-based network organisation.

16.4   Planning for internal marketing

There are a variety of situations when strategic thinking about competitive strategy should address the possible role of internal marketing:

- where performance in critical areas of customer service is unsatisfactory and not sufficient to establish a strong competitive position;
- where customer satisfaction is consistently low and complaints suggest that the underlying causes are employee attitudes and behaviour, rather than poor product standards or inadequate support systems;
- when market conditions and customer requirements have shifted, so that continuing the standards and practices of the past will no longer bring success;
- when new marketing strategies require new skills and ways of behaving – a 'stretch' strategy;
- when bridging the gap between planning and implementation has proved problematic in the past.

In such situations, we may wish to consider an internal marketing strategy with the following components.

Internal market orientation

Some attention has been given to internal market orientation as the foundation for success, in the same way that external market orientation has been linked to the effectiveness of external marketing strategies. The logic is that internal market orientation increases the effectiveness of a market-orientated company to external market conditions, because it allows management to better align external market objectives with internal capabilities. However, this symmetry relies on assessment of internal market orientation as a precursor to action (Gounaris, 2006). Lings and Greenley (2005) propose that assessing internal market orientation should encompass directly parallel measures to those associated with external market orientation, thus internal market orientation involves the generation and dissemination of intelligence pertaining to the wants and needs of employees, and the design and implementation of appropriate responses to meet those wants and needs.

Internal market strategy

In broad terms, this is what is needed to gain the successful implementation of an external market strategy. It is here that we need to confront the real implications of our external market strategy for the internal customer – the decision makers, managers, operatives and others without whose support, cooperation and commitment the external strategy will fail. This is the most critical question in the whole internal marketing exercise. It may be worth consulting the people directly concerned – doing internal market research. It is certainly worth incorporating some diversity of opinion. As we learn more, we can come back and redraft and rethink our conclusions here. It is here that we should take a view of what it is likely to cost us to achieve these things and the deadline for achieving them to implement the external marketing strategy on time.

Internal market segmentation

This is about identifying the targets in the internal marketplace around which we can build internal marketing programmes, which are different according to what we have to achieve and how we are going to do it. This may not be straightforward, but is the route to real insights into the internal market problem and effectiveness in how we cope with that problem. The most obvious way of identifying internal segments may be by role or function, or location, and this may be sufficient. It might be more productive to think who are the innovators and opinion leaders who will influence others? We might approach this more directly in terms of the role that different people will play in implementing the external strategy and the problems they may face in this, or simply how much different people will have to change to get the external strategy to work.

For example, one argument is that we should consider the employer as the brand, and then the same underlying bases can be used in segmenting employees as are used externally with consumers: potential profitability, product-feature preferences, influential reference groups, bargaining power, choice barriers. Then the internal market segmentation model will include:

- **Potential profitability** – employees who have the skills, experience or knowledge that is strategically important to the company, who should get resources for recruitment and retention.
- **Product-feature preferences** – employees grouped according to the career benefits they value most highly, to identify the bundles of benefits with most value to these groups.
- **Reference groups** – people generally want to work for companies with good reputations, as judged by the people whose opinions they value. This supports efforts to reinforce the brand with those who influence employee perceptions.
- **Bargaining power** – the power of some employees in negotiating terms of employment because of the rarity of their skills, level of seniority, relevant experience and qualifications. This suggests the need for richer benefits packages (not necessarily money).
- **Choice barriers** – the recruitment and pay policies set up by an employer to prevent people entering or leaving the firm. The goal of action here is to counter the bargaining power of some employee groups.

Although this example is specific to the 'employer brand', it illustrates nicely the use of segmentation principles in the internal market that are drawn directly from those used in the consumer market (Moroko and Uncles, 2009).

Internal marketing programmes

These specify which internal marketing programmes will be needed in each internal market segment to achieve the objectives we have set. In each area we need to collect our thoughts about the rational issues, but also the human and cultural issues. To us the product may be a new marketing plan that we need to inform people about (internal marketing communications), through formal presentations (internal marketing distribution), adjusting commission and evaluation systems as need be (internal marketing price). To the internal customer, the same plan may be about disruption and threat (product), loss of initiative and status (price), imposed without consultation by management (communication) and rigorously 'policed' through coercion (distribution). If internal marketing is about anything, it is about confronting and coping with this conflict. It is this confrontation that will drive us away from thinking about internal marketing as simply writing customer care brochures and doing great plan presentations, towards coping with the human and organisational realities of what strategic change involves and costs. This is also the stage to take a look at the cost implications of what we now see to be necessary in our internal marketing: does the internal marketing cost mean that the external market strategy is no longer attractive? Do we have to account for an internal marketing cost that is more than we expected, but bearable? Do we have to change the external strategy to reduce the internal marketing cost? Are there cheaper ways of achieving the critical internal marketing goals?

Internal marketing evaluation

This is what we can measure to see if we are getting there, ideally quantified and objective: for example, reduced customer complaint rates or higher customer satisfaction scores. This may be ambitious and we should not abandon important objectives because they are difficult to evaluate – we may have to settle for a subjective or qualitative evaluation, which is better than nothing.

However, the possible problems to be anticipated in implementing internal marketing strategy programmes effectively should not be underestimated. For example, Don Schultz suggests that many, if not most, internal marketing approaches fail, for the following reasons:

- **Lack of financial measures of internal marketing success** – not achieving the goal of linking measurable behavioural changes to financial returns for the business.
- **Weak management cohesion** – the organisational location of responsibility for internal marketing is confused and those responsible have no authority or responsibility for the people whose behaviours they are trying to change.
- **Lack of senior management support** – internal marketing is not perceived as a senior management issue, but the concern of middle managers with all the inherent problems of turf wars and organisational politics.
- **No connection between internal stakeholders and external customers** – the difficulty for employees in non-customer-facing roles to understand how internal marketing affects them, or how they affect the external customer.
- **Lack of a management calculus** – no clear ideas about the value or return of internal marketing and no effective internal marketing planning system.

For example, one initiative at Wells Fargo, the San Francisco bank, is the happy/grumpy ratio, to measure the proportion of cheery staff versus the less happy. The company believes that happy employees are more likely to do the right thing than unhappy people, so it measures the proportions. It reports that, over the course of five years, the ratio of happy to grumpy improved from 3.8:1 to 8:1, suggesting the effectiveness of the policy (Kellaway, 2015). That said, in 2016, Wells Fargo was accused of encouraging unethical practices among its sales staff, and numerous reports emerged of a negative performance-at-all-costs culture in the sales staff. This illustrates the point that companies need to align incentive structures and the like with any corporate culture initiatives. Just encouraging 'happiness' in itself is rarely enough to outweigh performance incentives that encourage the wrong types of behaviour.

Schultz (2004) suggests that we should apply the lessons of integrated marketing communications in internal as well as external marketing. However, the issue of integration has yet further practical aspects, as we see in the next section of the chapter.

16.5 Cross-functional partnership as internal marketing

16.5.1 Rationale for cross-functional partnership

Perhaps the greatest contemporary challenge for internal marketing is the achievement of the effective cross-functional partnerships required to deliver superior customer value. Two things are increasingly apparent.

First, delivering value results from a complex set of processes and activities inside the organisation and possibly also in a network of organisations in a strategic alliance (see Chapter 15). Many of the processes of defining, creating and delivering value to customers are not 'owned' or directly managed by marketing or sales departments. The challenge may be looking at different units as a form of strategic alliance, where benefits and costs should be carefully analysed (Campbell, 2006). Research suggests that organisations that collaborate well internally perform better in meeting customer needs, accommodating special customer requests and introducing new products, and as a result are perceived more favourably by customers (Wilding, 2006). *Second*, sophisticated customers will not accept anything less than seamless delivery of value on their terms – problems in the integration of processes in the seller's organisation are the seller's problem, not the buyer's (Hulbert *et al.*, 2003; Piercy and Lane, 2012).

The integration of the whole organisation around the drivers of customer value has become an imperative – all activities must work together, fit together and be seen to appear together by the customer. Nonetheless, many organisations appear to struggle with this imperative. The model in Figure 16.5 provides a framework for analysing the challenges in identifying and integrating the complex of functional specialisms and internal and external resource centres that impact on the operation of the value processes of value identification, creation and delivery (however these processes are labelled in a particular company).

We consider briefly the nature of each of the interfaces between marketing and other functional groups, which may provide internal marketing targets for internal alliance building.

16.5.2 Marketing and human resource management

It is now a considerable time since Glassman and McAfee (1992) called for the full-scale integration of marketing and human resource management departments. Their logic was that the two functions were both focused on 'people issues' (the one on customers and the other on employees), yet seemed unable to integrate their activities effectively. However, HRM in

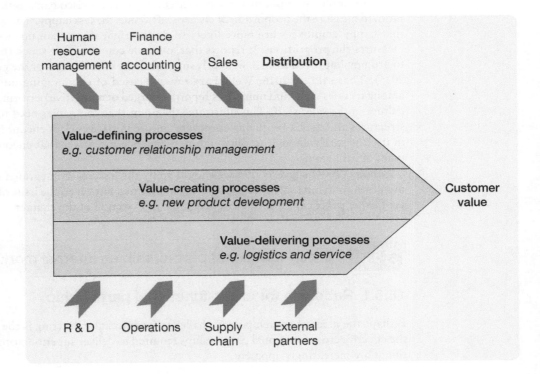

Figure 16.5
Cross-functional
contributions to
value processes

many organisations has moved towards a 'strategic human resource management' approach, with a primary concern for aligning the skills and capabilities of employees and managers with the requirements of business strategy. The processes usually managed in HRM are extremely relevant to the goals of marketing strategy: recruitment and selection, evaluation and reward system, training and development and other drivers of corporate culture. There is an opportunity for marketing to work with HRM in identifying the key elements of employee motivation, and the instigation of training and development programmes – but particularly in providing the research capabilities to evaluate the internal marketplace, including employees, channel partners and customer service providers (Schultz, 2002).

Some companies are making large efforts to ensure that marketing and HRM work together, to ensure that they communicate and deliver brand values to both internal and external audiences. The 'Everything is Possible' campaign at H-P Invest (formerly Hewlett-Packard) is aimed to be as inspirational for staff as it is for customers. Allied-Domecq sees its 'people brand' as one of its nine core brands. Some companies, such as Allied-Domecq and Sainsbury's, have appointed employer brand managers to bridge the gap between HR and marketing (Simms, 2003).

One view is that HR and marketing collaboration becomes critical when the priority is to maintain a coherent corporate brand and employer brand, and that the way forward is to: make internal brand management a strategic imperative; break down HR/marketing barriers; empower employees as brand ambassadors; establish and maintain aligned corporate and employer brands; and build internal brand management around brand-centred HR practices (Brown, 2014). Nonetheless, many company practices clearly fall short of this ideal.

An internal marketing agenda concerned with the contribution of HRM to value processes might include the following issues:

- the better alignment of employee and manager training and development processes with customer priorities;
- tracking and comparing employee satisfaction and customer satisfaction to understand the relationship between them;
- working on the links between customer satisfaction and retention issues, and employee training, reward and evaluation processes;
- looking at the way in which internal communications approaches support external market strategies (Piercy, 2009a).

The importance of the marketing/HRM link is such that, in many situations, major customers are increasingly playing a direct role in participating in the operation of suppliers' internal HRM processes, such as recruitment into sales and service jobs.

Indeed, more operational views of the interface between marketing and HRM issues focus on the link between HRM and relationship marketing strategies (Perrien *et al.*, 1993; Perrien and Ricard, 1995), and the need to direct HRM policies to focus on customer service and customer value (Cripe, 1994; Gubman, 1995). Sheth and Mittal (1996) have even examined the use of HRM skills in the management of customer expectations. Nonetheless, research suggests that the marketing/HRM relationship is frequently associated with conflict and poor interdepartmental communication, with a detrimental impact on strategy implementation (Chimhanzi, 2004).

16.5.3 Marketing and finance and accounting

The conflict between marketing and finance/accounting in the past has reflected the goal of accounting to cut costs and to increase reported short-term profit, compared to the objective of marketing to gain long-term investment in brands and market share. Conflicts have also centred on different views of pricing – the accounting model of cost-plus pricing produces very different outcomes to a marketing model of price based on customer value. However, these disputes have been rendered largely obsolete by two important factors. The first factor is the overwhelming pressure that marketing is under in a growing number of companies to 'prove' its added-value to the company and its shareholders (Ambler, 2003). Many of the metrics that marketing most needs in order to establish its shareholder value creation can only be achieved through collaboration with finance and accounting (Farris *et al.*, 2006). The second factor is the increasingly strategic view of business being taken by finance and accounting executives, which is likely to reduce the conflicts with marketing and sales. Moves towards internal alliances between marketing and finance/accounting are likely to be important in achieving the speed of change and market responsiveness required by modern customers.

16.5.4 Marketing and sales integration

In Chapter 14 we examined the growing role of the sales organisation in strategic customer management, and as a change agent inside the company. Nonetheless, for many companies the relationship between marketing and sales remains problematic. It has been noted 'the relationship between sales and marketing functions has persisted as one of the major sources of organisational conflict' (Webster, 1997), and that 'the marketing–sales relationship, whilst strongly interdependent, is reported as neither collaborative nor harmonious' (Dewsnap and Jobber, 2000). For these reasons, sales and marketing integration remains a high and very topical priority on the management agenda (Rouzies *et al.*, 2005). This question merits more detailed consideration, since it appears frequently to be one of the most critical obstacles to marketing strategy implementation.

The conventional literature often assumes that marketing departments and sales organisations are a single organisational unit, but they are frequently quite distinct functions in companies (Piercy and Lane, 2012). For example, in their 1998 study, Workman *et al.* suggest that 'it is highly significant that more than thirty years after the call to integrate sales and marketing activities under a CME [Chief Marketing Executive], we find no firms that had adopted this recommendation.' In fact, part of the reason is that marketing and sales should not be the same because the functions they perform are different (Shapiro, 2002). However, the new market conditions and strategic sales role we described in Chapter 14 place considerable importance on cross-functional collaboration and cooperation, which may align poorly with the traditional need for functional separation based on task specialisation.

What is far from well understood is which conflicts, or elements of conflict, actually have negative consequences for business performance and which do not (Deshpandé and Webster, 1989). While marketing and sales exist alongside each other as business functions, there are likely to be fundamental differences between them in perspective and priorities. However, in examining the coordination of these differentiated functions, Cespedes (1996) highlights an important dilemma: 'the solution is *not* to eliminate differences among these groups', but that 'paradoxically, there is virtue in *separating* and distinguishing functional roles in order to improve the cross-functional coordination needed' (Cespedes, 1995). The suggestion is that differences between marketing and sales may actually provide a much-needed breadth of perspective and richness of market understanding *because* of the differences between the functions. As collaboration and cooperation between marketing and sales grows in importance, this paradox provides an important insight – teamwork and joint-working has to accommodate differences in perspective and understanding, and to focus on enhanced business performance, not simply smooth team operation or harmonious interrelationships.

The marketing/sales interface

To other functions in the business, the marketing and sales functions look alike – they are both focused on the customer and the market – but aligning sales and marketing has proved difficult in practice and is likely to be even more difficult in the future. The importance of the issue is quite simply that poor cooperation between marketing and sales will lead to inconsistent and weak strategy, coupled with flawed and inefficient implementation (Shapiro, 2002).

When the customer base was homogeneous, simple and dominated by mid-sized accounts, marketing operated as a strategic function concentrating on product strategy, segmentation and competitive positioning, while sales executed the strategy in the field – selling to end-users and distributors. The easy separation of sales and marketing has come to an end in markets dominated by very large accounts with sophisticated buying teams, and multi-channel strategies to reach medium and small accounts. With the largest accounts, marketing and sales need to make joint decisions to achieve an integrated offer that meets the standards required by purchasers who can dictate many terms to their suppliers. Marketing executives need to acquire new understanding of individual customers, key account needs and the sales task – the reality is that 'as power shifted from the seller to the buyer, it also shifted from headquarters to the field' (Shapiro, 2002). With multi-channelling (for instance, a website, social media, online platforms such as Amazon and Alibaba, telesales, direct marketing and personal selling working alongside each other), effectiveness and profitability also require shared sales and marketing decisions on channel strategy and execution (Shapiro, 2002).

While relatively little solid empirical evidence is available, executive opinion and anecdote suggest the relationship between marketing and sales remains problematic in many companies, with conflict surrounding such issues as the division of responsibilities and demarcation lines, ownership of customer information, competition for resources, control of price and the short-term orientation of sales versus the long-term orientation of marketing. Differences in reward systems (volume-based in sales and margin-based in marketing), information needs (geographically and customer-based in sales and product/brand-orientated in marketing) and competencies underline the potential for conflict rather than collaboration between marketing and sales (Cespedes, 1993, 1994; Montgomery and Webster, 1997; Dewsnap and Jobber, 2000).

Underpinning the potential for market/sales conflict is what has been described as the existence of different 'mindsets' in marketing and sales – different perspectives on issues and approaches for addressing problems – which have been described as:

- *Customer versus product* – focus and rewards for sales are based on customers and territories, while marketing champions products and brands.
- *Personal relationships versus analysis* – sales may be more 'people-orientated' and relationship-focused, while marketing emphasises aggregations of data and abstractions.
- *Continuous daily activity versus sporadic projects* – sales is driven by constant daily tasks, while marketing is organised around longer-term projects.
- *Field versus office* – sales is under immediate customer and budget pressures, while marketing may be removed from this environment.
- *Results versus process* – sales lives by fast, direct results from its selling efforts, while marketing activities are less easily linked to short-term results, so may emphasise process and intermediate outcomes.
- *Short-term orientation versus long-term orientation* – sales emphasises month-to-month sales results, while marketing concentrates on long-term competitive position (Rouzies *et al.*, 2005).

Such differences in mindset provide the context in which marketing–sales collaboration must be achieved, but may provide important practical barriers.

The signs of poor marketing/sales integration

The pioneering study by Strahle *et al.* (1996) noted that sales managers frequently do not set sales objectives consistent with the strategy developed by marketing executives for a product, through poor communications and incompatibility between marketing and sales goals. They note also the attempts by marketing executives to mislead sales managers about product performance in an effort to manipulate their behaviour. Unsurprisingly, the result is feelings of distrust and resentment towards marketing on the part of sales managers. Other research also suggests that changes in marketing strategy do not lead to consistent modification of sales operations (Colletti and Chonko, 1997).

A checklist of signals that marketing and sales are not well aligned is provided by the following statements, which may be assessed by marketing and sales executives in their own operations:

- Your marketing strategies fail to affect sales operations, impeding effective implementation.
- New marketing strategies ignore customer and competitor insights developed by the salesforce.
- Managers in other functions misunderstand what sales can and should achieve.
- Conflicts between sales and marketing managers frequently spill over into acrimony.
- You are experiencing serious salesperson retention problems and escalating replacement costs.
- There are serious mismatches between the tasks that salespeople must perform to implement marketing strategy and the ways in which they are organised, evaluated and rewarded.
- Career paths for salespeople take the best performers away from customers and place them in administration or management.
- Your salespeople struggle to cope with the ambiguous roles they now play.
- Your company offers little support for salespeople to make the transition from transaction to relationship selling.
- Your salespeople are hostile to your other routes to market, such as the Internet.
- Your customer relationships are getting weaker, not stronger (Hulbert *et al.*, 2003).

Careful assessment of these statements may be useful in identifying the beginnings of marketing/sales rifts that would otherwise remain hidden until becoming serious barriers to effective cross-functional working.

The internal marketing challenge

Shapiro (2002) notes that the prerequisites for effective marketing/sales relationships are a common understanding of the need for integration, and that both sales and marketing focus on the productive sharing of power, information and resources, but also warns: 'there are many approaches to improving integration. They work best when they themselves are well integrated (big surprise!). . . the stress will be on "mixing and matching" the individual elements of coordination to get a robust, efficient program.' This need for understanding and alignment between marketing strategy and the sales organisation defines the internal marketing challenge. The challenge is to both marketing and sales, as we suggested when examining the underlying premises of the strategic sales organisation. Indeed, if organisations cannot do better in building partnership between marketing and sales, it does not bode well for marketing's ability to create alliances with other functional groups.

16.5.5 Marketing and operations functions: R&D, manufacturing and supply chain management

The relationship between marketing and R&D is most usually associated with effectiveness in areas such as new product development. The synergy achieved by linking R&D spend to customer value is clear. However, the role of R&D may be significant to value defining and value delivering processes, as well as the classic function of value creation (new products). For example, companies such as IBM and Xerox bring lead-customers into their R&D laboratories, to meet the challenge of translating technical advances into new business options and profitable products. On the other hand, in some high-technology businesses R&D is a major component of relationship marketing – working with suppliers and customers on technology innovation is a key component of buyer–seller relationships (Tzokas *et al.*, 1997). Indeed, in industries associated with an accelerating rate of innovation, poor integration of marketing and R&D has been linked to reducing customer loyalty and long-term profits – innovations may be pushed into the marketplace without adequate commercialisation and technology readiness, so while customers may buy the innovation, in the absence of superior quality and service they are ready to migrate to the next 'big idea' as soon as it appears from a rival (Donath, 1997). The building of firmer links between R&D and marketing poses a greater challenge than simply providing new product pipelines.

In the other 'technical' functions, modern thinking is dominated by supply chain strategy – in particular the promise of the 'lean' supply chain to 'banish waste and create wealth' (Womack and Jones, 1996). The supply chain model of identifying value streams for products and organising around flow and the demand pull of products has been enormously influential, because of the potential it offers for reducing storage and waste costs to a minimum. Nonetheless, from a marketing perspective, the weakness of the lean supply chain lies in its rigid definition of customer value in purely technical terms, and the desirability of reducing product choices to reduce supply chain costs. However, the strategic link between supply chain and marketing strategy lies in the relationship between supply chain advantage and marketing/brand advantage. Applying internal marketing efforts to enhancing the understanding and collaboration between supply chain strategy and marketing strategy is a new mandate for marketing executives.

Certainly, at the supply chain operations level, there is evidence that internal marketing efforts to stimulate the impact of frontline logistics workers on customer value creation can lead to higher job satisfaction and performance in distribution centre employees, and increased interdepartmental customer orientation (Keller *et al.*, 2006).

16.5.6 Marketing and external partners

It will very frequently be the case that the successful implementation of marketing strategy will rely on the efforts of partnered organisations operating externally – distributors at home and abroad, outsourced manufacturers, third-party suppliers of customer services and network members delivering the product or service for the supplier. We examined in Chapter 15 the growing role of alliances and networks, and the way in which in some sectors such as global air travel, competition is between networks rather than individual airlines. The challenge of achieving effective delivery of strategic goals through partnered organisations remains considerable in many situations. Networks are characterised by dependencies. These increasingly common situations define a new and possibly critical function for internal marketing: the positioning of strategic imperatives with partner organisations in the networks that have been formed to reach the marketplace.

16.5.7 A process-based role for internal marketing

The logic for this part of the chapter is based on the following premises: that increasingly the effective implementation of marketing strategies will rely on effectiveness in managing cross-functional relationships, and that the management of processes of collaboration and alliance-building in organisations (and extended alliance-based networks) extends the internal marketing agenda from simply planning implementation strategy to a process design and management role. The model in Figure 16.4 provides a basis for addressing the nature of the main value processes in an organisation and then identifying the actual or potential contributions of diverse functional specialisms to the effectiveness of the value processes. Once identified, the cross-functional integration and collaboration needs define the internal marketing role.

16.6　Implementation and internal marketing[*]

The approach we have taken in this chapter to strategy implementation and internal marketing attempts to emphasise that strategy cannot usefully be examined in isolation from execution – developing strategic ideas around a company's markets achieves effectiveness only when placed in the context of implementation. However, when we focus on implementation, it is clear that we face both long-term and short-term issues. The short-term issues are what has mainly occupied us so far – gaining the execution of a given plan or strategy. The longer-term issues are more concerned with management decisions aimed at avoiding the implementation problems we have considered here.

This suggests that there is a need to consider both process management and execution skills in implementation. The difference is that managing the strategy process has the goal of integrating implementation and change issues with marketing strategy, with the goal of avoiding the emergence of implementation barriers. On the other hand, execution skills are concerned with how to manage a way though the change problems and barriers, which stand in the way of marketing strategy. While these are different approaches, they are not mutually exclusive, and in most practical situations attention will need to be paid to both.

The underlying rationale is summarised in Figure 16.6. There are four implementation scenarios suggested: **weak implementation** – where the management of process and execution skills are inappropriate to drive a marketing strategy; **management-driven implementation** – where the emphasis is on leadership and control by management to put a strategy into effect and to overcome problems or barriers that may exist; **implementation-driven strategy** – where the emphasis is on exploiting the capabilities of the existing organisation and adapting strategies to 'fit' with this reality; and **integrated strategy and implementation** – which achieves implementation by both managing key processes and applying management execution skills. In facing the implementation challenges in a given situation, it can be useful to map positioning on this framework and to track the practical implications for an effective implementation strategy.

The weak implementation scenario is largely based on managers assuming that once plans and strategies are written, then people will go away and make them happen. Some managers make these assumptions implicitly in how they approach things, and fail to anticipate the problems when their edicts and commands are not put into effect or are implemented half-heartedly or haphazardly. Any marketing strategy that matters to an organisation deserves to have implementation taken more seriously than this.

Figure 16.6
Integrating strategy and implementation processes

[*] This section draws on more detailed coverage of this issue in Piercy (2017).

The management-driven implementation scenario is probably closest to the traditional view of how things should be managed. The emphasis is on line management to take charge, to overcome obstacles, to lead, to coerce and to make things happen – it relies on high-quality management execution skills to overcome implementation barriers. It is fast to put into practice and in the short term may achieve change, but the problem is it lacks longer-term effectiveness in sustaining change.

The implementation-driven strategy scenario is where the focus of market strategies is dominated by exploiting existing capabilities and skills in the organisation, mainly by adapting market strategies to 'fit' with the organisation's existing competencies. This is also fast to be put into effect, and will keep implementation costs low. It is weaker in achieving strategic change because the emphasis is on exploiting what we already have, not developing new capabilities – this is fine until the point when our capabilities do not provide what the market wants, thus our strategy becomes outdated by market change.

The integrated strategy and implementation scenario is the ideal to which we aspire. Implementation is not an issue because it is fully integrated with the market strategy, and we are not forced to cling to existing skills and processes because part of developing strategy is developing the appropriate processes, structures, skills and capabilities to drive the strategy. It is slower to achieve and expensive, and in the short term not outstandingly effective, but it is probably the only route to long-term sustained strategic change. It is also the scenario we understand least well, and rarely find in practice.

Understanding the reality of the implementation scenario faced and the implications of the approaches adopted by management provides insights into problems likely to be faced, and a foundation for planning a longer-term strategy to enhance implementation capabilities in a company.

Summary

The focus of this chapter is strategy implementation – the transition from plans to execution. Strategy implementation faces a variety of obstacles and poses several important challenges for marketing executives. Part of the challenge is to avoid the separation of strategy and implementation and to recognise their interdependence. We take the increasingly widespread view that part of thinking about implementing competitive marketing strategy should be concerned with managing the internal market (of employees, functional specialists, managers and so on), because this may enhance a company's ability to deliver its strategies to customers in the external market. In part, this view is based on the recognition of the importance of relationship management with partners, achieving competition differentiation through the skills of the 'part-time marketers' in the organisation and the role of internal branding to parallel external branding.

We saw that internal marketing may be traced back to early views about the synergy between the marketing concept and the 'human relations' concept, and to have developed operationally in a variety of ways. The scope of internal marketing was seen to encompass service quality enhancement, internal communications programmes, managing the adoption of innovations inside an organisation, cross-functional and cross-divisional supply of products and services and a framework for marketing implementation. Our interest here is primarily, though not exclusively, in strategic internal marketing as a framework for managing implementation.

In this area we saw that internal marketing offers a framework for evaluating the costs of change and for managing change that utilises the same concepts, terminology and techniques as planning external marketing. This provides a pragmatic model for guiding implementation choices and actions.

The last part of the chapter gave attention to the more process-based view of internal marketing, which focuses on integration of company efforts around customer value creation, and the challenges of forming cross-functional partnerships to deliver marketing strategy to the marketplace. We examined the potentials for internal marketing efforts to build closer ties and collaboration between marketing, human resource management, finance and accounting, sales, operations functions and external partners. We suggested that perhaps one of the most important roles of internal marketing goes beyond aligning employees' values and behaviours with strategies, and confronts the need to achieve superior customer value through seamlessness in strategy delivery. This role emphasises internal marketing to achieve cross-functional partnerships within the organisation, and crossing organisational boundaries to align external partners with the imperatives of marketing strategy.

The long-term approach to effective strategy implementation is likely to be one that balances process management and execution skills in order to produce an integrated strategy and implementation approach – one that enhances a company's implementation capabilities.

Case study

Inter Ikea's Torbjorn Loof: making the vision clear

By Richard Milne

The retailer's boss is transforming the business — and is prepared to make mistakes

Internal politics had supposedly never played much of a role in the tangled web of companies that makes up the world's largest furniture retailer. But when Inter Ikea, little-known owner of the brand and concept, acquired the product range, design and manufacturing businesses in 2016 from its more famous sister company, Ikea Group, Torbjorn Loof was struck by the infighting.

The chief executive of Inter Ikea says: 'In the midst of everything, we also saw a bit of what we call political behaviour in the company. In the beginning that surprised me. When you work in Ikea you don't know how to handle that because this was something new.'

The 53-year-old is running a franchise system that decides everything: from which products are on offer and what the stores look like, to the famous catalogues and flat-pack design. But rather than use his new-found power and influence, Mr Loof took a different approach.

'Of course, it's easier for the party who in our case acquired resources, acquired influence ... You need to understand and respect the partner that you are doing the deal with: to say what do you need and what's your perspective on this? You have almost to put yourself mentally in their shoes,' he adds, in an interview in the store in Almhult, the southern Swedish town that was the birthplace of Ikea 76 years ago.

Mr Loof was raised in the nearby hamlet of Pjatteryd, and has worked at Ikea for 30 years in a variety

Inter IKEA Chief Executive Torbjorn Loof speaks in Almhult, Sweden, June 7, 2017
Source: Anna Ringstrom/REUTERS.

of roles from purchaser and manager in Italy, to head of Ikea Sweden, the company at the heart of the empire that designs its products and was part of the 2016 deal.

That acquisition – completed a year after he became chief executive of Inter Ikea – was in large part designed to help the company deal with the external forces buffeting the company in common with other retailers: online shopping, reduced footfall in stores, and increased urbanisation.

Mr Loof is now engineering the biggest transformation Ikea has undertaken by changing its famed business model that has brought it so much success. Having giant out-of-town warehouses, where shoppers pick their own furniture and then build it at home, underpinned Ikea's solid profitability for seven decades.

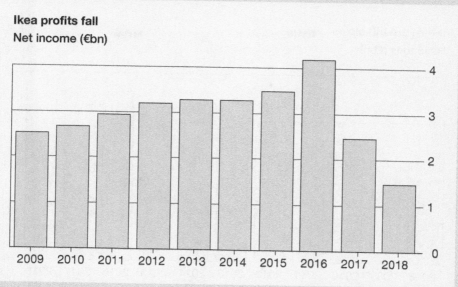

Ikea profits fall
Net income (€bn)

IKEA profit falls

Source: "Inter Ikea's Torbjorn Loof: making the vision clear" The Ft: February 3rd 2019, https://www.ft.com/content/6b250c0a-2486-11e9-b329-c7e6ceb5ffdf.

But now it is looking increasingly at city-centre stores, online shopping, home delivery and assembly, and more radical ideas such as leasing furniture and selling on websites such as Alibaba. Mr Loof says that challenging such a successful status quo is tricky, especially as the company does not have all the answers on what the new retail landscape will look like.

'You need to get people on board in the "why" part, why we are doing that, and also mobilise people to have energy in being part of this journey, not seeing it as "here we have an answer, OK, now I know what to do" – but actually you have to be part of this journey together with us.' He acknowledges that the company did not focus enough on the 'why' at the beginning, preferring to get on with things before realising it needed to do more communication. 'We made sure that the vision and the purpose were very, very clear. Not spending too much time on what sometimes is in the middle of things – all the strategies and plans, and all of that had to come later.'

Meetings of all the company's leaders were called several times a year, and all were allowed input on how their part of the business would change, rather than having 'a brilliant PowerPoint that says we [have] got the answers'. Mr Loof says it was important to put dates on when things would be decided, even if it was uncertain as to whether the solution was definitive. As a CEO used to delegating, he says it also became necessary for him to examine all proposals himself to stay on top of the details.

Doing the merger, changing the business model, and dealing with the decline and then death of founder Ingvar Kamprad was what he calls 'a perfect storm'. He says he misses Kamprad, who founded Ikea aged 17, and his advice. Mr Loof recalls one of the last times he saw him, together with some other Ikea managers. Kamprad said it was important to be long term and 'think about where should we be in 200 years?' The managers smiled at his exaggeration and asked him if that wasn't too much. 'Yes, of course,' he said, 'but then you make the short-term plan: that means the next 100 years.'

The Inter Ikea chief says that one of the toughest tasks is encouraging the entrepreneurship that characterised the company's early days. He concedes that the decade-long period of growth in the early part of this century stifled Ikea's creativity and recalls going to see Kamprad a few years ago when sales suddenly hit a bump.

'I was a little bit worried. I said to Ingvar: "sales are not growing", and then he looked at me and just smiled and he said: "wonderful! Crisis!" So, there is this kind of [attitude] to love the crisis because the opportunities in the crisis are that you get more creative,' he adds.

Since then, it has experimented more with what Mr Loof calls the 'phygital' – the place where the physical and digital worlds of shopping collide. It has released an augmented reality app to allow you to visualise how Ikea furniture would look in your house as well as a virtual reality kitchen in some stores to let customers test set-ups instantly.

The transformation has not been without its mistakes. Mr Loof early on championed a new store format, pick-up and order points, designed for places such as the Canary Islands where Ikea would not build a full-store warehouse. Successful in remote

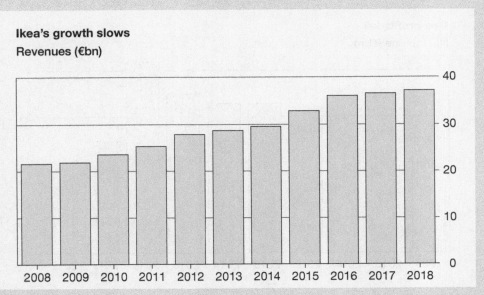

Ikea's growth slows
Revenues (€bn)

IKEA growth slows

Source: "Inter Ikea's Torbjorn Loof: making the vision clear" The Ft: February 3rd 2019, https://www.ft.com/content/6b250c0a-2486-11e9-b329-c7e6ceb5ffdf.

areas, it soon brought them to bigger cities in countries such as the UK where they became unpopular with customers for the additional costs and not offering the full product range.

Out of that, Mr Loof says the company realised it needed different shop sizes — so it developed warehouses of 5,000 and 10,000 square metres (the Almhult store is 35,000 square metres) that contain most products but much less inventory than a traditional warehouse.

He says Ikea will do numerous trials in the next few years: 'Even if we would be the best planners, we hire brilliant business analysts, the best strategists, I think we would not make it. So, we have to be the fastest learners. . . daring to test things and make mistakes, but also again correct them.'

Three questions for Torbjorn Loof

Who is your leadership hero?

I never thought of heroes in that way. But I have always been inspired by leaders that have big ambitions and a clear vision of what they want to accomplish. A leader that I had the privilege to work with was Ingvar Kamprad. His way to lead by being out in the business, talking to people and learning from reality was a big inspiration.

If you were not a CEO, what would you be?

I would either be a professional trumpet player or driving an excavator. Before I joined Ikea I played trumpet on a semi-professional basis. The career never took off but as they say, it's never too late. The last couple of years I have been driving an excavator on my farm and realised that it's a job I would love to do.

What was your first leadership lesson?

I was a newly appointed production leader in a factory at the age of 22. On my first day, my boss, a 64-year-old experienced production manager, came to me with a bucket of water. He put his hand in the water and said, do you know what this is? No, I said. That's you when you are here and you will take some space, like my hand in the water. He then pulled out his hand and the water filled the space of his hand. He then said, when you leave this is how much we will miss you. My first lesson was to always be humble and realise that once you leave, life goes on.

 Source: from 'Inter Ikea's Torbjorn Loof: making the vision clear', *Financial Times*, 03/02/19 (Milne, R.).

Discussion questions

1 What issues is Mr Loof trying to resolve?

2 How can internal marketing help Mr Loof in solving these issues?

3 Why doesn't Mr Loof mind making mistakes?

CHAPTER 17
CORPORATE SOCIAL RESPONSIBILITY AND ETHICS

'All too often, large companies see corporate social responsibility as something entirely separate from their business goals. As high unemployment, rising poverty, and dismay over corporate greed breed contempt for the capitalist market system. . . Serving the intersecting needs of business and the community is the only path to winning back respect.'

(Porter, 2010)

'The concept of shared value – which focuses on the connections between societal and economic progress – has the power to unleash the next wave of global growth. An increasing number of companies known for their hard-nosed approach to business – such as Google, IBM, Intel, Johnson & Johnson, Nestlé, Unilever, and Walmart – have begun to embark on important shared value initiatives. But our understanding of the potential of shared value is just beginning.'

(Porter and Kramer, 2011)

A 25-year battle to improve the image of McDonald's

Do you want ethics with that?

Source: McDonald's Art.

Every day McDonald's serves 69m customers, more than the population of Britain or France. The company has what is estimated to be the most valuable fast-food brand in the world, cherished as a cheap dining option for families.

But do consumers perceive McDonald's as a socially or environmentally responsible company? If they do not, it is in spite of the best efforts of Bob Langert. In 1988, he took a temporary assignment managing a furore over polystyrene 'clamshells' in which the company's burgers were served, and which were being damned for their contribution to America's litter problem. That turned into a 25-year career (he has since left the firm) dealing with the chain's various negative external effects.

It was a Herculean task, akin to being fashion consultant to Steve Bannon. Apart from litter, he had to deal with animal welfare, environmental destruction, obesity and workers' rights. When he began, the company's mascot was being dubbed 'Ronald McToxic' because of the clamshell problem. But he had more success than outsiders might think. His book *The Battle to Do Good: Inside McDonald's Sustainability Journey* is a must-read even for those who are cynical about the business of corporate social responsibility.

At times, the fast-food chain did not help itself. In the 1990s, it sued two Greenpeace activists for producing leaflets about its practices. The ensuing 'McLibel' trial gave the claims worldwide publicity and was described as the world's biggest corporate-PR disaster. Mr Langert tried to reduce the damage. The company consulted panels of independent experts and engaged with campaigning groups. On occasion it aimed to keep one step ahead of the activists – McDonald's took action even when there was little sign of public concern. Shaving one inch off the napkins saved 3m lbs of paper annually, for example, but few consumers noticed.

Environmentalists did attack the firm for its impact on the Amazon rainforest, saying trees were being cut down to make room for cattle pasture or the expansion of soy farming for cattle feed. In 1989 the company announced that it 'never has and never will buy beef from recently deforested rainforests' and it has also worked to limit the expansion of soy farming in the region. The rise of veganism amid doubts about the health effects of eating meat have given McDonald's new worries.

Accomplishing change is not just a matter of the company snapping its fingers. Most McDonald's restaurants are operated by franchisees and its goods are bought from a wide range of suppliers, so three or four layers may separate the McDonald's head office and the cattle-rancher who supplies the firm's beef.

In the late 1990s, after complaints from campaign groups about the living conditions of hens, Mr Langert visited an egg facility to find that conditions were indeed terrible. In August 2000 the firm said it would buy eggs only from suppliers that gave hens 72 square inches of space, compared with an industry average of 48 square inches. Suppliers resisted so strongly that McDonald's had to find new sources for its eggs. But those who complied found that the mortality rates of hens decreased and egg-laying rates increased, offsetting the extra costs.

Mr Langert found it took a long time to get agreement within the company on a particular subject and then to persuade suppliers to comply. But once he reached that stage, he had enormous clout; McDonald's is the largest purchaser of beef and pork in America, as well as the second-largest buyer of chicken. Another victory was persuading a supplier to phase out the use of gestation stalls for sows which make it impossible for the animals to move.

Human working conditions also caused the company trouble. One day Mr Langert got a call from a Catholic bishop who was concerned about the low wages paid to tomato-pickers. Another issue was the use of 'trans fats' to cook the restaurant's fries, which were deemed to increase the risk of heart disease; it took six years for the chain to phase out the practice. But the company has also added more salads and healthy options.

Was all the effort worth it? It seems likely that many of the people who care a lot about these issues would never eat a fast-food burger in the first place. But Mr Langert did more than most to reduce environmental waste and animal cruelty. A decent career record for an obviously decent man.

Source: from 'Do you want ethics with that?', *The Economist*, print edition/Business, 02/07/19 (Bartleby).

Discussion questions

1 What are the main issues raised here?

2 How is McDonald's addressing them?

Introduction

Considering corporate social responsibility (CSR) as an element of, or at the very least a major influence on, marketing strategy is now mandatory for executives in most organisations. This new imperative reflects the escalating importance of CSR in how companies manage their key processes and deliver customer value, and the seriousness with which these issues are viewed by our stakeholders all the way from shareholders and employees through to suppliers, distributors and end-customers. Indeed, one writer talks of the pressure on business to act with a social conscience and uses the term the 'Conscience Economy' to designate this imperative (Overman, 2014).

Certainly, it appears that in a post-recession environment when trust in business and professional institutions is seen by some to be at an all-time low, the scrutiny and judgement of corporate behaviour has reached unprecedented levels. Nowhere in the business is this likely to be more significant than in the marketing and sales actions at the front-end of the operation, where the company meets its markets.

In the past, it has been suggested that the marketing discipline has adopted a very partial perspective on CSR and that companies need a far broader view of the concept in the value chain (Vaaland et al., 2008). A starting point in developing that broader view is the Green Paper presented by the European Commission in 2001, which identifies corporate social responsibility as: 'a concept whereby companies integrate social and environmental concerns in their business operations and in their interaction with their stakeholders on a voluntary basis'. Moreover, the Green Paper identifies four factors underpinning the growing attention from executives to issues of corporate social responsibility:

1 The new concerns and expectations of consumers, public authorities and investors in the context of globalisation and industrial change.
2 Social criteria increasingly influencing the investment decisions of individuals and institutions.
3 Increased concern about the damage caused by economic and business activity to the physical environment.
4 Transparency of business activities brought about by media and new information and communication technologies.

It is increasingly clear that business norms across the world have moved CSR into the mainstream of business practice. Non-governmental organisations, such as the World Resources Institute (WRI), AccountAbility, Global Reporting Initiative (GRI), International Standards Organisation (ISO 14000) and the United Nations, all have major initiatives aimed at improving the social involvement and performance of the world's business community (Godfrey and Hatch, 2007). Indeed, there is an increasingly widespread view that sustainability is now the key driver of innovation for companies (Nidumolu et al., 2009). By 2014, more than 85 per cent of the companies in the FTSE 100 were reporting on social responsibility, and there was a clear expectation that companies should have a published strategy in place (Moore, 2014).

Indeed, Rosabeth Moss Kanter suggests that great companies think differently – they work to make money, but at the same time they think about building enduring institutions and investing in the future, while being aware of the need to build people and society. She claims that this social and institutional logic lies behind the practices of many widely admired, high-performing and enduring companies (Moss Kanter, 2011). The fundamental goal becomes one of focusing social initiatives onto alignment between a company's social and environmental activities and its business purpose and values (Rangan et al., 2015).

CSR, ethics and corporate reputation

In a world that is media-intensive and Internet-literate, where the scrutiny of business occurs with an unprecedented frequency and intensity, one important link for executives to consider is the one between a company's CSR and ethical positioning and its corporate reputation (Chun, 2005). Companies with strong positive reputations attract better staff, are perceived as providing better value, which allows a price premium, have more loyal customers and have advantages in financial markets. In economies where 70 to 80 per cent of market value comes from intangible assets such as brand equity and goodwill, companies are increasingly vulnerable to anything that damages their reputation (Eccles et al., 2007).

For example, one analysis links corporate reputation – having a good name – directly to share values. It estimates that if Coca-Cola had the more responsible reputation of Pepsi, the company would be worth $4 billion more. Similarly, it suggests that if Walmart had the superior corporate reputation for responsible behaviour enjoyed by Target, then its market value would be $9.7 billion higher (Engardio and Arndt, 2007). Relatedly, brand leaders across the world are investing heavily to regain the trust among consumers that they lost in the economic downturn because of the impact on brand value (Kiley and Helm, 2009). It appears corporate reputation, and in particular the impact of perceptions of social responsibility and ethical standards on reputation, should be part of executive evaluation of strategic choices.

While many damaging corporate crises are concerned with issues such as product defects (for example, the repeated recall of defective vehicles by Toyota and GM because of safety issues) and failure to deliver the product or service promised (such as the mishandling by G4S of security arrangements for the 2012 London Olympics), yet more are concerned with events that lead to public disapproval of the behaviour of companies related to trust, legitimacy and impact on society. There is a perception that businesses generally fall short in their ethical standards (Smith, 2015). Examples of such corporate crises that seriously damage reputations include:

- The 'horsemeat' scandal of 2012–13, when mislabelled meat was found in ready meals in the UK. This was probably less about the consumption of horsemeat and more about the perceptions of deception and unethical behaviour by a company such as Tesco in selling cheap meat without revealing the fact it was horsemeat, causing a major glitch in Tesco's competitive recovery strategy.
- Allegations of price fixing in 2013 in the petrol business, with raids on the offices of Shell, BP and Statoil, and the public's perception, encouraged by politicians, that they had been deceived and cheated. The issue was more about the companies' behaviour than the actual price of petrol.
- The same period saw the emergence of a public attack (which continues to this day) on the tax avoidance ploys of multinationals such as Amazon, Apple, Facebook and Starbucks, leading to them paying little or no tax in the UK. Anger and calls for boycotts emerged as the companies were seen to be cheating and behaving unethically (all such tax avoidance schemes are completely legal).
- The successful CEO of Abercrombie & Fitch, Mike Jeffries, committed what some have called brand suicide by his statements that his clothes were only for thin and attractive people, reflected in hiring only 'gorgeous' shop assistants and no clothes larger than size 10 to get 'cool, good-looking people' to wear the brand 'because they attract other cool kids'. He claimed once to have paid an unattractive customer not to wear his clothes. His statements were seen as offensive, discriminatory and arrogant. Celebrities in the USA showed their anger by defiantly giving A&F clothes to homeless people. Mr Jeffries left the company in 2014 amid falling sales and profits and circling activist investors.
- Accusations of bribery and unethical marketing practices have plagued companies such as GlaxoSmithKlein in the pharmaceuticals industry. GSK has been accused of bribing doctors and officials, paying rivals not to sell cheaper copies of its drugs in order to disadvantage customers such as the NHS, and promoting medicines beyond their approved uses. It has paid fines in response to some of these charges. The problem is that the perceived ethical violation is likely to outlast the impact of any financial penalties.
- The tragic clothing factory collapse disaster at Rana Plaza in Bangladesh in 2013 revealed the supply chain strategies of many clothing manufacturers and their reliance on low-wage workers operating in unsafe and foul conditions. Public judgements related both to the low-cost, low-price strategies of clothing retailers and also the level of integrity shown in their responses to the tragedy. The issue hinged on peoples' perceptions of right and wrong in employment conditions for workers in emerging countries.

Many of the most serious threats to corporate reputation come from perceptions of low ethical standards, poor executive behaviour and social and environmental damage.

The cost of failing to examine issues of ethical behaviour, social responsibility and the impact on corporate reputation may be lost sales and profits, but also longer-term loss of freedom of strategic flexibility – things you want to do and cannot because of reputational issues, and things you do not want to do, but have to.

What follows CSR?

It should be noted that while CSR and ethical mandates contribute a major topical issue in strategic decision making, and a very challenging one, executives should also be aware that thinking has not remained static, and there are emerging views of what follows CSR in changing corporate behaviours. This thinking may have a major impact in the future.

The last decade saw commentators identifying the 'new age of corporate responsibility' (Skapinker, 2005), and discussing what comes after the 'green corporation' (Engardio, 2007). However, an important article in 2011 by Porter and Kramer concerning the creation of shared value takes the vision much further. Porter and Kramer argue that the capitalist system itself is under siege and that, paradoxically, the more business has begun to embrace corporate responsibility the more it has been blamed for society's failures, suggesting that companies must take the lead in bringing business and society back together. They expand on the concept of shared values as 'policies and operating practices that enhance the competitiveness of a company while simultaneously advancing the economic and social conditions in the communities in which it operates', so that economic and social progress are both addressed through value principles (benefits relative to costs). They see a blurring of the profit/non-profit boundary. In their view, companies can create economic value by creating societal value through reconceiving products and markets, redefining productivity in the value chain and building supportive industry clusters at the company's locations. Shared value thus becomes an integral part of strategy.

While radical and visionary, it is likely that the shared value model will influence strategic thinking in many companies in the near future. By comparison, an even broader critique of the successes and failing of capitalism is provided by Philip Kotler in his book *Confronting Capitalism* (2015). Kotler identifies the underlying problems with capitalism, varying from poverty, income inequality and unemployment to failing to bring social values and happiness into the market equation, and indicates possible solutions to address these interrelated issues. The similarity with Porter and Kramer and the relevance to strategy decision makers is in requiring business and social problems to be addressed in combination, not separately, and for them to be addressed by company managers, not others. This represents a shift in thinking that goes beyond most current views of CSR, and is likely to be a recurring theme over the coming years.

In fact, the twenty-first century has seen issues of social responsibility and the morality and ethics of company practices become a key element of managing customer relationships, and in how companies are perceived and understood by their customers – how companies and their products are positioned competitively. However, for some time it has been suggested that an integrated approach to CSR in marketing is largely missing, both in theory and practice, and is overdue (Maignan *et al.*, 2005). Certainly, some attention has been given to the operational role of marketing in managing corporate social responsibility initiatives within companies, by expanding focus beyond consumers to include other stakeholders and integrating social responsibility initiatives (Maignan and Ferrell, 2004). These developments have been particularly associated with the development of social marketing, concerned with the contribution of marketing activities to socially desirable behaviours and goals (such as anti-smoking campaigns), and 'cause-related' marketing (for instance, the promotion of charitable donations to good causes). Some Australian companies are taking a stand against domestic violence, pioneering ways to tackle abuse at home and to support victims at work (Batty, 2015).

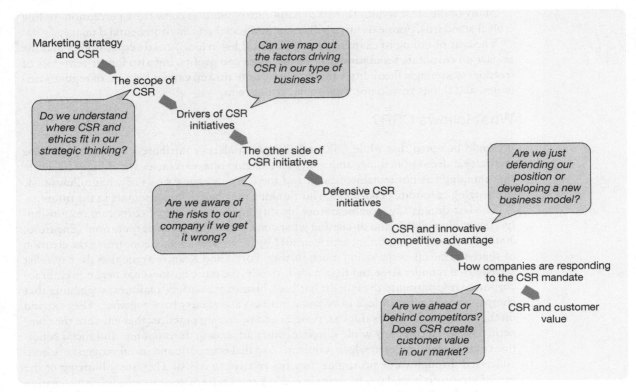

Figure 17.1 Key issues in assessing corporate social responsibility and marketing strategy

While the impact of social marketing on the social role attached to the marketing discipline has considerable social importance, our focus here is somewhat broader, and is concerned with the impact of the corporate social responsibility stance of the firm on its marketing and business strategy and performance. Social initiatives and ethical standards have become part of how companies compete and create value. The structure we are adopting to evaluate these issues and the key questions to address are summarised in Figure 17.1.

17.1 Marketing strategy and corporate social responsibility

At one time, the issue at stake was primarily a matter of 'corporate philanthropy' (Porter and Kramer, 2002), such as making donations of financial or other support to good causes, or entirely a question of moral obligation or pure altruism – for example when MAC cosmetics decided to donate all earnings from its Viva Glam lipstick range to HIV-related causes (Jack, 2008). However, corporate social responsibility (CSR) is now increasingly recognised as a source of competitive advantage (or disadvantage if we are weaker than others in this area), and thus a corporate resource, as well as an important part of how competitive relationships operate. Certainly, good corporate citizenship is a marketing asset that can yield benefits in customer loyalty and employee commitment and business performance, but corporate social responsibility is now seen as a strategic resource. Strength in this resource, as in any other, may bring competitive advantages; weakness in this resource, as in any other, may bring vulnerability (Branco and Rodrigues, 2006). Consider, for example, the following situations.

In 2007, Microsoft dropped one of its UK suppliers because that supplier failed to meet Microsoft's standards on employee diversity. Microsoft in the UK is one of a growing number of British companies that monitor suppliers to ensure that they employ a representative mix of women and ethnic minorities. The decision resulted from Microsoft's diversity audit at its 250 largest British suppliers (Taylor, 2007). In the USA, many large companies, including Microsoft, already insist on good diversity practices from suppliers, and are reducing or terminating the business they do with suppliers who fail to heed requests to diversify their workforces. Suppliers unable or unwilling to meet the social responsibilities defined by major customers stand the considerable risk of losing those customers.

In 2014, Apple extended its supply chain clean-up beyond Chinese factories that produce its devices, to pressure all its suppliers to make their own sourcing more ethical. The goal was to cut the amount of conflict resources ending up in iPhones and iPads sourced from mines in Africa (conflict resources are materials extracted in a conflict zone and sold to perpetuate and support the fighting). The company wants to stop using materials from mines that are unacceptable from a human rights perspective (Bradshaw, 2014).

Further concern extends to questions of ethics in executive behaviour, to which we will return, where inappropriate behaviours in managing buyer/seller relationships can cause expensive losses. The accusations of corruption and bribery levelled against Volkswagen and Siemens executives in Germany – for example, the alleged Siemens 'slush fund' to pay bribes to win international contracts – have been extremely damaging to both companies (Woodhead, 2007). Appositely, it should be noted that many practices regarded in the past as wholly acceptable – for example, 'corporate hospitality' – may now be enough to undermine or destroy buyer/seller relationships, not to mention the careers of individual executives. The impact is magnified by growing transparency and information availability, so dubious practices are more difficult to hide. A review of the 'integrity land-mines' faced by companies concludes:

> The changes in laws, regulations, stakeholder expectations, and media scrutiny that have taken place in the past decade can now make a major lapse in integrity catastrophic. Fines, penalties and settlements are counted in the hundreds of millions (or billions) of dollars. . . And worse, in some cases (as Enron and Arthur Andersen demonstrated) – a company can actually implode.
> (Heineman, 2007)

The management of business-to-business buyer–seller relationships has to be placed into this more demanding ethical context.

Moreover, at the level of the brand, questions of social responsibility and the ethics and morality of corporate behaviour are increasingly significant, posing both risks and opportunities. In 2007, the ethically minded coffee company Starbucks found itself in the midst of a damaging and intractable struggle over the legitimacy of coffee trademarking by the Ethiopian government. While the Ethiopian government – one of the world's poorest countries – wanted to trademark some of its most famous coffees, Starbucks objected to the trademarks as damaging to its own brand. The dispute was played out live on the video website YouTube. One commentator suggested that Starbucks was 'playing Russian roulette' with its brand (Rushe, 2007). Indeed, more recently, Starbucks' reputation has been further threatened by its tax avoidance policies – with its first-ever fall in UK sales after calls for a boycott from outraged consumers (Skapinker, 2014). Importantly, there may be an increasing number of trade-offs faced by companies between CSR and commercial goals.

There are important signs that consumers do indeed appear to be discriminating between brands and companies on issues of societal impact and ethical standards, although they may be less impressed by corporate posturing than some companies may believe. For example, consumers were less than amused to discover that Philips and Osram 'Eco' light bulbs were not actually 'green' and did not last longer – the makers claimed that 'Eco' stood for 'economy' not 'ecological' (Spencer, 2015a).

In fact, the real shift in attitudes towards consumption may be difficult to track – for example, while many consumers claim they would pay a 5–10 per cent premium for many ethical products, in practice such brands usually have tiny market shares (Grande, 2007b). Moreover, a five-country survey conducted by market research group GfK NOP suggested that consumers in five of the world's leading economies believe that business ethics have worsened in the past five years, and they are turning to 'ethical consumerism' to make companies more accountable (Grande, 2007a). Respondents believed that brands with 'ethical' claims – on environmental policies or treatment of staff or suppliers – would make business more answerable to the public, and that companies should 'promote ethical credentials more strongly' (Grande, 2007b).

Some commentators on branding have long suggested that ethical consumption is one of the most significant branding issues in modern markets, and underlies change in the automotive sector, food, retailing, technology, and health and beauty sectors. Its influence is behind the strong sales growth of hybrid cars, 'cruelty-free' beauty products and dramatic growth in sales of organic food. The position appears to be that ethical and environmental questions are being posed by growing numbers of consumers, but they are not always favourably impressed by companies' responses. Nonetheless, the impact of 'ethical consumerism' is likely to be large and of escalating significance.

The growing frequency of issues of this kind suggests that questions relating to corporate social responsibility initiatives and the ethical standards evidenced by companies are increasingly relevant to the decisions about marketing strategy and positioning relative to competitors, because:

- they represent a new kind of corporate resource that has implications for building a sustainable and defensible competitive position;
- the measurement and reporting of corporate social responsibility 'scores' (often computed with questionable methodologies) imposes new requirements for openness and transparency in company behaviour – the majority of the world's largest multinationals publish corporate social responsibility reports;
- reflecting the norms of behaviour determined by buyer organisations is increasingly mandatory in sustaining buyer–seller relationships in business-to-business markets (and is made yet more complex where those relationships are global in nature and span different cultures);
- failure to conform to or exceed the standards of behaviour defined by a media-influenced and Internet-literate consumer may undermine conventional efforts to establish the credentials of a brand and to build a position in a market;
- increasingly, employees and managers expect their companies to reflect emerging societal values as well as superior ethical standards, and the retention of critical talent in a company may be closely related to these perceptions and beliefs – indeed, companies such as Azco, one of the world's biggest chemicals businesses, and TNT and DSM in the Netherlands, have already started to roll out executive bonus schemes linked directly to meeting sustainability targets (Goodman, 2010; Milne, 2010);
- most telling of all, increasingly corporate social responsibility is not being viewed as purely altruistic, but as an element of competitive advantage (Porter and Kramer, 2006) – companies are challenged to 'outbehave' their competitors in corporate virtue to achieve advantage (Murphy, 2010).

This chapter addresses the evolving question of the impact of corporate social responsibility and ethical standards on marketing strategy and competitive positioning. First, we examine the scope of CSR, and the corporate drivers of CSR strategies. This is followed by a review of CSR as a defensive strategy, and then as a source of sustainable competitive advantage.

17.2 | The scope of corporate social responsibility

The modern marketplace increasingly is characterised by a variety of anti-business sentiments and activism. Examples include the anti-globalisation movement, shareholder activism and corporate governance reforms – indeed, some suggest that we are experiencing a climate of 'defiance' towards business (Maignan and Ferrell, 2004). Certainly, global business scandals, such as the accounting abuses uncovered at Enron and Arthur Andersen and the bribery accusations at VW and Siemens, plus the economic downturn and recession, have done little to improve perceptions of business (Piercy *et al.*, 2010a). Indeed, VW's position was further harmed by the 2015 scandal regarding the 'defeat software' fitted to millions of its diesel vehicles, specifically to cheat emissions tests.

Even at a trivial level, businesses of various kinds are under media-orchestrated attacks for their normal ways of doing business. Recent examples of these pressures include: public campaigns to complain and demand repayment of bank charges; protests about '4 × 4' (SUV) vehicles, inspired by global warming fears; the conditions under which the tobacco and alcohol industries now operate; demands that airlines should reduce the number of flights they operate and that, like cigarette packs, holiday packages should carry 'health warnings' related to fears about carbon emissions; the anti-obesity campaign pressure on food retailers and restriction of the advertising of junk food products to children; and anti-salt and sugar campaigns to persuade food manufacturers to reduce salt and sugar content in processed foods. There is growing evidence that the way in which products are marketed in many sectors is changing because consumer groups and public authorities believe business practices to be irresponsible.

Accordingly, the belief that consumers are more likely to buy from companies they perceive as socially responsible, and would switch brands to favour products and stores that show concern about the community, has led to growing pressure on firms to behave as good 'corporate citizens'. In contrast to the traditional view that the only responsibility of the firm is to make a profit (Friedman, 1970), companies have been encouraged to undertake activities that provide benefits to various groups: supportive work–family policies, ethics compliance programmes, corporate volunteerism and green marketing. In this sense, 'corporate citizenship' has become a term that describes the activities and processes adopted by businesses to meet their social responsibilities.

One link between these various trends and issues is the effect of inhibiting the ability of companies to develop effective marketing strategy, or to establish and defend their desired competitive positions, without making allowance for a societal dimension in their actions. Perhaps the most significant issue now in being a good 'corporate citizen' is not so much moral obligation, as a business case for initiatives that protect and provide new business opportunities.

The growth in corporate attention to CSR has not always been voluntary, instead reflecting surprise at public reaction to issues not previously thought to be their responsibility: Nike faced consumer boycotts after media reporting of abusive labour practices in its Indonesian suppliers' factories; fast-food and packaged-food companies are being held responsible for obesity problems and poor nutrition; and pharmaceutical companies are expected to respond to the AIDS pandemic in Africa, though it is far removed from their main product lines and markets (Porter and Kramer, 2006).

More positively, CSR may be associated with important and measurable benefits to companies. For example, cause-related projects may impact directly on income: if firms that create social gains realise cash value in terms of increased purchases by morally-conscious customers (or those customers are willing to pay higher prices), or in reduced costs. More broadly, CSR may have the impact of building long-term customer loyalty, legitimacy, trust or brand equity (Godfrey and Hatch, 2007). Indeed, some companies have made high-profile efforts to position themselves as socially responsible as a core part of their strategy, which may in part be a response to external critics, but also part of the underlying vision of what a business is about:

- Nike advertises its commitment to adopting 'responsible business practices that contribute to profitable and sustainable growth', having come through a decade or more of vocal condemnation of its employment practices in its overseas supplier workshops.
- The Body Shop was positioned from its outset as actively involved in social improvement projects throughout the world and opposed to practices such as animal-testing of cosmetics and toiletry products, which is thought to be one of the resources of the business that made it an attractive acquisition for the more traditional cosmetics company, L'Oréal.
- Furniture retailer IKEA has a strategy of purchasing wind farms – already in France, Germany, Poland and the USA, with other countries to follow – as part of efforts to reduce the carbon footprint of its furniture stores, and is pursuing a long-term goal of securing all its electricity needs from renewable sources.

Certainly, it has become increasingly important for strategic decision makers to understand the scope of corporate social responsibility (CSR) initiatives, both in developing possible defences against attacks on their competitive position and ability to compete, and also as potential sources of new types of competitive strength.

Scoping CSR possibilities involves initially considering the specific dimensions of CSR. Attention has been given to initiatives such as the support of charitable causes and the advent of 'cause-related marketing' (Barone *et al.*, 2000), as well as the protection of the natural environment as an influence on purchasing behaviour and marketing strategy.

In developing an integrative framework to examine CSR, Maignan and Ferrell (2004) provide a useful overview of how CSR has been understood, and how that understanding is changing. They distinguish between CSR as social obligation, as stakeholder obligation, as ethics-driven and as managerial process. These distinctions are useful in understanding the case for CSR and providing a managerial framework for addressing the strategic implications of CSR:

- **CSR as social obligation:** Since the 1950s onwards, there has been a strong link between CSR and the alignment of corporate actions with the objectives and values of society. This ethos is still found in contemporary marketing studies, particularly regarding the potential for both positive and negative consumer reactions to CSR initiatives of this type (Sen and Bhattacharya, 2001). Classically, Carroll (1979) distinguishes social obligations as: *economic obligations* – to be productive and economically viable; *legal and ethical obligations* – to follow the law and accepted values and norms; and *philanthropic obligations* – to actively give back to society.
- **CSR as stakeholder obligation:** The 1990s saw the emergence of the view that CSR as social obligation was too broad to allow the effective management of CSR (Clarkson, 1995), and the argument that businesses are not responsible to society as a whole, but only to those who directly or indirectly affect, or are affected by, the firm's activities – that is, the firm's stakeholders (Donaldson and Preston, 1995). Accordingly, stakeholders can be grouped into: *organisational* – employees, customers, shareholders, suppliers; *community* – local residents, special interest groups; *regulatory* – local authorities, legal controls; and *media* stakeholders (Henriques and Sadorsky, 1999).
- **CSR as ethics-driven:** Viewing CSR as either a social or stakeholder issue suggests that CSR is motivated only by corporate self-interests, enabling business to gain legitimacy with important external parties. It has been argued that such views fail to account for actions by companies that represent a positive commitment to society's interests that disregard self-interest and are genuinely altruistic (Swanson, 1995). Indeed, if CSR reflects only obligations, then it becomes difficult to evaluate whether business practices are or are not socially responsible, as opposed to simply reciprocal (Jones, 1995). An ethics-driven view of CSR is concerned with the rightness or wrongness of specific initiatives, independently of any social or stakeholder obligation. For example, justice-based ethics

would lead a company to attempt to systematically favour decisions that stimulate equality and fairness for its partners and associates.

- **CSR as managerial process:** The first three perspectives attempt to identify the factors that persuade businesses to undertake CSR initiatives. An additional view concerns CSR in terms of organisational processes (sometimes called 'corporate social responsiveness') (Ackerman, 1975). One view advocates that 'issues management' and 'environmental assessment' constitute managerial processes relevant to working towards a proactive responsibility stance (Wood, 1991). Others suggest the type of sequential management process useful to systematic development of CSR initiatives (Ackerman, 1975): monitoring and assessing environmental conditions; attending to stakeholder demands; and designing plans and policies aimed at enhancing the firm's impacts. Carroll earlier described the managerial processes of response to social responsibility as involving planning and social forecasting, organising for social response, controlling social activities and developing corporate social policy (Carroll, 1979).

The importance of Maignan and Ferrell's integration of these disparate conceptualisations of CSR is that it provides us with an overview of the issues likely to be raised by CSR initiatives, and suggests the importance of developing appropriate organisational processes for managing CSR. Scoping the existing and likely future impacts of the diverse pressures towards CSR is becoming an important challenge for management. In this context, Porter and Kramer (2006) suggest that management attention should focus on:

- **Identifying the points of intersection between the company and society** – including the ways in which the business impacts on society in the normal course of business (such as transport emissions), but also the way in which social conditions impact on the business (for example, regulatory standards). This involves mapping the social impact of the value chain, and also the social influences on the company's competitiveness.
- **Choosing which social issues to address** – selecting issues that intersect with the business and that present an opportunity to create shared value, rather than trying to solve all society's problems.
- **Creating a corporate social agenda** – looking beyond external expectations to achieve both social and economic benefits.

Although the ways in which it can be addressed will differ greatly between company situations, the framework in this section provides an initial approach to making CSR issues explicit and integrating them into thinking about marketing strategy.

17.3 Drivers of corporate social responsibility initiatives

Notwithstanding the links between corporate social responsibility and marketing strategy, it would be wrong to suggest that altruistic, corporate philanthropy is disappearing or diminishing in importance. Indeed, while traditional philanthropy has been criticised as ineffective, the birth of the 'social enterprise' movement represents a new model addressing issues of social justice, with approaches drawn from the business world. For example, Google.org is the philanthropic arm of the search engine company, established to invest in and support for-profit and not-for-profit groups that focus on energy, poverty and the environment. Certainly, charitable gifts by UK companies have soared since 2007 (Smith, 2014). Achieving social goals through business means – social enterprise – represents a new type of business model, fuelled by individuals such as Microsoft's Bill Gates, who do not simply want to donate money to good causes, but to bring their own philosophy and skills to managing it to achieve social return. Social enterprise aims to break down traditional barriers between business, government and charity in ventures that aim to combine innovation, market orientation and an objective to generate a public benefit (Jack, 2007). It is speculated by some that there may even be a move away from shareholder capitalism to a radically different enterprise model, in which social purpose is placed above profit, or profit is harnessed to social purpose (Smith and Ward, 2007).

However, while social enterprise is an important extension of traditional concepts of corporate philanthropy, and it may enhance the reputations of companies and leaders who devote resources to these ventures, our present interests are in the drivers of more conventional corporate social responsibility initiatives, and the links to business and marketing strategy in existing companies rather than new hybrid business models.

Porter and Kramer (2006), in their influential review of CSR, suggest that while CSR generally remains imbued with a strong moral imperative (as we saw in the previous section of the chapter), modern supporters of the CSR movement rely on four arguments to justify attention and resources for these initiatives:

- **Moral obligation**: the duty of a company to be a good citizen and to do 'the right thing'. However, there are many dilemmas faced in such questions – Google's entry to the China market created a major conflict between Western dislike for censorship and the legal requirements imposed by the Chinese government.
- **Sustainability**: emphasis on the environmental and community impact of the business. To an extent this may reflect enlightened self-interest – changes to packaging at McDonald's have reduced its solid waste by 30 per cent.
- **Licence to operate**: the tacit or explicit permission a company needs from governments, communities and other stakeholders to do business – this permission is being progressively withdrawn from the tobacco industry.
- **Reputation**: CSR initiatives to enhance a company's image, strengthen its brand, improve morale, or even raise share prices. Some organisations have a distinctive position based on an extraordinary long-term commitment to social responsibility – for example, Ben & Jerry's and The Body Shop.

Perhaps, to this list can be added the need to *respond to the CSR-based positioning of competitors*, who are seeking advantage through an enhanced franchise with the customer, and to *coping with explicit customer demands* for the standards they expect in, for example, their suppliers. Interestingly, Porter and Kramer note that 'all four schools of thought share the same weakness: they focus on the tension between business and society rather than their interdependence' (2006, p. 83).

Thomas Stewart (2006) underlines this point. He notes the contradiction between the classic argument that a company's only responsibility to society is to make as much money as it legally can, compared to the modern reality that a company that shunned society would be ostracised, in turn, to its cost. The opposite problem for executives may be the conflict between social initiatives and business goals – is there perhaps hypocrisy in the brewer urging consumers not to drink, or the oil company promoting fuel conservation? Stewart's point is that such views share a logical flaw: they assume that companies and society have opposing interests. Thus, it follows that starting from the premise that business and society are interdependent identifies CSR as a strategic opportunity that is of far greater importance than moral duty alone.

Importantly, CSR may be associated with significant and measurable benefits for companies. Indeed, Peter Senge and colleagues argue that after years of scepticism, big companies are genuinely acting to cut waste, cut carbon emissions, find sources of renewable energy and develop sustainable business models (Senge *et al.*, 2008). There is an increasingly widespread view that there is a business case for social initiatives – behind the drive for sustainability lies a growing belief that environmental and social projects not only improve corporate reputations, but also foster innovation, cut costs and open up new markets (Skapinker, 2008b). Unilever's Pureit machine is illustrative – it cleans water to provide drinking water without boiling or the use of mains electricity, and purifies water more cheaply than boiling. Developed by Hindustan Unilever in India, the social and health benefits of lower costs for clean drinking water are evident, but also the potential market for the product in the rural areas of developing countries is huge.

Indeed, some companies have made high-profile efforts to position themselves as socially responsible, as an explicit part of their strategy, which may in part be a response to external critics, but also part of the underlying vision of what a business is about. Some go even further in advocating the combination of business and social goals. Moss Kanter uses the term 'vanguard companies' to describe those that are 'ahead of the pack and potentially the wave of the future' because they aspire to be 'big but human, efficient but innovative, global but concerned about local communities [and] try to use their power and influence to develop solutions to problems the public cares about'. She concludes from her studies of companies such as IBM, Procter and Gamble, Publicis, Cemex and Diageo that 'humanistic values and attention to societal needs are a starting point for smart strategy in the global information age'. In particular, 'the leaders of a vanguard company espouse positive values and encourage their employees to embrace and act on them'. Social purpose creates strategic advantages, but only if those social commitments have an economic logic that attracts resources to the firm (Moss Kanter, 2009). The Moss Kanter concept of a 'vanguard company' reaches for a post-CSR setting of successful businesses sustained by moral purpose as well as economic achievement.

In 2010, Paul Polman, chief executive of Unilever, outlined his company's 'sustainable living plan' to City investors. His commitment to sustainability and a new type of business led to the statement:

> Unilever has been around for 100-plus years. We want to be around for several hundred more years. So if you buy into this long-term value-creation model, which is equitable, which is shared, which is sustainable, then come and invest with us. If you don't buy into this, I respect you as a human being, but don't put your money in our company.
> (Skapinker, 2010)

This is a very strong statement for a chief executive to make to investors, which underlines his determination to combine commercial and social goals. Nonetheless, some investors are nervous that Mr Polman's focus on sustainability and climate and social issues may be a distraction from strategy and performance (Daneshkhu, 2015). However, the success of 'purpose-driven' firms such as Patagonia and the like, across many business sectors, suggests that a large body of customers at least are very enthusiastic about such messages.

Nonetheless, there is wide recognition that firms face choices in their responsiveness to social responsibility (see section 17.7). This background provides the basis for examining the linkages between CSR and competitive advantage and strategic positioning in the marketplace, in ways that have not been fully recognised in earlier stages of the consideration of CSR initiatives. In particular, we distinguish between CSR as a *defence* against attacks that can undermine competitive position, and as a *strategy* that can provide new business opportunities. Prior to making that distinction, it is important to note that there are potential downsides to the innovation of CSR initiatives in companies.

17.4 The other side of corporate social responsibility initiatives

It is important that well-meant enthusiasm for combining social and commercial goals for the greater good of society and the business should not blind executives to the fact that there are vocal critics of CSR initiatives, and that not all CSR efforts have achieved their intended beneficial effects. There are risks to companies in CSR initiatives that misfire, as summarised in Figure 17.2.

Figure 17.2 The other side of CSR

Some suggest, for example, that 'ethical shopping' is no more than a middle-class indulgence that offers very limited benefits to the good causes espoused (Hattersley, 2008). Indeed, one commentator suggests that the deadliest greenhouse gas is actually the 'hot air of CSR' – inclining to the view that the truly responsible thing is to run a business competently, not to be involved in social causes (Stern, 2009). Similarly, others suggest that organic food is 'a tax on the gullible' (Lawson, 2009). It is perhaps telling that with economic downturn, many government environmental policies were quietly dropped amid business opposition and signs that voter priorities were changing (Pickard and Harvey, 2008). Others believe that the more focused concept of sustainability (in the sense of meeting current needs without harming future generations) will replace that of CSR in management thinking.

17.4.1 Criticisms of CSR initiatives

The development of CSR initiatives by businesses is not universally welcomed. For example, some managers talk about the 'little green lies' – challenging the notion that making a company environmentally friendly can be cost-effective and also profitable, and accusing advocates of these initiatives of 'empty boasting' (Elgin, 2007).

Cynics also point to the collapse of markets such as that for organic foods in the UK under the pressure of rising food prices and economic pressures on the consumer. Indeed, 2008 did see a 19 per cent fall in organic food sales, as consumers filled their shopping baskets with cheaper, non-organic food. Some believe that organic farming is now in decline in the UK (Daneshkhu, 2014). Certainly, there are strong signs that when times are difficult financially, the shopper is prepared to sacrifice 'green' credentials in favour of cheaper food (Rigby, 2008).

Critics also suggest that the rush to 'carbon credit' projects yielded few if any environmental benefits – some organisations are paying for emissions reductions that do not take place; others are making large profits from carbon trading for clean-ups that would have been made anyway. The 'green gold rush' of carbon trading stimulated by environmental concerns appears seriously flawed (Harvey and Fidler, 2007).

Indeed, some opponents argue that although CSR can improve a company's reputation (perhaps rebuilding goodwill in the wake of corporate scandals and regulatory scrutiny) and attract talent (from employees who expect their companies to be active in social issues), it costs too much (possibly at the expense of other priorities such as R&D), and is often misguided and ineffective (Grow *et al.*, 2005).

The tobacco industry provides an interesting illustration of the limitations of CSR. Notwithstanding vehement criticism by anti-smoking groups, and opponents such as the World Health Organisation – which categorically questions the very possibility of social responsibility in the tobacco industry – recent years have seen tobacco companies starting to position themselves as good corporate citizens. These moves include corporate philanthropy – such as donations to universities for research, and to environmental groups; CSR reporting – in annual reports and other publications; and self-regulation – for example, BAT, Philip Morris and Japan Tobacco launching an international voluntary code of marketing. However, research suggests that these moves are likely to be ineffective or even counter-productive: some scientific journals refuse to publish research sponsored by the tobacco industry, many stakeholder groups will not risk their own reputations by engaging with tobacco companies and CSR claims are regarded by many as window-dressing at best. While the tobacco industry can defend its position by showing integrity in its supply chain (such as by improving the working conditions of plantation employees), it is unable to demonstrate a contribution to the well-being of society (because of the addictive and lethally dangerous nature of its products) (Palazzo and Richter, 2005). While defensive CSR may offer some advantages to tobacco companies, a proactive stance is unlikely to be effective.

17.4.2 Exaggerated and misleading claims for CSR

Some companies have been accused of unscrupulous marketing ploys that use green propaganda to attract customers, and the Advertising Standards Authority (ASA) has already ruled against several spurious claims of 'greenery' (Hanlon, 2007). The ploy consists of aiming to sell more by making people feel guilty. For example, while British supermarkets compete aggressively to prove their green credentials (Goodman, 2006), groups such as the National Consumer Council suggest that they fail to live up to their claims when tested against objective criteria, such as making seasonal foods available, taking products from sustainable sources, stocking organic products and cutting waste (Harvey and Rigby, 2006). Certainly, the fact that Tesco's 'local' chickens go on a thousand-mile round trip before being put on sale suggests a cynical use of the term 'local' (Allen, 2008). Supermarkets, including Tesco and Sainsbury's in the UK, stand accused of 'greenwash' – making false 'eco' claims about their products to deceive consumers seeking a 'green' lifestyle (Poulter, 2010).

Similar controversy continues to surround the Fairtrade programme and brand. Although very successful – for example, from 2009 all Cadbury's chocolate carried the ethical logo, as well as all Tate & Lyle's retail sugar (Boyle, 2009; Beattie, 2008) – the Adam Smith Institute's report 'Unfair Trade' (Adam Smith Institute, 2008) concludes that Fairtrade: (1) helps only a very small number of farmers, while leaving the majority worse off; (2) favours producers from better-off nations such as Mexico rather than poorer African nations; (3) holds back economic development by rewarding the inefficient; (4) creates a situation where supermarkets profit more from the higher price of Fairtrade goods than do the farmers; and (5) that only a fifth of produce grown on Fairtrade-approved farms is actually purchased at its guaranteed fair price. For example, it was estimated in 2006 that of the £200 million spent on Fairtrade products in the UK, only £42 million went back to those in the developing world – supermarkets took 32p in every pound spent and the rest went to middlemen and the licensing fees charged by the Fairtrade organisation (Ebrahami, 2006). The 'Unfair Trade' report claims that 'At best, Fairtrade is a marketing device that does the poor little good. At worst, it may inadvertently be harming some of the planet's most vulnerable people.'

17.4.3 Doing bad through doing good

Other critics of CSR focus on the 'unintended consequences' of well-meaning social initiatives. For example, planting trees in Uganda to offset greenhouse gas emissions in Europe was an attractive idea, which became less appealing in the light of Ugandan farmers being evicted from their land at gunpoint to make room for a forest (Zizola, 2007). Similarly, fervent environmentalist support for biofuels has diminished somewhat as it has become clear that switching crops to biofuels has created food shortages in many emerging markets and contributed to rising food prices in the developed countries (Blas and Wiggins, 2007). More minor initiatives can also fail through their actual rather than intended consequences. In 2006, B&Q announced that it would cease selling environmentally-friendly roof top wind turbines, because they do not work in built-up areas and, worse, they create considerable noise pollution (Crooks, 2009).

A recent controversy surrounds diesel cars. For some 20 years, manufacturers have been urged by the 'global warming' lobby and encouraged by governments through tax concessions to persuade motorists to switch to diesel-powered vehicles to protect the environment. Research now suggests that diesel emissions are actually more damaging to the environment and more health-threatening than those from petrol-powered vehicles. Around half the new cars sold in the UK were diesels by 2015. One estimate is that diesel cars account for more than 5,000 premature deaths in the UK alone each year. The negative impact on the credibility of the green lobby and car manufacturers is considerable (Glover, 2015), not helped by the scandal of Volkswagen deliberately looking to cheat emissions tests. By 2018, governments in many countries (including the UK) had done an about-turn, suggesting that all new cars should be electric by the mid twenty-first century. They had little to say to the millions of customers who bought diesel cars based on governmental encouragement that they were more environmentally friendly.

Similarly, while countries in the West have seen escalating sales of solar panels, symbolising the drive for clean energy and greener lifestyle, the poisonous waste created in their production is blighting crops and water supplies. In China, the thriving renewable energy industry is accused of air, soil and water pollution, poor safety standards and causing withered crops and poisoned rivers around solar panel factories at the heart of the renewable energy revolution (Sheridan and Jones, 2010). The overall effect currently may even be negative, in spite of the best intentions of those who promote clean energy.

The well-meaning government incentives to persuade car drivers to adopt electric vehicles in Norway includes free access for electric cars to bus lanes. The result has been worse congestion as buses struggle to get around the additional extra electric cars in the restricted lanes, and a poorer service for those who leave their cars at home and take the bus (Jervell, 2014). This is not what was intended.

17.4.4 Countering intuition

Intuition (and some vocal opinion) would probably suggest that, generally, healthy food is 'good', traditional cloth babies' nappies are 'good', dishwashers are 'bad' and plastic carrier bags are 'bad'.

While consumers who favour healthier eating are likely also to dislike animal testing, in 2007 it was reported that the trend towards healthier eating had led to an increase of more than 300 per cent in laboratory experiments on animals for food additives, sweeteners and health supplements. Animals appear to have become the victims of the fad for health foods (Woolf, 2007). In 2008, the British government tried to suppress an embarrassing report finding that old-fashioned reusable nappies damage the environment more than disposables – the findings are upsetting for proponents of real nappies, who have claimed that they can help save the planet (Woolf, 2008).

Reckitt Benckiser is understandably making much of the fact that calculations show that using a dishwasher (with Reckitt's detergent of course) is more environmentally friendly than washing up by hand, which uses more energy and water (Harvey, 2007). Even the much-vilified supermarket plastic bag turns out to be 'greener' in some ways than the paper or hessian equivalents, which consume more energy and water and produce more pollution, though more expensive reusable bags are better for the environment than any disposable bag (Ball, 2009).

17.4.5 Do consumers really care about good causes?

The answer to this question probably is that some do and some do not, suggesting that the issue for executives to examine is which consumers care and whether they make a coherent target for marketing strategies relating to CSR. Environmentalists were disappointed, for example, to see US sales of gas-guzzling 4×4 SUVs and trucks recover with low oil prices – as fuel prices dropped, consumer enthusiasm for eco-friendly cars appeared to decline also

(Welch, 2008). Similarly, a survey in the UK by Pledge4Plastics revealed a high degree of consumer indifference to recycling initiatives (Hull, 2014).

The economic recession encouraged the view that a solid record in sustainability will not impress consumers unless there is a direct and easily identified benefit for them (Gary, 2013). While companies understand the value of green marketing and sustainability, there are signs that some consumers remain stubbornly indifferent or antagonistic about going green, suggesting the need for more efforts to promote sustainability-focused purchasing behaviours (Stafford and Hartman, 2013).

Certainly, a retail viewpoint suggests that consumers fall into four categories regarding ethics and social responsibility: (1) committed, cause-driven purchasers (8 per cent of the total); (2) those who want to purchase ethically but are not sure how to, and are looking for help (30–35 per cent); (3) those who feel the same but doubt their individual purchases can make much difference (30–35 per cent); and (4) those who are completely uninterested (the rest). Retailers have long commented on the 30:3 phenomenon (30 per cent of purchasers say that they thought about workers' rights, animal welfare and the planet when deciding what to buy, but sales figures show only 3 per cent of them act on those thoughts). However, the proportion of consumers buying ethically, or poised to do so, is now seen as much higher, and growing (Skapinker, 2007).

Interestingly, one recent US study concludes that companies that act in a socially responsible manner and advertise that fact may be able to charge more for their products. The researchers conclude that companies should segment their markets and make a particular effort to reach out to buyers with high ethical standards, because those are the customers who can deliver the biggest potential profit on ethically produced goods (Trudel and Cotte, 2008).

Nonetheless, while a company such as Primark has been severely criticised for the labour abuses in its supply chain, it achieved record sales in the economic downturn and recovery because of the ultra-low prices on its fashion clothing imports. Its customers appear to place a higher value on two T-shirts for £1 than ethical working conditions for those who make them. Similarly, ugly images of a seven-year-old boy working a 98-hour week in Delhi for 7p an hour to make Christmas decorations for British retailer Poundland seemed to have had little negative impact on Poundland's sales (Smith, 2010).

17.4.6 International differences

For the international business, research by Globescan underlines the point that CSR is judged differently in different parts of the world because peoples' top priorities vary. So, for example, to Chinese consumers the hallmark of social responsibility is safe, high-quality products, while in South Africa what matters most is a contribution to social needs such as healthcare and education. In countries including the USA, France, Italy and Switzerland, and much of South America, the highest priority is to treat employees fairly. In Australia, Canada, Indonesia and the UK, environmental protection is the highest priority. In Turkey, the most important indicator of corporate responsibility is charitable donation (Maitland, 2005).

There is an important need to balance global and local issues when examining the potential impact of CSR initiatives for a company operating across national and cultural boundaries. For example, it is clear that increasing global transparency is an unavoidable consequence of communications advances – so while Microsoft maintained a position of integrity and social awareness, as well as corporate philanthropy, in the developed world, paradoxically workers assembling its computer mice and webcams in China were working 15-hour shifts in poor conditions for 34p an hour (Hull and Sorrell, 2010).

17.4.7 Internal company barriers

In 2014, the *Financial Times* (Moore, 2014) reported that the number of business leaders supporting CSR had fallen, amid suggestions that share prices did not reflect investments in social initiatives. In a post-recession context, the search for business performance has reduced the emphasis on the environment and sustainability for managers in some companies (Murray, 2014).

An Arthur D. Little report entitled 'The Innovation High Ground' suggests that while it is important for social and environmental concerns to receive explicit attention when setting strategy and designing products, relatively few companies display this as a capability (Arthur D. Little, 2005). The report suggests that the main barriers to CSR initiatives are: a lack of understanding among strategists of the significance of social and environmental trends; internal and external scepticism, often combined with a perception that these activities involve high risk and uncertainty; an absence of appropriate business models, particularly for emerging markets; a tendency to use available capital for 'more of the same', rather than new business models; and an unwillingness to finance new projects, particularly at the bottom of the business cycle. Interestingly, this research was conducted among major international companies, including Sony, Dupont, HP and Vodafone.

Executives proposing strategic marketing programmes that rely on CSR-based positioning should be aware of the likely resistance and barriers from those who distrust CSR and do not understand it as a legitimate strategic tool. Moreover, the risks of damage to corporate reputation from unintended consequences and perceptions of insincerity should also be considered.

17.5   Defensive corporate social responsibility initiatives

Returning to the question of defensive versus strategic responses to CSR, if a firm is essentially defensive or accommodative in its stance to social responsiveness, then its primary concerns with CSR will be the protection of relationships – for example, with consumers, business-to-business customers, influential lobby or pressure groups, suppliers, employees and managers – and its relative position against competitors. This array of pressures towards defensive CSR is summarised in Figure 17.3. Currently, the evidence is that most firms concentrate their communications regarding CSR with their consumers, employees and shareholders, showing some neglect of their competitors and alliance partners (Snider et al., 2003).

For example, clothing company H&M (along with other Scandinavian retailers) suspended sales of items containing Angora wool in response to video footage distributed by animal rights activists showing the harvesting practices. The video was produced by the powerful People for the Ethical Treatment of Animals (PETA) lobby group and

Figure 17.3 Pressures driving defensive CSR strategies

showed hair being torn or plucked from Angora rabbits, leaving the animals in agony. The retailer response was defensive, to avoid damage by association with producer practices (Hansegard, 2013).

Porter and Kramer (2006) warn about defensive forms of CSR – particularly in terms of responding to the challenges of pressure groups – in that companies seeing CSR only as a way to placate pressure groups often find that this approach turns into a series of short-term public relations actions, with minimal social benefit and no strategic benefit for the business. They suggest the most common corporate responses to CSR have not been strategic and are often little more than cosmetic. Nonetheless, the risks in remaining inactive when social demands become severe are considerable.

The changing policies at Coca-Cola are illustrative. Coke has attracted a barrage of negative publicity over recent years: the alleged mistreatment of workers in Colombia; the use of water in drought-stricken parts of India; delaying acceptance of responsibility for contaminated product in Belgium in 1999; violently ejecting shareholder activists from the AGM; and playing a major role in fuelling the childhood obesity epidemic sweeping the developed world. Coke has been actively boycotted on university campuses throughout North America, and in parts of Europe. The company was in danger of replacing Nike and McDonald's as the chief corporate villain for the anti-globalisation movement. The problem, recognised by management, was the negative perceptions of the company that were progressively undermining the value of the brand. The new CEO of Coke mandated a proactive company approach to social issues, with a goal of making Coke the 'recognised global leader in corporate social responsibility'. The company has undertaken an audit of labour practices throughout its supply chain, launched several water-conservation projects, embraced industry guidelines restricting the sale of sugary drinks in schools and supported initiatives to encourage physical exercise among children. Nonetheless, critics still claim the company is pursuing these initiatives under pressure, not because it believes they are the right things to do (Ward, 2006). Certainly the company's recent attempt to present itself as an anti-obesity campaigner backfired badly, illustrating the difficult balancing act for food and drink companies in an increasingly health-conscious world (Rappeport, 2013).

The managerial goal in a defensive CSR mode should be to anticipate and develop appropriate responses to social demands from any source that threatens to undermine the value and credibility of brands, the attractiveness of the competitive position upon which the company's strategy depends and the viability of the marketing strategy itself. However, it is important that social initiative responses to these pressures should be carefully evaluated for likely effects, rather than constitute an unthinking knee-jerk reaction by management.

Management attention can usefully be given to examining the links between CSR stance and the impacts on consumers, business-to-business customers, investors, lobby groups, suppliers, employees and managers, and competitors. The goal should be to carefully evaluate the possible positive and negative impacts of CSR efforts on each of these groups.

17.5.1 Consumers and CSR

The adoption of social causes by organisations has often been based on the assumption that consumers will reward this behaviour (Levy, 1999). It is, however, unlikely that consumers will blindly accept social initiatives as sincere, and so may or may not reward the firm with positive attitudes and purchases (Becker-Olsen *et al.*, 2006). Indeed, research suggests that consumers will 'punish' firms that are perceived as insincere or manipulative in their social involvement (Becker-Olsen *et al.*, 2006). Nonetheless, there have been some research findings suggesting that there is a link between a company's social initiatives and positive consumer responses in attitudes, beliefs and behaviours, and positive associations have been found between social initiatives and price, perceived quality, corporate attitudes and purchase intentions (Becker-Olsen *et al.*, 2006). In fact, one study underlines that: customers will pay a premium for ethically produced goods; conversely, they will punish companies not seen as ethical (by demanding a lower price); the punishment exacted is greater than the premium customers are willing to pay; and companies do not need to be 100 per cent ethical to be rewarded (Trudel and Cotte, 2009).

Certainly, there is a strong argument that, to be effective, social initiatives must be consistent with a firm's operating objectives and values. Indeed, there is some evidence that when social initiatives are not aligned with corporate objectives and values, they may become a liability and diminish previously held beliefs about the firm. There is some priority for social initiatives and responses to be chosen carefully to reflect the firm's values and domain, so that consumers perceive initiatives as proactive and genuinely socially motivated (Becker-Olsen *et al.*, 2006).

Executives should be aware that the potential impact of ethical consumers may remain hidden for some time. One important concern is 'conflicted consumers' – they currently buy the product and on the face of things appear to have high satisfaction and display loyalty, but actually they would rather not buy from you and are poised to switch as soon as a viable alternative appears. They constitute a 'stealth segment' of apparently loyal customers who actually have major ethical concerns about your company (Fraser, 2007).

17.5.2 Business-to-business customers and CSR

The escalating demands of business-to-business customers for their suppliers to implement CSR policies and initiatives that are acceptable to the customer organisation have already been noted. For example, to reinforce its ethical credentials, jeans maker Levi Strauss & Co. now offers financial incentives to suppliers in Bangladesh and China to meet environmental, labour and safety standards, providing those suppliers with access to lower-cost working capital – publicised as adding 'ethical cred to street cred' for Levi's (Donnan, 2014).

The 'vendor compliance' programme at Target Corporation is illustrative. Target Corporation is a US retailer that prides itself on its high ethical standards and business principles, emphasising the protection of human rights, and extends these principles and standards to its suppliers. Target sources its purchases globally, through its Associated Merchandising Corporation subsidiary. Purchasing officers are required to uphold Target Corporation social responsibility standards wherever they buy in the world, even when these exceed the requirements of local laws – Target engineers do not just inspect suppliers' factories for product quality, but also for labour rights and employment conditions. Target operates a formal 'compliance organisation' for its purchasing, to enforce its vendor standards, focusing on vendor education and verification, with the following components:

● Implementation of a compliance audit programme, where audit staff conduct random visits to supplier manufacturing facilities, following which any compliance violations are subject to administrative probation or severance of the relationship.
● Limitation of subcontractors used by suppliers to only those approved by Target.
● Regular vendor evaluations, as well as formal audits.

Target is not unusual in its attention to the ethical and social responsibility standards it demands of its suppliers throughout the world. The introduction of formal social responsibility dimensions to supplier relationships is becoming the norm rather than the exception with large customers. These social responsibility mandates impact on supplier selection, and on the continuation of relationships with existing suppliers.

Customer-orientated social strategies directly influence supply chain relationships. In dealing with suppliers, Home Depot (one of the biggest buyers of wood products in the USA) demands that all its wood products come from suppliers who can provide evidence of sound forest-management practices. Organisational customers' evolving social responsibility requirements mandate effective responses. Certainly, one response may be that a customer's social responsibility demands reduce the attractiveness of that customer to the seller, and the business should be sacrificed. Nonetheless, the spread of vendor evaluation approaches, which make CSR demands on suppliers, requires continuous and systematic evaluation as the basis for an appropriate response.

17.5.3 Investors and CSR

There are growing signs that many corporate boards of directors are under shareholder pressure to adopt more acceptable environmental policies and keep a closer watch on environmental issues, reflecting investor concerns about global warming and shortages of natural resources. We noted earlier a growing trend for linking executive remuneration to sustainability targets. In major companies it is now commonly the case that sustainability has become an important part of the activities of every board of directors (Lublin, 2008).

The attitude of investors towards CSR initiatives, however, may be positive or negative. For example, it may be that from an investor perspective the case for sustainability is essentially a business case – initiatives are not about 'saving the planet', but about cutting waste, reducing costs and becoming more efficient. In 2006, Google launched a strategy to switch to renewable energy; while this reflects the personal beliefs of the founders of the business, it is also true that Google is a massive user of electricity, and renewable energy provides a way to cut costs (Senge *et al.*, 2008). Nonetheless, when Google announced its renewable energy strategy, one leading New York stock analyst downgraded the company's shares, despite clear indications that the initiative would cut costs – his view was that the company was no longer focusing on its real priorities (Witzel, 2008).

On the institutional investment front, there are active pressures towards 'responsible investing' – both exclusion in removing certain companies or sectors from an investment fund based on environmental, social or government criteria, and integration by including environmental, social and government factors in the traditional analysis conducted by fund managers. The divestment campaign against fossil fuels and the Pope's eco-encyclical have brought social investing into the spotlight. Globally, more than 30 per cent of institutionally managed stocks have a social mandate, accounting for $21.4 trillion in assets (Authers, 2015). The ability of a company to raise capital, and its attractiveness to investors, will be influenced in part by its social and ethical initiatives.

17.5.4 Lobby groups and CSR

There is strong evidence that companies with poor CSR records risk serious negative consequences, such as large-scale consumer boycotts, weaker brand image, or reduced sales. Part of this effect may be accounted for by the growth of consumer groups who actively promote awareness of what they believe to be company wrongdoing, and actively promote consumer boycotts (Snider *et al.*, 2003).

Certainly it appears that activist organisations have become far more aggressive and effective in bringing public pressure to bear on companies. They may target the most visible companies, to draw attention to the issue, even if the company in question has little impact on the problem. Nestlé is the world's largest seller of bottled water, and has become a major target in the global dilemma about access to fresh water. In fact, Nestlé's impact on world water usage and availability is relatively trivial – but it is a very convenient target (Porter and Kramer, 2006).

In another example, in 2015, animal rights protesters opposing the UK badger cull pressured Caffè Nero to stop selling milk from badger cull areas by threatening to target them in an 'anti-austerity' march. Interestingly, Caffè Nero then found itself on the end of vocal public criticisms from farmers' groups for threatening their livelihoods by giving in to blackmail. The CEO somewhat publicly lost his cool when asked to apologise to farmers. This is the type of situation where it is difficult for a company to emerge unscathed. The same

'Stop the Cull' protestors then moved on to Sainsbury's – sending pictures to the company's shareholders of bloody, wounded badgers shot to prevent the spread of bovine TB to cattle, and threatening to hijack Sainsbury's AGM. Unlike Caffè Nero, Sainsbury's chose to stand with the farmers and take the consequences (Petre and Elliott, 2015).

In a continuing anti-sugar campaign in the UK, doctors (via the British Medical Association) pressed for a tax on sugary drinks to fight the obesity crisis (Spencer, 2015b) – resulting in a tax on sugary drinks announced by the government in the Spring budget of 2016, to the acclaim of anti-sugar campaigners and the threats of legal action by the drinks companies. Yet, on the other hand, when Tesco decided to stop selling Ribena drinks cartons (the small cartons preferred for childrens' lunches and snacks) because of the sugar content, they faced a vocal consumer backlash of angry and Internet-literate customers who objected to being denied a favourite product (White, 2015). The long-term implications of sustained pressure on the food and drink industry are substantial and paradoxical.

One outcome of scoping CSR issues in the way we propose is to identify the issues that are likely to become high profile with different types of pressure groups. This provides some basis for responding effectively when they become live issues. Nonetheless, responses to external pressure groups have to be evaluated carefully for their potential 'unintended consequences' (Fry and Polonsky, 2004).

It is clear that lobby groups have the power to punish companies of which they disapprove. Pressured by PETA (People for the Ethical Treatment of Animals), 2008 saw companies from Timberland to H&M and Benetton banning Australian wool – PETA objects to the treatment of merino sheep in Australia, and as one European retailer noted: 'Who wants to be on PETA's radar screen?' (Capell, 2008). There is sound commercial logic that impels companies such as Walmart and Unilever to look to the Rainforest Alliance to help them certify the tea and coffee that they sell (Skapinker, 2008b).

Lobby and pressure groups may or may not represent issues of widespread concern, and they may or may not be legitimate in their activities. Responses to pressures from unmandated groups of dubious standing are unlikely to have positive effects for a company, and may bring additional dilemmas. For example, in the sustained attacks on the animal testing company, Huntingdon Life Sciences, animal rights protestors targeted not only HLS with violent threats and protests, but also its suppliers, including the company's banks. The dilemma facing the banks was whether to concede to the protestors' demands and cease trading with HLS, or to face violent actions against their own employees and premises. However, the first signs of concession to the protestors were met with criticisms from shareholders and the financial press that the banks had no right to cave in to the demands of animal rights protestors and their dubious tactics.

More broadly, influential lobby groups may shape public (consumer) opinion and drive government actions to control business actions. Increasingly, governments use their power to mandate social responsibility or create new legislative demands. For example, in the UK the government has pressured supermarkets to banish '2 for 1' deals on fresh food to reduce food waste – policy makers believe that 'bogoff' (buy one, get one free) offers are a main cause of the waste of a third of all food (Webster and Elliott, 2009). The same government has tried to prevent supermarkets from selling cheap alcohol, which is believed to encourage teenage drunkenness. When governments act on issues of social impact, the effect may be far more dramatic than would be voluntary compliance – for example, the UK domestic appliance industry was faced with a bill of more than £500 million to meet government plans for recycling, which was more than their combined annual profits (Willman, 2006).

Responding to outside pressures, particularly where they are vocal and well organised, in order to defend a company's competitive position may be an appropriate management action. On the other hand, it may not – it may be impossible or undesirable to respond to some pressure groups' demands. In either case, the effects of such responses need to be carefully considered in the context of the entire value chain, and attempts made to control the 'unintended consequences' of such actions.

17.5.5 Suppliers and CSR

The issue of CSR and ethical standards in a company's supply base is a direct reflection of the questions raised previously regarding the CSR-related demands made by major customers. Indeed, the ethical and social standards displayed by a seller's own suppliers may form part of a customer's CSR evaluation – as in the limitation of the use of subcontractors in the Target example. Increasingly, our major customers may require that we adopt a proactive CSR stance towards the entire value chain. Currently, food and agriculture are at the forefront of efforts to make producers more accountable, and in areas such as coffee, cocoa, palm oil and tea, the market share of sustainable commodities has escalated rapidly (Terazono, 2015).

While the general trend is clear, managers still face choices. If CSR-related demands cannot or will not be met by suppliers, then the choice becomes whether or not to continue the relationship – accepting that alternative suppliers will then have to be located and new value chain arrangements made. Conversely, if suppliers are prepared to concede new standards in their behaviour, then there are likely to be implications for the prices they charge, and hence for the company's cost structure and the prices it must ask of its own customers. This is likely to be a complex calculation. Careful evaluation is required.

17.5.6 Employees, managers and CSR

CSR is also seen as impacting on the perceptions of the employees and managers inside the company, and consequently on their motivation and commitment to the organisation. It is certainly apparent that many of the individuals now entering professional employment and providing the pool of talent from which future corporate leadership will be drawn, have important concerns about moral and ethical issues in business. The question is whether CSR initiatives will appeal to those concerns and generate the superior level of employee and manager commitment that should be associated with higher levels of job performance.

Research suggests two caveats to assuming that CSR will impact positively on employee beliefs and attitudes. First, employee attitudes and behaviours will be shaped in part by organisational culture and climate, and the impact of CSR will be influenced by whether initiatives are presented in terms of compliance or values, and whether such policies are integrated into business processes, or simply seen as 'window-dressing'. Secondly, the impact of CSR on employee motivation and commitment will be affected by the degree to which individuals can align their personal values with those of the organisation, by their perceptions of fairness and justice in the organisation, how CSR performance is rewarded and by their perceptions of top management attitudes towards CSR and performance (Collier and Esteban, 2007).

Nonetheless, a research study by McKinsey suggests that as many as 70 per cent of company managers believe there is room for improvement in the way large companies anticipate social pressure and respond to it. Managers see risks for their businesses in some social challenges – such as climate change, data privacy and healthcare – but opportunities in other challenges – such as the growing demand for more ethical, healthier and safer products (Maitland, 2006). Further indications of the importance of ethical and social responsibility issues are shown in studies of the perceptions of business school students – who will provide the next generation of managers. Business students appear to believe that companies should work harder towards the betterment of society, and want to find socially responsible employment in their careers (Knight, 2006).

17.5.7 Competitors and CSR

We commented earlier on the pressure to meet, equal or exceed CSR moves by competitors. The 'environmental arms race' between UK supermarkets, with each company trying to outdo the others on their environmental protection strategies, is illustrative. Certainly, CSR initiatives provide one way in which competitors attempt to differentiate themselves, even if this is swiftly countered by rivals.

It should also be recognised that some social issues are shared by all members of an industry, and joint or collaborative CSR initiatives may be to the benefit of all. For example, the Extractive Industries Transparency Initiative, initially based in London but now in Oslo, is a global collaboration including more than 90 major oil, gas and mining companies, who have agreed to work against corruption by using full public disclosure and verification of all company payments to governments in countries where they operate. The collective action by all the major companies makes it difficult for a government to undermine the social benefit of corruption-free trading by choosing not to deal with companies that disclose bribery payments.

There are clearly some risks for a company in adopting a wholly defensive approach to dealing with CSR issues. Failure to scope the CSR imperatives likely to be faced may be associated with ineffective short-term responses to social pressures. Nonetheless, in some cases a defensive stance may be all that is available, on some social issues. In such cases, initiatives should be carefully evaluated and implemented to avoid the risks of making the situation worse, of being perceived as insincere and cynical, or of undertaking actions with broader and potentially undesirable consequences for the company or for society as a whole.

17.6 Corporate social responsibility and innovative competitive advantage

From the perspective of marketing strategy, the important argument is that corporate social responsibility (CSR) provides a potential source of competitive advantage that is of increasing significance. For example, Michael Porter and Mark Kramer (2006) have made a compelling case for the position that businesses should not simply be taking corporate social responsibility seriously as an end in itself, but should be embedding it into their strategy to help build competitive advantage. They argue that conventional CSR approaches have often resulted in a mix of uncoordinated CSR initiatives and philanthropic activities that neither make meaningful social impact, nor strengthen the firm's long-term competitiveness. (We have earlier suggested the converse of this case: that companies neglecting issues of corporate social responsibility and ethical or moral standards may find themselves wrong-footed by competitors who position themselves partly on the basis of these resources.) The Porter and Kramer model is highly influential in management thinking, and it provides the underlying structure for this section of the chapter. Above all, Porter and Kramer link CSR directly to creating competitive advantage.

The logic linking corporate responsibility to competitive advantage follows these lines. Porter and Kramer (2006) argue that many prevailing approaches to CSR are fragmented and disconnected from business and strategy, while in fact the real challenge is for companies to analyse their social responsibility prospects using the same frameworks that guide their core business choices. The goal is to establish CSR not simply as corporate altruism, but as a source of opportunity, innovation and competitive advantage.

Porter and Kramer argue that companies should make choices about which social issues to address, from:

- *generic social issues* – things that are not affected by the company's operations, nor impacting on its long-term competitiveness;
- *value chain social impacts* – social issues that are affected by the company's activities in the normal course of business;
- *social dimensions of competitive context* – social issues in the external environment that significantly affect the underlying drivers of the company's competitiveness.

They suggest that a company should sort social issues into these three categories for each business unit and location, and then rank them in terms of potential impact. The category into which a given issue will fall will depend on the business and its location. For example, the AIDS pandemic in Africa might be a generic social issue for a retailer in the USA or Europe, a value chain impact for a pharmaceutical company and a competitive context issue for a mining company dependent on local labour in Africa for its operations.

The purpose of this ranking is to create an explicit corporate social agenda for a company, which 'looks beyond community expectations to achieve social and economic benefits simultaneously. It moves from mitigating harm to finding ways to reinforce corporate strategy by advancing social conditions' (Porter and Kramer, 2006, p. 85). Porter and Kramer reinforce the critically important distinction between responsive CSR and strategic CSR, suggesting it is through strategic CSR that a company can make the greatest social impact while also achieving the greatest competitive benefits. Their distinction is between two levels of CSR:

- **Responsive CSR**: involves acting as a good corporate citizen, reflecting the social concerns of stakeholders in the company, and also mitigating the existing or predicted adverse effects of business activities. The domain is generic social impacts and value chain social impacts. The limitation of many citizenship initiatives remains that however beneficial the social effects, such programmes tend to remain incidental to the company's business. The key to mitigating value chain social impacts is best practice, though competitive advantage through such endeavours is likely to be temporary.
- **Strategic CSR**: moves beyond good citizenship and value chain impacts to initiatives with large and distinctive effects. The goals are the transformation of value chain activities to benefit society, while at the same time reinforcing the company's strategy, and strategic moves that leverage corporate capabilities to improve areas of competitive context. Strategic CSR may involve the introduction of radically different new products – the Toyota Prius hybrid car and now electric cars respond to consumer concerns about car emissions pollution, and provide both competitive advantage for Toyota and other innovators such as Tesla, and environmental benefits. However, the broader goal of strategic CSR is to invest in social aspects of the company's context to strengthen company competitiveness. This is achieved, in part, by adding a social dimension to the company's value proposition and ways of doing business. Only a small number of the social issues that could be addressed have this potential to make a real difference to society and build competitive advantage.

As a framework for examining these distinctions and differences, the Porter and Kramer logic is summarised in Figure 17.4.

Further, using the example of Whole Foods Market in the USA (which has since been purchased by Amazon), Porter and Kramer underline the competitive strength created by creating a social dimension to the value proposition. They suggest that the heart of strategy is a value proposition that rests on the set of needs that a company can uniquely meet for its chosen customers. The most strategic CSR adds a dimension to the value proposition, such that social impact is central to strategy. The value proposition at Whole Foods Market is to sell natural, organic, healthy food products to consumers who are orientated to healthy eating and the environment. The company's stance on social issues is central to what makes them unique in food retailing and able to ask premium prices. For example: sourcing emphasises purchasing at store level from local farmers; buyers screen-out ingredients considered unhealthy or environmentally damaging; the company offsets its electricity consumption; spoilt produce goes to regional centres for composting; vehicles are being converted to run on bio-fuels; and cleaning products in stores are environmentally friendly. The effect is that every aspect of the company's value chain reinforces the social dimensions of its value proposition, and provides strong differentiation from its competitors. That said, the company has struggled somewhat with its image as an expensive store for middle-class foodies, and is sometimes known as 'whole paycheck' in the USA because of its high prices.

Figure
17.4 Responsive and strategic CSR

It's not entirely clear yet whether the purchase of Whole Foods by Amazon will herald a return to its roots as a health-food store rather than a source of 'foodie treats', but, either way, the company is performing strongly.

Porter and Kramer conclude that while not every company can be a Whole Foods, adding a social dimension to the value proposition adds a new frontier for our thinking about competitive positioning. They also note that the number of industries and companies whose competitive advantage can involve social value propositions is rapidly growing. Their conclusion is important to how we consider the resource profile of an organisation, and the ways in which it can leverage and strengthen that profile:

> Organisations that make the right choices and build focussed, proactive, and integrated social initiatives in concert with their core strategies will increasingly distance themselves from the pack. . . Perceiving social responsibility as building shared value rather than as damage control or as a PR campaign will require dramatically different thinking in business. We are convinced, however, that CSR will become increasingly important to competitive success.
> *(Porter and Kramer, 2006, pp. 91–112)*

A similar viewpoint is adopted by Andrew Savitz, who created the environmental practice at PwC and has worked on environmental issues with some of America's largest companies (Savitz and Weber, 2006). Savitz and Weber share the view that it makes financial sense for companies to anticipate and respond to society's emerging demands – anticipating reciprocal advantages in the longer term in that the sustainable company will be more profitable as a result of its responsiveness. In their terms, sustainability is about conducting business in such a way that it benefits employees, customers, business partners, communities and shareholders at the same time – it is 'the art of doing business in an interdependent world' (Savitz and Weber, 2006). They suggest that the best-run companies have identified 'sustainability sweet spots' – areas where shareholders' long-term interests overlap with those of society. They point, for example, to Unilever's Project Shakti in India, where 70,000 female Shakti entrepreneurs have been employed and trained to distribute Unilever products to rural communities, providing economic income in a deprived area, but at the same time gaining market access and penetration in a difficult market.

Indeed, *Fortune* magazine lists the companies identified as the world's top 'eco-innovators' – the businesses doing the most to make the world smarter and more sustainable. The list includes: Tesla, in electric cars; Nest, with intelligent automation for the home; SolarCity, pioneering solar leasing programmes for the home; Environmental Initiatives at Apple, addressing electronic waste and recycling old Apple products for free; and Broad Group, with energy-efficient cooling systems for commercial buildings (Dumaine, 2014). There are close links between sustainability and exciting product and technology innovation (see Chapter 12).

Nonetheless, on occasion, there may be major questions surrounding the balance between business and social benefits in some CSR initiatives of this kind. For example, some companies are benefiting commercially by asking 'green' consumers to pay them for cleaning up their own pollution. Similarly, Blue Source, a US offsetting company, invites consumers to offset their carbon emissions by investing in enhanced oil recovery (pumping carbon dioxide into depleted oil wells to bring up the remaining oil). In fact, Blue Source admits that this process is often profitable in itself, and the 'carbon credit' represents additional revenue (Harvey and Fidler, 2007). It is likely that such schemes will fail to deliver more than short-term financial benefits, rather than synergy between business and social benefits.

One example of the possibilities for large-scale competitive change around social benefit initiatives is provided by the MIT team, who said in 2004 they were going to overcome the digital divide between the rich and poor by making a $100 laptop for the poor children of the world – the One Laptop Per Child (OLPC) project. While initially dismissed simply as a charitable project, the MIT team's vision has underlined to the commercial IT sector the market power of the poor – the fact that the majority of the world's population does not have a computer will be one of the main drivers of growth for the sector. The effects on hardware and software companies have been dramatic in driving the industry towards providing ultra-cheap laptops in various forms. The OLPC project underlines the social benefits and the commercial opportunities in a cheap laptop, which was relatively easy to make using newer technologies, open source software and stripping out unneeded functions (Hille, 2007). The next socially driven innovation in this area, this time from the UK, was the Raspberry Pi – a minicomputer to help children learn programming skills, priced at £22 (Palmer, 2012).

Relatedly in this sector, an interesting example of a company leveraging its distinctive competitive competences to further initiatives with both business and social benefits was provided by Dell Inc in the early part of the 2000s. Dell used the strengths of its direct business model to generate collective efforts to reduce energy consumption and protect the environment. The initiative centred on improving the efficiency of IT products, reducing the harmful materials used in them and cooperating with customers to dispose of old products. Michael Dell's environmental strategy focused on three areas:

- Creating easy, low-cost ways for businesses to do better in protecting the environment – providing, for example, global recycling and product recovery programmes for customers, with participation requiring little effort on their part.
- Taking creative approaches to lessen the environmental impact of products from design to disposal – helping customers to take full advantage of new, energy-saving technology and processes, and advising on upgrades of legacy systems to reduce electricity usage.
- Looking to partnership with governments to promote environmental stewardship – for example, in Dell's 'Plant a Tree for Me' programme, offering customers the chance to offset emissions from the electricity their computers use by making a contribution to buying a tree when they buy a PC.

As a company, Dell committed efforts to enhancing operational efficiencies and reducing its carbon footprint through the use of renewable energy (Dell, 2007). Importantly, Dell's initiative started with the distinctive strengths of the company (the direct business-to-business model with corporate customers), applied these strengths to address an environmental issue (reduced pollution, lower energy use), but at the same time achieved business goals (reinforcing the company's leadership, strengthening customer relationships, faster take-up of newer, more efficient products and technologies). The link between this CSR initiative and the company's business model and value proposition is clear.

Similarly, Microsoft has partnered with governments in less developed countries to offer Microsoft Windows and Office software packages for a few dollars to governments that subsidise the cost of computers for schoolchildren. The potential business benefit for Microsoft is to double the number of PC users worldwide, and reinforce the company's market growth. The social benefit is the greater investment in technology in some of the poorest countries in the world, with the goal of improving living standards and reducing global inequality (*Financial Times*, 2007).

On the environmental front, General Electric – the largest company in the world – has its well-established 'Ecomagination' initiative. Ecomagination has grown out of GE's long-term investment in cleaner technologies, and places these technologies under a single brand. To qualify for Ecomagination branding, products must significantly and measurably improve customers' environmental and operating performance. However, the Ecomagination vision is driven by the principle that its green initiatives will have a positive impact on GE's competitive position and financial performance (Harvey, 2005; Hart, 2005).

CSR strategy at companies such as Dell Inc., Microsoft and GE may provide a prototype of linking CSR to competitive advantage that will influence management thinking.

17.7   How companies are responding to the CSR mandate

The ways in which companies are developing responses to the imperatives to display more ethical and socially acceptable policies are not well codified. Certainly, there is wide recognition that firms face choices in their responsiveness to social responsibility. For example, corporate social responsiveness may reflect models or philosophies, ranging from 'do nothing' to 'do much' (Carroll, 1979). However, responsiveness alone may not be the same as good corporate citizenship. For example, a responsive organisation may address social pressures by moving to a less demanding environment – consider the growing emphasis from tobacco companies on the relatively unregulated developing countries, where tobacco consumption remains socially acceptable. The simple prescription of responsiveness oversimplifies the complexity of the situations that companies face. The issue is how a company responds, and what its responses represent to its stakeholders. There is also potential insight from benchmarking and making comparisons with competitors.

Certainly, there is a dilemma for some companies if their existing business model relies on resources and capabilities that become questionable in terms of social responsibilities and duty. We noted earlier that Primark is a very successful British fashion retailer. The Primark business model relies on sourcing fashion items from low-cost manufacturing areas and turning catwalk trends into products in as little as two weeks at extremely low prices. The result is that Primark buys from suppliers whose workers are paid as little as 9p an hour, working 90 hours a week in extremely poor conditions. Notwithstanding the company's 'charm offensive' in the ethics and social responsibility field – and the company's efforts to stop buying from suppliers using child labour (Urry, 2008) – the dilemma is that the low-price, lean supply chain business model relies on low-cost suppliers. This dilemma is shared by other low-price fashion retailers, including Tesco and Asda.

The urgency of the issue is underlined by escalating transparency – for example, the growth in the use of new software packages that allow consumers and rivals to trace the provenance of products. Many companies have stopped using suppliers where there are suspicions of the use of forced or child labour, or conflict materials are present – not least because of the ease with which these facts can be identified by consumers. For example,

Figure 17.5 Corporate responses to CSR imperatives
Source: Adapted from Piercy and Lane (2009b).

GoodGuide provides an online database of verified information regarding the health, environmental and social impact of more than 250,000 common products (Tyrell, 2010).

Figure 17.5 presents a framework for evaluating the ways in which companies are responding to pressures encouraging the adoption of corporate social responsibility initiatives in business and marketing strategy. This model suggests that responses vary in extent, but also that the impact on customer value will depend in part on employee and manager perceptions of CSR, perceptions among other stakeholders such as supply chain partners and investors, and the company's 'social credibility' – essentially whether its history and actions mean that its social intentions are interpreted positively by different stakeholders. The framework assists in identifying the linkages between CSR and customer value.

17.7.1 Company CSR responses

It is clear that companies differ substantially in their stance on corporate social responsibility and ethical behaviour initiatives (Pohle and Hittner, 2008). Variation includes both the extent and direction of response – how much they change their behaviour and in what ways.

Denial/rejection

There is little doubt that some executives remain unconvinced that corporate social responsibility represents anything other than charitable giving, and that such initiatives are unconnected, or at best only loosely related, to customer value. Underpinning such responses and negative attitudes towards CSR is probably the residual belief among some managers and investors that it is simply not the role of business to pursue social goals, but rather to create the economic wealth that facilitates the pursuit of such objectives by public authorities and not-for-profit organisations. This is a legitimate and defensible position to take. CSR-related actions in this situation may amount to little more than meeting legal obligations and compliance with regulation in countries of production, operation and distribution, but the cost may be vulnerability to attack and missed opportunities.

Limited engagement

Philanthropy may involve some degree of alignment of charitable activities with social issues that support business objectives, although some charitable giving may be about 'doing good' rather than meeting business goals. However, even at the level of corporate giving to good causes, companies are increasingly choosing projects in which they can be actively involved and that encompass parts of their business model. This concept of 'strategic philanthropy' is gathering momentum alongside the idea of 'capitalist philanthropy', which suggests that charitable giving should be evaluated as an investment (Brewster, 2008).

Defensive approaches

If a firm is essentially defensive in its stance to social responsiveness, then its primary concerns with CSR will be the protection of relationships – for example, with consumers, business-to-business customers, influential lobby or pressure groups, suppliers, employees and managers, and relative position against competitors.

For example, when Greenpeace parodied Unilever advertisements, accusing the company of destroying Indonesian rainforests for palm oil (a key ingredient of the company's soaps and margarines), the company was quick to reverse its position and declare it would buy palm oil only from suppliers who can demonstrate they did not cut down forestry. As the world's largest seller of bottled water, Nestlé's response to environmental criticisms was more negative – they responded with a large advertising campaign linking soft drinks to obesity (Patrick, 2008).

Strategic moves

The underlying logic with more strategic approaches is that CSR provides a new growth platform, potentially bringing access to new markets, new partnerships and new types of product/service innovation that generate value – this represents a shift from compliance and defensiveness to integrating CSR into strategy to achieve revenue growth and brand differentiation (Pohle and Hittner, 2008). Increasingly, such strategic moves involve partnerships with non-government organisations (NGOs) to combine social and commercial activities. For example, Unilever has partnered with public health networks in Africa to promote its anti-bacterial Lifebuoy soap – the NGOs seek to promote handwashing to prevent the spread of disease, while Unilever aims to sell more soap (Jopson, 2007).

New business models

The compelling logic of the Porter and Kramer (2006) approach is that the real impact of corporate social responsibility imperatives is in encouraging the development of new business models that address both commercial and social needs at the same time. Porter and Kramer conclude that adding a social dimension to the value proposition adds a new frontier for our thinking about competitive positioning and competitive advantage in business and marketing strategy. They also note that the number of industries and companies whose competitive advantage can involve social value propositions is rapidly growing. We saw earlier that companies such as Whole Foods Market are illustrative of this.

For example, consider the emergence of 'eco-entrepreneurs' – transforming traditional business models with new technologies. Fast-moving 'eco-upstarts' may be better positioned than established companies to pursue social goals with commercial benefits. For example, PlanetTran is a chauffeur and airport shuttle service that uses only hybrid cars and aims to save the planet 'one car journey at a time'. Successful with the eco-conscious business community in Boston and San Francisco, PlanetTran supplies corporate clients with quarterly reports measuring the environmental benefits of using PlanetTran compared to traditional transport arrangements (Knight, 2008).

Or, look at the impact of the 'sharing economy' on traditional car companies – BMW has extended its DriveNow, pay-as-you-go car-sharing club to London after its successful origins in Germany, Austria and the United States. One estimate is that one sharing vehicle removes the need for 32 personal car purchases (Sharman, 2014).

17.7.2 Employee/manager perceptions

The impact of CSR initiatives on customer value perceptions is also likely to be moderated by a company's employee and manager perceptions of the initiatives and the relevance and importance of them. On the face of things, companies can often anticipate positive and supportive employee/manager perceptions of CSR that will enhance the impact on customer value. Nonetheless, questions may still be raised about the degree to which CSR initiatives shape interactions between company personnel and customers in ways that impact positively on customer value. Giving approval to CSR concepts may differ from changing the way work is done to reflect actual CSR initiatives. For example, consider the degree to which salespeople buy-in to CSR and the degree to which their selling efforts reflect CSR to enhance customer value – this appears often to be limited and a victim of salesperson cynicism (Piercy and Lane, 2011). Certainly, research suggests that high-performing companies fully engage their employees in their CSR objectives, rather than adopting a top-down approach (Pohle and Hittner, 2008).

17.7.3 Other stakeholder perceptions

Supply chain partners may be very significant in creating pressures towards more responsible behaviour. Walmart has, for example, led the way in asking suppliers to measure and report their greenhouse gas emissions, with the goal of helping suppliers to 'get the costs of carbon out of the system' (Harvey and Birchall, 2007). Recall also that we commented earlier on the impact of other stakeholders, such as investors, the government and regulators, and other stakeholders in the value chain.

17.7.4 Company social credibility

An additional complication is whether a company's corporate reputation supports CSR initiatives, in the sense that such initiatives are perceived externally as well-meaning and sincere (and likely to be reinforced and maintained), or alternatively as cynical and manipulative (and likely to be minimised or abandoned in favour of the next 'marketing gimmick').

The impact of social credibility (or the lack of it) may be profound. For example, US retailer Walmart has long had a reputation for aggression and ruthlessness in dealing with suppliers, competitors and employees – branded the 'merchant of shame' by critics of its labour policies (Berner, 2005). Nonetheless, in recent years, Walmart has focused considerable attention on employment diversity issues and environmental protection, and yet has failed to convince its environmental critics of the company's sincerity. To champion Walmart's social contributions, then-chief executive Lee Scott used his annual shareholder meeting to offer to partner with governments on issues from the environment to healthcare reform. Yet many still doubt the sincerity of Walmart's social change intentions (McWilliams and Zuckerman, 2008).

Similarly, as noted earlier, Coca-Cola continues to struggle to overcome the perception that its business model involves 'waste, pollution and questionable nutrition', and is working hard through water- and energy-saving projects to overcome criticisms, collaborating with environmental campaign groups such as Greenpeace (Wiggins, 2007). Establishing credibility as an ethical company may require overcoming perceptions of a company's history as well as initiating new CSR projects.

Indeed, company practices are not simply more visible as a result of aggressive questioning by customers, NGOs and advocacy groups, they face growing demands for transparency – taking the wraps off information once considered proprietary or confidential. Social credibility depends in part on developing information strategies that are relevant to customers' concerns, expectations and preferences – only the company that shares reliable information is likely to be perceived as a trustworthy 'partner in sustainability' by customers and other stakeholders (Pohle and Hittner, 2008).

The link between CSR efforts and customer value is likely to be moderated by the company's credibility as a social player, shaped by its history and corporate reputation. Low credibility may not be an absolute barrier to implementing useful CSR initiatives, but it may well reduce the impact of those initiatives on customer perceptions. When considering the impact of CSR on strategy and positioning choices, it is necessary to be realistic as well as visionary.

17.8   CSR and customer value

It follows from the last section, and is suggested in Figure 17.5, that from a strategic marketing perspective, the critical linkage is the one between CSR initiatives and customer value. This is not to deny the importance of CSR that simply does good in its own right, but rather emphasises value-creation through CSR, which resonates with the development of new business models that combine social and business goals.

The central strategic marketing question is thus how CSR impacts on the customer value proposition. While widely used and loosely defined, the value proposition describes the unique offer made to the customer, with all its hard and soft dimensions, and is at the centre of how a company aims to differentiate itself from competitors in its target market segments. In fact, there are indications that many companies have a poor understanding of their customers' real concerns about social and environmental issues surrounding their businesses, and few are asking them – leaving suppliers to rely on assumptions about what CSR means to their customers. High-performing companies show a deeper understanding of their customers' CSR expectations (Pohle and Hittner, 2008). Businesses need new sources of operational, supply chain and customer information to gain the new levels of insight required to meet objectives in areas such as sustainability (IBM, 2009).

In fact, in business-to-business marketing in particular, it is possible to identify three types of value proposition, providing an insightful framework for examining the link between CSR and the value proposition. Anderson *et al.* (2006) identify three kinds of value proposition:

1 **All benefits**: when asked to construct a value proposition, managers list all the benefits they believe their offering might deliver to target customers, with the risk they claim advantage from features that actually provide no benefit or value to target customers.
2 **Favourable points of difference**: recognising that customers have alternatives, this identifies what differentiates the offering from the next best alternative, which risks assuming that all favourable comparisons create value for the customer.
3 **Resonating focus**: concentrates on the one or two points of difference that deliver, and with improvement will continue to deliver, greatest value to target customers, though clearly this relies on deeper knowledge of what drives value for the customer.

The researchers conclude that customer value propositions with a resonating focus should be the gold standard (Anderson *et al.*, 2006).

The Anderson *et al.* framework is used in Figure 17.6 to suggest the questions that should be asked regarding the relationship between a selling or supplying company's CSR, and customer value perceptions. Questioning moves progressively from investigating what specific customer benefits are linked to a supplier's CSR, in the 'all benefits' value proposition, to

Types of value proposition	All benefits value proposition	Favourable points of difference value proposition	Resonating focus value proposition
	Lists all the benefits the customer will receive and why they should buy this offering	Identifies the favourable points of difference compared to the alternatives for the customer	Focuses on the one or two points of difference whose improvement will deliver the greatest value to the customer
	Risks asserting benefits that do not really create customer value	Risks assuming that favourable differences create value for the customer	Requires deeper kowledge of what drives value for the customer
Corporate social responsibility questions	What customer benefits are linked to our CSR initiatives?	In what ways does our CSR strategy make us more attractive to the customer than our competitors?	How do our CSR initiatives align with customer priorities and drive customer value?

Figure 17.6 CSR and customer value propositions

seeking the ways in which CSR strategy achieves 'favourable points of difference' compared to competitors, to examining how CSR initiatives align with customer priorities and thus drive value for the customer.

Consider the case of Philips' environmentally friendly Alto industrial lighting tubes. While containing less toxicity, the Alto product was more expensive than competing light tubes, and conventional suppliers sold on price and bulb life to purchasing officers. Telling buyers that the tube is more environmentally friendly (as part of an all benefits approach) or that it is more environmentally friendly than competitors' products (favourable points of difference) is unlikely to impress purchasing officers accustomed to evaluating alternatives on price and bulb life. However, appealing to, for example, shopping mall developers on the basis of reduced disposal costs (because the green product is less toxic) and environmental image (the cleaner lighting becomes part of their environmental appeal to consumers) was effective. Alto replaced more than 25 per cent of the US market for traditional fluorescent lamps (Kim and Mauborgne, 1999).

Summary

This chapter sets out to establish the impact of corporate social responsibility on marketing strategy and customer value. Social responsibility and ethical standards are closely linked to corporate reputation and thus a company's freedom of strategic positioning. This is an area that is evolving rapidly, and one that is turning out to be highly significant to the ability of a company to maintain its chosen competitive position and to compete effectively. Nonetheless, it is an area where precise definitions and analytical methodologies do not yet exist. Our approach suggests that companies should devote efforts to understanding better, through scoping or issue analysis, the social pressures that are likely to affect their ability to compete.

Company responses to social issues fall into several categories, ranging from altruistic company philanthropy and the concept of social enterprise, to defensive moves to protect competitive position, to strategic moves that aim to create competitive advantage through CSR initiatives. Our attention focuses on the latter areas: defensive CSR and creating competitive advantage through CSR. We place this into a strategic marketing context by examining the impact of CSR on customer value, and the varying ways in which companies appear to be responding to CSR imperatives.

Case study

Iceland Foods takes heat for bold environmental message

By Jonathan Eley

UK supermarket has not shied away from controversy with campaigns such as palm oil ban

The unveiling of Christmas television advertisements is an annual ritual in the UK's hugely competitive retail market. Yet the commercial judged to be the most effective in 2018 never made it on to the nation's TV screens.

Advertising agency Kantar Millward Brown conducts consumer research into the effectiveness of festive campaigns. It says the expensive effort by department store John Lewis featuring singer Elton John and a schmaltzy Sainsbury's supermarket advert about a school play both had less resonance than Iceland Foods' low-budget animated feature about an orangutan made homeless by deforestation.

Richard Walker, managing director of the frozen food chain, says the 'Rang-Tan' advert was originally made for Greenpeace, the environmental lobby group of which he is a member. 'They showed us a rough cut of this campaign video they had: it brought a tear to my eyes. We thought it would be great if we could use it as our Christmas advert,' he says.

Clearcast, the organisation controlled by broadcasters that approves adverts, had other ideas. It refused to clear the advert because it had previously appeared on the Greenpeace website and the group had some of the legal characteristics of a political organisation. Instead, the advert was released online – with a generous dose of 'the ad they tried to ban' publicity – and promptly went viral. It was viewed more than 70m times worldwide, while a petition launched in the UK urging Clearcast to reconsider received more than 1m signatures.

Walker is adamant Iceland did not plan for this turn of events as a cost-effective way to upstage bigger rivals. 'We thought debadging it would be enough to get it past Clearcast. I genuinely did not

think it would be banned.' He says the company had booked more than £600,000 of television advertising slots to air the commercial.

The advert refers to the clearing of forests in Indonesia and Malaysia to make way for palm oil plantations. According to Greenpeace, an area equivalent to 146 football pitches is cleared every day in Indonesia alone. 'Rainforests cover only 2 per cent of the planet's surface but account for half its biodiversity. They are the crown jewels,' says Walker, who in April 2018 pledged to remove palm oil from all Iceland's own-label products by last December to persuade the industry to stop clearing forests.

Iceland's choice of campaign theme might seem an odd one for a company that, since its foundation in 1970, has targeted customers at the value end of the shopping spectrum. It lacks the scale of other supermarkets – its annual revenue of £3bn is a fraction of the £51bn (excluding fuel) that UK market leader Tesco achieves, or the SFr91.4bn ($90.6bn) posted by food multinational Nestlé. Iceland's palm oil consumption for own-label products, about 500 tonnes a year, was inconsequential in a global context; consumer goods giant Unilever gets through 1.5m tonnes annually, and total world yearly production is 72m tonnes.

Walker acknowledges the move was at least partly a personal one. 'Were [customers] screaming down the aisles saying, "If only there was no palm oil"? No, but I am so proud that now some customers, some of whom only have £20 a week or so to spend on food, are talking about palm oil – where it comes from, the pros and cons,' he says.

Environmentalists such as Jonathan Porritt say UK retailers generally have a good record on palm oil – the World Wide Fund for Nature rates most of them highly on progress towards ensuring that record is sustainable, mostly via participation in the Roundtable on Sustainable Palm Oil (RSPO), an industry standards body.

But Iceland was the first to propose removing palm oil from its products altogether – a controversial move in many respects. It was derided by Porritt (who is an adviser to Sime Darby, a producer of sustainable palm oil) as 'an almost entirely meaningless gesture'. Other critics say switching to alternatives would have a catastrophic impact on the smallholders who cultivate palm oil.

Walker acknowledges such matters are rarely clear cut. Palm oil is a widely used ingredient because it is one of the cheapest vegetable fats and is much higher yielding than many alternatives. Sunflower or rapeseed, for instance, require far more land to produce the same volume. He says his objection is specifically to deforestation, and that 'it would be great' if improved sustainability meant he could remove the 'No Palm Oil' branding proliferating across Iceland's ranges.

The palm oil ban is not the first occasion Iceland has made a bold move in the name of the environment. Two decades before, it was the first UK supermarket to ban genetically modified (GM) ingredients. Previous initiatives have included recycling freezers containing ozone-depleting chemicals and removing artificial colourings and preservatives from foods.

The man behind many of those decisions was not Walker but his father, Sir Malcolm Walker, the company's founder and executive chairman, who claims to have coined the phrase 'Frankenstein foods'. 'Our business was about walking a tightrope between what people will spend on food and the absolute quality of the product,' Sir Malcolm wrote about GM foods in *Best Served Cold*, his 2013 autobiography. 'We had to compete but we also had to be ethical. Our customers were mainly on a low income but they had a right to a choice.'

Not that he minded the publicity such moves attracted. 'I wasn't embarrassed to shout about them and try to turn them into a point of difference. They were certainly good for sales and our constant high profile in the media brought in new customers.'

Richard Walker is more circumspect, saying there was no clear-cut evidence of a sales boost from the 'Rang-tan' advert. The company also incurred significant costs by helping its suppliers remove palm oil from its ranges, at a time when it is carrying a relatively high debt load and facing challenging trading conditions. Iceland's borrowings – more than five times its earnings – stem from a leveraged buyout of the group led by Sir Malcolm in 2012. The ratio of debt to earnings is below two at all the major UK supermarkets.

An even more complex undertaking is Iceland's pledge to remove all plastic from its own-label ranges by 2023, another area where rivals have followed its lead. Plastic, which is cheap and versatile, is integral to food packaging, but the BBC's Blue Planet wildlife documentaries have raised public awareness of its environmental effects.

Walker says there have been some early wins. Wrapping bananas in a cardboard girdle rather than bagging them has saved 10m plastic bags a year, for instance. 'We are a fifth of the way on the journey in terms of tonnage, though I'm not entirely happy. If you go into our shops now, it is still a wall of plastic,' he says.

Walker also admits there is a degree of contradiction in a company that owns a private jet lecturing others about environmentalism. 'There are contradictions in all our lives, but I don't think the answer is to live in a cave and never fly anywhere,' he says.

Rita Clifton, co-founder of BrandCap, a consultancy, says Iceland seemed to have overcome the 'radical at the research questionnaire but reactionary at the checkout' situation, where customers profess strong views about an issue but fail to act on them if that would mean bearing additional costs. Last December, Wilmar, the world's largest palm oil trader, said it would improve the monitoring of its suppliers, a decision Greenpeace described as 'a breakthrough moment'. The previous month, the RSPO had said it would commit to a no-deforestation policy.

It is impossible to know to what degree the advert influenced these changes, given that environmental organisations have lobbied food manufacturers and retailers for years to clean up their act on palm oil.

Clifton says it is easy to criticise the flaws in such initiatives, but adds: 'If they're nudging the peanut forward in the right way, they should be encouraged as well as monitored.'

Source: from 'Iceland Foods takes heat for bold environmental message', *Financial Times*, 14/03/19 (Eley, J.).

Discussion questions

1 What is the key impact of CSR on marketing strategy?

2 How does Iceland express its sustainability ambitions?

3 What could be drivers of CSR initiatives for supermarkets such as Iceland?

PART 6
CONCLUSIONS

Chapter 18 concludes *Marketing Strategy and Competitive Positioning* by looking ahead at what marketing strategies for the next decade of the twenty-first century might be. Significant changes in the business environment are highlighted and a number of building blocks are suggested for developing adaptive and flexible strategies for a rapidly changing world. These include: the need for organisations to have learning at their core, and an ability to capture, analyse, interpret and utilise information to create knowledge and action; the need for a clear market orientation, and a focus on creating superior value and high levels of satisfaction for customers; the need to base positioning strategies on marketing assets and competencies; the need to establish close relationships with key customers; and finally, the need to rethink the role of marketing within the organisation. A number of dimensions are discussed that can provide keys to positioning in the future. Price, quality, innovation, service, benefit differentiation and customisation are compared as fundamental positioning dimensions and strategies, and the competencies and assets required for each are explored.

The chapter, and the text as a whole, concludes by predicting that marketing will be seen more as a process for achieving a close fit between market requirements and company competencies and assets, rather than as a functional department within the firm. It is how this strategic, rather than operational or tactical, role for marketing will be fulfilled in the future that holds much excitement for the discipline of marketing.

CHAPTER 18
MARKETING IN THE TWENTY-FIRST CENTURY

'It is not the strongest of the species that survive, nor the most intelligent, but the ones most responsive to change.'

Charles Darwin, *On the Origin of Species* **(1853)**

'Prediction is very difficult, especially if it's about the future.'

Niels Bohr (Danish physicist, 1885–1962)

Apple ready to unveil big bet on television

By Tim Bradshaw in London and Anna Nicolaou in New York

The question is whether media companies will sign up to its TV platform

Steve Jobs told his biographer in 2011 that Apple had 'finally cracked' a winning formula for television. But eight years later, his successor Tim Cook is still trying to win a place in his customers' living rooms.

Chief executive Tim Cook is betting that Apple can position itself as an aggregator

Source: Justin Sullivan / Staff/Getty Images.

For more than a decade, Apple has toyed with the idea of making its own television sets and pitched cable companies on various kinds of software integrations and bundled services.

Now, after several false starts, Apple is ready to unveil its latest vision for TV, with an event at its Cupertino headquarters next week titled 'It's show time'.

Mr Cook's latest bet is that an acceleration in cord-cutting and the proliferation of streaming services has created a new role for Apple as aggregator. Apple wants to reinvent the TV guide with a personalised slate of programming drawn from a wide range of sources, including a few shows of its own.

Even getting as far as launching a new service is something of an achievement for Apple. Unlike the music and telecoms industries, which have been forced to cede control to Apple through the iPod and iPhone eras, pay-TV operators have proven able to cling on to their direct relationship with customers.

Instead of trying to reorient the TV experience around an iPhone-like grid of apps from the likes of Netflix, Disney or HBO, Apple's new TV platform is likely to put the focus on individual shows.

Services remain a small fraction of Apple's revenues

Share of total revenues (%)

■ Other   □ iPhone   ■ Services

Services remain a small fraction of Apple's revenues

Sources: Tim Bradshaw (2019), Apple ready to unveil big bet on television, The Financial Times.

Its existing 'TV' app, which is already available on iPhones and iPads as well as the Apple TV box itself, is designed around each individual viewer's favourite series, with personalised recommendations for other TV and movies drawn from a wide range of providers.

Until now, however, shows from key providers such as Netflix have been absent from Apple's TV guide.

With Hollywood still on the fence about teaming with the iPhone maker, Apple embarked on a radical change in its television strategy two years ago. It hired two well-regarded executives, Jamie Erlicht and Zack Van Amburg, from Sony Pictures TV. Armed with a billion-dollar budget, they began to commission its own original TV shows and now has more than 30 series in the works from big-name talents including Oprah Winfrey and Steven Spielberg.

Apple just needs one of those original shows to become a hit – perhaps its new drama starring Reese Witherspoon and Jennifer Aniston, a sci-fi epic based on Isaac Asimov's *Foundation* novels, or a mystery thriller from *Sixth Sense* director M Night Shyamalan – to pull in viewers to its TV app.

As it scouted for shows, Hollywood executives say that Apple has sought out high-quality content at a time when Netflix is chasing the mass market with a huge volume of original shows. 'Apple are taking a lot of pride in being very curated, with a smaller but higher-quality offering,' said one producer who has worked with both companies.

However, some in Hollywood have struggled to adjust to the secrecy and exacting standards with which Apple typically approaches all its products.

While Apple could show an 'abundance of caution at taking each little step,' the producer said, the company is also anxious not to develop a reputation that it is difficult to work with. 'They want the best creative talent to work there, not find [Apple] so maddening that they give up.'

Analysts estimate Apple could charge $10 to $15 a month for a subscription video service that includes its original shows. The company needs new sources of income to counteract the iPhone's recent declines and meet its $50bn services revenue target by 2020.

Some on Wall Street are sceptical that a video service can make a meaningful impact. Analysts at Goldman Sachs said in a note this week that even if 20m people sign up to a $15 monthly fee, by 2020 it would generate only $3.6bn in annual revenues – barely 1 per cent of Apple's $265.6bn total sales last year – and add less than half of 1 per cent to Wall Street's consensus earnings estimates.

To bolster the income from its own shows, Apple has also spent many months negotiating deals with television networks and film studios to offer their content too.

Viacom and CBS are in advanced talks to license programmes to Apple, while AT&T-owned HBO has also held talks, said people familiar with the matter. WarnerMedia's other content is not being discussed but could be in the future, these people said.

The pricing would mirror the structure of Amazon's Channels, in which Prime customers can pay an additional monthly fee for individual subscriptions to other streaming services, such as Nickelodeon's Noggin, aimed at pre-school kids. 'You basically have an easy flow of the content back and

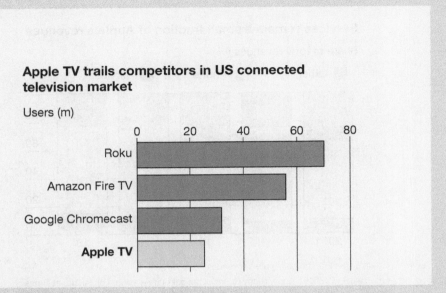

Apple TV trails competitors in the US connected television market
Source: Tim Bradshaw (2019), Apple ready to unveil big bet on television, The Financial Times.

forth between different brands,' said one person with knowledge of the plans.

Hollywood executives are tempted to team up with Apple because of its massive reach, but are also wary of the potential costs of further ceding control of their content to tech giants. Within Apple's ecosystem, they may not be privy to information about who their customers are or what they are watching. TV groups fear losing their longstanding control over pricing or user interface design, with their channel brands submerged behind a list of programmes and Apple acting as gatekeeper.

Netflix said at its own press event in Hollywood on Monday that it would not be joining Apple's new platform. 'We want to have people watch our content on our service,' Reed Hastings, Netflix chief executive, told reporters, Bloomberg reported.

For smaller companies such as Viacom and CBS, this is an easier decision. Viacom is not trying to build its own streaming service and is making good money by selling shows to tech companies, such as a reboot of MTV's *Real World* reality show for Facebook.

The decision is more complicated for AT&T and Disney, who have made mega acquisitions to build their content libraries and take on Netflix. 'There will be some content that [they] decide is probably best to keep,' said one person familiar with AT&T's strategy. 'The calculus is different now.'

Disney is gearing up to reveal plans for its own streaming service just two weeks after Apple's event. The media group has been outspoken about its plans, with chief executive Bob Iger dropping details during earnings calls through the past year.

By contrast, Apple has provided little information about the March 25 event, even to the studios whose shows will appear as part of its new video bundle. After waiting so long for the big unveiling, many in the television business still feel Apple has a lot to prove.

'They haven't illustrated a strategy,' said one TV network executive. 'It's Apple, but at the same time there are other places to go.'

This story has been updated since publication to include comments from Reed Hastings, Netflix chief executive.

 Source: from 'Apple ready to unveil big bet on television', *Financial Times*, 19/03/19 (Bradshaw, T. and Nicolaou, A.).

Discussion questions

1 What are the issues presented here?

2 How can Apple address them?

Introduction

The emphasis throughout *Marketing Strategy and Competitive Positioning* has been on developing robust marketing strategies and competitive positioning to enable organisations to survive and prosper in turbulent, competitive and frequently hostile markets. From the outset, the critical need to develop effective ways to cope with changing customer markets, and the ways in which companies go to market, has been stressed. This chapter reviews some of the major trends, and suggests ways in which new competitive strategies might be fashioned to exploit emerging opportunities. As Peter Drucker (1997) once said:

> In human affairs – political, social, economic, or business – it is pointless to try and predict the future. But it is possible – and fruitful – to identify major events that have already happened, irrevocably, and that will have predictable effects in the next decade or two. It is possible, in other words, to identify and prepare for the future that has already happened.

18.1   The changing competitive arena

Chapter 3 reviewed some of the significant changes taking place in today's markets. Here, we briefly summarise those changes.

18.1.1 Changes in the business environment

To claim that 'the only constant is change' is somewhat trite, but also true in today's business environment. A report by the Royal Society for the encouragement of Arts, Manufactures and Commerce (RSA) explored *Tomorrow's Company: The Role of Business in a Changing World*. The report identified a number of major changes taking place in business markets, and these were:

- The pace of economic change is accelerating. During the Industrial Revolution it took 60 years for productivity per person to double. China and South Korea have done the same in 10 years.
- There is an explosion in innovation and new knowledge generation that is accelerating. Every year, as much new knowledge is generated through research and development as the total sum of all human knowledge up to the 1960s.
- Competitive pressures are intensifying. Computer manufacturers, for example, need to reduce costs and improve product performance by around 30 per cent per annum to remain competitive.
- Manufacturing can now take place almost anywhere. Companies are constantly seeking more efficient manufacturing options, and that typically means sourcing from wherever makes economic sense.
- New organisational structures are emerging as firms seek to make themselves more competitive. Firms have reorganised, reduced overheads, de-layered, merged and created alliances and partnerships in attempts to create advantage in the marketplace.
- International trade is being liberalised through the World Trade Organization (WTO), but there are still massive regional trading blocs within which regional, national, ethnic and religious groupings seek to retain individual identity.
- Company actions are becoming increasingly visible, especially their effects on the environment. Customers are demanding more both economically and environmentally.

All of these factors are relevant and important for modern businesses and, to a large extent, drive many of the sleepless nights experienced by business owners and managers.

A small detail that has been deliberately omitted thus far, however, is the publication date of the report. . . 1994! It is comforting to know that the strategic issues faced by modern businesses are not totally new challenges, but it is perhaps the new and novel formats and contexts through which they present themselves that make the potentially negative impacts no smaller or less problematic.

The broad trends listed have all continued, and in many ways accelerated in the 25-plus years since the report was published. The economic shocks and aftershocks of the recent global recession, coupled with increased concerns over climate change and sustainability, have served to drive companies to look increasingly at efficiency, and how costs can be reduced.

At the macro-level, changes can be grouped into economic, technological, social, legal and political issues. Just as water supply companies cannot change weather patterns, most macro-environmental factors are outside the control of individual firms. Few companies have the ability to influence political, economic, social and technological processes significantly, but most need to try and understand and predict changes. Water companies need to predict both weather patterns (supply of water) and demand (water usage), so that they can then put strategies in place to meet that demand.

A once very well-known company that failed to grasp the significance of crucial change in its market was Encyclopaedia Britannica (EB). EB went from peak profits to severe difficulties in the 1990s, as it failed to anticipate and appreciate the impact of technology (specifically the CD-ROM) on its business. The business had been built through a highly motivated and successful salesforce selling encyclopaedias to middle-class families (often bought by parents for their children's education) at around $1,500 each.

Then along came home computers, with CD-ROM players and encyclopaedias such as Encarta at around $50. The new entrants may not have had the depth of coverage of EB, but they were in a format children enjoyed using, offered the opportunities for multi-media display (video and audio clips and animations), could be more easily updated and, perhaps most crucially, offered middle-class parents a justification for the purchase of often expensive home computer systems, which in many cases were used primarily for games purposes!

With the advent of the 'information superhighway', the World Wide Web/Internet and cloud storage, holding large amounts of data on individual PCs has, for many, become a thing of the past – posing potential problems (and of course opportunities) for marketers of CD-ROM-based encyclopaedias. In particular, the advent of open access, user-built encyclopaedias such as Wikipedia have significantly impacted on the CD-based products. Rapidly updated, and relying on users to submit, update and expand on the content, these are essentially free at the point of use (making their money out of advertising links), rapidly expanding in content and do not take up local storage space on hard disk or other media (see **www.wikipedia.org**). More recently, EB has made its encyclopaedia available online to subscribers (**http://www.britannica.com/**), recognising that a key advantage lies in its expert editorial staff. While Wikipedia relies on random contributors with minimal editorial control to check for accuracy, EB trades on its expert contributors and the constant updating available online.

Similarly, Hoover and Electrolux suffered greatly from the overnight success of the Dyson bagless vacuum cleaner – both losing a great deal of market share to the innovation. However, an often-forgotten nuance of this story is that both were offered (prior to Dyson going to market with his own product) the rights to the new and innovative bagless technology. The issue was not that Hoover and Electrolux did not see the innovation coming, indeed they knew about it in advance, but rather they both had a vested interest in preserving the status quo.

It is also easy to underestimate the practical realities of rapid accelerations in the speed and disruptive impact of change. For example, consider the unfolding impact of Internet telephony. While it took 50 years for the telephone to gain widespread diffusion, it took less than a decade for the mobile phone to do the same. It is expected that Internet telephony will reach critical mass in only a few years. Similarly, in the photography market, the disruptive and pervasive impact of digital technology demanded rapid transformation in business models by existing players such as Kodak. The failure of Kodak to understand the speed of change and rapid decline in demand for traditional cameras and film led to major financial losses, extensive lay-offs and plant closures for the company.

No company can ever hope to predict every aspect of the macro-environment in which it operates, but organisations should aim to achieve profound understanding of their core markets (the micro level). There will always be surprises and shocks as new technological breakthroughs emerge, or political discontinuities occur. However, successful companies are able to identify what is important and respond to trends and changes more effectively than competitors. Shocks are less for those companies prepared to think the 'unthinkable' and to challenge the status quo in their strategising.

Importantly, disruptive changes have the potential to make deep changes in the structure of a market, which may disadvantage existing competitors but offer important opportunities to others.

18.1.2 Changes in markets

A number of trends can be seen in modern markets that are likely to continue into the future (see Figure 18.1).

First, customers are becoming increasingly demanding of the products and services they buy. Customers demand, and expect, reliable and durable products with quick, efficient service at reasonable prices. They also expect the products and services they buy to meet their needs. Different customers have different wants and needs, and hence companies have an opportunity to select segments where their offerings most closely align with those needs, and where they can focus activities to create competitive advantage. What is more, there is little long-term stability in customer demands. A relatively strong market position may be achieved through offering superior customer value, and yet without constant improvement value is likely to be eroded by competitive actions.

A second major trend, and one that has particularly differentiated the early part of the twenty-first century, is that customers are less prepared to pay a substantial premium for products or services that do not offer demonstrably greater value – possibly exacerbated by very challenging global economic conditions. While it is undeniable that well-developed and well-managed brands can generally command higher prices than unbranded products in many markets, the differentials commanded are now much less than they were, and customers increasingly question the extra value they get for the extra expense incurred.

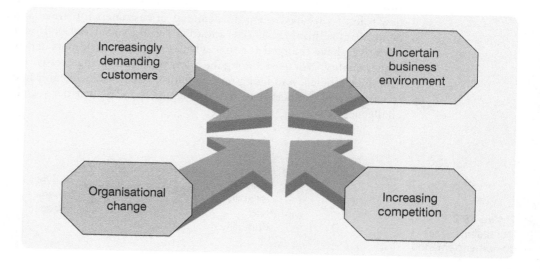

Figure 18.1
Pressures on
marketing

New strategic thinking has to consider that customers are more sophisticated and more marketing-literate than ever before. Price comparison sites, such as **Gocompare.com** and **Confused.com**, allow customers to compare not only product features, but also retail prices of the same product in different outlets. There are now also comparison websites that compare the information available on comparison websites, and comparison websites for business-to-business markets. Phone apps also contribute to this issue, allowing customers to scan barcodes while in store, and to see instantly whether the same product is cheaper elsewhere, online or locally. Other similar apps abound, and all offer customers more information regarding 'the market' for particular products or services than ever before. As a result, customers are now less likely to buy (or continue to buy) cheap products of low quality. Equally, they are unlikely to be won by image-based advertising alone. The implication is clear: differentiation needs to be based on clearly demonstrating superior value to customers (see Figure 18.2). To do this effectively, companies must be aware of the value they create in any given market and the ways in which customer perceptions of value might be affected or change. As a result, a deep knowledge of 'the market' and its customers is essential, and an ongoing ability to derive accurate and useful insights from customer and market data is of central importance.

A third major trend is in both the level and nature of competition. Competition is becoming more intense and more global in nature. Firms generally (recent geo-political 'issues' aside) face tougher international competition at home and increased opportunities abroad. Time and distance are shrinking rapidly as communications become near instantaneous. Firms are increasingly thinking global in their strategies, especially as cross-national segments are beginning to emerge for products and services, from fast foods through toys to computers and automobiles. The increasingly widespread use of the Internet for promoting and marketing products and services now means that communications are largely unaffected by national boundaries, other than those operating within strict political guidelines. Not only are markets becoming more competitive through more players emerging in them, those firms that survive and thrive in these more competitive conditions are, by their very nature, tougher competitors. Weak firms are being shaken out of markets where they do not have clear positions and attendant capabilities. The implication of heightened, more aggressive competition, both domestic and international, is that firms will need to look even more closely at their scope of operations and targeting in the future.

And yet, the executive must confront the central paradox in all this. As markets become harsher in their judgements, and in the level of competitiveness faced, companies are under growing pressure to collaborate with and partner others. Increasingly, collaboration is taking place, with suppliers, customers and even competitors. The clear demarcation lines of the past are blurring, and executives have to deal with more ambiguous new roles. As we have seen, the demands of customers for firms (and their suppliers) to demonstrate ethical credentials and to undertake social and environmentally responsible initiatives, have emerged at a time where those same customers demand lower prices and higher quality. Not least among the many problems facing executives is that of achieving economic efficiency and long-term viability, while also being able to demonstrate clearly to various stakeholders that they are helping to tackle broader social and environmental challenges.

Figure 18.2
Increasing
customer demands

Higher standards of reliability and durability ⟶ ⟵ At ever lower prices

18.1.3 Organisational change

While 'downsizing' is still very much a part of the commercial landscape and lexicon, many firms have come to terms with the notion that there is only so much 'fat' that can be removed before you damage the muscle, and too much aggressive slimming can lead to *anorexia industrialis* (the excessive desire to be leaner and fitter, leading to total emaciation and eventual death). The impact on organisational structures has been far broader, and this is manifest in two main directions: first, there is the impact within the firm; second, there is the impact on inter-firm relations.

Within firms, boundaries between functional areas are becoming more blurred. Where firms were once organised with clear-cut divisions between marketing, finance and operations, it is now recognised that 'functional silos' can result in myopic operations and sub-optimal strategies. Although it would be misleading to suggest that all firms have tackled this issue successfully, in market-leading firms, functional boundaries are softened and replaced, or augmented by process teams that view the operations of the organisation in broad/holistic terms and are not hampered by petty rivalries between functions. This is representative of a more result/outcome-based organisational logic, as opposed to a more traditional inward-looking, structurally convenient approach.

At the same time, the role of marketing in organisations is being challenged. Marketing departments can get in the way of serving customers for two main reasons. The first is territorial, and connects with the traditional approach mentioned earlier. Marketers might see dealing with customers as their 'preserve', and wish to retain the power and influence that goes with that connection. Second, however, is that the very presence of a marketing department or team may encourage others in an organisation to offload responsibility to them for customer building, retention and overall customer experience. This creates a dangerous norm or perception that 'others' (those not designated as marketing people) should not concern themselves with customers, or issues relating to customer experience, as someone else will take care of it. One view is that the days of traditional marketing are over, and the challenge is to design and implement better ways of managing the process of going to market – a process that is likely to cut across traditional functional boundaries, as well as external boundaries with partners.

The boundaries between firms and their suppliers are also increasingly blurred. Boundaries with suppliers, distributors and customers are changing as more businesses understand the need to manage the entire value chain, from raw materials through to customers, and to work more closely with partner firms to achieve added value throughout the chain.

Successful strategy initiatives may increasingly rely on finding ways around a lack of responsiveness and slow movement of traditional functional bureaucracies. Organisations that fail to address these important issue may not survive – there is a compelling need for change!

In fact, these changes require businesses to reassess their strategy in general, and marketing strategy in particular. The strategies that will be successful in the future will need to create organisations that are responsive and adaptable, rather than those that are rigid and fixed. The key will be in creating an organisational context where learning can take place, market changes can be identified and capabilities can be fashioned to ensure a strategic fit between market and the firm. In short, the development of organisations that are dynamic, flexible and adaptable will become more critical.

18.2   Fundamentals of strategy in a changing world

Figure 18.3 illustrates a number of factors that are important for organisations competing in complex and changing markets.

Figure 18.3
Fundamentals
of strategy in a
changing world

18.2.1 The learning organisation

Central to developing a sustainable competitive advantage in rapidly changing and often unpredictable circumstances is the capability to learn and adapt (Prokesch, 1997; Sinkula *et al.*, 1997; Morgan *et al.*, 1998). The competitive dynamics of markets with new entrants, substitute technologies and shifts in customer preferences can swiftly erode static advantages built on 'generic' strategies of cost leadership or product differentiation (McKee and Varadarajan, 1995). Organisational learning, however, offers the potential both to respond to and act on opportunities in the markets of the firm. Indeed, it has been suggested that the ability to learn faster than competitors may be the *only* real source of sustainable competitive advantage (Dickson, 1992), echoing the quote from Charles Darwin at the start of this chapter.

Learning is manifest in the knowledge, experience and information held in an organisation (Mahoney, 1995). It resides in both people and technical systems. Learning involves the acquisition, processing, storing and retrieval (dissemination) of knowledge. A major challenge for many organisations is to create the combination of culture and climate to maximise learning (Slater and Narver, 1995). At the human level, managerial systems need to be established to create and control knowledge. At the technical level, systems need to be established to facilitate the accumulation and storage of relevant information in a manner that makes it readily accessible to those who need to access it.

Much of an organisation's knowledge base typically resides in the heads of managers and workers. When personnel leave through retirement, 'downsizing' or recruitment by competitors, that knowledge may be lost or, more damagingly, gained by a competitor. Employment contracts of key personnel increasingly are including 'golden handcuffs', which prohibit critical managers from taking their knowledge to competitors. Organisations increasingly are also looking for ways of extracting the knowledge of key people and transmitting it to others in the organisation through expert systems and training processes, so that the knowledge is more secure and embedded in the fabric of the organisation.

Of particular importance in the context of marketing strategy is the development of knowledge and skills in how to create superior customer value. Slater and Narver (1995) show that a primary focus of market orientation is to create superior customer value and that, in turn, needs to be based on knowledge derived from customer and competitor analysis, together with knowledge gleaned from suppliers, businesses in different industries, government sources, universities, consultants and other potential sources. They conclude that learning organisations continually acquire, process and disseminate knowledge about markets, products, technologies and business processes based on experience, experimentation, information from customers, suppliers, competitors and other sources. This learning enables them to anticipate and act on opportunities in turbulent and fragmented markets.

And yet, developing learning capabilities need not be complex and sophisticated. Superior learning capabilities may be as much about market sensing and understanding as they are about utilising technology. Indeed, research at the Marketing Science Institute has found that, of ten market-based capabilities, market sensing displayed the strongest impact on business process performance (Ramaswami *et al.*, 2004).

While the central requirement for competing in the future is learning, a number of other more specific building blocks can be suggested as important ingredients in fashioning competitive strategy.

18.2.2 Heightened market orientation and focus on creating superior customer value

In increasingly crowded and competitive markets there is no substitute for being market orientated. Put simply, a market orientation focuses the firm's activities on meeting the needs and requirements of customers better than competitors. This, in turn, requires finding out what will give customers value and ensuring that the firm's energies are directed towards providing that. Identifying ways of providing superior customer value is one of the central challenges of management for the twenty-first century.

A market orientation does not imply over-sophisticated marketing operation. Indeed, it has been argued by some that marketing departments can themselves get in the way of providing superior customer value.

In the quest to provide superior customer value, no firm can stand still. What may offer better value than competitors today, might be considered standard tomorrow. Innovation – the constant improving of the offering to customers – is essential for sustained competitive advantage.

The focus of activities in firms that are truly market-orientated and intent on creating superior value for their customers is on finding solutions to those customers' problems. Rather than a focus on selling the firm's own existing products, it sets out first to identify current and future customer problems and then to find solutions to them. Solutions may involve creating new products and services, integrating the offerings of other providers (through alliances), and even in some instances accepting that customers cannot be well served and recommending alternative suppliers. After exhausting all other options, a truly market-orientated firm can gain more customer goodwill (and ultimately more long-term business) by admitting that it cannot provide exactly what the customer wants, rather than trying to persuade the customer to accept second best, or even pretending that the solution offered is appropriate.

18.2.3 Positioning built on marketing assets, capabilities and competencies

Much of the strategy literature available today refers to, and is more often than not based on, the 'resource-based theory' of the firm (see Chapter 6). This emphasises the need for strategies to be based on the resources and capabilities of the firm, rather than merely chasing customers irrespective of the ability of the firm to serve them. Resource-based theorists, however, are in danger of losing sight of the fact that resources are valuable *only when they are translated into providing something that customers want*. This is the essence of the 'resource-based marketing' approach espoused in this text.

Markets change, and so too must resources such as assets and competencies. They need to be constantly improved and developed if the firm is to thrive. An essential task for marketing management is to identify and, to an extent, predict and champion competencies and assets that are likely to be needed, as well as those that are needed today, so that they can be built or acquired in advance.

As discussed in Chapter 6, marketing resources are any properties or processes that can be exploited in the marketplace to create or sustain a competitive advantage. They range from recognised brand names, through unique use of distribution channels, to information and quality control systems. These assets are the resource endowments the business has created or acquired over time and now has available to deploy in the market. Competencies are the skills that are used to deploy the assets to best effect in the market.

These definitions are in line with early resource-based theorists such as Barney (1991), who suggest that it is management that is the most important resource because they make use of the assets and other resources available to them based on their knowledge of the market acquired through their previous learning.

As we saw in Chapter 6, Day (1994) goes on to identify three main types of competencies: outside-in, inside-out, and spanning and integrating competencies. Outside-in competencies are those skills and abilities that enable a business to understand its customers and create closer linkages with them. Inside-out competencies are the internal capabilities of the firm and its employees that can be deployed in the marketplace to provide better products and services to customers. Spanning and integrating competencies bring together the inside-out and the outside-in to ensure delivery of appropriate products and services to customers.

More recently, RBV theorists have argued the need for dynamic capabilities (Menguc and Auh, 2006; Helfat *et al.*, 2007). Dynamic capabilities represent 'the capacity of an organisation to purposefully create, extend, or modify its resource base' (Helfat *et al.*, 2007, p. 4). Menguac and Auh (2006) show how dynamic capabilities can be built through capitalising on market orientation and innovativeness. They demonstrate empirically how the effect of market orientation on firm performance is enhanced when firms demonstrate a high degree of innovation.

Not all assets and capabilities may be vested in the focal firm. Increasingly, companies are creating alliances and networks with others that enable them to leverage further assets and competencies of partner firms (see Chapter 15). Alliances can offer four main sets of assets and competencies – that is, access to new markets, access to managerial competence, access to technological competence and economic benefits.

There are, however, problems in realising the advantages offered by alliances and networks of collaborating firms, and many alliances that appear to be an excellent and complementary idea at the time, fail. Understanding of the dynamics of alliances and the critical executive skills required by these new organisations is sadly limited (see Chapter 15).

Taken together, marketing assets and competencies/capabilities are the basis on which competitive positioning is built. Ideally, firms should seek to build a strategic position on the basis of assets and competencies that are superior to those of competitors, and difficult to duplicate. They should also seek to create or acquire assets and competencies that can be exploited in many other situations (such as extending brand name(s) into new markets, exploiting technology in new industries and allowing networks to be used differently). In future, a critical issue is likely to be how the different assets and competencies might be combined to create new products and services (Hamel and Prahalad, 1994).

18.2.4 Establishing closer relationships with key customers

In Chapter 14 we discussed the ways in which firms can build closer relationships with their customers. Fundamental issues include which customers to build those relationships with and how to build them.

Relationship marketing (Payne and Frow, 2005) has been one of the most significant ideas in marketing of recent years. While it has been recognised as important in some markets for some time and under different labels (such as the personal account managers in financial services), it is now generally agreed that customer retention through superior service and relationship building is widely applicable and relevant.

In consumer markets, relationships can be built initially through branding and reputation creation. In the past, relationships in business markets have been stereotyped as between individuals – the salesperson and purchasing officer. However, in modern business-to-business markets the pressure is for team-based selling and relationship building across the whole spectrum of internal departments. The challenge is to become the 'outsource of preference' by understanding customer's business and adding value in excess of cost (Chally, 2006). Similarly, Simon (1996) stresses that the relationships that endure in business markets are those based on sound economic and business grounds, rather than ephemeral personal/social bases. Relationships and reputations can be far harder for competitors to copy than possibly transitory product features, special offers or deals.

Not all customers, however, place great value on ever-closer relationships with their suppliers. Similarly, the costs of creating closer relationships with some customers (in terms of time, effort and financial resource) may well outweigh the long-term commercial benefits. What will become increasingly important will be for firms to decide the optimum intensity of relationship with each customer or customer group, and then find an effective and efficient means of establishing that level. It is likely that any firm will be operating in a number of different marketing modes depending on the customers served. For some key accounts, a heavy emphasis on one-to-one close relationship building to create 'partners' might be applicable, while at the same time other groups are marketed less intensively so as to create 'advocates' rather than partners. For yet other customers of the same firm, a mass marketing approach might be applicable to secure their business in the first place. *Multimode marketing*, the adoption of different marketing approaches for different customers or customer groups, is likely to take the place of more uniform marketing to all customers.

18.2.5 Rethinking the role of marketing in the organisation

The ideas covered so far lead to the inevitable conclusion that the role and function of marketing within the organisation (or within the 'virtual network') needs to be redefined and reasserted.

Fundamental to this is being able to escape from the notion that marketing is essentially a business function, or a department on an organisational chart. Increasingly, marketing is seen as a process within the value chain, and a process responsible for ensuring the creation of value for customers in both the short and long term. Structures need to be created that facilitate rapid response and flexibility rather than hinder it. Indeed, it is interesting to note that many successful companies do not have specifically named 'marketing departments', yet few would dispute that they are close to their customers, and attentive and reactive to their needs.

Brown (1995) notes:

> There are now two types of corporation: those with a marketing department and those with a marketing soul. Even a cursory glance at the latest Fortune 500 shows that the latter are the top performing companies, while the former, steeped in the business traditions of the past, are fast disappearing.

Simon (1996) also notes that many of the firms in his sample of 'hidden champions' do not have marketing departments. However, they share two main traits. First, they are extremely close to their customers and ensure that all employees recognise their role in serving them. Second, they focus on solving customers' problems through innovation, in order to improve their market offerings and to continuously improve their customer value. These two traits are the essence of a market orientation, but can be achieved without the trappings of a marketing department.

It is important, in defining the role of marketing for the future, to recognise that marketing operates at two main levels: strategic and operational. At the operational level, brand managers and marketing managers deal with day-to-day marketing tasks such as liaison with market research companies, advertising and public relations agencies and so on. In fast-moving consumer goods (FMCG) companies, trade and consumer promotions, special deals, competitions and so on can occupy a lot of time.

At the strategic level, however, marketing is more concerned with decisions as to which markets to operate in, and how to compete successfully in them. At this level, marketing is not a functional activity, but requires input of alternative perspectives and skills from across the organisation. As noted earlier, the challenge is to manage the process of going to market to build superior customer value, through a complex mix of resources, capabilities and relationships that make up the overall offering.

Marketing needs to become, and remain, flexible and responsive to change. That entails distinguishing the philosophy from the trappings. At a strategic level, everyone in the organisation should place customers at the forefront of their minds.

In the highly competitive markets envisaged for the foreseeable future, the ability to assimilate and act on knowledge, to create strategies based on assets and competencies, to establish close, deep relationships with chosen market segments and, finally, the ability to redefine the scope and role of marketing within the organisation will be the bases for creating competitive advantage.

18.3 Competitive positioning strategies

As has been argued already, competitive positioning is about making choices that ensure a fit between chosen market targets and the competencies and assets the firm can deploy to serve those chosen targets more effectively than competitors. While there are, in reality, an infinite number of different ways in which firms might position themselves in their markets, these can be summarised on the basis of the emphasis they give to six main dimensions of differentiation.

Figure 18.4 shows these six dimensions. Positioning could be based on *price*, technical *quality* (or more correctly, grade), *service*, *innovation*, benefit *differentiation* or *customisation*.

While individual firms may choose to position on more than one dimension simultaneously, they may find that these are contradictory. For example, offering a higher grade of product is generally incongruent with keeping costs (and hence prices) as low as possible. Indeed, charging low prices for a high-grade product may create confusion in the minds of customers. The key to creating sustainable positions is to ensure that they are built on the marketing assets and competencies of the firm.

Figure 18.4
Basic positioning
options

18.3.1 Price positioning

Costs must be kept in check. By this we mean at least as low (or preferably lower) than competitors', in order for a low-price position to be achievable or sustainable. If there is no cost advantage, price wars may put the instigator at a financial disadvantage and the whole positioning strategy may not be sustainable. Positioning as the low-price supplier requires strong inside-out and spanning capabilities. Effective cost-control systems (through activity-based costing) are needed, not only within the firm's own operations but also within suppliers' operations. Procurement of raw materials and other factor inputs is organised around keeping costs to a minimum. Distribution logistics are similarly managed for minimum cost (see Figure 18.5).

While the low-price position is a viable option for some firms, there is a constant need to work at keeping costs down, especially when new competitors enter the market with new operating methods or unique assets that can be used to undercut the costs of incumbents.

For a price positioning strategy to be successful in the marketplace, the existence of a viable, price-sensitive customer segment is also required. In most markets there are customers who will buy primarily on price. Also, in most markets, price-sensitive customers have been very much present of late, given the global economic conditions. Price positioning can be successful where there is a clearly defined, price-sensitive sector of the market and the firm has a cost advantage in serving that market.

Nonetheless, reliance purely on low-price-based positioning also carries risks. Those adopting this approach must be constantly mindful of opportunities to reduce costs and very defensive of any (no matter how small) increase. Ryanair (the low-cost Irish airline) is a good example of an organisation that ruthlessly pursues cost reduction and cost control. It is very clear regarding the value it creates for the customers it serves, and also the value it needs to create. Additionally, it has aligned its systems and processes throughout the value delivery chain to deliver just that.

Some firms position at the other end of the price spectrum. They deliberately price their products and services more highly than competitors to create exclusivity for their offerings. High-price positions are usually accompanied by higher-quality, branded offerings requiring strong reputations and clearly superior images (such as that of Harrods department store in Knightsbridge). The competencies required for high-price (premium) positions to be effective are focused on the ability to create a superior or exclusive image that customers are willing to pay a premium to be associated with. Brand assets, in particular, need to be built through the use of creative promotional campaigns and associations.

18.3.2 Quality positioning

Positioning as a high technical-quality (grade) supplier also requires effective internal control systems, especially quality assessment and quality assurance. Beyond control, however, it

Figure 18.5
Low-price
positioning

also requires technical competence, particularly in engineering and manufacturing, where physical products are produced. Most significantly, it requires a clear view of what constitutes 'quality' in the eyes of the customer, which entails the outside-in capabilities of market sensing and customer bonding (see Figure 18.6).

Also important in delivering high-quality products and services is supply chain management – ensuring that the inputs are of the required quality, not simply the cheapest available. While its business model is typified by high-profile peaks and troughs in performance, Marks & Spencer has a deserved reputation for building long-term, demanding relationships with its suppliers to ensure that the products it puts its labels on are of the required quality. M&S now sources more widely, but still keeps a close eye on the quality of the inputs used in its products.

There are four 'Betty's Tea Rooms' in Yorkshire and one 'Taylor's'. Together they sell 2 million cups of tea each year. They don't advertise, but people flock in their thousands and are prepared to queue for seats. The atmosphere is elegant and sophisticated, and waiters and waitresses are formally dressed in the style of Victorian servants. The tea is perfect and the cakes are delicious (I assure you!). The pastries range from exotic Amadeus Torte to local Yorkshire curd tarts. The company was started in Harrogate by a Swiss confectioner, Frederick Belmont, in 1919. The company's bakers and confectioners still train in Lucerne. The company has built on its brand asset by opening related gift shops on the premises, selling confectionery suited to the tourists who visit. It also sells its products by mail order. More recently, it has marketed Yorkshire Tea, which has become a major brand in the beverages market (Kotler *et al.*, 1996).

Often critical to a quality positioning are the marketing assets of brand image and reputation, as demonstrated in the previous example. Image and reputation can take years to create and, once established, need to be nurtured and defended vigorously when necessary.

To customers, quality is manifest through better reliability, durability and aesthetic appearance. For quality positions to be viable, customers must be prepared to pay for superior quality as there are usually, although not always, higher costs associated with offering a higher-quality product. In the automotive industry, German manufacturers such as Mercedes-Benz, BMW and Audi have successfully positioned themselves at the high-quality end of the spectrum through superior design, technical engineering skills (as Audi famously stated 'Vorsprung durch Technik' – leading through technology) and attention to quality control throughout the manufacturing process.

We should bear in mind in all this, however, that quality and value are judged by customers, not by engineers in the factory or advertising executives in the marketing department.

18.3.3 Innovation positioning

Where markets are changing rapidly, especially as a result of technological developments, there may be opportunities to position on the basis of innovativeness, or speed to market

Figure 18.6
Premium-quality
positioning

Figure 18.7
Innovation
positioning

(see Figure 18.7). Hamel and Prahalad (1991) suggest that firms should encourage 'fast failure' – that is, encourage the test launch of new products, in the recognition that many may fail but that some will succeed. Fast failure, they argue, is preferable to smothering new ideas at birth or delaying their launch through over-elaborate screening systems.

Similarly, the successes of Samsung Electronics in the 2000s, and more recently Huawei, are based on organisational cultures that have research and development and innovation at their cores. In both examples, market leadership was (and has been) pursued through innovation, technology and design. The key competencies required include excellent new product development skills, together with technical and creative abilities. These are combinations of inside-out and spanning competencies. Once new product ideas are developed, it is important to test them out on customers to avoid the launch of highly innovative but essentially unwanted products. There are many high-profile examples of products that have failed throughout history: the Ford Edsel (1950s), Sony Betamax (1970s), 'New' Coke (1980s), Microsoft Bob (1990s), Google Glass (although still in development, the original Google Glass launch has been viewed as a failure by many) and Burger King 'Satisfries' (2000s), along with many, many others!

An academic study of first-to-market firms concluded that for many firms a more successful strategy is to be a fast follower. Under this approach, firms learn from the mistakes of the pioneers and capitalise on the growth phase of the market without incurring the costs of establishing the market (Tellis and Golder, 1996). Moore (1991, 2014), in his study of innovation in high-technology markets, concludes that the critical aspect of new product success is bridging the 'chasm' between innovators (those who will be attracted to an innovation because of its innovative nature) and the early majority who represent the beginnings of the mass market. It is this chasm that, in Moore's opinion, accounts for the failure of many new products.

James Dyson is an inventor who has successfully positioned his firm as the provider of innovative solutions to everyday problems. In January 1997, he won the European Design Award for his innovative vacuum cleaner. Dyson started inventing at the age of 28 when he recognised a design fault in conventional wheelbarrows. When full, the barrow, with a single, thin wheel at the front, was prone to tipping over. He replaced the wheel with a large red ball, which solved the problem. When he set up in business the 'ball barrow' was an immediate success, selling over 60,000 per year. Following that success, he designed a new garden roller that was light and manoeuvrable when not in use, but heavy enough to roll lawns flat. His innovation was to use a hollow plastic roller that could be filled with water when in use but drained when not in use. Bagless vacuum cleaners followed, and Dyson has since launched hand dryers, hair dryers and an award-winning range of room fans and heaters that have won numerous design and innovation awards. The success of the £3.5 billion-plus turnover company has been based on innovation, being first to market with revolutionary designs of everyday products and offering superior value to customers.

18.3.4 Service positioning

Positioning on the basis of offering superior service, or rather service clearly tailored to the needs of the target market, is increasingly being used. Variations in the nature and level of service offered, coupled with differences in requirements across customer groups, means that service positioning can be viable and attractive for more than one company in a market. Critical to providing superior service are: market sensing skills that can identify what level/ type of service is required; customer bonding skills that build closer relationships with key customers; service systems that assist the service providers in delivering service to customers; and monitoring skills that can regularly assess the customer satisfaction with the level and type of service provided. However, most critical to providing superior service are the people or staff who actually provide the service. Selection, training, motivation and reward of service staff are areas that need high priority in firms seeking to establish a competitive edge through service provision (see Figure 18.8).

Firms seeking to create a service edge to position themselves as offering superior service to that of competitors need first to understand how customers judge service, what dimensions are important to them and how these are manifest. They then need to put in place strategies and systems to ensure their staff can deliver superior service (see Chapter 13).

Otis (best known for making elevators) recognised the importance of providing excellent service in the elevator business. Customers preferred to deal directly with Otis rather than go through an intermediary, and hence the company set up the OTISLINE through which customers are able to contact a service centre 24 hours a day. The service has been used to market the firm's offerings and to give customers confidence in them. It also formed the basis for the company's making further improvements in information systems, including REM (remote elevator monitoring) to identify problems before lifts break down. The system improved response times through better call management and improved diagnostic capabilities, and strengthened the service team by providing them with better communications. The result has been significant increases in customer satisfaction levels (Armistead and Clark, 1992).

18.3.5 Differentiated benefits positioning

Differentiated benefits positioning rests on clearly identifying alternative benefit segments within markets and then focusing on providing what they want (see Figure 18.9). As discussed in Chapter 9, segmenting markets on the basis of the benefits customers seek can help identify new market opportunities and suggest ways in which marketing efforts can be more effectively targeted.

Figure 18.8
Superior-service
positioning

Figure 18.9
Differentiated
positioning

Positioning on this basis is dependent on having well-developed outside-in competencies to identify the benefits customers seek, and to segment the market creatively into meaningful but commercially viable sectors. It can also require effective new product/service development skills to ensure that the benefits sought are actually delivered to customers through incorporating relevant features.

In the US mouthwash market, for example, P&G successfully challenged the incumbent market leader Listerine with a better-tasting alternative (branded 'Scope'), taking significant market share away very quickly. Surprisingly, mouthwashes were once advertised as being good because they tasted 'bad', connecting with a belief that mouthwashes had to taste bad in order to work effectively. Indeed, in an early television commercial for Listerine, the closing phrase was: 'Listerine. The taste you hate twice a day.' Clearly, a better-tasting alternative that promised the same benefits as the bad-tasting incumbent was particularly attractive to consumers. Fairy Liquid is a washing-up liquid that has been consistently positioned on the basis of the twin benefits it provides to users – that is, clean dishes *and* smooth hands for the washer-up. The product was test launched in Birmingham, UK, in 1959 when the market was in its infancy, with only 17 per cent of consumers using washing-up liquid – the remainder relying on soap powders or household soap to wash their dishes. The national launch in 1960 involved a massive door-to-door programme that delivered 15 million sample bottles to 85 per cent of houses in the UK. The launch platform stressed that the product was strong enough to remove dirt and grease from plates and dishes, but was mild on hands.

By 1980, 1 billion bottles of Fairy Liquid had been sold. Product improvements in 1982 enabled the advertisements to demonstrate a 20 per cent improvement in the volume of dishes that could be washed with one bottle (a 20 per cent 'mileage' improvement), and the brand had reached 27 per cent market share. Further continuous product improvement followed with the launch of a lemon-scented variant in 1984–85 (share climbed to 32 per cent) and further increased mileage in 1988 (by 15 per cent) and 1992 (by a further 50 per cent, signalled by a change of name to Fairy Excel), taking market share above 50 per cent for the first time. In 1993 Fairy Excel Plus replaced Fairy Excel, offering yet another 50 per cent mileage improvement but still retaining the mildness effect on hands. One manager was quoted as saying that 'the heritage of the brand is so linked with mildness it [putting anything less mild on the market] would be regarded as treachery by the consumer'.

Yamaha was world market leader in fine upright and grand pianos. Globally, the company held 40 per cent of the market, but the market was in decline at around 10 per cent per annum. Market research showed that many pianos were seldom played, gathered dust and were out of tune. Using its competencies in digital music technology (the firm had pioneered electronic keyboards), the firm set about offering additional benefits in the pianos it sold. It developed the 'disklavier', which was a traditional piano (upright and grand) that could be played normally but also had an additional feature. Attached to the piano was an electronic device that enabled the owner to play pre-recorded music on their own piano. The device accepted a 3.5-inch disk, similar to a computer floppy disk, which contained the recorded music and played it on the piano. On its launch in Japan the product was an immediate success, rising to 20 per cent market share within three years. The firm also worked on the possibilities of retro-fitting existing pianos with the device in order to expand the market potential even further.

Interestingly, the concept was not completely new. In 1930s America, 'pianolas' (pianos that could play rolls of punched paper when pedalled) were very popular!

Positioning based on benefits sought by customers is conventionally associated with consumer markets. In fact, the same is true of the strategies of successful firms in business-to-business markets. In both cases, benefit segments provide a powerful basis on which to build positioning directly related to the requirements of customers.

18.3.6 Customised positioning (one-to-one marketing)

Perhaps the ultimate in targeting and positioning is the attempt to offer products that are customised to the requirements of individual customers. While this has been practised in many business-to-business markets for some time, it is now available to others, and consumer markets in particular (see Figure 18.10).

German car manufacturer Porsche produces around 150 cars a day from its assembly line in Stuttgart. Each car is customised, so that customers have more than 1 billion combinations to choose from. They can choose interiors, seats, dashboards, engine types, body styles and colours. In fact, Porsche will paint the car any colour the customer desires (for a price!), as will other leading quality manufacturers.

The important skills for customised positioning are a combination of outside-in competencies to enable the firm to identify what the customer wants, and to establish relationships with customers, with inside-out competencies of flexible production capability. Recent advances in manufacturing make it increasingly possible for firms to enjoy the cost and efficiency advantages of mass production while at the same time tailoring their offerings to individual customer requirements.

The clearest examples of customised positioning, however, are generally found in both consumer and business services, where the service provider can tailor the offer to the specific requirements of individual customers. Financial consultants offer tailored analysis of investment needs, accountants offer tailored accounts packages, hairdressers offer tailored haircuts and architects can offer individual house designs.

Customised positioning rests on being able to understand individual rather than market segment needs, and also being flexible enough to meet those needs, at a price the customer

Figure 18.10
Customised
positioning

is willing to pay. While technology, such as the use of the Internet, can play an important role in enabling economically viable customisation, the process has to be market-led rather than technology-driven. Increasingly, companies are looking to create synergies through the use of new technology to respond to customer demands.

Levi Strauss now offers customised blue jeans – tailored to the tight fit required by customers – by taking measurements in the shop that are sent electronically to the factory to produce a unique garment (and will store the data for repeat purchases). The same type of customer offer is made by some shoe suppliers in the USA, who respond to customer preferences for unique products by using technology to achieve this at a reasonable cost.

Amazon has millions of customers but delivers the experience of one-to-one marketing in a highly effective manner. The firm is very successful at tracking what customers do (what they look at and purchase) and, using that information, sending emails to them with information about new products similar or related to those they have purchased or viewed. This customised information service has helped Amazon achieve good levels of customer retention and repeat purchase.

These alternative approaches to positioning are not necessarily exclusive of each other. They constitute, however, the basic alternatives open to firms. The creative application of those alternatives offers an almost infinite variety of ways that firms might build competitive advantage in modern markets. The task of marketing is to select among the alternatives, basing the choice firmly on the competencies and capabilities of the firm.

Summary

Business is changing and so is marketing. Successful strategies for the future will be based on creating a fit between the requirements of the chosen market and the resources of the firm, and its ability to meet those requirements.

Marketing increasingly will be seen more as an approach or methodology for achieving this type of fit, rather than a functional specialisation or department. For organisations to focus on the process of going to market rather than conventional marketing structures, offers a chance to enhance the role of customers as a driving force for the company, and to finally achieve operationally the goal that 'marketing's future is not as a function of business, but as the function of business' (Haeckel, 1997). The new processes of marketing will require us to learn new ways of doing business in unfamiliar organisational forms.

Neither resources nor markets are fixed. We may by now be well used to the notion of market requirements changing over time and the need to monitor those changes. We are perhaps less aware of the need, explicitly and constantly, to examine and develop our resources and capabilities over time. New capabilities must be developed or otherwise acquired (through alliances, mergers or acquisitions) to enable organisations to compete effectively in the future. At the same time, firms should examine how they can use their current set of capabilities and assets in different markets, or combine existing capabilities in innovative ways to create new opportunities (as Yamaha did with its digital pianos).

Fundamentally, we can expect firms to be more selective and narrower in their choice of markets and customers to serve, but to concentrate efforts on creating deeper relationships with those chosen, to ensure long-term value creation through long-term relationships. There is, of course, an infinite number of ways in which a firm can create relationships with its customers.

Marketers must also dare to think differently about their role and the strategies they pursue. Ideas that have been in the collective consciousness since the advent of formalised theories of marketing have to now be challenged. Indeed, some of the notions and frameworks expressed in this text, while still very much relevant, may well be less so in the very near future. Sheth and Sisodia (2006) incorporate these ideas when they state:

Forget all the old ideas about marketing warfare, customer conquest and capture, or aggressive marketing tactics of any kind. Indeed aggressive sentiments and mindsets have no place in marketing. Marketing must be about pursuing desirable ends (delighted customers, undamaged societal interests, fair returns to shareholders) through desirable means.

They then expand on this and list a number of virtues that they believe must be embedded in marketing practice, such as truth, integrity, authenticity, trust, respect, good manners and humility. Many of these words are not often associated with marketing or marketing strategy and, while this may be unfair, it is at the heart of the issue. The challenge for marketing and marketing practice in the coming decade of the twenty-first century, is to achieve positive outcomes (that can be justified and demonstrated), not only for the organisations deploying the resource, but also for all associated stakeholders such as employees, customers, suppliers, society and government. In this way, issues of marketing strategy and competitive positioning can continue to be central to successful strategic decision making in modern, forward-thinking businesses.

Case study

Twitter builds on its character

By David Gelles in San Francisco

Twitter has taken its fair share of criticism in the four years since its launch. Users complained it was unreliable; critics called tweets frivolous; analysts warned the micro-blogging website was not serious about making money.

In the past week, however, the San Francisco-based company has done much to answer its would-be detractors. It unveiled its revenue-making model, released impressive statistics about its size, and introduced a bevy of new products.

At Chirp, Twitter's first ever conference for software developers, which began in San Francisco on Tuesday, users and analysts said Twitter was growing up before their eyes, transforming from a 'start-up' to a 'big company'.

But at the same time, Twitter, which allows users to post short messages known as 'tweets', has provoked serious new questions about its direction, and raised tensions with both users and third-party developers who have been so crucial to its success.

Most in the Twitter community believe the service, which now boasts 106m registered users, is still in the early days of its growth. 'I think there's going to be more opportunity now than ever,' said Bijan Sabet, a partner at Spark Capital and an early investor. 'Getting to half a billion users, that's the next step.'

Twitter's most significant move this week was the unveiling of its revenue model – an advertising system similar to Google's highly profitable AdWords. Twitter will allow businesses to bid on keywords

New direction: co-founder Evan Williams outlines his vision at Twitter's first conference for software developers
Source: Chip Chipman/Bloomberg/Contributor/Getty Images.

and have their 'promoted tweets' appear at the top of search results.

This is relatively unobtrusive as online advertising goes. Yet among Twitter's notoriously fickle community, some users have been rankled by the idea of the site bearing ads at all.

The business plan will also potentially hurt at least one developer. Just a day before Twitter unveiled promoted tweets, Bill Gross, a seasoned entrepreneur credited with inventing search advertising, disclosed his TweetUp service, which was relying on a near identical model.

This highlights a line in the sand that Twitter has drawn with its developers, who have built more than 100,000 applications that operate on the site and interact with tweets.

Twitter, said co-founder Evan Williams, will focus on the 'core experiences' – keeping the platform up and running and implementing an advertising system. Developers should put their efforts into building specified products for niche audiences, such as applications that serve business customers, or harness the film and music communities.

But even this line between the host and the apps is blurring. One of the most fruitful areas of third-party development has been in apps that allow users to manage their tweets on a desktop or mobile phone. Indeed, 75 per cent of Twitter's traffic happens not on **Twitter.com**, but through the likes of the Tweetdeck, Seesmic and Echofon apps.

Last week, however, Twitter shocked the developer community, saying it had purchased the maker of Tweetie, the most popular iPhone client, and had developed its own app for BlackBerry smartphones.

This prompted an outcry from developers, who complained Twitter had pivoted from benevolent platform to aggressive competitor.

'The strength of the reaction is a testament to the naiveté of the community,' said Mike Hirschland, a partner at Polaris Venture Partners who has invested in Twitter developers. 'At some point the platform is going to get deadly serious about making money, and you better get out of the way.'

That time seems to have arrived. Mr Williams said Twitter was now focused on making money from its 55m daily tweets. 'It's a high priority for us.'

To developers nervous that the platform for which they are building software might compete with them, Mr Williams would give no reassurances. 'That's part of the game,' he said.

 Source: from 'Twitter builds on its character', *Financial Times*, 15/04/10 (Gelles, D.).

Discussion questions

1. Why did developers react so negatively to Twitter's purchase of the maker of Tweetie? What changes does this vignette illustrate?
2. Why did Twitter change its business model?
3. What fundamentals of strategy could Twitter adopt to become more sustainable?

REFERENCES

Aaker, D.A. (1991), *Managing Brand Equity*, New York: The Free Press.

Aaker, D.A. and Moorman, C. (2017), *Strategic Market Management*, 11th edn, New York: Wiley.

Abell, D.F. (1978), 'Strategic windows', *Journal of Marketing*, 42(3), 21–6.

Aberdeen Group (2011), Sales and marketing alignment: The new power couple (December).

Achrol, R. (1991), 'Evolution of the marketing organisation: New forms for turbulent environments', *Journal of Marketing*, 55(October), 77–93.

Achrol, R. (1997), 'Changes in the theory of interorganisational relations in marketing: Toward a network paradigm', *Journal of the Academy of Marketing Science*, 25(1), 56–71.

Ackerman, R.W. (1975), *The Social Challenge in Business*, Cambridge, MA: Harvard University Press.

Act-On Software, Sales and Marketing Alignment (2015), June 15, www.act-on.com/whitepaper/introduction-to-sales-and-marketing-alignment/, accessed 2019.

Adam Smith Institute (2008), *Unfair Trade*, London: Adam Smith Institute.

Adamson, B., Dixon, M. and Toman, N. (2013), 'Dismantling the sales machine', *Harvard Business Review*, November, 102–9.

Agrawal, M., Kumaresh, T.V. and Mercer, G.A. (2001), 'The false promise of mass customisation', *McKinsey Quarterly*, 1, 31–43.

Ahuja, G. and Katila, R. (2004), 'Where do resources come from? The role of idiosyncratic situations', *Strategic Management Journal*, 25, 887–907.

Airline Industry Information (2007), 'Boeing and Lockheed Martin form strategic alliance', *Airline Industry Information*, January 23, 1.

Al Bawaba (2006), 'Dell/EMC extend multi-billion dollar strategic alliance until 2011', *Al Bawaba*, September 18, 1.

Alexander, L.D. (1991), 'Strategy implementation: Nature of the problem', in D. Hussey (ed.), *International Review of Strategic Management*, 2(1), 74.

Allen, V. (2008), '1,000-mile chicken', *Daily Mail*, 19 March, p. 35.

Allison, K. and Waters, R. (2007), 'Hewlett-Packard comes back fighting', *Financial Times*, 30 April, p. 27.

Allison, K. (2008), 'Apple unveils iPhone grand plan', *Financial Times*, 10 March, p. 23.

Almeida, P., Dokko, G. and Rosenkopf, L. (2003), 'Startup size and the mechanisms of external learning: Increasing opportunity and decreasing ability?', *Research Policy*, 32(2), 301–15.

Almquist, E., Senior, J. and Bloch, N. (2016), 'The Elements of Value', *Harvard Business Review*, September, 46–53.

Alsem, K.J., Leeflang, P.S.H. and Reuyl, J.C. (1989), 'The forecasting accuracy of market share models using predicted values of competitive marketing behavior', *International Journal of Research in Marketing*, 6(3), 183–98.

AMA (2008), 'American Marketing Association releases new definition of marketing', Ad Age, https://adage.com/article/btob/american-marketing-association-releases-definition-marketing/270184, accessed 2019.

Ambler, T. (2000), *Marketing and the Bottom Line: The New Metrics of Corporate Wealth*, Hemel Hempstead: Prentice Hall.

Ambler, T. (2003), *Marketing and the Bottom Line*, 2nd edn, Hemel Hempstead: Prentice Hall.

Ambrosini, V. and Bowman, C. (2009), 'What are dynamic capacities and are they a useful construct in strategic management?', *International Journal of Management Reviews*, 11(1), 29–49.

Ambrosini, V., Bowman, C. and Collier, N. (2009), 'Dynamic capabilities: An exploration of how firms renew their resource base', *British Journal of Management*, 20, S9–S24.

American Salesman (2002), 'Shift to value-added selling is biggest challenge in sales', *American Salesman*, November, 13.

Amit, R. and Shoemaker, P.J.H. (1993), 'Strategic assets and organisational rent', *Strategic Management Journal*, 14, 33–46.

Ancona, D. and Bresman, H. (2007), *X-Teams: How to Build Teams That Lead, Innovate and Succeed*, Boston, MA: Harvard Business School Press.

Anderlini, J., Jack, A. and Parker, G. (2014), 'China hits at GSK's "systemic" bribery"', *Financial Times*, 2014, May 15, p. 1.

Anderson, E.W. and Sullivan, M.W. (1993), 'The antecedents and consequences of customer satisfaction for firms', *Marketing Science*, 12(2), 125–43.

Anderson, E. and Trinkle, B. (2005), *Outsourcing the Sales Function: The Real Costs of Field Sales*, Mason, OH: Thomson.

Anderson, J.C., Narus, J.A. and van Rossum, W. (2006), 'Customer value propositions in business markets', *Harvard Business Review*, March, 91–9.

Anderson, L. (2008), 'Finding a true heart in business', *Financial Times*, April 21, p. 17.

Andrew, J. and Waldmeir, P. (2013), 'Bribery fears infect drug dealings in China', *Financial Times*, September 24, 19.

Ansoff, H.I. (1984), *Implanting Strategic Management*, London: Prentice Hall.

Anthony, S.C., Eyring, M. and Gibson, L. (2006), 'Mapping your innovation strategy', *Harvard Business Review*, 84(5), 104–13.

Armistead, C.G. and Clark, G. (1992), *Customer Service and Support*, London: Pitman Publishing.

Arndt, M. and Einhorn, B. (2010), 'The 50 most innovative companies', *Bloomberg BusinessWeek*, April 25, pp. 34–40.

Arnold, M. (2014), 'Banks failing to shed aggressive sales culture, report warns', *Financial Times*, November 26, p. 2.

Arrington, M. (2007), 'AT&T piles on Yahoo', www.TechCrunch.com, March 9.

Arruñada, B. and Vázquez, X.H. (2006), 'When your contract manufacturer becomes your competitor', *Harvard Business Review*, September, 135–44.

Arthur D. Little (2005), *The Innovation High Ground*, New York: Arthur D. Little.

Ashton, J. (2005), 'Marconi up for grabs', *Daily Mail*, May 4, p. 64.

Ashton, J. and Watts, R. (2008), 'Good payers face being axed by credit card firms', *Sunday Times*, February 3, p. S1, 7.

Aufreiter, N.A., Lawler, T.L. and Lun, C.D. (2000), 'A new way to market', *The McKinsey Quarterly*, (2), 52–61.

Authers, J. (2015), 'Vice versus nice', *Financial Times*, June 26, p. 11.

Backaler, J. and Shankman, P. (2018), *Digital Influence: Unleash the Power of Influencer Marketing to Accelerate Your Global Business*, Basingstoke, UK: Palgrave Macmillan.

Baghai, M., Coley, S. and White, D. (2000), *The Alchemy of Growth: Practical Insights for Building the Enduring Enterprise*, New York: Perseus Books.

Baker, M.J. (1992), *Marketing Strategy and Management*, 2nd edn, London: Macmillan.

Baldauf, A., Cravens, D.W. and Piercy, N. (2001a), 'Examining business strategy, sales management, and salesperson antecedents of sales organisation effectiveness', *Journal of Personal Selling & Sales Management*, 21, 123–34.

Baldauf, A., Piercy, N. and Cravens, D.W. (2001b), 'Examining the consequences of sales management control strategies in European field sales organisations', *International Marketing Review*, 18, 474–508.

Baldauf, A., Cravens, D.W. and Piercy, N. (2005), 'Sales management control research – synthesis and an agenda for future research', *Journal of Personal Selling & Sales Management*, 25(1), 7–26.

Ball, J. (2009), 'The upside to a plastic bag', *Wall Street Journal*, June 16, p. 12.

Bamford, J., Ernst, D. and Fubini, D.G. (2004), 'Launching a world-class joint venture', *Harvard Business Review*, February, 90–100.

Barnes, S.J., Bauer, H.H., Neumann, M.M. and Huber, F. (2007), 'Segmenting cyberspace: A customer typology for the internet', *European Journal of Marketing*, 41(1/2), 71–93.

Barney, J.B. (1991), 'Firm resources and sustained competitive advantage', *Journal of Management*, 17(1), 99–120.

Barney, J.B. (1997), 'Looking inside for competitive advantage', in A. Campbell and K.S. Luchs (eds), *Core Competency-Based Strategy*, London: International Thomson Business Press.

Barnett, M. (2018), 'How brands are finally realising the full potential of personalisation', *Marketing Week*, November, 13.

Barone, M.J., Miyazaki, A.D. and Taylor, K.A. (2000), 'The influence of case-related marketing on consumer choice: Does one good turn deserve another?', *Journal of the Academy of Marketing Science*, 28(2), 248–62.

Barwise, P. and Meehan, S. (2004), *Simply Better: Winning and Keeping Customers by Delivering What Matters Most*, Boston MA: Harvard Business School Press.

Bass, F.M. (1969), 'A new product forecasting model for consumer durables', *Marketing Science*, 15(2), 215–27.

Batty, R. (2015), 'Taking a corporate stand against domestic violence', *Financial Times*, February 12, p. 14.

Baumwoll, J.P. (1974), 'Segmentation research: The Baker vs the Cookie Monster', in *Proceedings, American Marketing Association Conference*, 3–20.

BCG (2019), 'The most innovative companies 2019', March 21, https://www.bcg.com/publications/collections/most-innovative-companies-2019-artificial-intelligence-platforms-ecosystems.aspx, accessed 2019.

Beattie, A. (2005), 'Unchained malady: Business is becoming ever more exposed to supplier problems', *Financial Times*, August 25, p. 13.

Beattie, A. (2008), 'Tate & Lyle sugar adopts Fairtrade label', *Financial Times*, February 23/24, p. 17.

Becker-Olsen, K.L., Cudmore, B.A. and Hill, R.P. (2006), 'The impact of perceived corporate social responsibility on consumer behavior', *Journal of Business Research*, 59, 46–53.

Bell, E. (1996), '"Bastards" are losing out to Mr Clean', *Observer*, June 30.

Bell, E. (2015), 'How Red Bull became the world's most popular energy drink', *Vinepair.com*, September 11.

Bennett, J. and Ramsey, M. (2011), 'Ford, Toyota to team on hybrids', *Wall Street Journal*, August 23, p. 1.

Bensimon, S. (1999), 'Strategic alliances', *Executive Excellence*, 16(10), 9.

Berfield, S. and Baigorri, M. (2013), 'Zara's fast-fashion edge', *Bloomberg Businessweek*, November 15, www.businessweek.com/articles/2013-11-14/2014-outlook-zaras-fashion-supply-chain-edge, accessed 2019.

Berman, D. (2012), 'Google's challenge: A Motorola strategy', *Wall Street Journal*, April 11, p. 21.

Berner, R. (2005), 'Can Walmart fit into a white hat?', *BusinessWeek*, October 23, pp. 73–5.

Bernhardt, D. (ed.) (1993), *Perfectly Legal Competitor Intelligence*, London: Pitman Publishing.

Bernoth, A. (1996), 'Companies show they care', *Sunday Times*, December 8.

Berry, L.L. and Parasuraman, A. (1991), *Marketing Services: Competing Through Quality*, New York: The Free Press.

Berstell, G. and Nitterhouse, D. (2005), 'Letting the customer make the case', *Strategy and Innovation*, March–April, 3–6.

Birchall, J. (2010), 'Open innovation powers growth', *Financial Times*, December 28, p. 10.

Birchall, J. (2010), 'P&G goes online to compete for sales', *Financial Times*, May 20, p. 20.

Black, H. (2015), 'Loyal customers leaving Barclays after being told they're too poor', *Daily Mail*, February 11, p. 41.

Blas, J. and Wiggins, J. (2007), 'Surge in biofuel production pushes up food prices', *Financial Times*, July 16, p. 7.

Bohr, N. (1991), as quoted in H. Rosovsky, *The University: An Owners' Manual*, New York: W.W. Norton & Company, p. 147.

Bonoma, T.V. (1985), *The Marketing Edge: Making Strategies Work*, New York: Free Press.

Bonoma, T.V. (1990), 'Employees can free the hostages', *Marketing News*, March 19.

Booz, Allen and Hamilton (1982), *New Products Management for the 1980s*, New York: Booz, Allen and Hamilton Inc.

Borden, N. (1964), 'The concept of the marketing mix', *Journal of Advertising Research*, 4, 2–7.

Boston Consulting Group (1979), *Specialisation*, Boston, MA: BCG.

Bowen, D.E. and Lawler, E.E. (1992), 'The empowerment of service workers: What, why, how and when', *Sloan Management Review*, Spring, 31–9.

Bowman, C. and Ambrosini, V. (2003), 'How the resource-based and dynamic capabilities views of the firm inform corporate-level strategy', *British Journal of Management*, 14, 289–303.

Boyle, C. (2009), 'Fairtrade chocolate sales set to treble as Cadbury's Dairy Milk carries ethical logo', *Times*, July 22, p. 39.

Boyle, M. (2011), 'Who's really stocking your grocer's shelf', *Bloomberg BusinessWeek*, March 20–April 3, pp. 34–5.

Bradley, U. (1987), *Applied Marketing and Social Research*, 2nd edn, Chichester: John Wiley.

Brady, J. and Davis, I. (1993), 'Marketing's mid-life crisis', *The McKinsey Quarterly*, 2(2), 17–28.

Bradshaw, T. (2014), 'Apple in supply-chain purge at Africa mines', *Financial Times*, February 14, p. 20.

Branco, M.C. and Rodrigues, L.L. (2006), 'Corporate social responsibility and resource-based perspectives', *Journal of Business Ethics*, 69, 111–32.

Brewster, D. (2008), 'Smart solution for corporate philanthropists', *Financial Times*, October 1, p. 14.

Brittan, Sir L. (1990), 'A compelling reality', *Speaking of Japan*, February, 10(110), 18–24.

Broadbent, S. (ed.) (1983), *Advertising Works 2*, London: Holt, Reinhart and Winston.

Brown, A. (1995), 'The fall and rise of marketing', *Marketing Business*, February, 25–8.

Brown, S. (1995), *Postmodern Marketing*, London: Routledge.

Brown, T. (2104), 'Connecting brand promise and people', *The Marketer*, December, p. 15.

Brummer, A. (2005), 'Marconi crisis is a disaster for UK PLC', *Daily Mail*, May 11, p. 67.

Bruni, D.S. and Verona, G. (2009), 'Dynamic marketing capabilities in science-based firms: An exploratory investigation in the pharmaceutical industry', *British Journal of Management*, special issue, 20, S101–S17.

Bucklin, L.P. and Sengupta, S. (1993), 'Organising successful co-marketing alliances', *Journal of Marketing*, April, 32–46.

Buffington, B.I. and Frabelli, K.F. (1991), 'Acquisitions and alliances in the communications industry', in H.E. Glass (ed.), *Handbook of Business Strategy*, 3rd edn, New York: Warren Gorman and Lamont.

Butler, S. (2019), 'Half of UK retail sales will be online within 10 years, report predicts', The Guardian, July 9, https://www.theguardian.com/business/2019/jul/09/half-of-uk-retail-sales-will-be-online-within-10-years-report-predicts (accessed October 2019).

BusinessWeek (2009), 'The joys and perils of "reverse innovation"', *BusinessWeek*, October 5, p. 12.

Buzzell, R.D. and Gale, B.T. (1987), *The PIMS Principles*, New York: The Free Press.

Byron, E. (2008), 'A new odd couple: Google and P&G swap workers to spur innovation', *Wall Street Journal*, September 20, pp. 16–17.

Cable, D.M. (2007), *Change to Strange: Create A Great Organisation by Building A Strange Workforce*, Philadelphia, PA: Wharton School Publishing.

Calder, B.J. (1994), 'Qualitative marketing research', in Richard P. Bagozzi (ed.), *Principles of Marketing Research*, Boston, MA: Blackwell.

Campbell, A. (2006), 'Why in-house collaboration is so difficult', *Financial Times*, February 13, p. 14.

Cano, C.R., Rodriguez, Francois, A.C. and Jamarillio, F. (2004), 'A meta-analysis of the relationship between market orientation and business performance: Evidence from five continents', *International Journal of Research in Marketing*, 21(2), 179–200.

Capell, K. (2008), 'The wool industry gets bloodied', *BusinessWeek*, July 14 and 21, p. 31.

Capizzi, M.T. and Ferguson, R. (2005), 'Loyalty trends for the twenty-first century', *Journal of Consumer Marketing*, 22(2), 72–80.

Capon, N. (2001), *Key Account Management and Planning*, New York: The Free Press.

Carey, T. (1989), 'Strategy formulation in banks', *International Journal of Bank Marketing*, 7(3), 4–44.

Carroll, A. and Shabana, K.M. (2010), 'The business case for corporate social responsibility: A review of concepts, research and practice', *International Journal of Management Reviews*, 12(1), 85–105.

Carroll, A.B. (1979), 'A three-dimensional conceptual model of corporate performance', *Academy of Management Review*, October, 497–505.

Carroll, D.J., Green, P.E. and Schaffer, C.M. (1986), 'Interpoint distance comparisons in correspondence analysis', *Journal of Marketing Research*, 23, 271–80.

Carroll, D.J., Green, P.E. and Schaffer, C.M. (1987), 'Comparing interpoint distances in correspondence analysis: A clarification', *Journal of Marketing Research*, 24, 445–50.

Caruana, A., Ewing, M. and Ramaseshan, B. (2000), 'Assessment of the three-column format SERVQUAL', *Journal of Business Research*, 49, 57–65.

Cave, F. (2005), 'Surging costs put more pressure on manufacturers', *Financial Times*, July 12, p. 4.

Central Statistical Office (1995), *Annual Abstract of Statistics*, London: HMSO.

Cespedes, F.V. (1993), 'Coordinating sales and marketing in consumer goods firms', *Journal of Consumer Marketing*, 10(2), 37–55.

Cespedes, F.V. (1994), 'Industrial marketing: Managing new requirements', *Sloan Management Review*, Spring, 45–60.

Cespedes, F.V. (1995), *Concurrent Marketing: Integrating Product, Sales and Service*, Cambridge, MA: Harvard Business School Press.

Cespedes, F.V. (1996), 'Beyond teamwork: How the wise can synchronise', *Marketing Management*, 5(1), 25–37.

Cespedes, F.V. (2014), 'Putting sales at the centre of strategy', *Harvard Business Review*, October, 23–5.

Cespedes, F.V. and Piercy, N.F. (1996), 'Implementing marketing strategy', *Journal of Marketing Management*, 12, 135–60.

Chally Group, H.R. (1996), *The Customer Selected World Class Sales Excellence Report*, Dayton, OH: H.R. Chally Group.

Chally, H.R. (2006), *The Chally World Class Sales Excellence Research Report*, Dayton, OH: H.R. Chally Group.

Chandy, R.K. and Tellis, G.J. (1998a), *Organising for Radical Product Innovation*, Boston, MA: Marketing Science Institute, Report, 98–102.

Chandy, R.K. and Tellis, G.J. (1998b), 'Organising for radical product innovation: The overlooked role of willingness to cannibalise', *Journal of Marketing Research*, November, 474–87.

Chang, J.J. and Carroll, J.D. (1969), 'How to use MDPREF: A computer program for multidimensional analysis of preference data', unpublished paper, Murray Hill, NJ: Bell Laboratories.

Chang, J.J. and Carroll, J.D. (1972), 'How to use PREFMAP and PREFMAP 2 – programs which relate preference data to multidimensional scaling solutions', unpublished paper, Murray Hill, NJ: Bell Laboratories.

Chang, J. (2005), 'From the inside out', *Sales & Marketing Management*, August, 8.

Chao, L. (2012), 'Lenovo keeps production in-house as foes outsource', *Wall Street Journal*, July 10, pp. 14–15.

Chartered Institute of Marketing (2011), 'Marketing and sales fusion', https://www.cim.co.uk/media/4887/1259ri_wp_mktgsalesfusion_web.pdf, accessed 2019.

Chattopadhyay, A., Nedungadi, P. and Chakravarti, D. (1985), 'Marketing strategy and differential advantage – a comment', *Journal of Marketing*, 49(2), 129–36.

Chesbrough, H.W. (2006), *Open Business Models: How to Thrive in the New Innovation Landscape*, Boston, MA: Harvard Business School Press.

Chimhanzi, J. (2004), 'The impact of marketing/HR interactions on marketing strategy implementation', *European Journal of Marketing*, 38(1/2), 73–98.

Christensen, C. and Bower, J. (1996), 'Customer power, strategic investment and the failure of leading firms', *Strategic Management Journal*, 17(3), 197–218.

Christensen, C.M. (1997), *The Innovator's Dilemma: When New Technologies Cause Great Firms to Fail*, Boston, MA: Harvard Business School Press.

Christensen, C.M., Anthony, S.D., Berstell, G. and Nitterhouse, D. (2007), 'Finding the right job for your product', *MIT Sloan Management Review*, 6(38), 2–11.

Christensen, C., Anthony, S.D. and Roth, E.A. (2004), *Seeing What's Next: Using the Theories of Innovation to Predict Industry Change*, Boston, MA: Harvard Business School Press.

Christensen, C., Cook, S. and Hall, T. (2005), 'Marketing malpractice: The cause and the cure', *Harvard Business Review*, 83(12), 74–83.

Christensen, C.M., Kaufman, S.P. and Shih, W.C. (2008), 'Innovation killers', *Harvard Business Review*, January, 98–105.

Christensen, C.M. and Raynor, M.E. (2003), *The Innovator's Solution: Creating and Sustaining Successful Growth*, Boston, MA: Harvard Business School Press.

Chu, J. (2002), 'What top-performing retailers know about satisfying customers: Experience is key', IBM Institute for Business Value.

Chun, R. (2005), 'Corporate reputation: Meaning and measurement', *International Journal of Management Reviews*, 7(2), 91–109.

Clark, P. (1986), 'The marketing of margarine', *European Journal of Marketing*, 20(5), 52–65.

Clarkson, M.B.E. (1995), 'A stakeholder framework for analyzing and evaluating corporate social performance', *Academy of Management Review*, 20(1), 92–117.

Clausewitz, C. von (1908), *On War*, London: Routledge & Kegan Paul.

Clavell, J. (ed.) (1981), *The Art of War by Sun Tzu*, London: Hodder and Stoughton.

Clegg, A. (2014), 'Maverick developers on the edge', *Financial Times*, January 7, p. 10.

Coad, T. (1989), 'Lifestyle analysis – opportunities for early entry into Europe with effective customer targeting', Institute of International Research Conference on Customer Segmentation and Lifestyle Marketing, London, December 11–12.

Collack, L. and Armstrong, R. (2014), 'Alibaba', *Financial Times*, September 10, p. 11.

Colletti, J.A. and Chonko, L.B. (1997), 'Change management initiatives: Moving sales organisations from obsolescence to high performance', *Journal of Personal Selling & Sales Management*, 17(Spring), 1–30.

Collier, J. and Esteban, R. (2007), 'Corporate social responsibility and employee commitment', *Business Ethics*, 16(1), 19–29.

Collis, D.J. and Montgomery, C.A. (1995), 'Competing on resources: Strategy for the 1990s', *Harvard Business Review*, 73(4), 118–28.

Collis, D.J. and Montgomery, C.A. (1997), *Corporate Strategy: Resources and the Scope of the Firm*, Chicago, IL: McGraw-Hill.

Columbus, L. (2016), 'Ten ways Big Data is revolutionizing marketing and sales', *Forbes*, May 9.

Colvin, G. (2007), 'Power: A cooling trend', *Fortune*, December 10, pp. 37–51.

Colvin, G. (2006), 'The imagination economy', *Fortune*, July 10, p. 29.

Commission of the European Communities (2001), 'Green Paper: Promoting a European framework for corporate social responsibility', Strasbourg: COM, July.

Conlin, M. and Greene, J. (2007), 'How to make a micro-serf smile', *BusinessWeek*, September 10, pp. 57–9.

Cook, G. (2019), 'The Clean Beauty Boom', *Financial Times*, February 13.

Cook, V.J. (1983), 'Marketing strategy and differential advantage', *Journal of Marketing*, 47(2), 68–75.

Cook, V.J. and Mindak, W.A. (1984), 'A search for constants: The heavy user revisited', *Journal of Consumer Research*, 1(4), 80.

Cookson, C. (2006), 'How Big Pharma is made to pay', *Financial Times*, November 8, p. 29.

Coy, P. (2015), 'What's in the innovation sandwich?', *BusinessWeek*, January 19–25, pp. 49–51.

Coye, R.W. (2004), 'Managing customer expectations in the service encounter', *International Journal of Service Industry Management*, 15(4), 54–71.

Coyles, S. and Gokey, T.C. (2005), 'Customer retention is not enough', *Journal of Consumer Marketing*, 22(2), 101–5.

Cravens, D.W. (1995), 'The changing role of the sales force', *Marketing Management*, Fall, 17–32.

Cravens, D.W., Greenley, G., Piercy, N.F. and Slater, S. (1997), 'Integrating contemporary strategic management philosophy', *Long Range Planning*, 30(4), 493–506.

Cravens, D.W., Greenley, G., Piercy, N.F. and Slater, S. (1998), 'Mapping the path to market leadership', *Marketing Management*, Fall, 29–39.

Cravens, D.W. and Piercy, N.F. (2012), *Strategic Marketing*, 10th edn, New York: McGraw-Hill/Irwin.

Cravens, K., Piercy, N. and Cravens, D.W. (2000), 'Assessing the performance of strategic alliances: Matching metrics to strategies', *European Management Journal*, 18(5), 529–41.

Cravens, D.W., Piercy, N.F. and Low, G.S. (2002), 'The innovation challenges of proactive cannibalisation and discontinuous technology', *European Business Review*, 14(4), 257–67.

Cravens, D.W., Piercy, N.F. and Shipp, S.H. (1996), 'New organisational forms for competing in highly dynamic environments: The network paradigm', *British Journal of Management*, 7, 203–18.

Cravens, D.W., Shipp, S.H. and Cravens, K.S. (1993), 'Analysis of co-operative interorganisational relationships, strategic alliance formation, and strategic alliance effectiveness', *Journal of Strategic Marketing*, March, 55–70.

Crimp, M. (1990), *The Marketing Research Process*, 3rd edn, Hemel Hempstead: Prentice Hall.

Crimp, M. and Wright, L.T. (1995), *The Marketing Research Process*, 4th edn, Hemel Hempstead: Prentice Hall.

Cripe, E.J. (1994), 'Upgrading the service level of HR', *Human Resources Professional*, 7(3), 7–11.

Croft, M. (2007), 'Training and development: Brand ambassadors', *Marketing Week*, March 8, p. 39.

Crooks, E. (2009), 'B&Q halts sales of rooftop turbines', *Financial Times*, February 7–8, p. 2.

Crooks, E. (2015), 'Off the grid', *Financial Times*, January 14, p. 9.

Cross, J., Hartley, S.W., Rudelius, W. and Vassey, M.J. (2001), 'Sales force activities and marketing strategies in industrial firms: Relationships and implications', *Journal of Personal Selling & Sales Management*, 21(3), 199–206.

Crouch, S. and Housden, M. (1996), *Marketing Research for Managers*, 2nd edn, Oxford: Butterworth-Heinemann.

Crouch, S. and Housden, M. (2003), *Marketing Research for Managers*, 3rd edn, London: Butterworth-Heinemann.

Culliton, J. (1948), *The Management of Marketing Costs*, Boston, MA: Harvard University Graduate School of Business Administration, Research Division.

Cumbo, J. (2012), 'Private banks give marching orders to clients who are not rich enough', *Financial Times*, August 11–12, p. 1.

Czaplewski, A.J., Ferguson, J.M. and Milliman, J.F. (2001), 'Southwest Airlines: How internal marketing pilots success', *Marketing Management*, Sept/Oct, 14–17.

d'Astous, A. and Boujbel, L. (2007), 'Positioning countries on personality dimensions: Scale development and implications for country marketing', *Journal of Business Research*, 60, 231–9.

Dabholkar, P.A., Thorpe, D. and Rentz, J. (1996), 'A measure of service quality for retail stores: Scale development and validation', *Journal of the Academy of Marketing Science*, 24(1), 3–16.

Daily Telegraph (1997), 'Laura Ashley may defeat superman', 27 August.

Daneshkhu, S. (2014), 'Organic farming in decline despite rising sales', *Financial Times*, March 13, p. 2.

Daneshkhu, S. (2015), 'Unilever investors call for sale of Flora', *Financial Times*, March 2, p. 21.

Danneels, E. (1996), 'Market segmentation: Normative model versus business reality', *European Journal of Marketing*, 30(6), 36–51.

Dartnell Corporation (1999), *Dartnell's 30th Sales Force Compensation Survey: 1998–1999*, Chicago, IL: Dartnell Corporation.

Darwin, C. (1859), *On the Origin of Species*, London: John Murray.

Davidson, A. (2010), 'Guru who puts workers first, customers second', *Sunday Times*, May 9, pp. 3–6.

Davidson, H. (1983), 'Putting assets first', *Marketing*, November 17.

Davies, E., Eccles, L. and Groves, J. (2015), '6m cold calls from just one firm', *Daily Mail*, March 13, p. 8.

Dawar, N. (2018), 'Marketing in the Age of Alexa', *Harvard Business Review*, May–June.

Day, G. (2000), 'Tying in an asset', in *Understanding CRM*, London: Financial Times.

Day, G.S. (1992), 'Marketing's contribution to the strategy dialogue', *Journal of the Academy of Marketing Science*, 20(4), 37–52.

Day, G.S. (1994), 'The capabilities of market-driven organisations', *Journal of Marketing*, 58(3), 37–52.

Day, G.S. (1997), 'Aligning the organisation to the market', in D.R. Lehmann and K.E. Jocz (eds), *Reflections on the Futures of Marketing*, Cambridge, MA: Marketing Science Institute.

Day, G.S. (1999), 'Misconceptions about market orientation', *Journal of Market Focused Management*, 4(1), 5–16.

Day, G.S. (2003), 'Feeding the growth strategy', *Marketing Management*, November–December, 15–21.

Day, G.S. (2007), 'Is it real? Can we win? Is it worth doing?', *Harvard Business Review*, December, 110–20.

Day, G.S., Shocker, A.D. and Srivastava, R.K. (1979), 'Customer-oriented approach to identifying product markets', *Journal of Marketing*, 43(4), 8–19.

De Boer, L., Labro, E. and Morlacci, O. (2001), 'A review of methods supporting supplier selection', *European Journal of Purchasing and Supply Management*, 7(2), 75–89.

de Burton, S. (2019), 'Can hybrid watches hijack the ascent of the smartwatch?' *Financial Times*, 21 March.

de Chernatony, L. and MacDonald, M.H.B. (1992), *Creating Brands*, Oxford: Butterworth-Heinemann.

Deise, M.V., Nowokow, C., King, P. and Wright, A. (2000), *Executive's Guide to e-Business*, New York: John Wiley and Sons.

Delios, A., Inkpen, A.C. and Ross, J. (2004), 'Escalation in international strategic alliances', *Management International Review*, 44(4), 457–79.

Dell, M. (2007), 'Everyone has a choice', *Financial Times Digital Business – Special Report*, April 18, p. 1.

Deloitte Touche (2005), *Strategic Sales Compensation Survey*, New York: Deloitte Touche Development LLC.

Delves Broughton, P. (2012), 'Selling deserves a corner office', *Financial Times*, May 1, p. 14.

Deshpandé, R., Farley, J.U. and Webster, F.E. (1993), 'Corporate culture, customer orientation and innovativeness in Japanese firms: A quadrad analysis', *Journal of Marketing*, 57, 23–7.

Deshpandé, R. and Webster, F.E. (1989), 'Organisational culture and marketing: Defining the research agenda', *Journal of Marketing*, 53(January), 3–15.

Dewar, R. and Schultz, D. (1989), 'The product manager: An idea whose time has gone', *Marketing Communications*, May, 28–35.

Dewsnap, B. and Jobber, D. (2000), 'The sales–marketing interface in consumer packaged goods companies: A conceptual framework', *Journal of Personal Selling & Sales Management*, 2, 109–19.

Dibb, S. and Simkin, L. (1994), 'Implementation problems in industrial market segmentation', *Industrial Marketing Management*, 23, February, 55–63.

Dickson, P.R. (1992), 'Towards a general theory of competitive rationality', *Journal of Marketing*, 56, January, 69–83.

Dierickx, I. and Cool, K. (1989), 'Asset stock accumulation and sustainability of competitive advantage', *Management Science*, 35, 1,504–51.

Divita, S. (1996), 'Colleagues are customers, market to them', *Marketing News*, October 21.

Dixon, M., Freeman, K. and Toman, N. (2010), 'STOP trying to delight your customers', *Harvard Business Review*, July–August, 116–22.

Dixon, N.F. (1976), *On the Psychology of Military Incompetence*, London: Futura.

Donaldson, T. and Preston, L.E. (1995), 'The stakeholder theory of the corporation: Concepts, evidence and implications', *Academy of Management Review*, 29(January), 65–91.

Donath, B. (1997), 'Marketers of technology make promises they can't keep', *Marketing News*, October 13, p. 5.

Donath, B. (2000), 'Big customers may cause bigger dilemmas', *Marketing News*, September 11, p. 16.

Done, K. (2003), 'Ryanair swoops to land buzz in £15 million deal', *Financial Times*, February 1/2, p. 1.

Donnan, S. (2014), 'Levi Strauss adds ethical cred to street cred by rewarding responsible suppliers', *Financial Times*, November 5, p. 17.

Dorsch, M.J., Swanson, S.R. and Kelley, S.W. (1998), 'The role of relationship quality in the stratification of vendors as perceived by customers', *Journal of the Academy of Marketing Science*, 26(2), 128–42.

Dowdy, C. (2001), 'Internal branding', *Financial Times*, November 6, p. 4.

Downes, L. and Nunes, P. (2013), 'Big Bang disruption', *Harvard Business Review*, 44–56.

Doyle, P. (1995), 'Marketing in the new millennium', *European Journal of Marketing*, 29(13), 23–41.

Doyle, P. (1997), 'Go for robust growth', *Marketing Business*, April, 53.

Doyle, P. (2000), *Value Based Marketing*, Chichester: John Wiley & Sons.

Doyle, P. (2008), *Value Based Marketing*, 2nd edn, London: John Wiley and Sons.

Doyle, P., Saunders, J.A. and Wong, V. (1986), 'A comparative study of Japanese and British marketing strategies in the UK market', *Journal of International Business Studies*, 17(1), 27–46.

Doyle, P. and Stern, P. (2006), *Marketing Management and Strategy*, 4th edn, Harlow: Pearson Education.

Drake, S.M., Galman, M.J. and Roberts, S.M. (2005), *Light Their Fire: Using Internal Marketing to Ignite Employee Performance and Wow Your Customers*, Wokingham: Kaplan Business.

Drucker, P. (1954), *The Practice of Management*, New York: Harper & Row.

Drucker, P. (1973), *Management: Tasks, Responsibilities and Practices*, New York: Harper & Row.

Drucker, P. (1997), 'The future that has already happened', *Harvard Business Review*, 75(5), 20–4.

Dumaine, B. (2014), 'The world's top 25 eco-innovators', *Fortune*, May 19, pp. 46–51.

Durman, P. and Box, D. (2005), 'Cut off', *Sunday Times*, 1 May, 3:5.

Dwek, R. (1997), 'Losing the race', *Marketing Business*, March.

Easterby-Smith, M., Lyles, M.A. and Peteraf, M.A. (2009), 'Dynamic capabilities: Current debates and future directions', *British Journal of Management*, special issue, 20, S1–S8.

Ebrahami, H. (2006), 'How supermarkets are squeezing fat profits from Fairtrade brands', *Financial Mail*, September 24, p. 3.

Eccles, R.G., Newquist, S.C. and Schatz, R. (2007), 'Reputation and its risks', *Harvard Business Review*, February, 104–14.

Economist, The (1994), 'Death of the brand manager', April 9, 79–80.

Economist, The (2007), 'Globalisation's offspring', Economist.com, April 4.

Economist, The (2012), '*Economist* Fashion Forward; Inditex', March 24, 63–4.

Edmunds, M. (2000), 'Your wish is on my database,' *Financial Times*, February 28, p. 16.

Eisenhardt, K.M. and Martin, J.A. (2000), 'Dynamic capabilities: What are they?', *Strategic Management Journal*, 21, 1,105–21.

Eisenstat, R., Foote, N., Galbraith, J. and Miller, D. (2001), 'Beyond the business unit', *McKinsey Quarterly*, (1), 54–63.

Elgin, B. (2007), 'Little green lies', *BusinessWeek*, October 29, pp. 45–52.

Elkington, J. (1994), 'Towards the sustainable corporation: Win–win–win business strategies for sustainable development', *California Management Review*, 36(2), 90–100.

Engardio, P. (2004), 'Scouring the world for brainiacs', *BusinessWeek*, October 11, pp. 62–6.

Engardio, P. (2007), 'Beyond the green corporation', *BusinessWeek*, January 29, pp. 50–64.

Engardio, P. (2009), 'Why NCR said, "let's go back home"', *BusinessWeek*, August 24 and 31, p. 19.

Engardio, P. and Arndt, M. (2007), 'What price reputation?', *BusinessWeek*, July 9 and 16, pp. 70–79.

English, J. (1989), 'Selecting and analyzing your customer/market through efficient profile modeling and prospecting', Institute of International Research Conference on Customer Segmentation and Lifestyle Marketing, London, 11–12 December.

Ernst, D. and Bamford, J. (2005), 'Your alliances are too stable', *Harvard Business Review*, June, 133–41.

Evans, F.B. (1959), 'Psychological and objective factors in the prediction of brand choice', *Journal of Business*, 32, October, 340–69.

Evans, P.B. and Wurster, T.S. (1997), 'Strategy and the new economics of information', *Harvard Business Review*, 75 (5), 71–82.

Fahy, J. and Hooley, G.J. (2002), 'Sustainable competitive advantage in e-business: Towards a contingency perspective on the resource-based view', *Journal of Strategic Marketing*, 10 (4), 1–13.

Fairtrade (2010), 'Fairtrade fortnight: Sales reach double digit growth', February 23, http://www.fdin.org.uk/2010/02/fairtrade-fortnight-sales-reach-double-digit-growth/, accessed 2019.

Farris, P.W. and Moore, M.J. (2004), *The Profit Impact of Marketing Strategy Project: Retrospect and Prospects*, Cambridge, UK: Cambridge University Press.

Farris, P.W., Bendle, N.T., Pfeifer, P.E. and Reibstein, D.J. (2006), *Marketing Metrics: 50 Metrics Every Executive Should Master*, Upper Saddle River, NJ: Wharton School Publishing.

Feintzeig, R. (2014), 'When the boss says "make more friends"', *Wall Street Journal*, February 14–16, p. 25.

Felsted, A. (2010), 'Amazon to muscle in on Ocado's territory', *Financial Times*, July 8, p. 18.

Felsted, A. (2011), 'Alliance Boots extends Procter & Gamble tie-up', *Financial Times*, October 31, p. 20.

Felton, A.P. (1959), 'Making the marketing concept work', *Harvard Business Review*, 37(4), 55–65.

Ferrell, O.C. and Lucas, G.H. (1987), 'An evaluation of progress in the development of a definition of marketing', *Journal of the Academy of Marketing Science*, 15(3), 12–23.

Field, A. (2017), *Discovering Statistics Using IBM SPSS Statistics*, 5th edn, New York: SAGE Publishing.

Financial Times (2007), 'Footing the bill: Gates offers $3 software to poor', *Financial Times*, April 20, p. 1.

Financial Times (2016), 'Laura Ashley shares fall 9.3% as profits wilt', *Financial Times*, March 23

Financial Wire (2006), 'AT&T, Yahoo hit 5-year mark with broadband partnership', *Financial Wire*, November 22, p. 1.

Fink, R.C., Edelman, L.F. and Hatten, K.J. (2007), 'Supplier performance improvements in relational exchanges', *Journal of Business and Industrial Marketing*, 22(1), 29–40.

Fiol, C.M. and Lyles, M.A. (1985), 'Organisational learning', *Academy of Management Review*, 10, 803–13.

Fishburn, D. and Green, S. (eds) (2002), *The World in 2003*, London: Economist Newspapers Ltd.

Fitzgerald, D. (2012), 'Google to cut 20% of Motorola staff', *Wall Street Journal*, April 14, p. 19.

Fitzhugh, K.L.M. and Piercy, N.F. (2006), 'Integrating marketing intelligence sources: Reconsidering the role of the salesforce', *International Journal of Market Research*, 48, 699–716.

Fletcher, K. (1996), *Marketing Management and Information Technology*, 2nd edn, London: Prentice-Hall International.

Fogel, S., Hoffmeister, D., Rocco, R. and Trunk, D.P. (2012), 'Teaching sales', *Harvard Business Review*, July–August, 94–100.

Foley, A. and Fahy, J. (2004), 'Towards a further understanding of the development of market orientation in the firm: A conceptual framework based on market-sensing capability', *Journal of Strategic Marketing*, 12, 219–30.s

Forbis, J.L. and Mehta, N.T. (1981), 'Value-based strategies for industrial products', *Business Horizons*, 24(3), 32–42.

Ford, J.E. (2018), 'Social media marketing for the future: Strategies for 2020 and beyond: Stay ahead of the competition', Leverage Changing Online Trends to Grow Your Business (For Facebook, Twitter, Instagram +More)', independently published, October 22.

Fortune (2015), 'Change the world list', *Fortune*, September 1.

Foster, R.N. (1986a), *Innovation: The Attacker's Advantage*, London: Macmillan.

Foster, R.N. (1986b), 'Attacking through innovation', *The McKinsey Quarterly*, Summer, 2–12.

Frank, R.E., Massey, W.F. and Wind, Y. (1972), *Market Segmentation*, Englewood Cliffs, NJ: Prentice-Hall.

Fraser, K. (2007), 'Conflicted consumers', *Harvard Business Review*, February, 35–6.

Freedman, M. (2003), 'The genius is in the implementation', *Journal of Business Strategy*, March/April, 26–31.

Friedman, L.G. (2002), *Go To Market Strategy*, Woburn, MA: Butterworth-Heinemann Business Books.

Friedman, M. (1970), 'The social responsibility of business is to increase its profits', *New York Times Magazine*, 12 September, pp. 122–6.

Frosch, R. (1996), 'The customer for R&D is always wrong!', *Research-Technology Management*, Nov–Dec, 22–7.

Fry, M.-L. and Polonsky, M.J. (2004), 'Examining the unintended consequences of marketing', *Journal of Business Research*, 57, 1,303–6.

Fulmer, W.E. and Goodwin, J. (1988), 'Differentiation: Begin with the customer', *Business Horizons*, 31(5), 55–63.

Galea, C. (2006), 'What customers really want', *Sales & Marketing Management*, May, 11.

Gallagher, L. (2015), 'Why employees love Marriott', *Fortune*, March 5, pp. 39–44.

Gallo, A. (2015), 'A refresher on economic value to the customer', *Harvard Business Review*, May 7, 2–6.

Gapper, J. (2014), 'Mergers threaten golden age of television', *Financial Times*, July 24, p. 13.

Gapper, J. (2015), 'Software is steering the car industry', *Financial Times*, February 19, p. 11.

Gardner, N. (1997), 'Defining your class is as easy as ABC', *Sunday Times*, February 9, p. 7.

Gary, R. (2013), 'What's in it for me?', *The Marketer*, July/August, 33–6.

Giamanco, B. and Gregoire, K. (2012), 'Tweet me, friend me, make me buy', *Harvard Business Review*, July–August, 88–94.

Gibbs, R. and Humphries, A. (2009), *Strategic Alliances & Marketing Partnerships: Gaining Competitive Advantage Through Collaboration and Partnering*, London: Kogan Page.

Giles, C. and Tricks, H. (2005), 'Suppliers' woes could provide limitation to retailer's ambitions', *Financial Times*, June 3, p. 24.

Gilly, M.C. and Wolfinbarger, M. (1996), *Advertising's Second Audience: Employee Reactions to Organisational Communications*, Cambridge, MA: Marketing Science Institute.

Glassman, M. and McAfee, B. (1992), 'Integrating the personnel and marketing functions: The challenge of the 1990s', *Business Horizons*, 35(3), 52–9.

Glover, S. (2015), 'It's an inconvenient truth, but the global warming zealots are to blame for the deadly diesel fiasco', *Daily Mail*, September 24, p. 14.

Gluck, F. (1986), 'Strategic planning in a new key', *McKinsey Quarterly*, Winter, 173–83.

Godfrey, P.C. and Hatch, N.W. (2007), 'Researching corporate responsibility: An agenda for the 21st century', *Journal of Business Ethics*, 70, 87–8.

Goodman, M. (2006), 'The green grocers', *Sunday Times*, September 24, p. 3.5.

Goodman, M. (2010), 'Azko's fresh basis for bonus', *Sunday Times*, June 27, p. 3.9.

Gounaris, S.P. (2006), 'Internal-market orientation and its measurement', *Journal of Business Research*, 59(4), 432–48.

Govindarajan, V. and Trimble, C. (2012), *Reverse Innovation: Create Far from Home and Win Everywhere*, Cambridge MA: Harvard Business Review Press.

Gowers, A., de Jonquieres, G. and Fifield, A. (2005), 'When the cutting edge frightens the customers', *Financial Times*, October 14, p. 14.

Grande, C. (2005), 'Marconi's technology fails the price test', *Financial Times*, May 4, p. 23.

Grande, C. (2007a), 'Businesses behaving badly, say consumers', *Financial Times*, February 20, p. 24.

Grande, C. (2007b), 'Ethical consumption makes mark on branding', *Financial Times*, February 20, p. 24.

Grant, A.M. (2011), 'Customers can rally your troops', *Harvard Business Review*, July, 96–103.

Grant, J. (2005), 'Mr Daley's mission: To reach 6bn shoppers and make money', *Financial Times*, July 15, p. 32.

Grant, J. and Foster, L. (2005), 'McDonald's woos its "burger flippers"', *Financial Times*, April 15, p. 29.

Grant, R.M. (1995), *Contemporary Strategy Analysis*, 2nd edn, Cambridge, MA: Basil Blackwell.

Gratton, L. (2007), *Hot Spots: Why Some Companies Buzz With Innovation – And Others Don't*, Harlow: FT/Prentice Hall.

Green, J. (2013), 'The new Willy Loman survives by staying home', *Bloomberg BusinessWeek*, January 14–20, pp. 16–18.

Green, P., Carroll, J. and Goldberg, S. (1981), 'A general approach to product design optimisation via conjoint analysis', *Journal of Marketing*, 43, 17–35.

Green, P.E., Carmone, F.J. and Smith, S.M. (1989), *Multidimensional Scaling: Concepts and Applications*, Boston, MA: Allyn and Bacon.

Greene, J., Carey, J., Arndt, M. and Port, O. (2003), 'Reinventing corporate R&D', *BusinessWeek*, September 22, pp. 72–3.

Greenley, G.E. and Foxall, G.R. (1996), 'Consumer and non-consumer stakeholder orientation in UK firms', *Journal of Business Research*, 35, 105–16.

Greenley, G.E. and Foxall, G.R. (1997), 'Multiple stakeholder orientation in UK companies and the implications for company performance', *Journal of Management Studies*, 34, 259–84.

Greyser, S.A. (1997), 'Janus and marketing: The past, present and prospective future of marketing', in D.R. Lehmann and K.R. Jocz (eds), *Reflections on the Futures of Marketing*, Cambridge, MA: Marketing Science Institute.

Griffiths, B. (2014), 'Glaxo fined £297m as bribery probes go on', *Daily Mail*, September 20, p. 107.

Griffiths, B. (2014), 'GSK hurt by sales collapse in China', *Daily Mail*, October 24, p. 85.

Grönroos, C. (1994), 'From marketing mix to relationship marketing: Towards a paradigm shift in marketing', *Management Decision*, 32(2), 4–32.

Grow, B., Hamm, S. and Lee, L. (2005), 'The debate over doing good', *BusinessWeek*, September 5/12, pp. 78–80.

Gubman, E.L. (1995), 'Aligning people strategies with customer value', *Compensation and Benefits Review*, 27(1), 15–22.

Gulati, R., Sytch, M. and Mehotra, P. (2007), 'Preparing for the exit: When forming a business alliance, don't ignore one of the most crucial ingredients: How to break up', *Wall Street Journal (Special Report)*, March 3, R1.

Gummesson, E. (1987), 'The new marketing – developing long-term interactive relationships', *Long Range Planning*, 20(4), 10–20.

Gummesson, E. (1990), *The Part-Time Marketer*, University of Karlstad, Research Report, 90(3).

Gummesson, E. (1994), 'Service management: An evaluation and the future', *International Journal of Service Industry Management*, 5(1), 77–96.

Gummesson, E. (2008), *Total Relationship Marketing*, 3rd edn, Oxford: Butterworth-Heinemann.

Gupta, A.K., Raj, S.P. and Wilemon, D. (1986), 'A model for studying R&D/marketing interface in the product innovation process', *Journal of Marketing*, 50, 7–17.

Haeckel, S. (1997), 'Preface', in D.R. Lehmann and K.R. Jocz (eds), *Reflections on the Futures of Marketing*, Cambridge, MA: Marketing Science Institute.

Hagel, J. (2016), 'Strategy made simple, the three core strategy questions', *The Journal of Marketing*, October, 27.

Hagel, J. III and Seely-Brown, J. (2005), *The Only Sustainable Edge: Why Business Strategy Depends on Productive Friction and Dynamic Specialisation*, Boston, MA: Harvard Business School Press.

Hair, J.F., Anderson, R.E., Black, W.C. and Babin, B. (2018), *Multivariate Data Analysis*, 8th edn, Andover, UK: Cengage Learning EMEA.

Haley, R.I. (1968), 'Benefit segmentation: A decision-oriented tool', *Journal of Marketing*, July, 30–5.

Haley, R.I. (1984), 'Benefit segmentation – 20 years on', *Journal of Consumer Marketing*, 5–13.

Hall, R. (1992), 'The strategic analysis of intangible resources', *Strategic Management Journal*, 13, 135–44.

Hall, R. (1993), 'A framework for linking intangible resources and capabilities to sustainable competitive advantage', *Strategic Management Journal*, 14, 607–18.

Hamel, G. (1996), 'Strategy as revolution', *Harvard Business Review*, 74(4), 9–82.

Hamel, G. (2000), *Leading the Revolution*, Boston, MA: Harvard Business School Press.

Hamel, G. and Prahalad, C.K. (1989), 'Strategic intent', *Harvard Business Review*, 67(3), 63–76.

Hamel, G. and Prahalad, C.K. (1991), 'Corporate imagination and expeditionary marketing', *Harvard Business Review*, 69(4), 81–92.

Hamel, G. and Prahalad, C.K. (1994), *Competing for the Future*, Boston, MA: Harvard Business School Press.

Hamel, G. and Välikangas, L. (2003), 'The quest for resilience', *Harvard Business Review*, September, 52–63.

Hamm, S. (2005), 'Beyond blue', *BusinessWeek*, April 18, pp. 36–42.

Hamm, S. (2006), 'Speed demons', *BusinessWeek*, March 27, pp. 67–76.

Hamm, S. (2008), 'Big blue goes for the big win', *BusinessWeek*, March 10, pp. 63–5.

Hammermesh, R.G., Anderson, M.J. and Harris, J.E. (1978), 'Strategies for low market share businesses', *Harvard Business Review*, 50(3), 95–102.

Han, J.K., Kim, N. and Srivastava, R.K. (1998), 'Market orientation and organisational performance: Is innovation the missing link?', *Journal of Marketing*, 62, 30–45.

Hanlon, M. (2007), 'The great green con?', *Daily Mail*, July 23, pp. 30–31.

Hansegard, J. (2013), 'H&M suspends output of angora-wool items', *Wall Street Journal*, November 29–December 1, p. 18.

Hanssesns, D.M. and Dekimpe, M.G. (2012), in V. Shankar and G.S. Carpenter (eds), *Handbook of Marketing Strategy*, London: Edward Elgar Publishing Ltd, pp. 457–69.

Harris, L. and Goode, M. (2004), 'The four levels of loyalty and the pivotal role of trust', *Journal of Retailing*, 80, 139–58.

Harris, L.C. (1996), 'Cultural obstacles to market orientation', *Journal of Marketing Practice: Applied Marketing Science*, 4(2), 36–52.

Harris, L.C. (1998), 'Cultural domination: The key to a market-oriented culture', *European Journal of Marketing*, 32(3/4), 354–73.

Harrison, J.S. and St John, C.H. (1994), *Strategic Management of Organisations and Stakeholders*, St Paul, MN: West.

Harrison, M. (2007), 'To what extent is the UK market research industry a world leader?', ESOMAR world research report.

Harrison, M., Cupman, J., Truman, O. and Hague, P. (2016), *Market Research in Practice: An Introduction to Gaining Greater Market Insight*, 3rd edn, London: Kogan Page.

Hart, C.W.L., Heskett, J.L. and Sasser, W.E. (1990), 'The profitable art of service recovery', *Harvard Business Review*, 68(2), 148–56.

Hart, S. (2005), *Capitalism at the Crossroads: The Unlimited Business Opportunities in Solving the World's Most Difficult Problems*, Philadelphia, PA: Wharton School Publishing.

Harvey, F. (2007), 'Reckitt's plan to green-up its customers', *Financial Times*, November 1, p. 23.

Harvey, F. and Birchall, J. (2007), 'Walmart in greenhouse gas initiative', *Financial Times*, September 24, p. 25.

Harvey, F. and Fidler, S. (2007), 'Industry caught in "carbon credit" smokescreen', *Financial Times*, April 27, p. 1.

Harvey, F. (2005), 'GE looks out for a cleaner profit', *Financial Times*, July 1, p. 13.

Harvey, F. and Rigby, E. (2006), 'Supermarkets' green claims challenged', *Financial Times*, September 14, p. 6.

Hathi, S. (2007), 'Using blogs to involve', *Strategic Communication Management*, February/March, 8.

Hattersley, G. (2008), 'Does it really make any difference?', *Sunday Times*, April 2, p. 4.3.

He, H.W. and Balmer, J.M.T. (2006), 'Alliance brands: Building corporate brands through strategic alliances?', *Journal of Brand Management*, 13(4/5), 242–56.

Heineman Jnr, B.W. (2007), 'Avoiding integrity land mines', *Harvard Business Review*, April, 100–108.

Helfat, C.E., Finkelstein, S., Mitchell, W., Peteraf, M.A., Singh, H., Teece, D.J. and Winter, S.G. (2007), *Dynamic Capabilities: Understanding Change in Organisations*, Oxford: Blackwell Publishing.

Helm, B. (2008), 'How to sell luxury to penny-pinchers', *BusinessWeek*, November 10, p. 80.

Helm, B. and Arndt, M. (2007), 'It's not a McJob, it's a McCalling', *BusinessWeek*, June 4, p. 13.

Henriques, I. and Sadorsky, P. (1999), 'The relationship between environmental commitment and managerial perceptions of stakeholder importance', *Academy of Management Journal*, 42(1), 89–99.

Henry, D. (2006), 'Creativity pays: Here's how much', *BusinessWeek*, April 24, p. 76.

Heskett, J.L., Sasser, W.E., Jr and Schlesinger, L.A. (2003), *The Value Profit Chain: Treat Employees like Customers and Customers like Employees*, New York: The Free Press.

Hill, A. (2014), 'Corporate storytellers best left on the shelf', *Financial Times*, March 18, p. 12.

Hill, A. (2014), 'The serial adultery of the modern customer', *Financial Times*, February 4, p. 12.

Hill, R. (1979), 'Weak signals from the unknown', *International Management*, 34(10), 55–60.

Hille, K. (2007), 'The race for the $100 laptop', *Financial Times*, April 9, p. 8.

Hindle, T. and Thomas, M. (1994), *Pocket Marketing*, 2nd edn, Harmondsworth: The Economist Books.

Homburg, C. and Pflesser, C. (2000), 'A multiple layer model of market-oriented organisational culture: Measurement issues and performance outcomes', *Journal of Marketing Research*, 37, 449–62.

Homburg, C., Workman, J.P. and Jensen, O. (2000), 'Fundamental changes in marketing organisation: The movement toward a customer-focused organisational structure', *Journal of the Academy of Marketing Science*, 28(4), 459–78.

Homburg, C., Workman, J.P. and Jensen, O. (2002), 'A configurational perspective on key account management', *Journal of Marketing*, April, 38–60.

Hooley, G.J. (1980), 'Multidimensional scaling of consumer perceptions and preferences', *European Journal of Marketing*, 14(7), 436–80.

Hooley, G.J. (1982), 'Directing advertising creativity through benefit segmentation', *Journal of Advertising*, 1, 375–85.

Hooley, G.J., Cox, A.J. and Adams, A. (1992), 'Our five-year mission – to boldly go where no man has gone before', *Journal of Marketing Management*, 8(1), 35–48.

Hooley, G.J., Fahy, J., Cox, A.J., Beracs, J., Fonfara, K. and Snoj, B. (2000), 'Market orientation in the transition economies of central Europe', *Journal of Business Research*, 50(3), 273–85.

Hooley, G.J., Greenley, G., Cadogan, J.W. and Fahy J. (2005), 'The performance impact of marketing resources', *Journal of Business Research*, 58(1), 18–27.

Hooley, G.J. and Hussey, M.K. (eds) (1999), *Quantitative Methods in Marketing*, 2nd edn, London: Thomson Press.

Hooley, G.J., Möller, K. and Broderick, A.J. (1998), 'Competitive positioning and the resource-based view of the firm', *Journal of Strategic Marketing*, 6(2), 97–115.

Horobin, W. (2014), 'New French trains too wide for stations', *Wall Street Journal*, May 22, p. 3.

Hrebiniak, L.G. (2006), 'Obstacles to effective strategy implementation', *Organisational Dynamics*, 35(1), 12–31.

Huber, G.P. (1991), 'Organisational learning: The contributing processes and the literatures', *Organisational Science*, 2, 88–115.

Huff, T. (2014), 'How Starbucks crashes it on social media', *SocialMediaToday*, August 23.

Hughes, J. and Kirk, S. (2013), 'Li & Fung', *Financial Times*, January 24, p. 9.

Hughes, J. and Weiss, J. (2007), 'Simple rules for making alliances work', *Harvard Business Review*, November, 122–31.

Hulbert, J.M., Capon, N. and Piercy, N.F. (2009), *Total Integrated Marketing: Breaking the Bounds of the Function*, New York: The Free Press.

Hulbert, J.M., Capon, N. and Piercy, N.F. (2003), *Total Integrated Marketing: Breaking the Bounds of the Function*, New York: The Free Press.

Hull, L. (2014), 'Recycling? 60% of Us Don't Care', *Daily Mail*, September 8, p. 27.

Hull, L. and Sorrell, L. (2010), 'Too tired to stay awake: Microsoft's Chinese workforce earning only 34p an hour', *Daily Mail*, April 17, p. 31.

Hussey, M.K. and Hooley, G.J. (1995), 'The diffusion of quantitative methods into marketing management', *Journal of Marketing Practice: Applied Marketing Science*, 1(4), 13–31.

IBM (2005), *The Strategic Agenda for Customer Management in the Consumer Products Industry*, New York: IBM Institute for Business Value Executive Brief.

IBM (2009), *Leading a Sustainable Enterprise*, Somers, NY: IBM Institute for Business Value.

Ihlwan, M. (2010), 'Sony and Samsung's strategic split', *BusinessWeek*, January 18, p. 52.

Imai, M. (1986), *KAIZEN: The Key to Japan's Competitive Success*, Maidenhead: McGraw-Hill.

IMI plc (2010), *IMI plc – Key Themes*, https://www.imiplc.com/about-imi.aspx, accessed 2019.

Immelt, J.R., Govindarajan, V. and Trimble, C. (2009), 'How GE is disrupting itself', *Harvard Business Review*, October, 56–65.

Ingram, T.N., LaForge, R.W. and Leigh, T.W. (2002), 'Selling in the new millennium: A joint agenda', *Industrial Marketing Management*, 31, 559–67.

Jack, A. (2007), 'Beyond charity? A new generation enters the business of doing good', *Financial Times*, April 5, p. 13.

Jack, A. (2008), 'An unusual model for good causes', *Financial Times*, June 5, p. 16.

Jackson, S. (2007), 'Market share is not enough: Why strategic market positioning works', *The Journal of Business Strategy*, 28(1), 18–25.

Jackson, T. (1997), 'Dare to be different', *Financial Times*, June 19.

Jacobs, E. (2013), 'Old hands steered by the young', *Financial Times*, November 21, p. 16.

Jain, S.C. (1990), *Marketing Planning and Strategy*, 3rd edn, Cincinnati, OH: South Western.

James, B.J. (1984), *Business Wargames*, London: Abacus.

Janal, D. (2000), *Dan Janal's Guide to Marketing on the Internet*, New York: Wiley.

Janda, S. and Seshandri, S. (2001), 'The influence of purchasing strategies on performance', *Journal of Business and Industrial Marketing*, 16(4), 294–306.

Japan Corporate News Network (2006), 'Honda and Hong Kong Disneyland form strategic alliance', *Japan Corporate News Network*, July 12, p. 1.

Jaworski, B.J. and Kohli, A.K. (1993), 'Market orientation: Antecedents and consequences', *Journal of Marketing*, 57 (July), 53–70.

Jervell, E.E. (2014), 'In a Nordic power trip, bus drivers in Oslo mount an assault on batteries', *Wall Street Journal*, May 22, p. 31.

Jobs, S. (2008), quoted in *Fortune*, March 17.

Johnson, G. and Scholes, K. (1988), *Exploring Corporate Strategy*, 2nd edn, Hemel Hempstead: Prentice Hall International.

Johnson, G., Whittington, R., Scholes, K., Angwin, D. and Regner, P. (2017), *Exploring Corporate Strategy: Text and Cases*, 11th edn, Harlow, UK: Pearson.

Jones, E., Brown S.P., Zoltners, A.A. and Weitz, B.A. (2005), 'The changing environment of selling and sales management', *Journal of Personal Selling & Sales Management*, 25(2), 10–11.

Jones, R. (2000), *The Big Idea*, London: HarperCollins Business.

Jones, T.M. (1995), 'Instrumental stakeholder theory: A synthesis of ethics and economics', *Academy of Management Review*, 20(2), 404–37.

Jones, T.O. and Sasser, W.E. (1995), 'Why satisfied customers defect', *Harvard Business Review*, 73(6), 88–99.

Jopson, B. (2007), 'Unilever looks to clean up in Africa', *Financial Times*, November 15, p. 20.

Kale, P., Singh, H. and Perlmutter, H. (2000), 'Learning and protection of proprietary assets in strategic alliances: Building relational capital', *Strategic Management Journal*, 21, 217–37.

Kale, S. (2004), 'CRM failure and the seven deadly sins,' *Marketing Management*, 13(April), 42–6.

Kalligianis, K., Iatrou, K. and Mason, K. (2006), 'How do airlines perceive that strategic alliances affect their individual branding?', *Journal of Air Transportation*, 11(2), 3–21.

Kanner, B. (1996), 'In search of brand loyalty', *Sunday Business*, June 30, p. 11.

Kapelianis, D., Walker, B.A., Hutt, M.D. and Kumar, A. (2005), 'Those winning ways: The role of competitive crafting in complex sales', Working Paper, Arizona State University.

Kaplan, R.S. and Norton, D.P. (1996), *Translating Strategy into Action: The Balanced Scorecard*, Boston, MA: Harvard Business School Press.

Kavanagh, M. (2011), 'Premier Foods feels punch from retail woes', *Financial Times*, July 1, p. 18.

Kawasaki, G. (2012), *Enchantment: The Art of Changing Hearts, Minds and Actions – How to Woo, Influence and Persuade*, London: Portfolio/Penguin.

Kay, J. (1993), *Foundations of Corporate Success*, Oxford: Oxford University Press.

Kay, J. (2009), 'Innovation is not about wearing a white coat', *Financial Times*, December 16, p. 17.

Keegan, J. (1993), *A History of Warfare*, London: Hutchinson.

Keith, R.J. (1960), 'The marketing revolution', *Journal of Marketing*, 24(1), 35–8.

Kellaway, L. (2015), 'No need to "lean in" when laziness can be just as effective', *Financial Times*, February 23, p. 16.

Kellaway, L. (2015), 'Wells Fargo happy/grumpy ratio is no way to audit staff', *Financial Times*, February 9, p. 14.

Keller, S.B., Lynch, D.F., Ellinger, A.E., Ozment, J. and Calantone, R. (2006), 'The impact of internal marketing efforts in distribution service operations', *Journal of Business Logistics*, 27(1), 109–39.

Kerrigan, R., Roegner, E.V., Swinford, D.D. and Zawada, C.C. (2001), 'B2Basics', *McKinsey Quarterly*, (1), 45–53.

Khoo, P.C. (1992), *Sun Tzu and Management*, Petaling Jaya, Malaysia: Pelanduk.

Kiley, D. and Helm, B. (2009), '100 best global brands: The great trust offensive', *BusinessWeek*, September 28, pp. 38–60.

Kilmann, R.H. (1996), 'Management learning organisations: Enhancing business education for the 21st century', *Management Learning*, 27, 203–38.

Kim, W.C. and Mauborgne, R. (1997), 'Value innovation: The strategic logic of high growth', *Harvard Business Review*, January–February, 102–13.

Kim, W.C. and Mauborgne, R. (1998), 'Pioneers strike it rich', *Financial Times*, August 11, p. 11.

Kim, W.C. and Mauborgne, R. (1999), 'Creating new market space', *Harvard Business Review*, January–February, 83–93.

Kim, W. C. and Mauborgne, R. (2014), *Blue Ocean Strategy, Expanded Edition: How to Create Uncontested Market Space and Make the Competition Irrelevant*, Harvard Business Review Press, 2014.

Kinnear, T.C., Taylor, J.R. and Ahmed, S.A. (1974), 'Ecologically concerned consumers: Who are they?', *Journal of Marketing*, 38(2), 20–4.

Klump, E. and Reed, S. (2010), 'How BP's spill tarred Anadarko', *BusinessWeek*, July 26–August 1, pp. 18–20.

Knight, R. (2006), 'Business students portrayed as ethically minded in study', *Financial Times*, October 25, p. 9.

Knight R. (2008), 'Green entrepreneurs with the drive to transform travel', *Financial Times*, September 26, p. 16.

Knox, S., Maklan, S., Payne, A., Peppard, J. and Ryals, L. (2003), *Customer Relationship Management: Perspectives from the Marketplace*, Oxford: Butterworth-Heinemann.

Koerner, L. (2005), 'Conducting an organisational assessment of your SAM programme', Presentation at Strategic Account Management Association Conference, Paris.

Kohli, A.K. and Jaworski, B.J. (1990), 'Market orientation: The construct, research propositions and managerial implications', *Journal of Marketing*, 54(2), 1–18.

Kotler, P. (2015), *Confronting Capitalism: Real Solutions for a Troubled Economic System*, New York: American Management Association.

Kotler, P., Kartajaya, H. and Setiawan, I. (2017), *Marketing 4.0: Moving from Traditional to Digital*, Hoboken, NJ: Wiley.

Kotler, P., Kartajaya, H. and Setiawan, I. (2018), 'Marketing 4.0', *The Marketing Journal*, May 5.

Kotler, P. and Keller, K.L. (2007), *A Framework for Marketing Management*, 3rd edn, Hemel Hempstead, UK: Pearson/Prentice Hall.

Kotler, P. and Keller, K. (2008), *Marketing Management*, 13th edn, Hemel Hempstead, UK: Pearson/Prentice Hall.

Kotler, P. and Keller, K. (2016), *Marketing Management*, 15th edn, Harlow, UK: Pearson.

Kotler, P.C. (1997), *Marketing Management: Analysis, Planning, Implementation and Control*, 9th edn, Hemel Hempstead, UK: Prentice Hall International.

Kotler, P.C., Armstrong, G., Saunders, J.A. and Wong, V. (1996), *Principles of Marketing: The European Edition*, Hemel Hempstead, UK: Prentice Hall.

Kotler, P.C., Fahey, L. and Jatusritpitak, S. (1985), *The New Competition*, Hemel Hempstead, UK: Prentice Hall.

Kotler, P.C. and Sarkar, C. (2019), 'Ecosystem marketing: The future of competition', *The Marketing Journal*, February 21.

Kotler, P.C. and Singh, R. (1981), 'Marketing warfare in the 1980s', *Journal of Business Strategy*, 1(3), 30–41.

Krohmer, H., Homburg, C. and Workman, J.P. (2002), 'Should marketing be cross-functional? Conceptual development and international empirical evidence', *Journal of Business Research*, 35, 451–65.

Kruskal, J.B., Young, F.W. and Seery, J.B. (1973), 'How to use KYST: A very flexible program to do multidimensional scaling', Multidimensional Scaling Program Package of Bell Laboratories, Murray Hill, NJ: Bell Laboratories.

Kumar, V., Jones, E., Venkatesan, R. and Leone, R.P. (2011), 'Is market orientation a source of sustainable competitive advantage or simply the cost of competing?', *Journal of Marketing*, 75(1), 16–30.

Lafferty, B.A. and Hult, G.T.M. (2001), 'A synthesis of contemporary market orientation perspectives', *European Journal of Marketing*, 35(1/2), 92–109.

Laing, H. (1991), *Brand Advertising Targeting System*, London: Laing Henry.

Lambert, D.M., Emmelhainz, M.A. and Gardner, J.T. (1996), 'So you think you want to be a partner?', *Marketing Management*, Summer, 25–41.

Lambert, D.M., Marmorstein, H. and Sharma, A. (1990), 'Industrial salespeople as a source of market information', *Industrial Marketing Management*, 17(May), 111–18.

Langerak, F. (2001), 'Effects of market orientation on the behaviours of salespersons and purchasers, channel relationships and the performance of manufacturers', *International Journal of Research in Marketing*, 18, 221–34.

Lashinsky, A. (2006), 'Chaos by design', *Fortune*, October 2, pp. 34–42.

Lawson, D. (2009), 'Organic food is just a tax on the gullible', *Sunday Times*, August 9, p. 1.16.

Leadbeater, C. (2014), *The Frugal Innovator: Creating Change on a Shoestring Budget*, London: Palgrave Macmillan.

Leahy, J. (2007), 'Time for India's IT outsourcers to take a fresh look at the data', *Financial Times*, December 28, p. 20.

Leahy, J. (2009), 'Wipro begins to outsource its Indian workload', *Financial Times*, November 12, p. 25.

Leahy, J. (2010), 'Marriages of convenience', *Financial Times*, September 30, p. 15.

Lee, N. and Lings, I.N. (2008), *Doing Business Research: A Guide to Theory and Practice*, Thousand Oaks, CA: SAGE Publications Ltd.

Lehmann, D.R. and Winer, R.S. (1991), *Analysis for Marketing Planning*, 2nd edn, Homewood, IL: Irwin.

Leigh, T.W. and Marshall, G.W. (2001), 'Research priorities in sales strategy and performance', *Journal of Personal Selling & Sales Management*, 21(Spring), 83–94.

Leonard-Barton, D. (1992), 'Core capabilities and core rigidities: A paradox in managing new product development', *Strategic Management Journal*, 13(Summer Special Issue), 111–25.

Levitt, T. (1960), 'Marketing myopia', *Harvard Business Review*, 38(4), 45–56.

Levitt, T. (1986), *The Marketing Imagination*, New York: The Free Press.

Levy, R. (1999), *Give and Take*, Cambridge, MA: Harvard Business School Press.

Lilien, G.L. and Kotler, P.C. (1983), *Marketing Decision Making: A Model-Building Approach*, London: Harper & Row.

Lilien, G.L., Kotler, P. and Moorthy, K.S. (1992), *Marketing Models*, Hemel Hempstead: Prentice Hall International.

Lings, I.N. and Greenley, G.E. (2005), 'Measuring internal market orientation', *Journal of Service Research*, 7(3), 290–305.

Lippman, S. and Rumelt, R.P. (1982), 'Uncertain inimitability: An analysis of inter-firm differences in efficiency under competition', *Bell Journal of Economics*, 13, 418–53.

Little, J.D.C. (1979), 'Decision support systems for marketing management', *Journal of Marketing*, 43(3), 9–26.

Lockett, A., Thompson, S. and Morgenstern, U. (2009), 'The development of the resource-based view of the firm: A critical appraisal', *International Journal of Management Reviews*, 11(1), 9–28.

Lombardi, L.J. (2005), 'Managing strategic customer relationships as assets', *LIMRA'S MarketFacts Quarterly*, 24(1), 23–5.

Loroz, P.S. and Helgeson, J.G. (2013), 'Boomers and their babies: An exploratory study comparing psychological profiles and advertising appeal effectiveness across two generations', *Journal of Marketing Theory & Practice*, Summer, 21(3), 289–306.

Lublin, J.S. (2008), 'Environmentally friendly corporate boards', *Wall Street Journal*, August 11, p. 30.

Lusch, R.F., Vargo, S.L. and Malter, A.J. (2006), 'Marketing as service exchange: Taking a leadership role in global marketing management', *Organisational Dynamics*, 35(3), 264–78.

Lynn, M. (2015), 'The dismal decline of W.H. Smith', *Management Today*, October 21.

MacArthur, K. (2005), 'McD's strategy hinges on "balance"', *Advertising Age*, 76(2), 6.

McDonald, M. and Dunbar, I. (2012), *Market Segmentation: How to Do It, How to Profit From It*, 3rd edn, Oxford, UK: Butterworth-Heinemann.

McDonald, M. (2017), 'Market segmentation: Still the bedrock of commercial success', *The Marketing Journal*, October 17.

Mackintosh, J. and Simon, B. (2005), 'Ford to focus on business from "key suppliers"', *Financial Times*, September 30, p. 32.

Mackintosh, J. (2005), 'VW takes a hard line with parts suppliers', *Financial Times*, June 24, p. 30.

MacLeod, D. and Brady, C. (2007), *The Extra Mile: How to Engage Your People and Win*, Hemel Hempstead: FT Prentice Hall.

Mahoney, J.T. (1995), 'The management of resources and the resource of management', *Journal of Business Research*, 33(2), 91–101.

Mahoney, J.T. and Pandian, J.R. (1992), 'The resource-based view of the firm within the conversation of strategic management', *Strategic Management Journal*, 13, 363–80.

Maier, J. and Saunders, J.A. (1990), 'The implementation of segmentation in sales management', *The Journal of Personal Selling and Sales Management*, 10(1), 39–48.

Maignan, I. and Ferrell, O.C. (2004), 'Corporate social responsibility and marketing: An integrative framework', *Journal of the Academy of Marketing Science*, 32(1), 3–19.

Maignan, I., Ferrell, O.C. and Ferrell, L. (2005), 'A stakeholder model for implementing social responsibility in marketing', *European Journal of Marketing*, 39(9/10), 956–77.

Maitland, A. (2005), 'A responsible balancing act', *Financial Times*, June 1, p. 11.

Maitland, A. (2006), 'The frustrated will to act for public good', *Financial Times*, January 25, p. 15.

Mallaby, S. (2013), 'American industry is on the move', *Financial Times*, January 9, p. 13.

Mallett, V. and Crabtree, J. (2015), 'The American connection', *Financial Times*, May 25, p. 12.

Marketing Week (2003) 'Survey reveals "inadequate" state of internal marketing', *Marketing Week*, July 3, p. 8.

Marketing Week (2006), 'Marketing capability – blend for flexibility', *Marketing Week,*, July 17, p. 30.

Marketing Week (2012), 'The Uses of Research' – Segmentation: Microsoft', *Marketing Week*, August 1, https://www.marketingweek.com/the-uses-of-research-segmentation-microsoft/, accessed 2019.

Marketing Week (2018), 'Localised marketing, GDPR, digital skills: 5 killer stats to start your week', *Marketing Week*, September 24.

Mars (2019), 'The Five Principles', https://www.mars.com/about/five-principles, accessed 2019.

Marsh, P. (2007), 'Back on a roll in the business of bearings', *Financial Times*, February 7, p. 10.

Marsh, P. (2009), 'Complexity is key to overcoming recession', *Financial Times*, July 28, p. 3.

Marshall, G.W., Moncrief, W.C., Rudd, J.M. and Lee, N. (2013), 'Revolution in sales: The impact of social media and related technology on the selling environment', *Journal of Personal Selling and Sales Management*, September 23, 349–63.

Martin, R. (2011), 'The innovation catalysts', *Harvard Business Review*, June, 82–7.

Martin, R.L. (2010), 'The execution trap', *Harvard Business Review*, July–August, 64–71.

Matlack, C. (2013), 'Electrolux's holy trinity', *BusinessWeek*, November 4–10, 55–6.

Mattu, R. (2011), 'Expanded spheres of influence', *Financial Times*, November 29, p. 16.

Maunder, S., Harris, A., Bamford, J., Cook, L. and Cox, A. (2005), 'O2: It only works if it works – how troubled BT Cellnet was transformed into thriving O2', in A. Hoad (ed.), *Advertising Works 13: Proving the Effectiveness of Marketing Communications*, Henley-on-Thames: World Advertising Research Centre.

Mazur, L. (2000), 'The changing face of sales', *Marketing Business*, May, 31.

McGregor, J. (2007), 'Most innovative companies', *BusinessWeek*, May 14, pp. 52–64.

McKee, D. and Varadarajan, P.R. (1995), 'Introduction: Special issue on sustainable competitive advantage', *Journal of Business Research*, 33(2), 77–9.

McKitterick, J.B. (1957), 'What is the marketing management concept?', AMA Teachers' Conference, Philadelphia.

McWilliams, G. and Zuckerman, A. (2008), 'Walmart reached out', *Wall Street Journal*, June 9, p. 8.

Menguc, B. and Auh, S. (2006), 'Creating firm-level dynamic capability through capitalising on market orientation and innovativeness', *Journal of the Academy of Marketing Science*, 34(1), 63–73.

Menn, J. (2009), 'Schmidt's move is sign of the times', *Financial Times*, August 4, p. 17.

Miles, R.E. and Snow, C.C. (1984), 'Fit, failure, and the hall of fame', *California Management Review*, Spring, 10–28.

Miller, A.I. (1996), *Insight of Genius*, New York: Springer-Verlag.

Miller, D. (2002), 'Successful change leaders: What makes them? What do they do that is different?', *Journal of Change Management*, 2(4), 359–68.

Millman, T. and Wilson, K. (1989), 'Processual issues in key account management: Underpinning the customer-facing organisation', *Journal of Business & Industrial Marketing*, 14(4), 328–37.

Milne, R. (2008), 'Homesick producers lose taste for going overseas', *Financial Times*, June 5, p. 24.

Milne, R. (2010), 'Drive to link pay to sustainability begins', *Financial Times*, February 24, p. 22.

Milne, R. (2019) 'Ikea to trial furniture leasing in business overhaul', *Financial Times*, February 3.

Mitchell, A. (1995), 'Changing channels', *Marketing Business*, February, 10–13.

Mitchell, A. (1997), 'Speeding up the process', *Marketing Business*, March.

Mitchell, A. (2008), 'If you want to be loved, just do it right', *Financial Times*, March 27, p. 16.

Mitchell, R.K., Agle, B.R. and Wood, D.J. (1997), 'Toward a theory of stakeholder identification and salience: Defining the principle of who and what really counts', *Academy of Management Review*, 22, 853–86.

Mitchell, T. (2014), 'Carmakers "printing cash" in China', *Financial Times*, June 12, p. 21.

Mol, M.J. and Birkinshaw, J. (2007), *Giant Steps in Management: Innovations That Change the Way We Work*, Harlow: FT/Prentice Hall.

Montgomery, D.B. and Webster, F.E. (1997), 'Marketing's interfunctional interfaces: The MSI workshop on management of corporate fault zones', *Journal of Market-Focused Management*, 2, 7–26.

Moon, Y. (2005), 'Break free from the product life cycle', *Harvard Business Review*, May, 87–94.

Moore, E. (2014), 'Enthusiasm may wane as companies pursue growth', in *Responsible Business, Financial Times*, July 8, p. 2.

Moore, G.A. (1991), *Crossing the Chasm*, New York: HarperCollins.

Moore, G.A. (2014), *Crossing the Chasm*, 3rd edn, New York: Collins Business Essentials.

Moore, G.A. (2004), 'Innovating within established enterprises', *Harvard Business Review*, July–August, 86–92.

Moore, G.A. (2006), *Dealing with Darwin: How Great Companies Innovate at Every Phase of their Evolution*, Chichester: Capstone.

Moorman, C. and Lehman, D.R. (2004), *Assessing Marketing Strategy Performance*, Boston, Cambridge, MA: Marketing Science Institute.

Morgan, J. (2014), 'A simple explanation of the "Internet of Things"', *Forbes*, May 13.

Morgan, R.E., Katsikeas, C.S. and Appiah-Adu, K. (1998), 'Market orientation and organisational learning', *Journal of Marketing Management*, 14, 353–81.

Morgan, R.M. and Hunt, S.D. (1994), 'The commitment–trust theory of relationship marketing', *Journal of Marketing*, 58(3), 20–38.

Morgan, R.E. (2004), 'Business agility and internal marketing', *European Business Review*, 16(5), 464–72.

Moroko, L. and Uncles, M.D. (2009), 'Employer branding: Companies have long divided consumers into segments; they should do the same with potential – and current – workers', *Wall Street Journal*, March 23, R7.

Morrison, S. and Waters, R. (2005), 'Time comes to "think different"', *Financial Times*, June 7, p. 25.

Moss Kanter, R. (2009), *Supercorp: How Vanguard Companies Create Innovation, Profits, Growth and Social Good*, London: Profile Books.

Moss Kanter, R. (2011), 'How great companies think differently', *Harvard Business Review*, November, 66–79.

Moutinho, L. (1991), *Problems in Marketing*, London: Paul Chapman Publishing.

Murphy, J. (1991), *Brand Valuation*, 2nd edn, London: Business Books Ltd.

Murphy, P.E. and Staples, W.A. (1979), 'A modernized family life cycle', *Journal of Consumer Research*, June, 12–22.

Murphy, R.R. (2010), 'Why doing good is good for business', *Fortune*, February 8, pp. 59–62.

Murray, S. (2014), 'Search for growth hits progress on environment', *Sustainable Business, Financial Times*, May 22, p. 1.

Narayanda, D. (2005), 'Building loyalty in business markets', *Harvard Business Review*, September.

Narver, J.C. and Slater, S.F. (1990), 'The effect of a market orientation on business profitability', *Journal of Marketing*, 54(4), 20–35.

Nayar, V. (2010), *Employees First, Customers Second: Turning Conventional Management Upside Down*, Cambridge, MA: Harvard Business Press.

Neslin, S.A., Grewal, D., Leghorn, R., Shankar, V., Teerling, M.L., Thomas, J.S. and Verhoef, P.C. (2006), 'Challenges and opportunities in multichannel customer management', *Journal of Service Research*, 9(2), 95–112.

Nidumolu, R., Prahalad, C.K. and Rangaswami, M.R. (2009), 'Why sustainability is now the key driver of innovation', *Harvard Business Review*, September, 56–64.

Nussmaum, B. (2005), 'The evolution of the creative company', *BusinessWeek*, August 8/15, pp. 52–3.

O'Brien, N. and Ford, J. (1988), 'Can we at last say goodbye to social class?', *Journal of Market Research Society*, 16(2), 43–51.

O'Connell, D. (2003), 'Cassani throws a book at men who failed go', *Sunday Times*, October 26, pp. 3–11.

O'Connell, D. (2009), 'Rolls-Royce flies high despite airlines' nosedive', *Sunday Times*, August 2, p. 3.6.

O'Shaughnessy, J. (1995), *Competitive Marketing*, 3rd edn, London: Routledge.

Ogbuchi, A.O. and Sharma, V.M. (1999), 'Redefining industrial salesforce roles in a changing environment', *Journal of Marketing Theory and Practice*, 7(1), 64–71.

Ogden, S. and Watson, R. (1999), 'Corporate performance and stakeholder management: Balancing shareholder and customer interests in the UK privatized water industry', *Academy of Management Journal*, 42, 526–38.

Ohmae, K. (1982), *The Mind of the Strategist*, Harmondsworth: Penguin Books.

Ohmae, K. (1990), *The Borderless World*, New York: Harper Business.

Olins, R. (1997a), 'Wilting', *The Sunday Times*, August 24, p. 3.

Olins, R. (1997b), 'W.H. Smith stalls on the road to nowhere', *Sunday Times*, August 31, p. 5.

Olson, E.M., Cravens, D.W. and Slater, S.F. (2001), 'Competitiveness and sales management: A marriage of strategies,' *Business Horizons*, March/April, 25–30.

Opresnik, M.O., Kotler, P. and Hollensen, S. (2017), *'Social Media Marketing: A Practitioner Guide'*, 3rd edn, Lübeck, Germany: Opresnik Management Consulting.

Orme, B. (2005), *Getting Started with Conjoint Analysis*, Madison, WI: Research Publishers LLC.

Overell, S. (2005), 'Good ideas to generate more good ideas', *Financial Times*, June 28, p. 16.

Overman, S. (2014), *The Conscience Economy: How a Mass Movement for Good is Great*, Boston MA: Bibiomotion.

Oxx, C. (1972), 'Psychographics and life style', *Admap*, October, 303–5.

Ozretic-Dosen, D., Skare, V. and Krupka, Z. (2007), 'Assessments of country of origin and brand cues in evaluating a Croatian, western and eastern European food product', *Journal of Business Research*, 60(2), 130–6.

Palazzo, G. and Richter, U. (2005), 'CSR business as usual? The case of the tobacco industry', *Journal of Business Ethics*, 61, 387–401.

Palmatier, R. and Sridhar, S. (2017), *Marketing Strategy: Based on First Principles and Data Analytics*, Basingstoke, UK: Palgrave Macmillan.

Palmer, M. (2012), 'Raspberry Pi Minicomputer sells out', *Financial Times*, March 1, p. 2.

Palmisano, S.J. (2007), 'The globally integrated enterprise', *Foreign Affairs*, 85(3), 127–38.

Pansiri, J. (2005), 'The influence of managers' characteristics and perceptions in strategic alliance practice', *Management Decision*, 43(9), 1,097–13.

Parasuraman, A. and Colby, C.L. (2001), *Techno-Ready Marketing: How and Why Your Customers Adopt Technology*, New York: Free Press.

Parasuraman, A., Zeithaml, V.A. and Berry, L.L. (1985), 'A conceptual model of service quality and the implications for further research', *Journal of Marketing*, Fall, 41–50.

Parasuraman, A., Zeithaml, V.A. and Berry, L.L. (1988), 'SERVQUAL: A multiple-item scale for measuring customer perceptions of service quality', *Journal of Retailing*, 64(1), 12–40.

Parasuraman, A., Zeithaml, V.A. and Berry, L.L. (1994), 'Reassessment of expectations as a comparison standard in measuring service quality: Implications for further research', *Journal of Marketing*, 58(1), 111–24.

Parasuraman, A., Zeithaml, V. and Malhotra, A. (2005), 'E-S-QUAL: A multiple item scale for assessing electronic service quality', *Journal of Service Research*, 7(3), 213–33.

Pardo, C. (1997), 'Key account management in the business-to-business field: The key account's point of view', *Journal of Personal Selling & Sales Management*, 17(4), 17–26.

Pascale, R., Millman, M. and Gioja, L. (1997), 'Changing the way we change', *Harvard Business Review*, November/December, 127–39.

Patrick, A.O. (2008), 'As water sales dry up, Nestlé pans soda', *Wall Street Journal*, November 13, p. 4.

Payne, A. (1993), *The Essence of Services Marketing*, London: Prentice Hall.

Payne, A. (ed.) (1995), *Advances in Relationship Marketing*, London: Kogan Page.

Payne, A. and Frow, P. (2005), 'A strategic framework for customer relationship management', *Journal of Marketing*, October, 167–76.

Payne, A., Christopher, M., Clark, M. and Peck, H. (1995), *Relationship Marketing for Competitive Advantage*, Oxford: Butterworth-Heinemann.

Penrose, E.T. (1959), *The Theory of the Growth of the Firm*, New York: Wiley.

Perrien, J., Filiatraut, P. and Line, R. (1993), 'The implementation of relationship marketing in commercial banking', *Industrial Marketing Management*, 22(2), 141–8.

Perrien, J. and Ricard, L. (1995), 'The meaning of a marketing relationship', *Industrial Marketing Management*, 24(1), 37–43.

Petre, J. and Elliott, V. (2015), 'Sainsbury's shareholders targeted by badger cull extremists', *Daily Mail*, June 7, p. 17.

Pfeifer, S. (2008), 'Rolls-Royce reaps the rewards of client care', *Financial Times*, June 2, p. 22.

Pickard, J. and Harvey, F. (2008), 'Wilting agenda', *Financial Times*, May 28, p. 12.

Piercy, N., Low, G.S. and Cravens, D.W. (2004a), 'Consequences of sales management's behavior and compensation-based control strategies in developing countries', *Journal of International Marketing*, 12, 30–57.

Piercy, N., Low, G.S. and Cravens, D.W. (2004b), 'Examining the effectiveness of sales management control practices in developing countries', *Journal of World Business*, 39, 255–67.

Piercy, N.F. (1995), 'Customer satisfaction and the internal market: Marketing our customers to our employees', *Journal of Marketing Practice: Applied Marketing Science*, 1(1), 22–44.

Piercy, N.F. (2016), *Market-Led Strategic Change: Transforming the Process of Going to Market*, 5th edn, Abingdon, UK: Routledge.

Piercy, N. (2017), *Market-Led Strategic Change: Everything Has Changed, But Everything is the Same*, Abingdon, UK: Routledge.

Piercy, N.F. (1998), 'Marketing implementation: The implications of marketing paradigm weakness for the strategy execution process', *Journal of the Academy of Marketing Science*, 26(3), 222–36.

Piercy, N.F. (2002), *Market-Led Strategic Change: A Guide to Transforming the Process of Going to Market*, 3rd edn, Oxford: Butterworth-Heinemann.

Piercy, N.F. (2009a), *Market-Led Strategic Change: Transforming the Process of Going to Market*, 4th edn, Oxford: Butterworth-Heinemann.

Piercy, N.F. (2009b), 'Walmart's European adventure', in Nigel F. Piercy, *Market-Led Strategic Change: Transforming the Process of Going to Market*, 4th edn, Oxford: Butterworth-Heinemann, p. 39.

Piercy, N.F. (2009c), 'The clouds raining on the computer business', in N.F. Piercy, *Market-Led Strategic Change: Transforming the Process of Going to Market*, 4th edn, Oxford: Butterworth-Heinemann, pp. 162–7.

Piercy, N.F. (2009d), 'Ryanair: The master of non-service strategy', in N.F. Piercy, *Market-Led Strategic Change: Transforming the Process of Going to Market*, 4th edn, Oxford: Butterworth-Heinemann, pp. 46–48.

Piercy, N.F. (2016a), 'Privacy: The new product for the 21st century', in N.F. Piercy, *Market-Led Strategic Change: Transforming the Process of Going to Market*, 5th edn, London: Routledge.

Piercy, N.F. (2016b), 'Reinventing the healthcare business: An apple a day keeps the doctor away, but only if you throw it very hard indeed', in N.F. Piercy, *Market-Led Strategic Change: Transforming the Process of Going to Market*, 5th edn, London: Routledge.

Piercy, N.F. and Cravens, D.W. (1996), 'The network paradigm and the marketing organisation', *European Journal of Marketing*, 29(3), 7–34.

Piercy, N.F., Cravens, D.W. and Lane, N. (2010a), 'Marketing out of the recession: Recovery is coming, but things will never be the same again', *Marketing Review*, 10(1), 3–23.

Piercy, N.F., Cravens, D.W. and Lane, N. (2010b), 'Peek-a-boo: Finding and connecting with your customers', *Marketing Week*, Summer, pp. 18–24.

Piercy, N.F., Harris, L.C. and Lane, N. (2002), 'Market orientation and retail operatives' expectations', *Journal of Business Research*, 55(4), 261–73.

Piercy, N.F. and Lane, N. (1996), 'Marketing implementation: Building and sustaining a real market understanding', *Journal of Marketing Practice: Applied Marketing Science*, 2(3), 15–18.

Piercy, N.F. and Lane, N. (2006a), 'The underlying vulnerabilities in key account management strategies', *European Management Journal*, 24(2–3), 151–82.

Piercy, N.F. and Lane, N. (2006b), 'The hidden risks in strategic account management strategy', *Journal of Business Strategy*, 27(1), 18–26.

Piercy, N.F. and Lane, N. (2007), 'Ethical and moral dilemmas associated with strategic relationships between business-to-business buyers and sellers', *Journal of Business Ethics*, 72, 87–102.

Piercy, N.F. and Lane, N. (2009a), *Strategic Customer Management: Strategizing the Sales Organisation*, Oxford: Oxford University Press.

Piercy, N.F. and Lane, N. (2009b), 'Corporate social responsibility: Impacts on strategic marketing and customer value', *The Marketing Review*, 9(4), 335–60.

Piercy N.F. and Lane, N. (2011), 'Corporate social responsibility initiatives and strategic marketing imperatives', *Social Business*, 1(Winter), 325–45.

Piercy, N.F. and Lane, N. (2012), 'The evolution of the strategic sales organisation', in D.W. Cravens, K.L.M. Fitzhugh and N. Piercy (eds), *The Oxford Handbook of Selling and Sales Management*, Oxford: Oxford University Press, pp. 19–50.

Piercy, N.F. and Morgan, N.A. (1993), 'Strategic and operational market segmentation: A managerial analysis', *Journal of Strategic Marketing*, 1, 123–40.

Pine, B.J. (1993), *Mass Customisation: The New Frontier in Business Competition*, Boston, MA: Harvard Business School Press.

Pink, D. (2006), *A Whole New Mind: Why Right-Brainers Will Rule in the Future*, London: Cyan Books.

Plank, R.E. (1985), 'A critical review of industrial market segmentation', *Industrial Marketing Management*, 14, 79–91.

Plimmer, G. (2015), 'Outsourcing rises sharply under the coalition', *Financial Times*, May 1, p. 4.

Pohle, G. and Hittner, J. (2008), *Attaining Sustainable Growth Through Corporate Social Responsibility*, IBM Institute for Business Value, February.

Popper, M. and Lipschitz, R. (1998), 'Organisational learning mechanisms: A structural and cultural approach to organisational learning', *Journal of Applied Behavioural Science*, 34, 161–79.

Porter, M.E. (1980), *Competitive Strategy*, New York: The Free Press.

Porter, M.E. (1985), *Competitive Advantage*, New York: The Free Press.

Porter, M.E. (1987), 'From competitive advantage to corporate strategy', *Harvard Business Review*, 65(3), 43–59.

Porter, M.E. (1996), 'What is strategy?', *Harvard Business Review*, 74(6), 61–78.

Porter, M.E. (2001), 'Strategy and the Internet', *Harvard Business Review*, 79, 63–78.

Porter, M.E. (2010), 'How big business can help itself by helping its neighbors', *BusinessWeek*, May 31–June 6, p. 56.

Porter, M.E. and Kramer, M.R. (2002), 'The competitive advantage of corporate philanthropy', *Harvard Business Review*, December, 57–68.

Porter, M.E. and Kramer, M.R. (2006), 'Strategy and society: The link between competitive advantage and corporate social responsibility', *Harvard Business Review*, December, 78–92.

Porter, M.E. and Kramer, M.R. (2011), 'Creating shared value', *Harvard Business Review*, January–February, 62–77.

Poulter, S. (2010), 'Greenwashed!', *Daily Mail*, April 29, p. 33.

Poulter, S. (2014a), 'Ghost town Britain', *Daily Mail*, October 9, p. 12.

Poulter, S. (2014b), 'Relentless march of the internet shopping army', *Daily Mail*, December 9, p. 11.

Poulter, S. (2014c), 'Shops give out 1bn more plastic bags than four years ago', *Daily Mail*, July 16, p. 29.

Pounsford, M. (1994), 'Nothing to lose: Is internal communications adding value in today's organisations?', *Internal Communication Focus*, September, 6–8.

Powell, W.W. (1990), 'Neither market nor hierarchy: Network forms of organisation', *Research in Organisational Behavior*, 12, 295–336.

Prahalad, C.K. and Hamel, G. (1990), 'The core competence of the corporation', *Harvard Business Review*, 68(3), 79–91.

Prahalad, C.K. and Krishnan, M.S. (2008), *The New Age of Innovation: Driving Co-Created Value Through Global Networks*, Maidenhead: McGraw-Hill Professional.

Price, B. and Jaffe, D. (2008), *The Best Service Is No Service: How to Liberate Your Customers From Customer Service, Keep them Happy and Control Costs*, San Francisco, CA: Jossey Bass.

Priem, R.L. and Butler, J.E. (2001), 'Is the resource-based theory a useful perspective for strategic management research?', *Academy of Management Review*, 26(1), 22–40.

Prokesch, S.E. (1997), 'Unleashing the power of learning: An interview with British Petroleum's John Browne', *Harvard Business Review*, 75(5), 146–68.

Punj, G. and Stewart, D.W. (1983), 'Cluster analysis in marketing research: Review and suggestions for applications', *Journal of Marketing Research*, 20(May), 135–48.

Quinn, J. (2005a), 'Suppliers turn the screw on Rover', *Daily Mail*, April 8, p. 89.

Quinn, J. (2005b), 'Gillette deal to put P&G ahead by a close shave', *Daily Mail*, January 29, p. 105.

Quinn, J.B. (1992), *Intelligent Enterprise*, New York: Free Press.

Radjou, N. and Prabhu, J. (2015), *Frugal Innovation: How to do More with Less*, London: Profile Books/*The Economist*.

Radjou, N., Prabhu, J. and Ahuja, S. (2012), *Jugaad Innovation: Think Frugal, Be Flexible, Generate Breakthrough Growth*, Chichester: Wiley.

Ramaswami, S., Bharghava, M. and Srivasta, R. (2004), *Market-Based Assets and Capabilities, Business Processes, and Financial Performance*, Cambridge, MA: Report No. 04-102, Marketing Science Institute.

Rangan, V., Kasturi, L.C. and Karim, S. (2015), 'The truth about CSR', *Harvard Business Review*, January–February, pp. 40–49.

Rankine, K. (1996), 'Not a happy house', *The Daily Telegraph*, October 5, B2.

Rappeport, A. (2013), 'Out for the calorie count', *Financial Times*, January 26–27, p. 9.

Reed, J. (2008), 'Electric cars: How plug-in cars picked up speed and credibility,' *Financial Times*, January 8, p. 11.

Reed, J. (2010), 'Buyers loath to pay more for electric cars', *Financial Times*, September 20, p. 24.

Reed, J. (2012), 'Nissan and Daimler in engine tie-up', *Financial Times*, January 9, p. 17.

Reed, R. and DeFillippi, R.J. (1990), 'Causal ambiguity, barriers to imitation and sustainable competitive advantage', *Academy of Management Review*, 15, 88–102.

Reichheld, F. (1993), 'Loyalty-based management', *Harvard Business Review*, 71(2), 64–73.

Reichheld, F. and Sasser, W.E. (1990), 'Zero defections: Perfecting customer retention and recovery', *Harvard Business Review*, 68(5), 105–11.

Ries, A. and Trout, J. (1982), *Positioning: The Battle for Your Mind*, New York: McGraw-Hill.

Ries, A. and Trout, J. (2001), *Positioning: The Battle for Your Mind*, 2nd edn, New York: McGraw-Hill.

Ries, A. and Trout, J. (1986), *Marketing Warfare*, New York: McGraw-Hill.

Rigby, D.K., Reichheld, F.F. and Schafter, P. (2002), 'Avoid the four perils of CRM,' *Harvard Business Review*, February, 101–9.

Rigby, E. (2008), 'Shoppers fill baskets with cheaper food', *Financial Times*, September 6/7, p. 4.

Rigby, E. and Felsted, A. (2010a), 'Alliance Boots and P&G sign deal on European skincare business', *Financial Times*, May 8–9, p. 17.

Rigby, E. and Felsted, A. (2010b), 'Pessina to boost Alliance Boots skincare brands', *Financial Times*, April 27, p. 19.

Robertson, D.C. and Nicholson, N. (1996), 'Expressions of corporate social responsibility in UK firms', *Journal of Business Ethics*, 15(10), 1,095–106.

Robinson, S.J.Q., Hichens, R.E. and Wade, D.P. (1978), 'The directional policy matrix – tool for strategic planning', *Long Range Planning*, 11(3), 8–15.

Roch, J. and Mosconi, E. (2016), 'The use of social media tools in the product life cycle phases: A systematic literature review', 49th Hawaii International Conference on System Sciences.

Rogers, C. (2017), 'The shrinking and emerging demographics that marketers need to know', *Marketing Week*, March 13.

Rogers, C. (2018), 'How direct-to-consumer brands are reshaping marketing', *Marketing Week*, August 20.

Rogers, C. (2018), 'Iceland's banned Christmas ad is a festive masterstroke', *Marketing Week*, November 13.

Rogers, C. (2019), 'Why behaviour beats demographics when it comes to segmentation', *Marketing Week*, April 16.

Rogers, E.M. (2003), *Diffusion of Innovations*, New York: The Free Press.

Rouzies, D., Anderson, E., Kohli, A.K., Michaels, R.E., Weitz, B.A. and Zoltners, A.A. (2005), 'Sales and marketing integration: A proposed framework', *Journal of Personal Selling & Sales Management*, 25(2), 113–22.

Rowe, A.J., Mason, R.D., Dickel, K.E. and Synder, N.H. (1989), *Strategic Management: A Methodological Approach*, 3rd edn, Wokingham: Prentice Hall.

Rowley, T.J. (1997), 'Moving beyond dyadic ties: A network theory of stakeholder influences', *Academy of Management Review*, 22, 887–910.

RSA (1994), *Tomorrow's Company: The Role of Business in a Changing World*, London: RSA (Royal Society for the Encouragement of Arts, Manufactures and Commerce).

Rudd, J.M., Greenley, G.E., Beatson, A.T. and Lings, I.N. (2008), 'Strategic planning and performance: Extending the debate', *Journal of Business Research*, 61(2), 99–108.

Rushe, D. (2007), 'Starbucks stirs up a storm in a coffee cup', *Sunday Times*, March 2, 3.7.

Rust, R.T. and Zahorik, A.J. (1993), 'Customer satisfaction, customer retention and market share', *Journal of Retailing*, 69(2), 193–215.

Sabnis, G. and Grewal, R., 'Competition and its implications for marketing strategy', in V. Shankar and G.S. Carpenter (eds) (2012), *Handbook of Marketing Strategy*, Cheltenham: Edward Elgar Publishing Ltd, Chapter 5.

Sales Educators, The (2006), *Strategic Sales Leadership: Breakthrough Thinking for Breakthrough Results*, Mason, OH: Thomson.

Salmon, A.-M. (1997), 'Transforming a brand with energy: Lucozade in sickness and in health', *British Brands*, 4(Summer), 3.

Sammuels, G. (1994), 'CD-ROM's first big victim', *Forbes*, February 28, pp. 42–4.

Sarkar, C. and Kotler, P. (2019), 'Ecosystem marketing: The future of competition', *The Marketing Journal*, February 21.

Saunders, J.A. (1990), 'Brands and valuations', *International Journal of Forecasting*, 8(2), 95–110.

Saunders, J.A. (1999), 'Cluster analysis', in G.J. Hooley and M.K. Hussey (eds), *Quantitative Methods in Marketing*, 2nd edn, London: International Thomson Business Press.

Saunders, J., Stern, P., Wensley, R. and Forrester, R. (2000), 'In search of the lemmus, lummus: An investigation into convergent competition', *British Journal of Management*, 11, S81–S94.

Savitz, A. and Weber, K. (2006), *The Triple Bottom Line: How Today's Best-Run Companies are Achieving Economic, Social and Environmental Success and How You Can Too*, San Francisco, CA: Pfeiffer Wiley.

Schmitt, B.H. (2007), *Big Think Strategy: How to Leverage Bold Ideas and Leave Small Thinking Behind*, Boston, MA: Harvard Business School Press.

Schultz, D.E. (2002), 'Study internal marketing for better impact', *Marketing News*, 14, 8.

Schultz, D.E. (2004), 'Building an internal marketing management calculus', *Interactive Marketing*, 6(2), 111–29.

Schultz, D.E. (2006), 'Definition of internal marketing remains elusive', *Marketing News*, January 15, p. 6.

Segnit, S. and Broadbent, S. (1973), 'Life-style research: A case history in two parts', *European Research*, January, 62–8.

Seidenschwartz, W. (2005), 'A model for customer enthusiasm: Connecting the customer with internal processes', Strategic Account Management Association Conference, February, Paris.

Selnes, F., Jaworski, B.J. and Kohli, A.J. (1996), 'Market orientation in the United States and Scandinavian companies: A cross-cultural view', *Scandinavian Journal of Management*, 12(2), 139–57.

Sen, S. and Bhattacharya, C.B. (2001), 'Does doing good always lead to doing better? Consumer reactions to corporate social responsibility', *Journal of Marketing Research*, 38(May), 225–43.

Senge, P., Smith, B., Kruschwitz, N., Laur, J. and Schley, S. (2008), *The Necessary Revolution: How Individuals and Organisations Are Working Together to Create a Sustainable World*, London: Nicholas Brealey Publishing.

Sengupta, S. and Bucklin, L.P. (1994), *To Ally or Not to Ally*, Cambridge, MA: Marketing Science Institute.

Sevastopulo, D. (2014), 'Strategy to make the maths work', *Financial Times*, June 3, p. 14.

Shapiro, B.P. (2002), *Creating the Customer-Centric Team: Coordinating Sales & Marketing*, Harvard Business School, Note 9-999-006.

Shapiro, B.P. and Bonoma, T.V. (1990), 'How to segment industrial markets', in R.J. Dolan (ed.), *Strategic Marketing Management*, Cambridge, MA: Harvard Business School Press.

Shapiro, B.P., Slywotsky, A.J. and Doyle, S.X. (1998), *Strategic Sales Management: A Boardroom Issue*, Note 9-595-018, Cambridge, MA: Harvard Business School.

Sharman, A. (2014), 'BMW's pay-as-you-go heads to London', *Financial Times*, December 1, p. 20.

Sheridan, M. and Jones, R. (2010), 'Toxic fallout of China's solar panel boom', *Sunday Times*, October 3, pp. 1–30.

Shermach, K. (1995), 'Portrait of the world', *Marketing News*, August 28, 20.

Shervani, T. and Zerrillo, P.C. (1997), 'The albatross of product innovation', *Business Horizons*, January–February, 57–62.

Sheth, J.N. (1994), 'Relationship marketing: A customer perspective', keynote address, Relationship Marketing Conference, Emory University.

Sheth, J.N. and Mittal, B. (1996), 'A framework for managing customer expectations', *Journal of Market-Focused Management*, 1, 137–58.

Sheth, J.N. and Sisodia, R.S. (eds) (2006), 'The image of marketing', in *Does Marketing Need Reform? Fresh Perspectives on the Future*, New York: M.E. Sharpe Inc.

Shubber, K. (2015), 'Supermarkets battle to mop up excess space', *Financial Times*, May 29.

Siguaw, J.A., Brown, G. and Widing, R.E. (1994), 'The influence of the market orientation of the firm on sales force behavior and attitudes', *Journal of Marketing Research*, 31, 106–16.

Simms, J. (2003), 'HR or marketing: Who gets staff on side?', *Marketing*, July 24, p. 23.

Simon, B. (2005), 'Suppliers reorder priorities for survival', *Financial Times*, June 10, p. 28.

Simon, H. (1996), *Hidden Champions*, Boston, MA: Harvard Business School Press.

Simon, H. (2015), *Confessions of the Pricing Man: How Price Affects Everything*, Basel: Springer International Publishing, Switzerland.

Simonian, H. (2010), 'Nestlé to target less well-off in Europe', *Financial Times*, October 7, p. 24.

Simons, R. (2014), 'Choosing the right customer', *Harvard Business Review*, March, pp. 48–55.

Simonson, I. and Rosen, E. (2014), *Absolute Value: What Really Influences Customers in the Age of (Nearly) Perfect Information*, London: HarperBusiness.

Sinkula, J.M. (1994), 'Market information processing and organisational learning', *Journal of Marketing*, 58(1), 35–45.

Sinkula, J.M., Baker, W.E. and Noorewier, T. (1997), 'A framework for market-based organisational learning: Linking values, knowledge and behaviour', *Journal of the Academy of Marketing Science*, 25, 305–18.

Skapinker, M. (2003), 'Awkward customers', *Financial Times*, February 12, p. 12.

Skapinker, M. (2005), 'Nike ushers in a new age of corporate responsibility', *Financial Times*, April 20, p. 11.

Skapinker, M. (2007), 'There is a good trade in ethical retailing', *Financial Times*, September 11, p. 15.

Skapinker, M. (2008a), 'Corporate responsibility is not quite dead', *Financial Times*, February 12, p. 15.

Skapinker, M. (2008b), 'Why companies and campaigners collaborate', *Financial Times*, July 8, p. 15.

Skapinker, M. (2010), 'Long-term corporate plans may be lost in translation', *Financial Times*, November 23, p. 15.

Skapinker, M. (2014), 'Starbucks backlash was not just froth', *Financial Times*, May 15, p. 12.

Slater, S.F. (1997), 'Developing a customer value-based theory of the firm', *Journal of the Academy of Marketing Science*, 25(2), 162–7.

Slater, S.F. (1998), 'Customer-led and market-oriented: Let's not confuse the two', *Strategic Management Journal*, 19, 1,001–6.

Slater, S.F. and Narver, J.C. (1994), 'Does competitive environment moderate the market orientation–performance relationship?', *Journal of Marketing*, 58(1), 46–55.

Slater, S.F. and Narver, J.C. (1995), 'Market orientation and the learning organisation', *Journal of Marketing*, 59(July), 63–74.

Slywotzky, A. (1996), *Value Migration*, Boston, MA: Harvard Business School Press.

Smith, A. (1997), 'Brand-builders perceive pattern', *Financial Times*, June 23, p. 14.

Smith, A. (2014), 'Companies' charitable gifts soar since 2007', *Financial Times*, August 14, p. 3.

Smith, A. (2015), 'Businesses fall short of the mark on ethics', *Financial Times*, January 19, p. 22.

Smith, D.J. (2003), 'Strategic alliances and competitive strategies in the aerospace industry: The case of BMW and Rolls-Royce GmbH,' *European Business Review*, 15(4), 262–76.

Smith, N. (2010), 'Lost and scared: The boy on 7p an hour', *Sunday Times*, July 11, p. 1.25.

Smith, N.C. and Ward, H. (2007), 'Corporate social responsibility at a crossroads?', *Business Strategy Review*, 18(1), 16–21.

Smith, S.M. (1990), *PC MDS Version 5.1: Multidimensional scaling package*, Provo, UT: Brigham Young University.

Smith, W.R. (1956), 'Product differentiation and market segmentation as alternative marketing strategies', *Journal of Marketing*, July, 3–8.

Smyth, C. (2009), 'We sell junk, says Whole Foods chief', *Times*, August 6, p. 18.

Snider, J., Hill, R.P. and Martin, D. (2003), 'Corporate social responsibility in the 21st century: A view from the world's most successful firms', *Journal of Business Ethics*, 48(2), 175–87.

Soper, T. (2014), 'Former Microsoft CEO Steve Ballmer offers advice for young entrepreneurs', *GeekWire*, March 7.

Sorger, S. (2013), *Marketing Analytics: Strategic Models and Metrics*, Scotts Valley, CA: CreateSpace Independent Publishing Platform.

Sorrell, J. (1989), 'Power tools', *Marketing*, November 16, 45.

Spencer, B. (2015a), '"Eco" bulbs that aren't green and only last weeks', *Daily Mail*, January 24, p. 46.

Spencer, B. (2015b) 'Slap 20% tax on sugary drinks', *Daily Mail*, July 13, 1.

Spenner, P. and Freeman, K. (2012), 'To keep your customers, keep it simple', *Harvard Business Review*, (May), 108–14.

Spethman, B. (1992), 'Category management multiples', *Advertising Age*, May 11, 42.

Stafford, E.R. and Hartman, C.L. (2013), 'Promoting the value of sustainably minded purchase behaviours', *Marketing News*, January, 29–33.

Stalk, G. (1988), 'Time – the next source of competitive advantage', *Harvard Business Review*, 66(4), 41–51.

Stephens, H. (2003), 'The H.R. Chally Group', Presentation at the American Marketing Association Summer Educators' Conference, August.

Stern, S. (2009), 'The deadliest greenhouse gas? The hot air of CSR', *Financial Times*, February 3, p. 14.

Stern, S. (2008), 'How to get staff to care about their work', *Financial Times*, January 31, p. 14.

Stewart, T.A. (2006), 'Corporate social responsibility: Getting the logic right', *Harvard Business Review*, December, 14.

Stewart, T.A. (2006), 'The top line', *Harvard Business Review*, July–August, 10.

Stock, K. (2014), 'Big blue apple', *Bloomberg Business-Week*, July 21–27, p. 23.

Strahle, W.M., Spiro, R.L. and Acito, F. (1996), 'Marketing and sales: Strategic alignment and functional implementation', *Journal of Personal Selling & Sales Management*, 16(Winter), 1–20.

Straub, D. and Klein, R. (2001), 'e-Competitive transformations', *Business Horizons*, 44(3), 3–12.

Strelsin, S.C. and Mlot, S. (1992), 'The art of strategic sales alignment', *Journal of Business Strategy*, 13(6), 41–7.

Sull, D. (2005), 'Strategy as active waiting', *Harvard Business Review*, September, 120–9.

Sull, D., Homkes, R. and Sull, C. (2015), 'Why strategy execution unravels – and what to do about it', *Harvard Business Review*, (March), 58–67.

Svendsen, A. (1997), 'Building relationships with micro-communities', *Marketing News*, June 9, 13.

Swain, C.D. (1993), 'Competitive benchmarking', in D. Bernhardt (ed.), *Perfectly Legal Competitor Intelligence*, London: Pitman Publishing.

Swanson, D.L. (1995), 'Addressing a theoretical problem by reorienting the corporate social performance model', *Academy of Management Review*, 20(1), 43–64.

Tabachnik, B.G. and Fidell, L.S. (2014), *Using Multivariate Statistics*, 6th edn, Harlow, UK: Pearson.

Tallman, S. (2003), 'Dynamic capabilities', in D.O. Faulkner and A. Campbell (eds), *The Oxford Handbook of Strategy (Volume 1): A Strategy Overview and Competitive Advantage*, Oxford: Oxford University Press.

Talluri, S. and Narasimhan, R. (2004), 'A methodology for strategic sourcing', *European Journal of Operational Research*, 154(1), 236–50.

Tam, P.-W. (2006), 'System reboot – Hurd's big challenge at H-P', *Wall Street Journal*, April 3, A.1.

Tapscott, D. and Williams, A. (2007), *Wikinomics: How Mass Collaboration Changes Everything*, London: Atlantic Books.

Taylor, A. (2005), 'An operations perspective on strategic alliance success factors', *International Journal of Operations & Production Management*, 25(5), 469–90.

Taylor, A. (2007), 'Microsoft drops supplier over diversity policy', *Financial Times*, March 24/25, p. 5.

Taylor, P., Waters, R. and Palmer, M. (2007), 'Will Android be Google's transformer?', *Financial Times*, November 7, p. 20.

Taylor, W. and LaBarre, P. (2008), *Mavericks at Work: Why the Most Original Minds in Business Win*, London: Harper.

Teece, D.J., Pisano, G. and Shuen, A. (1997), 'Dynamic capabilities and strategic management', *Strategic Management Journal*, 18, 509–33.

Teinowitz, I. (1988), 'Brand managers: 90s dinosaurs?', *Advertising Age*, December 19, 19.

Tellis, G. and Golder, P. (1996), 'First to market, first to fail: Real causes of enduring market leadership', *Sloan Management Review*, 37(2).

Terazono, E. (2015), 'Sustainability creeps up the supply chain', *Financial Times*, April 21, p. 36.

Tett, G. (2015), 'How impatience hampers long-term growth', *Financial Times*, February 20, p. 11.

The Marketing Journal (2016), 'Scaling trust: marketing in a new key – an interview with John Hagel III', *The Marketing Journal*, January 15.

Thomas, N., Wells, P. and Wuild, J. (2015), 'Ryanair profits rise as caution prevails', *Financial Times*, May 27, p. 20.

Tighe, C. (1997), 'Lean sales machine', *Financial Times*, June 25, p. 26.

Timmers, P. (1999), *Electronic Commerce*, Chichester: John Wiley and Sons.

Todeva, E. and Knoke, D. (2005), 'Strategic alliances and models of collaboration', *Management Decision*, 43(1), 1,230–148.

Toffler, A. (1981), *The Third Wave*, London: Pan Books.

Tovey, A. (2015), 'Fracturing airline alliances could signal wave of industry consolidation', *The Telegraph*.

Trai, C.C. (1991), *Chinese Military Classic: The Art of War*, Singapore: Asiapac Books.

Treacy, M. and Wiersema, F. (1995), *The Discipline of Market Leaders*, London: HarperCollins.

Trudel, R. and Cotte, J. (2008), 'Does being ethical pay?', *Wall Street Journal*, May 13, pp. R2 & R8.

Trudel, R. and Cotte, J. (2009), 'Does it pay to be good?', *Sloan Management Review*, (Winter), 61–8.

Tull, D.S. (1967), 'The relationship of actual and predicted sales and profit in new product introductions', *Journal of Business*, 40(3), 233–50.

Tull, D.S. and Hawkins, D.I. (1993), *Marketing Research: Measurement and Method*, 6th edn, Englewood Cliffs, NJ: Prentice Hall.

Tyrell, P. (2010), 'Technology lets buyers unravel the ethics behind the brand', *Financial Times*, September 16, p. 16.

Tzokas, N., Saren, M. and Brownlie, D. (1997), 'Generating marketing resources by means of R&D activities in high technology firms', *Industrial Marketing Management*, 26, 331–40.

Ulrich, D. (1992), 'Strategic and human resource planning: Linking customers and employees', *Human Resource Planning*, 15(2), 47–62.

Ulwick, A.W., (2016), *Jobs to be Done: Theory to Practice*, Idea Bite Press.

Urry, M. (2008), 'Primark takes action on child labour', *Financial Times*, June 17, p. 20.

US Bureau of Labor Statistics (2013), 'International Labor Comparisons Report', August, http://www.bls.gov/fls/, accessed 2019.

Vaaland, T.I., Heide, M. and Gronhaug, K. (2008), 'Corporate social responsibility: Investigating theory and research in the marketing context', *European Journal of Marketing*, 42(9/10), 927–53.

Van Alstyne, M.W., Parker, G.G. and Choudary, S.P. (2016), 'Pipelines, platforms, and the new rules of strategy', *Harvard Business Review*, April, 54–62.

Varadarajan, P.R. (1992), 'Marketing's contribution to the strategy dialogue: The view from a different looking glass', *Journal of the Academy of Marketing Science*, 20(4), 335–44.

Varadarajan, R. (2012), 'Strategic marketing and marketing strategy', in *Handbook of Marketing Strategy*, V. Shankar, and G.S. Carpenter (eds), Cheltenham, UK: Edward Elgar Publishing, pp. 9–27.

Vargo, S.L. and Lusch, R.F. (2004), 'Evolving to a new dominant logic for marketing', *Journal of Marketing*, 68(January), 1–17.

Vence, D.L. (2007), 'Just a variation on a theme', *Marketing News*, February 1, 18–20.

Verhoef, P.C., Kannan, P.K. and Inman, J.J. (2015), 'From multi-channel retailing to omni-channel retailing: Introduction to the "Special Issue on Multi-Channel Retailing"', *Journal of Retailing*, 91(2), 174–81.

Vizard, S. (2018), 'Nike "proud" of Colin Kaepernick ad as campaign drives "record engagement"', *Marketing Week*, September 26.

Wagstyl, S. (2011), 'Replicators no more', *Financial Times*, January 6, p. 11.

Wall Street Journal (2012), 'GM and Peugeot strike Europe car partnership', March 1, p. 1.

Walsh, J. and Godfrey, S. (2000), 'The Internet: A new era in customer service', *European Management Journal*, 18(1), 85–92.

Wang, C.L. and Ahmed, P.K. (2007), 'Dynamic capabilities: A review and research agenda', *International Journal of Management Reviews*, 9(1), 31–51.

Waples, J. (2008), 'Overhaul that put the beans back into Heinz', *Sunday Times*, September 7, pp. 3–9.

Ward, A. (2006), 'Coke joins the battle for the brand corporate responsibility', *Financial Times*, November 21, p. 10.

Ward, A. (2015), 'Rush to snap up assets in cancer drugs race', *Financial Times*, April 8, p. 17.

Ward, A. and Waldmeir, P. (2014), 'Big Pharma fights back from China scandal', *Financial Times*, April 3, p. 21.

Ward, M.K. and Dahl, D.W. (2014), 'Should the devil sell Prada? Retail rejection increases aspiring consumers' desire for the brand', *Journal of Consumer Research*, 41(3), 590–609.

Ward, J. (1963), 'Hierarchical grouping to optimize an objective function', *Journal of the American Statistical Association*, 58, 236–44.

Warner, W.L. (1960), *Social Class in America*, New York: Harper and Row.

Warrington, P. and Eastlick, M. (2003), 'Quality value perceptions and satisfaction in an e-shopping environment', *Academy of Marketing Science Conference Proceedings*, p. 75.

Waters, R. and Taylor, P. (2007), 'Google mobile strategy steals a march on rivals', *Financial Times*, November 6, p. 1.

Waters, R. (2006), 'Computer pack top dogs lose their bite', *Financial Times*, June 5, p. 19.

Waters, R. (2001), 'Never forget to nurture the next big idea', *Financial Times*, May 15.

Webster, B. and Elliott, V. (2009), '2 for 1 deals face axe', *Times*, August 11, p. 1.

Webster, F.E. (1992), 'The changing role of marketing in the corporation', *Journal of Marketing*, 56(4), 1–17.

Webster, F.E. (1997), 'The future role of marketing in the organisation', in D.R. Lehmann and K.E. Jocz (eds), *Reflections on the Futures of Marketing*, Cambridge, MA: Marketing Science Institute, pp. 39–66.

Weintraub, A. (2007), 'Will Pharma finally have to fess up?', *BusinessWeek*, October 8, p. 36.

Weintraub, A. (2008), 'Just say no to drug reps', *BusinessWeek*, February 4, p. 69.

Weitzman, H. (2011), 'Boeing's 787 ready for take-off after three-year delay', *Financial Times*, July 19, p. 22.

Welch, D. (2008), 'The SUV is rising from the dead', *BusinessWeek*, December 8, p. 63.

Wells, K. (1994/5), 'The road ahead', *Marketing Business*, December–January, 18–20.

Wells, W.D. and Gubar, G. (1966), 'Life cycle concepts in marketing research', *Journal of Marketing Research*, 3(4), 355–63.

Wernerfelt, B. (1984), 'A resource-based view of the firm', *Strategic Management Journal*, 5(2), 171–80.

Wernerfelt, B. (1995), 'The resource-based view of the firm: Ten years after', *Strategic Management Journal*, 16, 171–80.

Weyer, M.V. (1997), 'The shop that time forgot', *Daily Telegraph*, August 30, p. 16.

Wheatcroft, P. (1997), 'Bright new look from Persil man', *Financial Mail on Sunday*, February 9, p. 9.

White, G.L. and Chazan, G. (2008), 'BP keeps TNK-BP stake but Russians gain clout', *Wall Street Journal*, September 5–7, p. 1.

White, J. (2015), 'A ban on Ribena? It's the last straw', *Daily Mail*, July 30, p. 31.

Wieczner, J. (2015), 'Tesla investors do the electric slide', *Fortune*, April 1, pp. 24–5.

Wierenga, B. (2010), 'Marketing and artificial intelligence: Great opportunities, reluctant partners', in J. Casillas and F.J. Martinez-Lopez (eds), *Marketing Intelligent Systems Using Soft Computing (Studies in Fuzziness and Soft Computing)*, Berlin: Springer, Volume 258, pp. 1–8.

Wiggins, J. (2007), 'Coke develops a thirst for sustainability', *Financial Times*, July 2, p. 26.

Wiggins, J. (2009), 'Heinz develops appetite for fresh outlets', *Financial Times*, July 27, p. 19.

Wilding, R. (2006), 'Playing to the tune of shared success', *Financial Times Report: Understanding Collaboration*, November 10, pp. 2–3.

Willman, J. (2006), 'Business fears recycling will cost £500m', *Financial Times*, June 6, p. 2.

Wilmott, M. (1989), 'Whose lifestyle is it anyway?', Institute of International Research Conference on Customer Segmentation and Lifestyle Marketing, London, December, 11–12.

Wind, Y. (1978), 'Issues and advances in segmentation research', *Journal of Marketing Research*, 15(3), 317–37.

Wind, Y. and Mahajan, V. (1981), 'Designing product and business portfolios', *Harvard Business Review*, 59(1), 155–65.

Wind, J. and Rangaswamy, A. (2001), 'Customerisation: The next revolution in mass customerisation', *Journal of Interactive Marketing*, 15(1), 13–32.

Winter, S.G. (2003), 'Understanding dynamic capabilities', *Strategic Management Journal*, 24, 991–5.

Wissema, J.G., Van der Pol, H.W. and Messer, H.M. (1980), 'Strategic management archetypes', *Strategic Management Journal*, 1(1), 37–47.

Witzel, M. (2008), 'The business case for more sustainability', *Financial Times*, July 3, p. 16.

Witzel, M. (2005a), 'An alliance that can supply a competitive edge', *Financial Times*, June 13, p. 14.

Witzel, M. (2005b), 'Big spenders are a boon – but don't forget the little guy', *Financial Times*, August 8, p. 14.

Wolfinbarger, M. and Gilly, M. (2003), 'Etailq: Dimensionalizing, measuring and predicting etail quality', *Journal of Retailing*, 79, 183–98.

Womack, J.P. and Jones, D.T. (1996), *Lean Thinking: Banish Waste and Create Wealth in Your Corporation*, London: Simon and Schuster.

Womack J.P. and Jones, D.T. (2005), 'Lean consumption', *Harvard Business Review*, March, 58–68.

Wood, D.J. (1991), 'Corporate social performance revisited', *Academy of Management Review*, 16(4), 691–718.

Woodhead, M. (2007), 'Dirty rotten business', *Sunday Times*, January 28, p. 3.5.

Woodhead, M. (2007), 'German firms retreat from eastern front', *Sunday Times*, November 25, pp. 3–12.

Woolf, M. (2007), 'Health food fads spark huge rise in animal testing', *Sunday Times*, December 30, p. 1.1.

Woolf, M. (2008), 'Blow to the image of the "green" nappy', *Sunday Times*, October 19, p. 1.7.

Workman, J.P., Homburg, C. and Gruner, K. (1998), 'Marketing organisation: An integrative framework of dimensions and determinants', *Journal of Marketing*, 62(July), 21–41.

Workman, J.P., Homburg, C. and Jensen, O. (2003), 'Intraorganisational determinants of key account management effectiveness', *Journal of the Academy of Marketing Science*, 31(1), 3–21.

Wright, P., Kroll, M., Pray, B. and Lado, A. (1990), 'Strategic orientations, competitive advantage and business performance', *Journal of Business Research*, 33, 143–51.

Yanklovich, D. and Meer, D. (2006), 'Rediscovering market segmentation', *Harvard Business Review*, 84(2), 122–31.

Yeh, A. (2006), 'McDonald's seeks heavy traffic fast-food expansion', *Financial Times*, June 21, p. 12.

Yoon, E. and Deeken, L. (2013), 'Why it pays to be a category creator', *Harvard Business Review*, March, 21–3.

Young, D. (1996), 'The politics behind market segmentation', *Marketing News*, October 21, p. 17.

Young, S., Off, F. and Fegin, B. (1978), 'Some practical considerations in market segmentation', *Journal of Marketing Research*, 15(August), 405–12.

Zahra, S.A. and George, G. (2002), 'Absorptive capacity: A review, reconceptualisation and extension', *Academy of Management Review*, 27(2), 185–203.

Zander, I. and Zander, U. (2005), 'The inside track: On the important (but neglected) role of customers in the resource-based view of strategy and firm growth', *Journal of Management Studies*, 42(8), 1,519–48.

Zielke, A. and Pohl, M. (1996), 'Virtual vertical integration: The key to success', *McKinsey Quarterly*, (3), 160–3.

Zizola, F. (2007), 'The other side of carbon trading', *Fortune*, September 3, pp. 67–74.

Zollo, M. and Winter, S.G. (2002), 'Deliberate learning and the evolution of dynamic capabilities', *Organisation Science*, 13(3), 339–51.

Zoltners, A.A., Sinha, P. and Lorimer, S.E. (2004), *Sales Force Design for Strategic Advantage*, New York: Palgrave Macmillan.

https://www.supplychainbrain.com/articles/1097-top-25-third-party-logistics-providers-extend-their-global-reach

www.luxottica.com/en/company/quick_view

INDEX